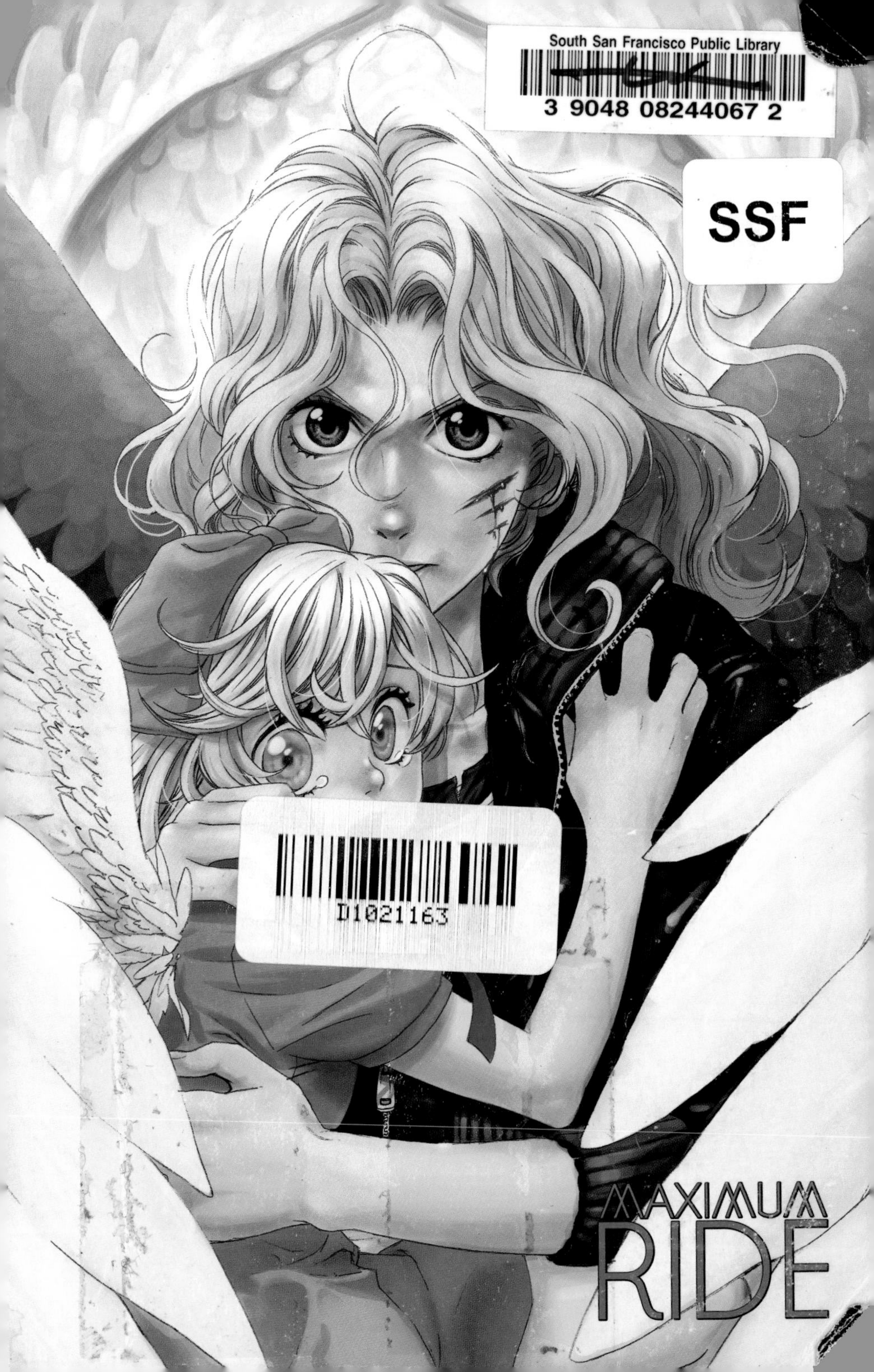
MAXIMUM
RIDE

MAXIMUM RIDE

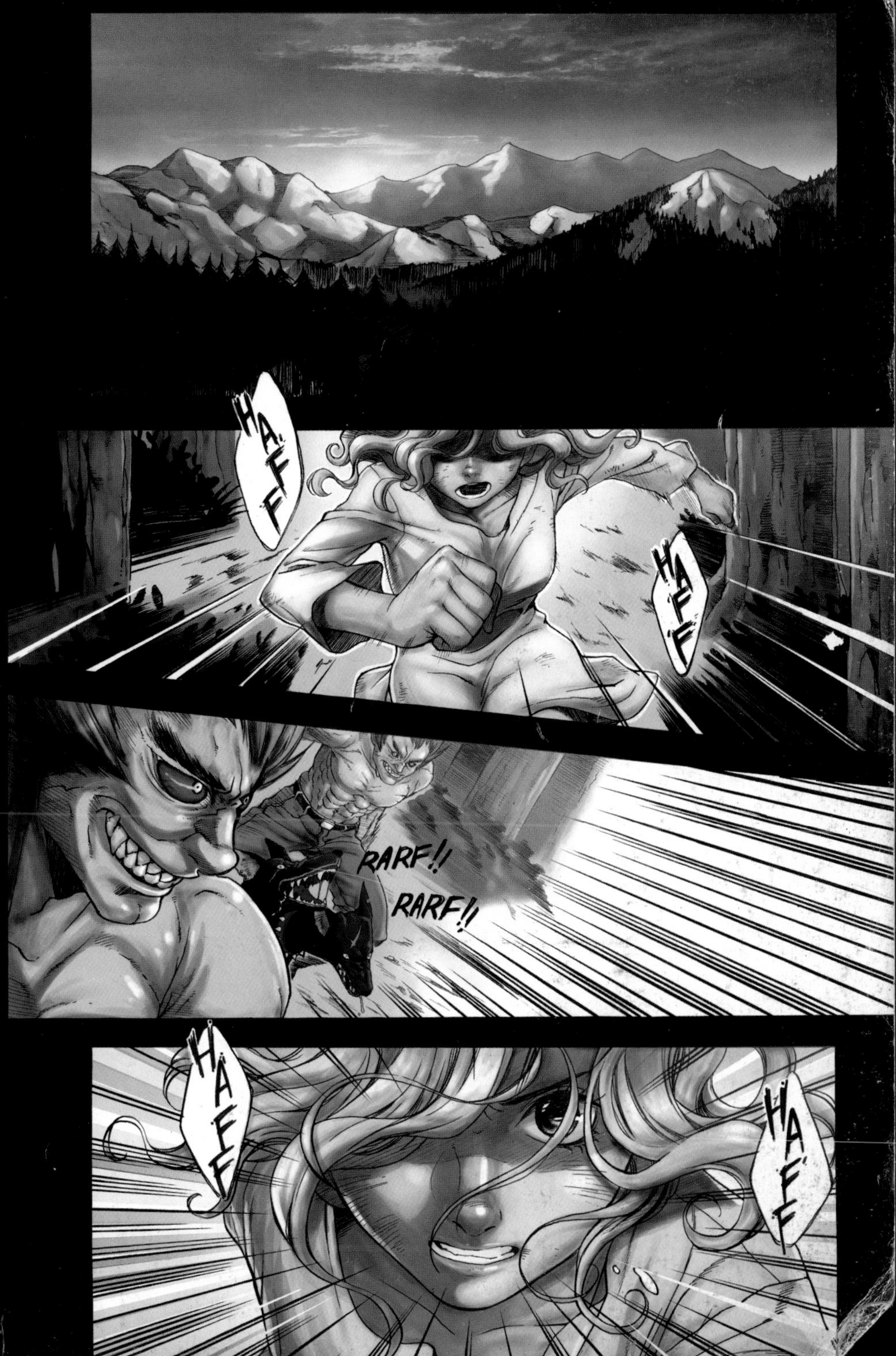
HAFF
HAFF
RARF!!
RARF!!
HAFF
HAFF

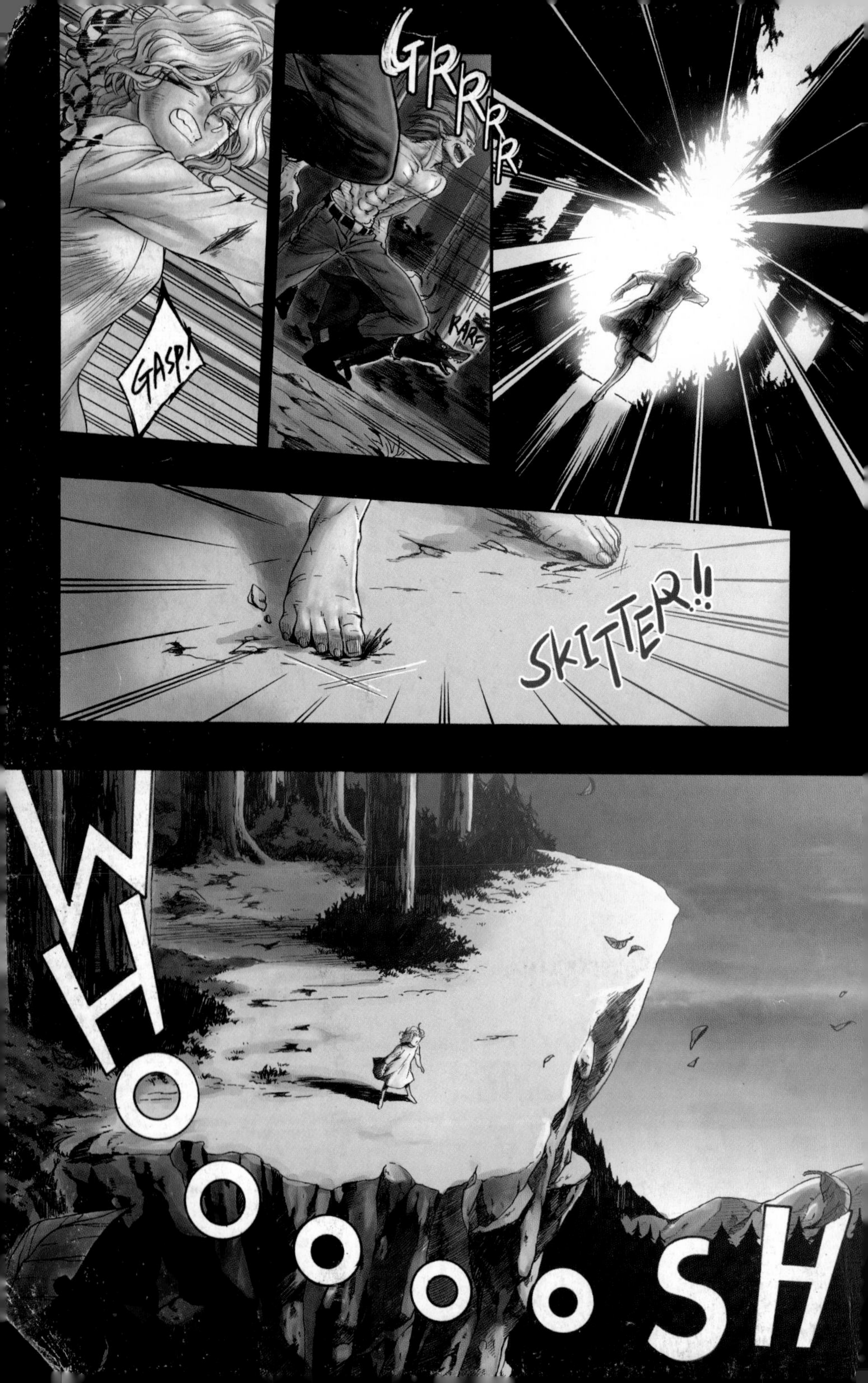
GASP!
GRRRRR
RARF
SKITTER!!
WHOOOOOOSH

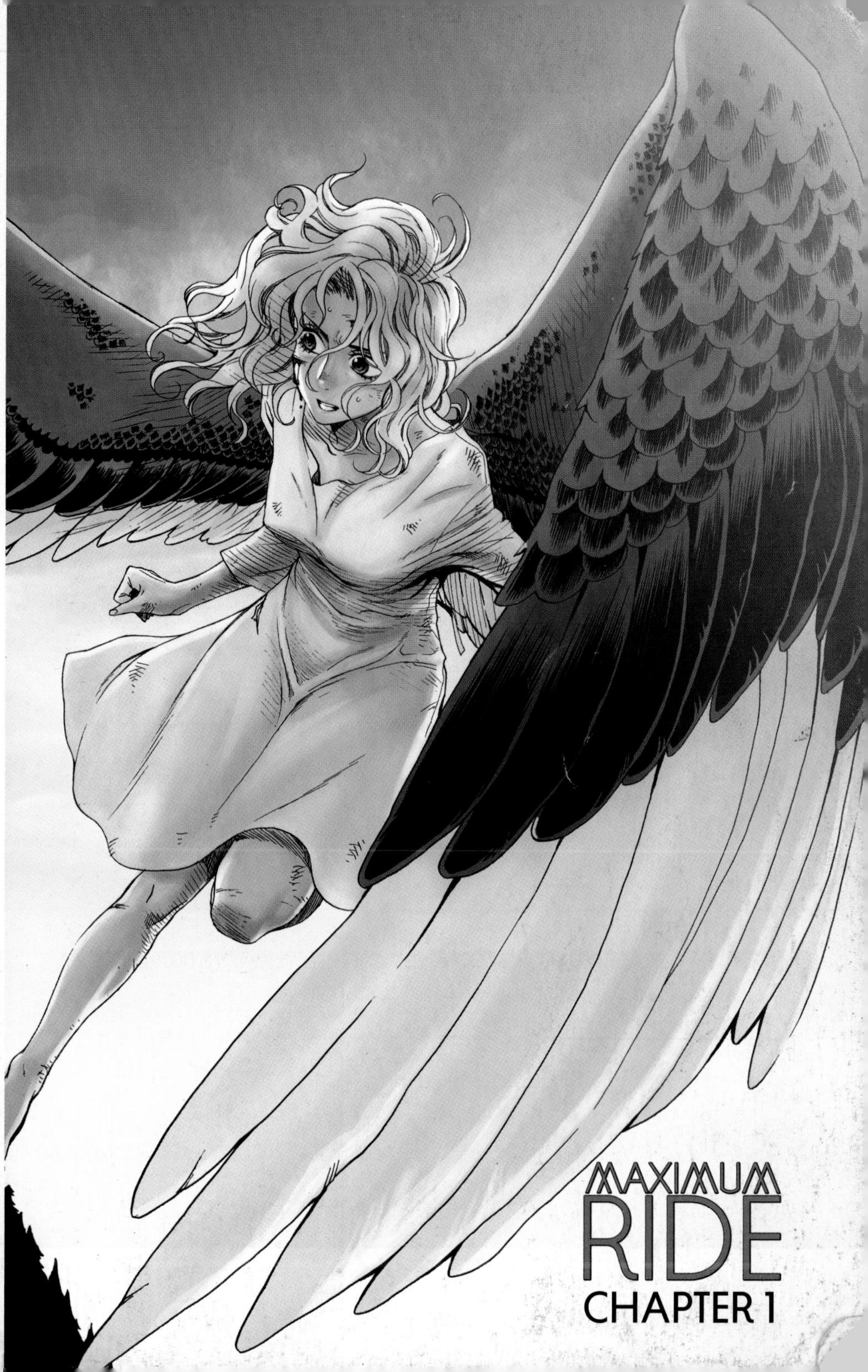

MAXIMUM RIDE
CHAPTER 1

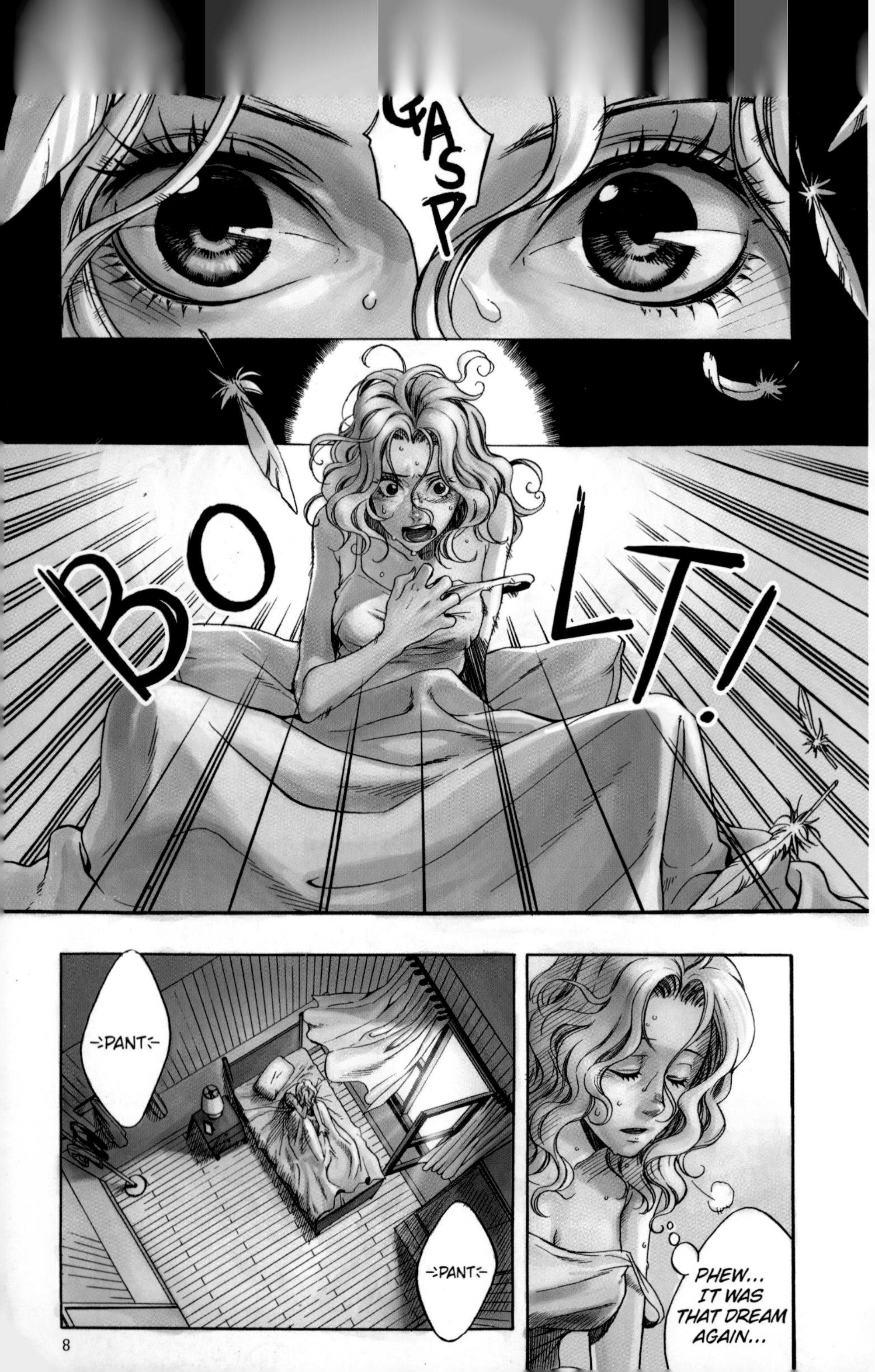
GASP
BOLT!
PANT
PANT
PHEW... IT WAS THAT DREAM AGAIN...

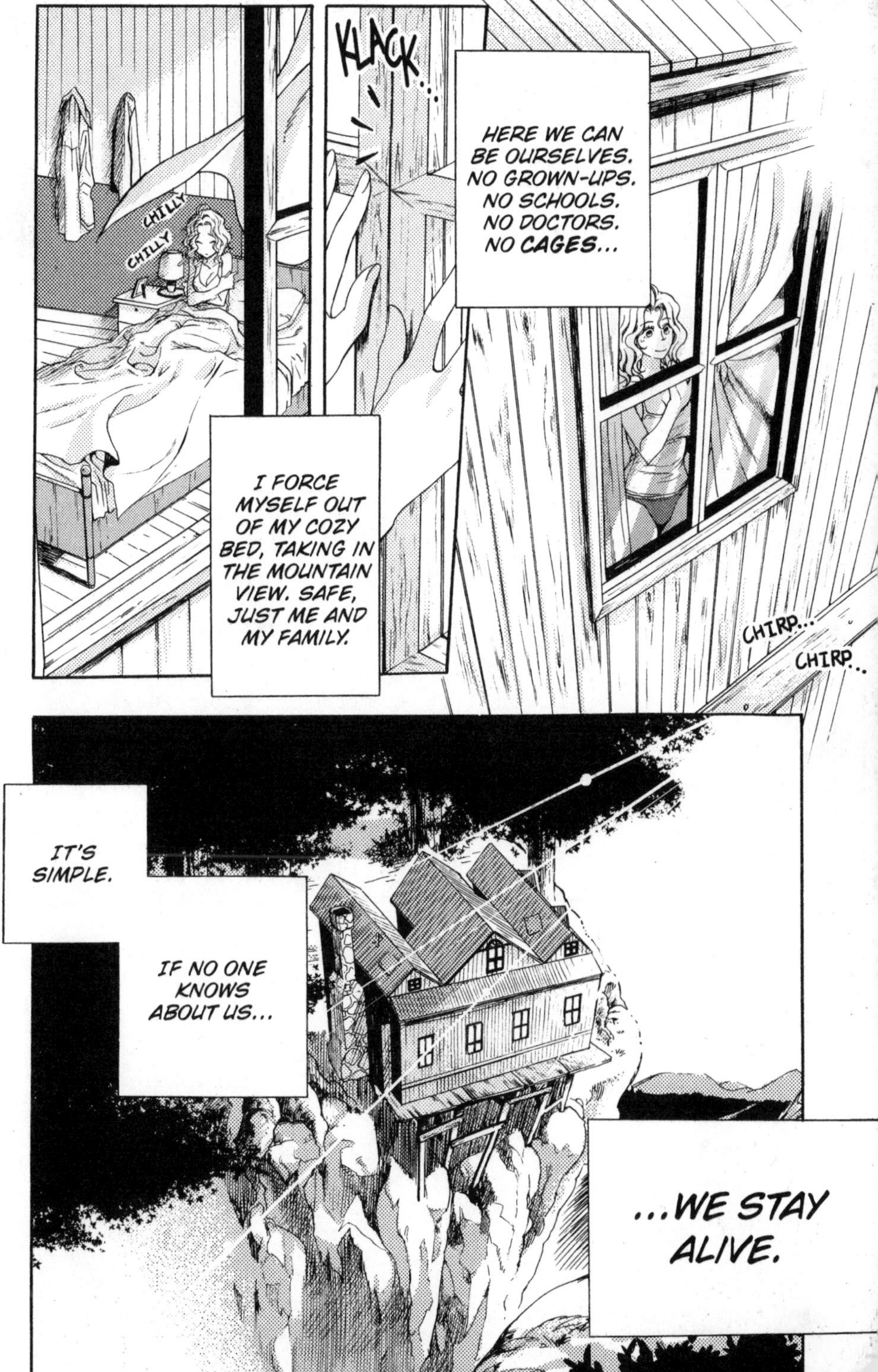
CHILLY
CHILLY
KLACK...
I FORCE MYSELF OUT OF MY COZY BED, TAKING IN THE MOUNTAIN VIEW. SAFE, JUST ME AND MY FAMILY.
HERE WE CAN BE OURSELVES. NO GROWN-UPS. NO SCHOOLS. NO DOCTORS. NO CAGES...
CHIRP...
CHIRP...
IT'S SIMPLE.
IF NO ONE KNOWS ABOUT US...
...WE STAY ALIVE.

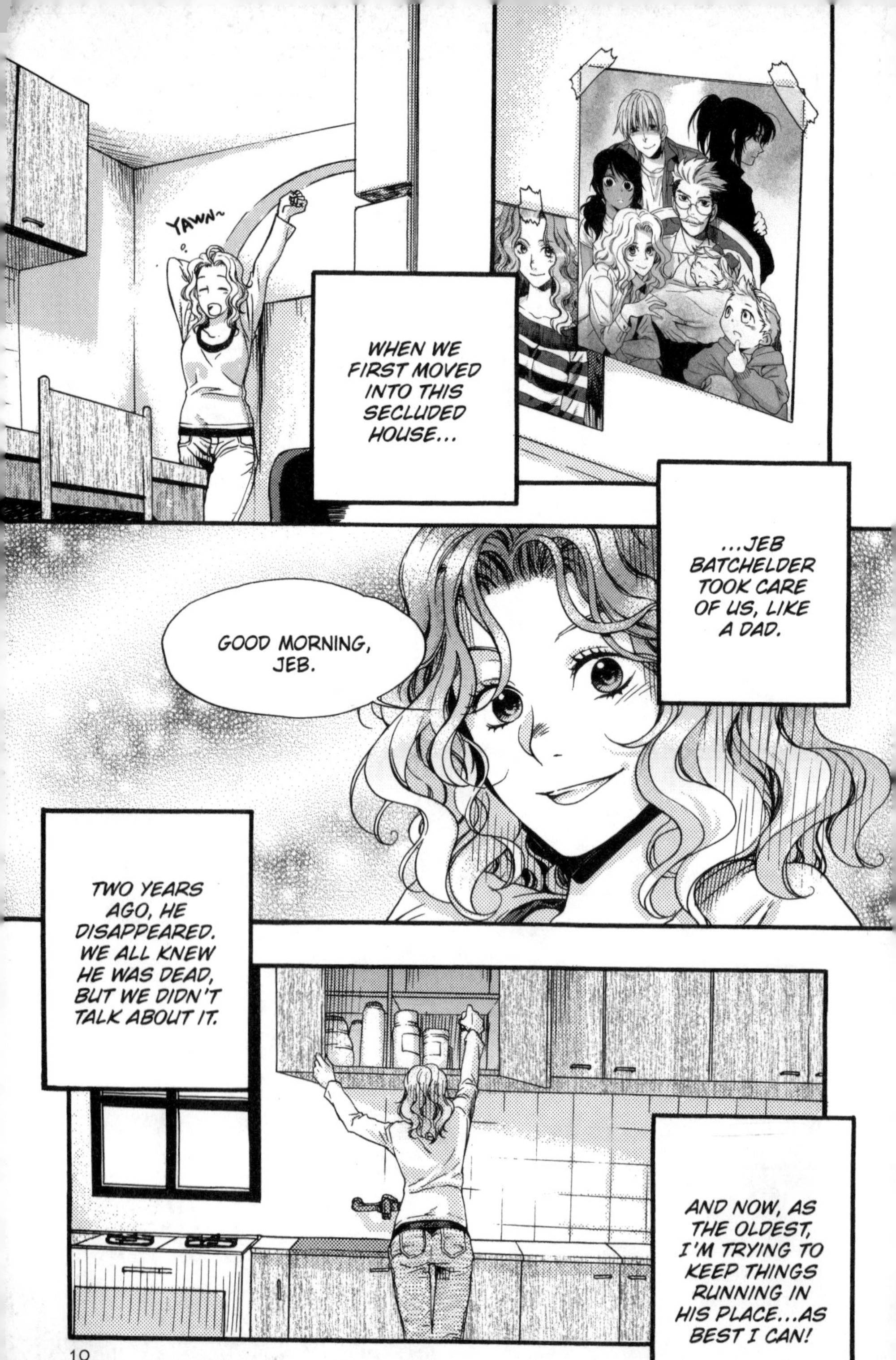
YAWN~
WHEN WE FIRST MOVED INTO THIS SECLUDED HOUSE...
...JEB BATCHELDER TOOK CARE OF US, LIKE A DAD.
GOOD MORNING, JEB.
TWO YEARS AGO, HE DISAPPEARED. WE ALL KNEW HE WAS DEAD, BUT WE DIDN'T TALK ABOUT IT.
AND NOW, AS THE OLDEST, I'M TRYING TO KEEP THINGS RUNNING IN HIS PLACE...AS BEST I CAN!

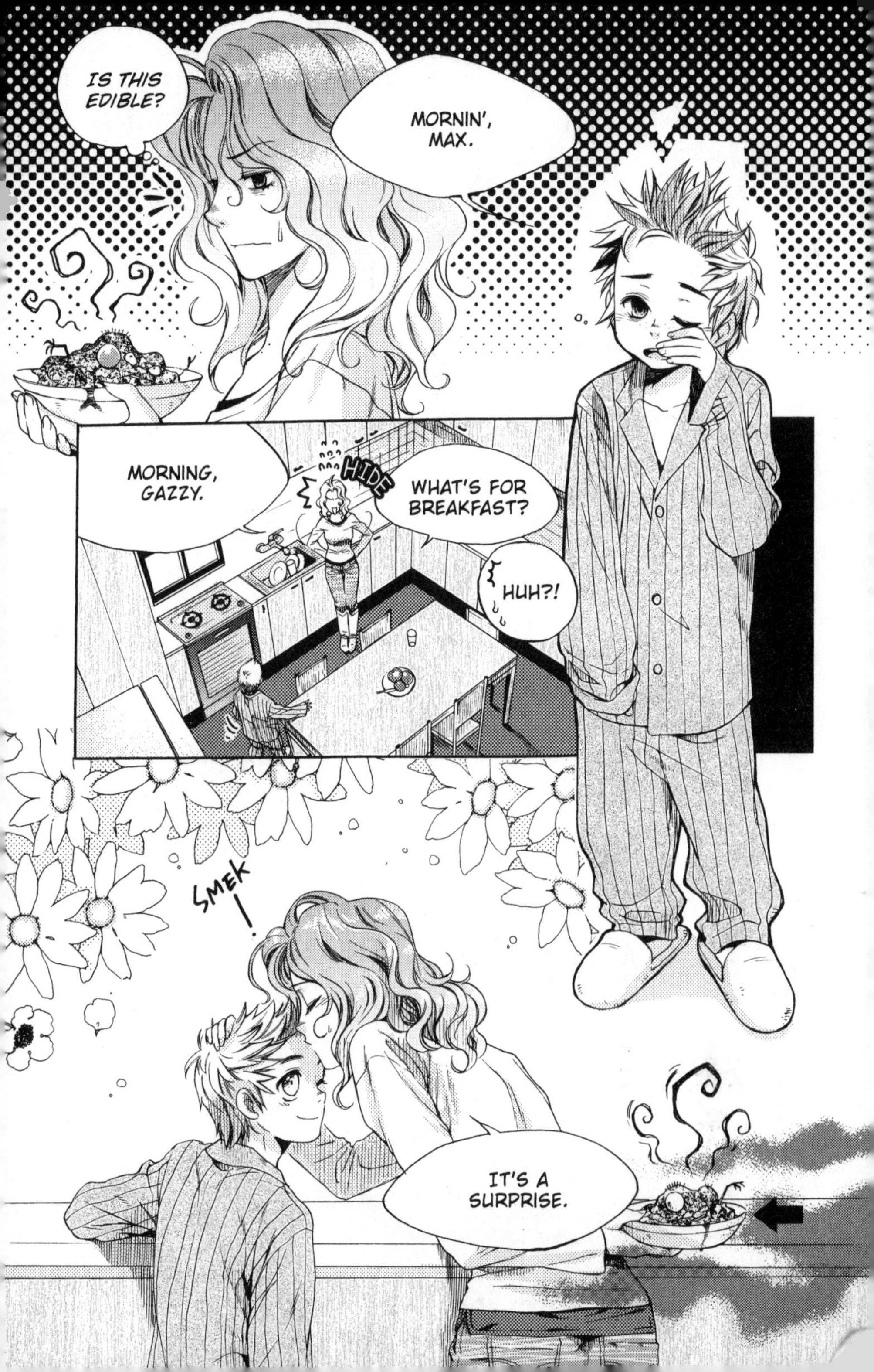
IS THIS EDIBLE?
MORNIN', MAX.
MORNING, GAZZY.
HIDE
WHAT'S FOR BREAKFAST?
HUH?!
SMEK
IT'S A SURPRISE.

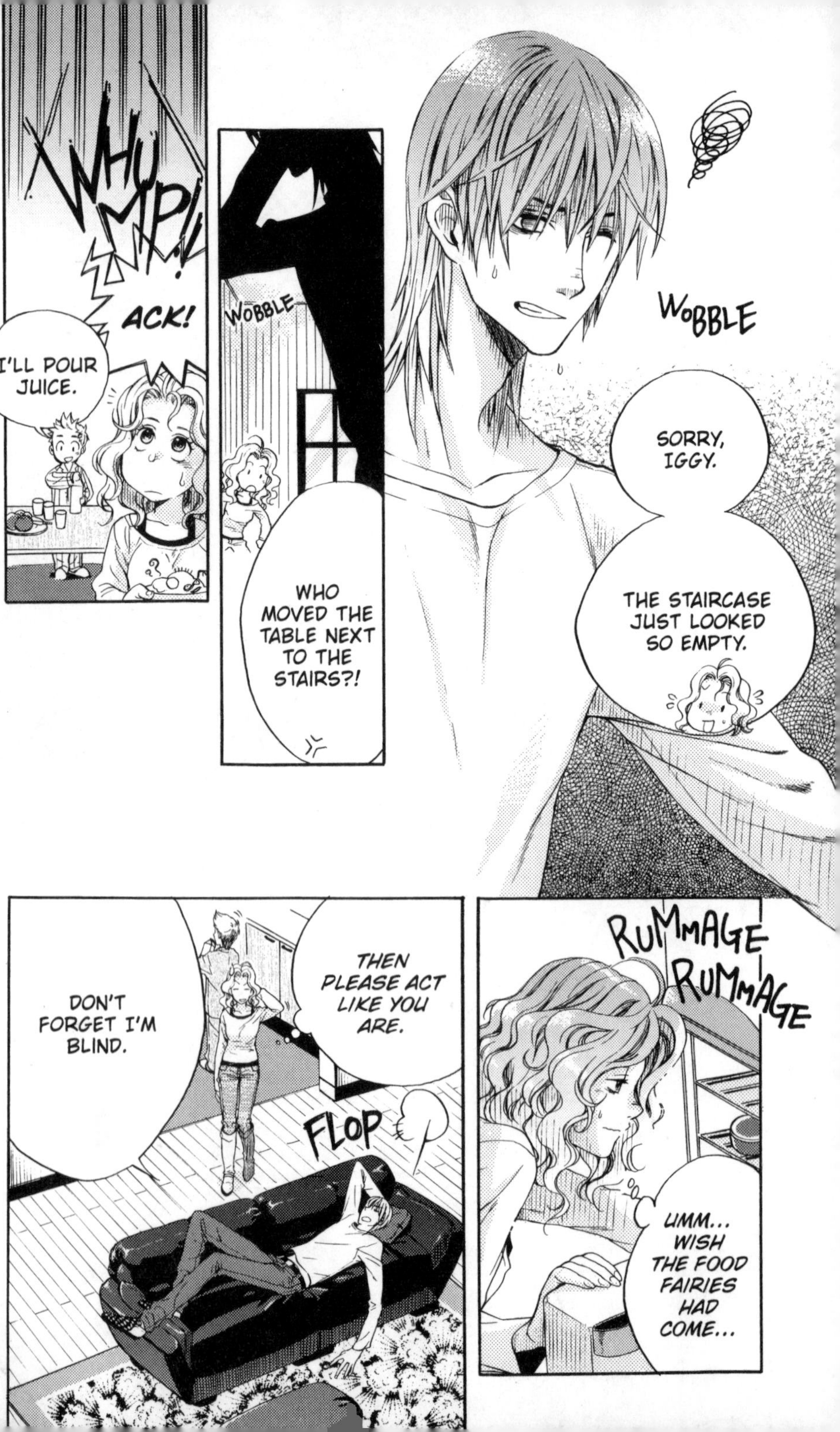
WHUMP!!
ACK!
I'LL POUR JUICE.
WOBBLE
WHO MOVED THE TABLE NEXT TO THE STAIRS?!
WOBBLE
SORRY, IGGY.
THE STAIRCASE JUST LOOKED SO EMPTY.
DON'T FORGET I'M BLIND.
THEN PLEASE ACT LIKE YOU ARE.
FLOP
RUMMAGE RUMMAGE
UMM... WISH THE FOOD FAIRIES HAD COME...

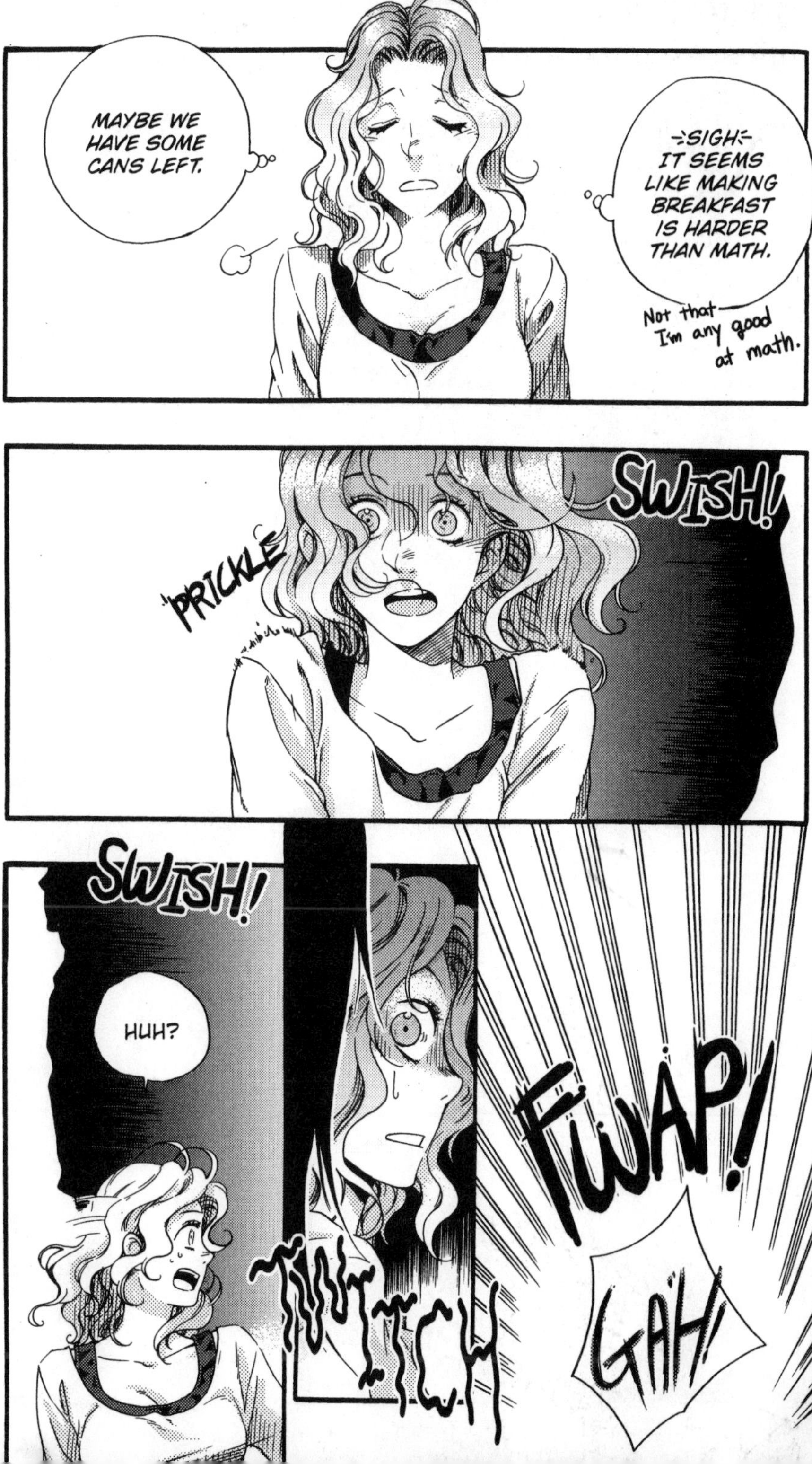
MAYBE WE HAVE SOME CANS LEFT.
=SIGH= IT SEEMS LIKE MAKING BREAKFAST IS HARDER THAN MATH.
Not that I'm any good at math.
PRICKLE
SWISH!
SWISH!
HUH?
TWITCH
FWAP!
GAH!

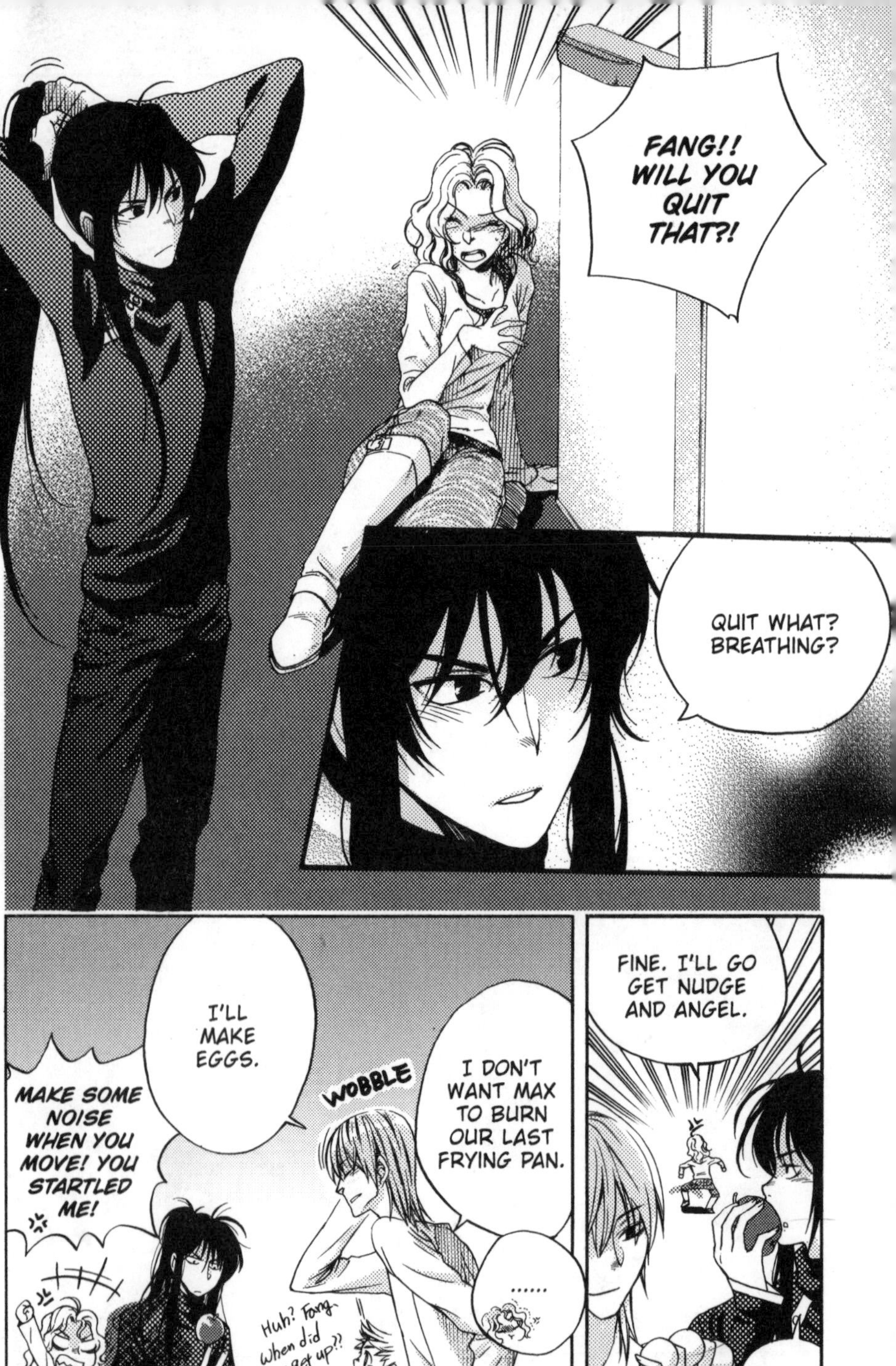
FANG!! WILL YOU QUIT THAT?!
QUIT WHAT? BREATHING?
MAKE SOME NOISE WHEN YOU MOVE! YOU STARTLED ME!
I'LL MAKE EGGS.
WOBBLE
I DON'T WANT MAX TO BURN OUR LAST FRYING PAN.
......
Huh? Fang~ When did you get up??
FINE. I'LL GO GET NUDGE AND ANGEL.
......

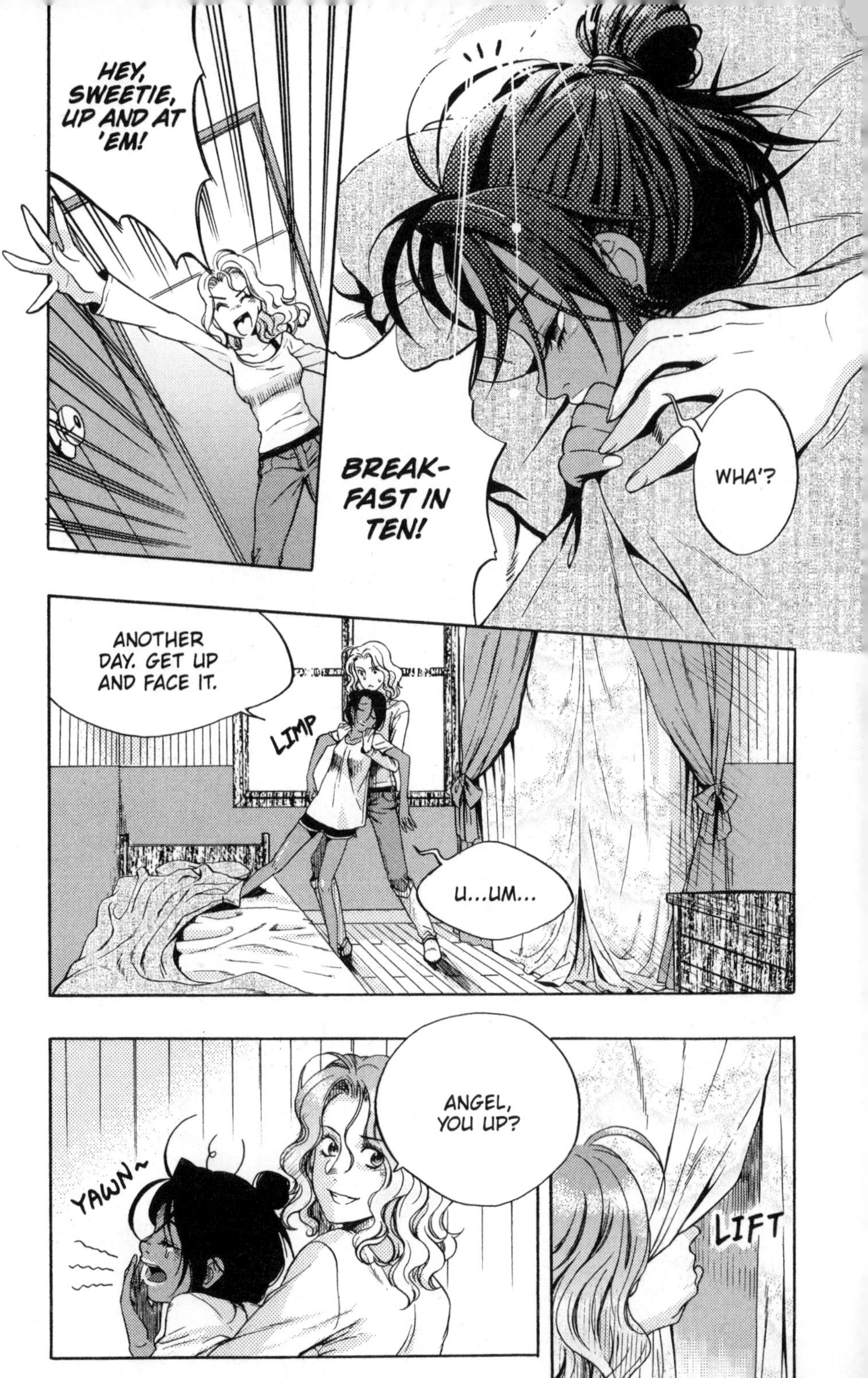
HEY, SWEETIE, UP AND AT 'EM!
BREAK-FAST IN TEN!
WHA'?
ANOTHER DAY. GET UP AND FACE IT.
LIMP
U...UM...
YAWN~
ANGEL, YOU UP?
LIFT

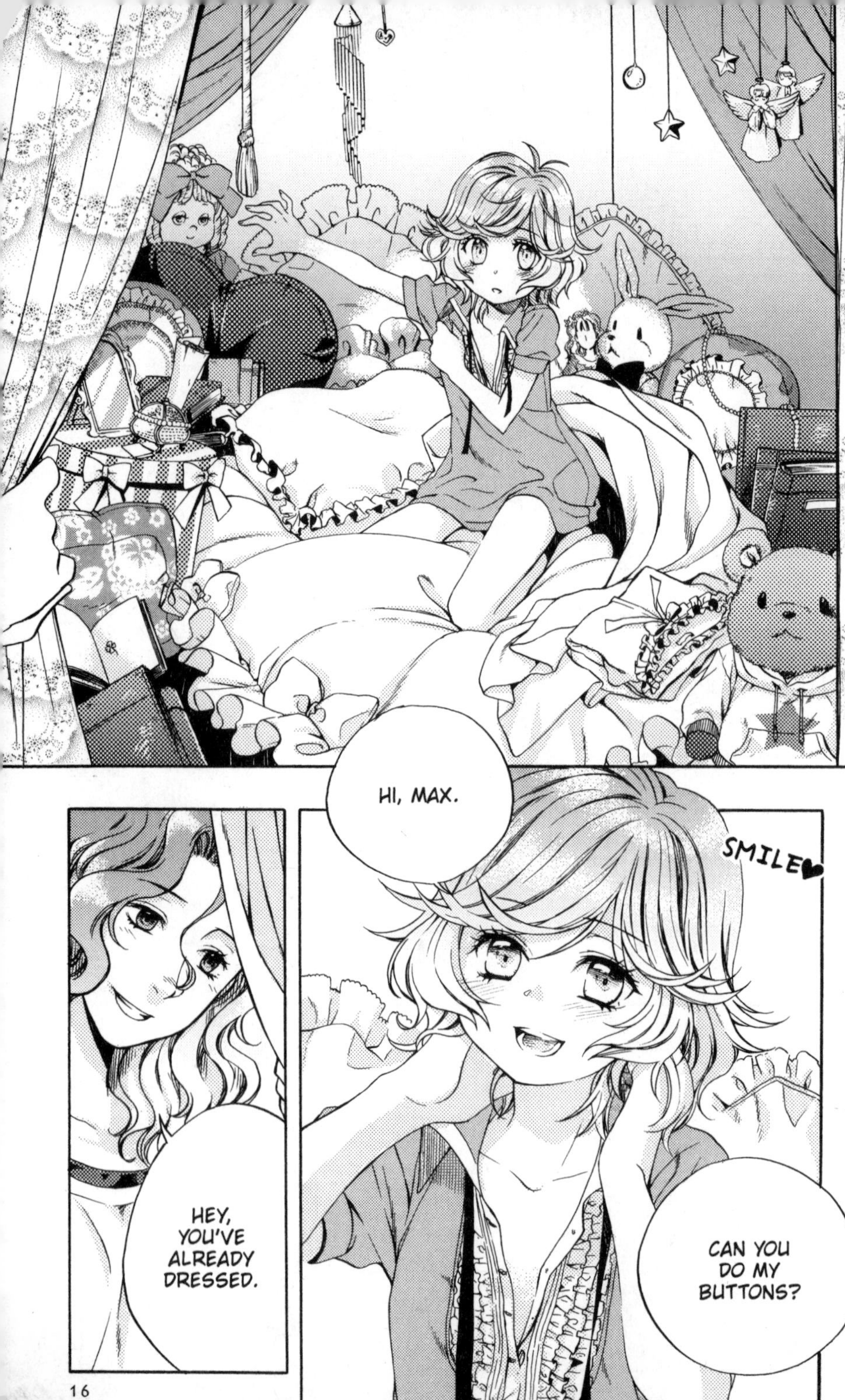
HI, MAX.
HEY, YOU'VE ALREADY DRESSED.
SMILE♥
CAN YOU DO MY BUTTONS?

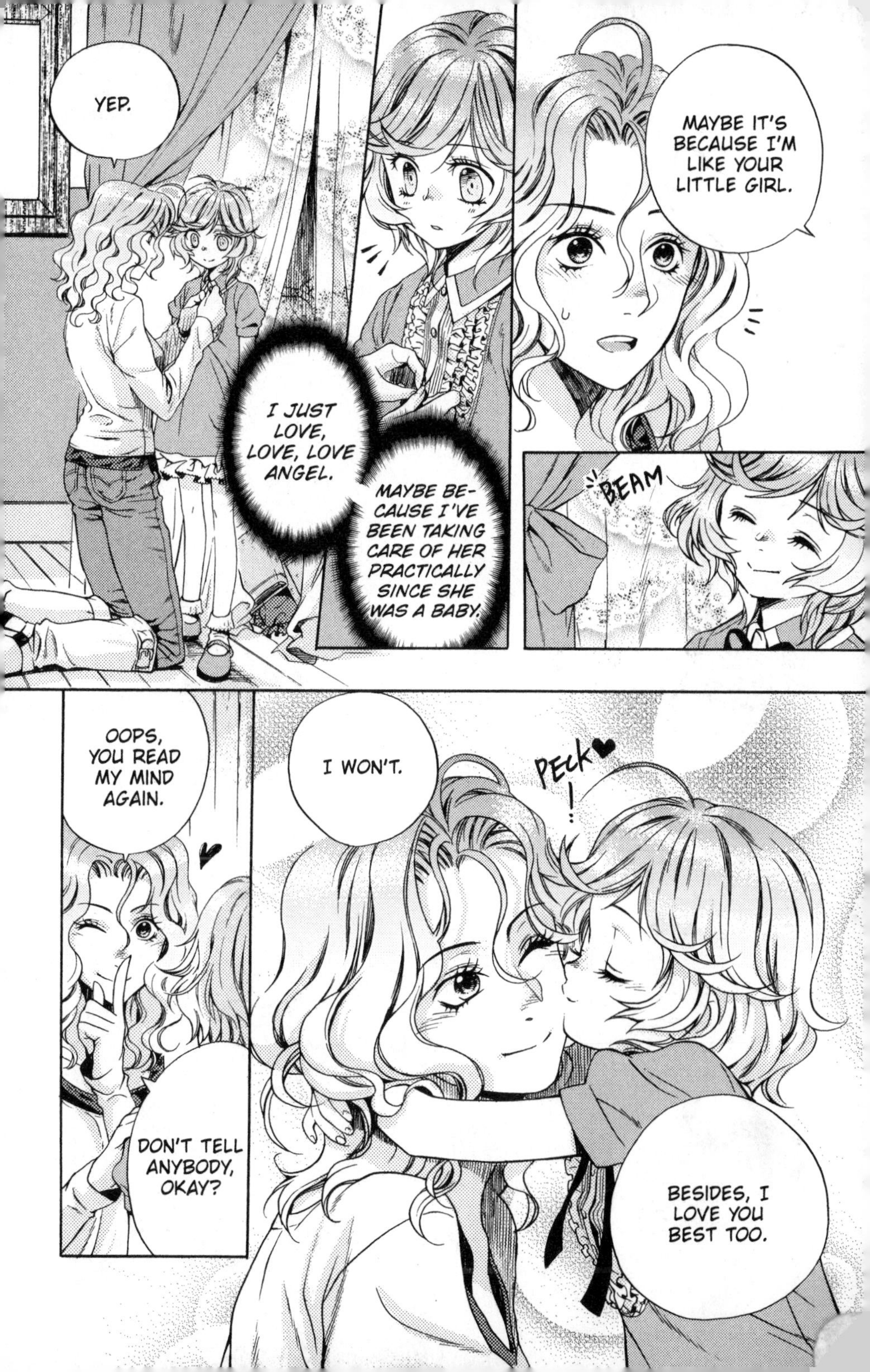
YEP.
I JUST LOVE, LOVE, LOVE ANGEL.
MAYBE BE-CAUSE I'VE BEEN TAKING CARE OF HER PRACTICALLY SINCE SHE WAS A BABY.
MAYBE IT'S BECAUSE I'M LIKE YOUR LITTLE GIRL.
BEAM
OOPS, YOU READ MY MIND AGAIN.
DON'T TELL ANYBODY, OKAY?
I WON'T.
PECK
BESIDES, I LOVE YOU BEST TOO.

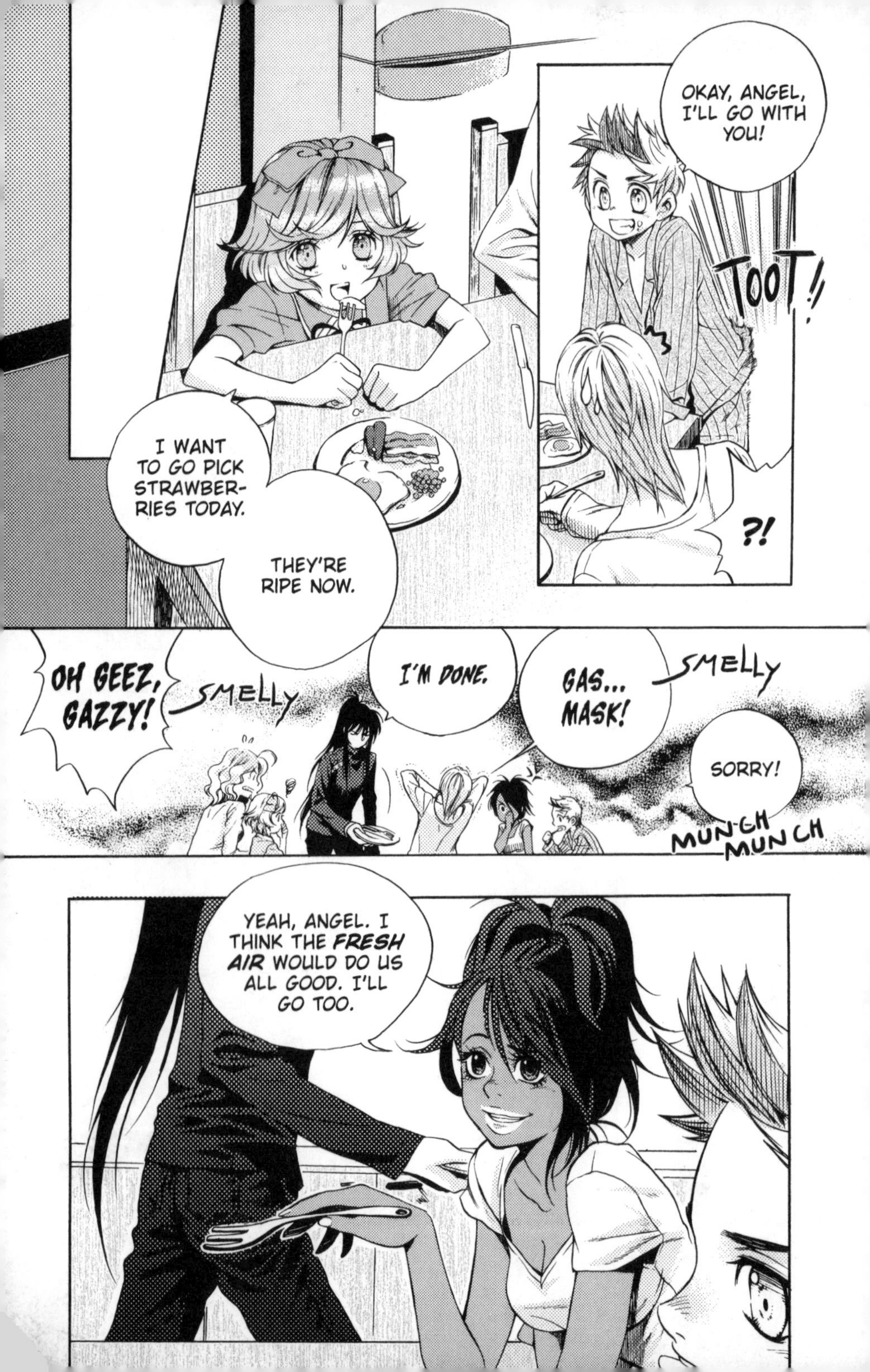
I WANT TO GO PICK STRAWBER-RIES TODAY.
THEY'RE RIPE NOW.
OKAY, ANGEL, I'LL GO WITH YOU!
TOOT!!
?!
OH GEEZ, GAZZY!
SMELLY
I'M DONE.
GAS... MASK!
SMELLY
SORRY!
MUNCH MUNCH
YEAH, ANGEL. I THINK THE *FRESH AIR* WOULD DO US ALL GOOD. I'LL GO TOO.

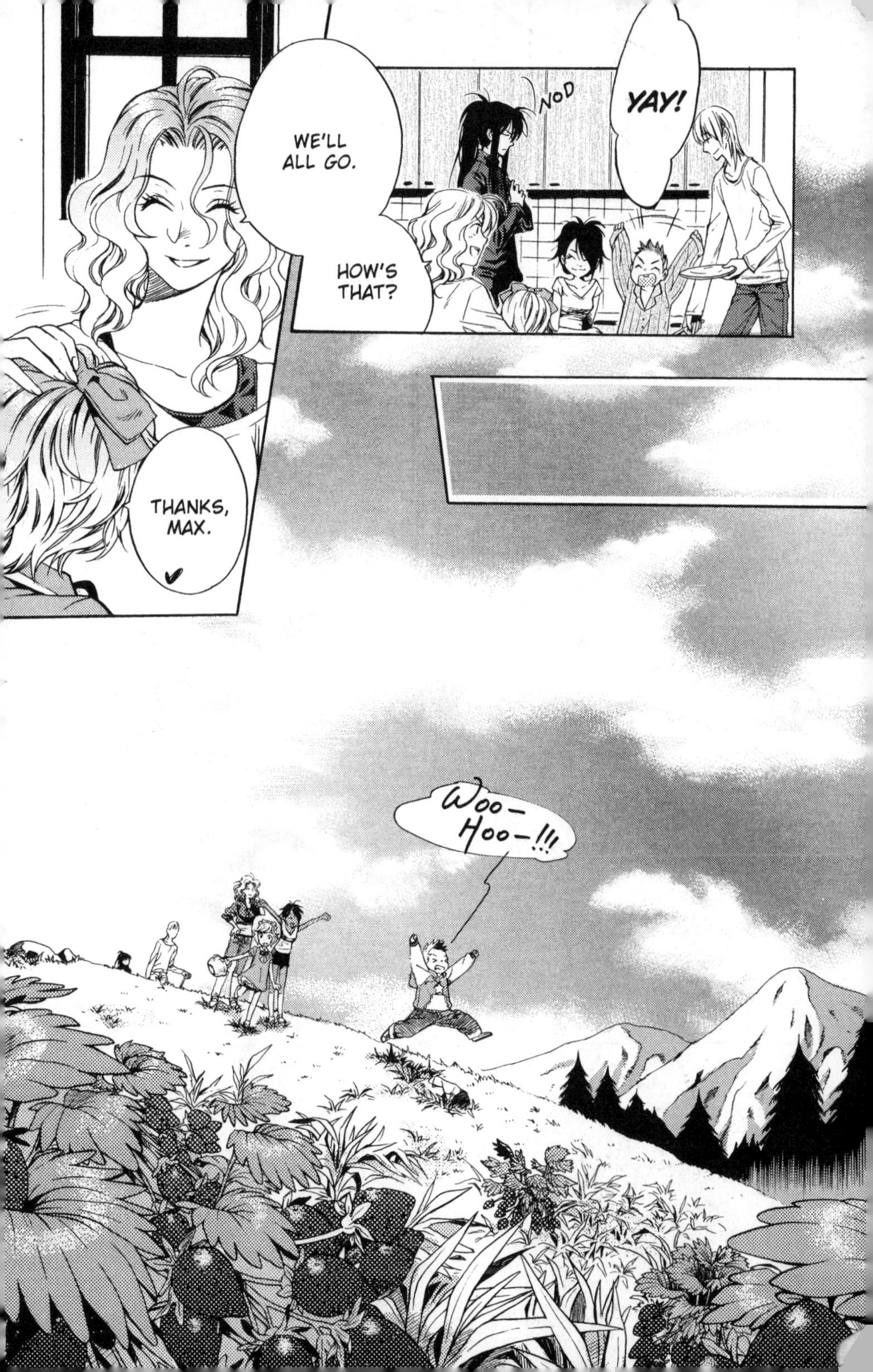
WE'LL ALL GO.
HOW'S THAT?
THANKS, MAX.
NOD
YAY!
Woo-Hoo-!!!

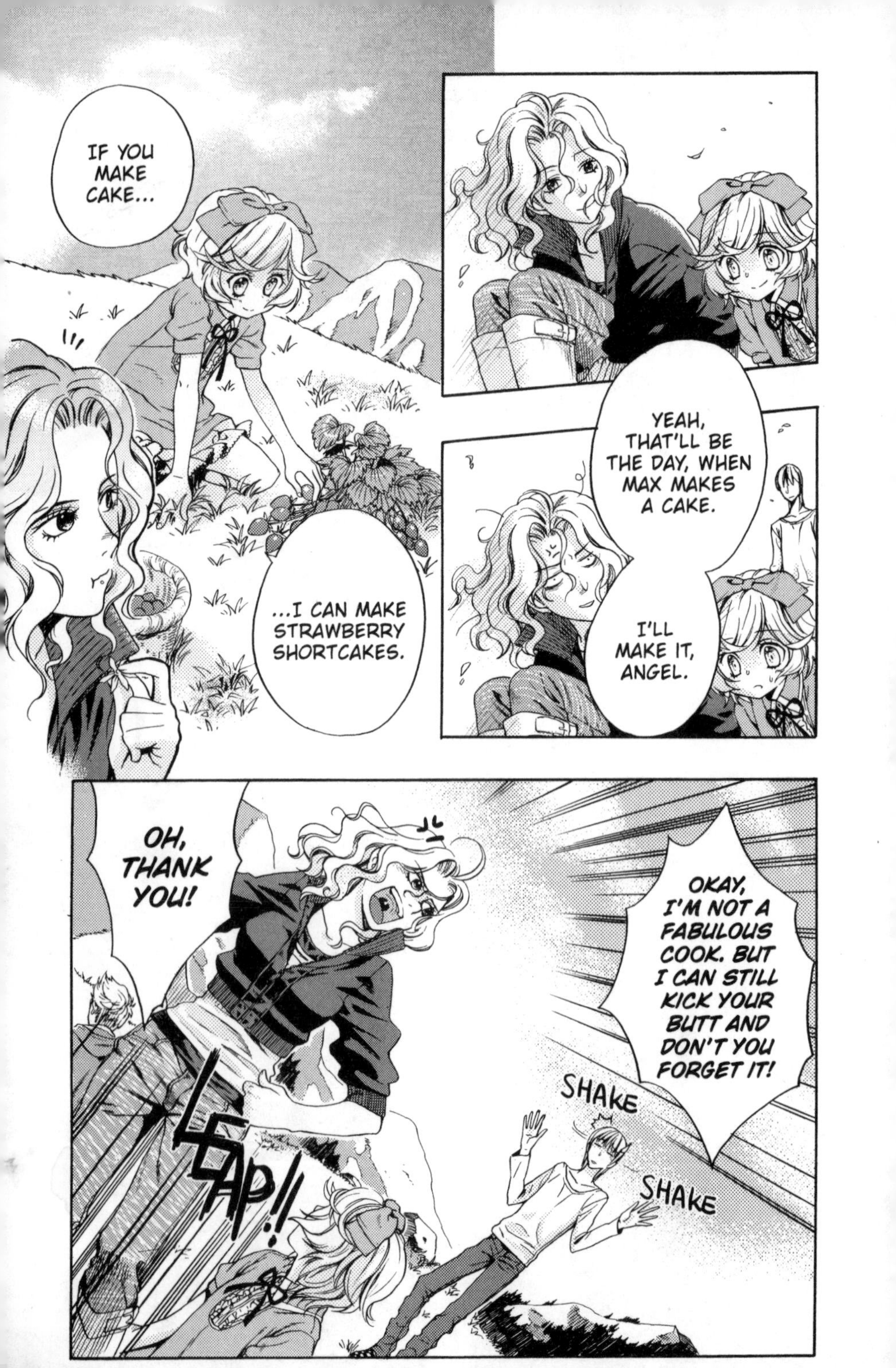
IF YOU MAKE CAKE...
...I CAN MAKE STRAWBERRY SHORTCAKES.
YEAH, THAT'LL BE THE DAY, WHEN MAX MAKES A CAKE.
I'LL MAKE IT, ANGEL.
OH, THANK YOU!
LEAP!!
OKAY, I'M NOT A FABULOUS COOK. BUT I CAN STILL KICK YOUR BUTT AND DON'T YOU FORGET IT!
SHAKE
SHAKE

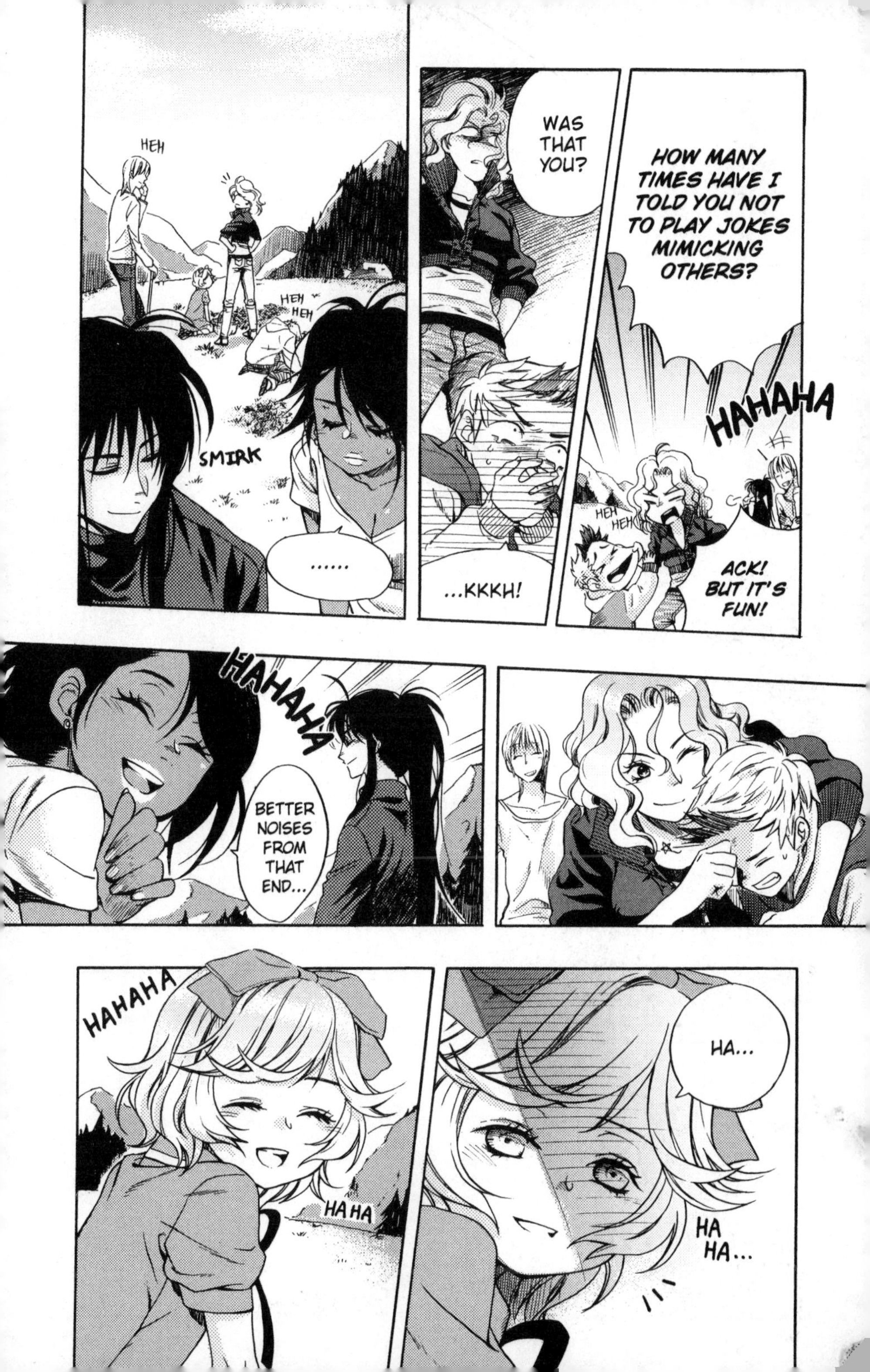
HEH
HEH HEH
SMIRK
......
WAS THAT YOU?
...KKKH!
HOW MANY TIMES HAVE I TOLD YOU NOT TO PLAY JOKES MIMICKING OTHERS?
HAHAHA
HEH HEH
ACK! BUT IT'S FUN!
HAHAHA
BETTER NOISES FROM THAT END...
HAHAHA
HA HA
HA...
HA HA...

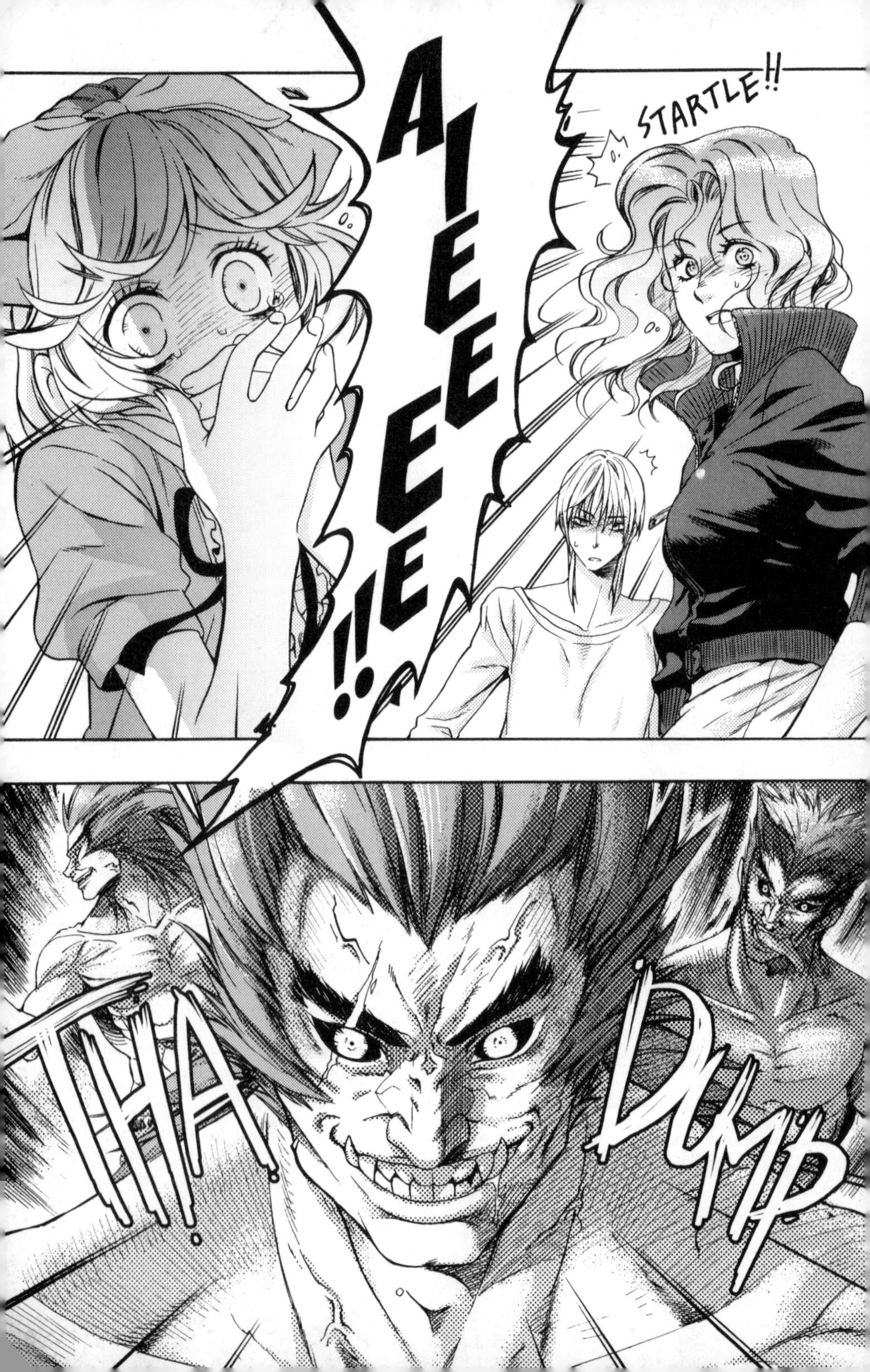
AIEEEEE!!
STARTLE!!
THA-DUMP

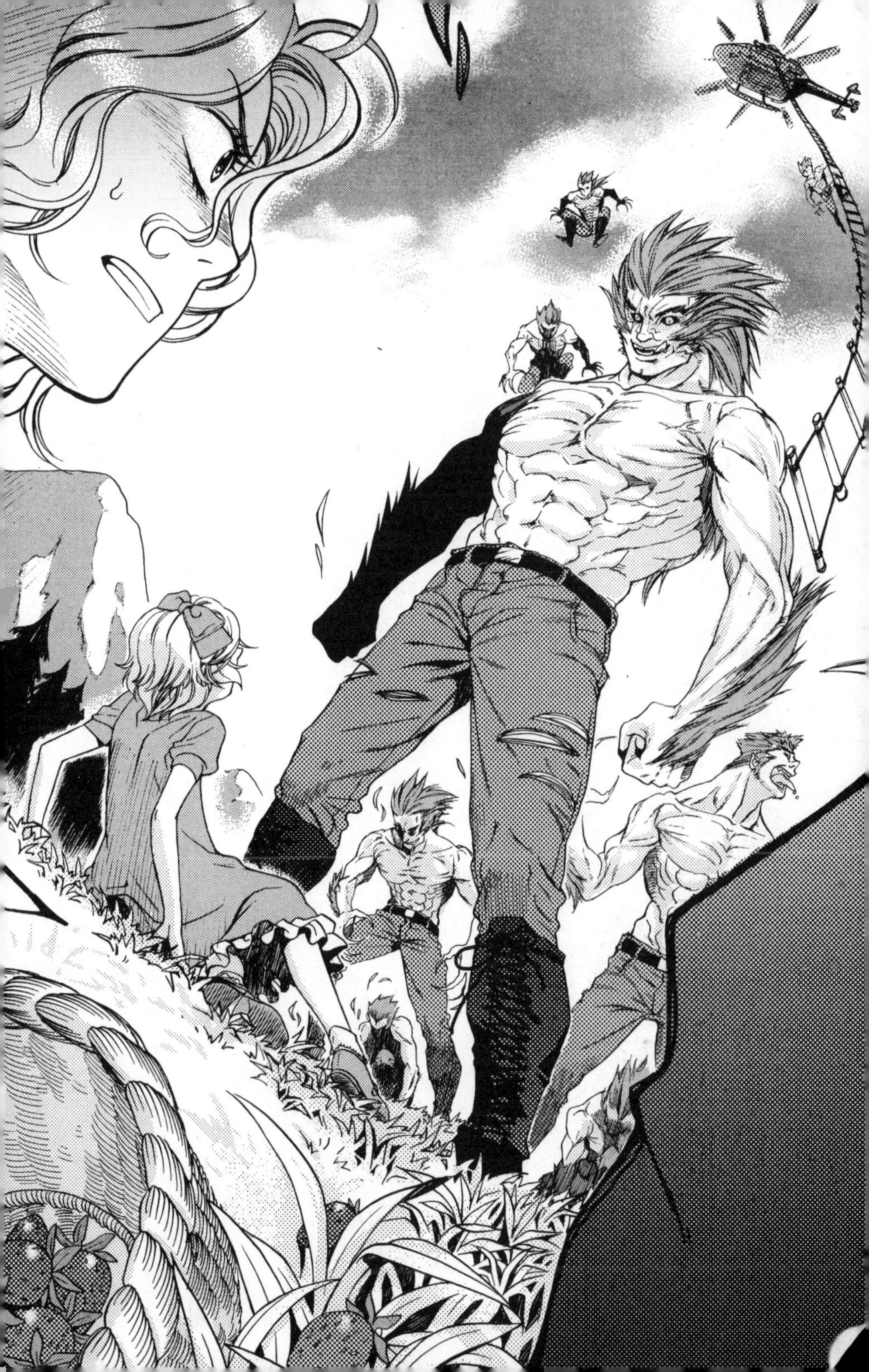

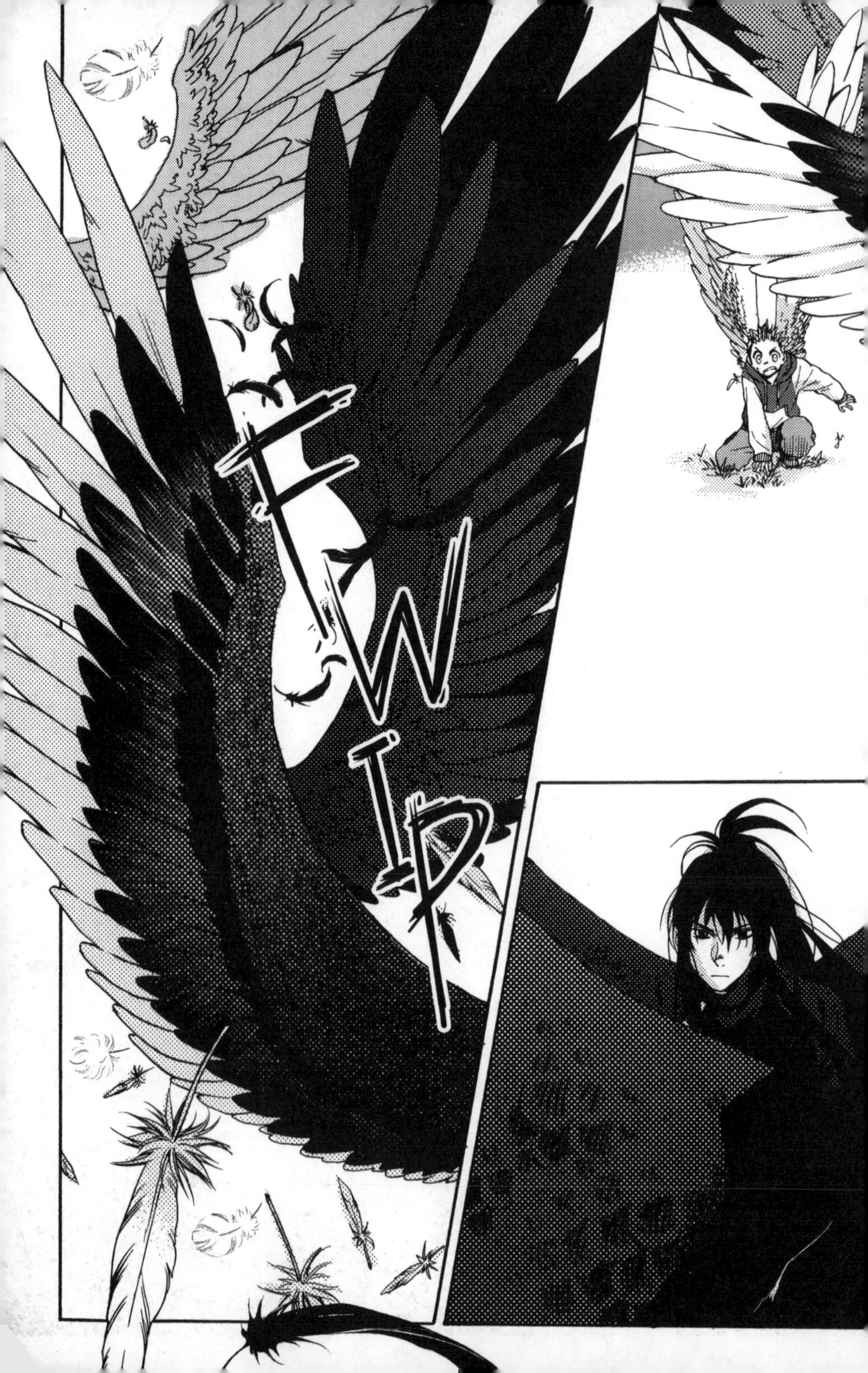
FWIP

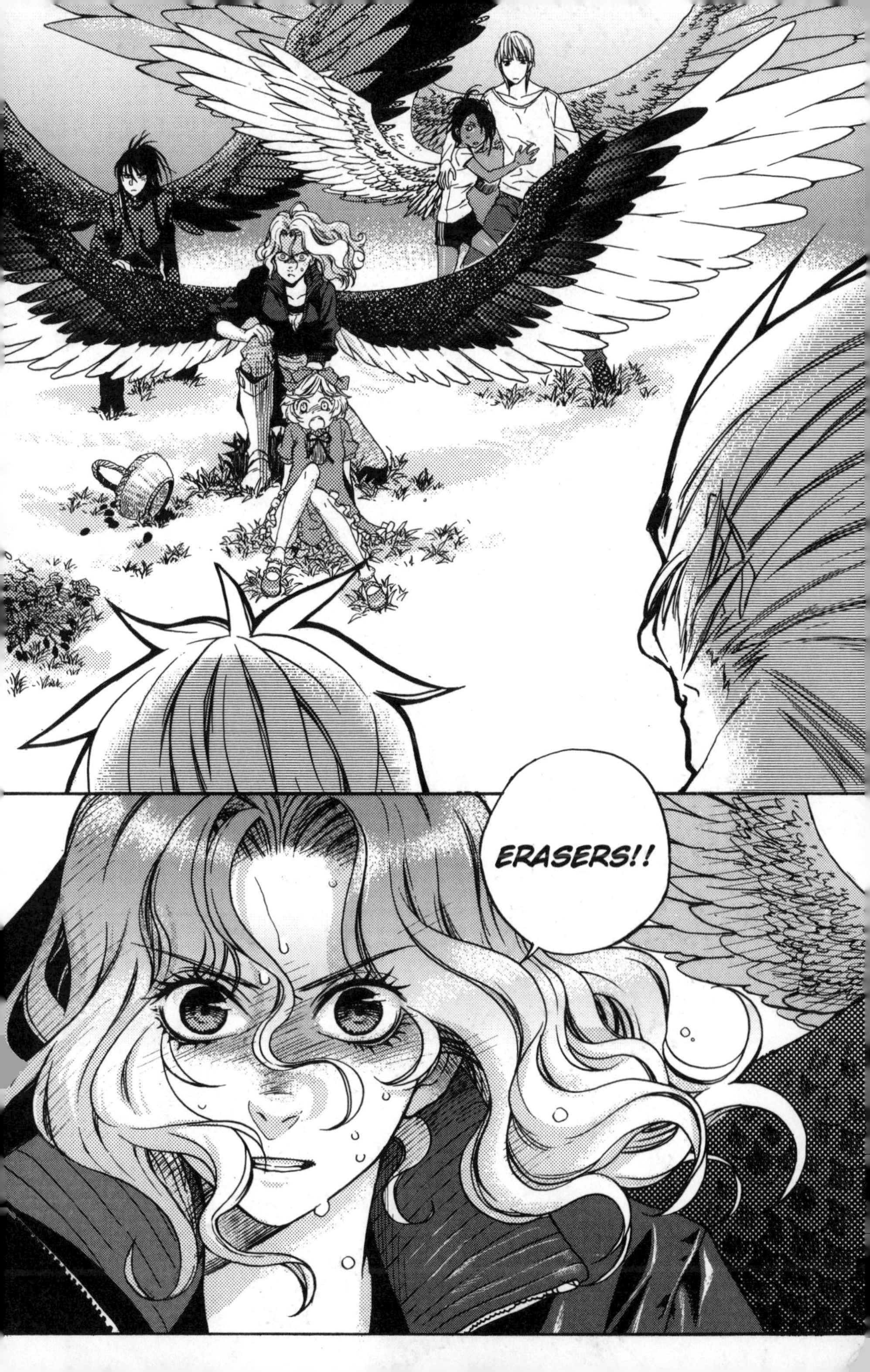
ERASERS!!

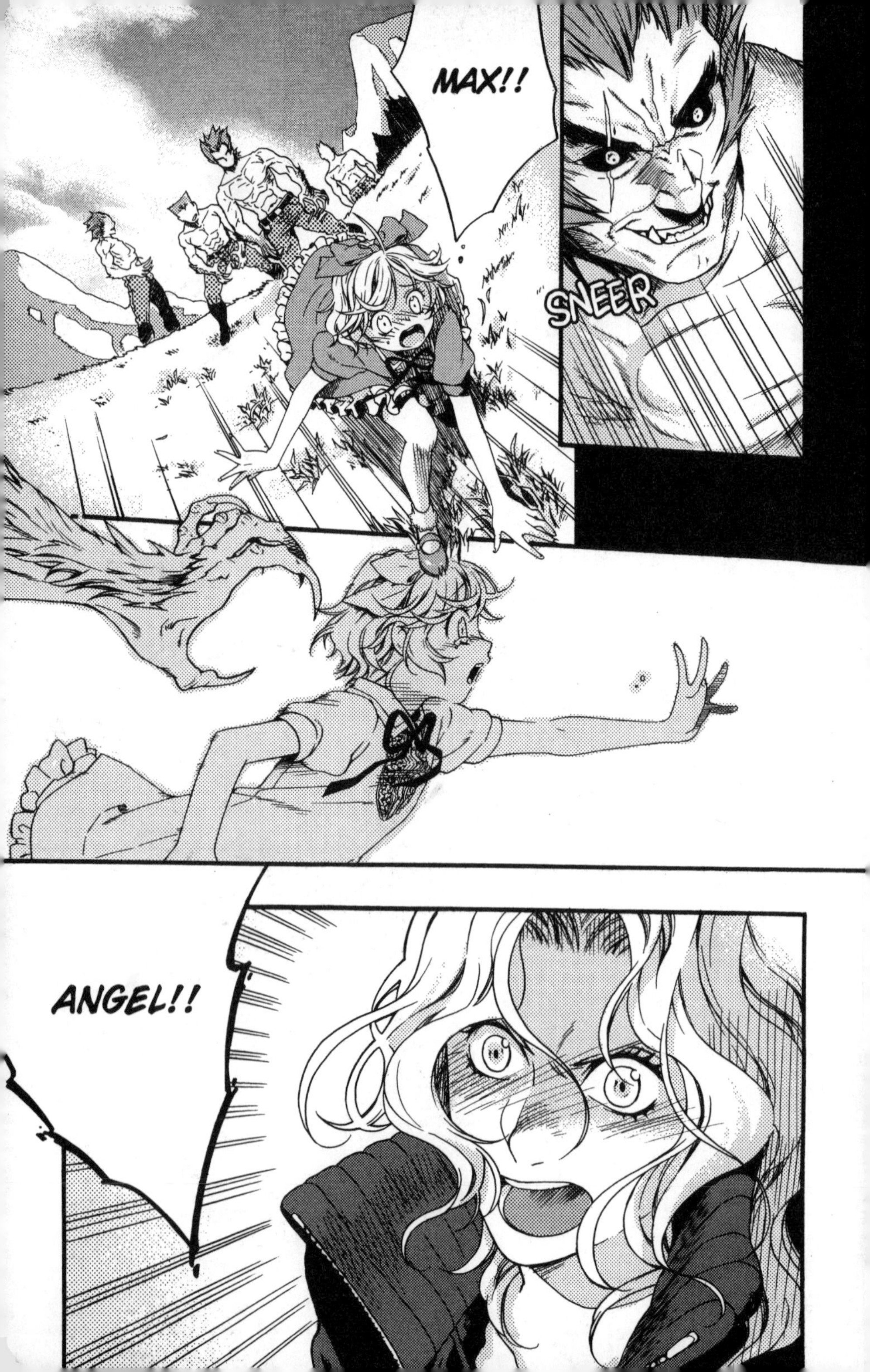
MAX!!
SNEER
ANGEL!!

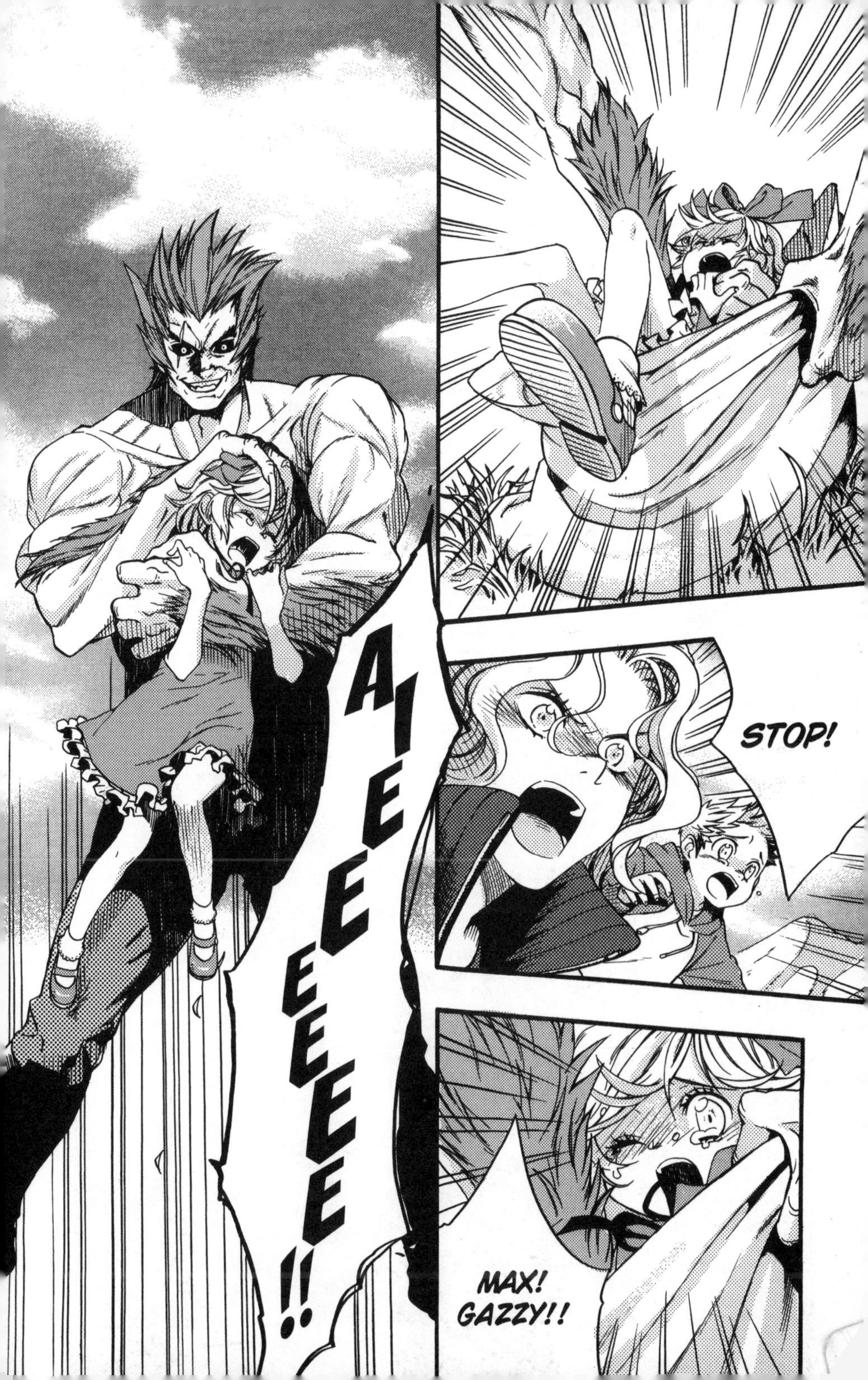
AIEEEEEEE!!
STOP!
MAX! GAZZY!!

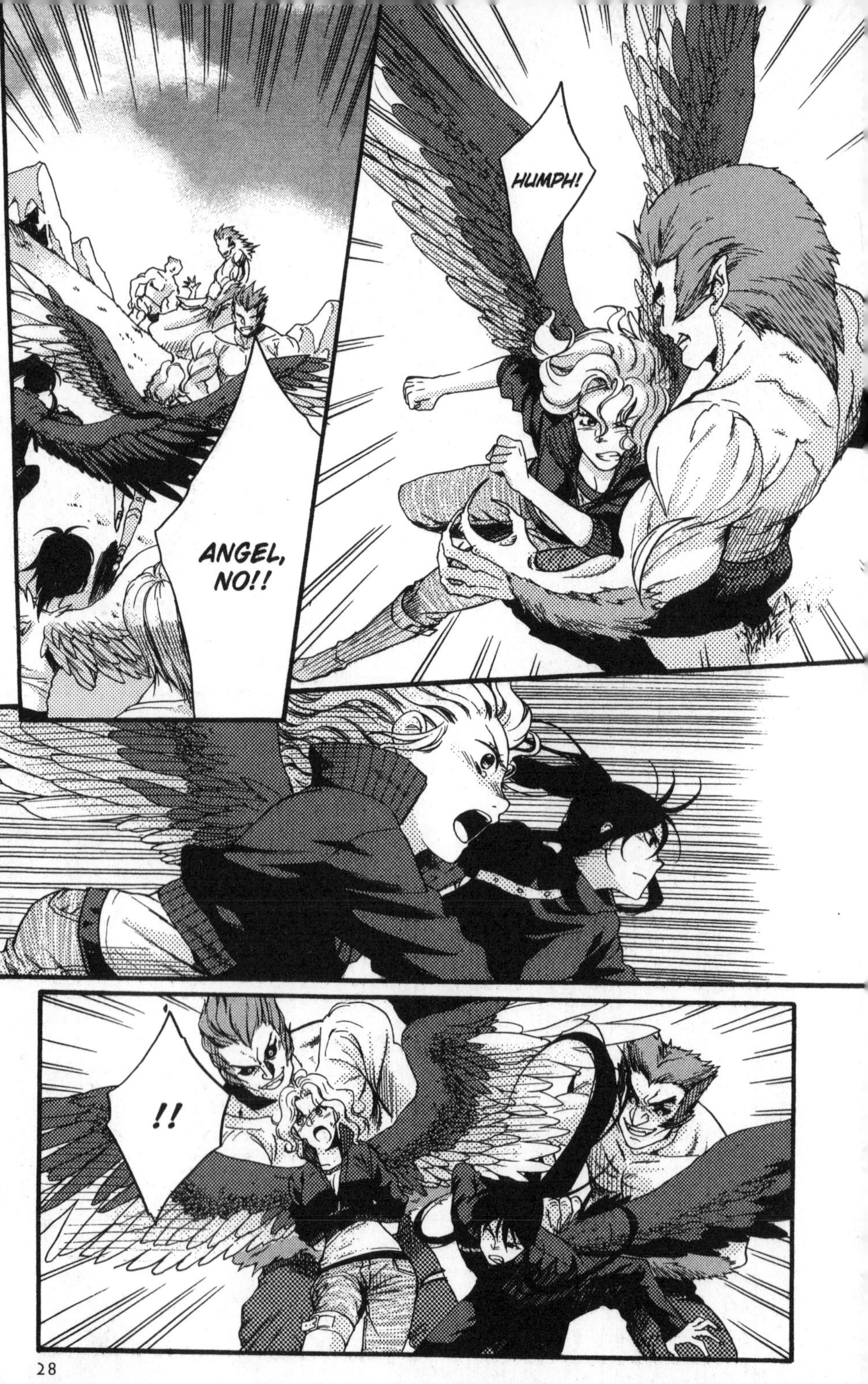
ANGEL, NO!!
HUMPH!
!!

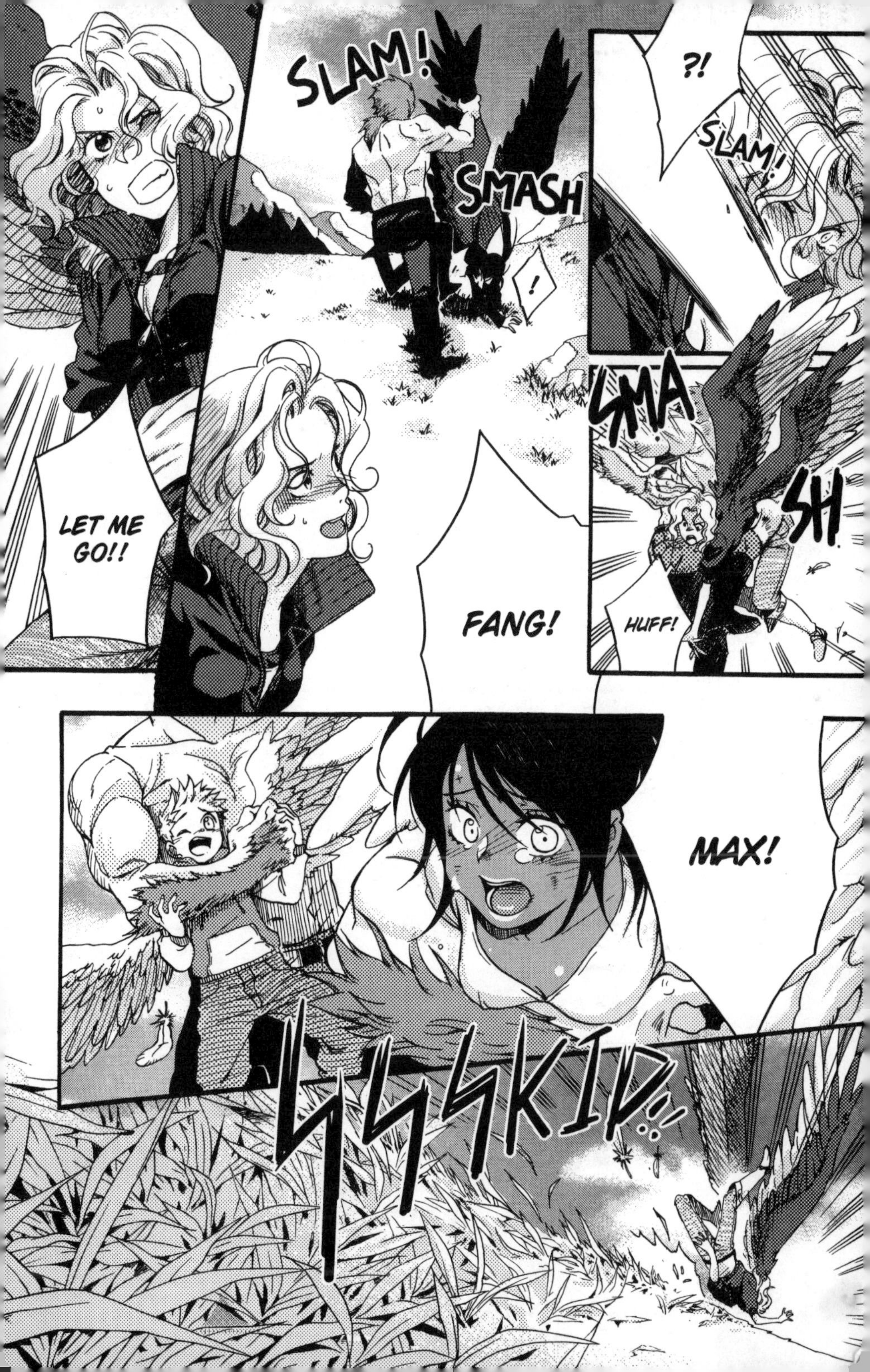
LET ME GO!!
SLAM!
SMASH
!
FANG!
?!
SLAM!
SMASH
HUFF!
MAX!
SSSKID!!

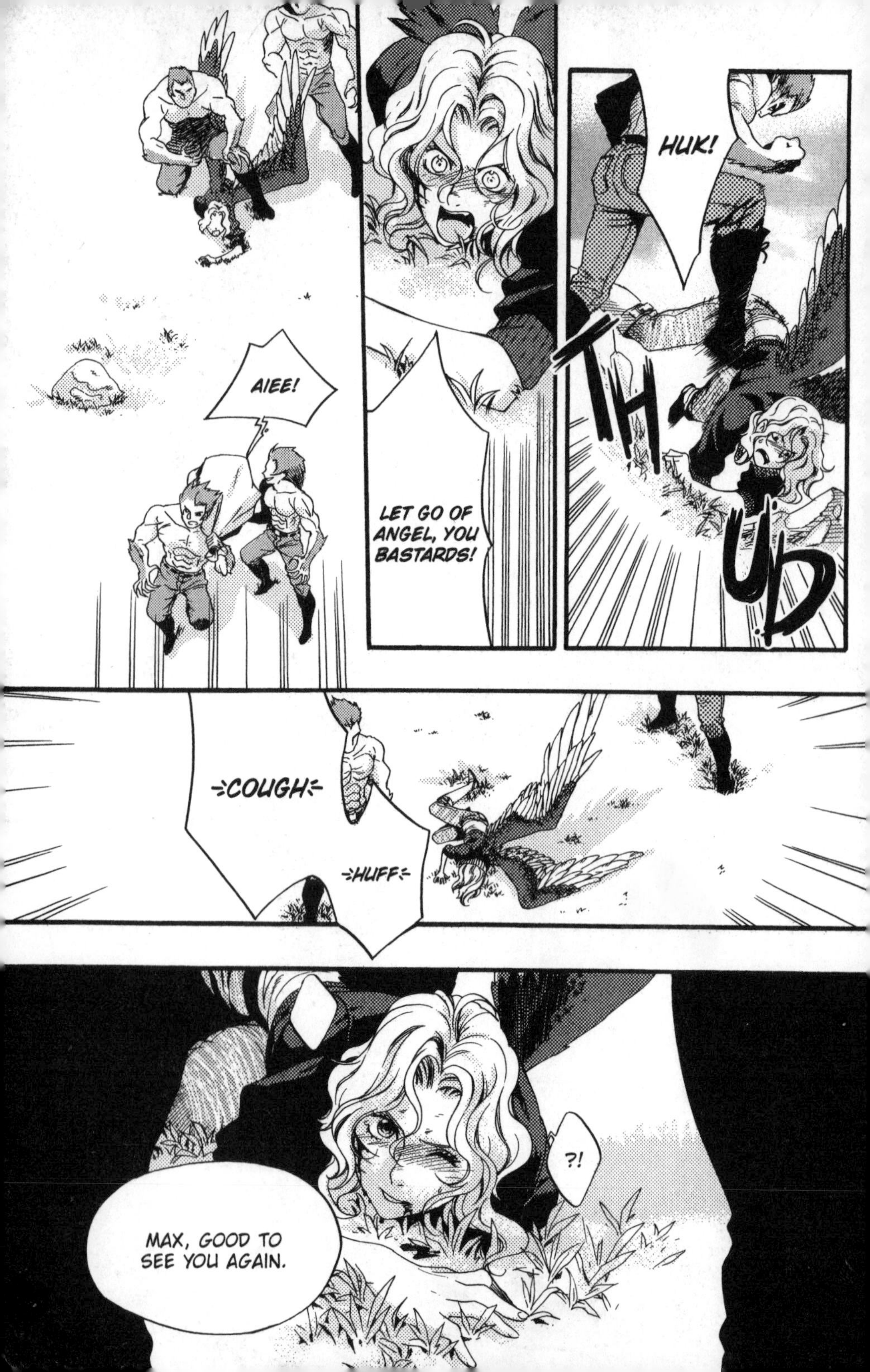
AIEE!
LET GO OF ANGEL, YOU BASTARDS!
HUK!
THUD
-COUGH-
-HUFF-
?!
MAX, GOOD TO SEE YOU AGAIN.

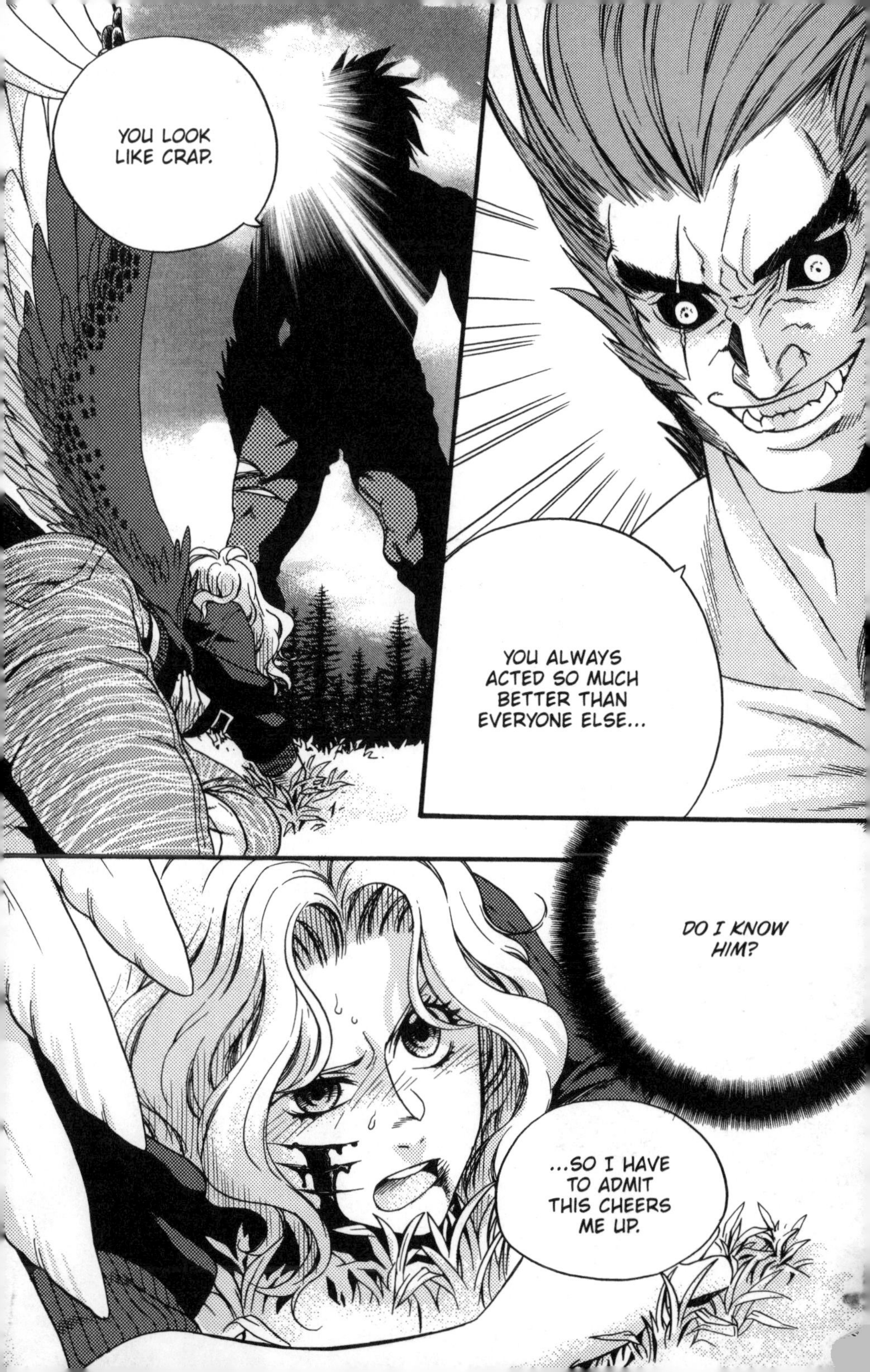
YOU LOOK LIKE CRAP.
YOU ALWAYS ACTED SO MUCH BETTER THAN EVERYONE ELSE...
DO I KNOW HIM?
...SO I HAVE TO ADMIT THIS CHEERS ME UP.

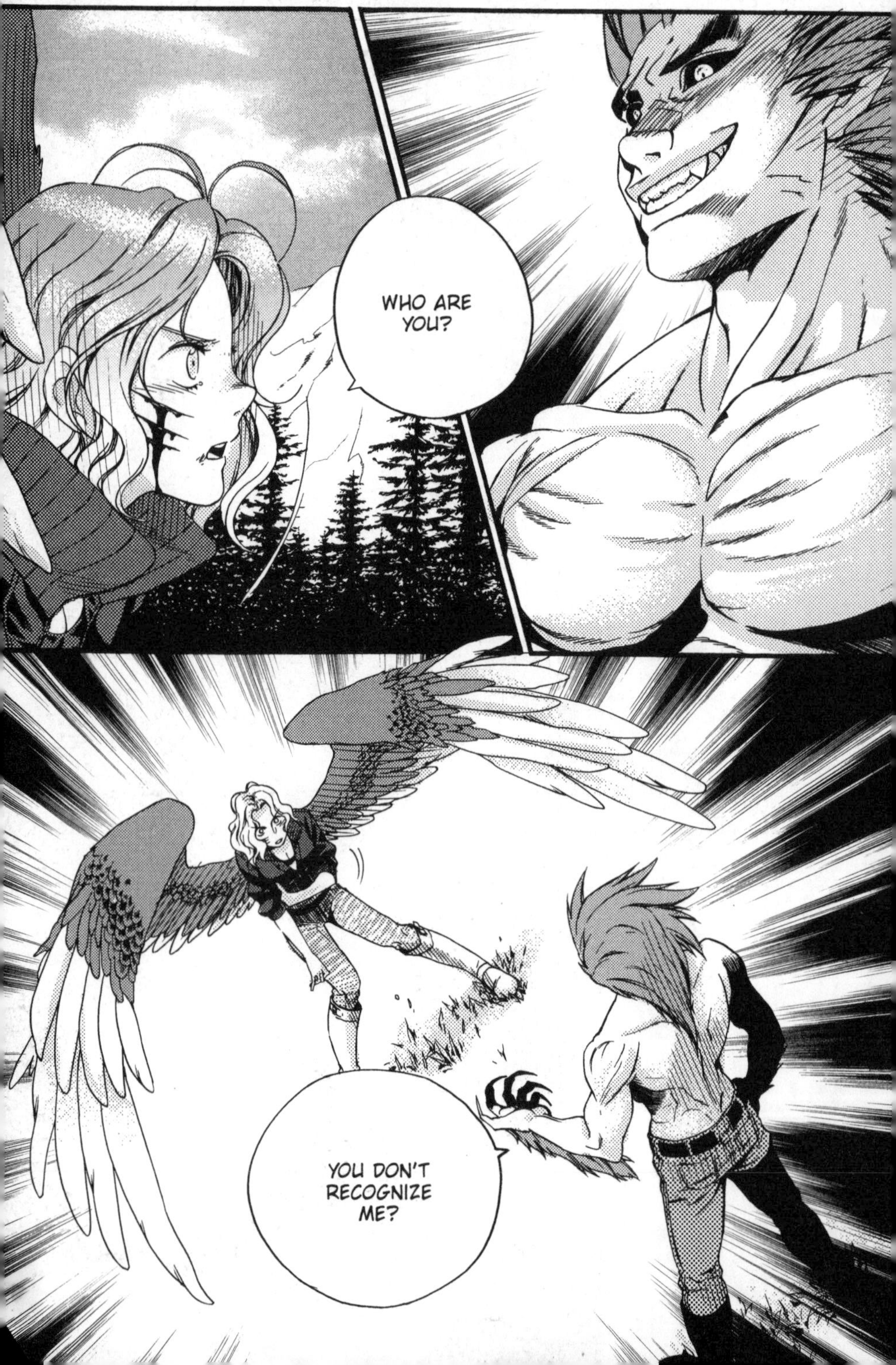
WHO ARE YOU?
YOU DON'T RECOGNIZE ME?

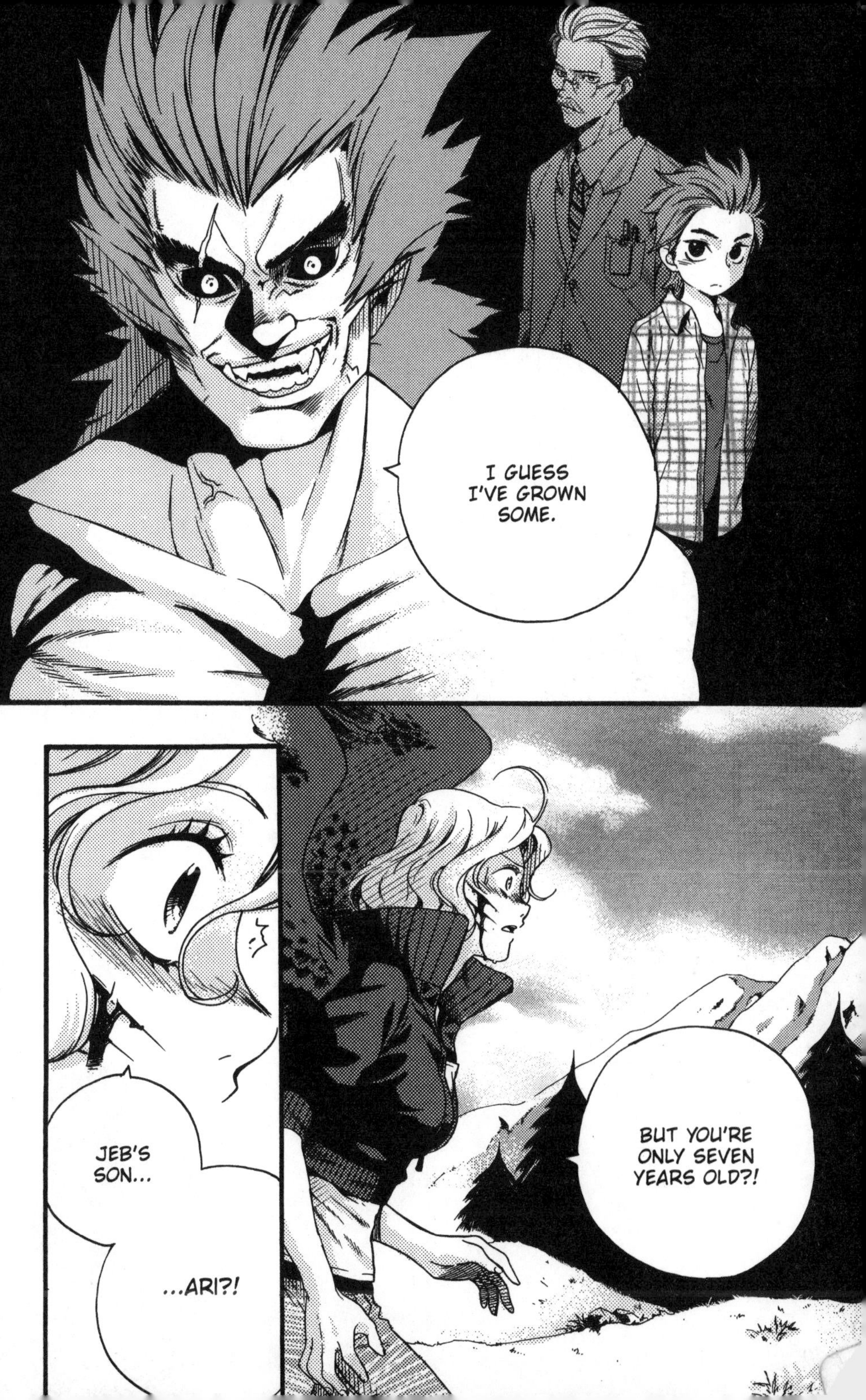
I GUESS I'VE GROWN SOME.
JEB'S SON...
...ARI?!
BUT YOU'RE ONLY SEVEN YEARS OLD?!

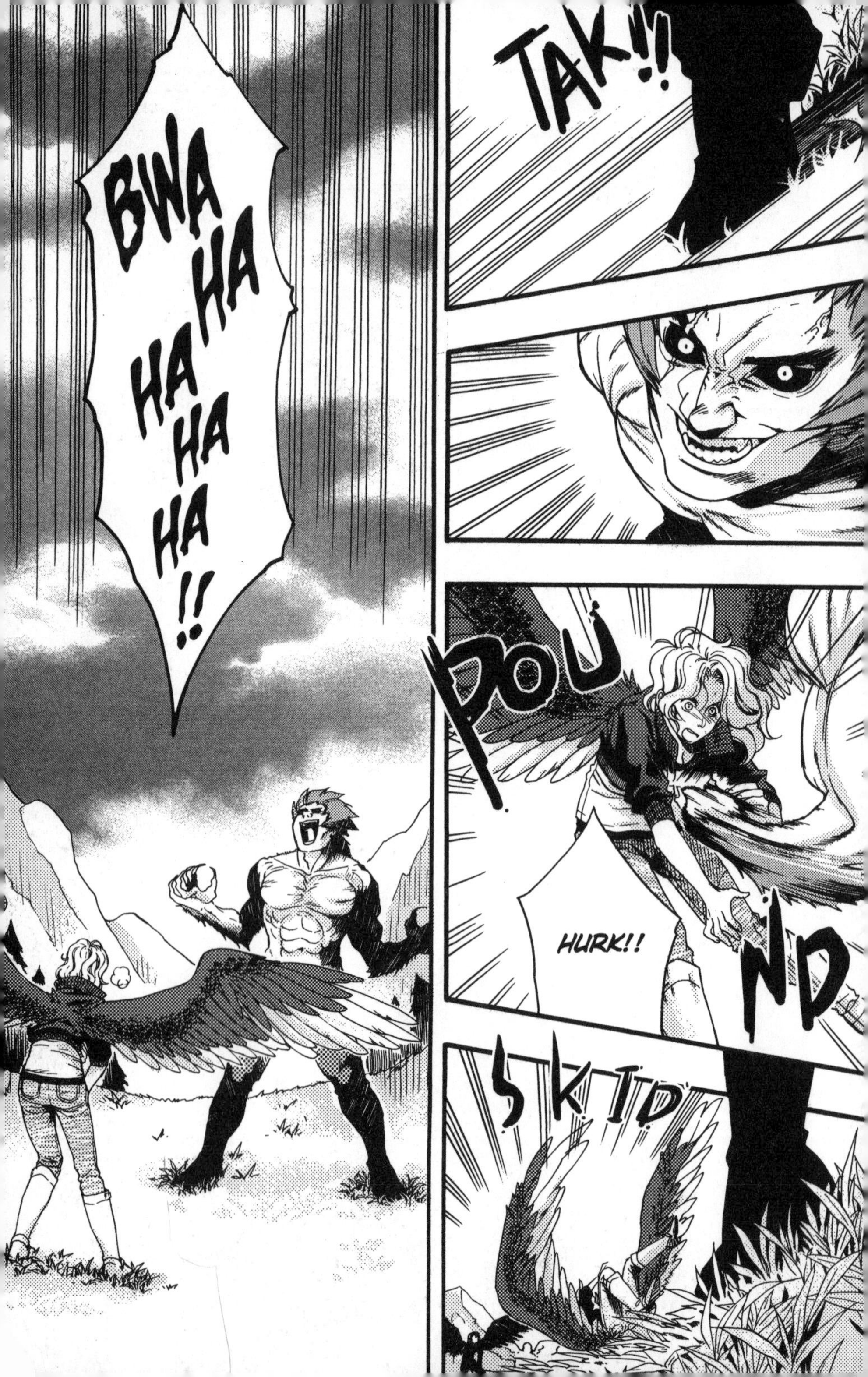
BWA HA HA HA HA HA!!
TAK!!
POUND
HURK!!
SKID

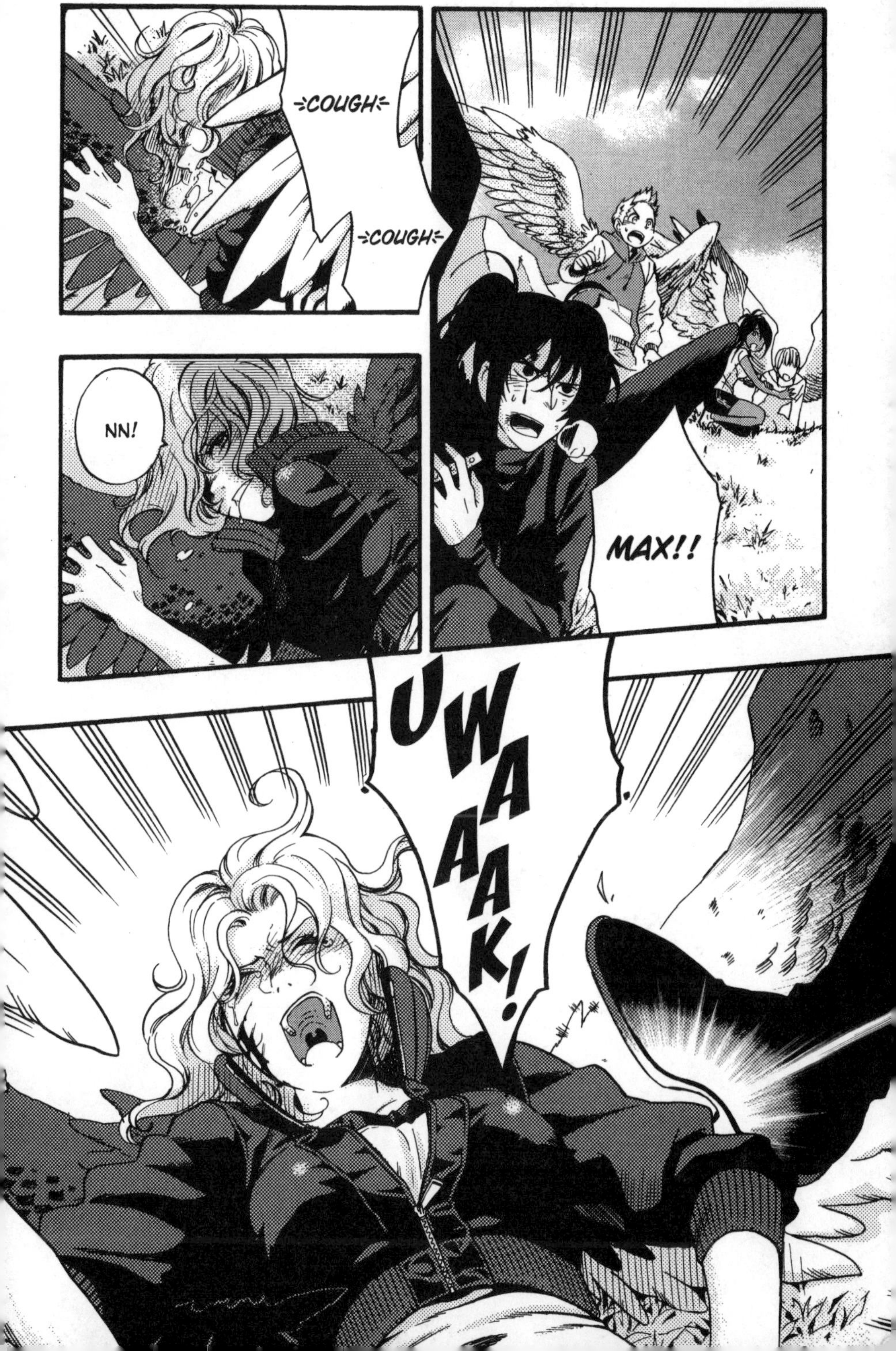
=COUGH=
=COUGH=
MAX!!
NN!
UWAAAK!

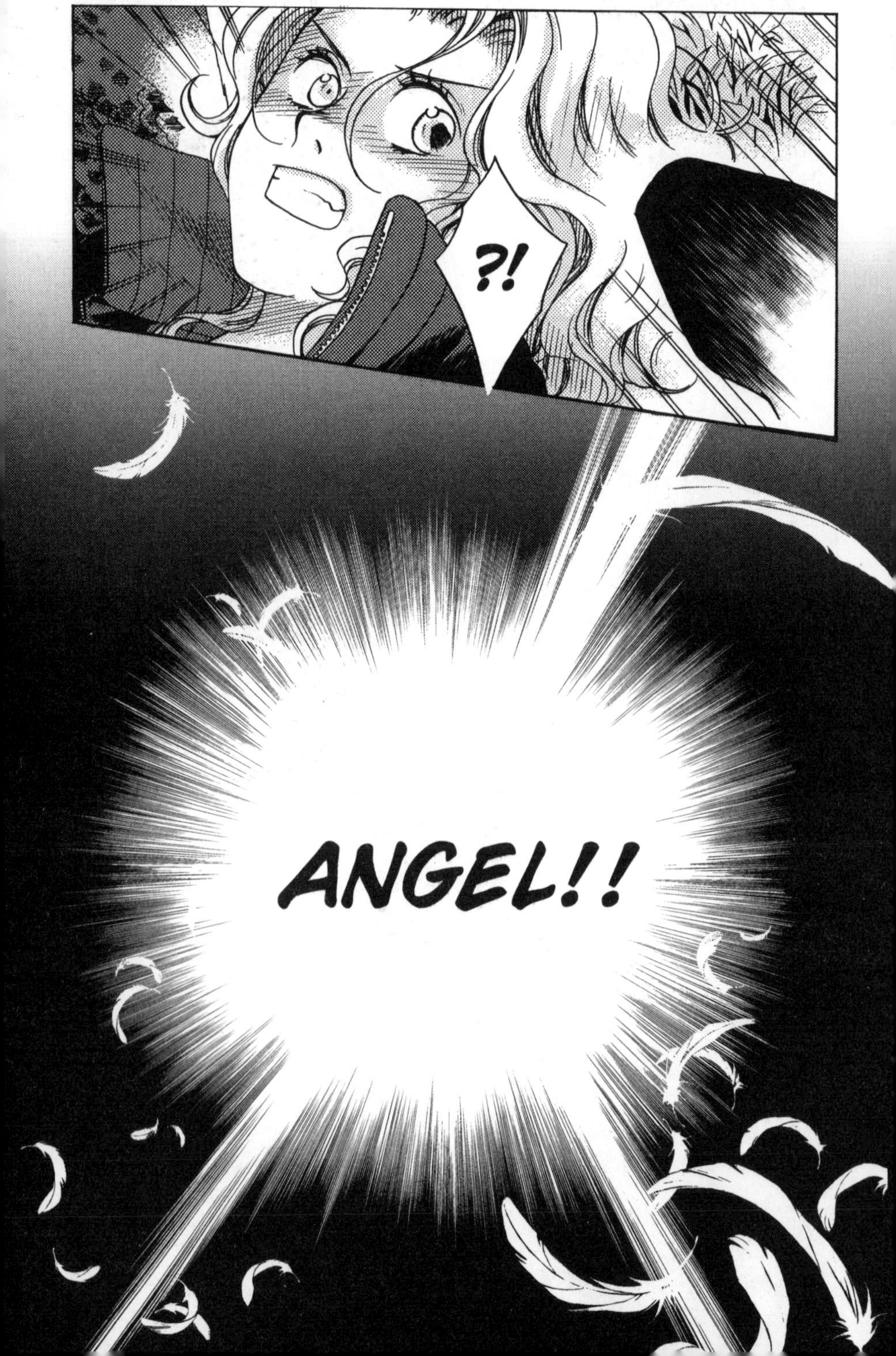
?!
ANGEL!!

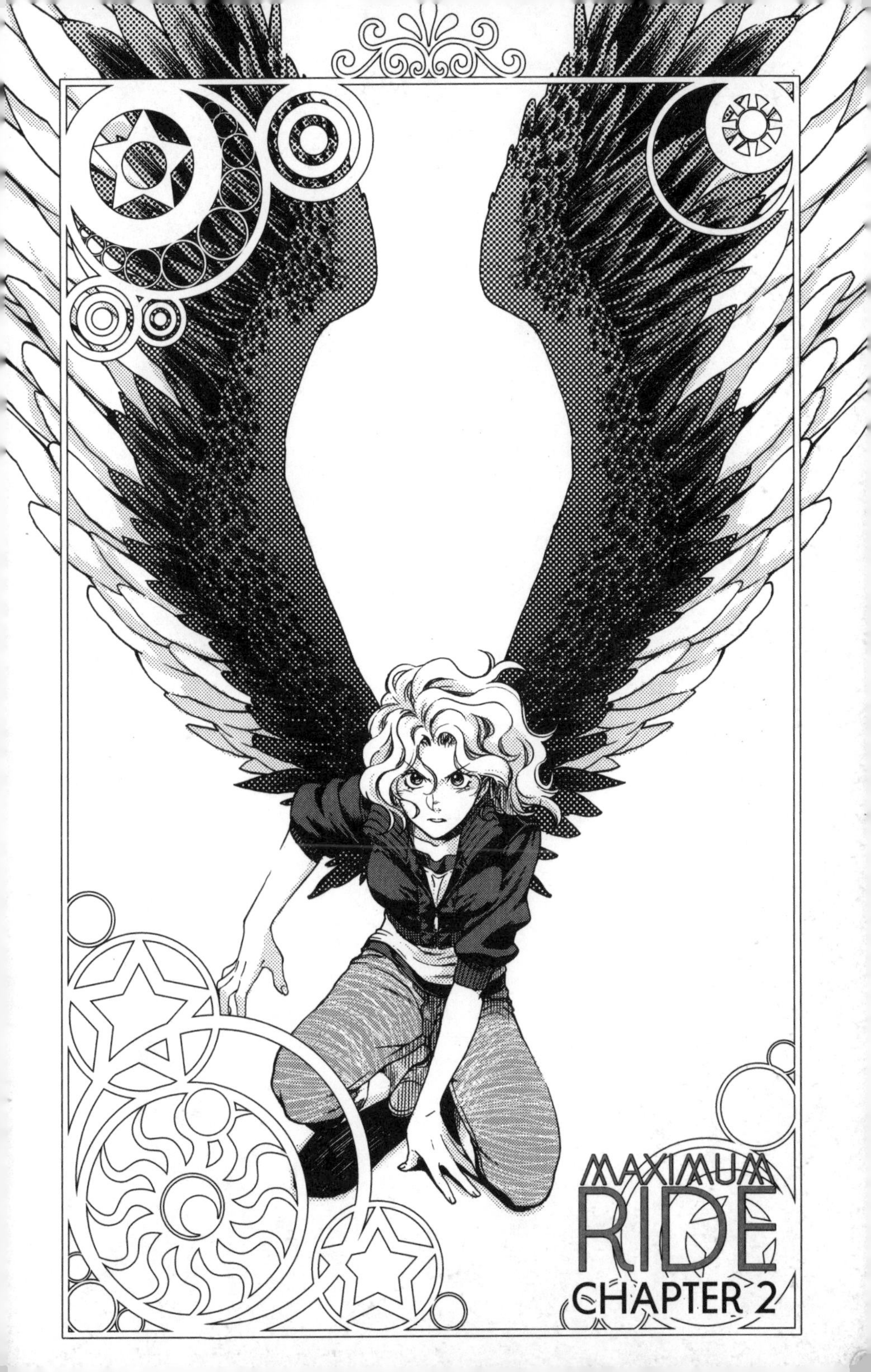
MAXIMUM
RIDE
CHAPTER 2

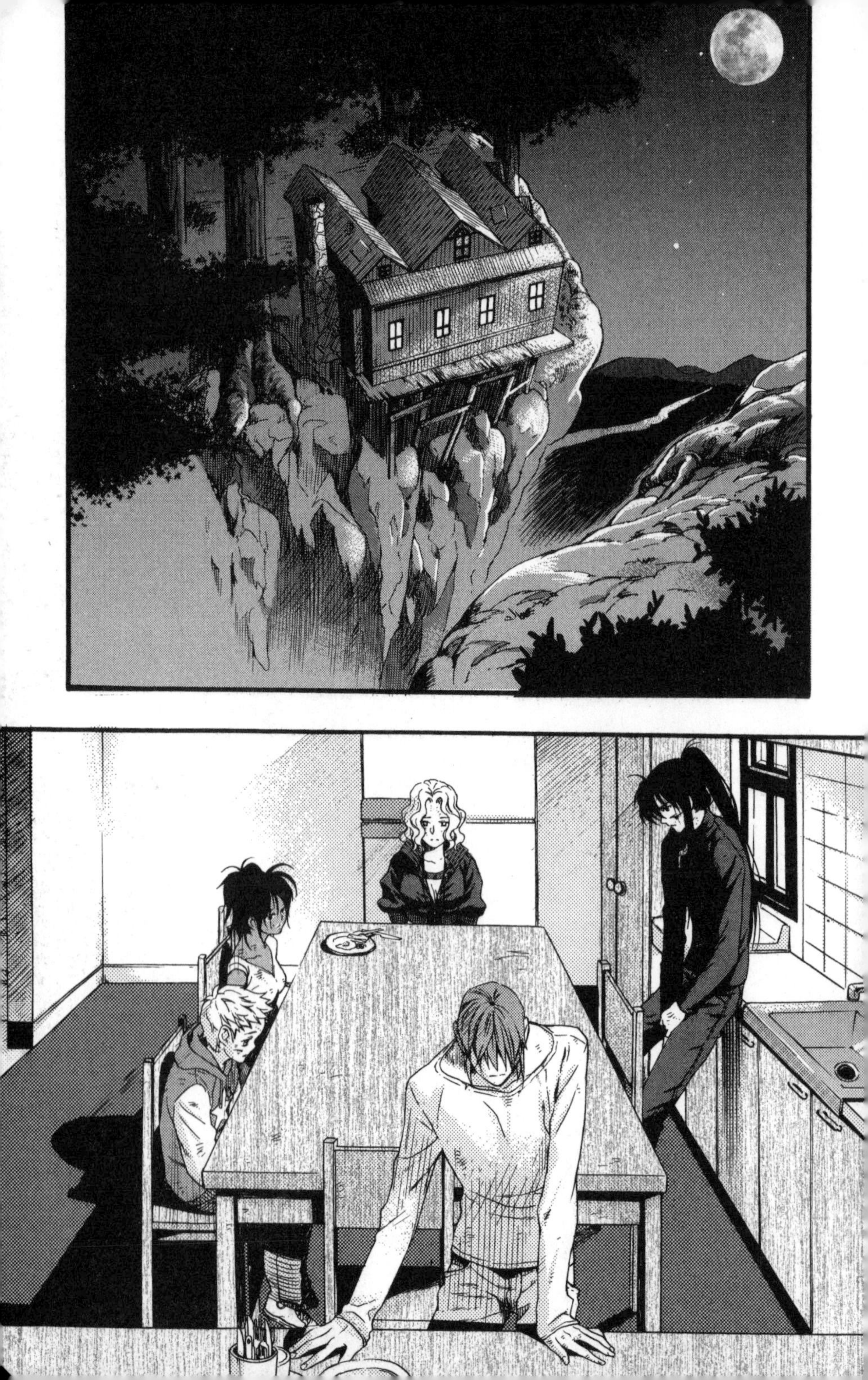

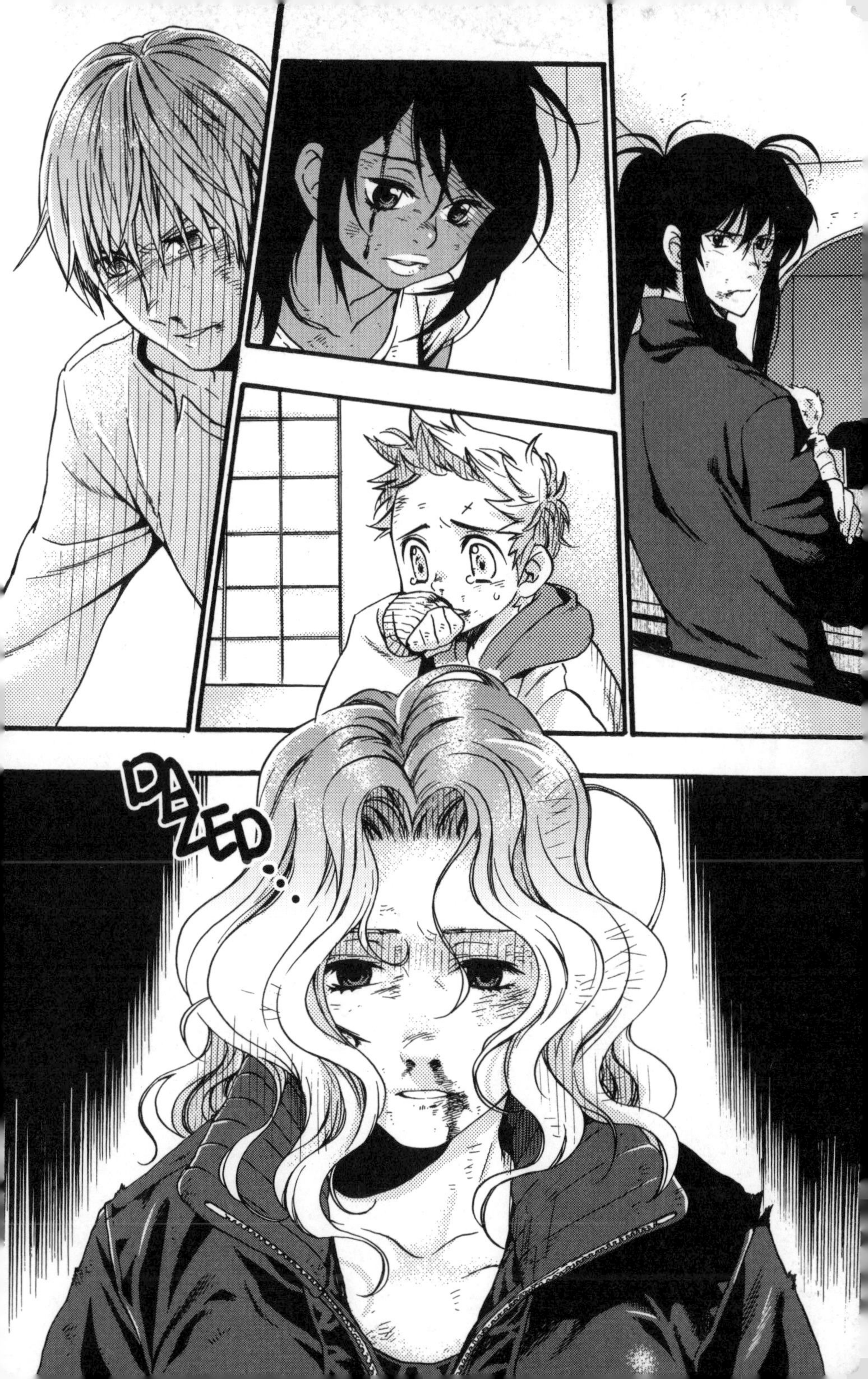
DAZED

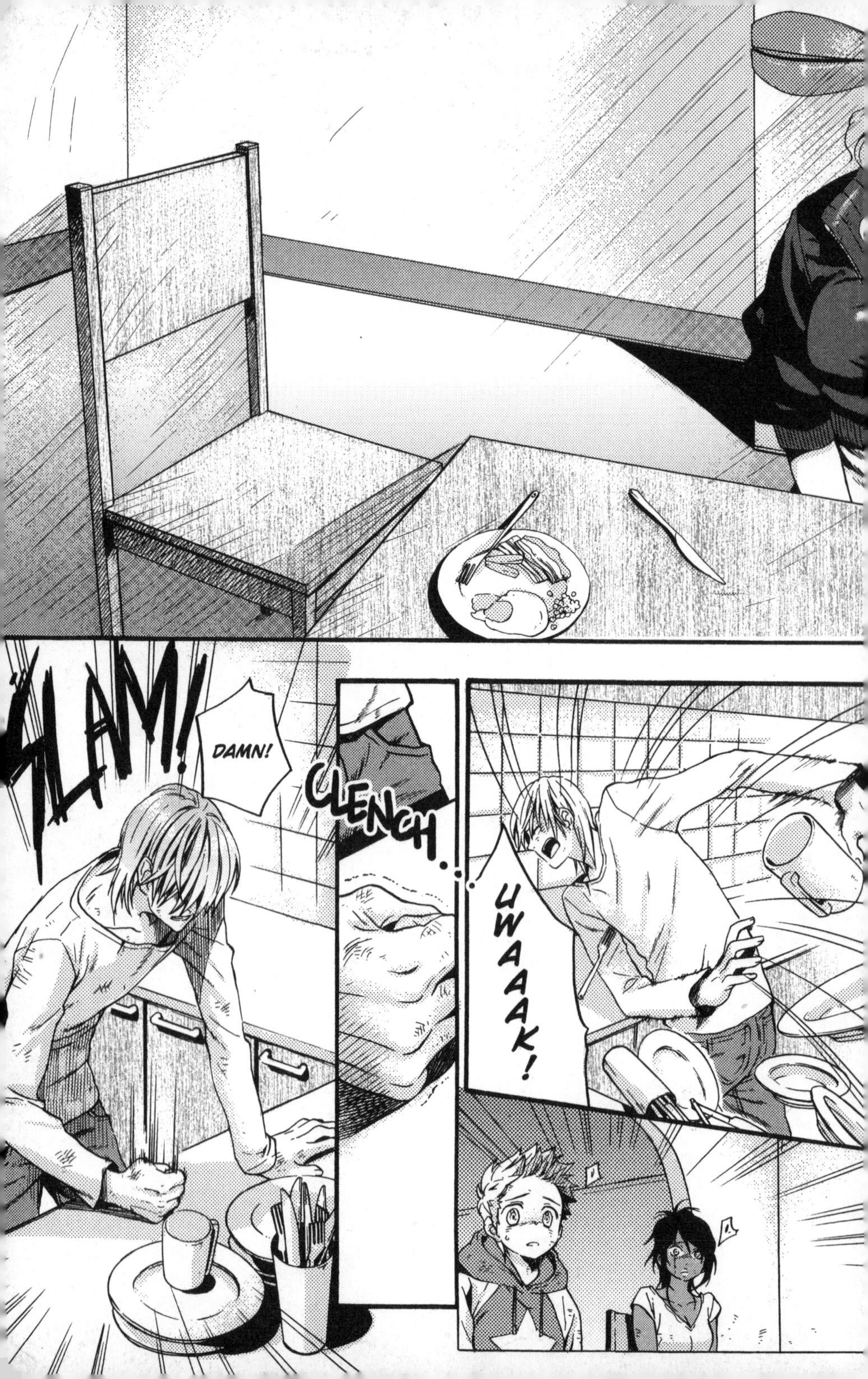
SLAM!
DAMN!
CLENCH...
UWAAAK!

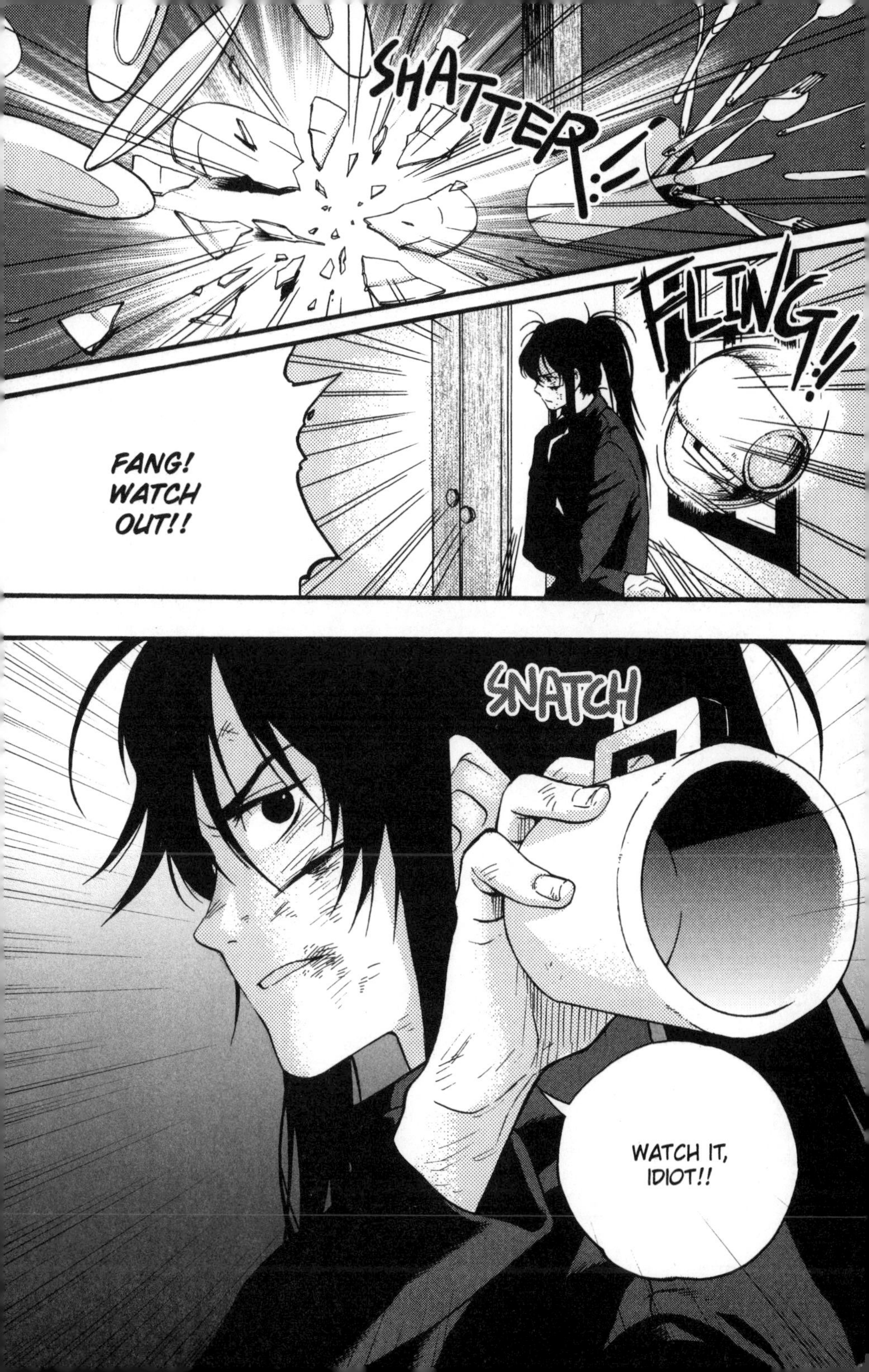
SHATTER!!
FLING!!
FANG! WATCH OUT!!
SNATCH
WATCH IT, IDIOT!!

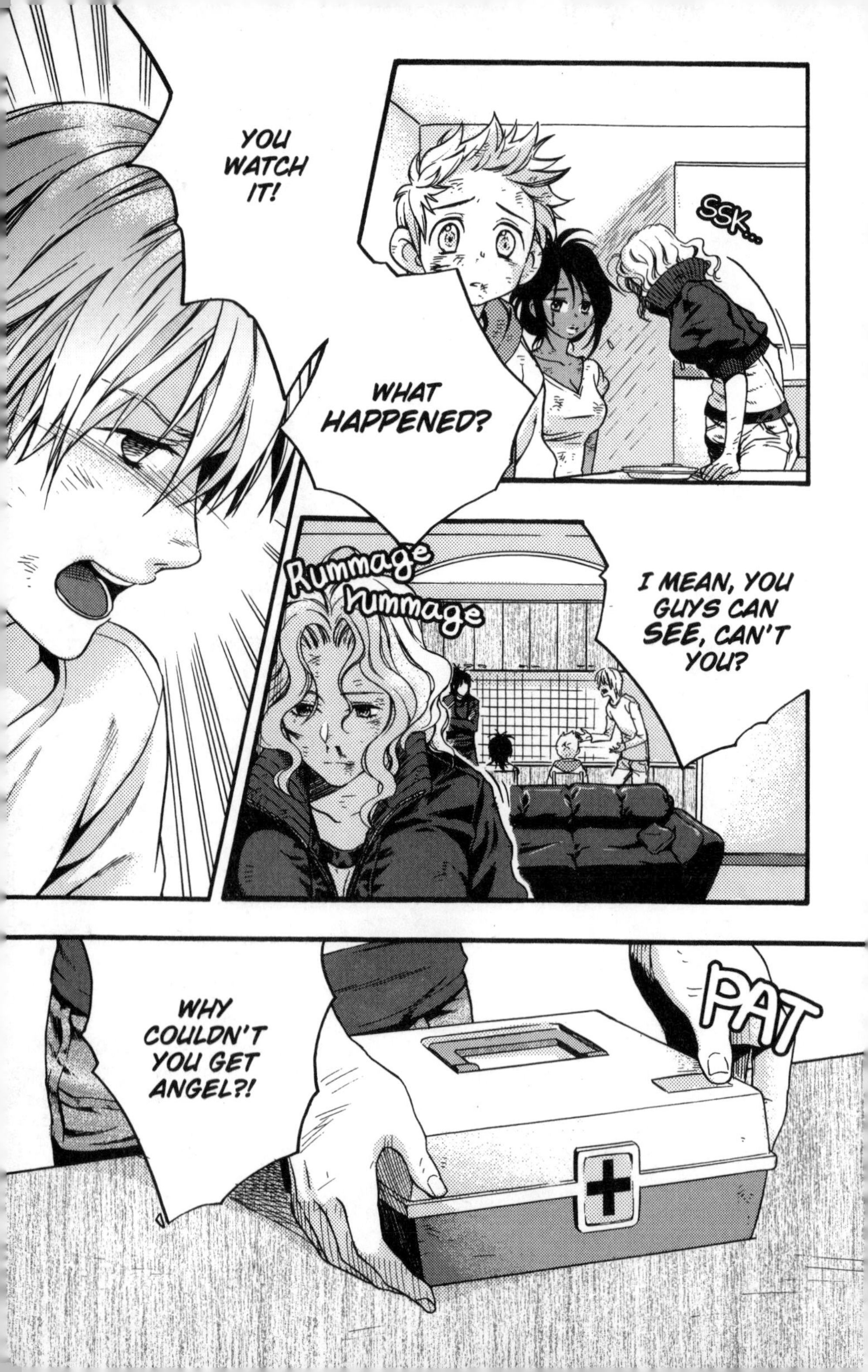
YOU WATCH IT!
WHAT HAPPENED?
SSK...
Rummage rummage
I MEAN, YOU GUYS CAN SEE, CAN'T YOU?
WHY COULDN'T YOU GET ANGEL?!
PAT

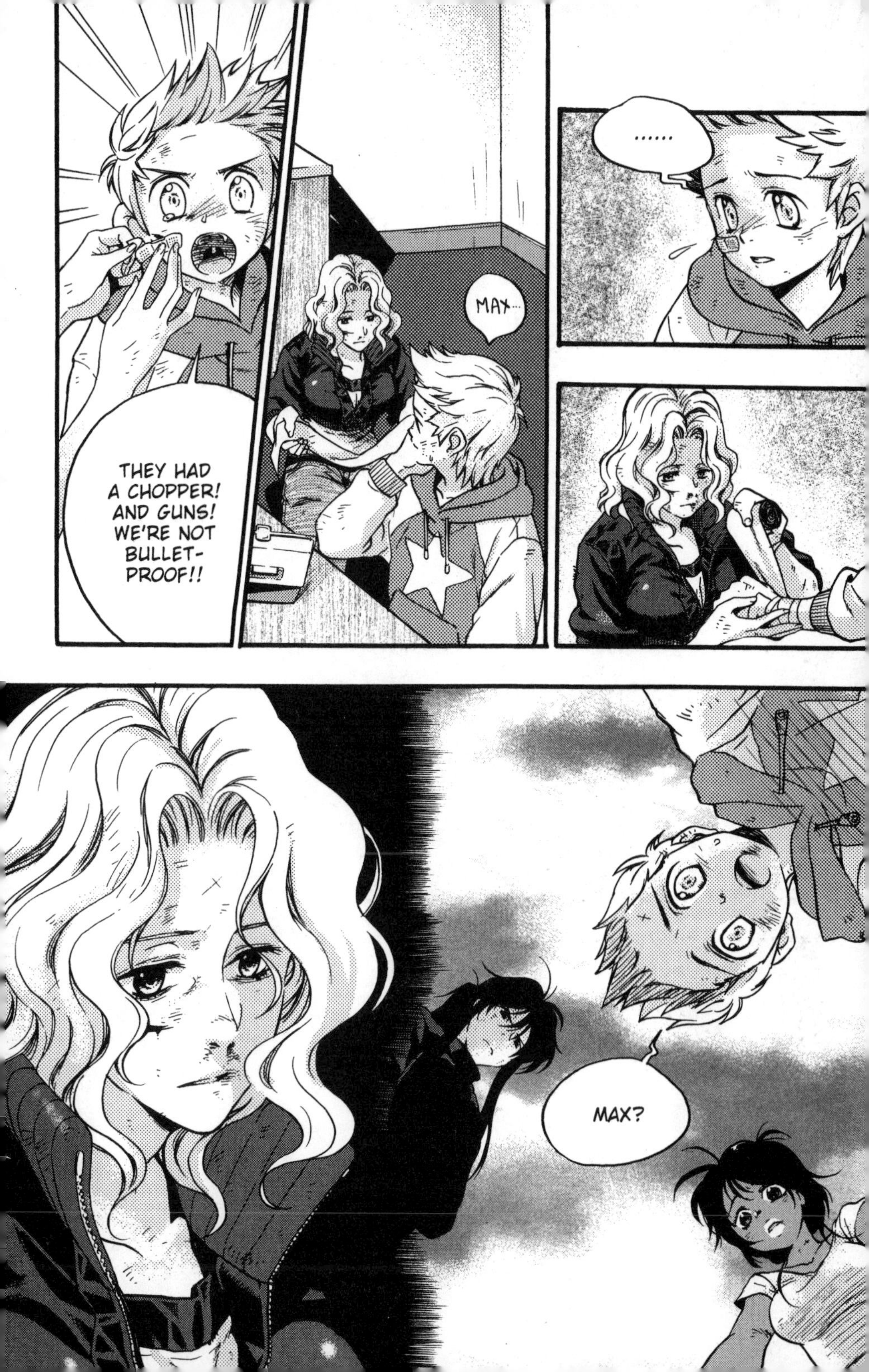
THEY HAD A CHOPPER! AND GUNS! WE'RE NOT BULLET-PROOF!!
MAX...
....
MAX?

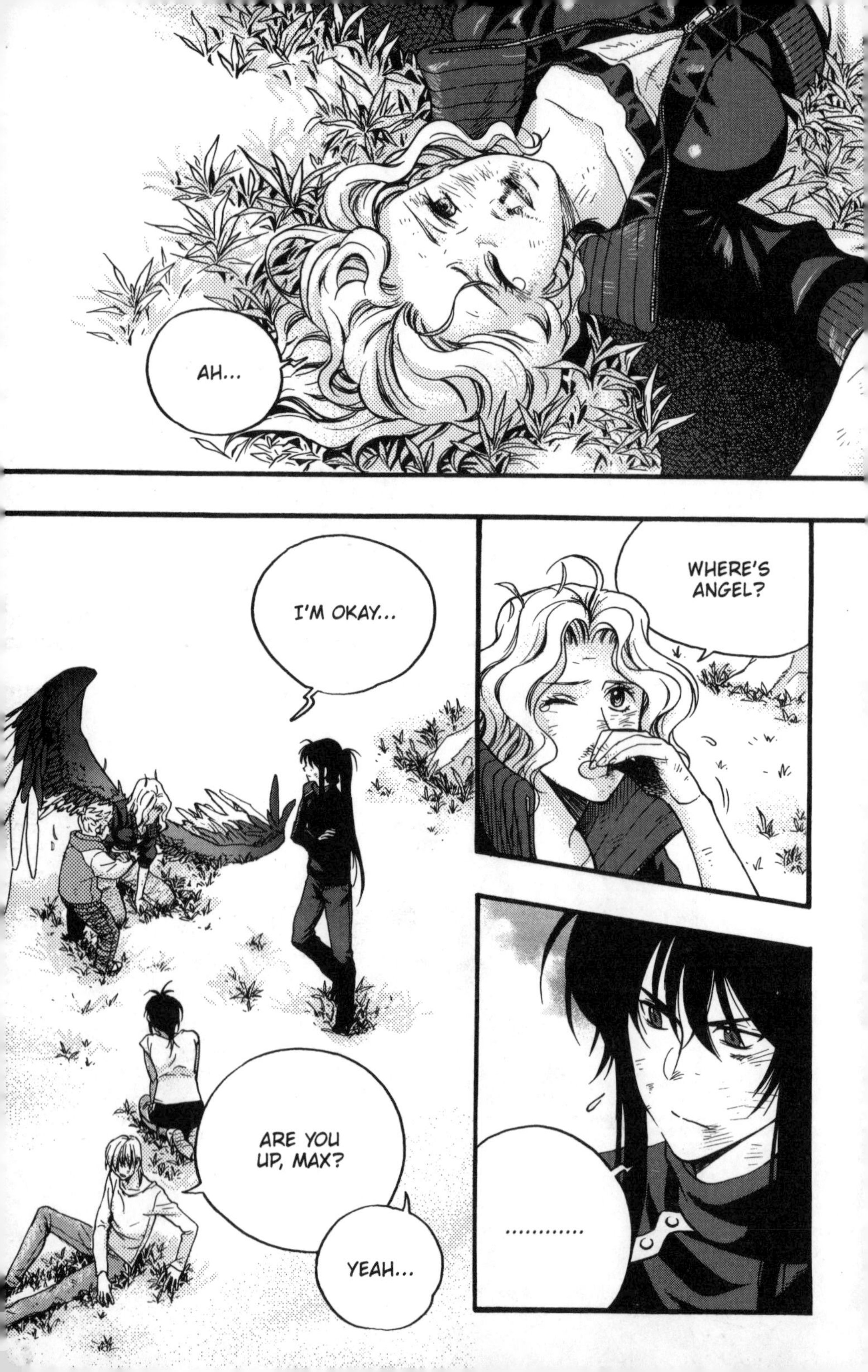
AH...
I'M OKAY...
ARE YOU UP, MAX?
YEAH...
WHERE'S ANGEL?
....

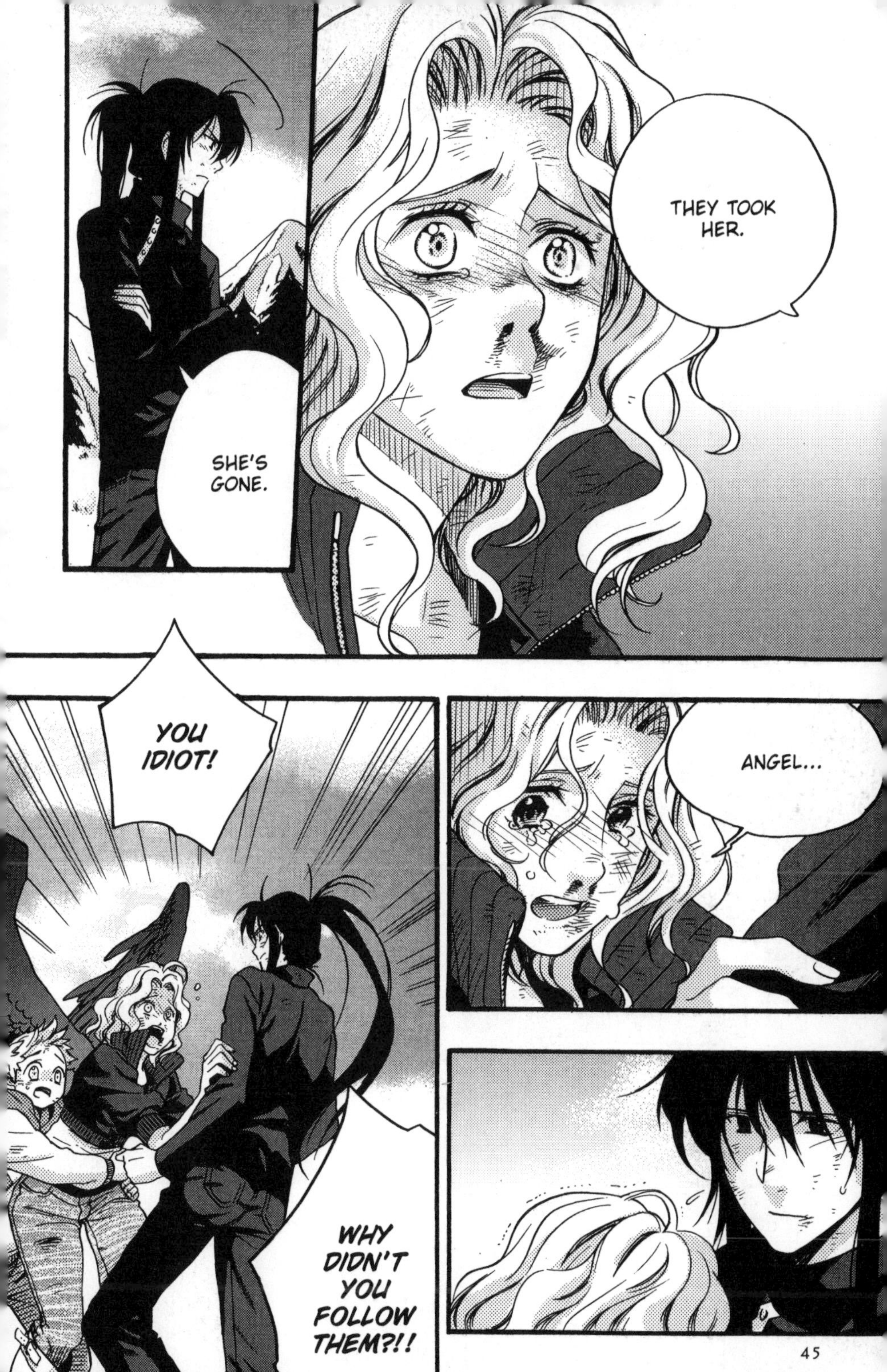
SHE'S GONE.
THEY TOOK HER.
YOU IDIOT!
WHY DIDN'T YOU FOLLOW THEM?!!
ANGEL...

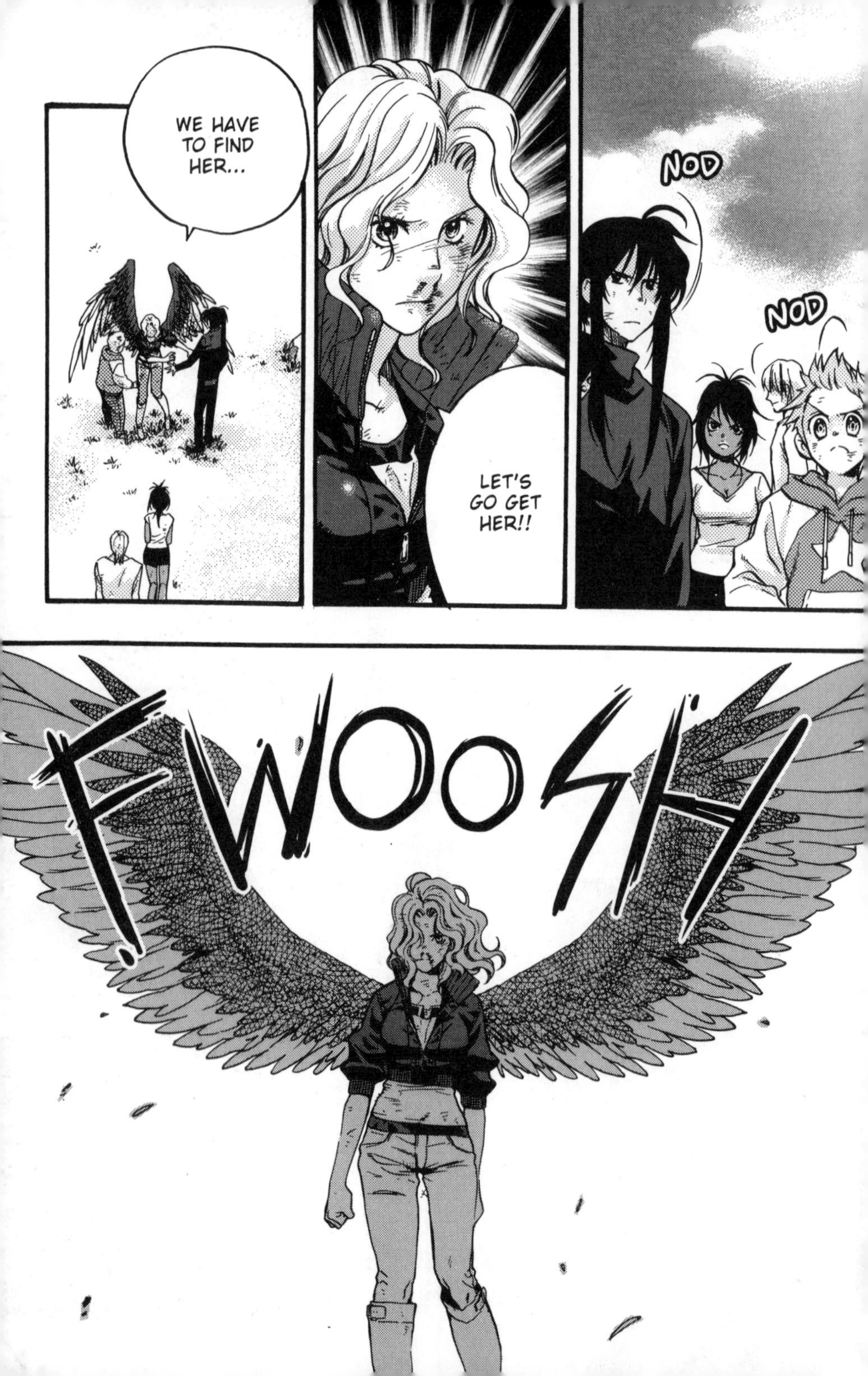
WE HAVE TO FIND HER...
LET'S GO GET HER!!
NOD
NOD
FWOOSH

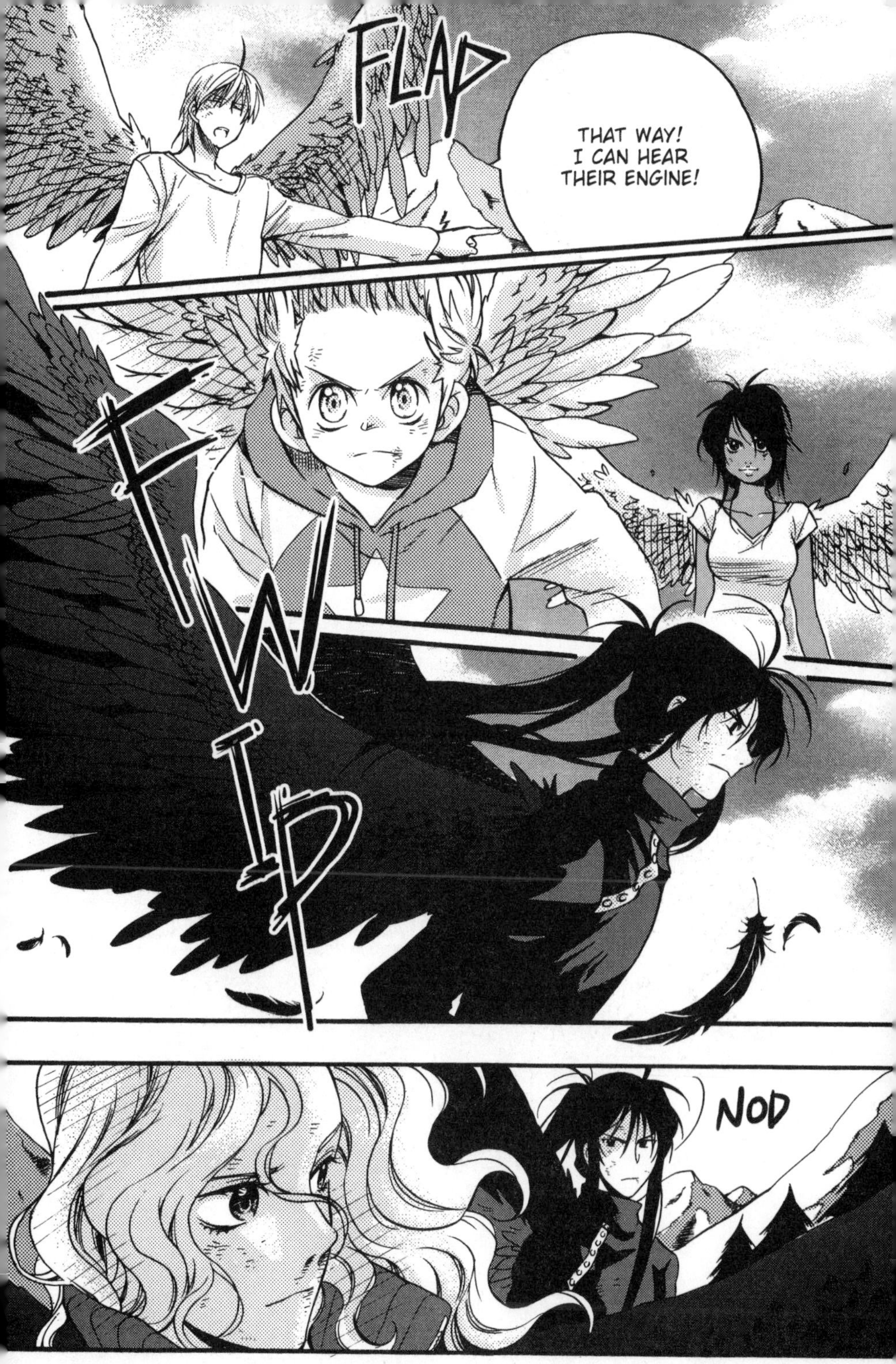
FLAP
THAT WAY! I CAN HEAR THEIR ENGINE!
FWIP
NOD

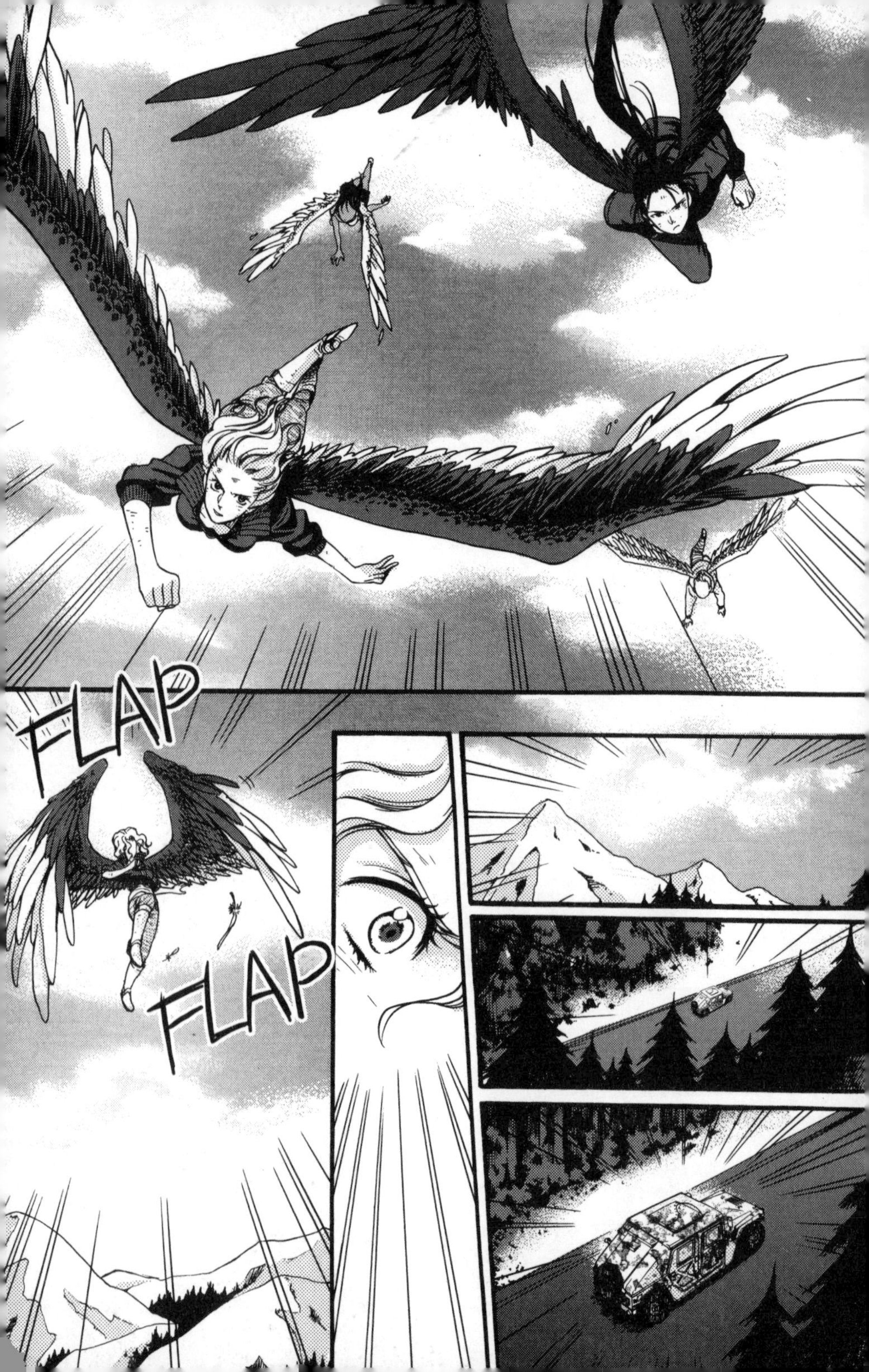
FLAP
FLAP

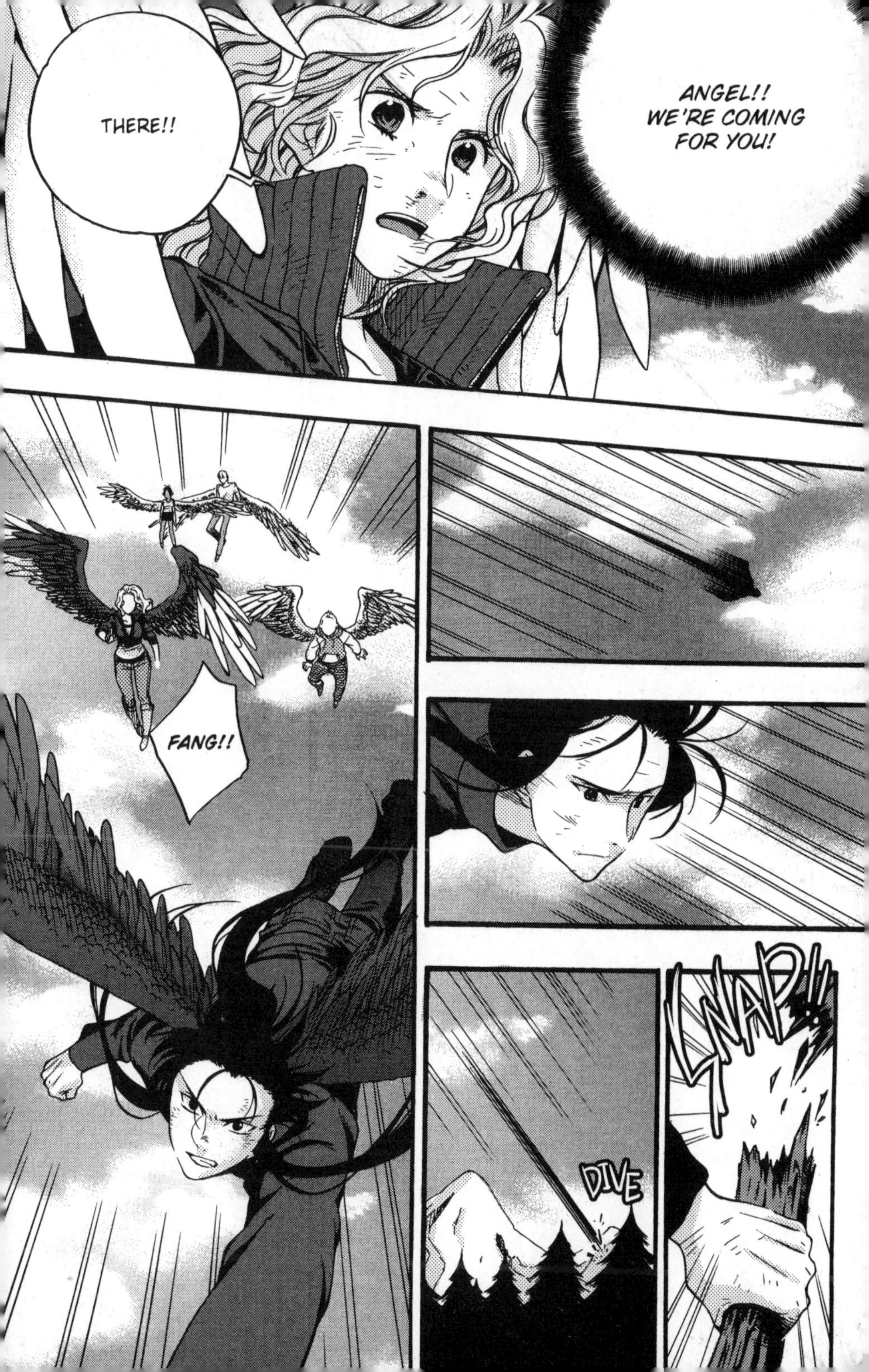
THERE!!
ANGEL!! WE'RE COMING FOR YOU!
FANG!!
DIVE
SNAP!!

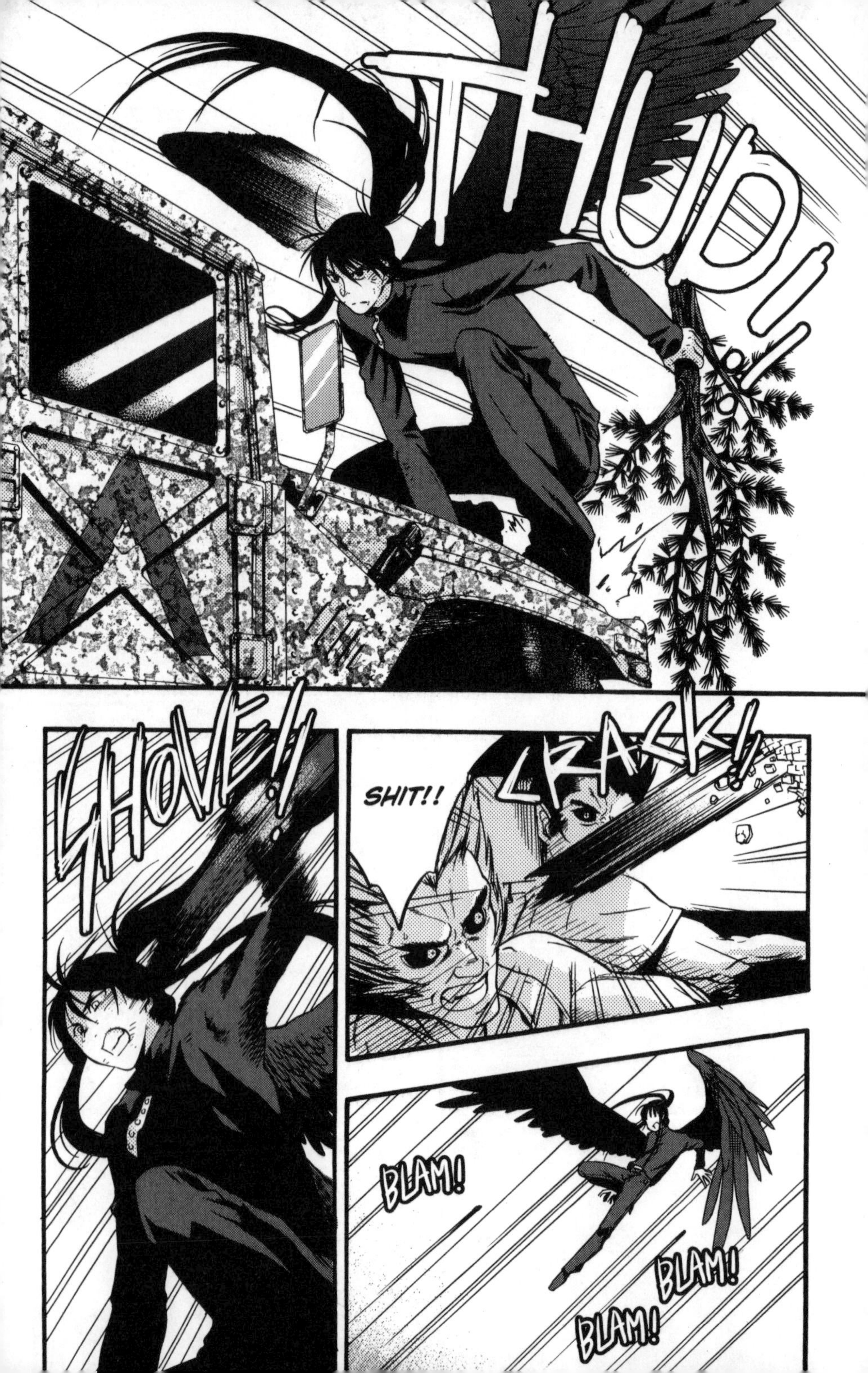
THUD!!
SHOVE!!
SHIT!!
CRACK!!
BLAM!
BLAM!
BLAM!

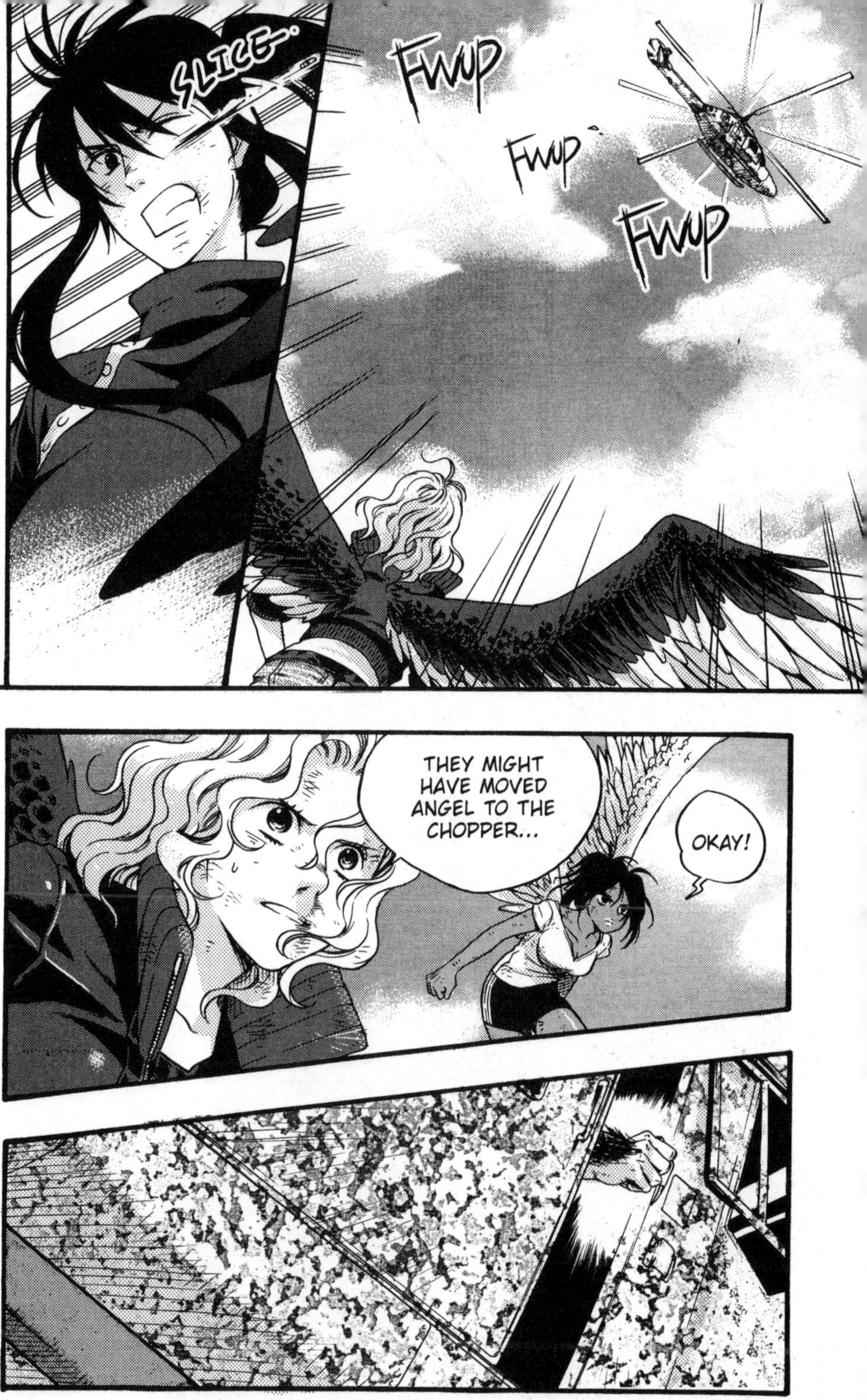
SLICE-
FWUP
FWUP
FWUP
THEY MIGHT HAVE MOVED ANGEL TO THE CHOPPER...
OKAY!

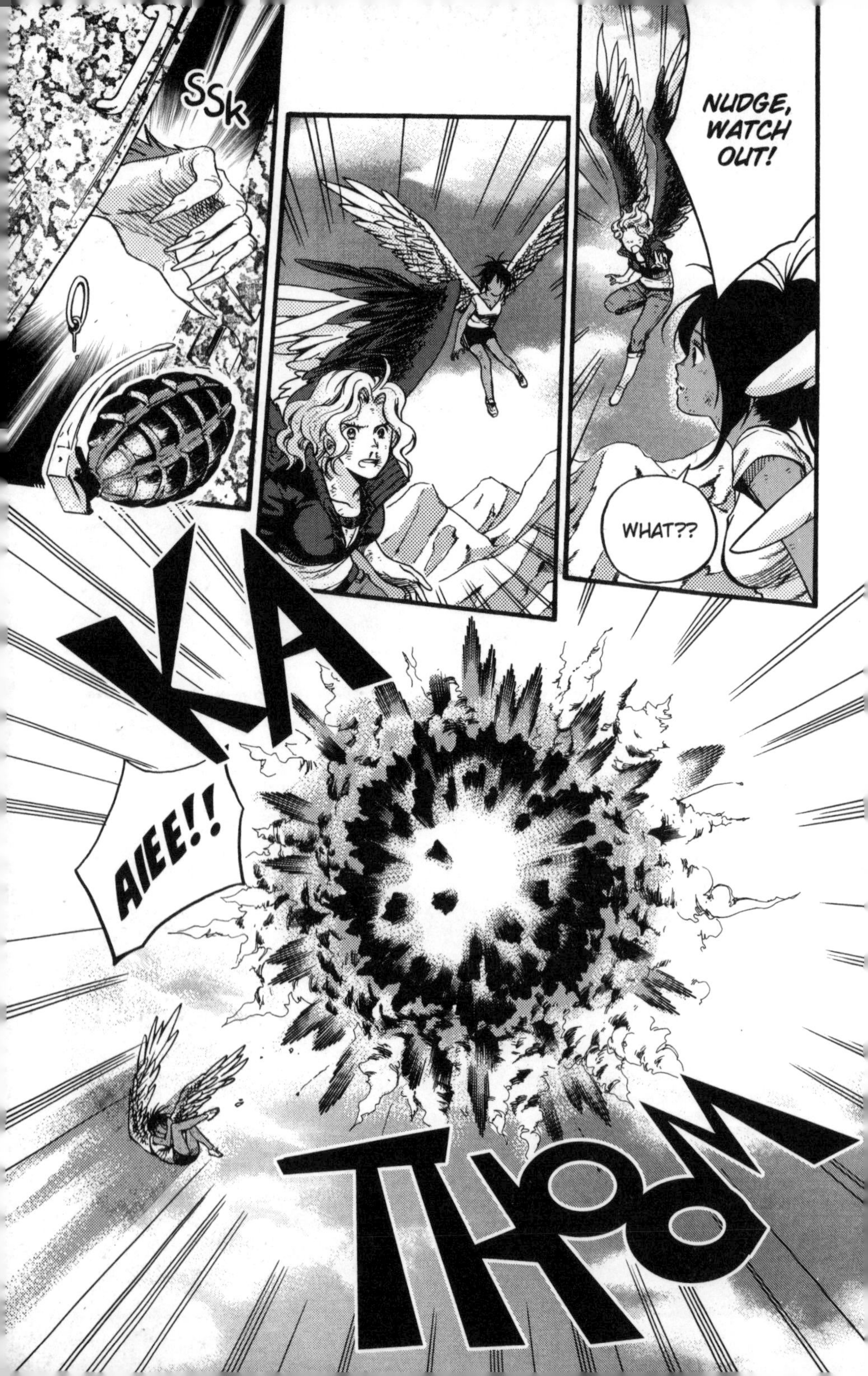
SSk
NUDGE, WATCH OUT!
WHAT??
KA
AIEE!!
THOOM

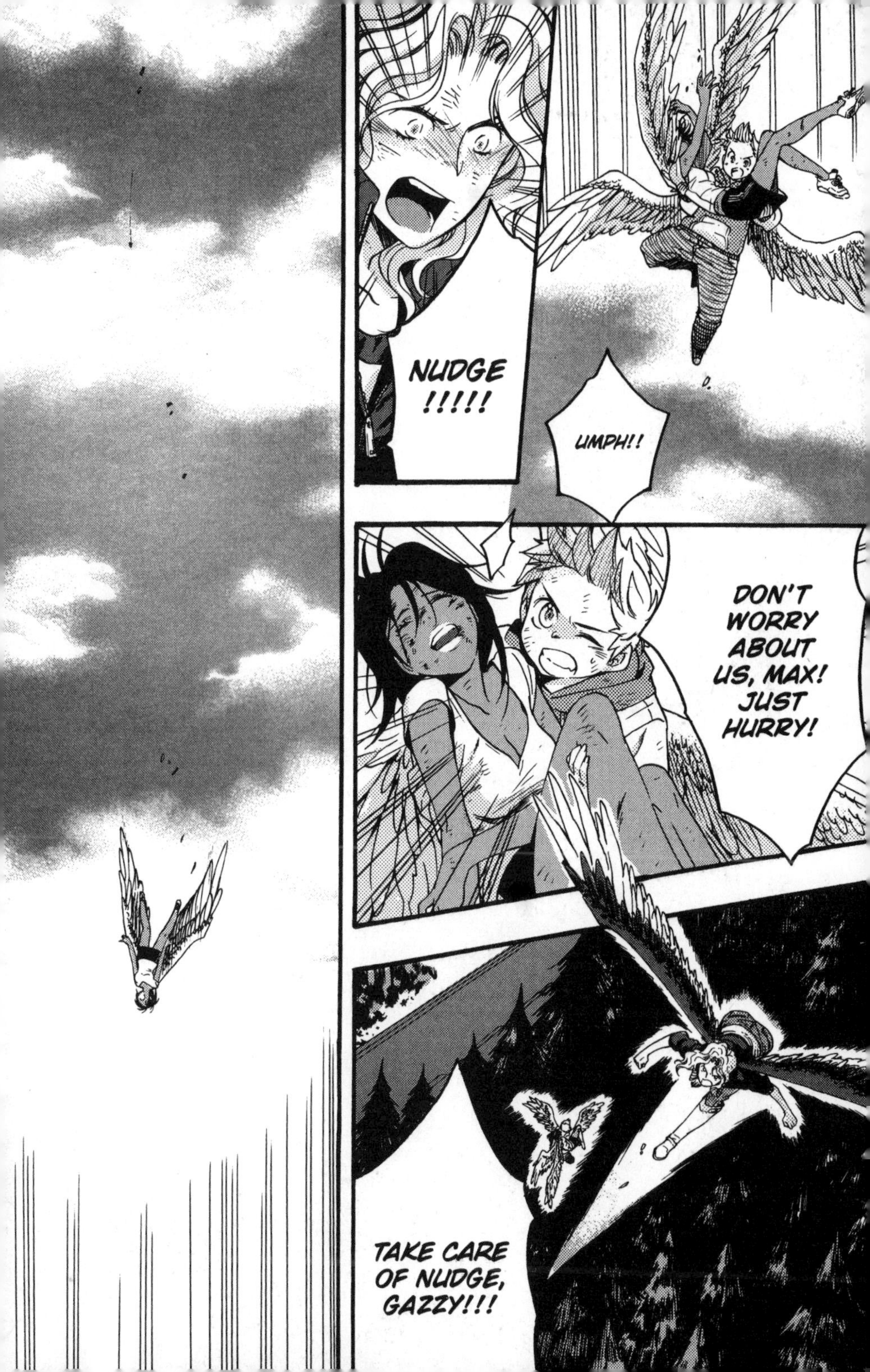
NUDGE !!!!!
UMPH!!
DON'T WORRY ABOUT US, MAX! JUST HURRY!
TAKE CARE OF NUDGE, GAZZY!!!

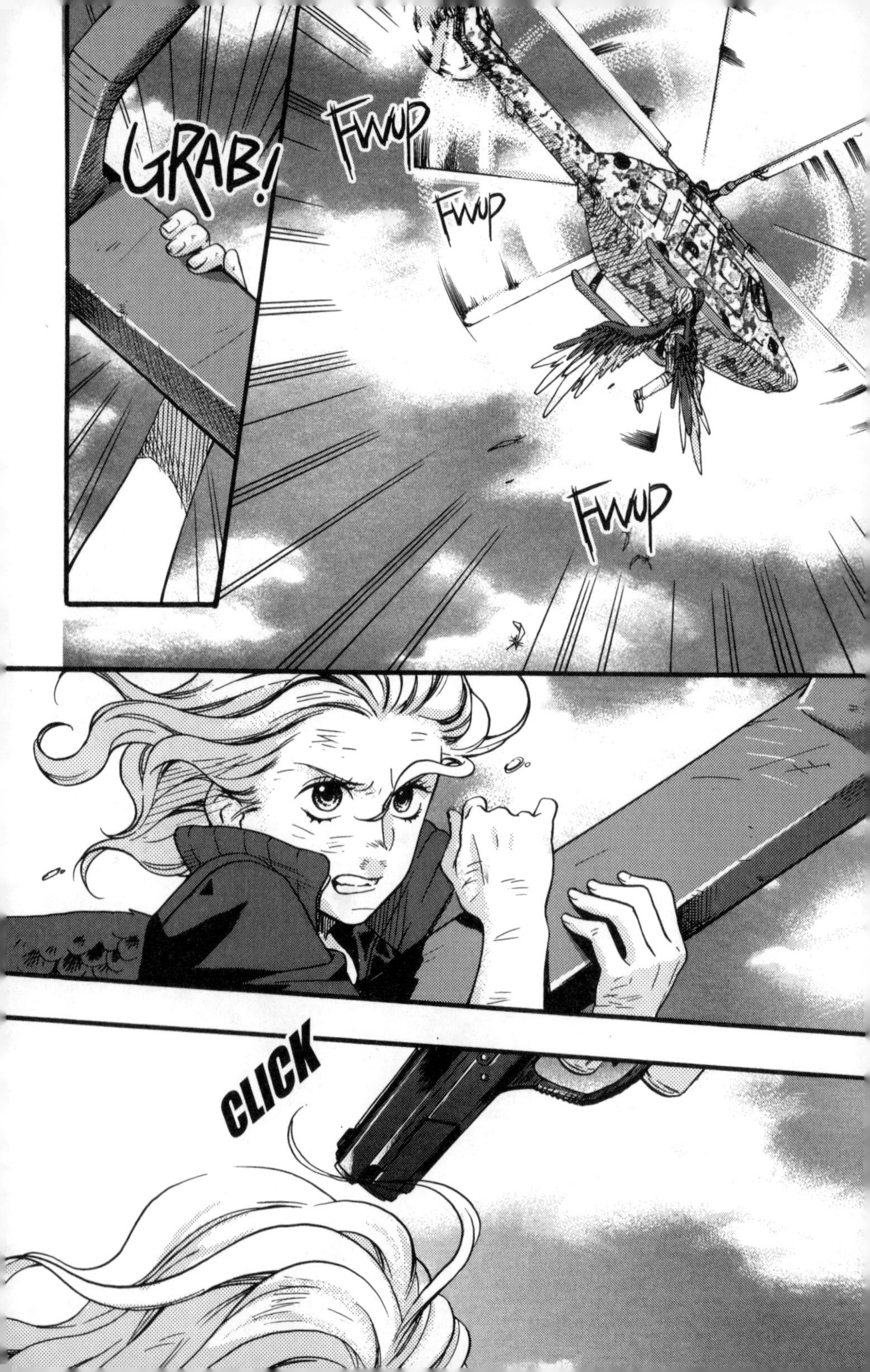
GRAB!
FWUP
FWUP
FWUP
CLICK

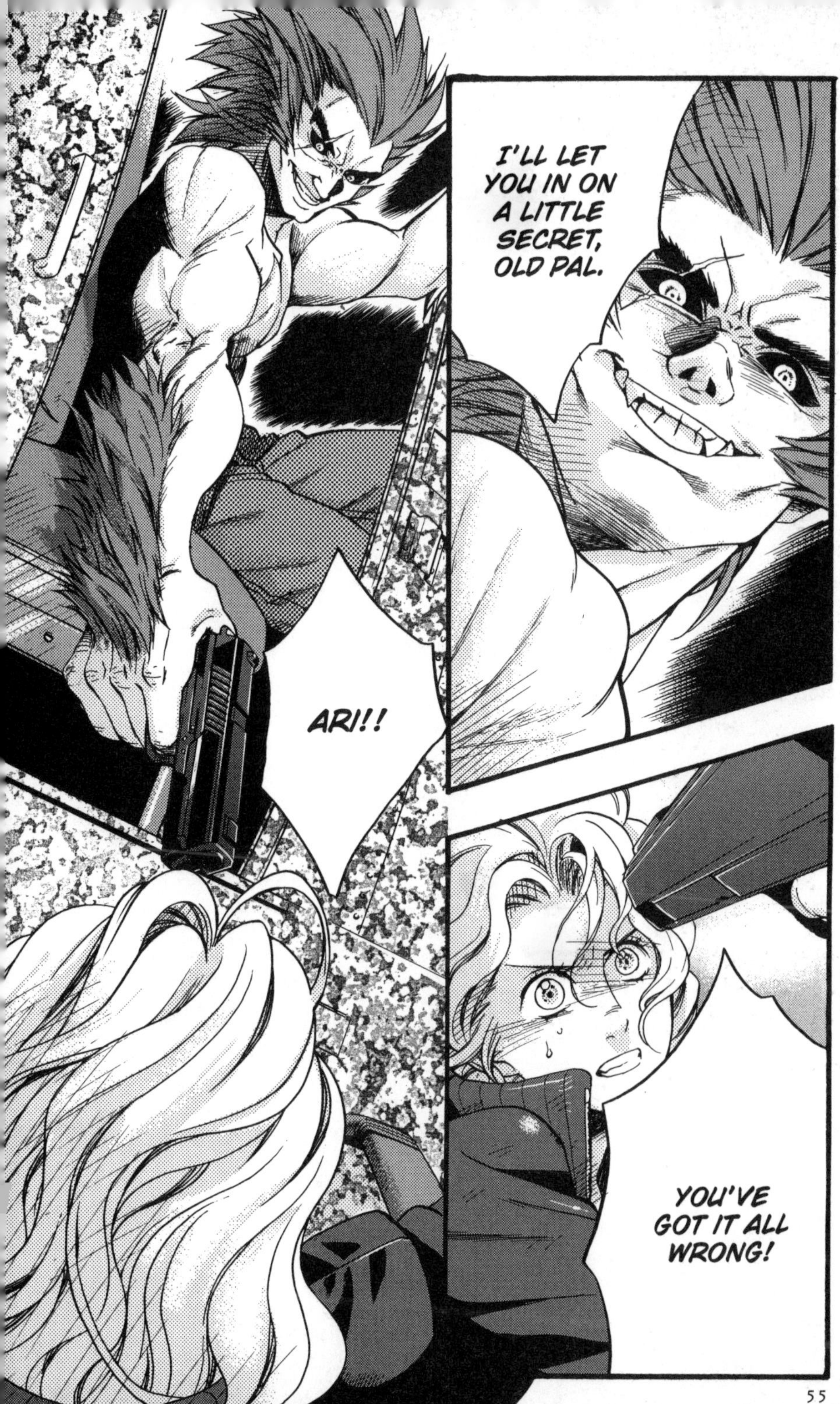
ARI!!
I'LL LET YOU IN ON A LITTLE SECRET, OLD PAL.
YOU'VE GOT IT ALL WRONG!

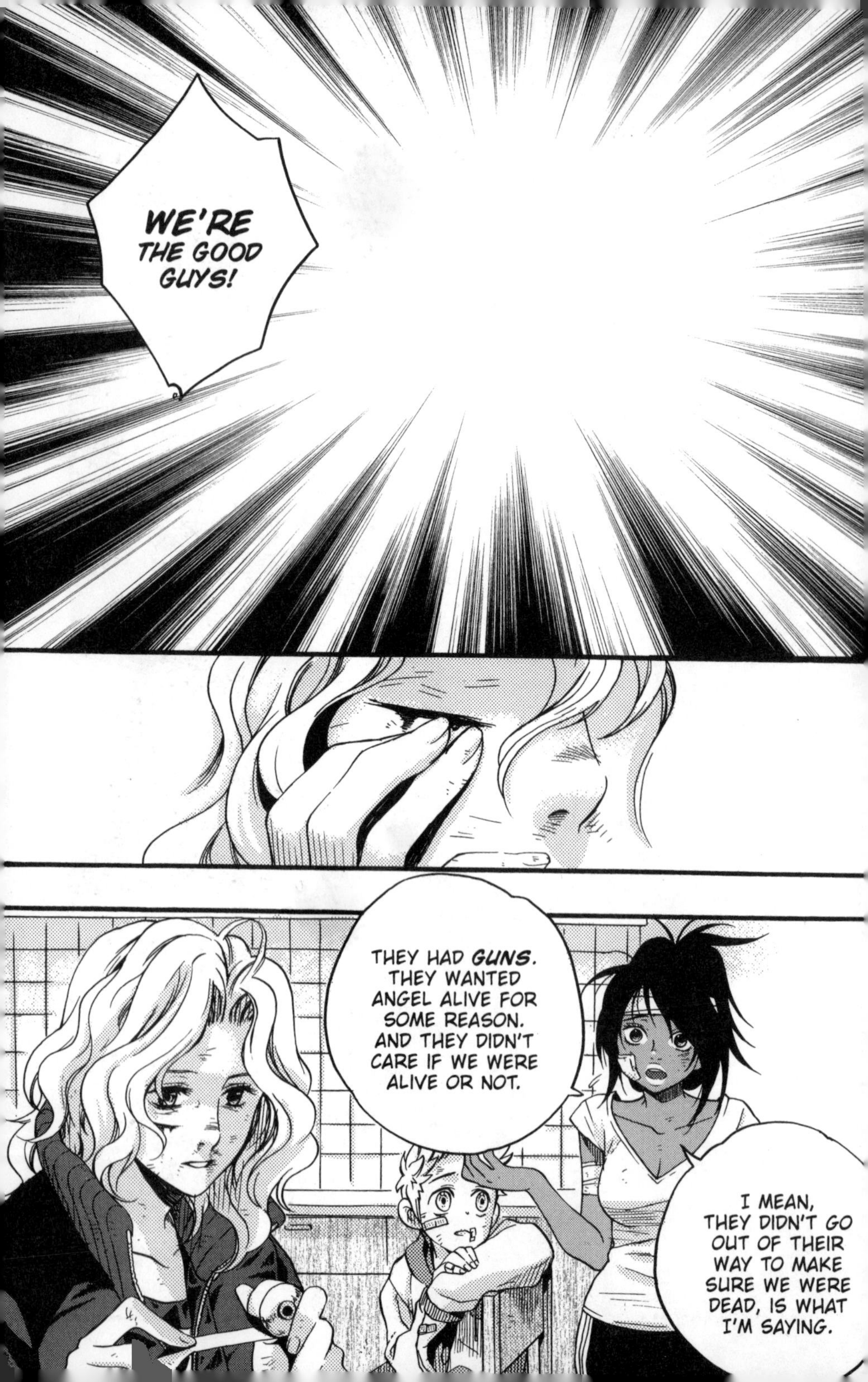
WE'RE THE GOOD GUYS!
THEY HAD **GUNS**. THEY WANTED ANGEL ALIVE FOR SOME REASON. AND THEY DIDN'T CARE IF WE WERE ALIVE OR NOT.
I MEAN, THEY DIDN'T GO OUT OF THEIR WAY TO MAKE SURE WE WERE DEAD, IS WHAT I'M SAYING.

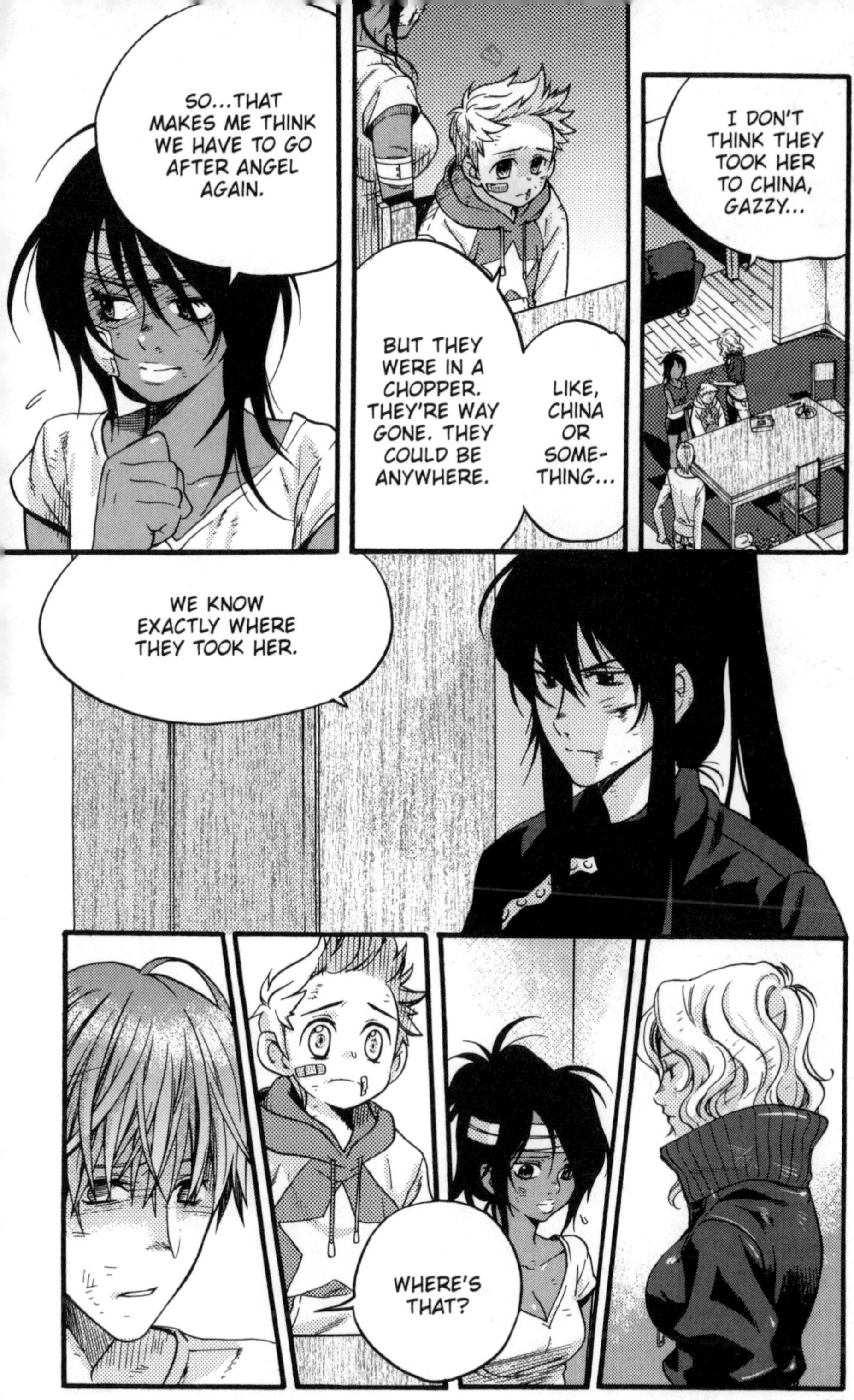
SO...THAT MAKES ME THINK WE HAVE TO GO AFTER ANGEL AGAIN.
BUT THEY WERE IN A CHOPPER. THEY'RE WAY GONE. THEY COULD BE ANYWHERE.
LIKE, CHINA OR SOME-THING...
I DON'T THINK THEY TOOK HER TO CHINA, GAZZY...
WE KNOW EXACTLY WHERE THEY TOOK HER.
WHERE'S THAT?

THE SCHOOL.

THEY TOOK ANGEL BACK TO THE SCHOOL?!

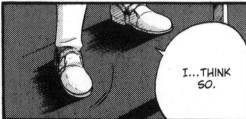

I...THINK SO.

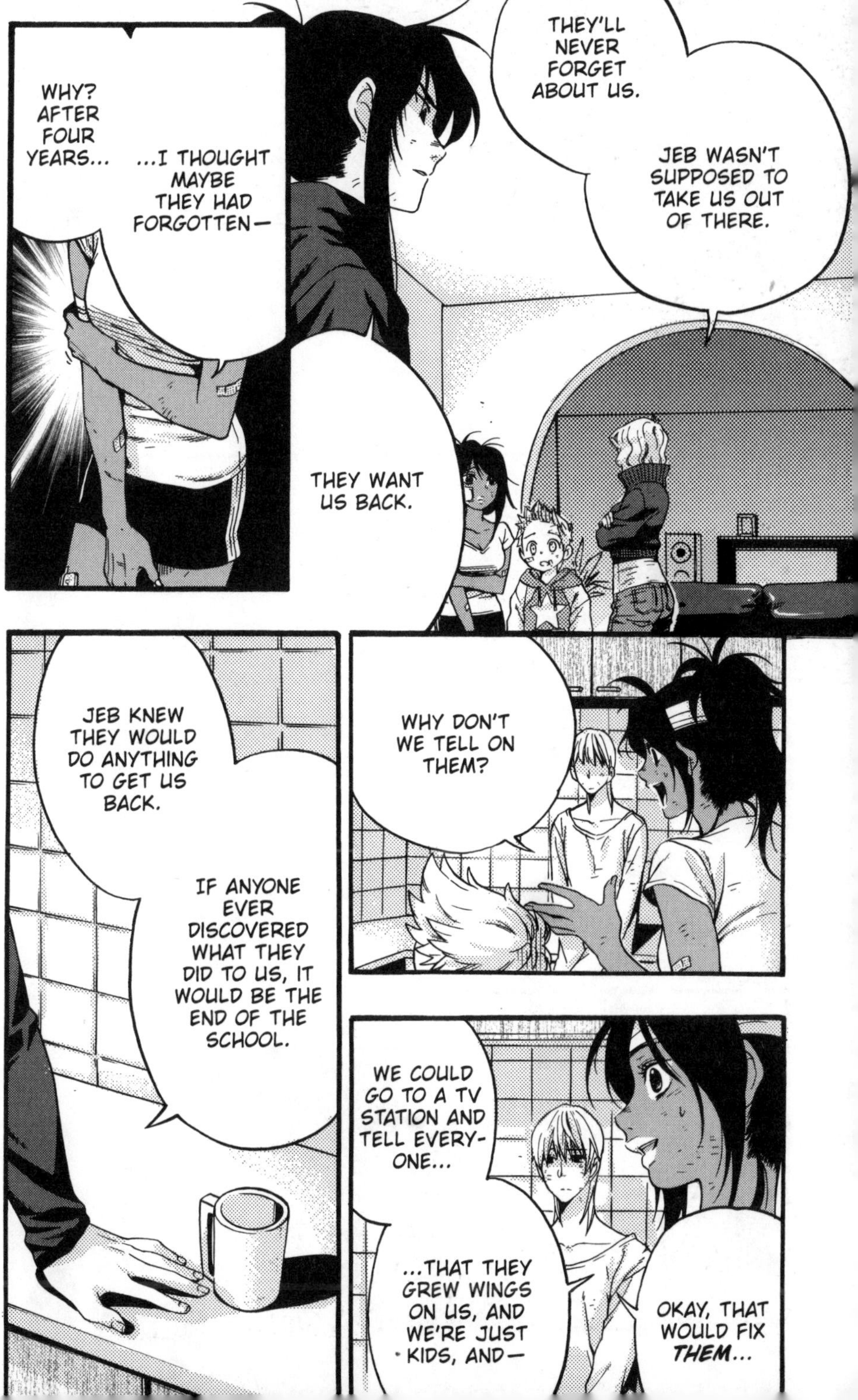
WHY? AFTER FOUR YEARS...
...I THOUGHT MAYBE THEY HAD FORGOTTEN—
THEY'LL NEVER FORGET ABOUT US.
JEB WASN'T SUPPOSED TO TAKE US OUT OF THERE.
THEY WANT US BACK.
JEB KNEW THEY WOULD DO ANYTHING TO GET US BACK.
IF ANYONE EVER DISCOVERED WHAT THEY DID TO US, IT WOULD BE THE END OF THE SCHOOL.
WHY DON'T WE TELL ON THEM?
WE COULD GO TO A TV STATION AND TELL EVERY-ONE...
...THAT THEY GREW WINGS ON US, AND WE'RE JUST KIDS, AND—
OKAY, THAT WOULD FIX *THEM*...

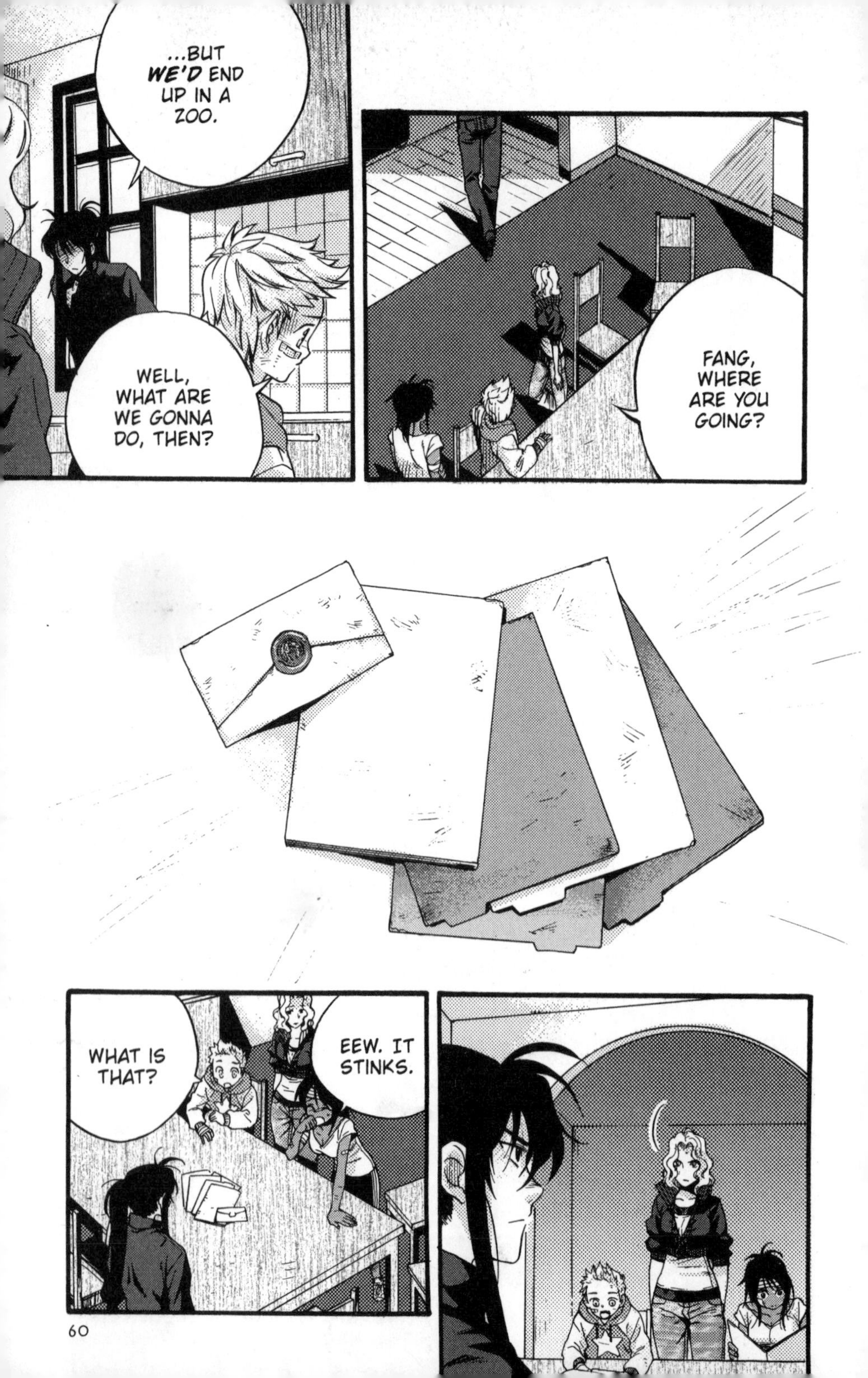
...BUT *WE'D* END UP IN A ZOO.
WELL, WHAT ARE WE GONNA DO, THEN?
FANG, WHERE ARE YOU GOING?
WHAT IS THAT?
EEW. IT STINKS.

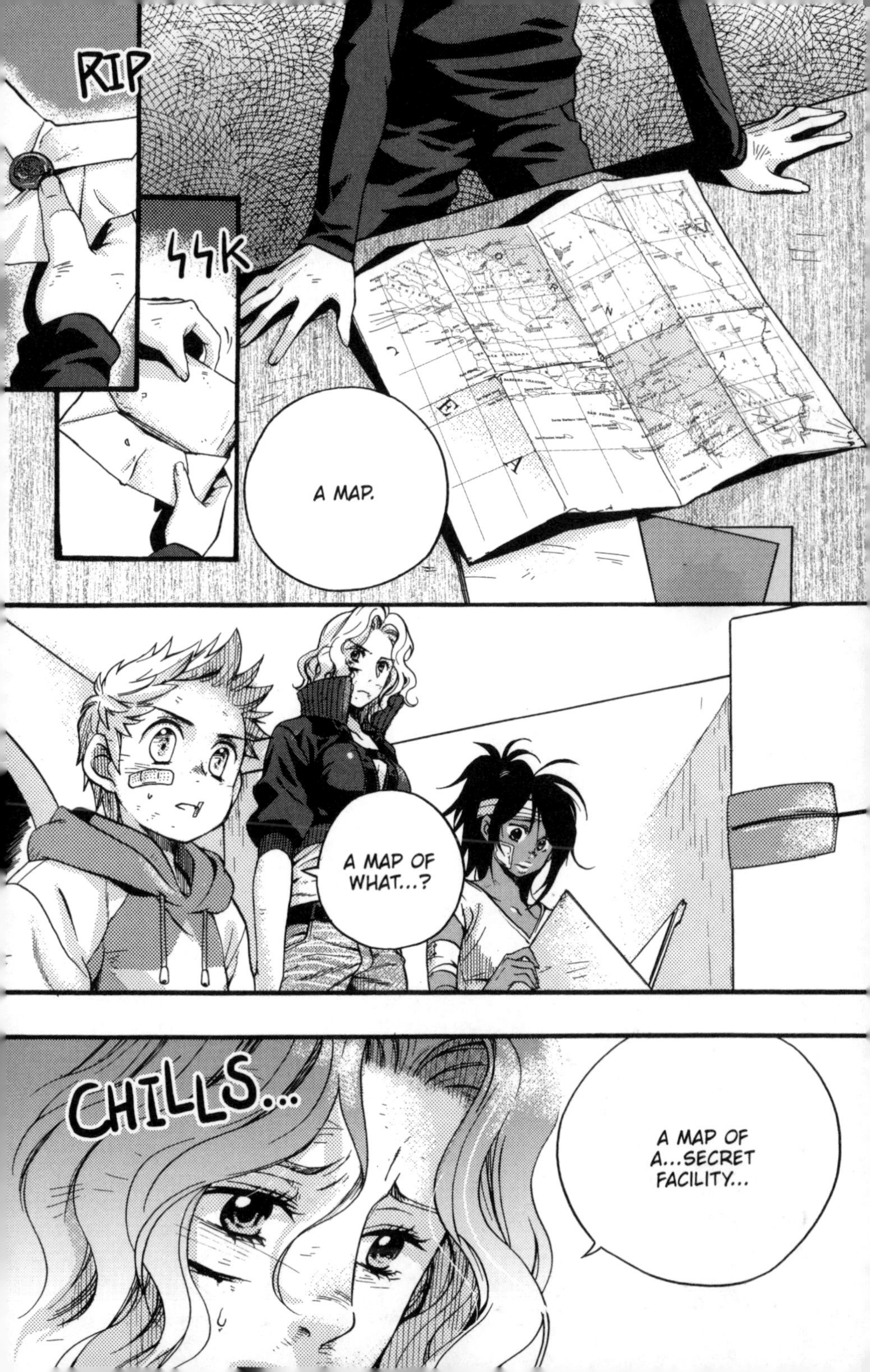
RIP
SSK
A MAP.
A MAP OF WHAT...?
CHILLS...
A MAP OF A...SECRET FACILITY...

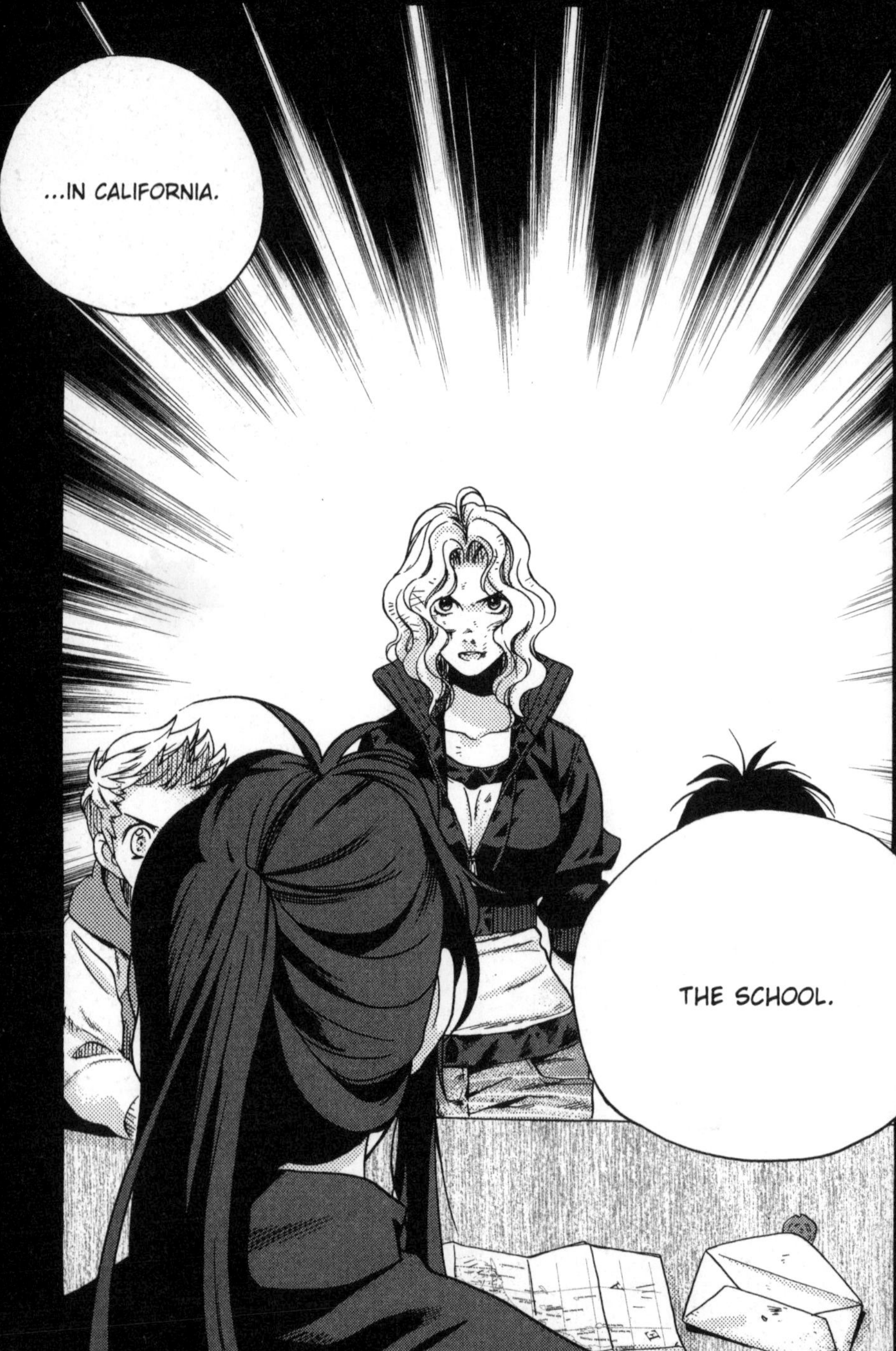
...IN CALIFORNIA.
THE SCHOOL.

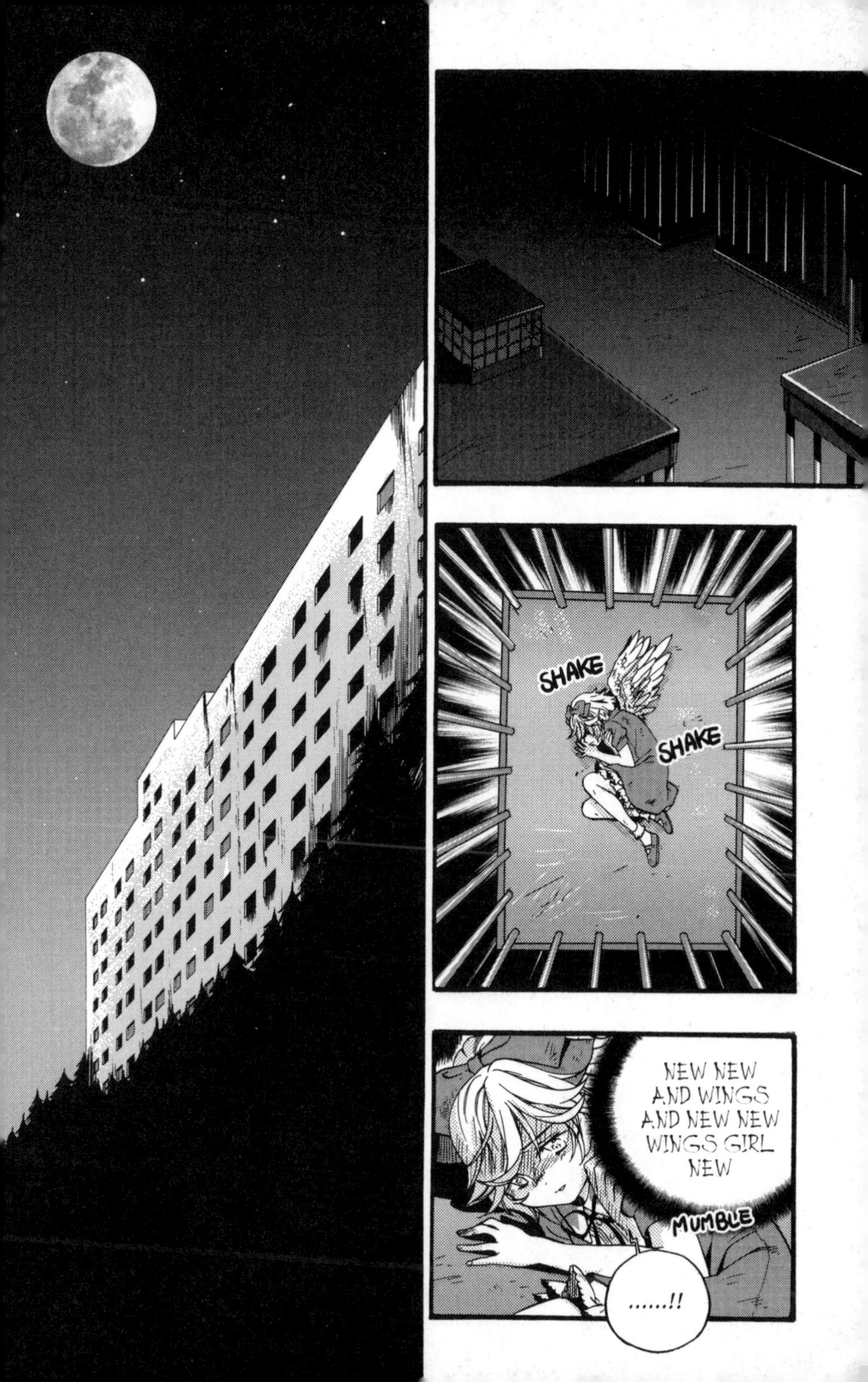
SHAKE
SHAKE
NEW NEW AND WINGS AND NEW NEW WINGS GIRL NEW
MUMBLE
......!!

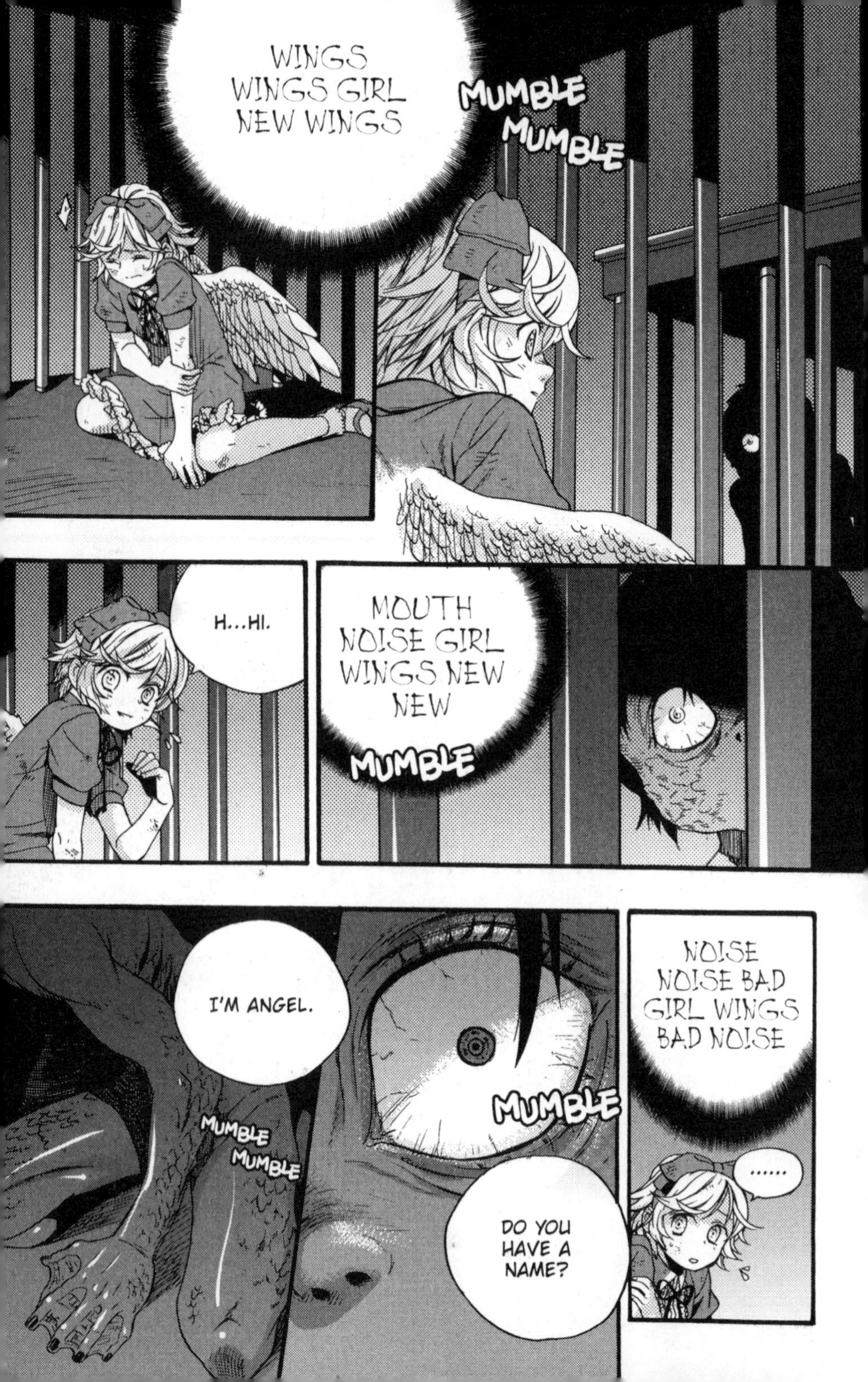
WINGS WINGS GIRL NEW WINGS
MUMBLE MUMBLE
H...HI.
MOUTH NOISE GIRL WINGS NEW NEW
MUMBLE
I'M ANGEL.
MUMBLE MUMBLE
NOISE NOISE BAD GIRL WINGS BAD NOISE
MUMBLE
DO YOU HAVE A NAME?
......

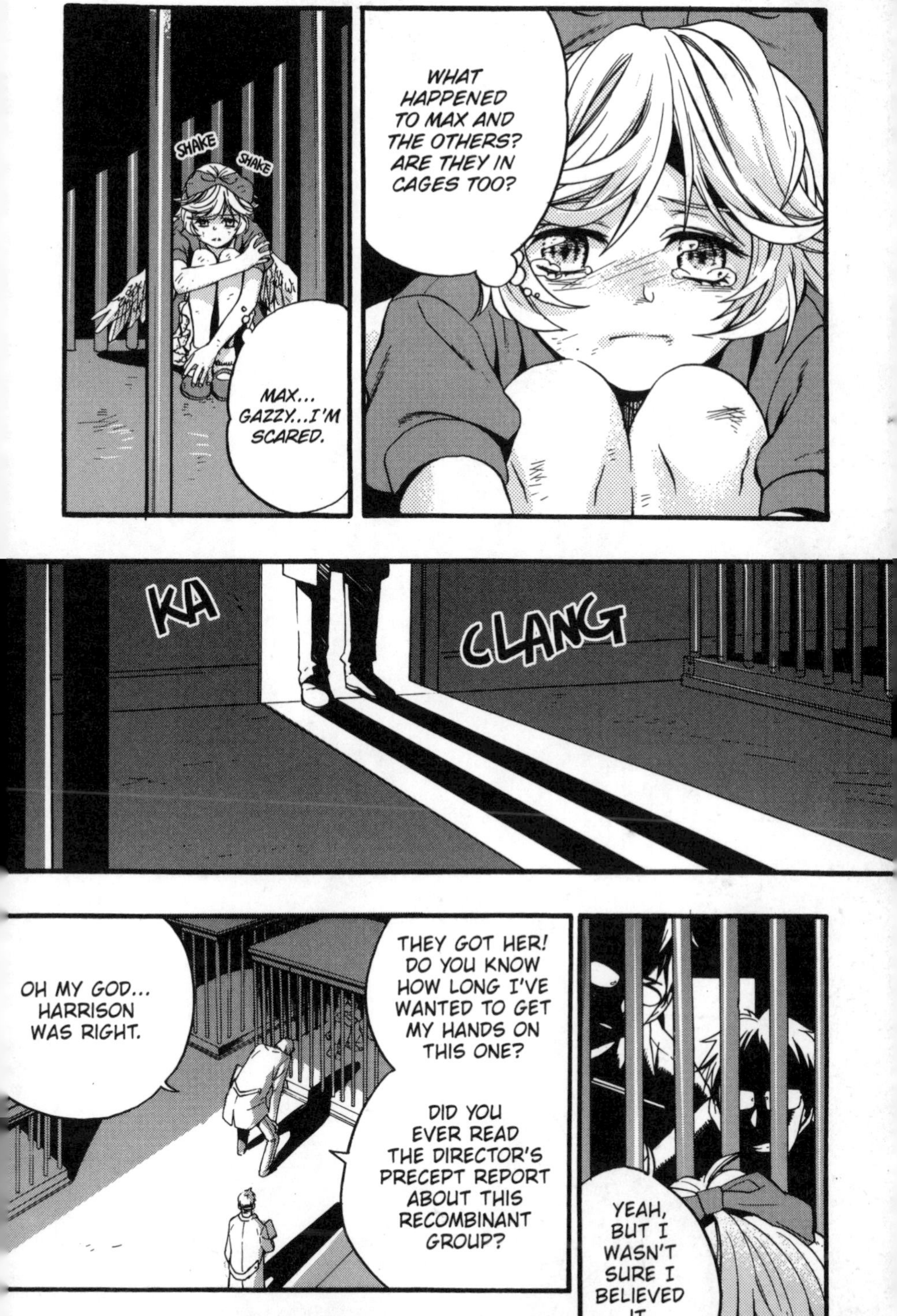
SHAKE
SHAKE
MAX... GAZZY...I'M SCARED.
WHAT HAPPENED TO MAX AND THE OTHERS? ARE THEY IN CAGES TOO?
KA
CLANG
OH MY GOD... HARRISON WAS RIGHT.
THEY GOT HER! DO YOU KNOW HOW LONG I'VE WANTED TO GET MY HANDS ON THIS ONE?
DID YOU EVER READ THE DIRECTOR'S PRECEPT REPORT ABOUT THIS RECOMBINANT GROUP?
YEAH, BUT I WASN'T SURE I BELIEVED IT.

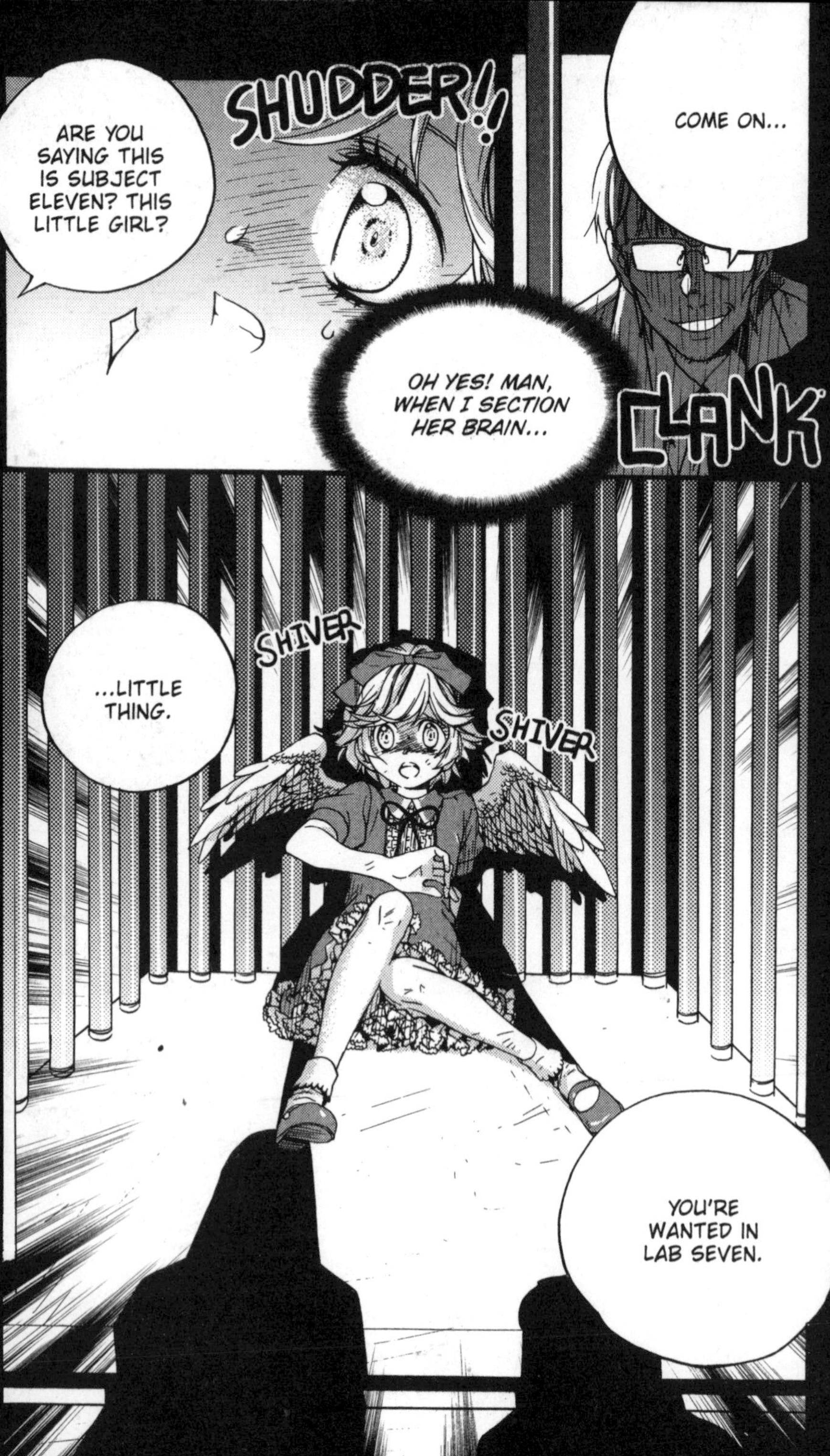
COME ON...
CLANK
SHUDDER!!
ARE YOU SAYING THIS IS SUBJECT ELEVEN? THIS LITTLE GIRL?
OH YES! MAN, WHEN I SECTION HER BRAIN...
SHIVER
SHIVER
...LITTLE THING.
YOU'RE WANTED IN LAB SEVEN.

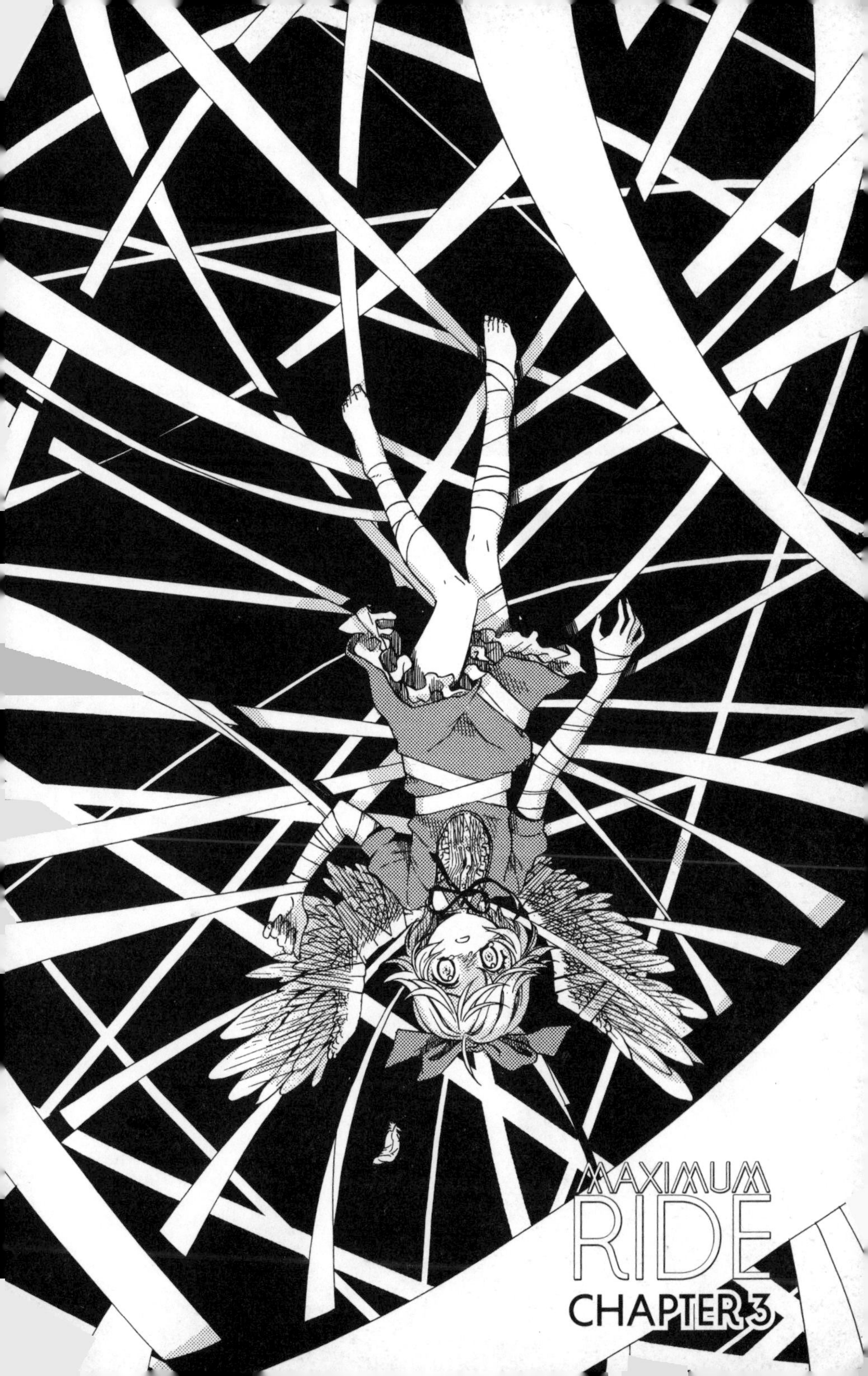
MAXIMUM
RIDE
CHAPTER 3

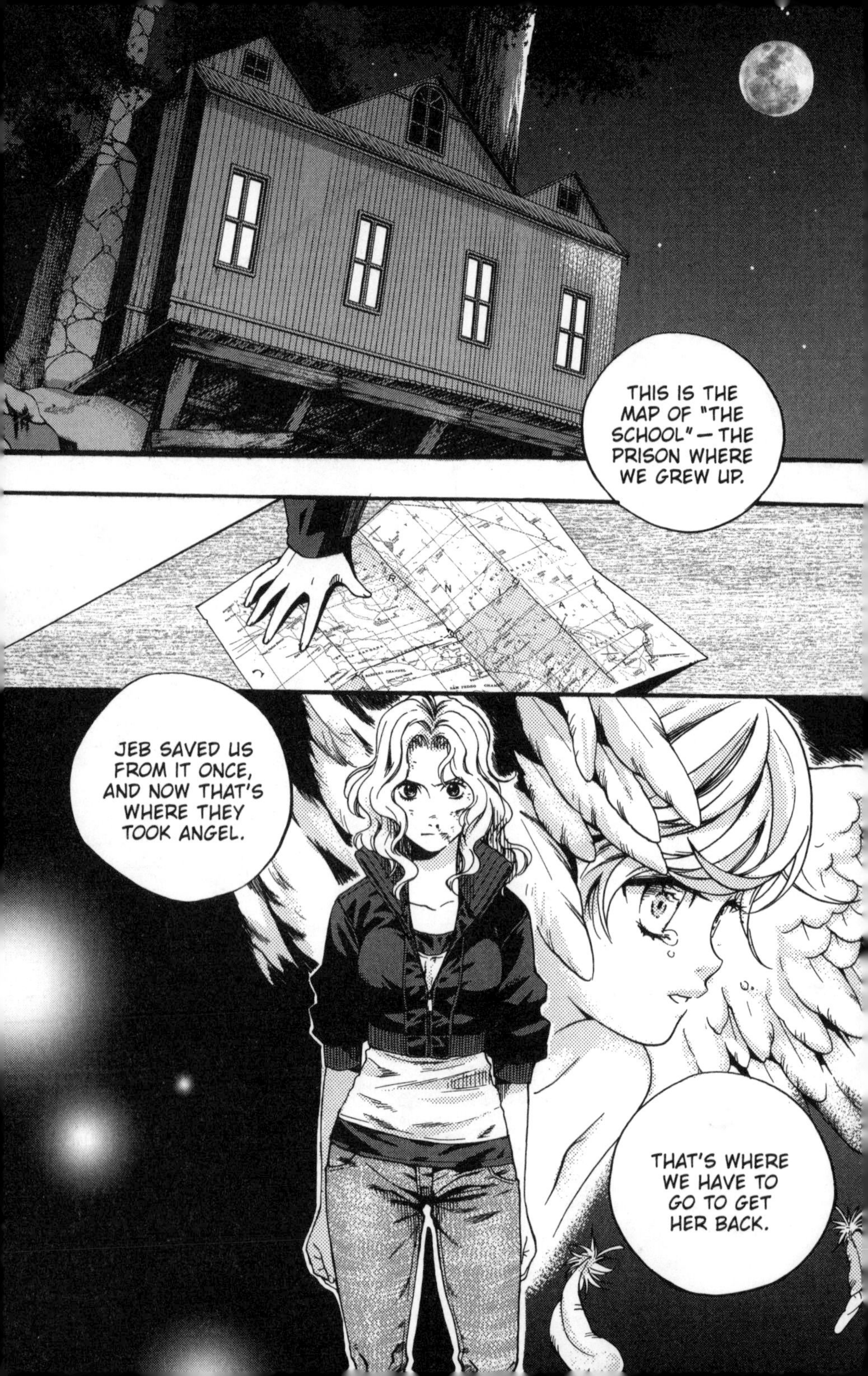
THIS IS THE MAP OF "THE SCHOOL"—THE PRISON WHERE WE GREW UP.
JEB SAVED US FROM IT ONCE, AND NOW THAT'S WHERE THEY TOOK ANGEL.
THAT'S WHERE WE HAVE TO GO TO GET HER BACK.

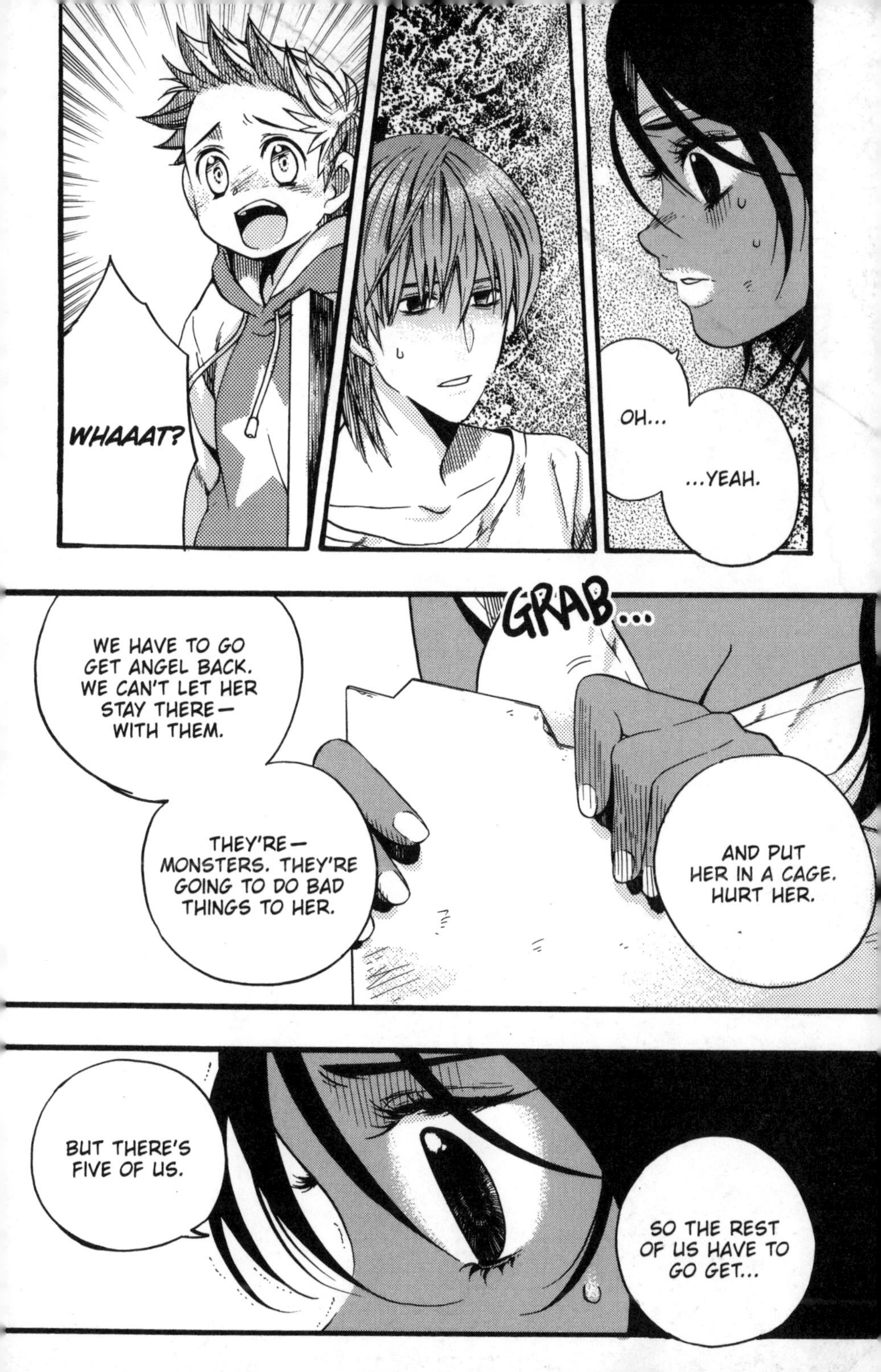
WHAAAT?
OH...
...YEAH.
WE HAVE TO GO GET ANGEL BACK. WE CAN'T LET HER STAY THERE—WITH THEM.
THEY'RE—MONSTERS. THEY'RE GOING TO DO BAD THINGS TO HER.
GRAB...
AND PUT HER IN A CAGE. HURT HER.
BUT THERE'S FIVE OF US.
SO THE REST OF US HAVE TO GO GET...

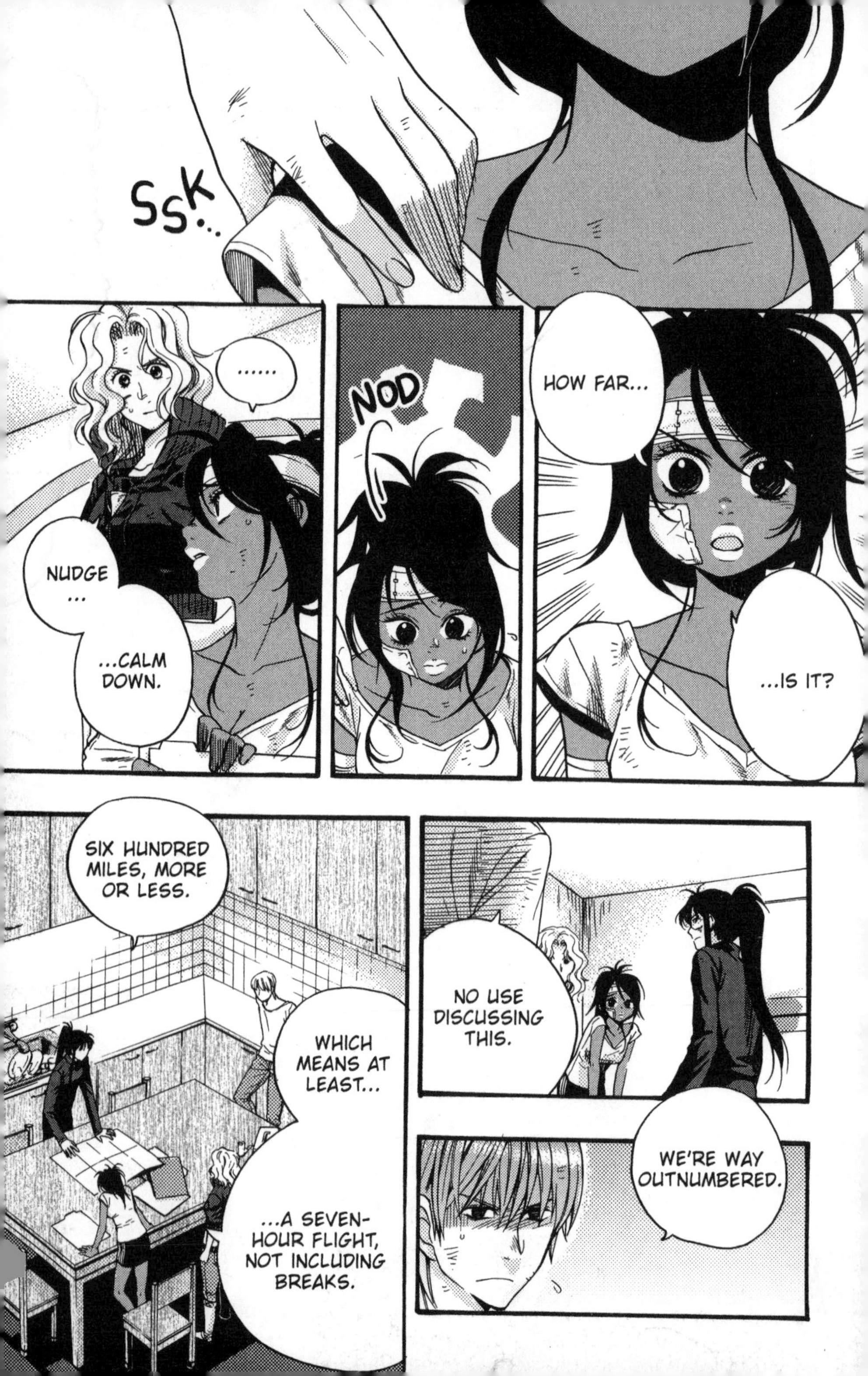
SSK...
......
NUDGE...
...CALM DOWN.
NOD
HOW FAR...
...IS IT?
SIX HUNDRED MILES, MORE OR LESS.
WHICH MEANS AT LEAST...
...A SEVEN-HOUR FLIGHT, NOT INCLUDING BREAKS.
NO USE DISCUSSING THIS.
WE'RE WAY OUTNUMBERED.

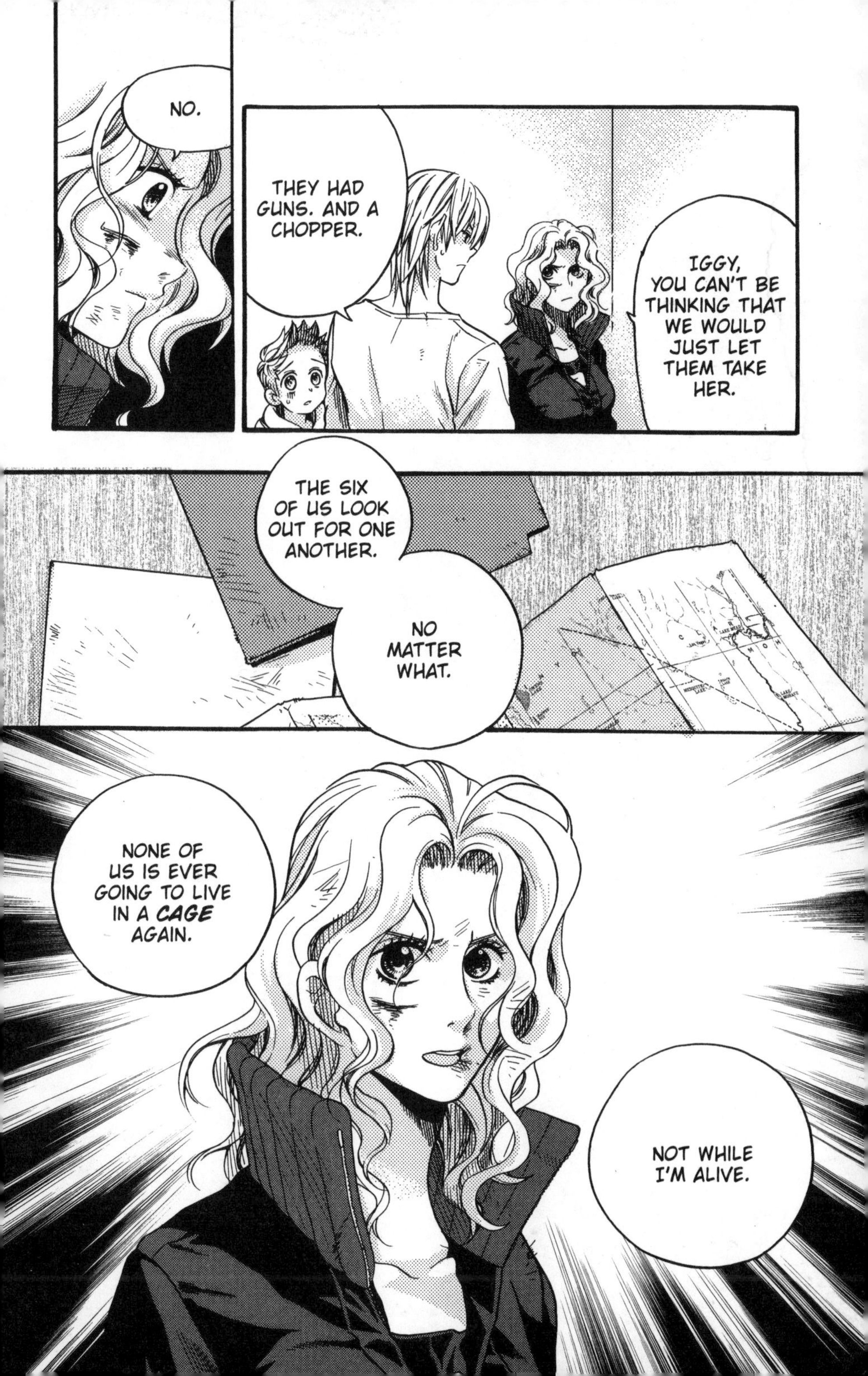
NO.
THEY HAD GUNS. AND A CHOPPER.
IGGY, YOU CAN'T BE THINKING THAT WE WOULD JUST LET THEM TAKE HER.
THE SIX OF US LOOK OUT FOR ONE ANOTHER.
NO MATTER WHAT.
NONE OF US IS EVER GOING TO LIVE IN A *CAGE* AGAIN.
NOT WHILE I'M ALIVE.

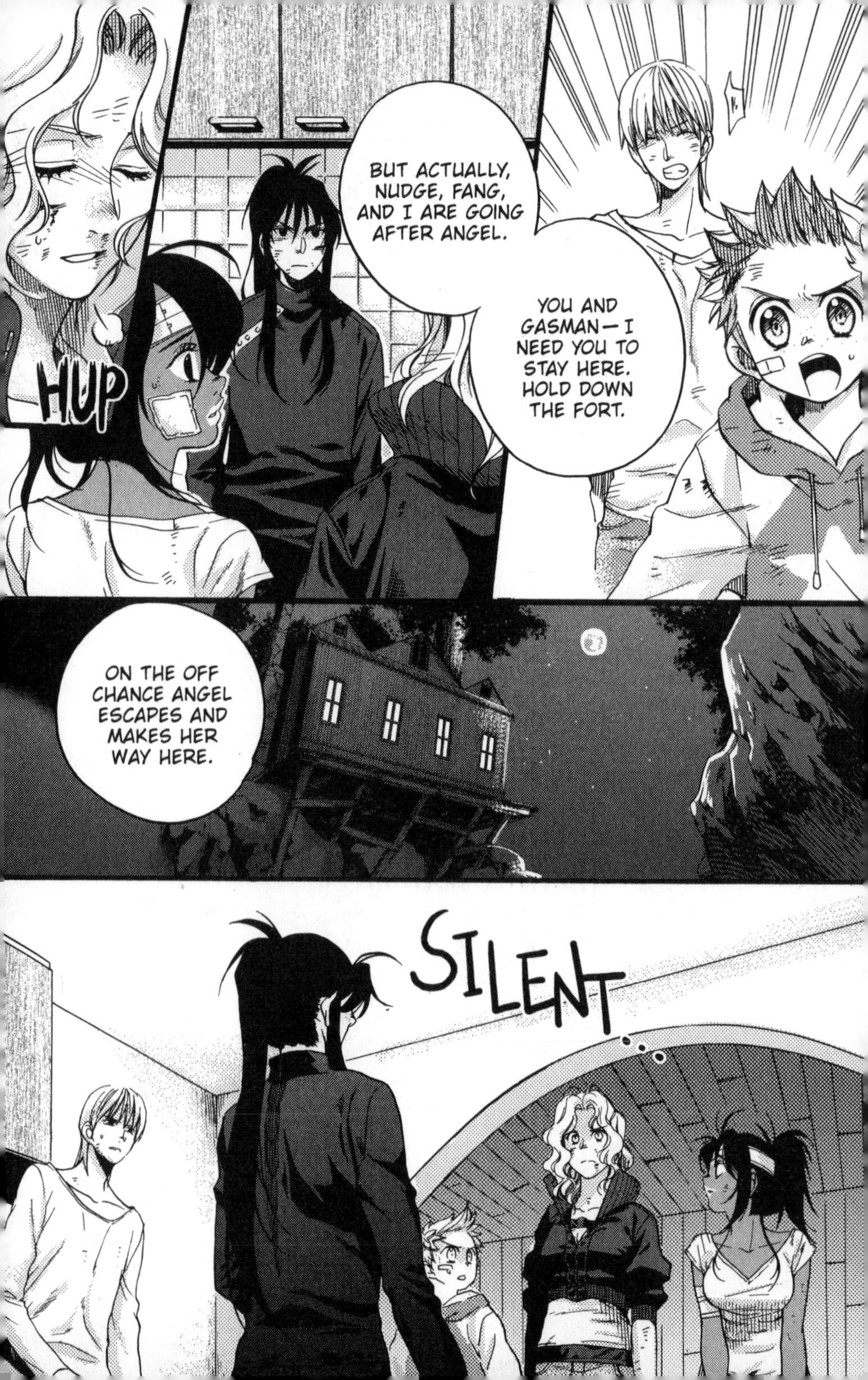
HUP
BUT ACTUALLY, NUDGE, FANG, AND I ARE GOING AFTER ANGEL.
YOU AND GASMAN—I NEED YOU TO STAY HERE. HOLD DOWN THE FORT.
ON THE OFF CHANCE ANGEL ESCAPES AND MAKES HER WAY HERE.
SILENT

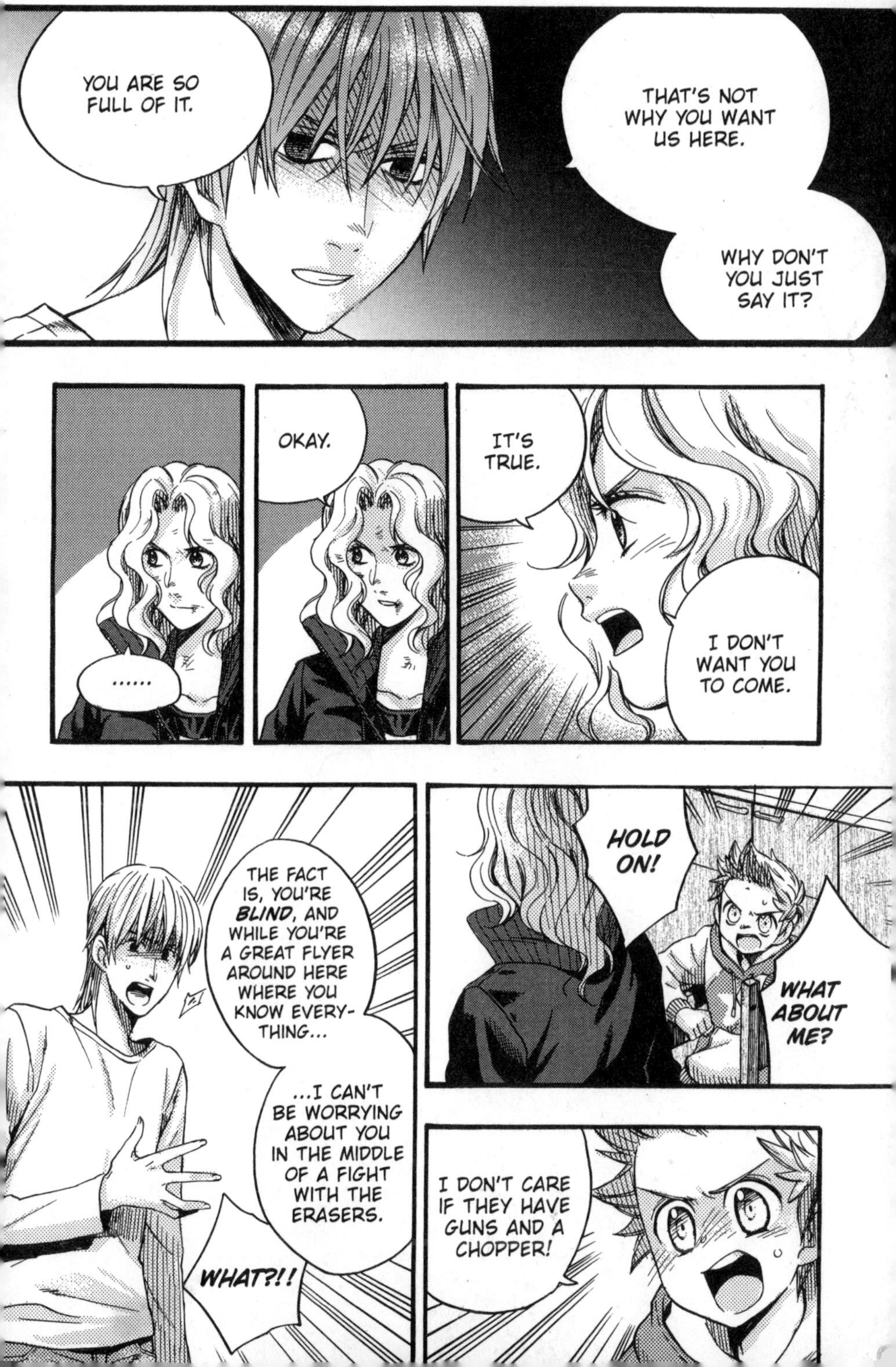
YOU ARE SO FULL OF IT.
THAT'S NOT WHY YOU WANT US HERE.
WHY DON'T YOU JUST SAY IT?
......
OKAY.
IT'S TRUE.
I DON'T WANT YOU TO COME.
THE FACT IS, YOU'RE *BLIND*, AND WHILE YOU'RE A GREAT FLYER AROUND HERE WHERE YOU KNOW EVERY-THING...
...I CAN'T BE WORRYING ABOUT YOU IN THE MIDDLE OF A FIGHT WITH THE ERASERS.
WHAT?!!
HOLD ON!
WHAT ABOUT ME?
I DON'T CARE IF THEY HAVE GUNS AND A CHOPPER!

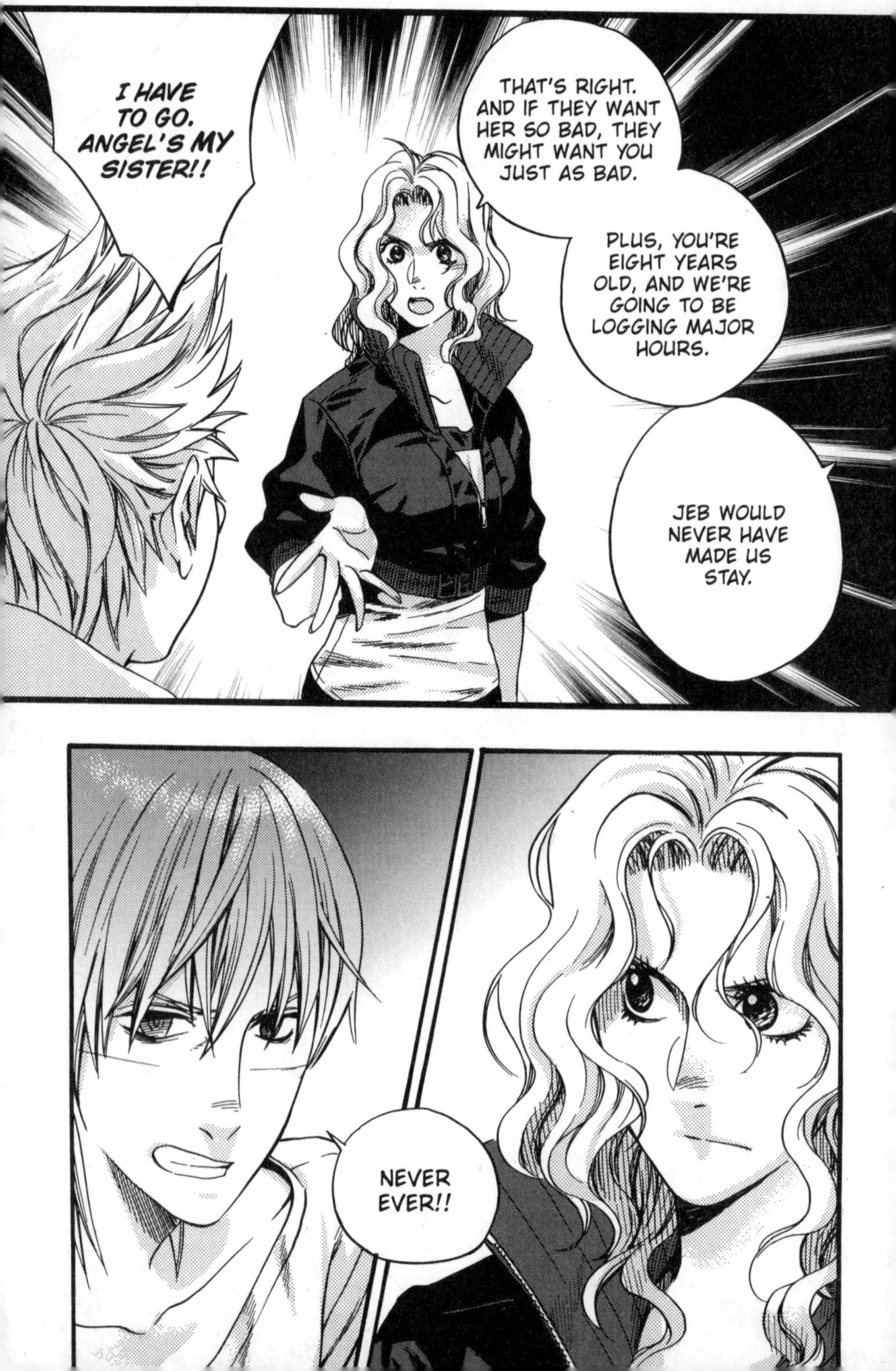
I HAVE TO GO. ANGEL'S MY SISTER!!
THAT'S RIGHT. AND IF THEY WANT HER SO BAD, THEY MIGHT WANT YOU JUST AS BAD.
PLUS, YOU'RE EIGHT YEARS OLD, AND WE'RE GOING TO BE LOGGING MAJOR HOURS.
JEB WOULD NEVER HAVE MADE US STAY.
NEVER EVER!!

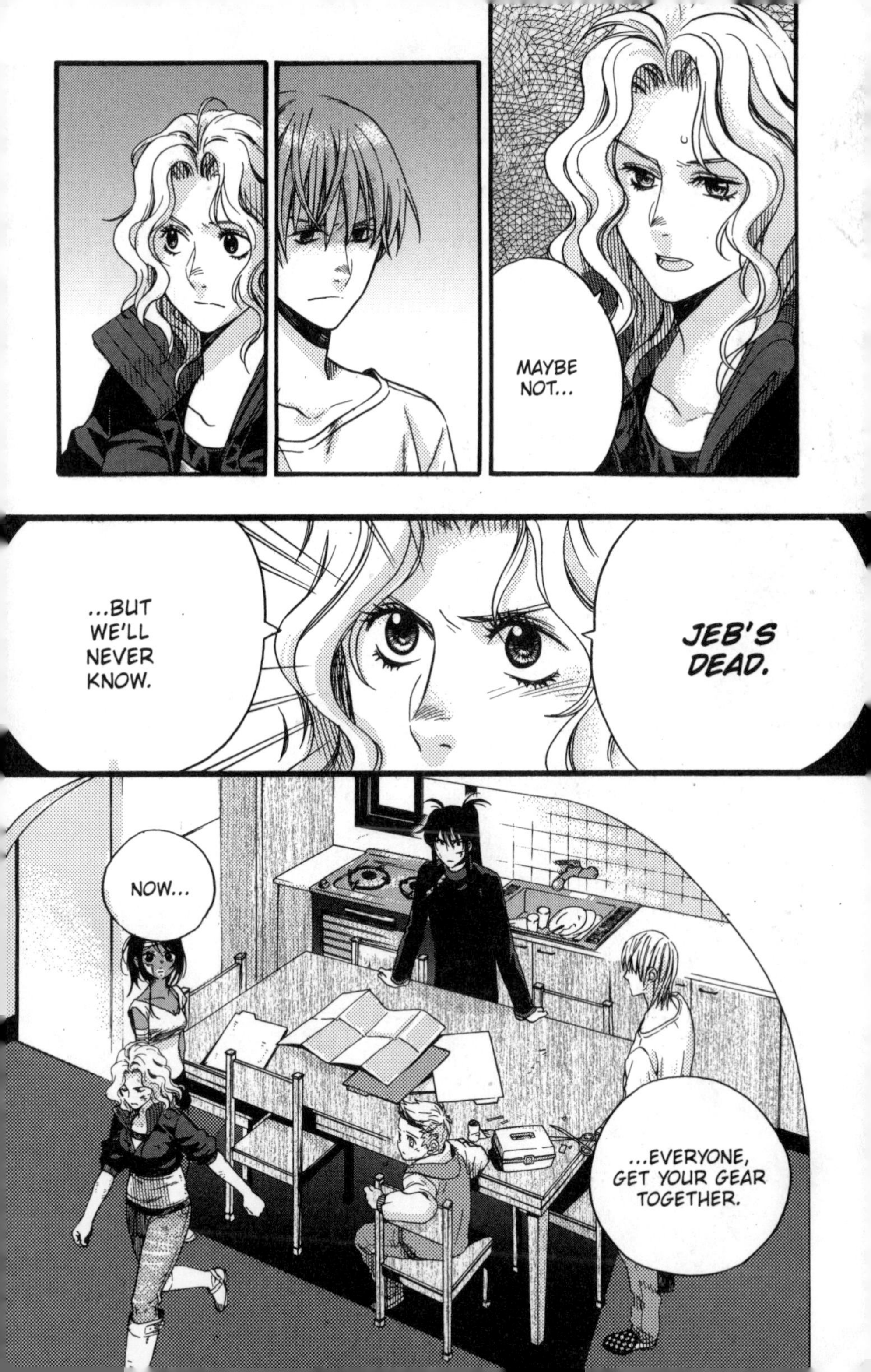
MAYBE NOT...
...BUT WE'LL NEVER KNOW.
JEB'S DEAD.
NOW...
...EVERYONE, GET YOUR GEAR TOGETHER.

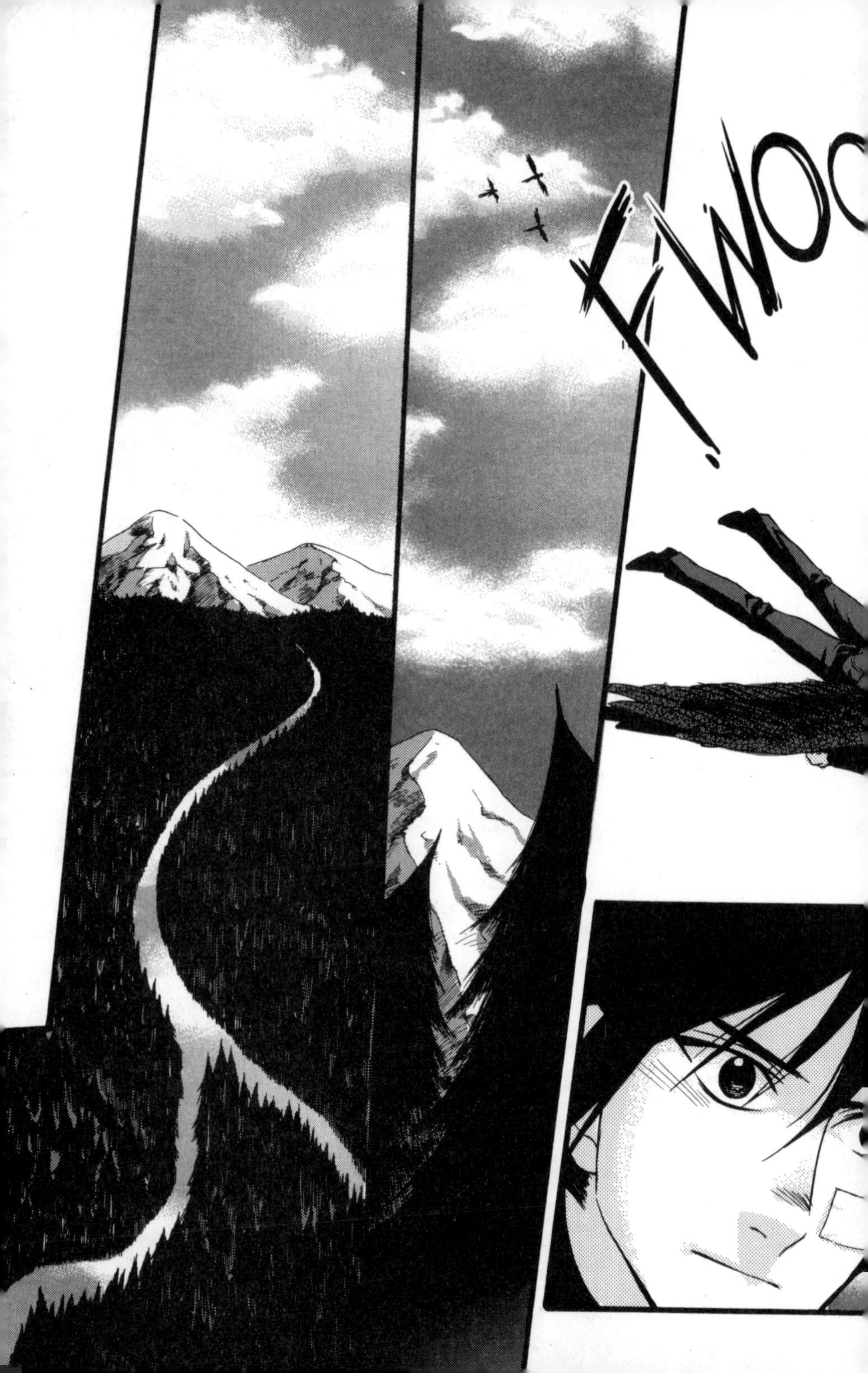
FWOO

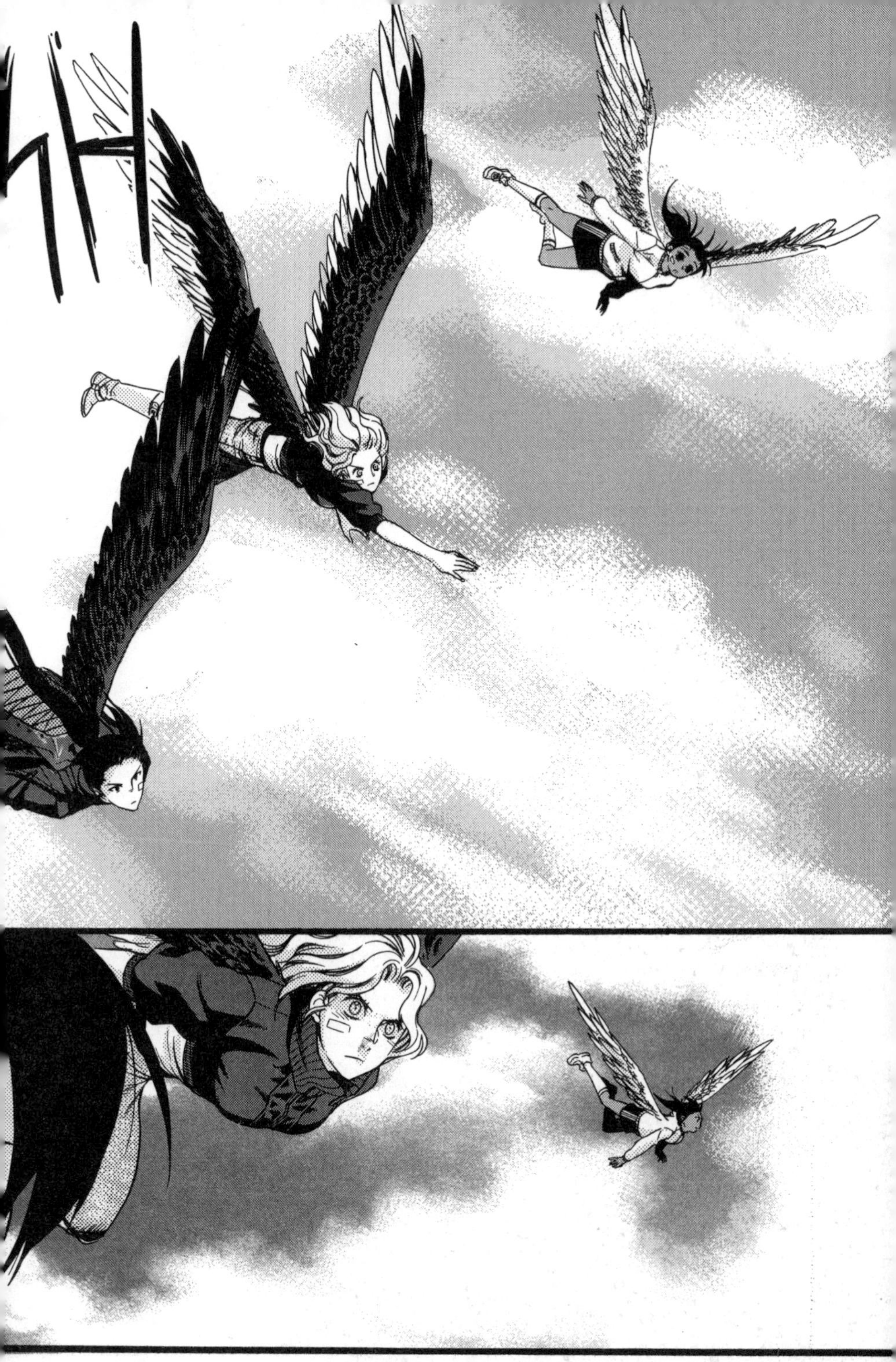

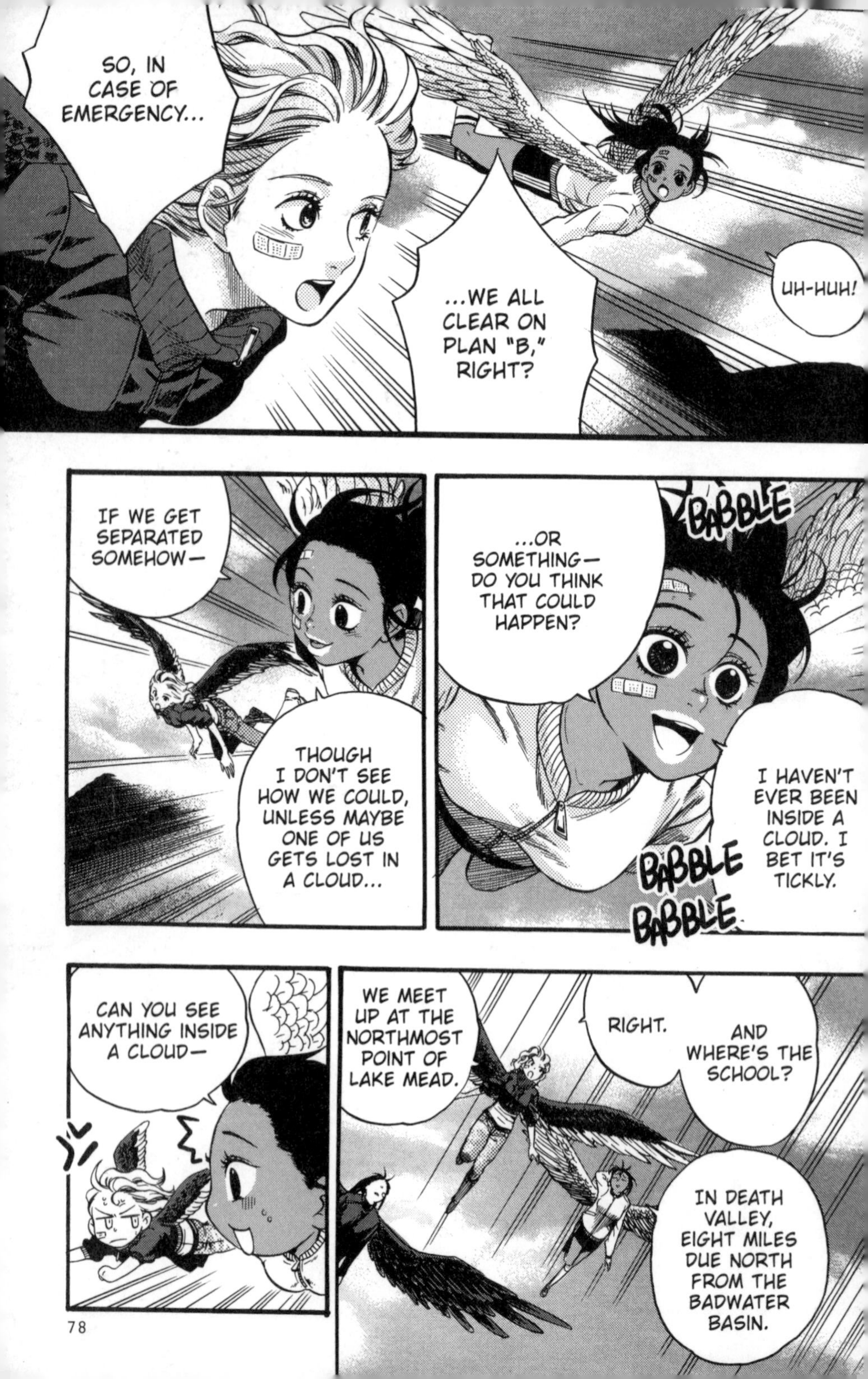
SO, IN CASE OF EMERGENCY...
...WE ALL CLEAR ON PLAN "B," RIGHT?
UH-HUH!
IF WE GET SEPARATED SOMEHOW—
THOUGH I DON'T SEE HOW WE COULD, UNLESS MAYBE ONE OF US GETS LOST IN A CLOUD...
BABBLE
...OR SOMETHING— DO YOU THINK THAT COULD HAPPEN?
I HAVEN'T EVER BEEN INSIDE A CLOUD. I BET IT'S TICKLY.
BABBLE
BABBLE
CAN YOU SEE ANYTHING INSIDE A CLOUD—
WE MEET UP AT THE NORTHMOST POINT OF LAKE MEAD.
RIGHT.
AND WHERE'S THE SCHOOL?
IN DEATH VALLEY, EIGHT MILES DUE NORTH FROM THE BADWATER BASIN.

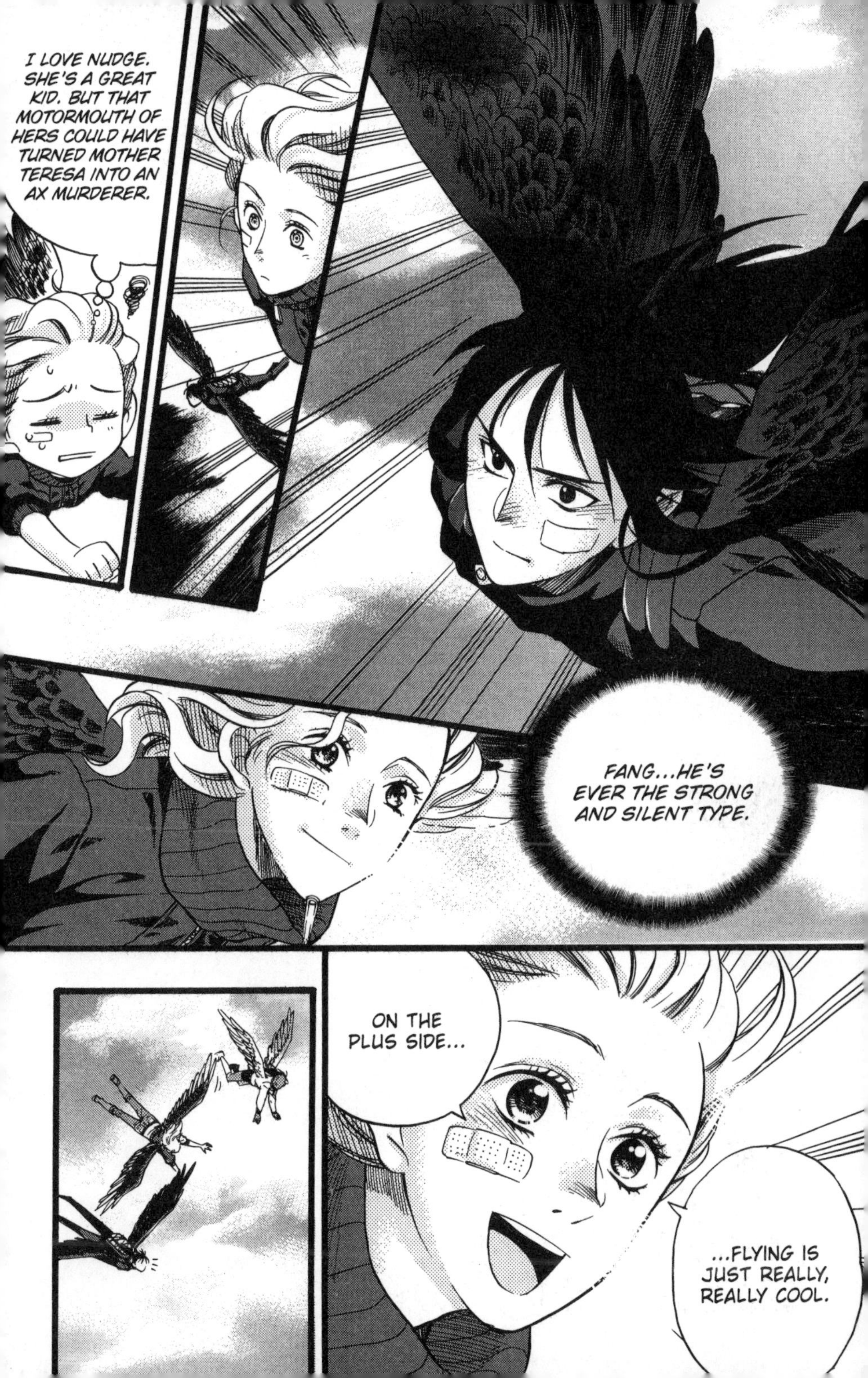
I LOVE NUDGE. SHE'S A GREAT KID. BUT THAT MOTORMOUTH OF HERS COULD HAVE TURNED MOTHER TERESA INTO AN AX MURDERER.
FANG...HE'S EVER THE STRONG AND SILENT TYPE.
ON THE PLUS SIDE...
...FLYING IS JUST REALLY, REALLY COOL.

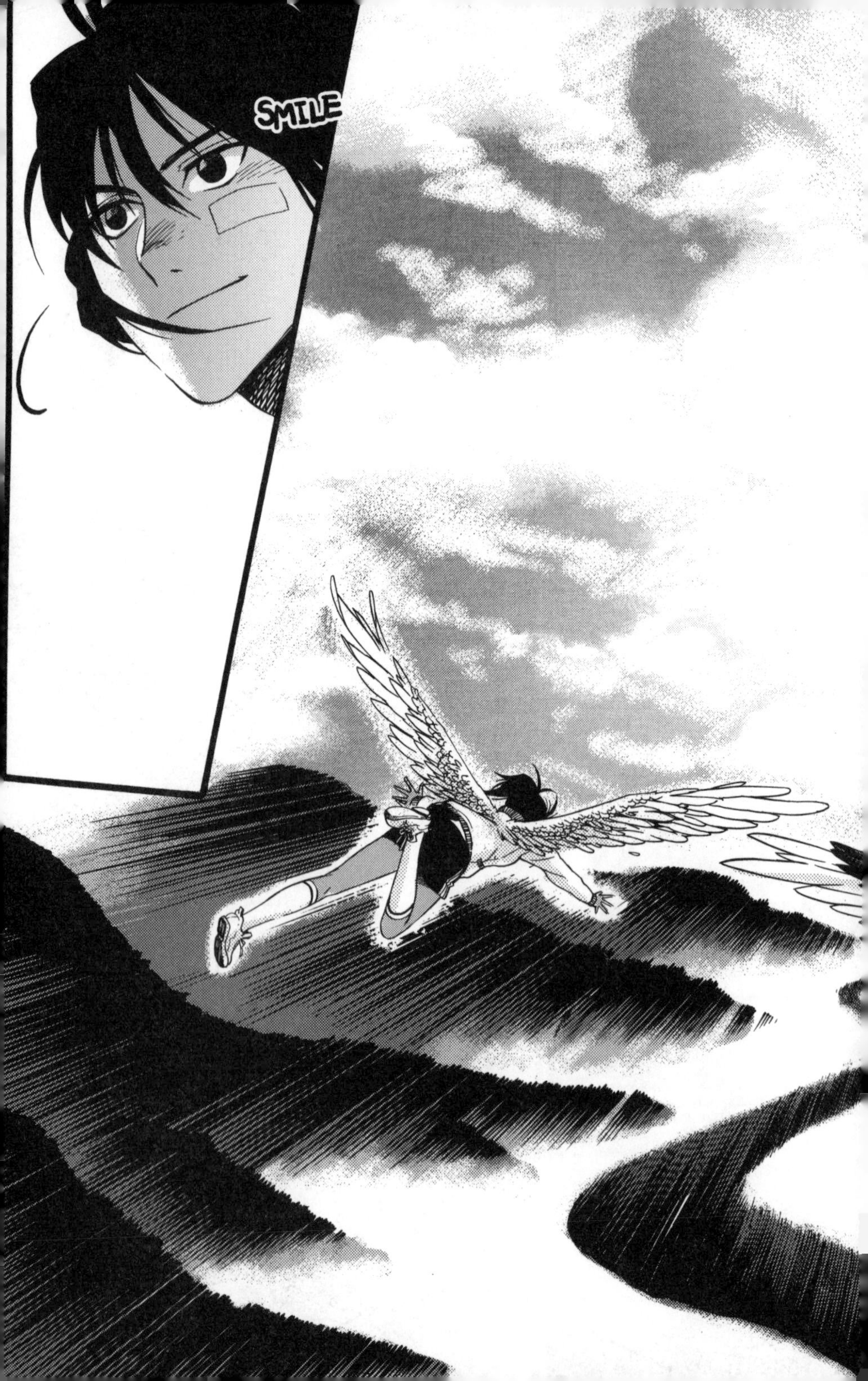
SMILE

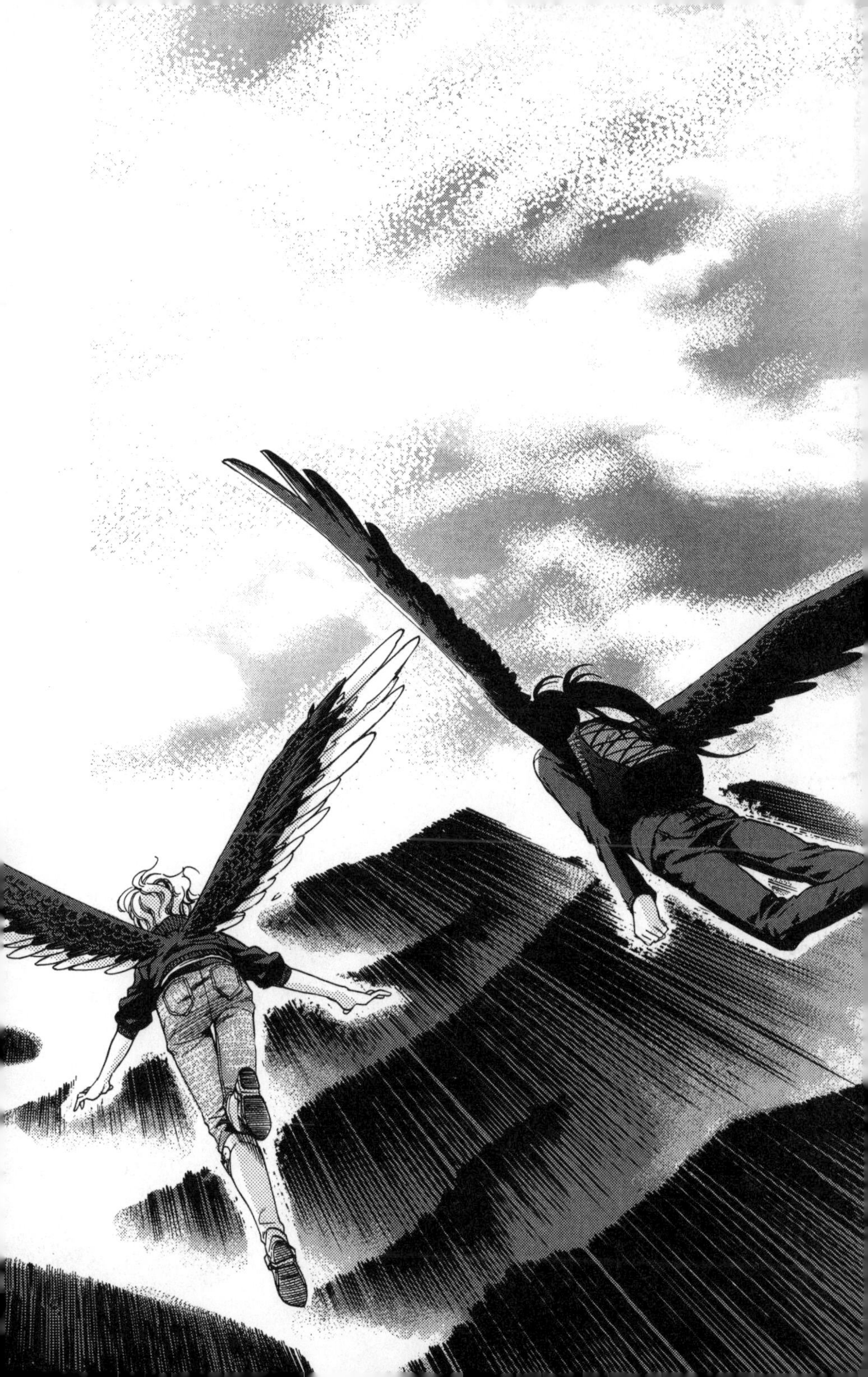

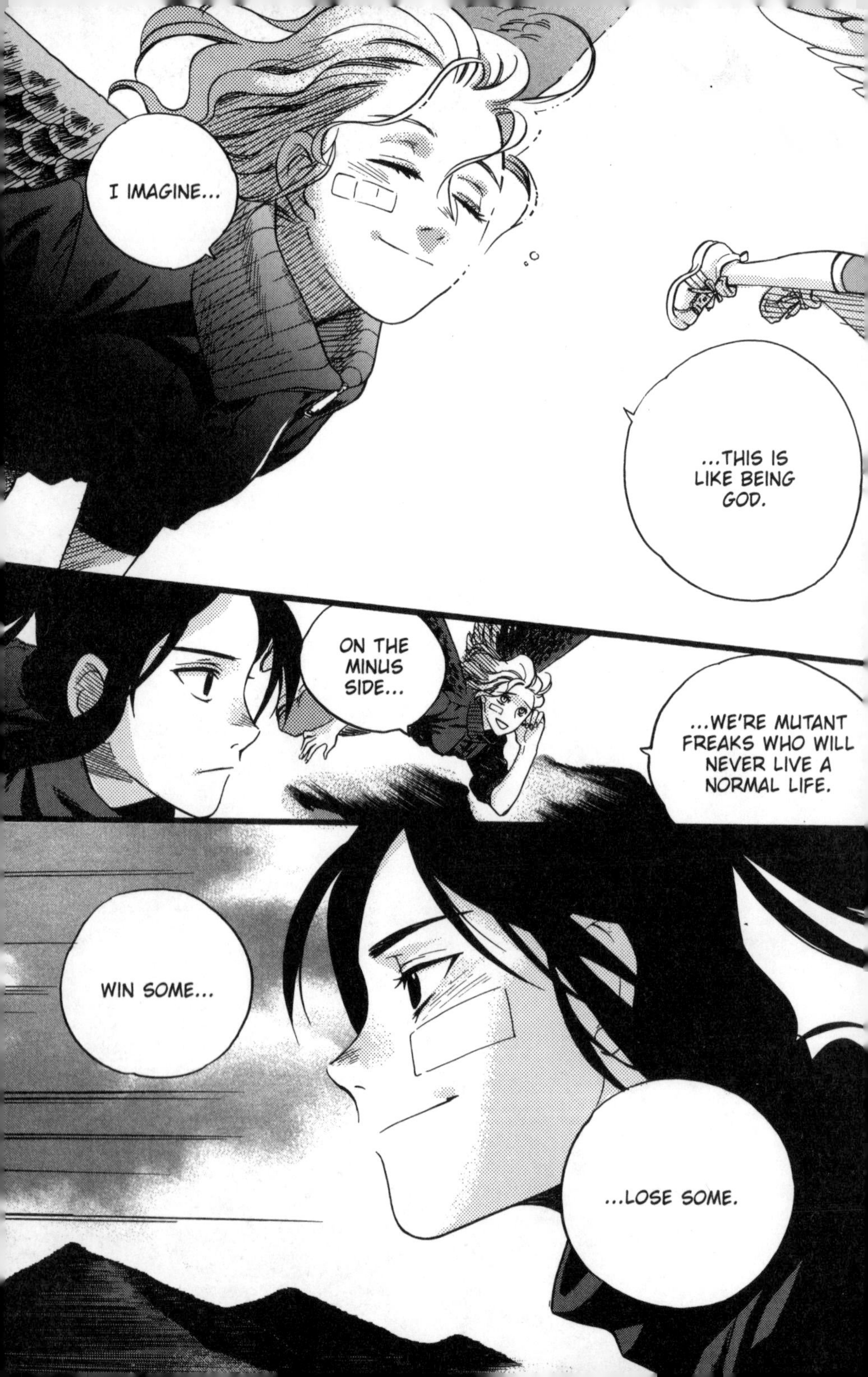
I IMAGINE...
...THIS IS LIKE BEING GOD.
ON THE MINUS SIDE...
...WE'RE MUTANT FREAKS WHO WILL NEVER LIVE A NORMAL LIFE.
WIN SOME...
...LOSE SOME.

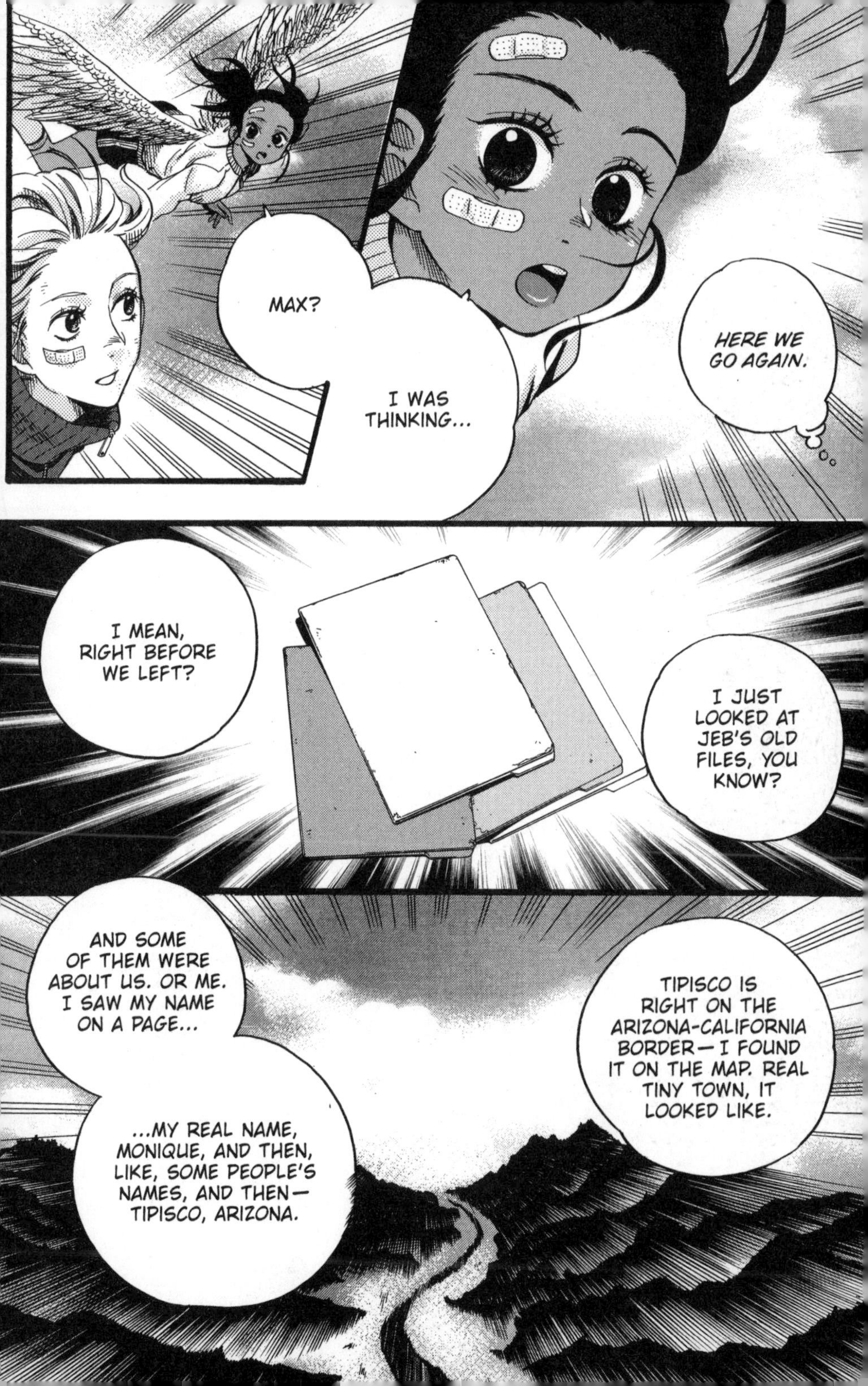
MAX?
I WAS THINKING...
HERE WE GO AGAIN.
I MEAN, RIGHT BEFORE WE LEFT?
I JUST LOOKED AT JEB'S OLD FILES, YOU KNOW?
AND SOME OF THEM WERE ABOUT US. OR ME. I SAW MY NAME ON A PAGE...
...MY REAL NAME, MONIQUE, AND THEN, LIKE, SOME PEOPLE'S NAMES, AND THEN— TIPISCO, ARIZONA.
TIPISCO IS RIGHT ON THE ARIZONA-CALIFORNIA BORDER—I FOUND IT ON THE MAP. REAL TINY TOWN, IT LOOKED LIKE.

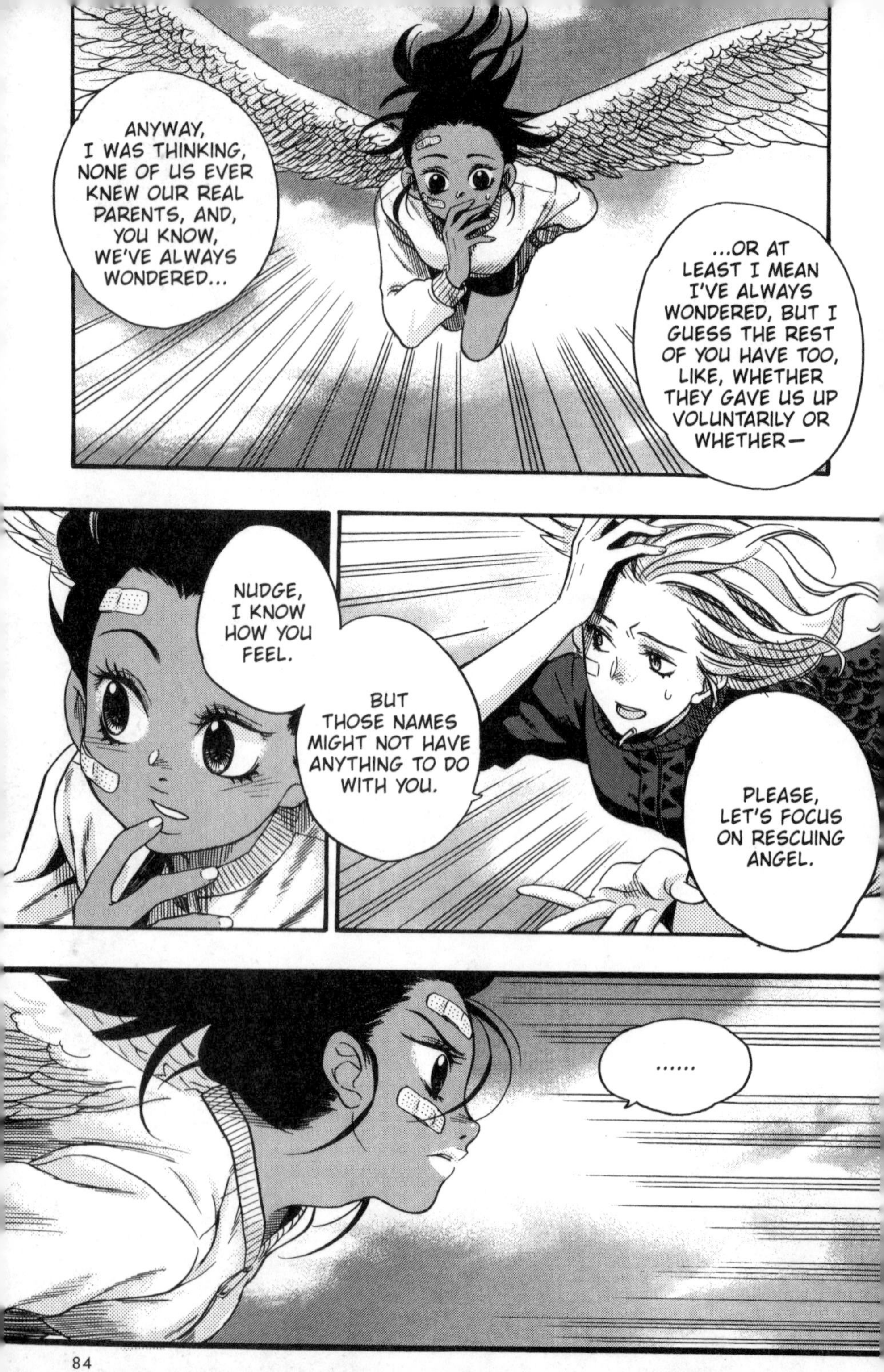
ANYWAY, I WAS THINKING, NONE OF US EVER KNEW OUR REAL PARENTS, AND, YOU KNOW, WE'VE ALWAYS WONDERED...
...OR AT LEAST I MEAN I'VE ALWAYS WONDERED, BUT I GUESS THE REST OF YOU HAVE TOO, LIKE, WHETHER THEY GAVE US UP VOLUNTARILY OR WHETHER—
NUDGE, I KNOW HOW YOU FEEL.
BUT THOSE NAMES MIGHT NOT HAVE ANYTHING TO DO WITH YOU.
PLEASE, LET'S FOCUS ON RESCUING ANGEL.
......

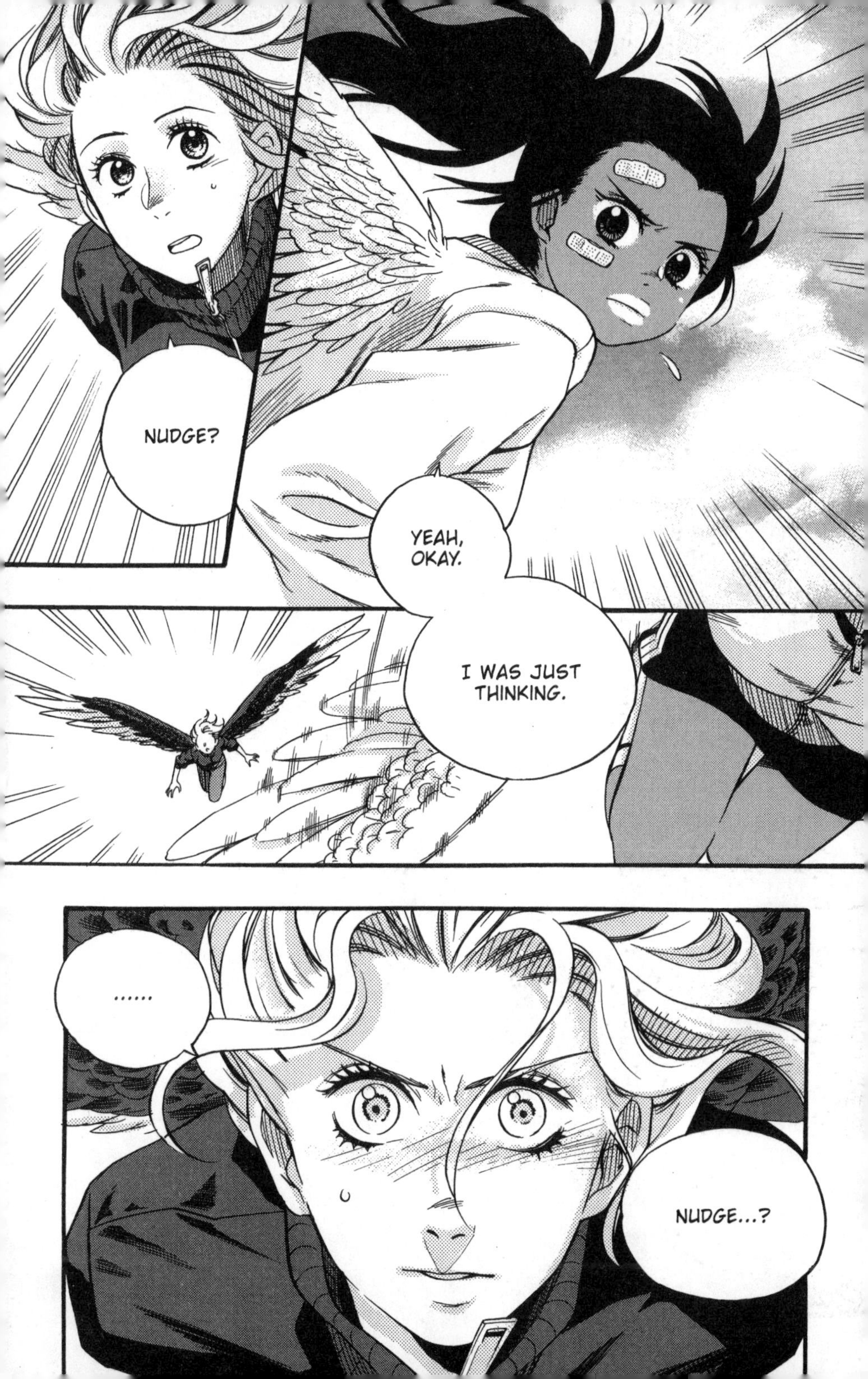
NUDGE?
YEAH, OKAY.
I WAS JUST THINKING.
......
NUDGE...?

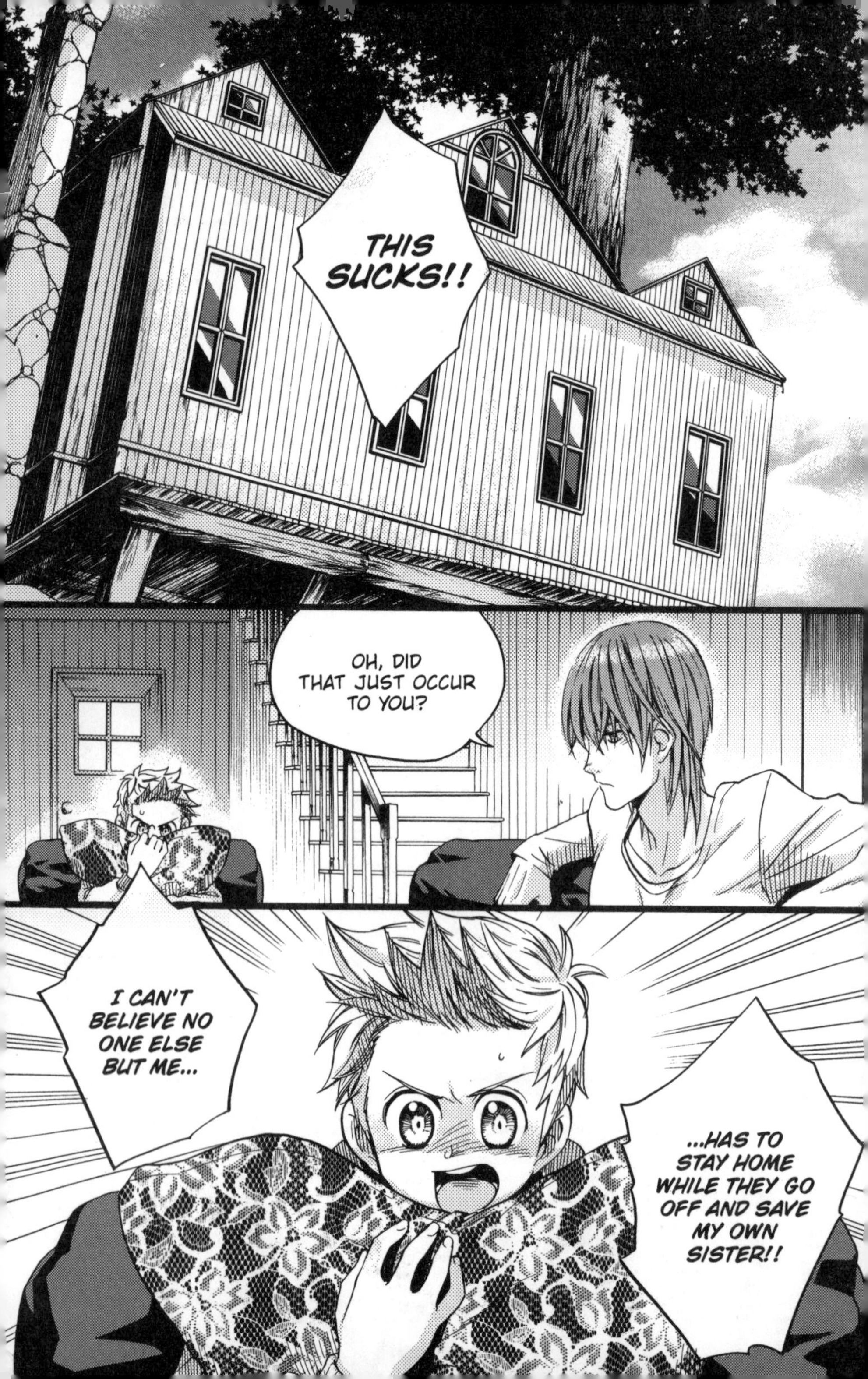
THIS SUCKS!!
OH, DID THAT JUST OCCUR TO YOU?
I CAN'T BELIEVE NO ONE ELSE BUT ME...
...HAS TO STAY HOME WHILE THEY GO OFF AND SAVE MY OWN SISTER!!

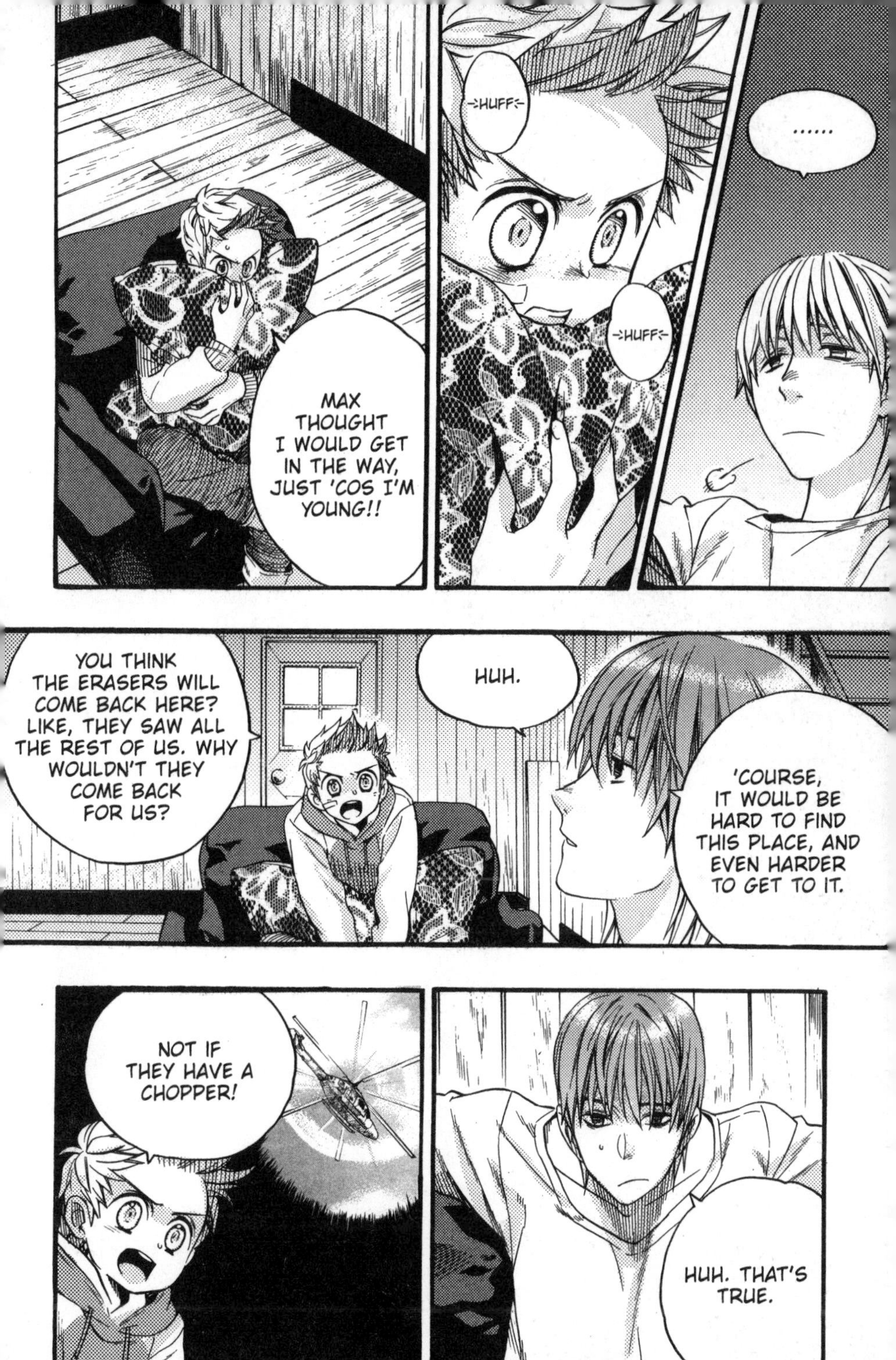

MAX THOUGHT I WOULD GET IN THE WAY, JUST 'COS I'M YOUNG!!
HUFF
HUFF
......
YOU THINK THE ERASERS WILL COME BACK HERE? LIKE, THEY SAW ALL THE REST OF US. WHY WOULDN'T THEY COME BACK FOR US?
HUH.
'COURSE, IT WOULD BE HARD TO FIND THIS PLACE, AND EVEN HARDER TO GET TO IT.
NOT IF THEY HAVE A CHOPPER!
HUH. THAT'S TRUE.

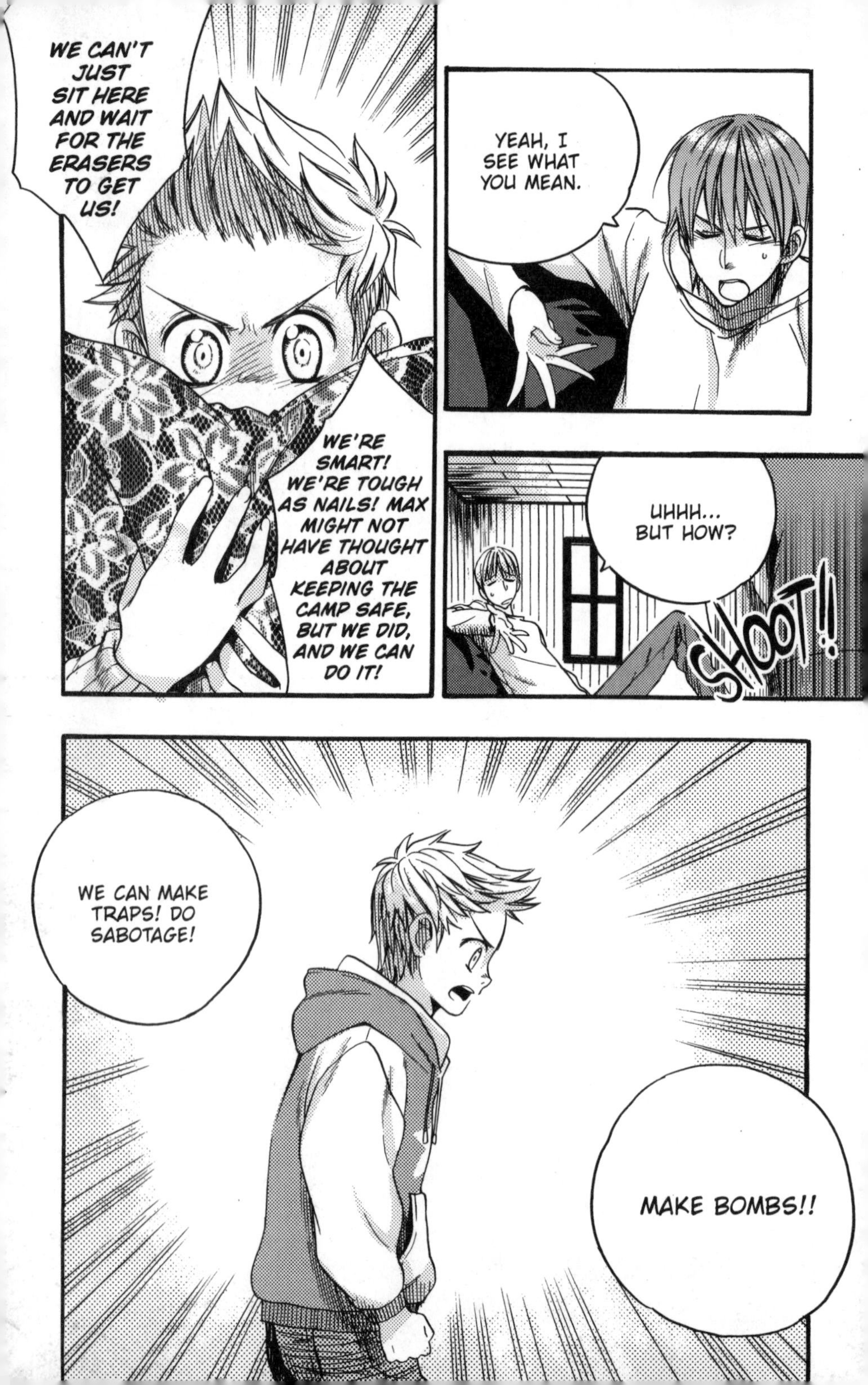
WE CAN'T JUST SIT HERE AND WAIT FOR THE ERASERS TO GET US!
WE'RE SMART! WE'RE TOUGH AS NAILS! MAX MIGHT NOT HAVE THOUGHT ABOUT KEEPING THE CAMP SAFE, BUT WE DID, AND WE CAN DO IT!
YEAH, I SEE WHAT YOU MEAN.
UHHH... BUT HOW?
SHOOT!!
WE CAN MAKE TRAPS! DO SABOTAGE!
MAKE BOMBS!!

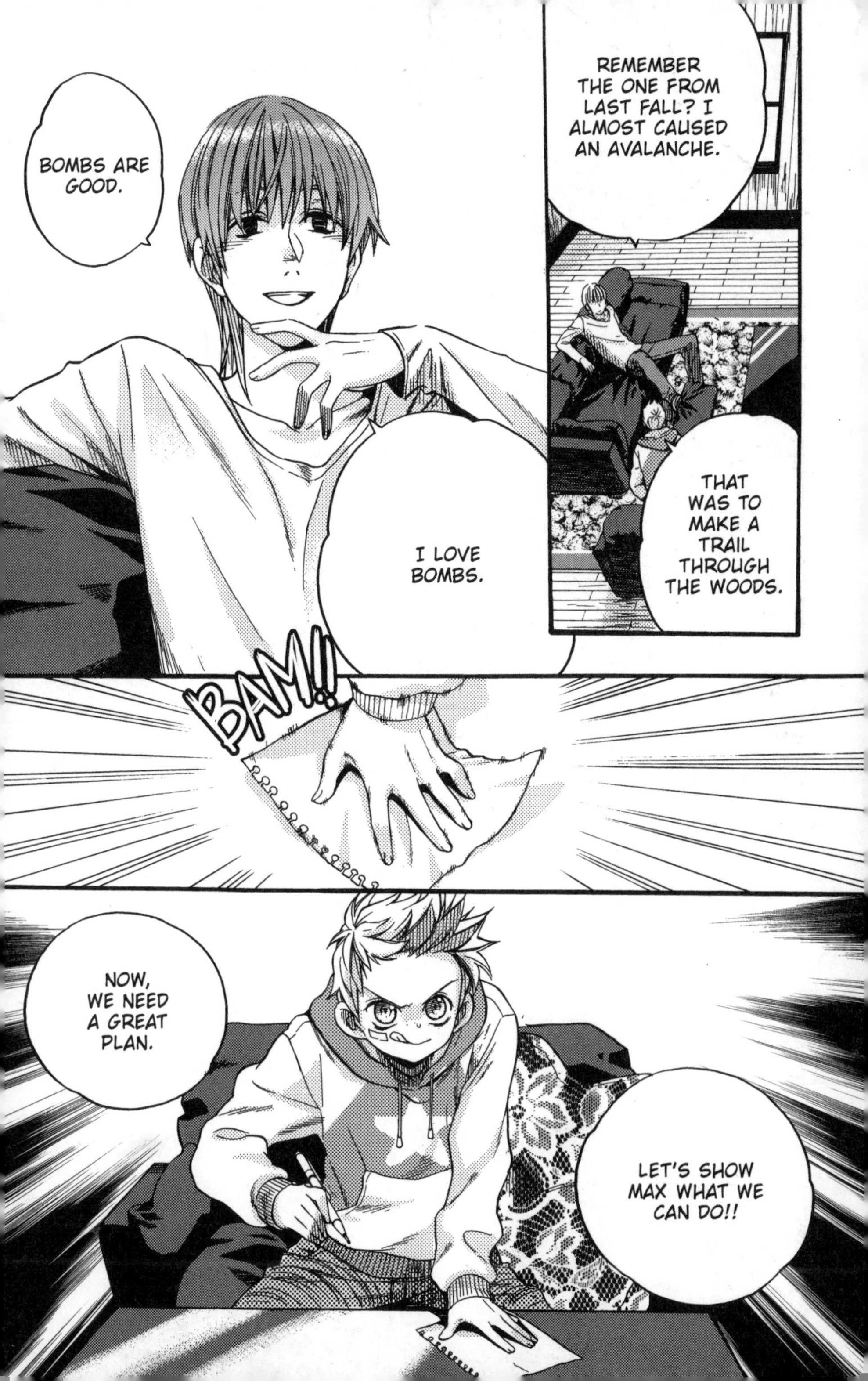
BOMBS ARE GOOD.
I LOVE BOMBS.
REMEMBER THE ONE FROM LAST FALL? I ALMOST CAUSED AN AVALANCHE.
THAT WAS TO MAKE A TRAIL THROUGH THE WOODS.
BAM!!
NOW, WE NEED A GREAT PLAN.
LET'S SHOW MAX WHAT WE CAN DO!!

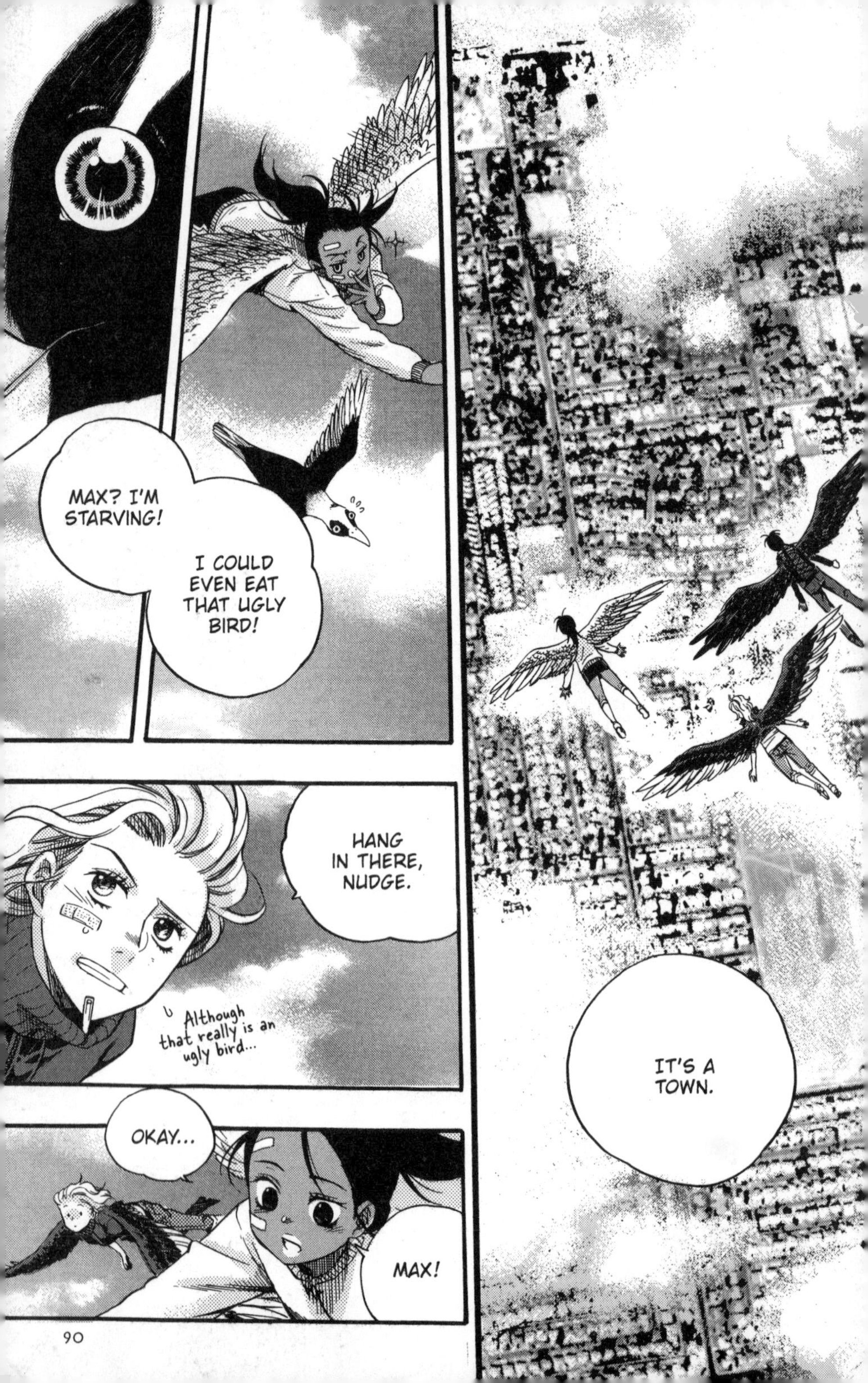

MAX? I'M STARVING!
I COULD EVEN EAT THAT UGLY BIRD!
HANG IN THERE, NUDGE.
Although that really is an ugly bird...
OKAY...
MAX!
IT'S A TOWN.

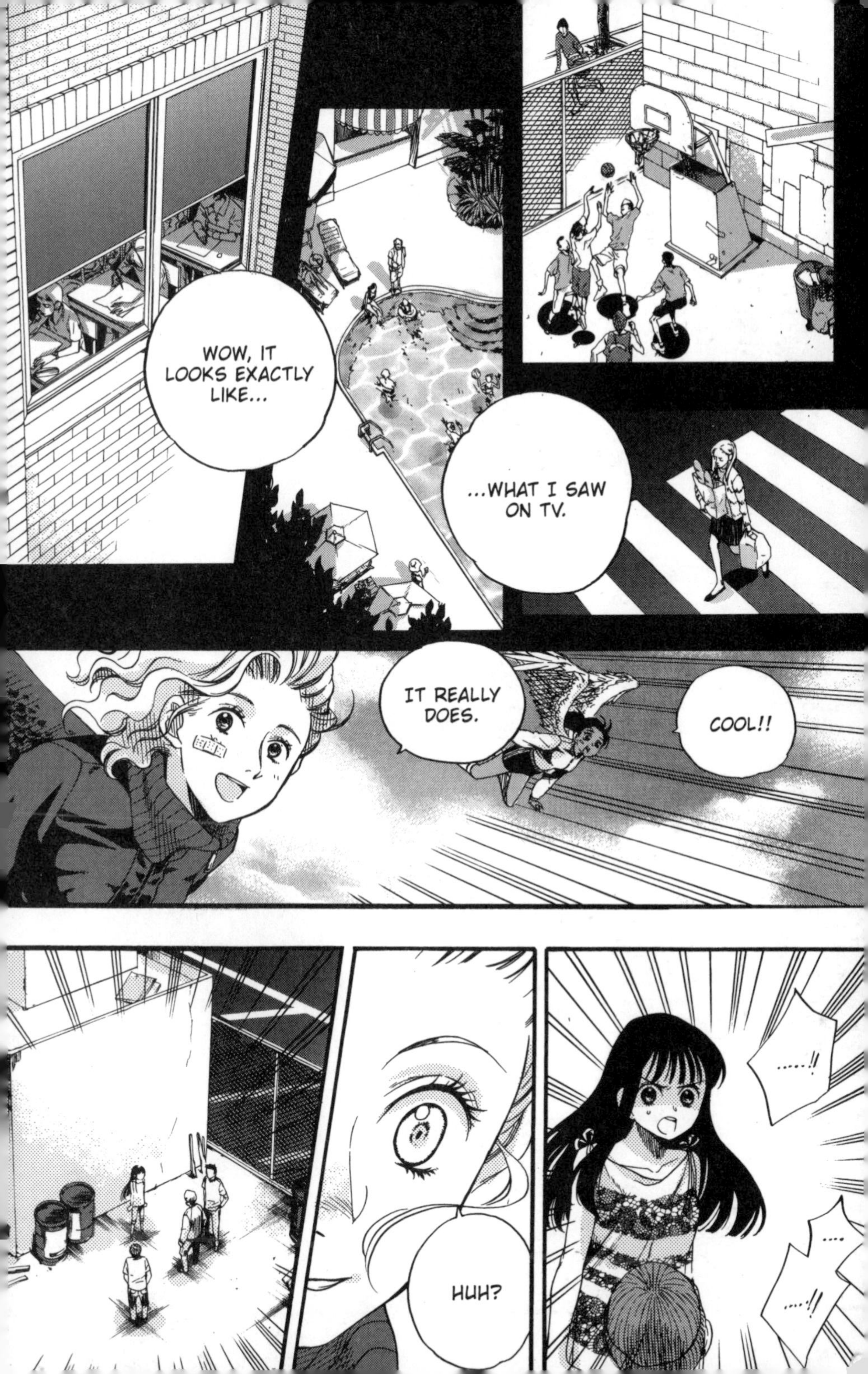
WOW, IT LOOKS EXACTLY LIKE...
...WHAT I SAW ON TV.
IT REALLY DOES.
COOL!!
HUH?
.....!!
....
....!!

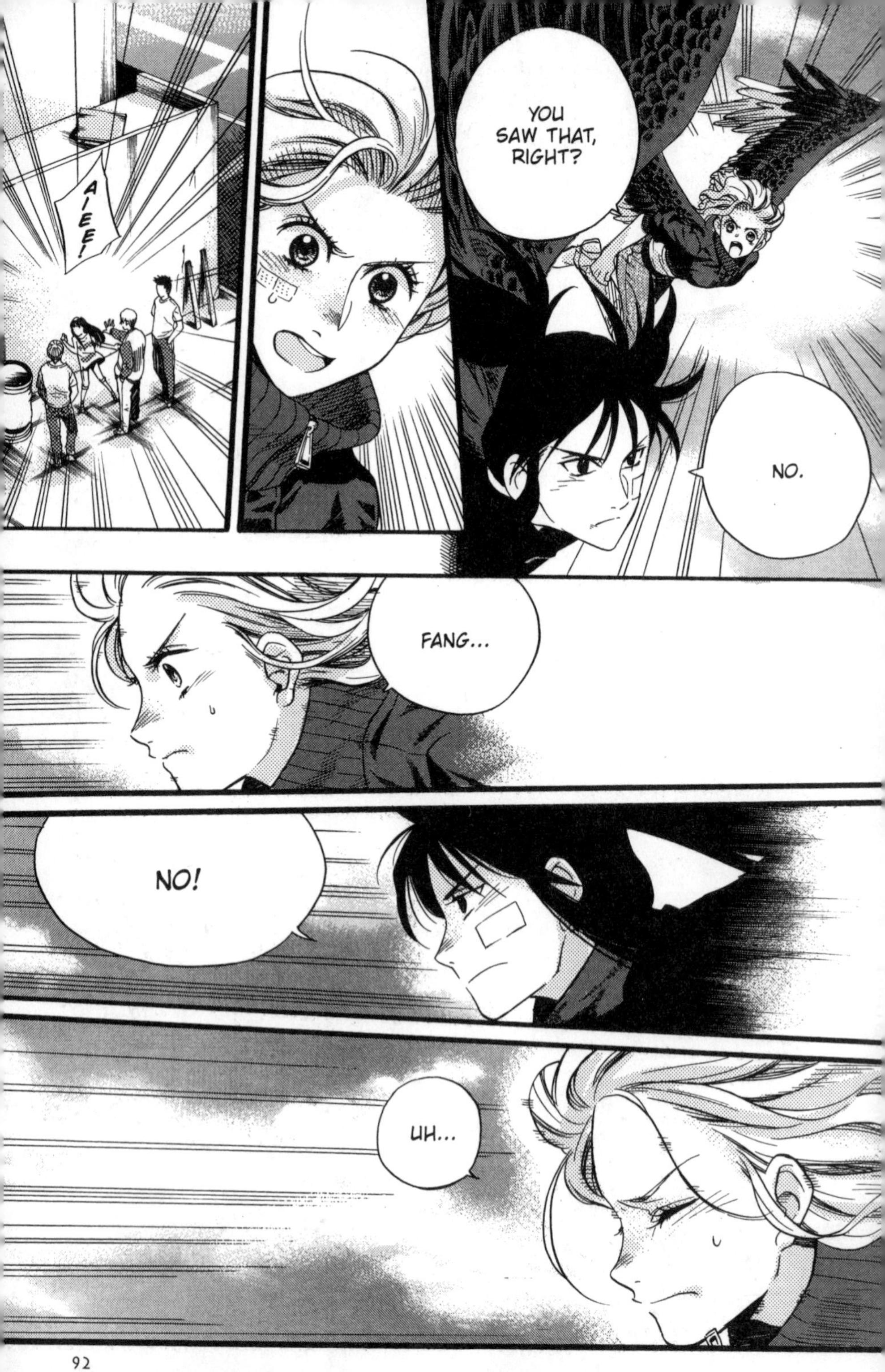
AIEEE!
YOU SAW THAT, RIGHT?
NO.
FANG...
NO!
UH...

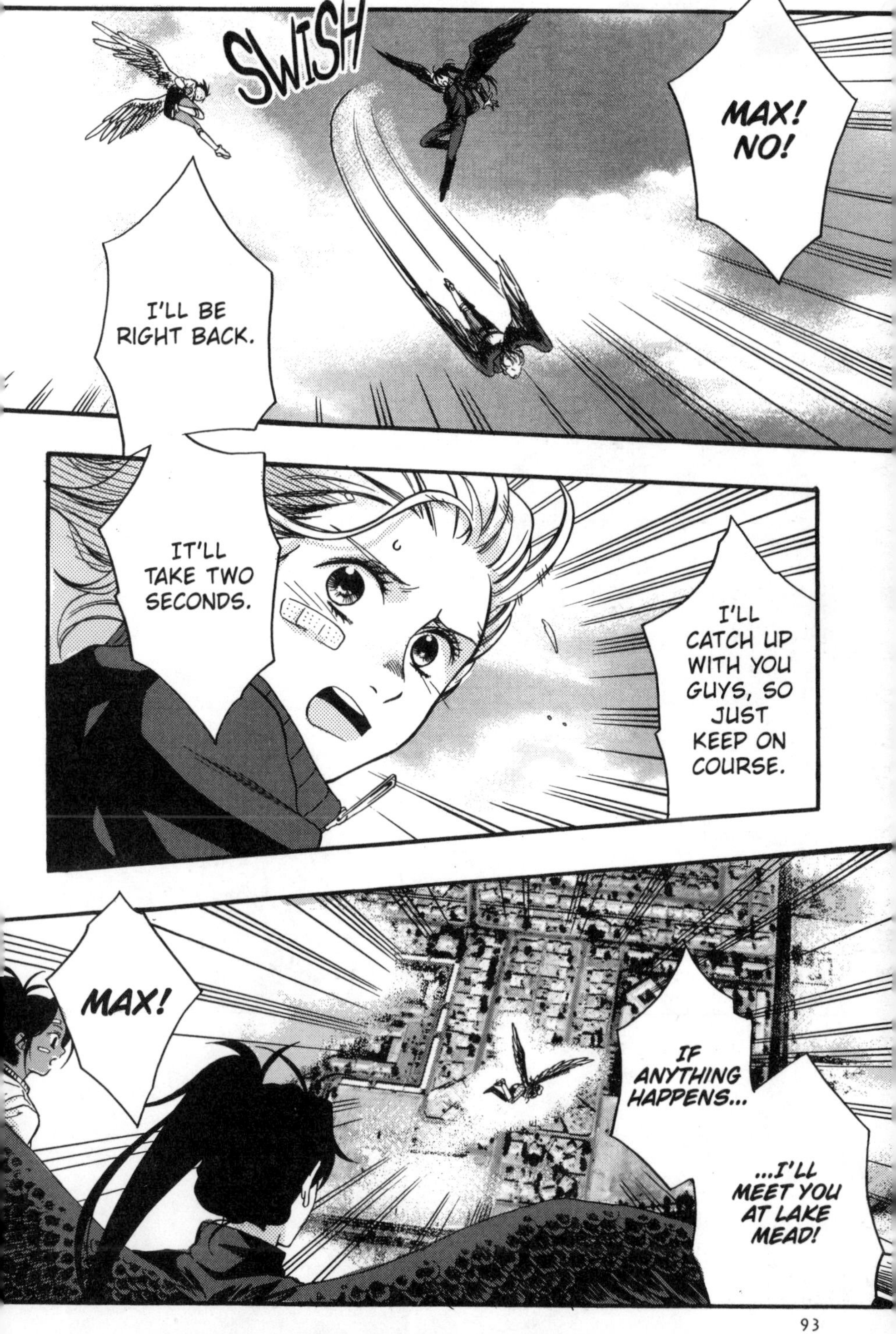
SWISH
MAX! NO!
I'LL BE RIGHT BACK.
IT'LL TAKE TWO SECONDS.
I'LL CATCH UP WITH YOU GUYS, SO JUST KEEP ON COURSE.
MAX!
IF ANYTHING HAPPENS...
...I'LL MEET YOU AT LAKE MEAD!

TAP

SSK

SO, WHAT HAVE YOU GOT TO SAY FOR YOURSELF?

IS THERE ANY REASON I SHOULDN'T TEACH YOU A LESSON TOO?

WITH MY WINGS FOLDED LIKE THIS...

...I SHOULD LOOK PERFECTLY NORMAL.

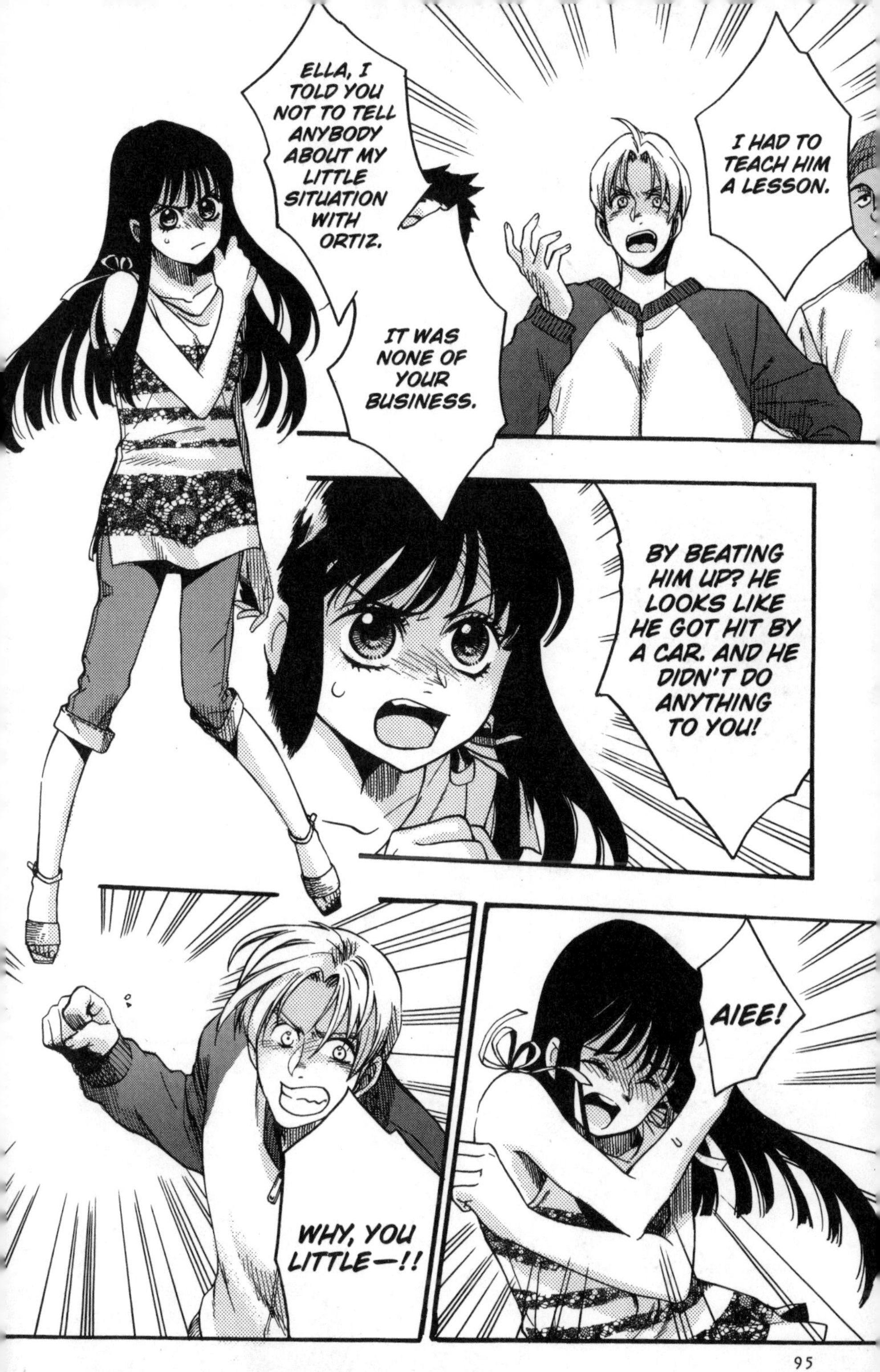
ELLA, I TOLD YOU NOT TO TELL ANYBODY ABOUT MY LITTLE SITUATION WITH ORTIZ.
IT WAS NONE OF YOUR BUSINESS.
I HAD TO TEACH HIM A LESSON.
BY BEATING HIM UP? HE LOOKS LIKE HE GOT HIT BY A CAR. AND HE DIDN'T DO ANYTHING TO YOU!
WHY, YOU LITTLE—!!
AIEE!

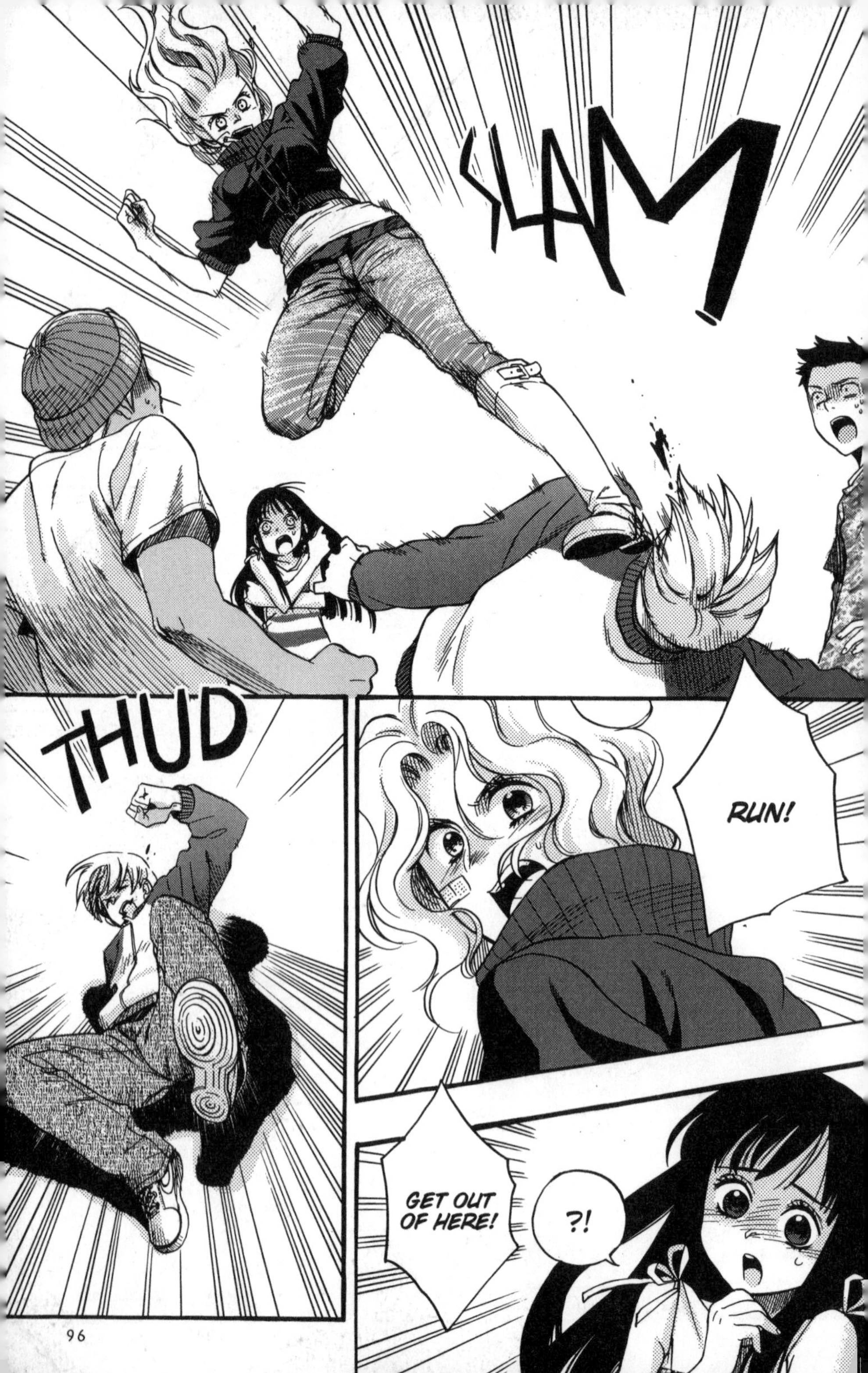
SLAM
THUD
RUN!
GET OUT OF HERE!
?!

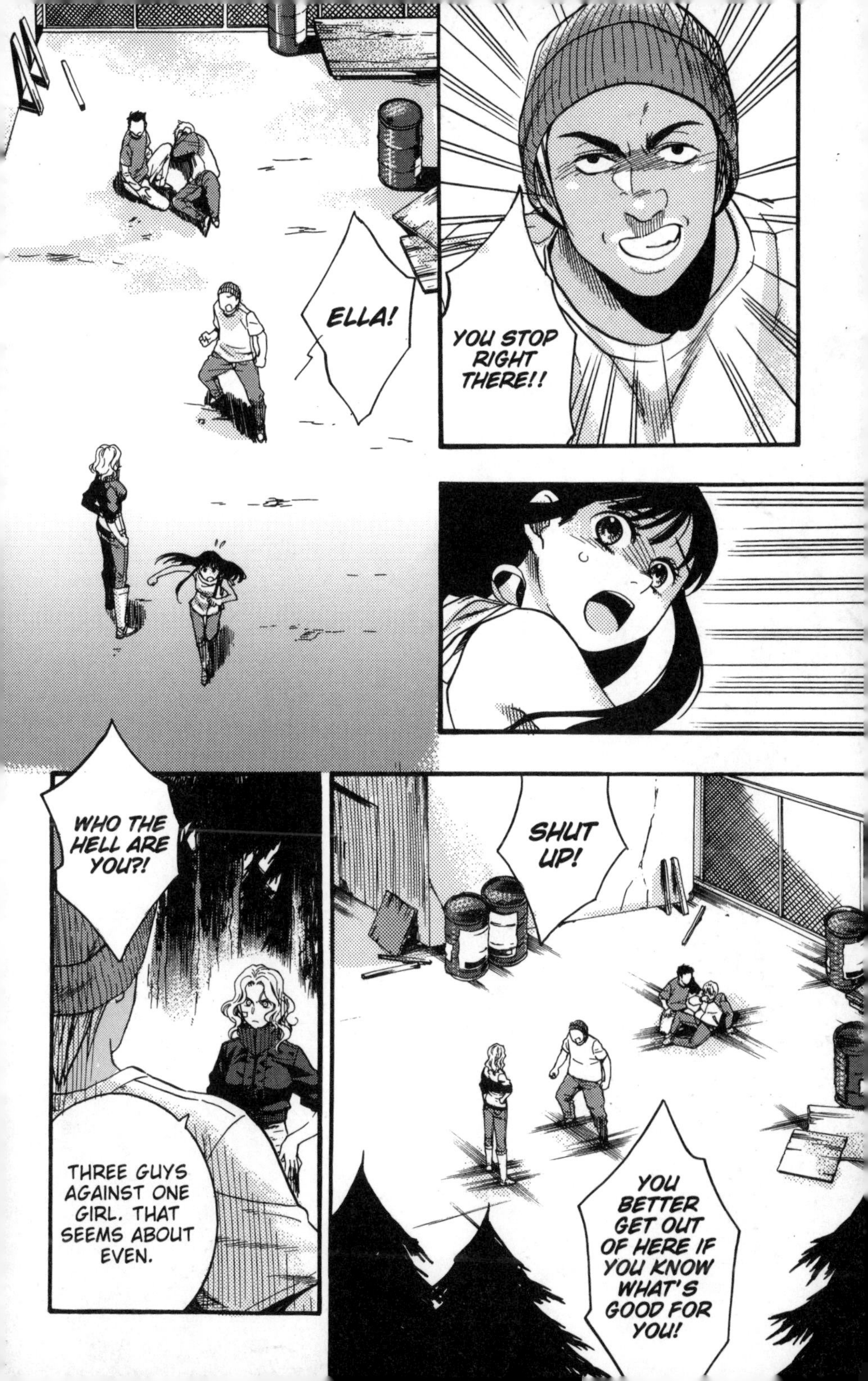
ELLA!
YOU STOP RIGHT THERE!!
WHO THE HELL ARE YOU?!
THREE GUYS AGAINST ONE GIRL. THAT SEEMS ABOUT EVEN.
SHUT UP!
YOU BETTER GET OUT OF HERE IF YOU KNOW WHAT'S GOOD FOR YOU!

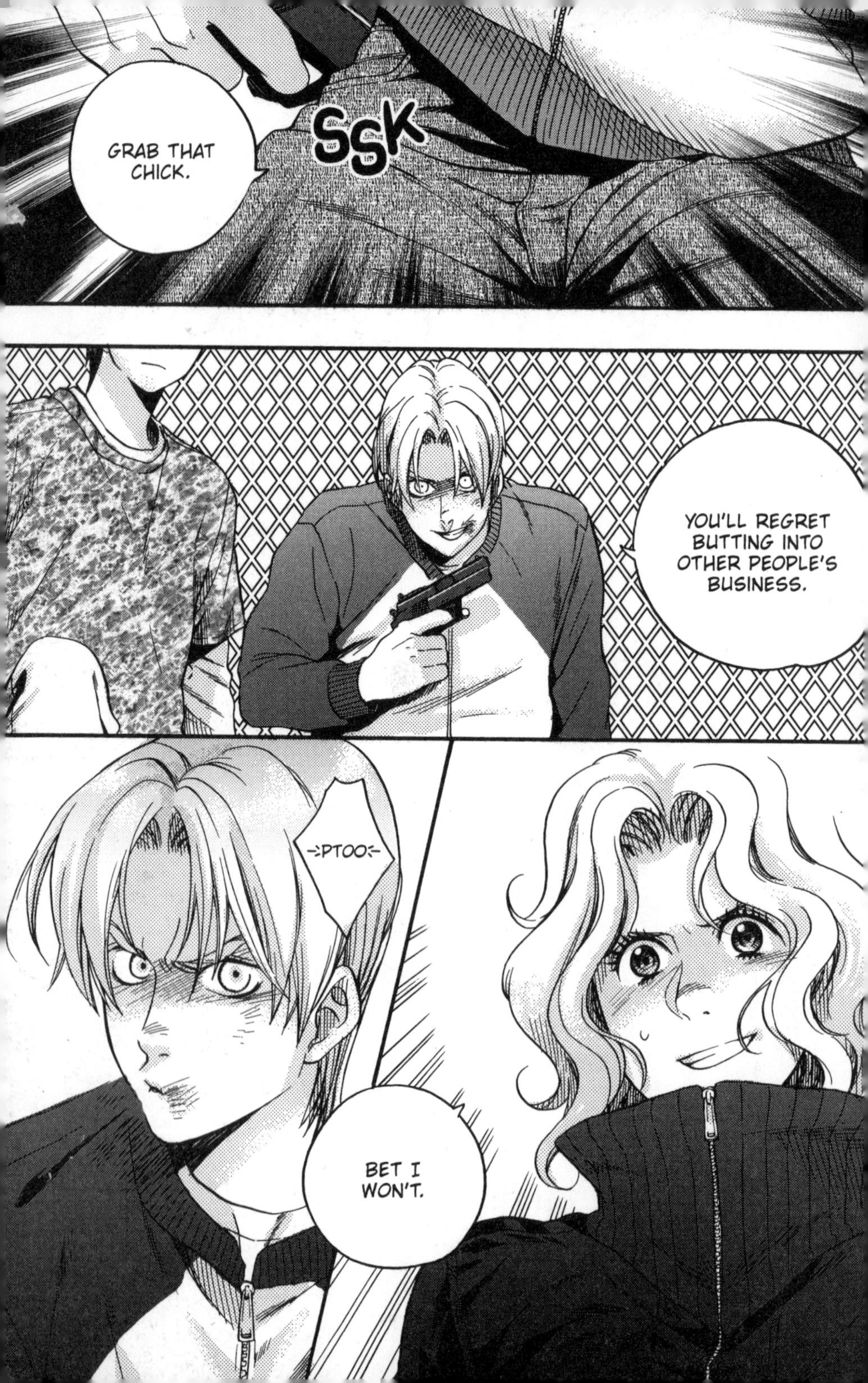
GRAB THAT CHICK.
SSK
YOU'LL REGRET BUTTING INTO OTHER PEOPLE'S BUSINESS.
PTOO
BET I WON'T.

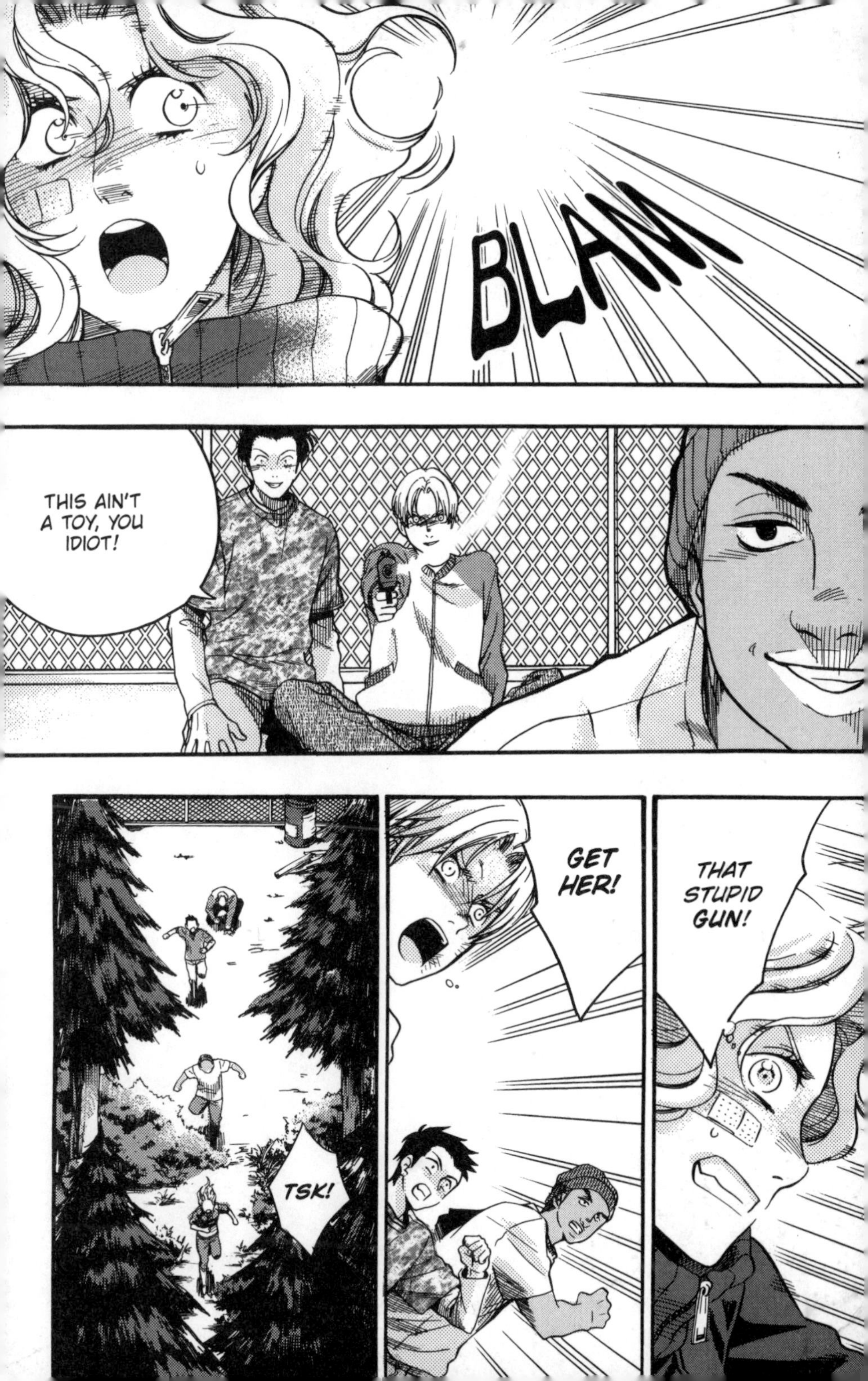
BLAM
THIS AIN'T A TOY, YOU IDIOT!
TSK!
GET HER!
THAT STUPID GUN!

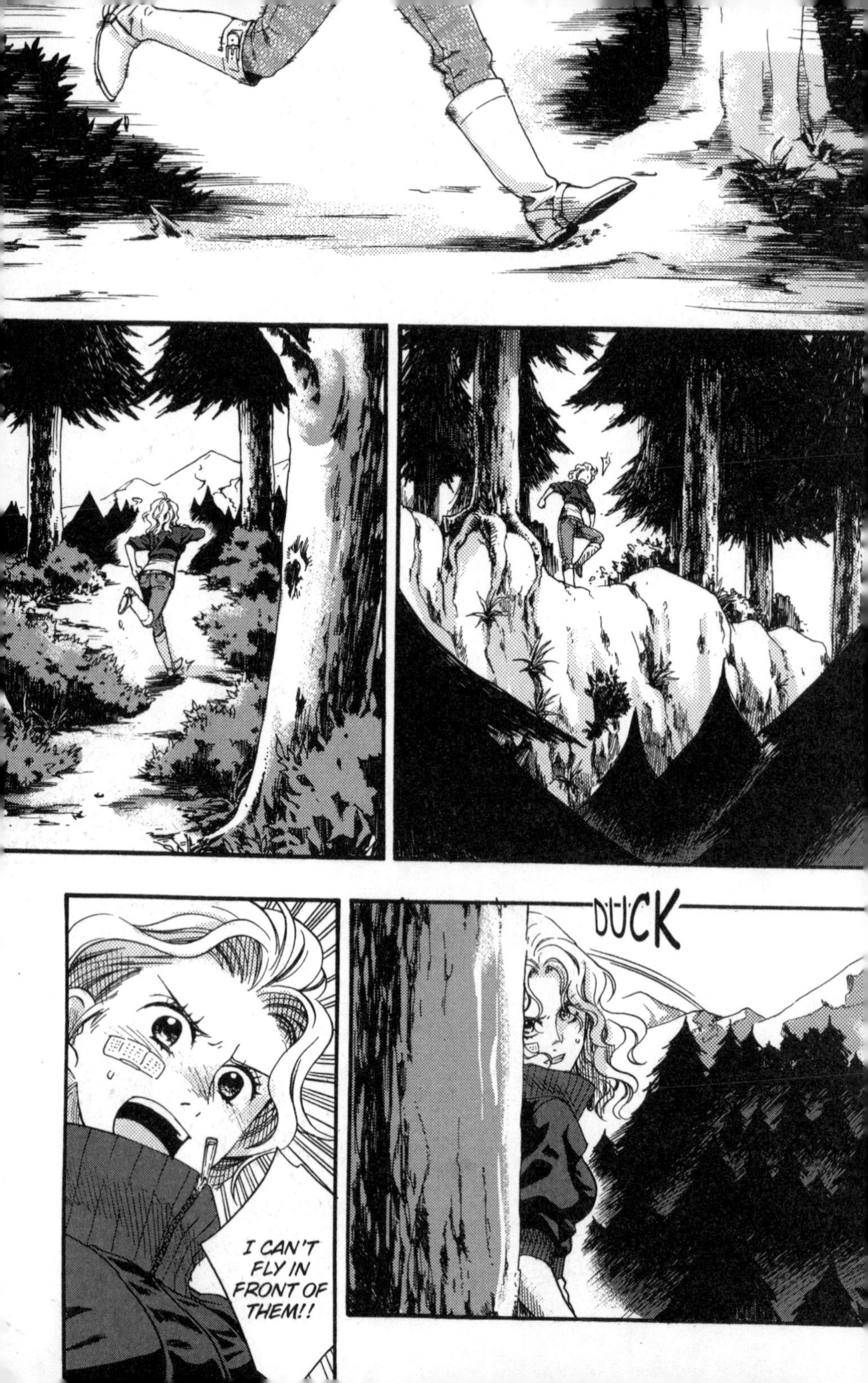
I CAN'T FLY IN FRONT OF THEM!!
DUCK

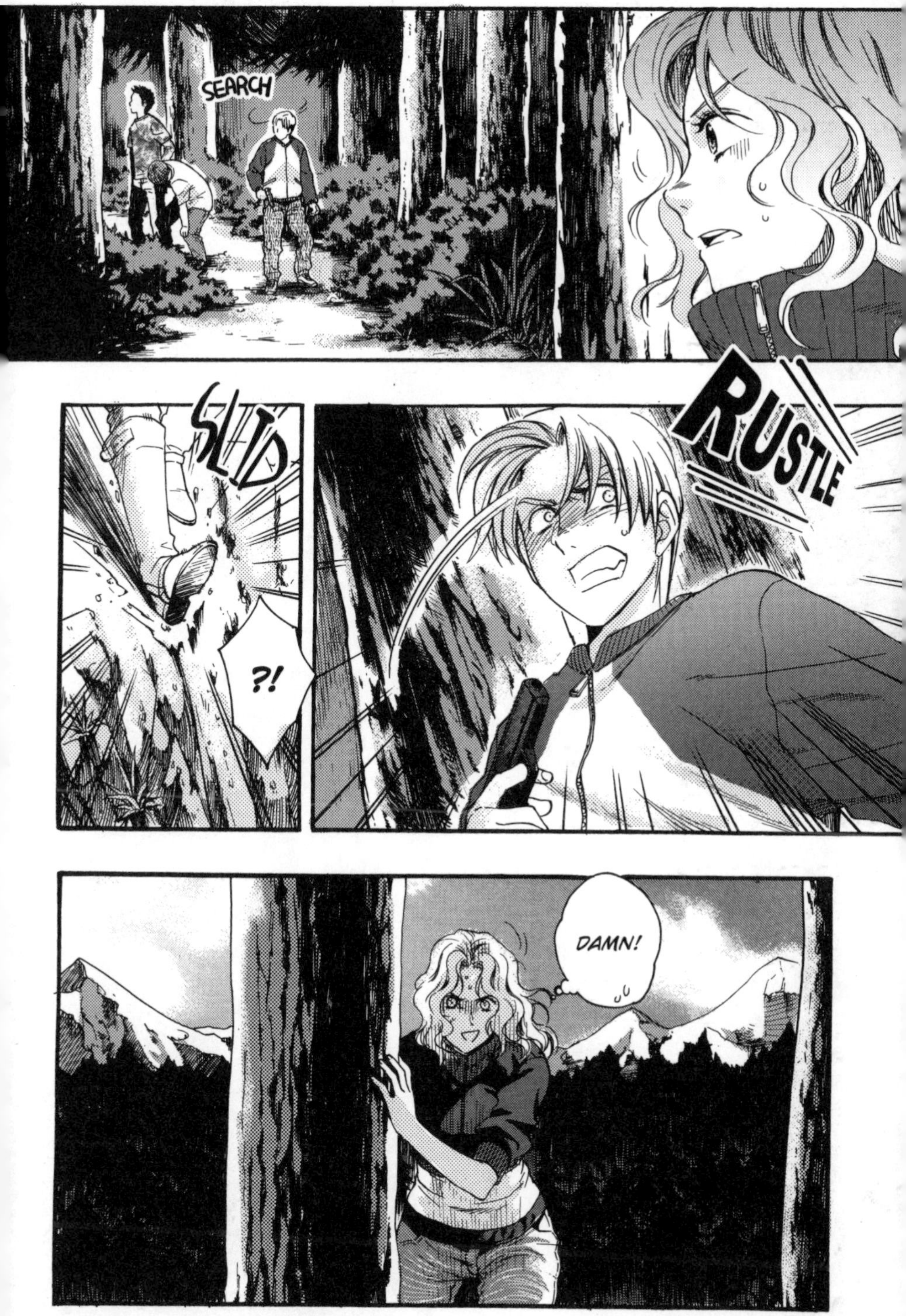
SEARCH
SLID
?!
RUSTLE
DAMN!

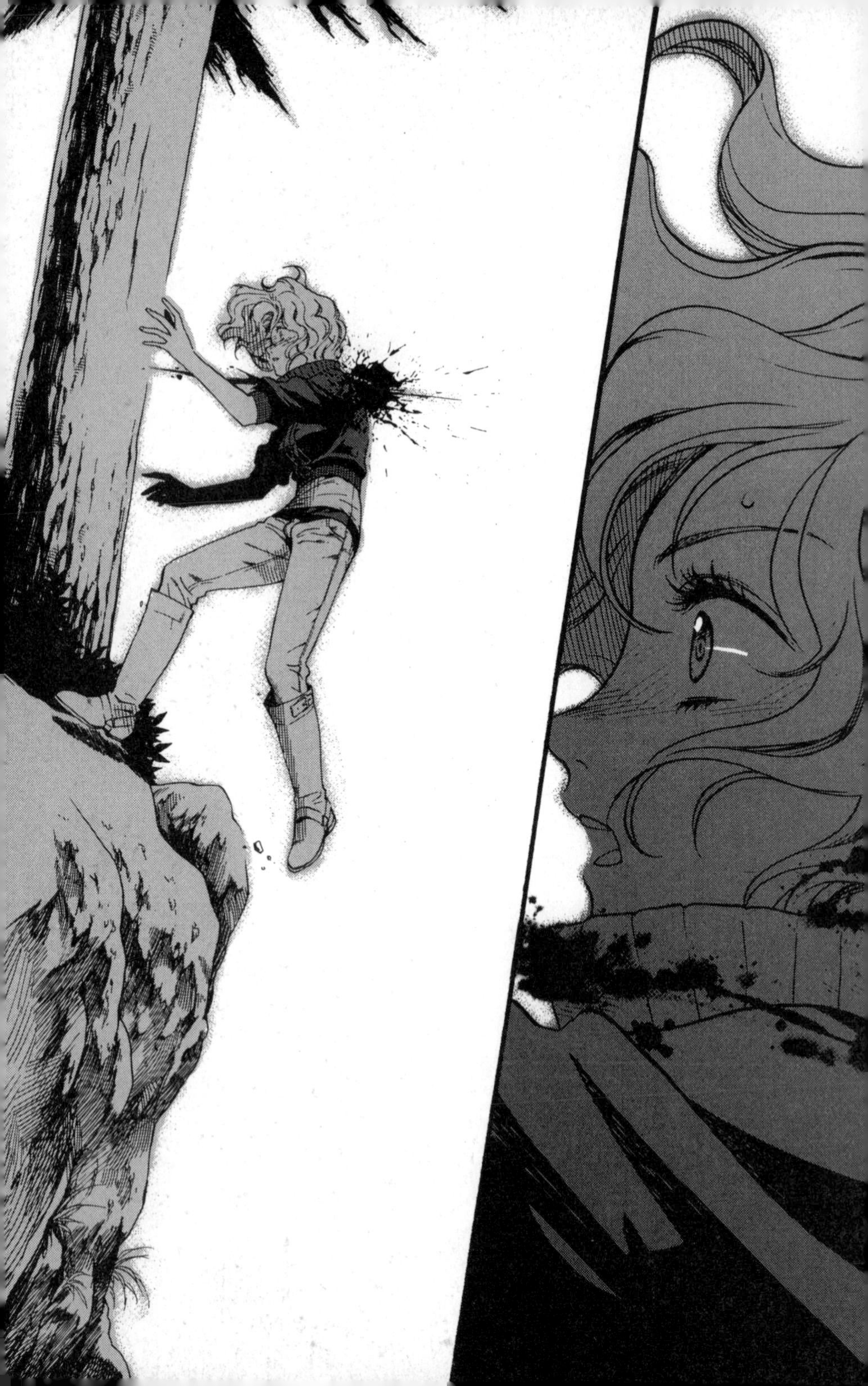

MAXIMUM
RIDE

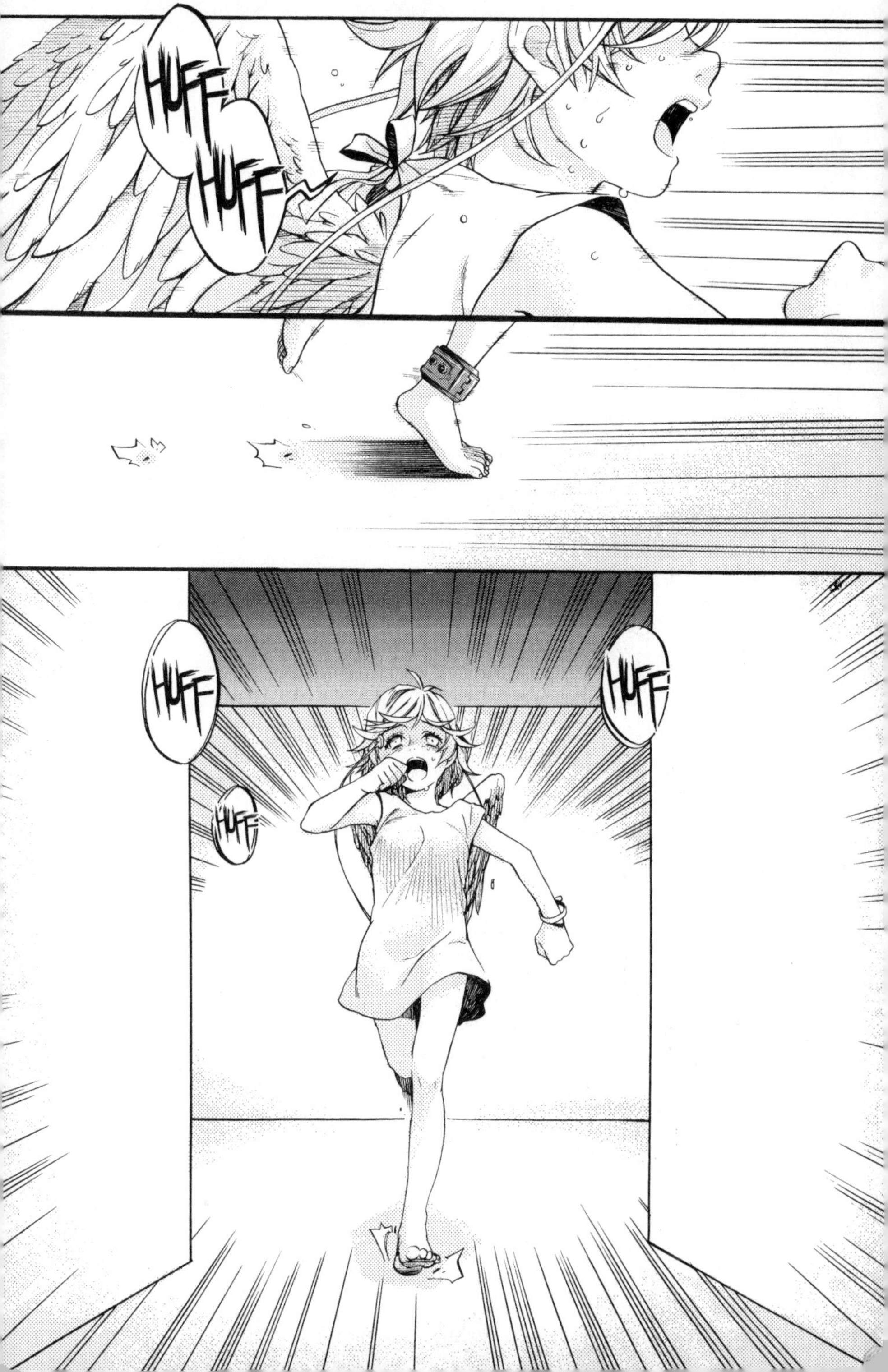
HUFF
HUFF
HUFF
HUFF
HUFF

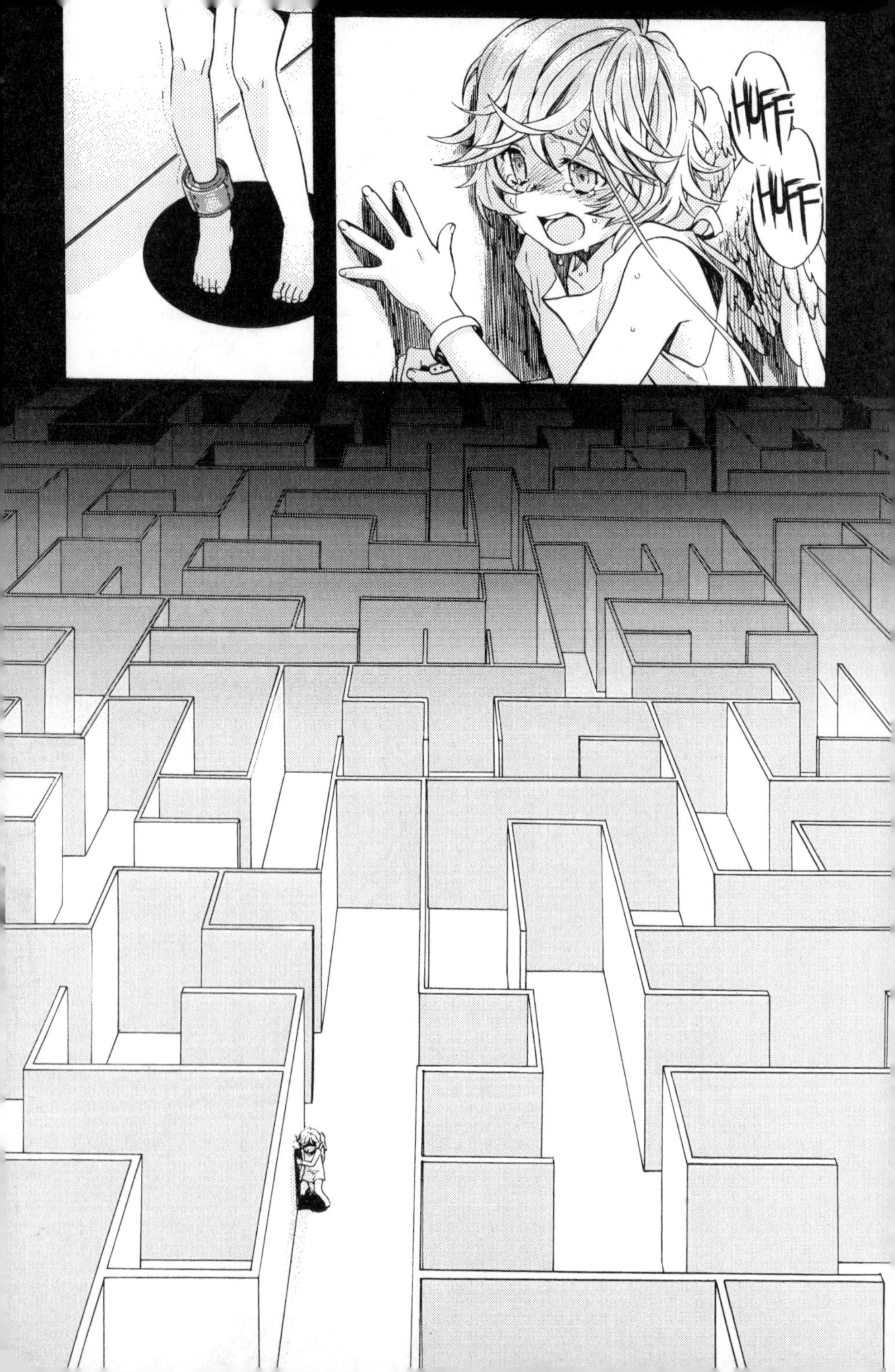
HUFF
HUFF

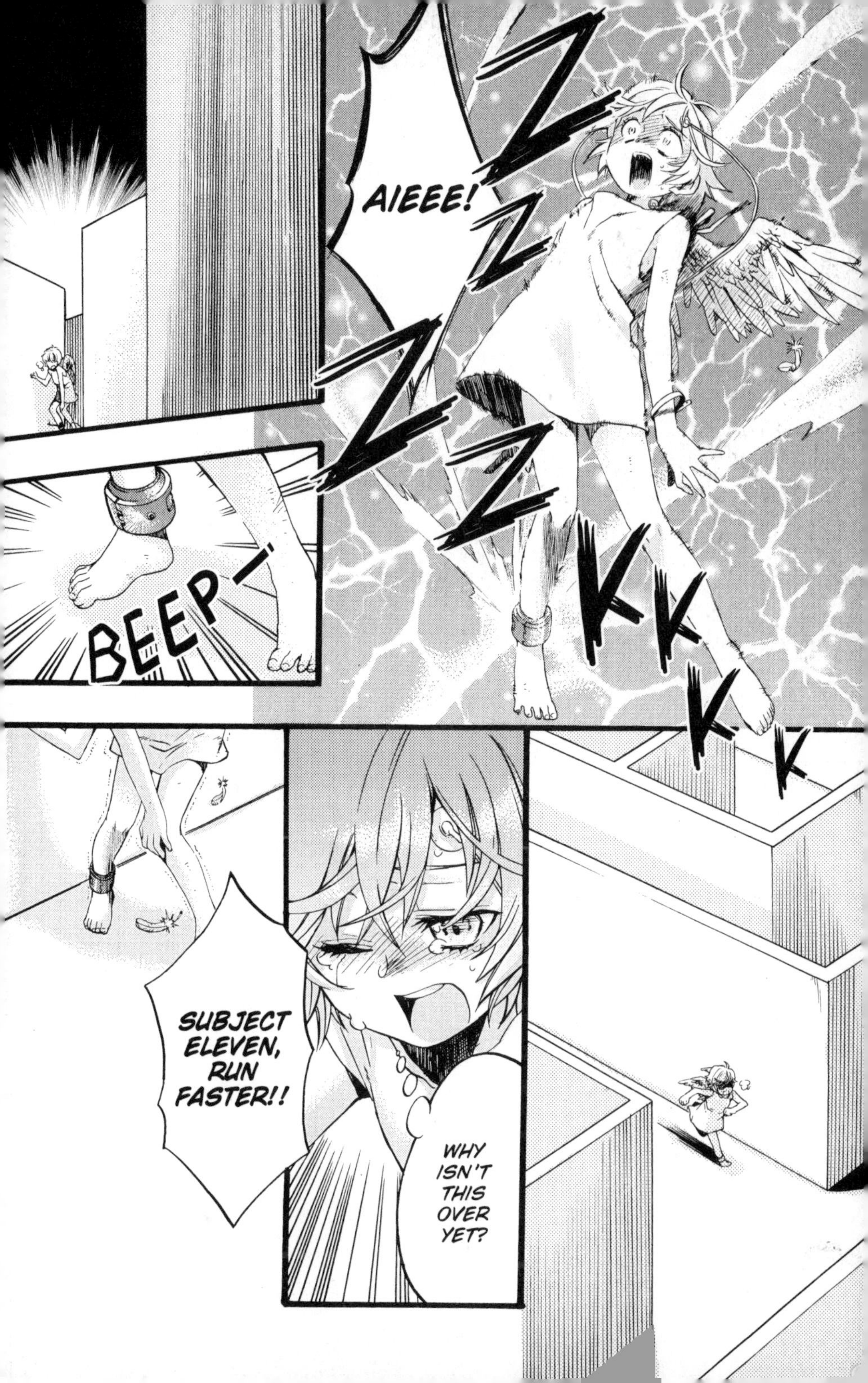
BEEP
AIEEE!
ZZZZKKKK
SUBJECT ELEVEN, RUN FASTER!!
WHY ISN'T THIS OVER YET?

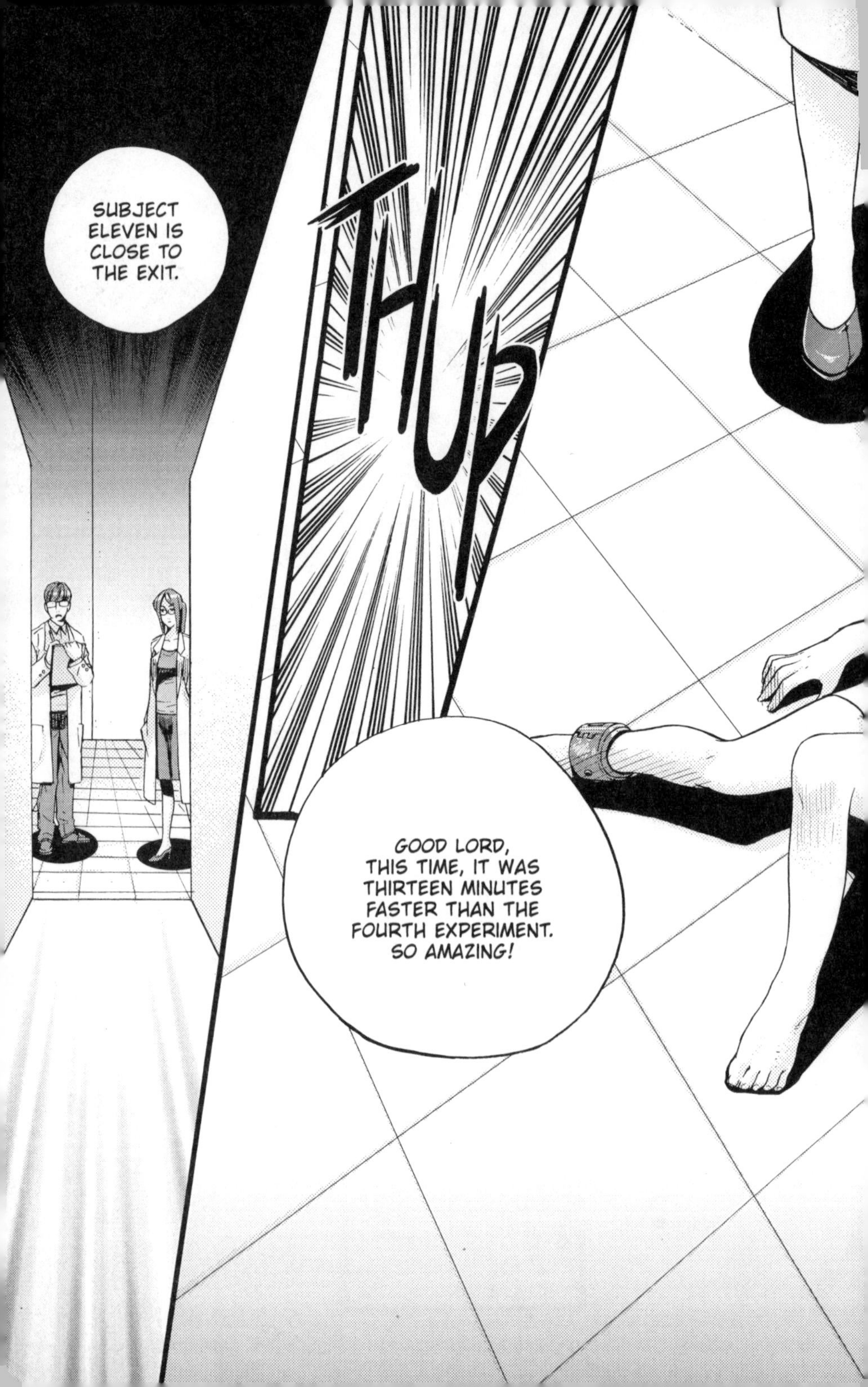
SUBJECT ELEVEN IS CLOSE TO THE EXIT.
THUD
GOOD LORD, THIS TIME, IT WAS THIRTEEN MINUTES FASTER THAN THE FOURTH EXPERIMENT. SO AMAZING!

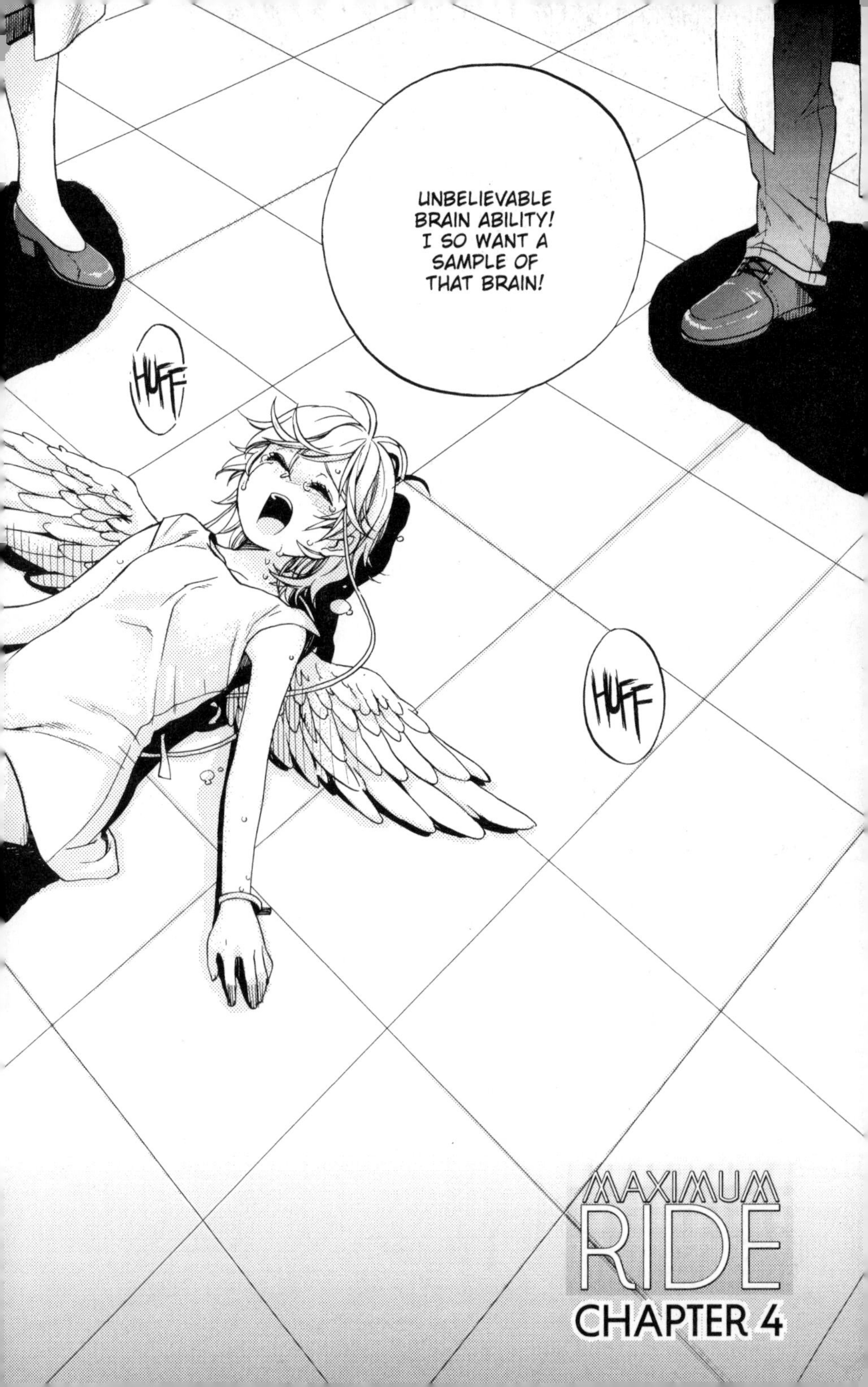
UNBELIEVABLE BRAIN ABILITY! I SO WANT A SAMPLE OF THAT BRAIN!
HUFF
HUFF
MAXIMUM RIDE
CHAPTER 4

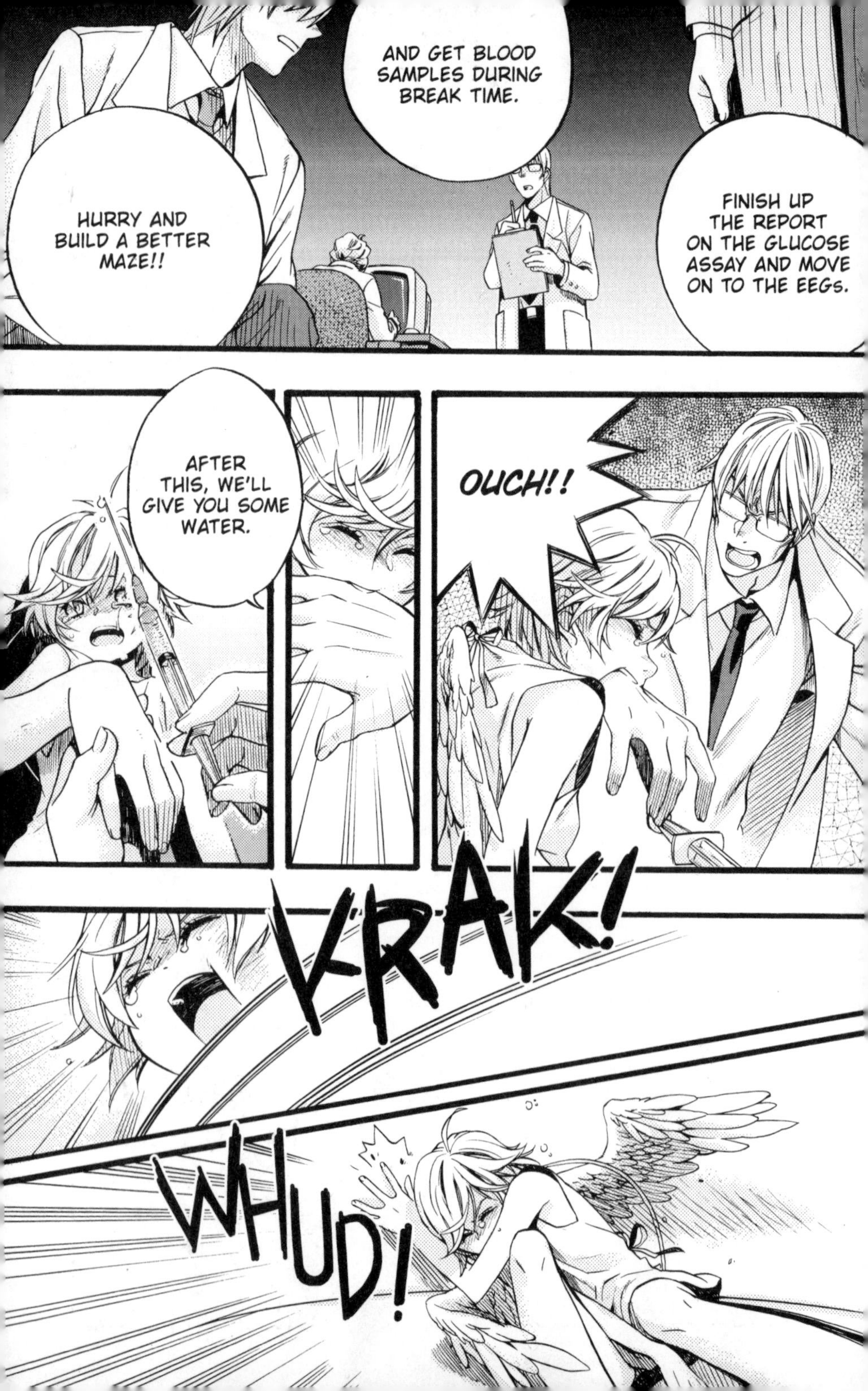
HURRY AND BUILD A BETTER MAZE!!
AND GET BLOOD SAMPLES DURING BREAK TIME.
FINISH UP THE REPORT ON THE GLUCOSE ASSAY AND MOVE ON TO THE EEGs.
AFTER THIS, WE'LL GIVE YOU SOME WATER.
OUCH!!
KRAK!
WHUD!

WHAT HAPPENED, REILLY?!

PANT PANT

WHAT'S GOING ON HERE?!!

IT BIT REILLY'S HAND AND HE HIT IT!!

DON'T YOU REALIZE HOW UNIQUE THIS "SUBJECT" IS?

THIS IS SUBJECT ELEVEN. DON'T YOU KNOW HOW LONG WE'VE BEEN LOOKING FOR IT? DO NOT DAMAGE THE MERCHANDISE!

I'M NOT A SUBJECT! AND I'M NOT MERCHANDISE EITHER!!

I'M SORRY.

GO TREAT YOUR HAND.

I'LL TAKE OVER HERE.

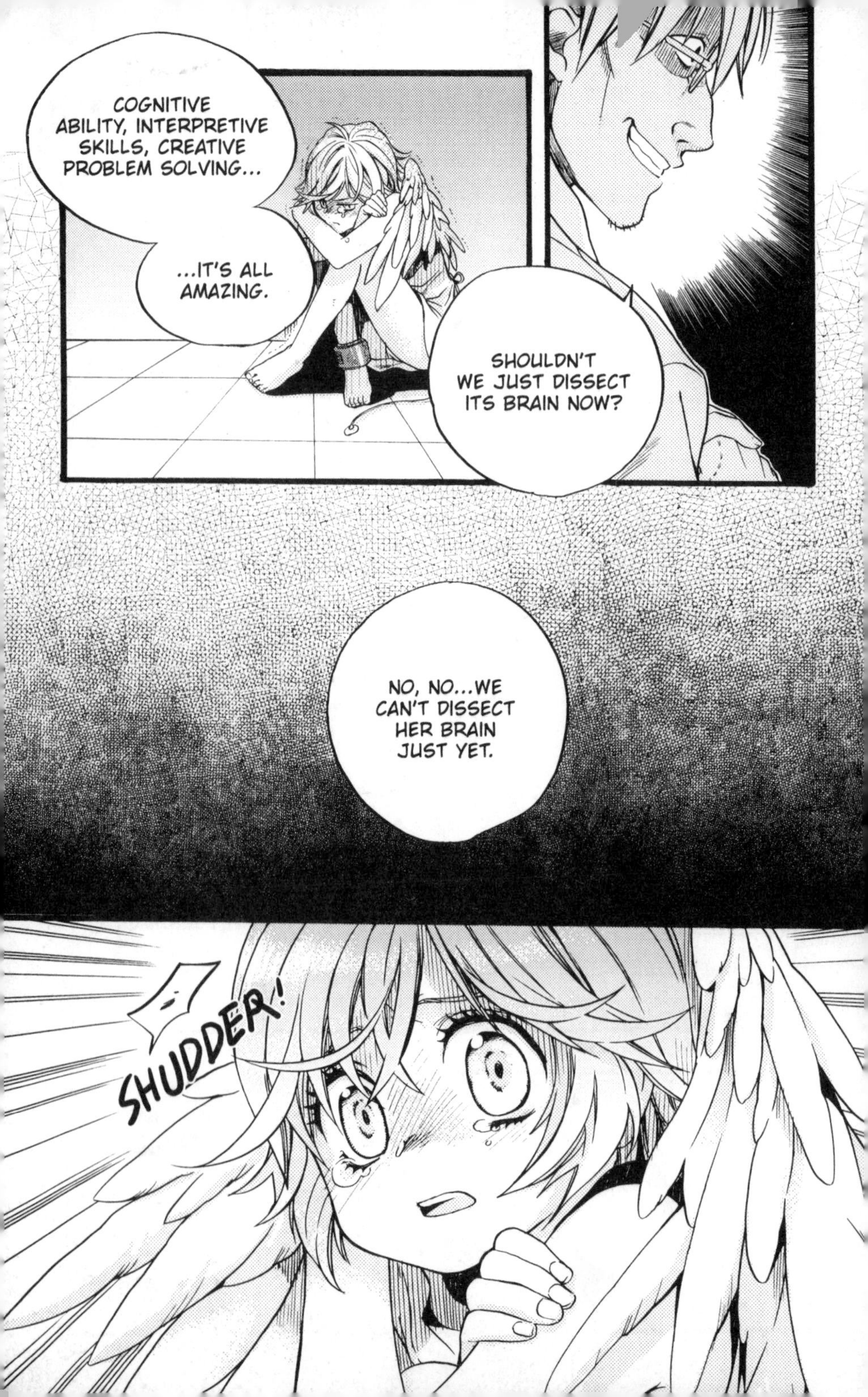
COGNITIVE ABILITY, INTERPRETIVE SKILLS, CREATIVE PROBLEM SOLVING...
...IT'S ALL AMAZING.
SHOULDN'T WE JUST DISSECT ITS BRAIN NOW?
NO, NO...WE CAN'T DISSECT HER BRAIN JUST YET.
SHUDDER!

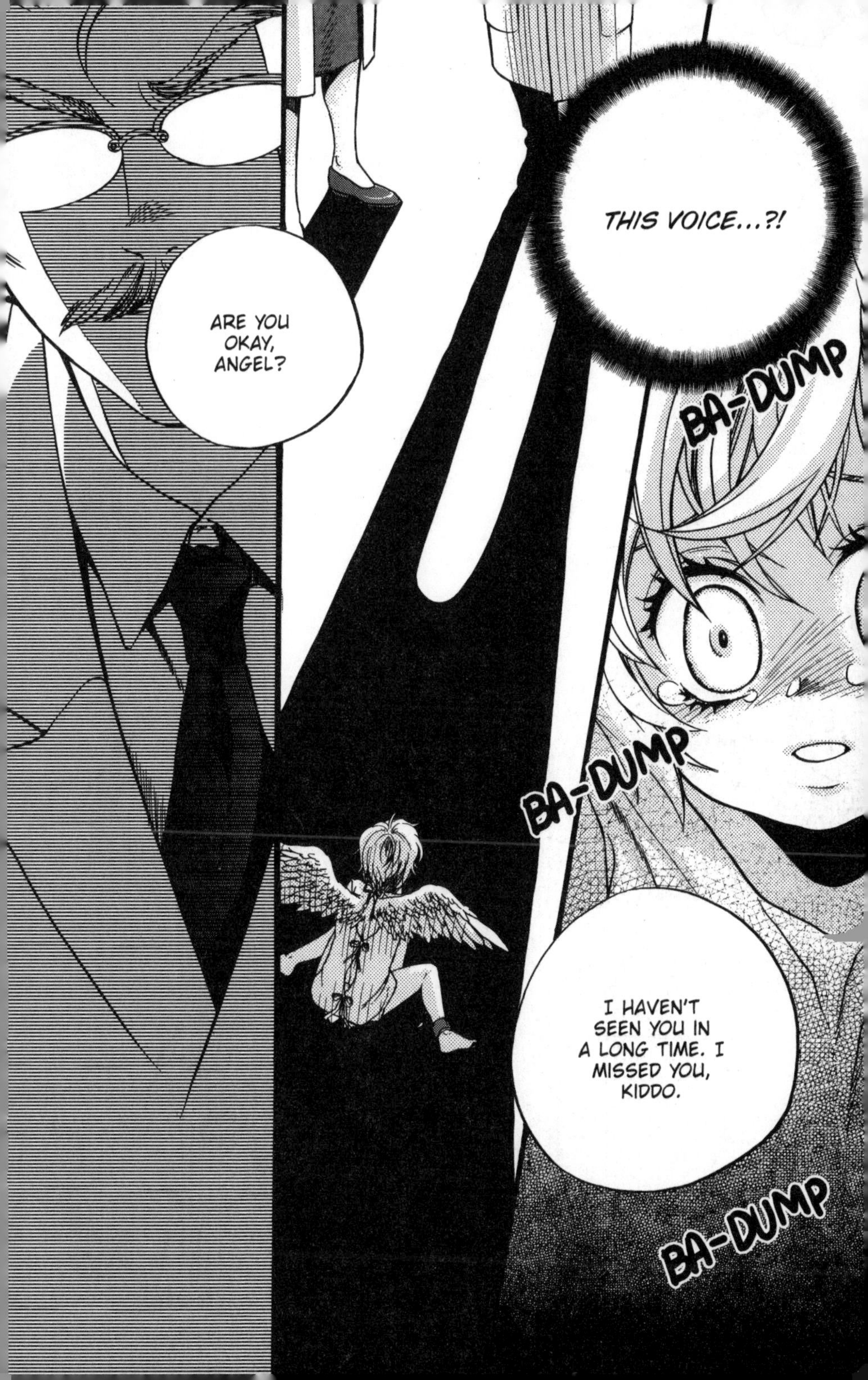
ARE YOU OKAY, ANGEL?
THIS VOICE...?!
BA-DUMP
BA-DUMP
I HAVEN'T SEEN YOU IN A LONG TIME. I MISSED YOU, KIDDO.
BA-DUMP

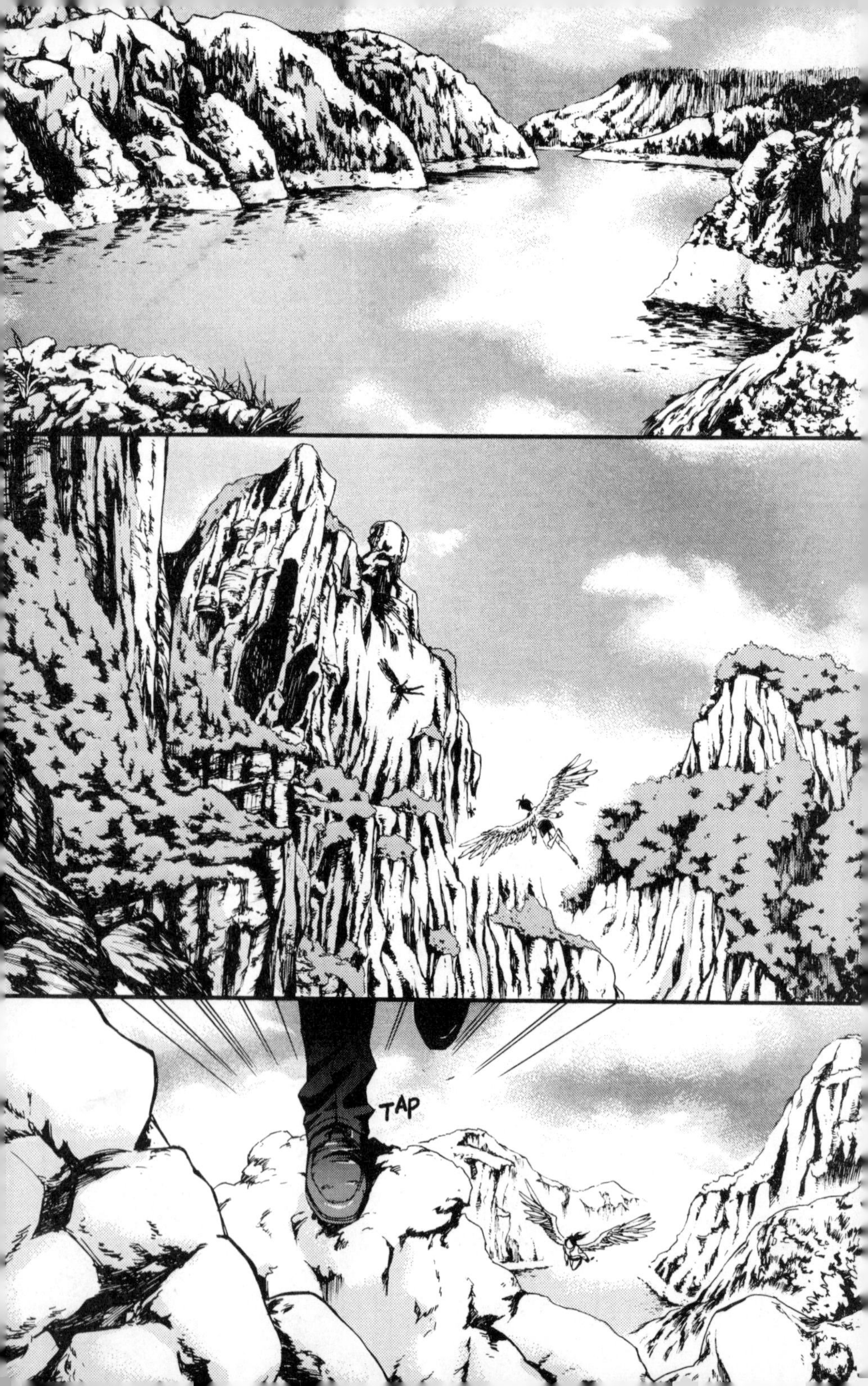
TAP

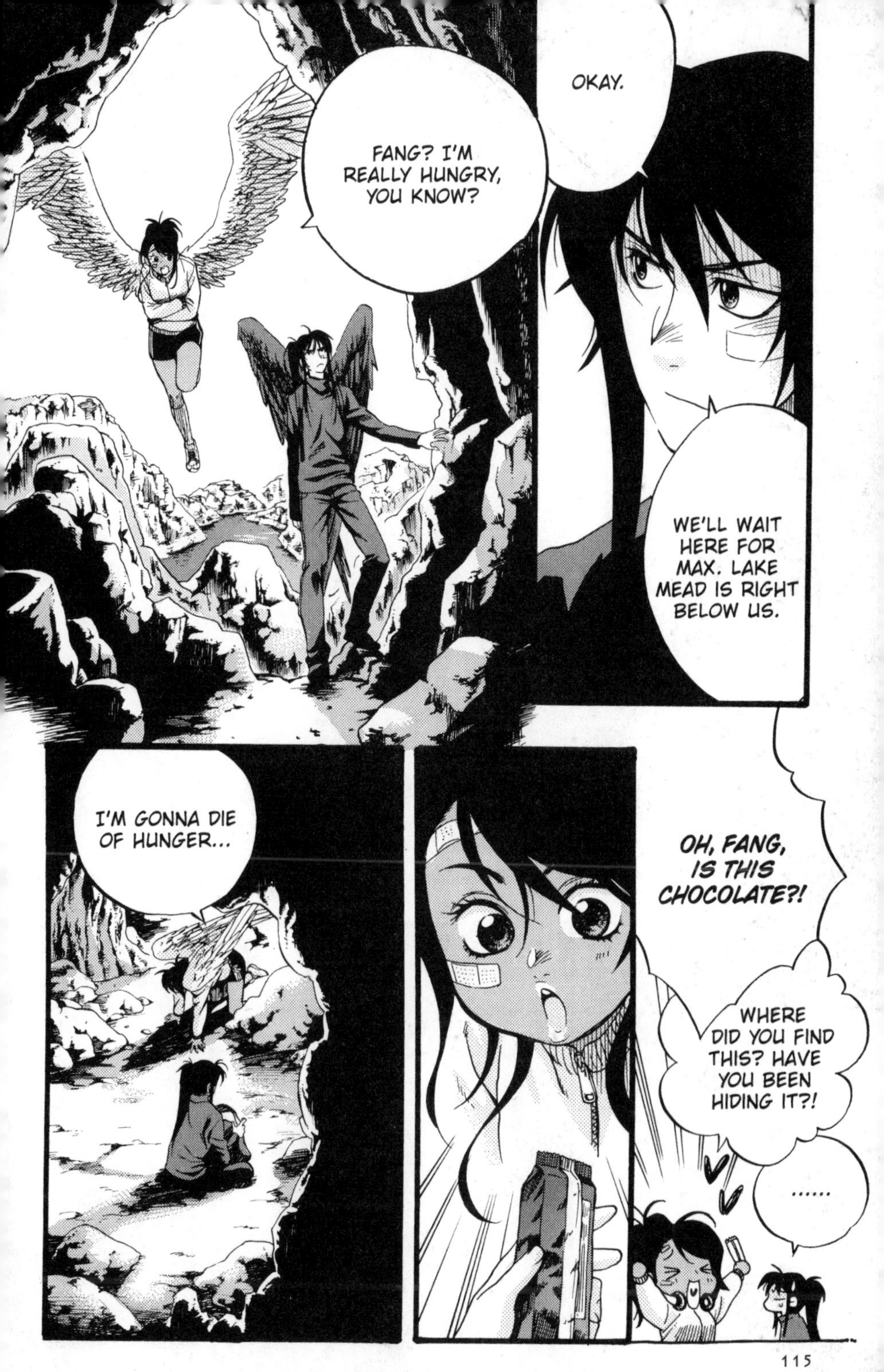
FANG? I'M REALLY HUNGRY, YOU KNOW?
OKAY.
WE'LL WAIT HERE FOR MAX. LAKE MEAD IS RIGHT BELOW US.
I'M GONNA DIE OF HUNGER...
OH, FANG, IS THIS CHOCOLATE?!
WHERE DID YOU FIND THIS? HAVE YOU BEEN HIDING IT?!
......

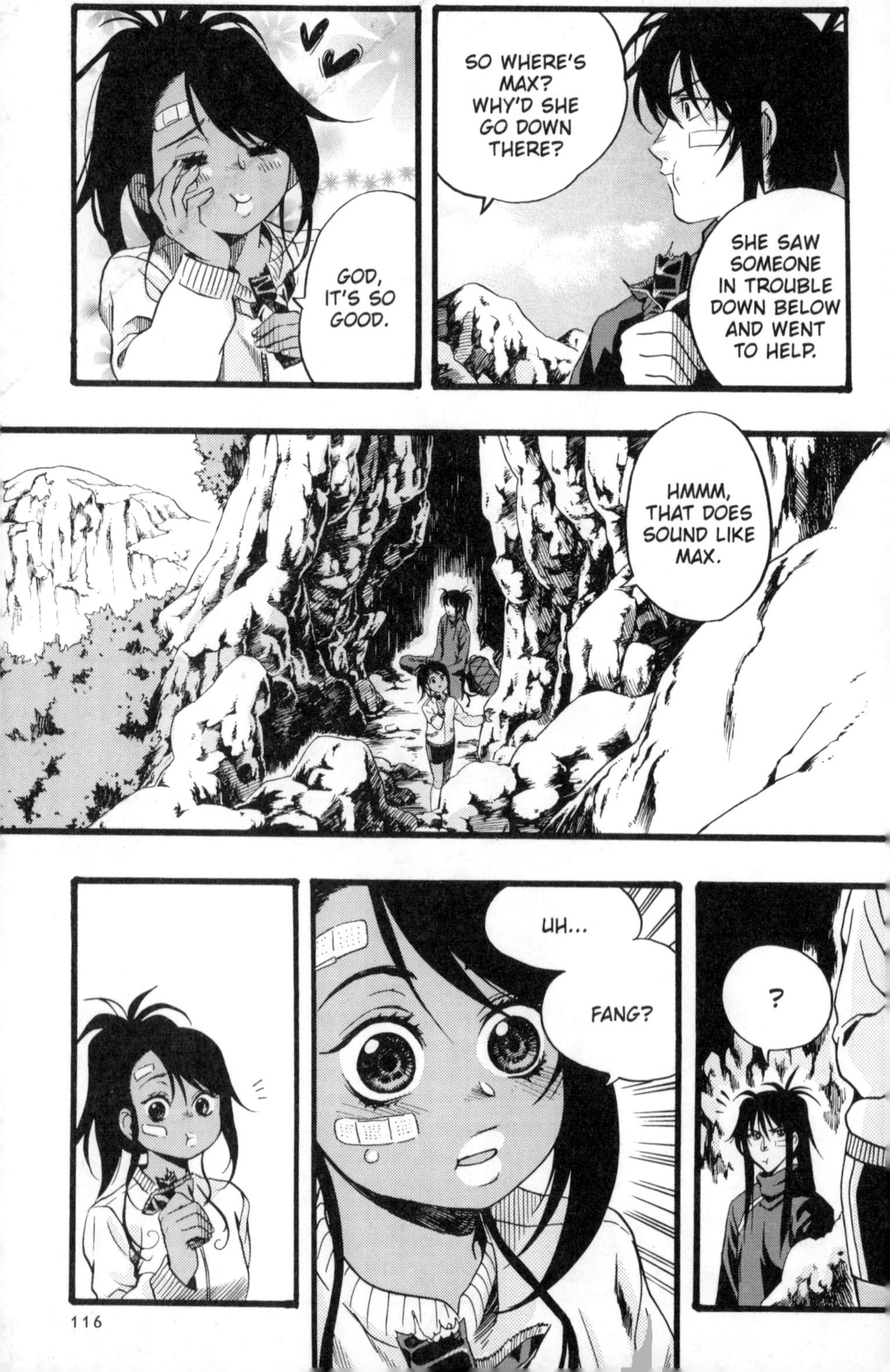
GOD, IT'S SO GOOD.
SO WHERE'S MAX? WHY'D SHE GO DOWN THERE?
SHE SAW SOMEONE IN TROUBLE DOWN BELOW AND WENT TO HELP.
HMMM, THAT DOES SOUND LIKE MAX.
UH...
FANG?
?

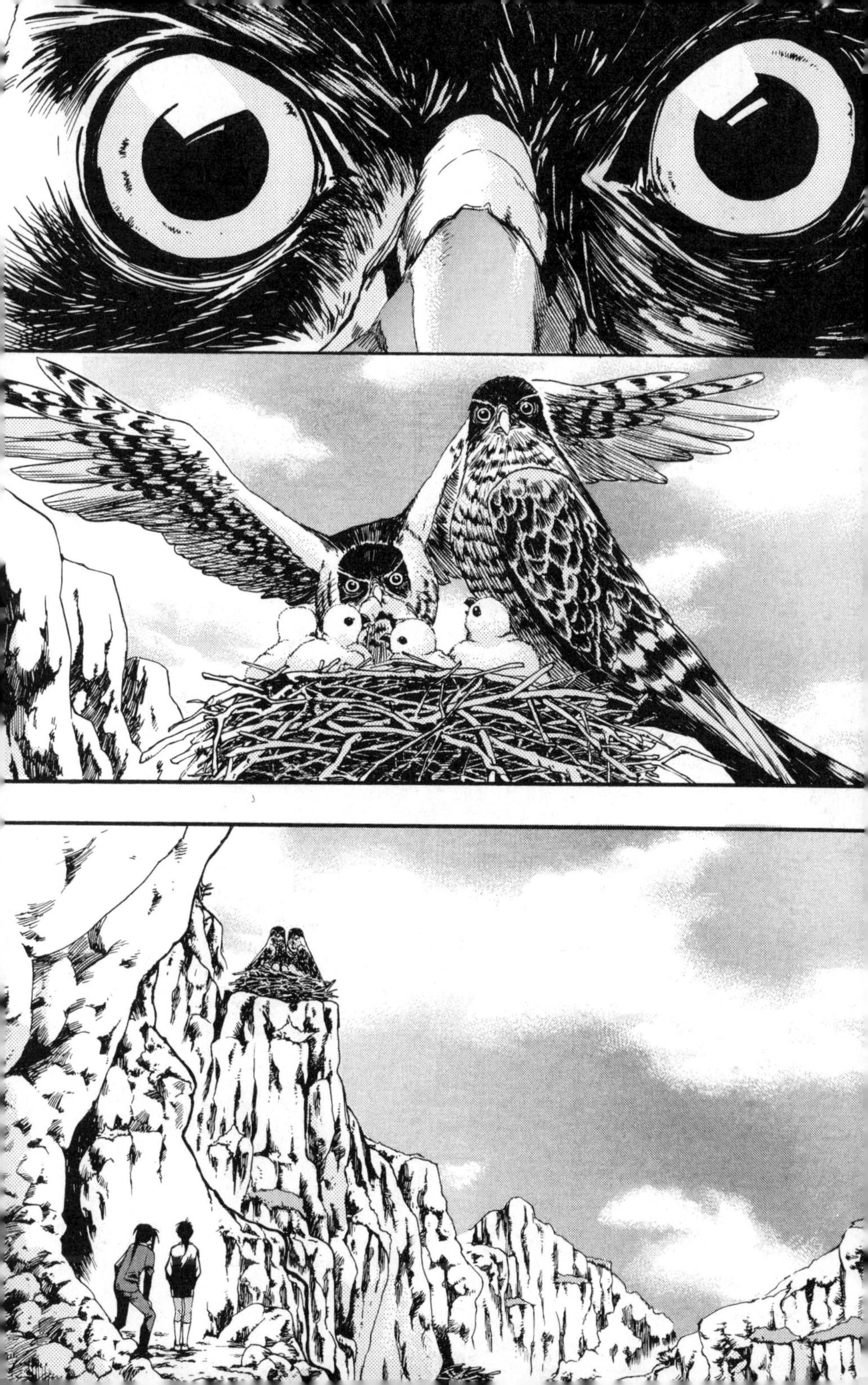

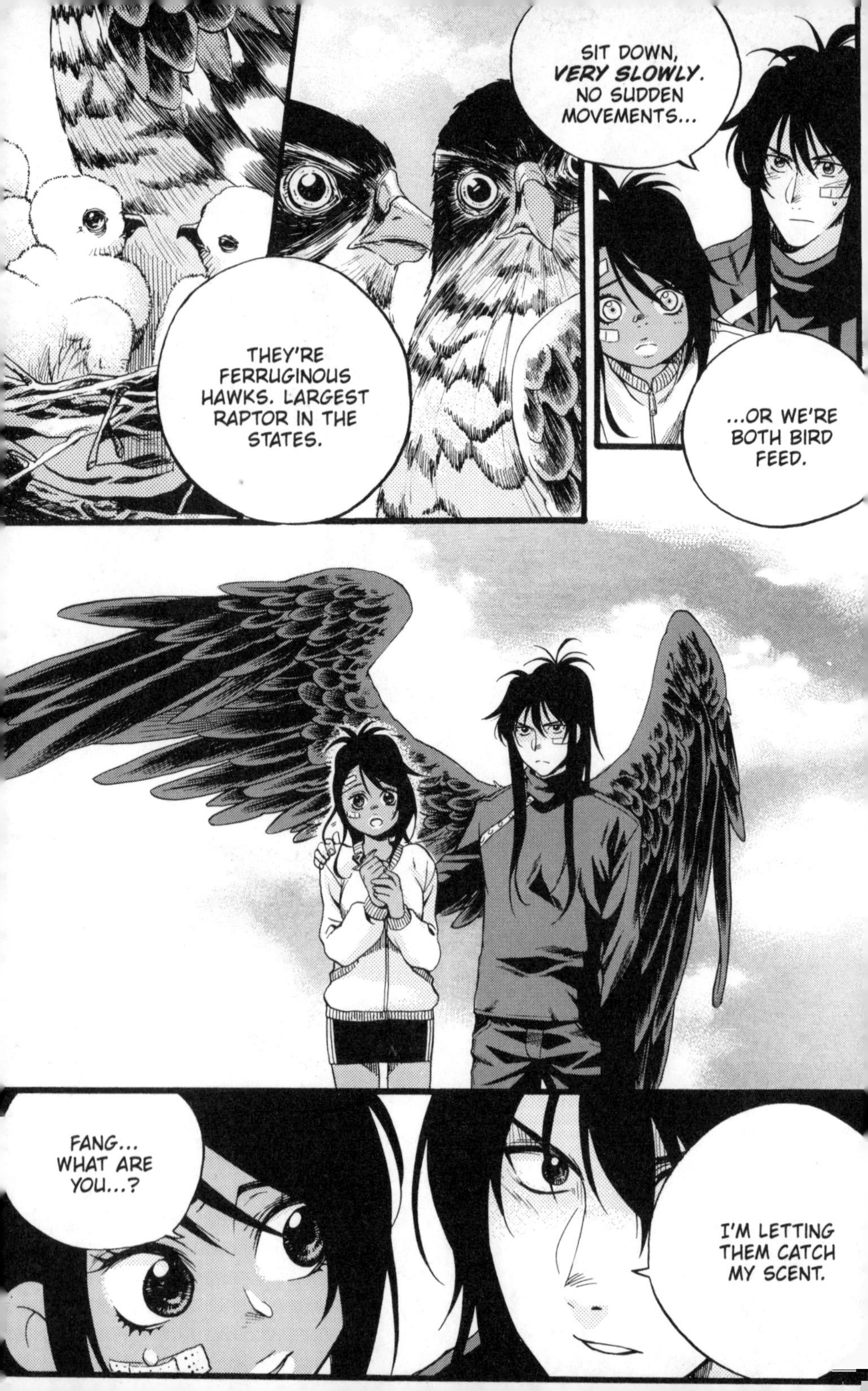
THEY'RE FERRUGINOUS HAWKS. LARGEST RAPTOR IN THE STATES.
SIT DOWN, ***VERY SLOWLY.*** NO SUDDEN MOVEMENTS...
...OR WE'RE BOTH BIRD FEED.
FANG... WHAT ARE YOU...?
I'M LETTING THEM CATCH MY SCENT.

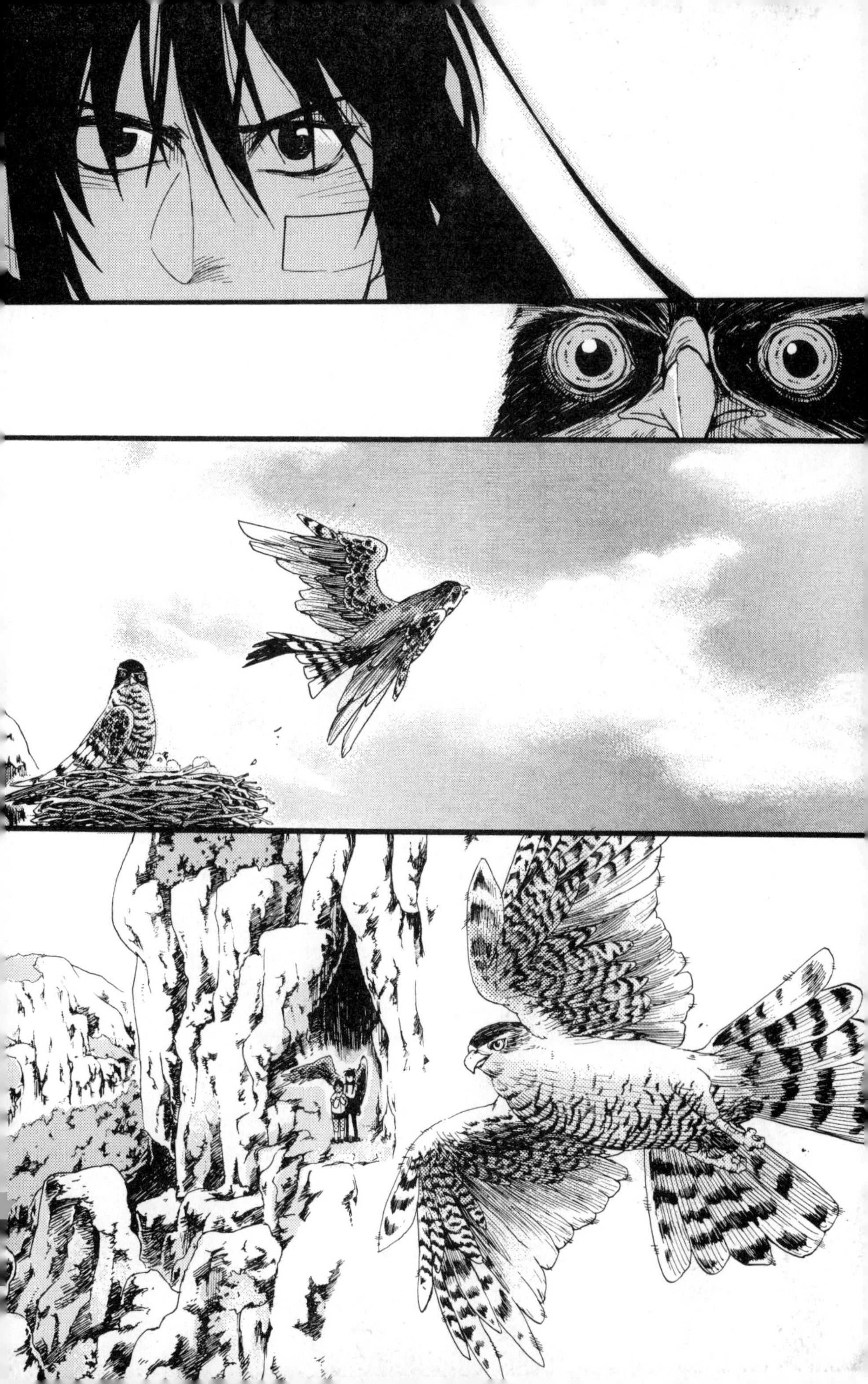

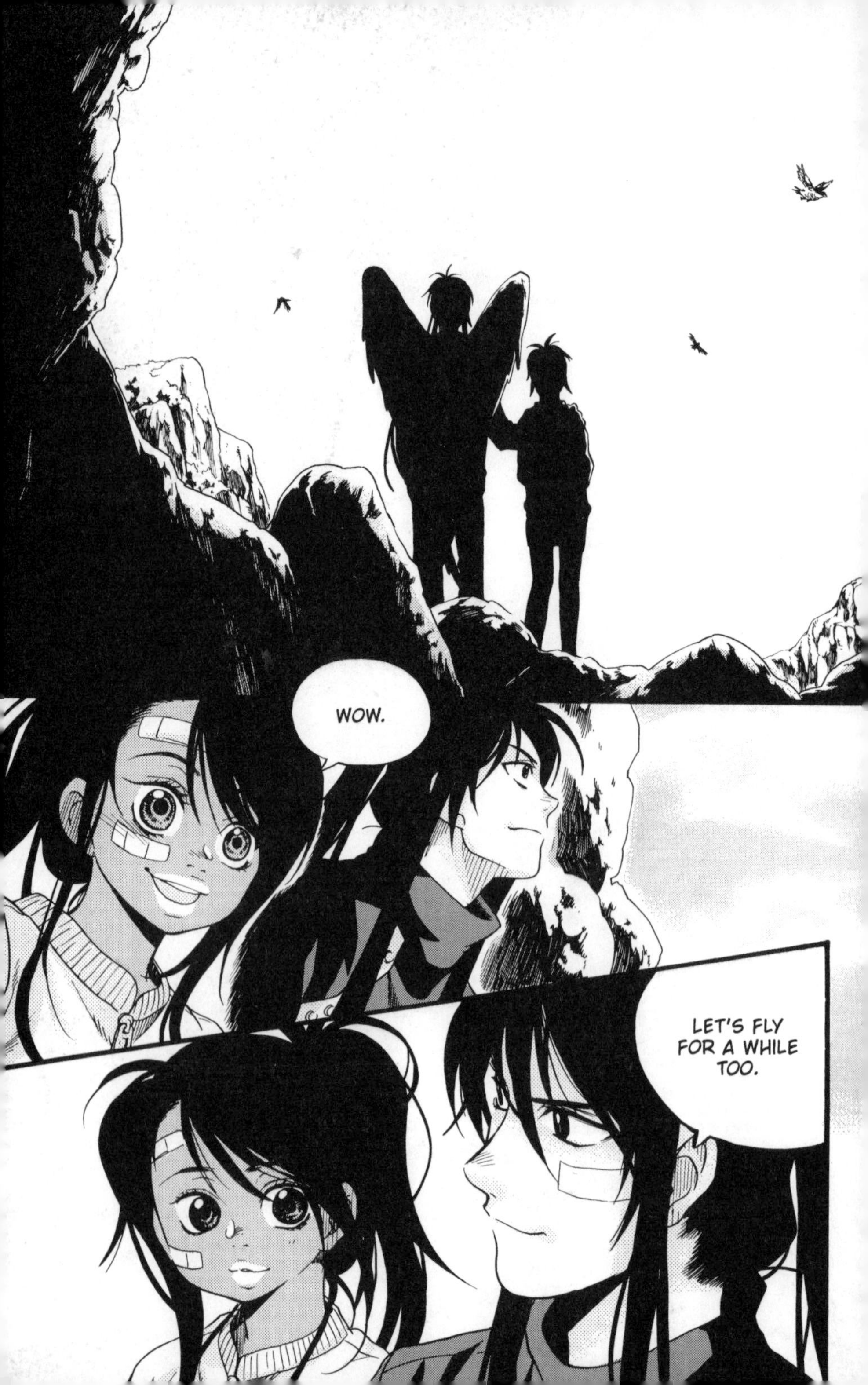
WOW.
LET'S FLY FOR A WHILE TOO.

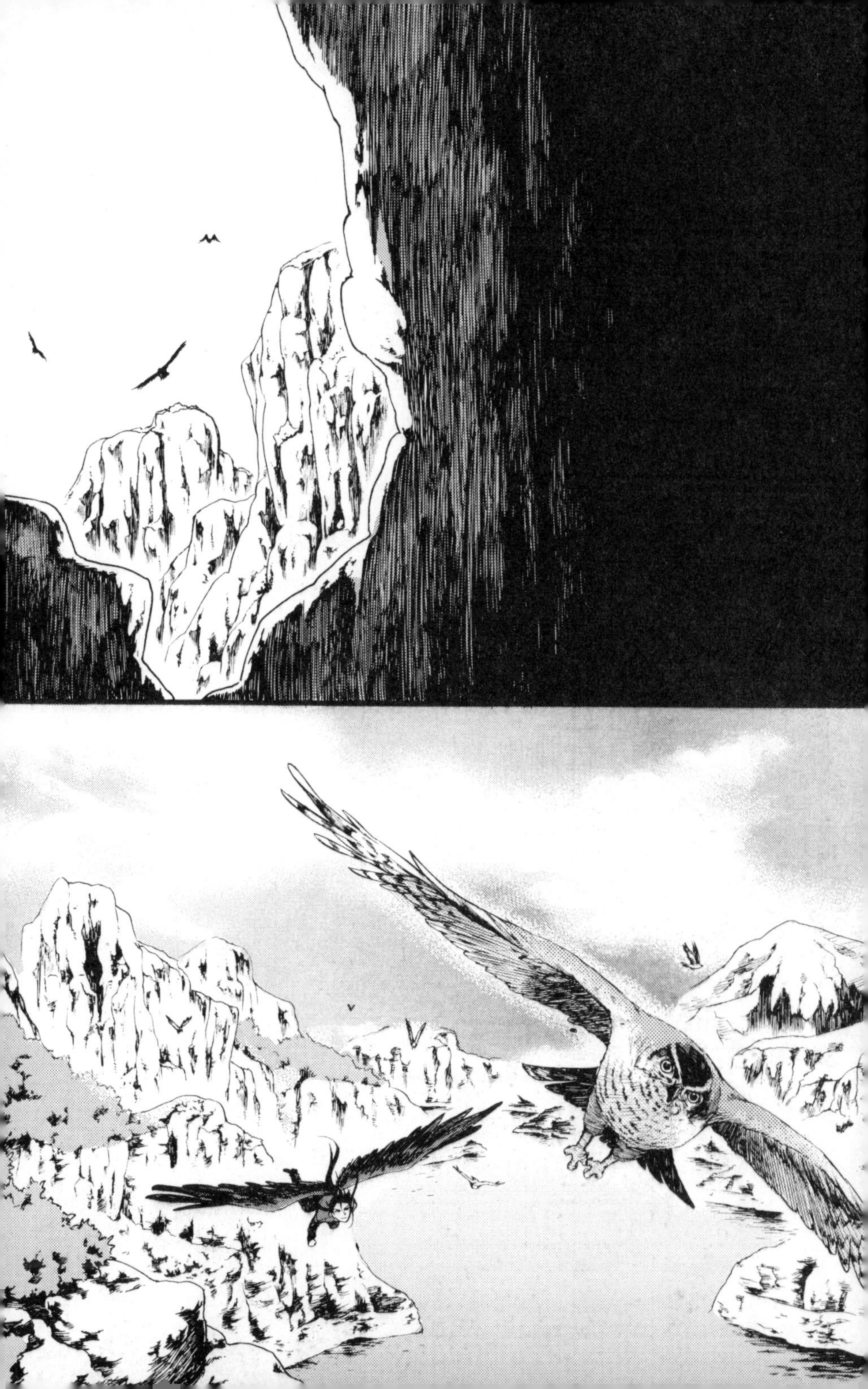

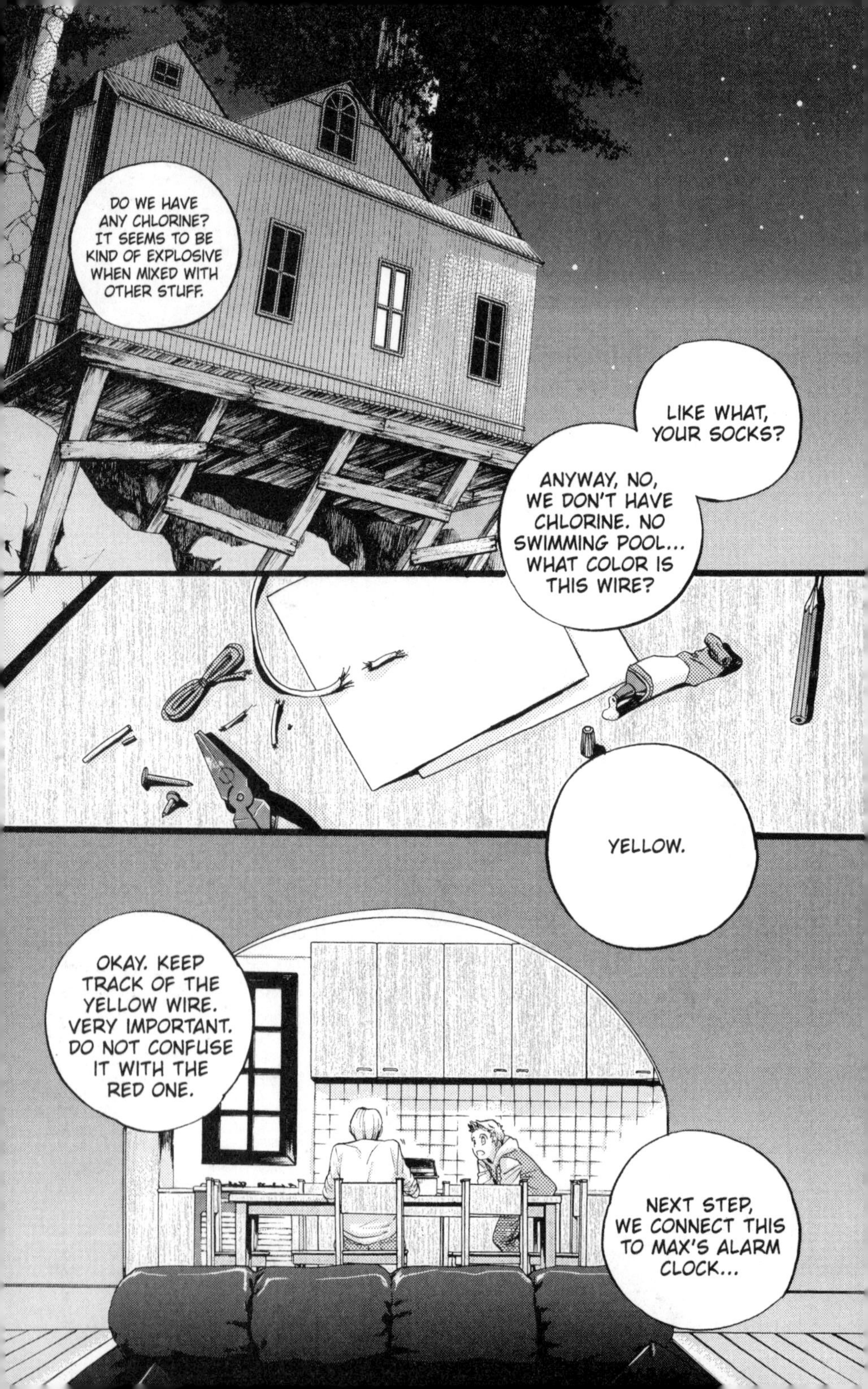
DO WE HAVE ANY CHLORINE? IT SEEMS TO BE KIND OF EXPLOSIVE WHEN MIXED WITH OTHER STUFF.
LIKE WHAT, YOUR SOCKS?
ANYWAY, NO, WE DON'T HAVE CHLORINE. NO SWIMMING POOL... WHAT COLOR IS THIS WIRE?
YELLOW.
OKAY. KEEP TRACK OF THE YELLOW WIRE. VERY IMPORTANT. DO NOT CONFUSE IT WITH THE RED ONE.
NEXT STEP, WE CONNECT THIS TO MAX'S ALARM CLOCK...

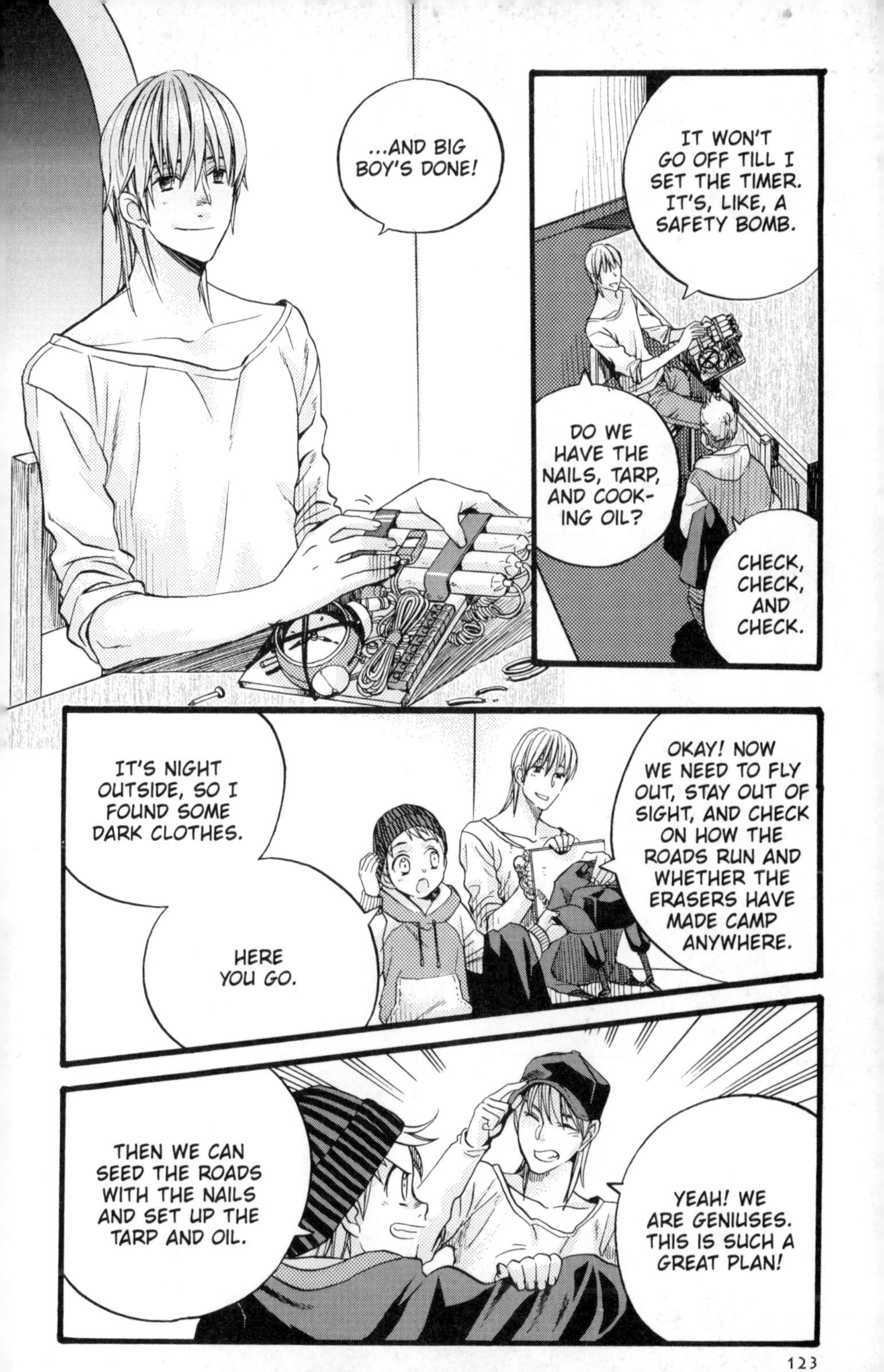
...AND BIG BOY'S DONE!
IT WON'T GO OFF TILL I SET THE TIMER. IT'S, LIKE, A SAFETY BOMB.
DO WE HAVE THE NAILS, TARP, AND COOK-ING OIL?
CHECK, CHECK, AND CHECK.
IT'S NIGHT OUTSIDE, SO I FOUND SOME DARK CLOTHES.
HERE YOU GO.
OKAY! NOW WE NEED TO FLY OUT, STAY OUT OF SIGHT, AND CHECK ON HOW THE ROADS RUN AND WHETHER THE ERASERS HAVE MADE CAMP ANYWHERE.
THEN WE CAN SEED THE ROADS WITH THE NAILS AND SET UP THE TARP AND OIL.
YEAH! WE ARE GENIUSES. THIS IS SUCH A GREAT PLAN!

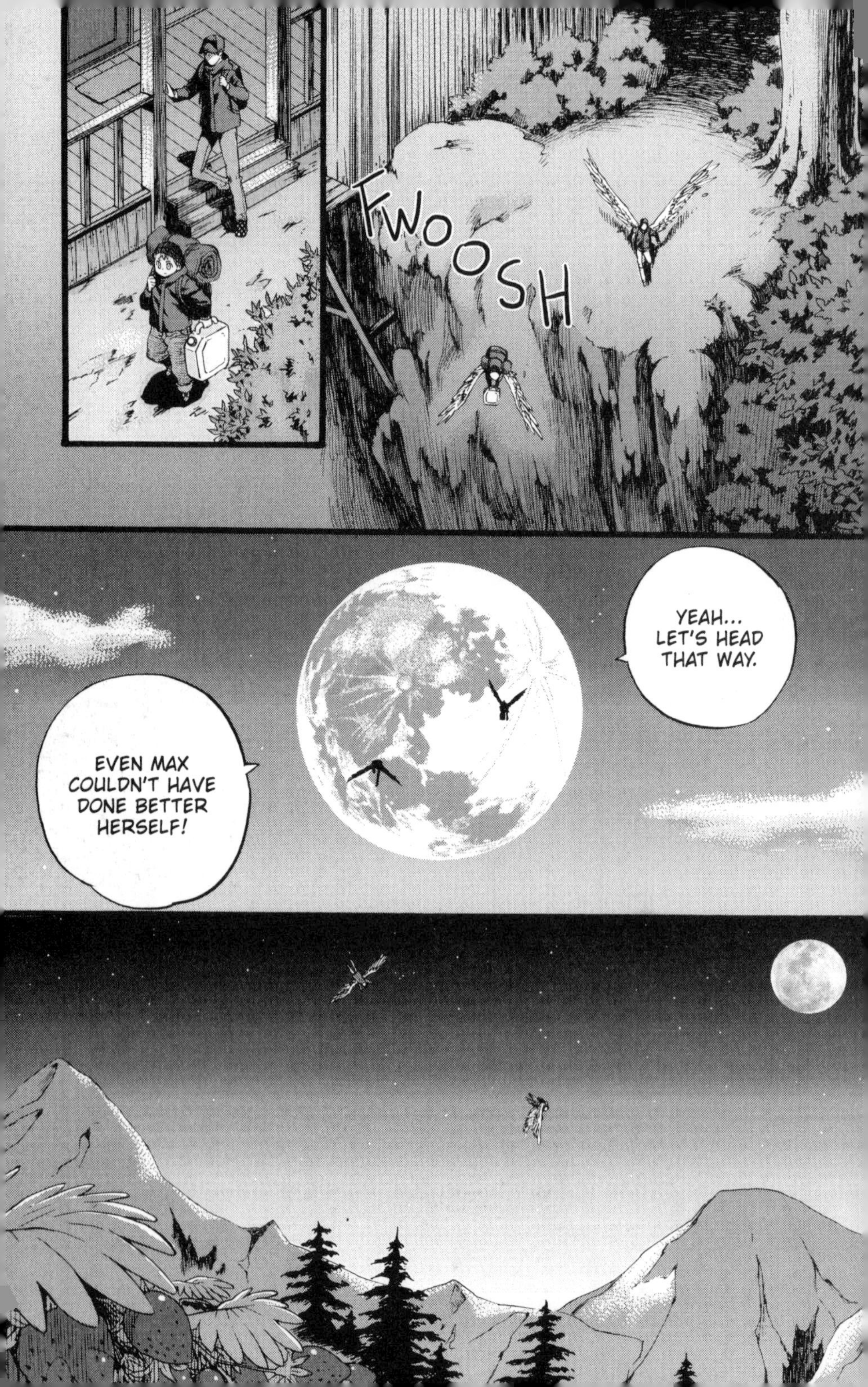
FWOOSH
YEAH... LET'S HEAD THAT WAY.
EVEN MAX COULDN'T HAVE DONE BETTER HERSELF!

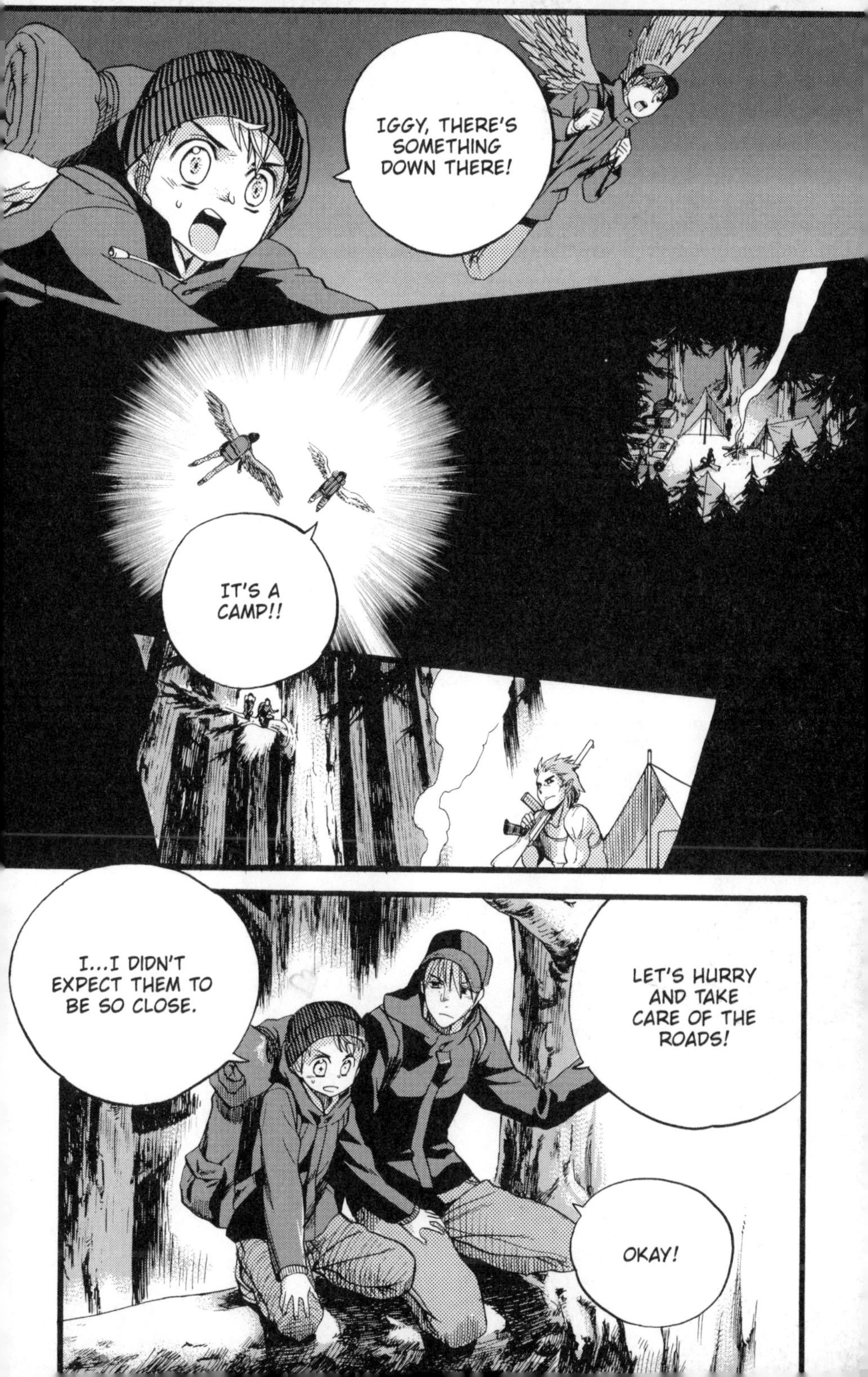
IGGY, THERE'S SOMETHING DOWN THERE!
IT'S A CAMP!!
I...I DIDN'T EXPECT THEM TO BE SO CLOSE.
LET'S HURRY AND TAKE CARE OF THE ROADS!
OKAY!

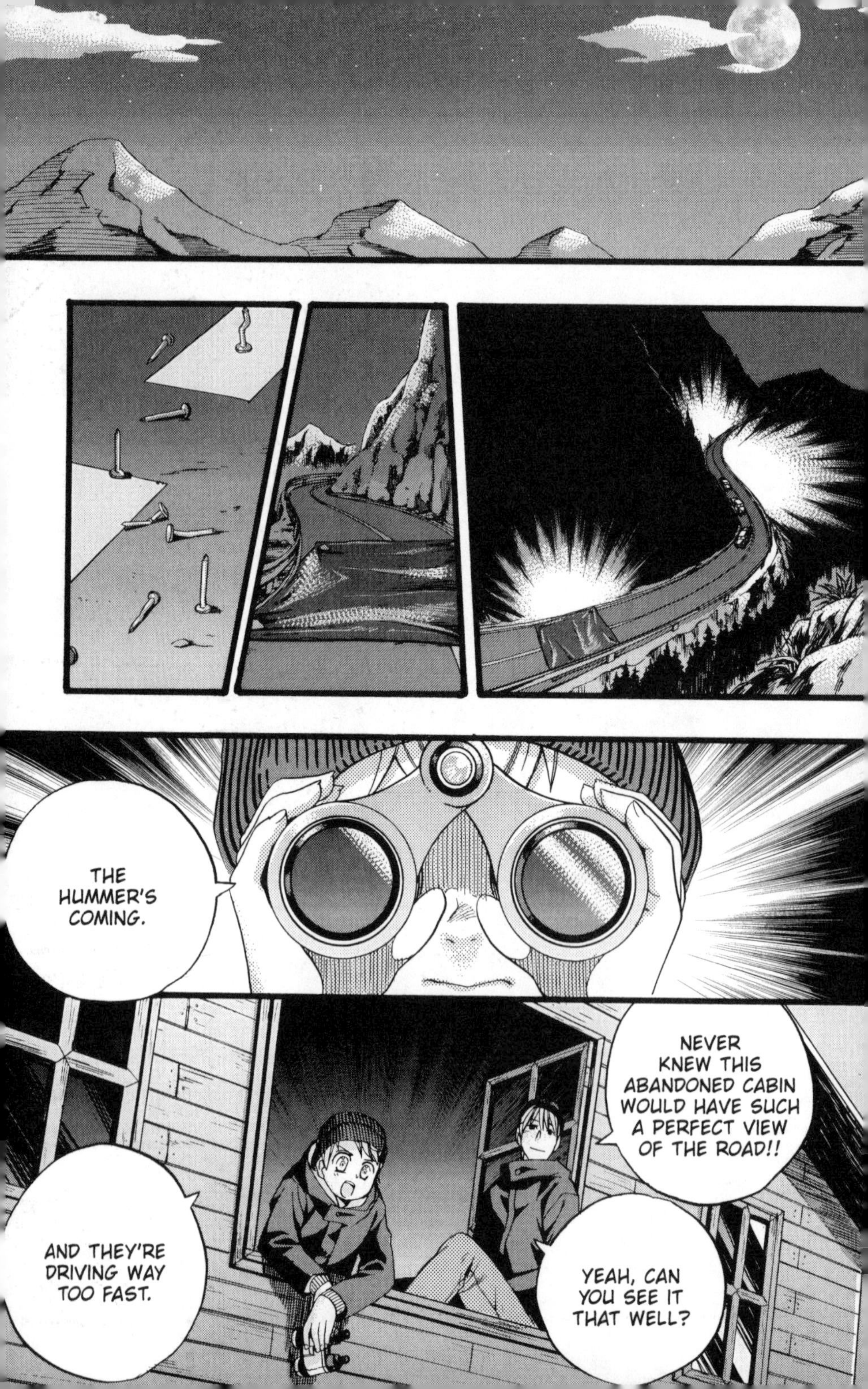
THE HUMMER'S COMING.
NEVER KNEW THIS ABANDONED CABIN WOULD HAVE SUCH A PERFECT VIEW OF THE ROAD!!
AND THEY'RE DRIVING WAY TOO FAST.
YEAH, CAN YOU SEE IT THAT WELL?

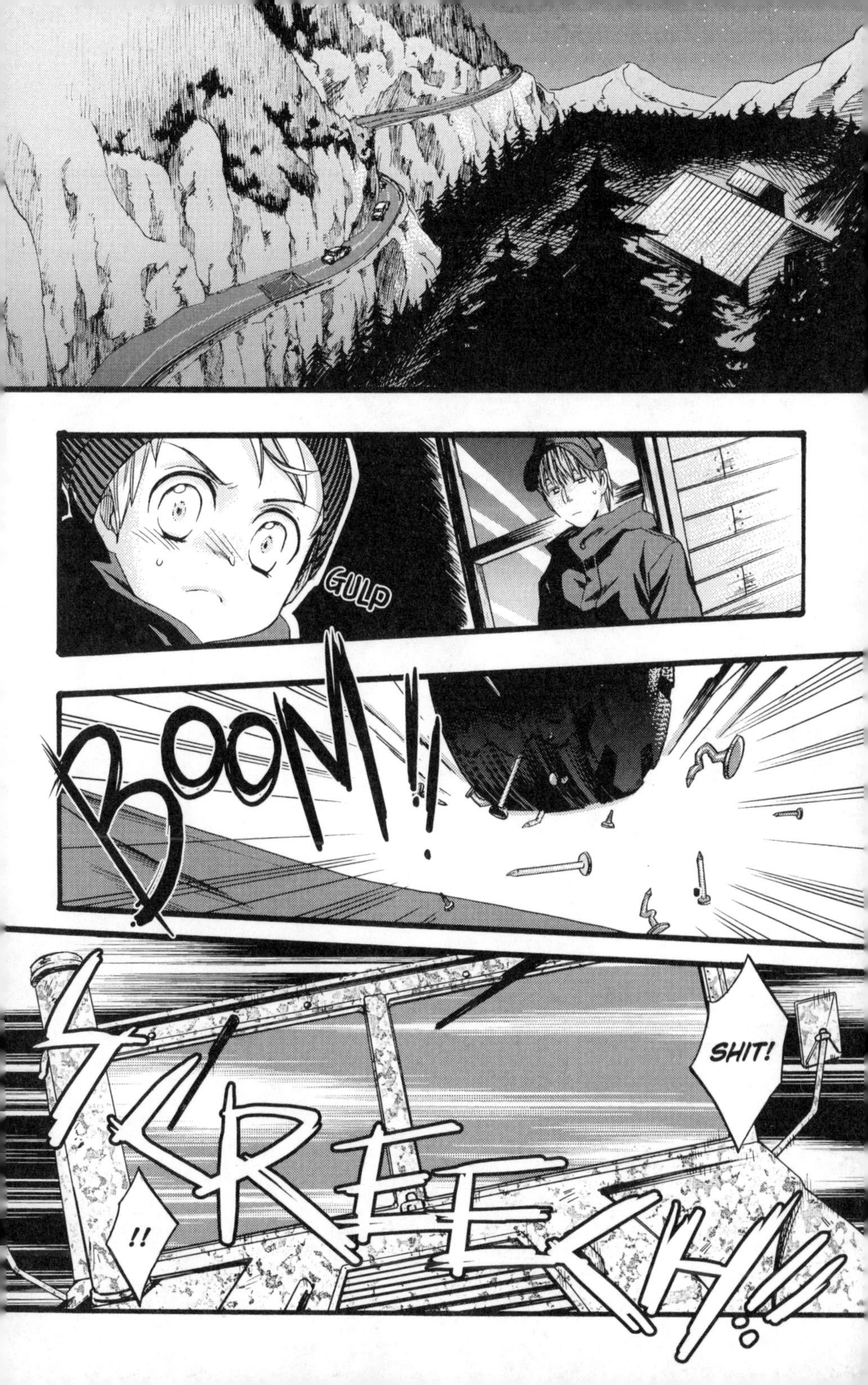
GULP
BOOM!!
SHIT!
!!
SKREECH!!

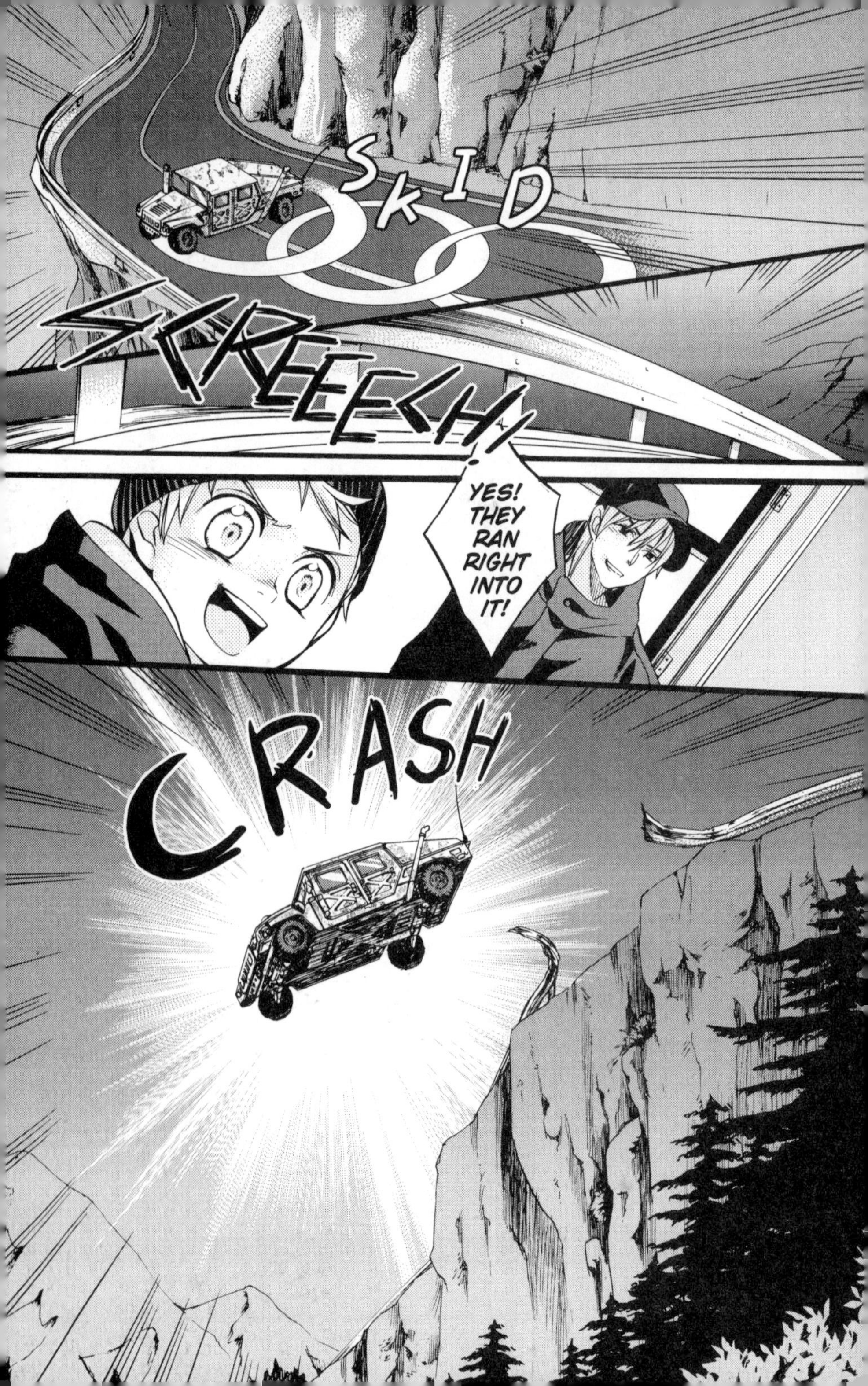
SKID
SKREEECH!
YES! THEY RAN RIGHT INTO IT!
CRASH

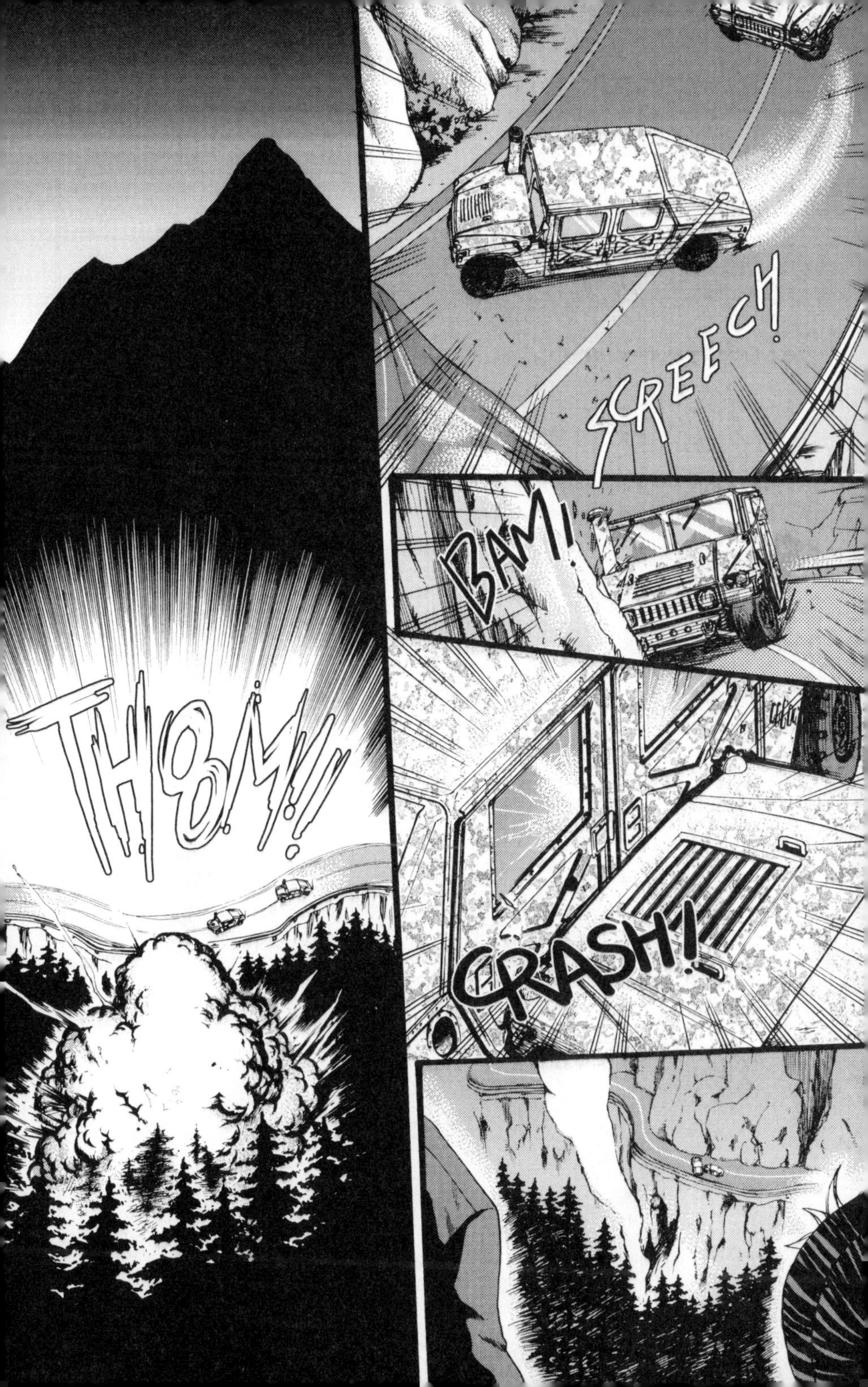
THOOM!!
SCREECH!
BAM!
CRASH!

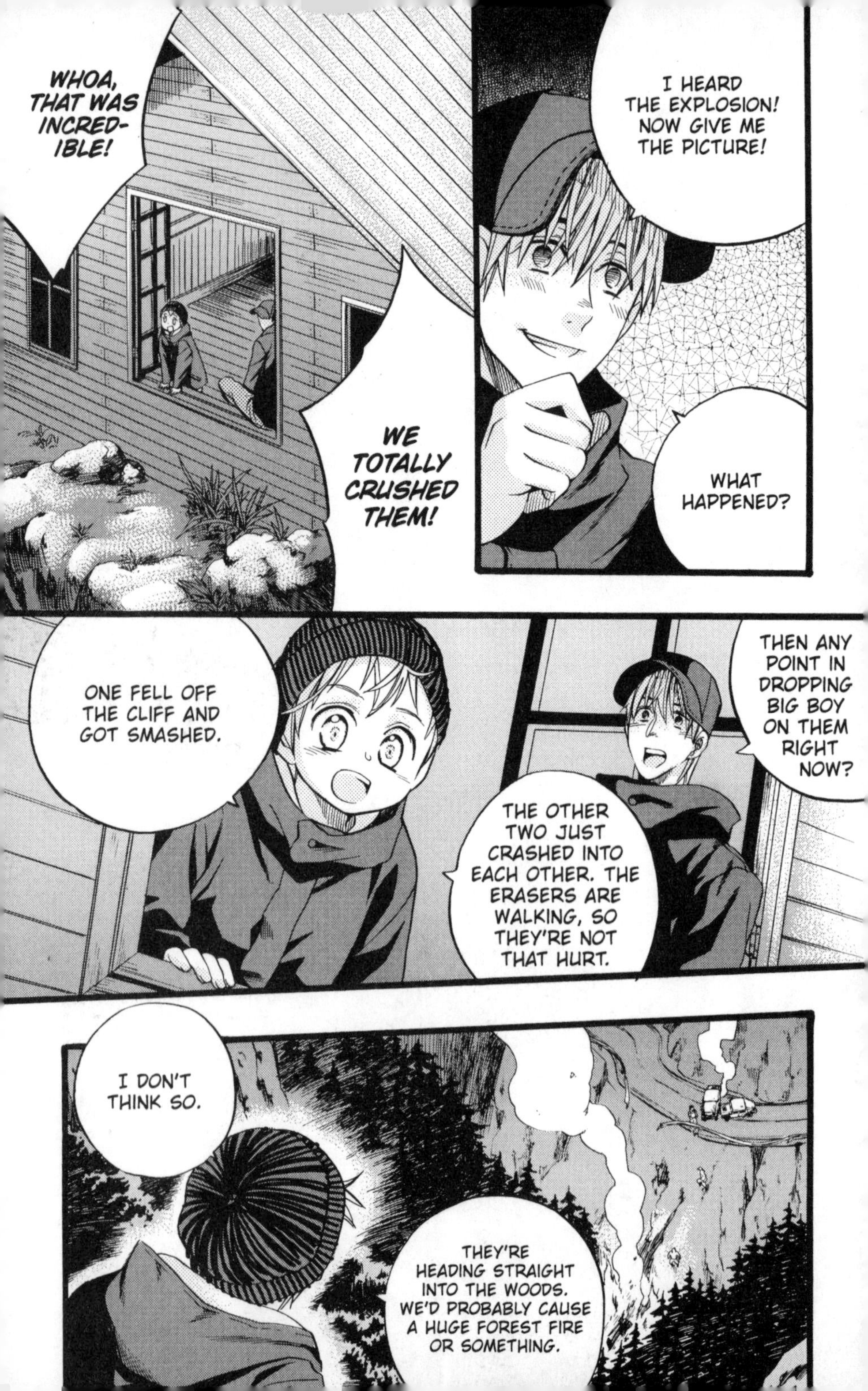
WHOA, THAT WAS INCREDIBLE!
WE TOTALLY CRUSHED THEM!
I HEARD THE EXPLOSION! NOW GIVE ME THE PICTURE!
WHAT HAPPENED?
ONE FELL OFF THE CLIFF AND GOT SMASHED.
THE OTHER TWO JUST CRASHED INTO EACH OTHER. THE ERASERS ARE WALKING, SO THEY'RE NOT THAT HURT.
THEN ANY POINT IN DROPPING BIG BOY ON THEM RIGHT NOW?
I DON'T THINK SO.
THEY'RE HEADING STRAIGHT INTO THE WOODS. WE'D PROBABLY CAUSE A HUGE FOREST FIRE OR SOMETHING.

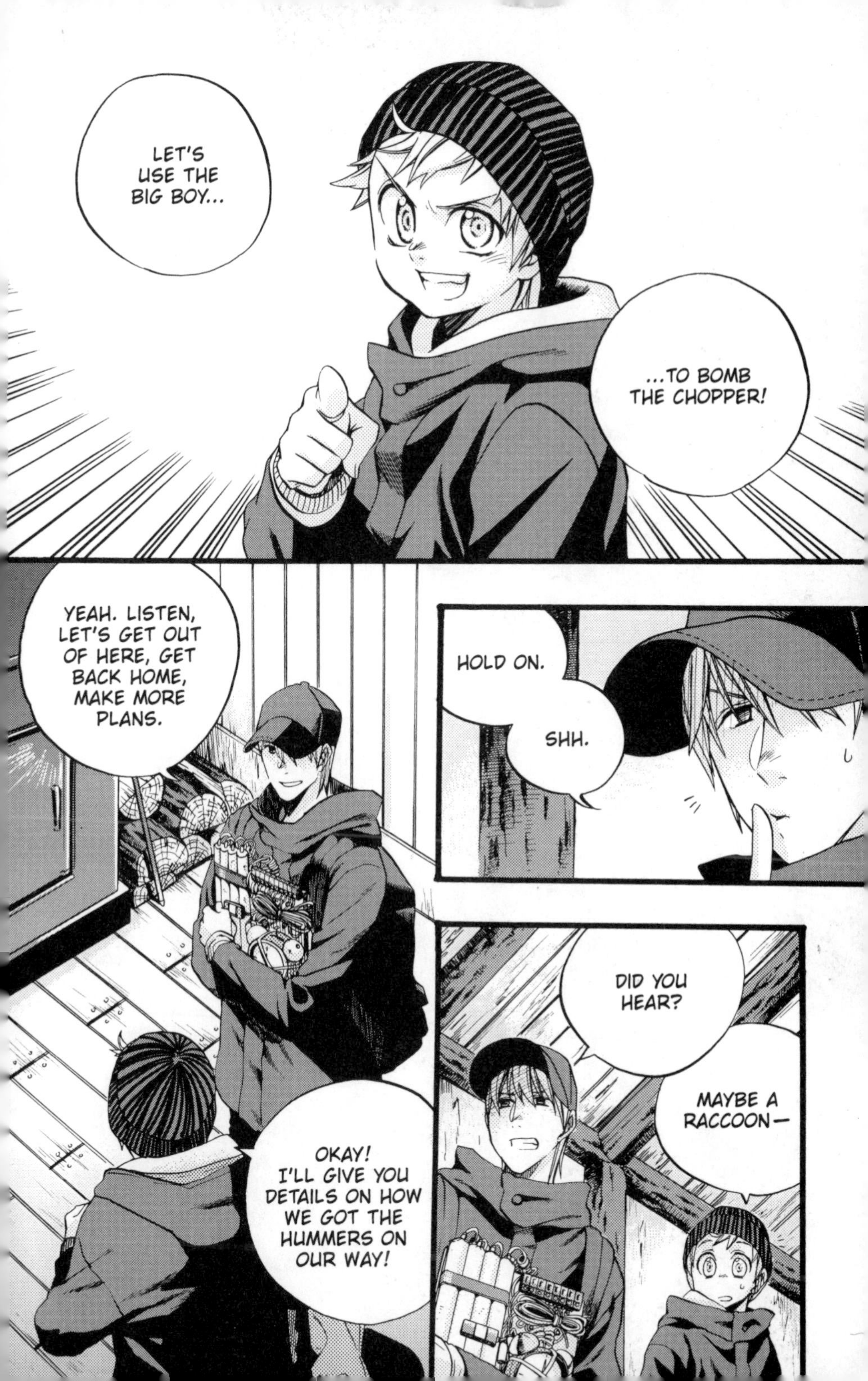
LET'S USE THE BIG BOY...
...TO BOMB THE CHOPPER!
YEAH. LISTEN, LET'S GET OUT OF HERE, GET BACK HOME, MAKE MORE PLANS.
OKAY! I'LL GIVE YOU DETAILS ON HOW WE GOT THE HUMMERS ON OUR WAY!
HOLD ON.
SHH.
DID YOU HEAR?
MAYBE A RACCOON—

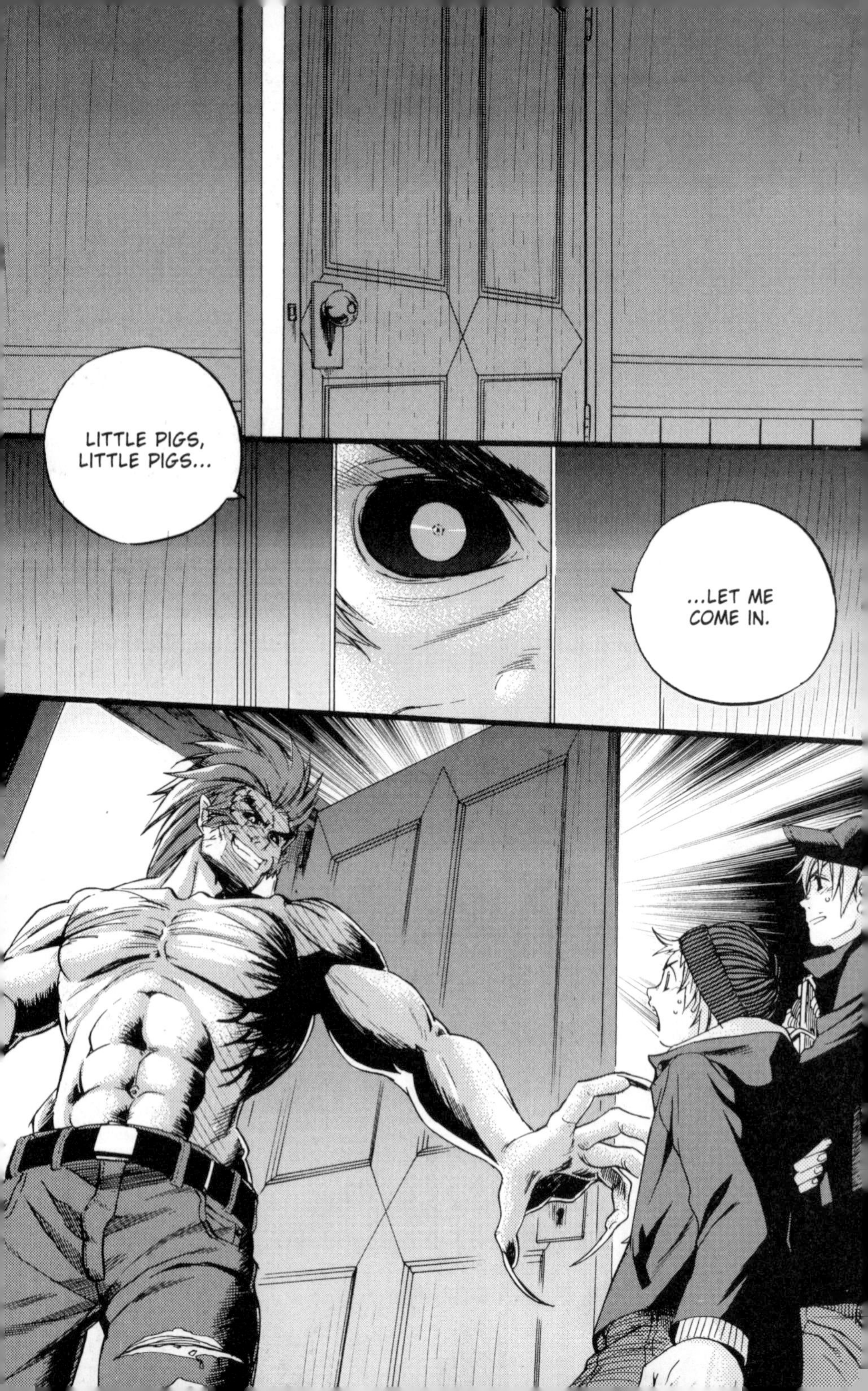
LITTLE PIGS,
LITTLE PIGS...
...LET ME
COME IN.

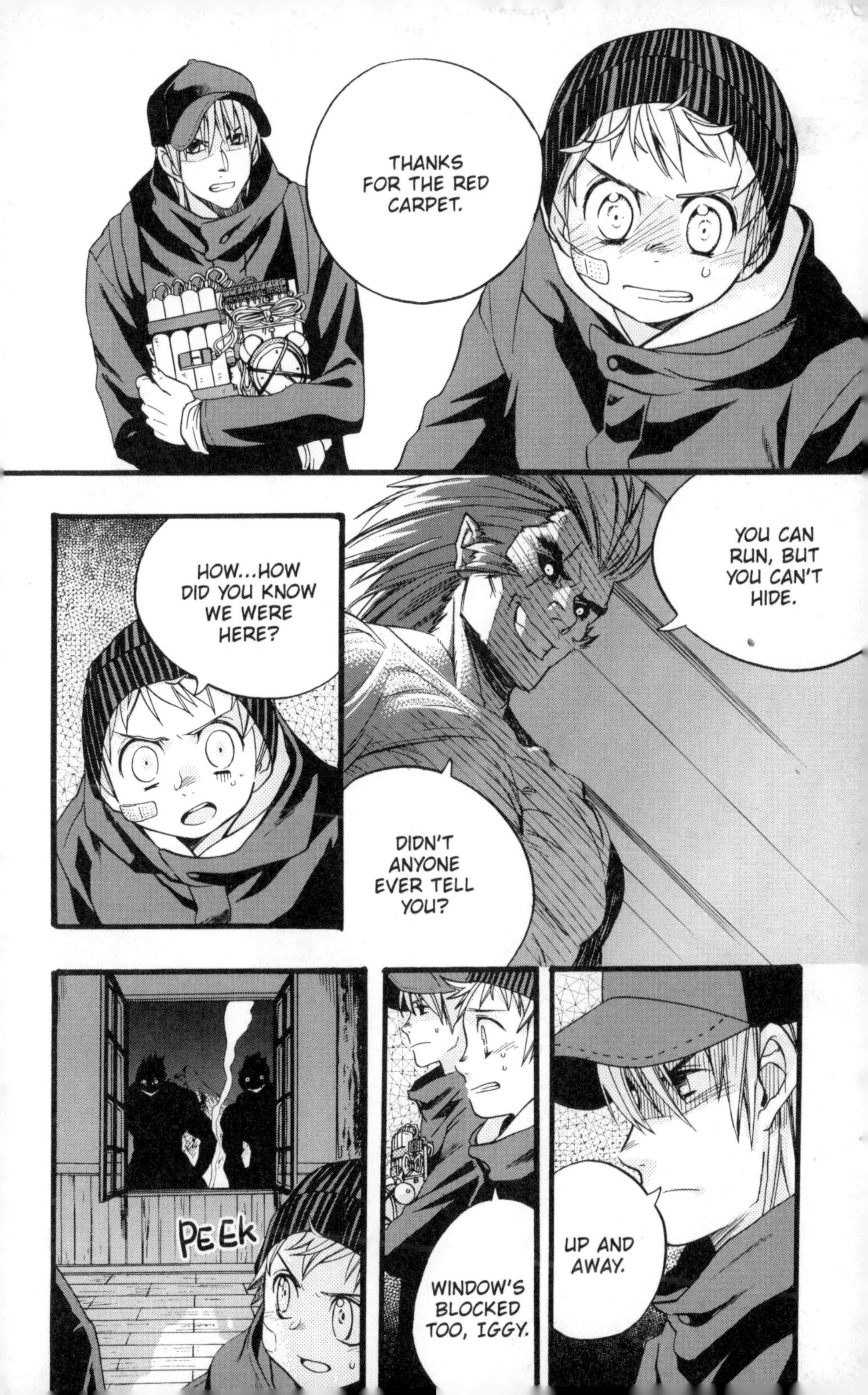
THANKS FOR THE RED CARPET.
HOW...HOW DID YOU KNOW WE WERE HERE?
YOU CAN RUN, BUT YOU CAN'T HIDE.
DIDN'T ANYONE EVER TELL YOU?
PEEK
WINDOW'S BLOCKED TOO, IGGY.
UP AND AWAY.

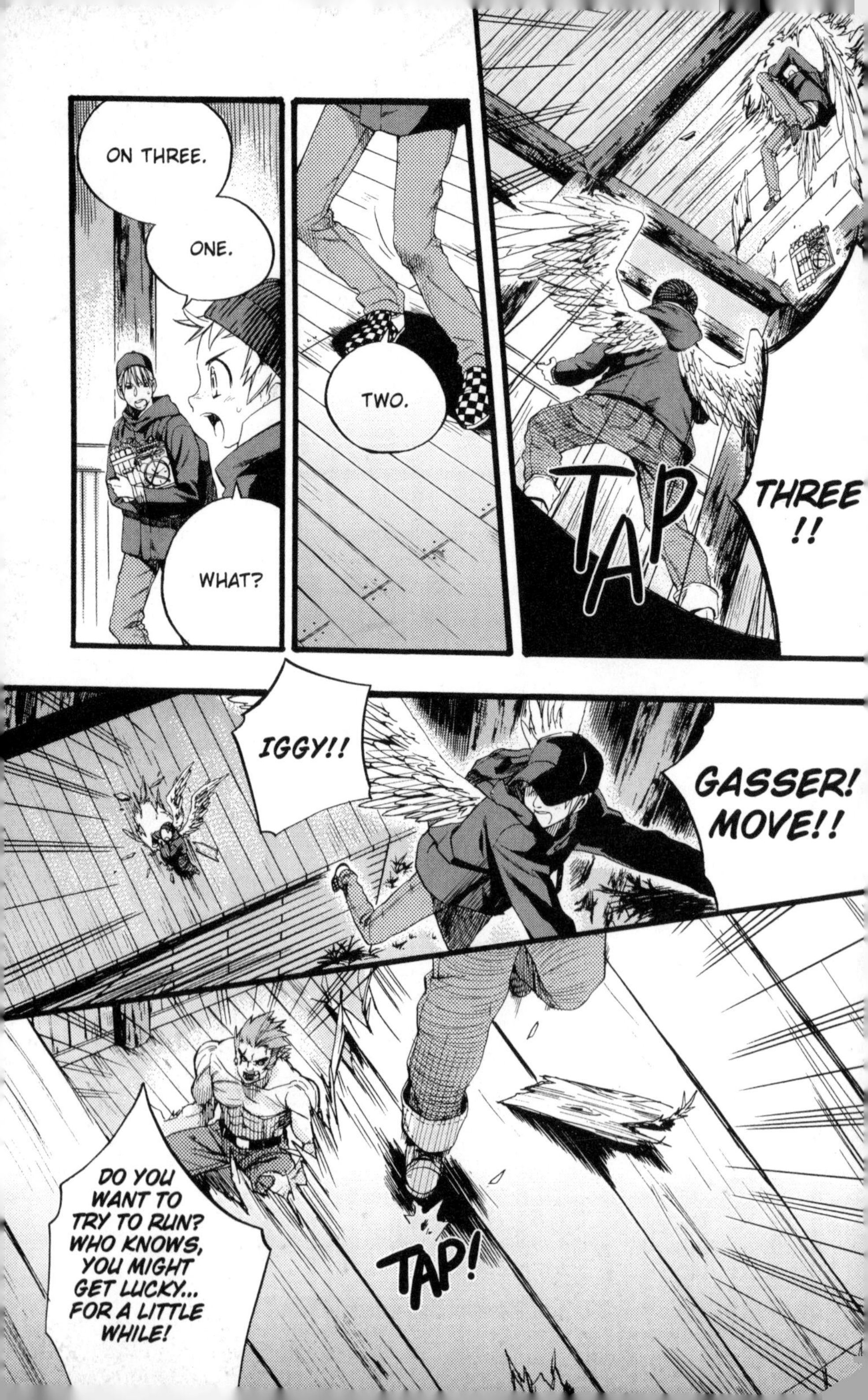
ON THREE.
ONE.
WHAT?
TWO.
TAP
THREE !!
IGGY!!
GASSER! MOVE!!
DO YOU WANT TO TRY TO RUN? WHO KNOWS, YOU MIGHT GET LUCKY... FOR A LITTLE WHILE!
TAP!

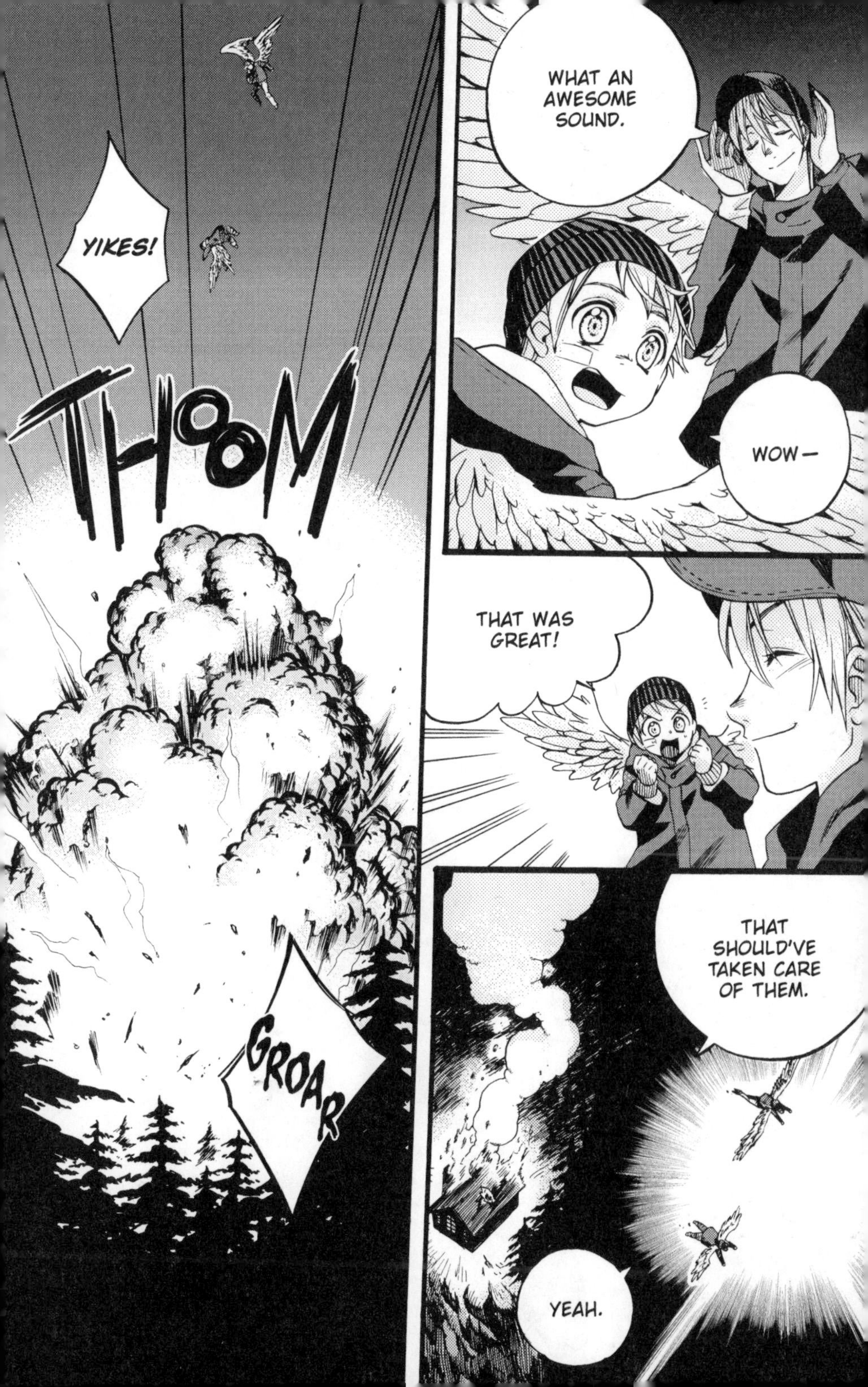
YIKES!
THOOM
GROAR
WHAT AN AWESOME SOUND.
WOW—
THAT WAS GREAT!
THAT SHOULD'VE TAKEN CARE OF THEM.
YEAH.

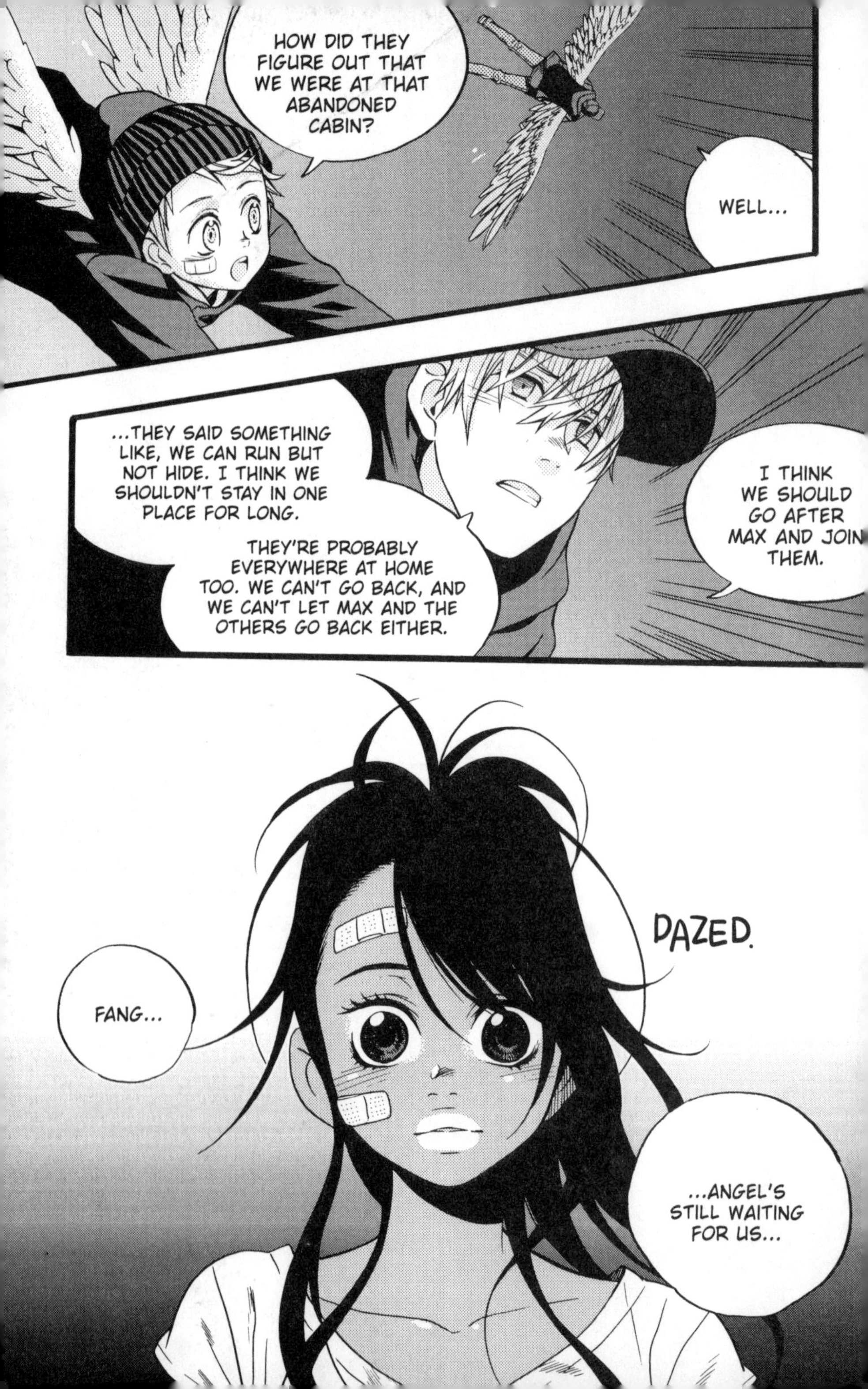
HOW DID THEY FIGURE OUT THAT WE WERE AT THAT ABANDONED CABIN?
WELL...
...THEY SAID SOMETHING LIKE, WE CAN RUN BUT NOT HIDE. I THINK WE SHOULDN'T STAY IN ONE PLACE FOR LONG.
THEY'RE PROBABLY EVERYWHERE AT HOME TOO. WE CAN'T GO BACK, AND WE CAN'T LET MAX AND THE OTHERS GO BACK EITHER.
I THINK WE SHOULD GO AFTER MAX AND JOIN THEM.
DAZED.
FANG...
...ANGEL'S STILL WAITING FOR US...

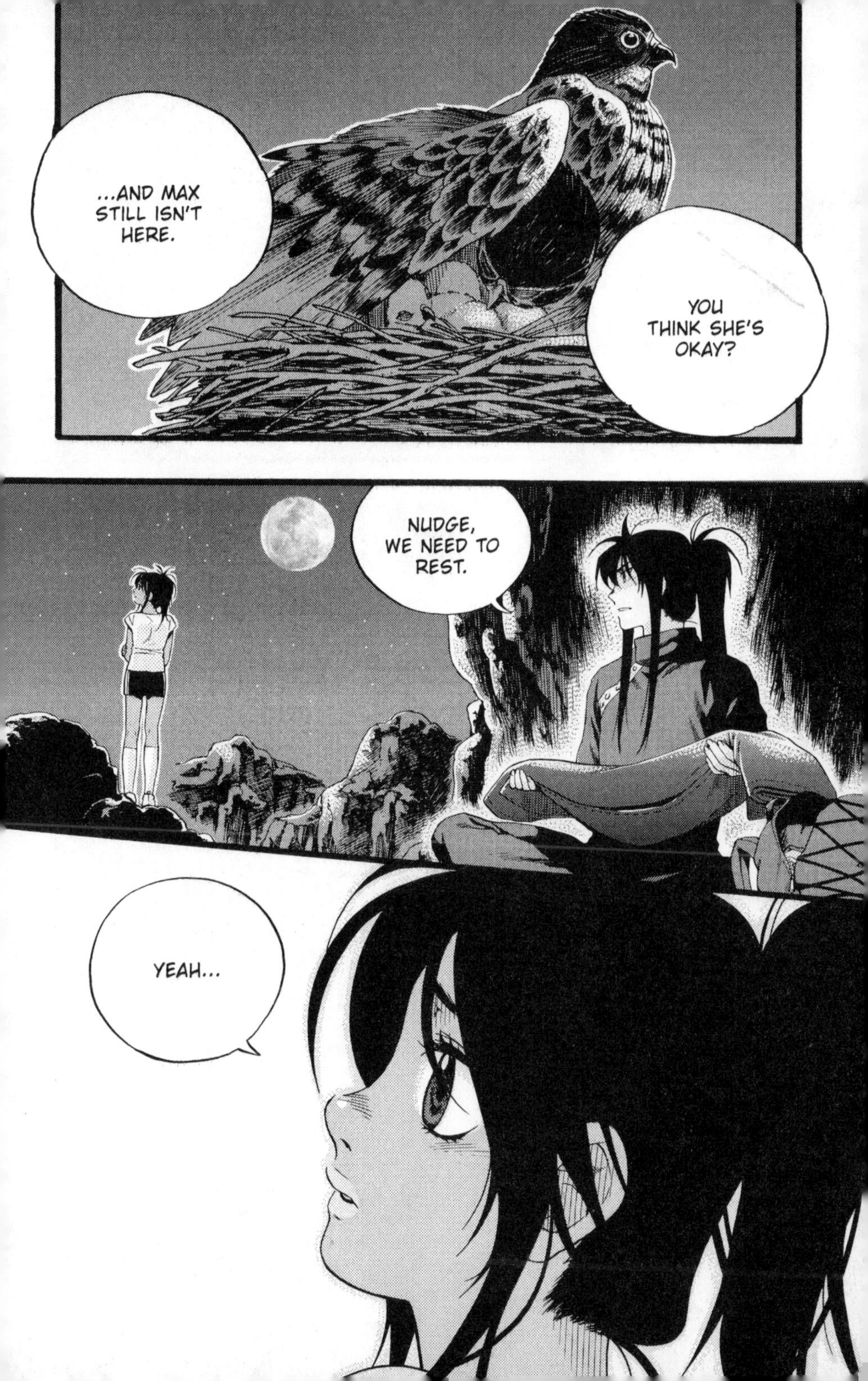
...AND MAX STILL ISN'T HERE.
YOU THINK SHE'S OKAY?
NUDGE, WE NEED TO REST.
YEAH...

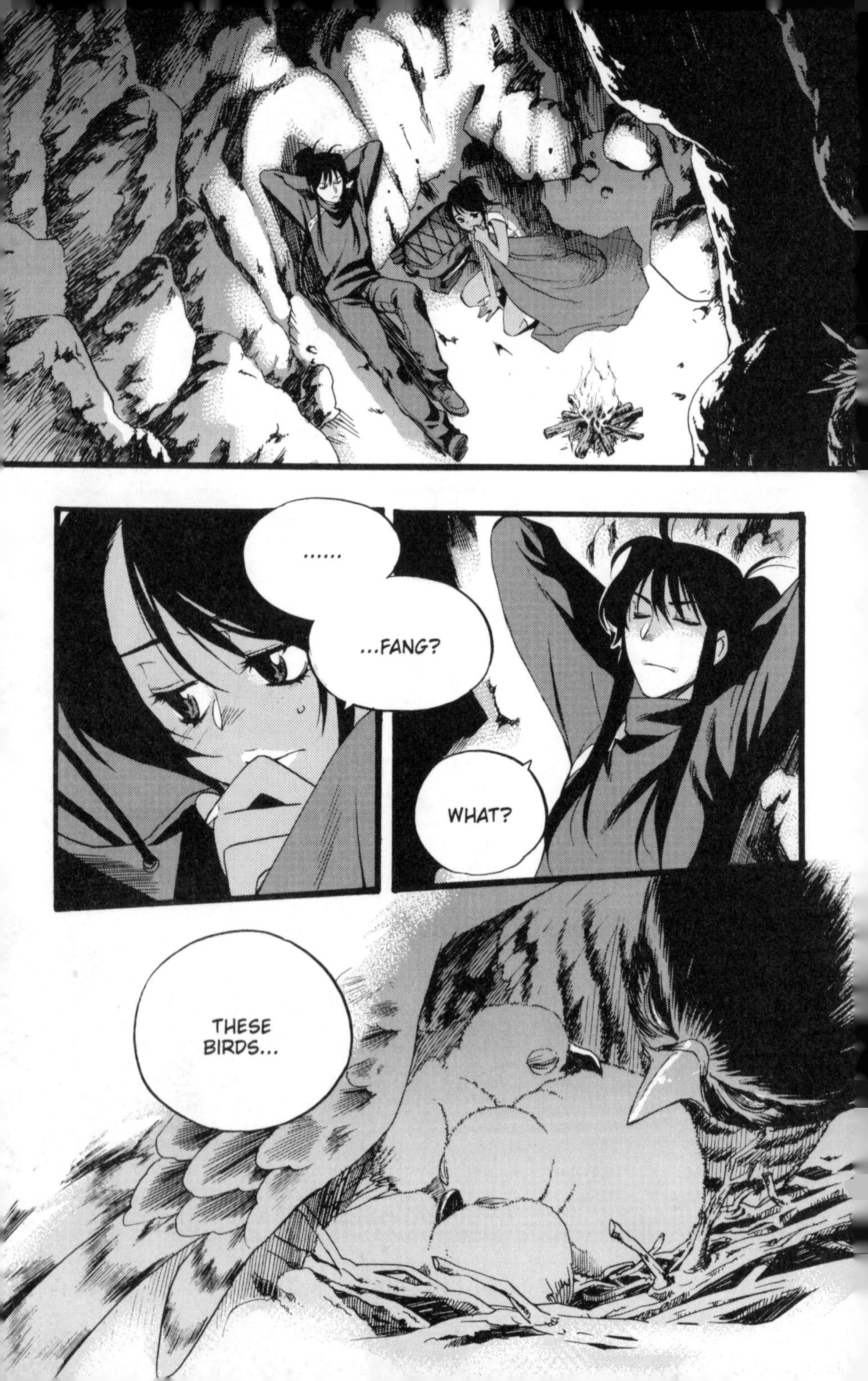
......
...FANG?
WHAT?
THESE BIRDS...

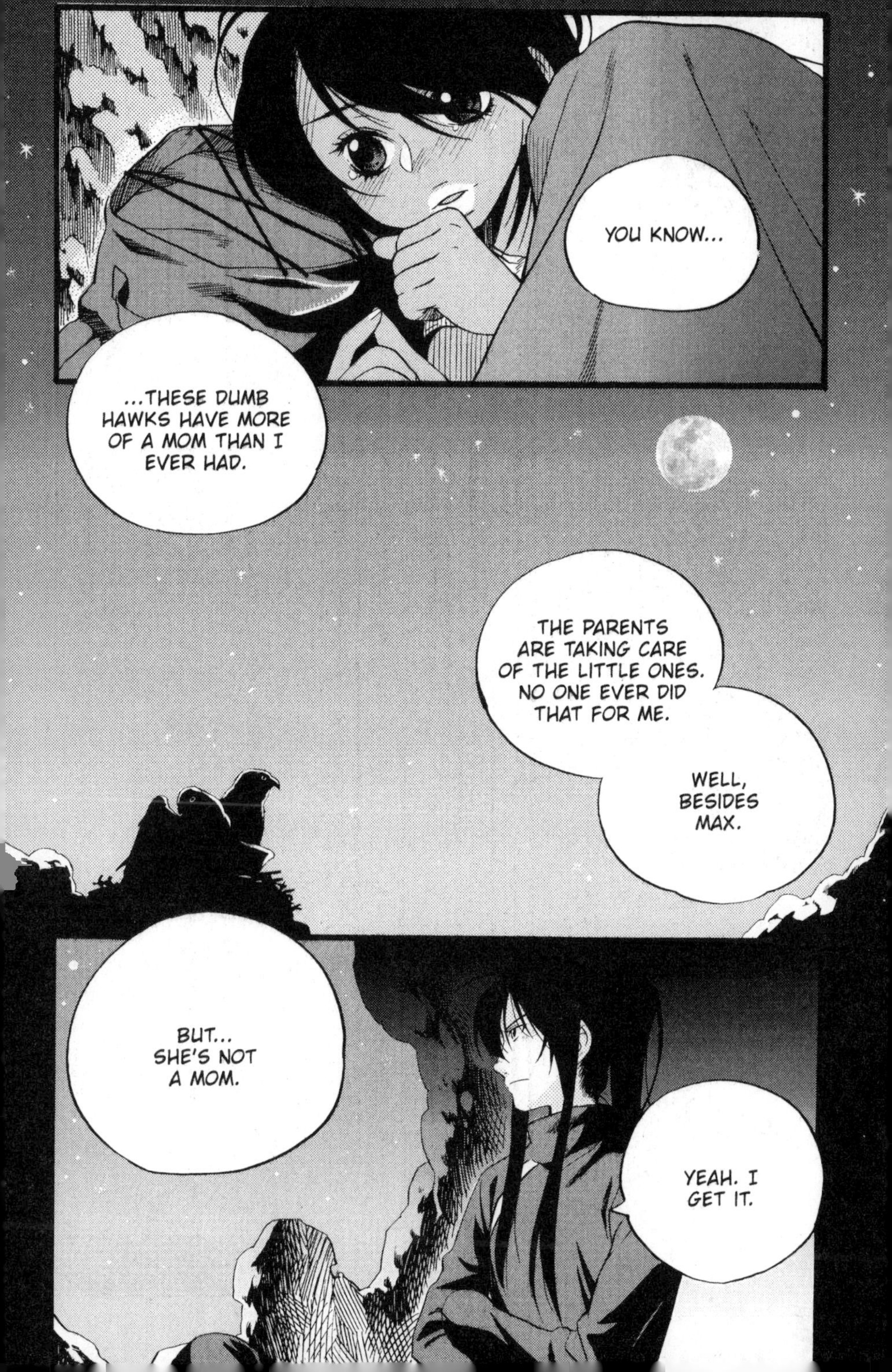
YOU KNOW...
...THESE DUMB HAWKS HAVE MORE OF A MOM THAN I EVER HAD.
THE PARENTS ARE TAKING CARE OF THE LITTLE ONES. NO ONE EVER DID THAT FOR ME.
WELL, BESIDES MAX.
BUT... SHE'S NOT A MOM.
YEAH. I GET IT.

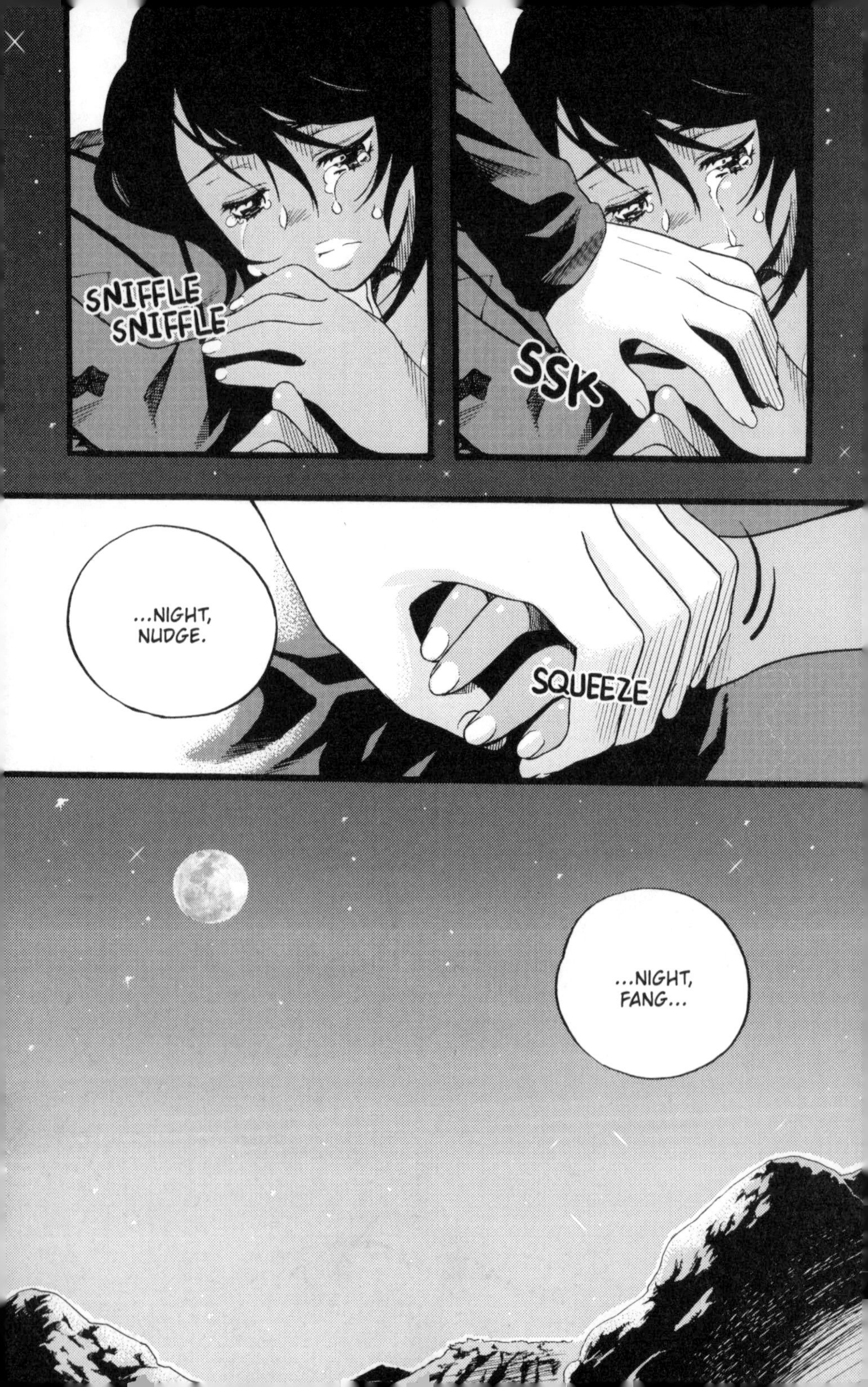
SNIFFLE SNIFFLE
SSK
...NIGHT, NUDGE.
SQUEEZE
...NIGHT, FANG...

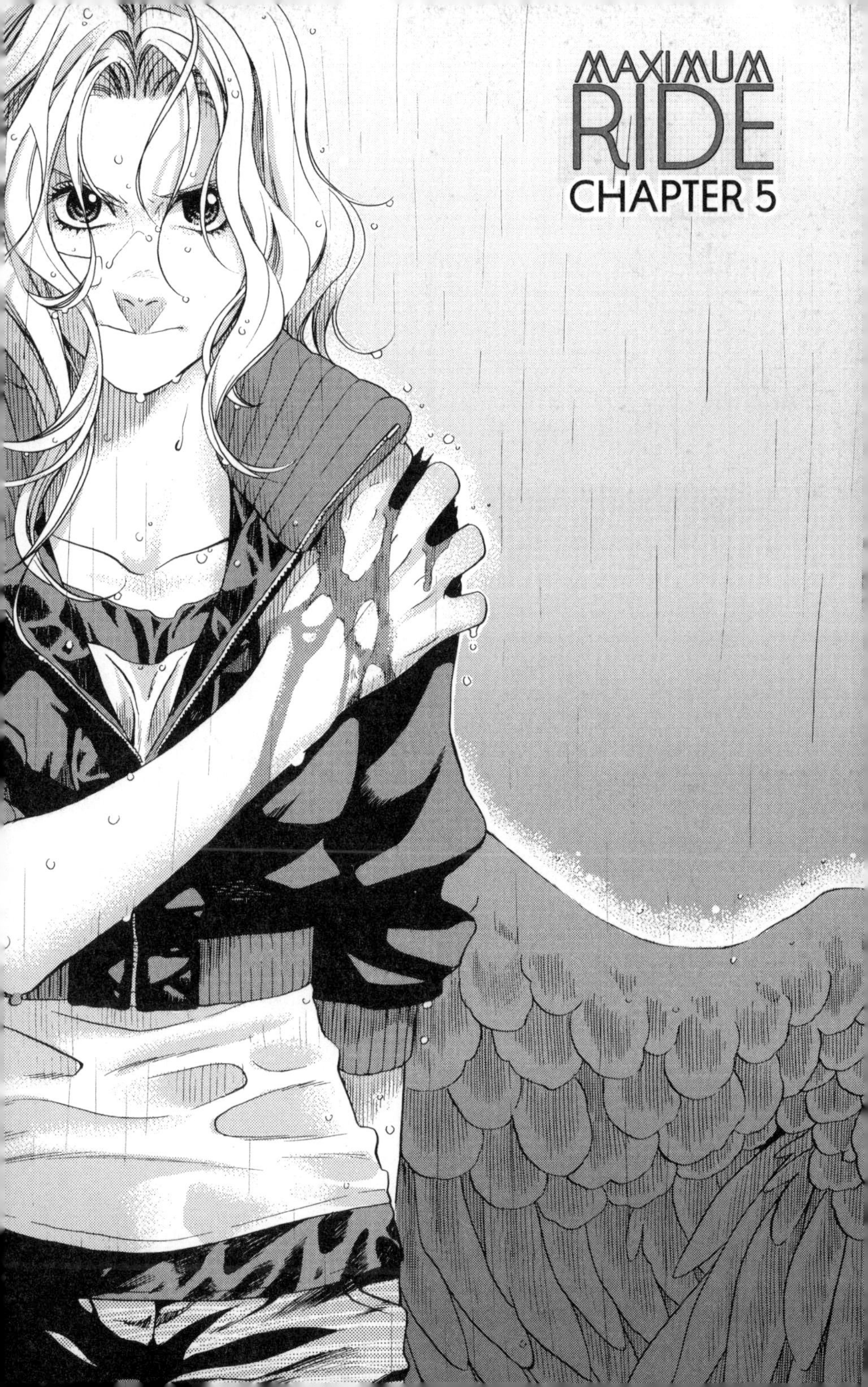
MAXIMUM
RIDE
CHAPTER 5

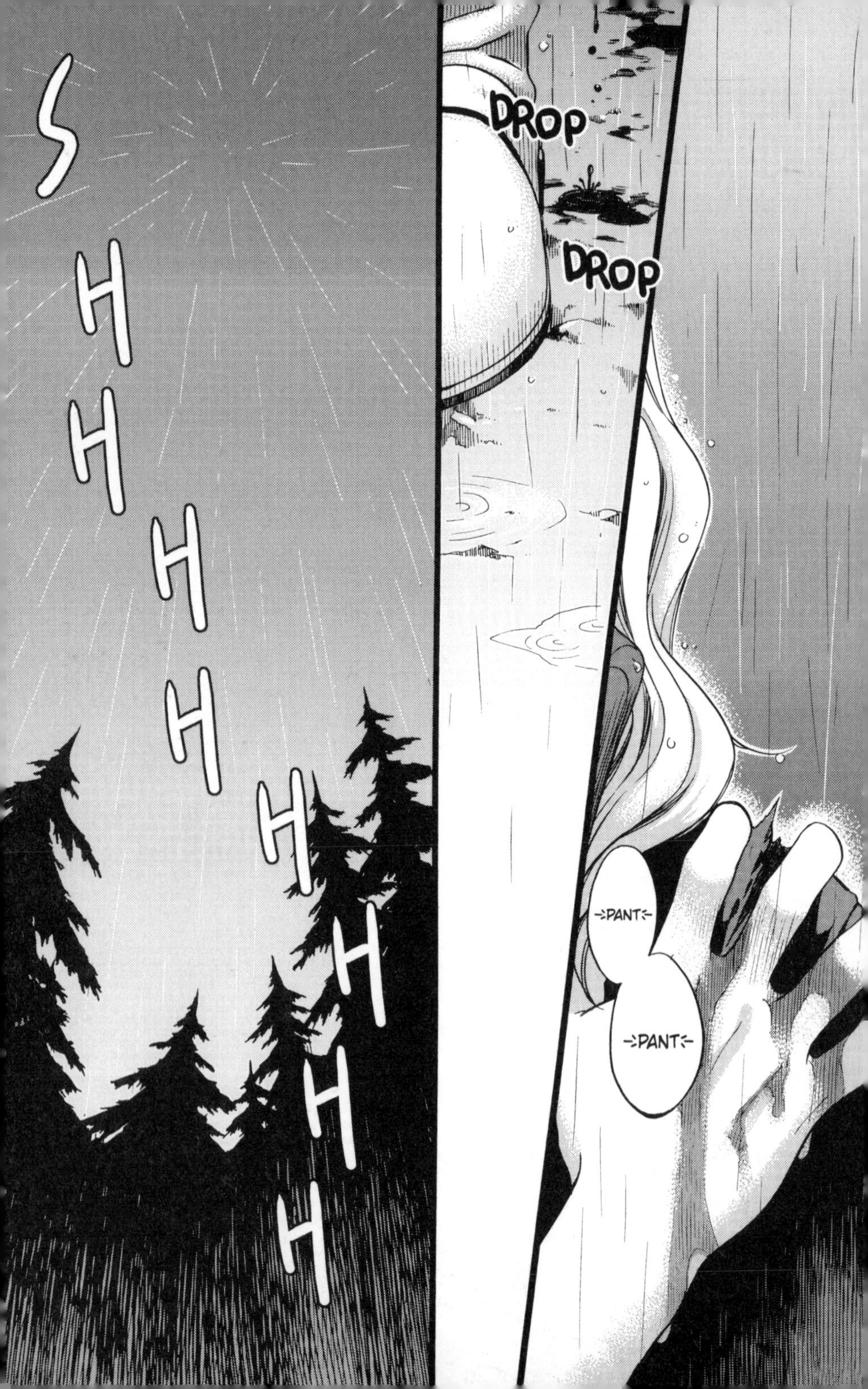
SHHHHHHHHH
DROP
DROP
PANT
PANT

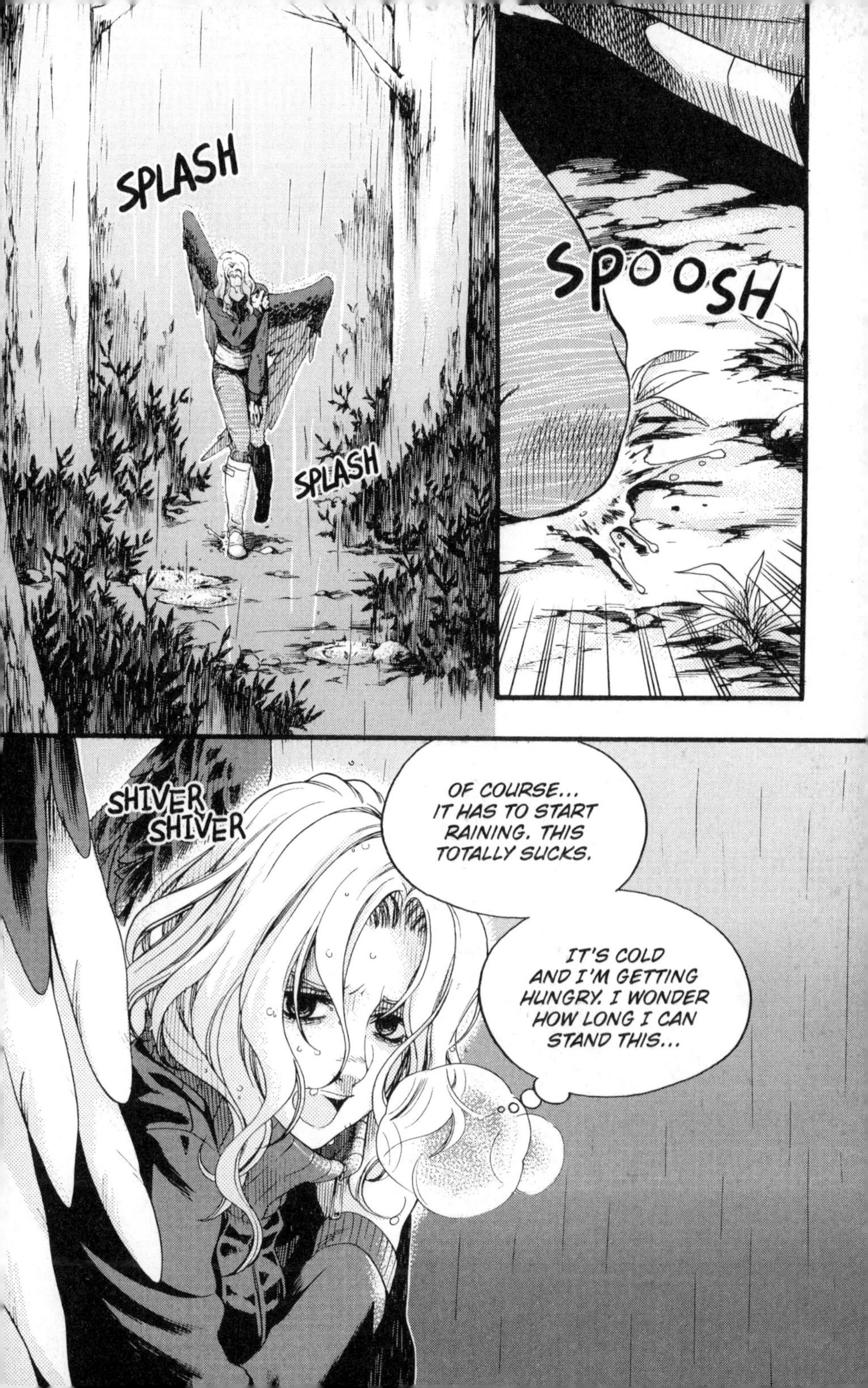
SPLASH
SPLASH
SPOOSH
SHIVER SHIVER
OF COURSE... IT HAS TO START RAINING. THIS TOTALLY SUCKS.
IT'S COLD AND I'M GETTING HUNGRY. I WONDER HOW LONG I CAN STAND THIS...

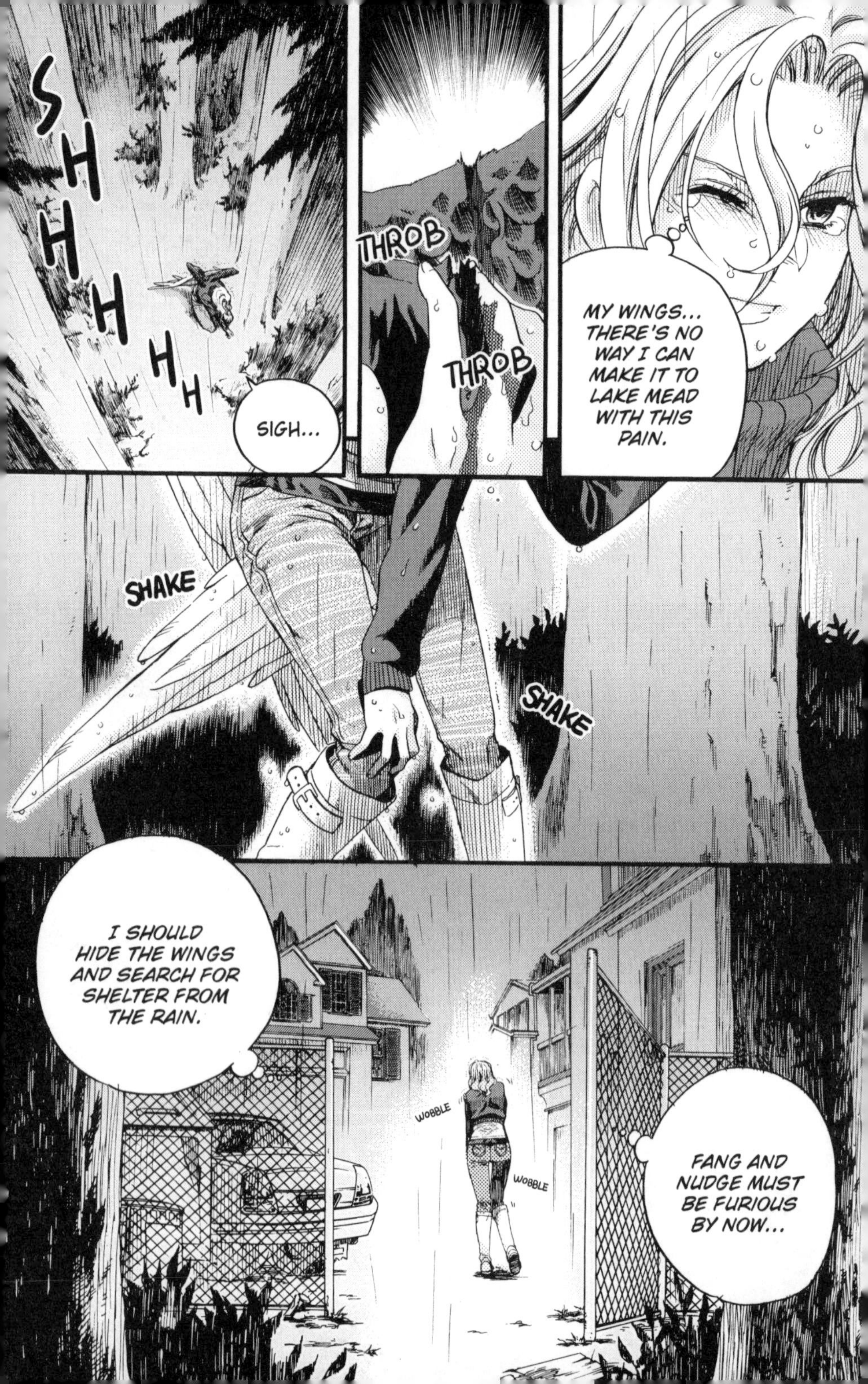
SHHHHHH
SIGH...
THROB
THROB
MY WINGS... THERE'S NO WAY I CAN MAKE IT TO LAKE MEAD WITH THIS PAIN.
SHAKE
SHAKE
I SHOULD HIDE THE WINGS AND SEARCH FOR SHELTER FROM THE RAIN.
WOBBLE
WOBBLE
FANG AND NUDGE MUST BE FURIOUS BY NOW...

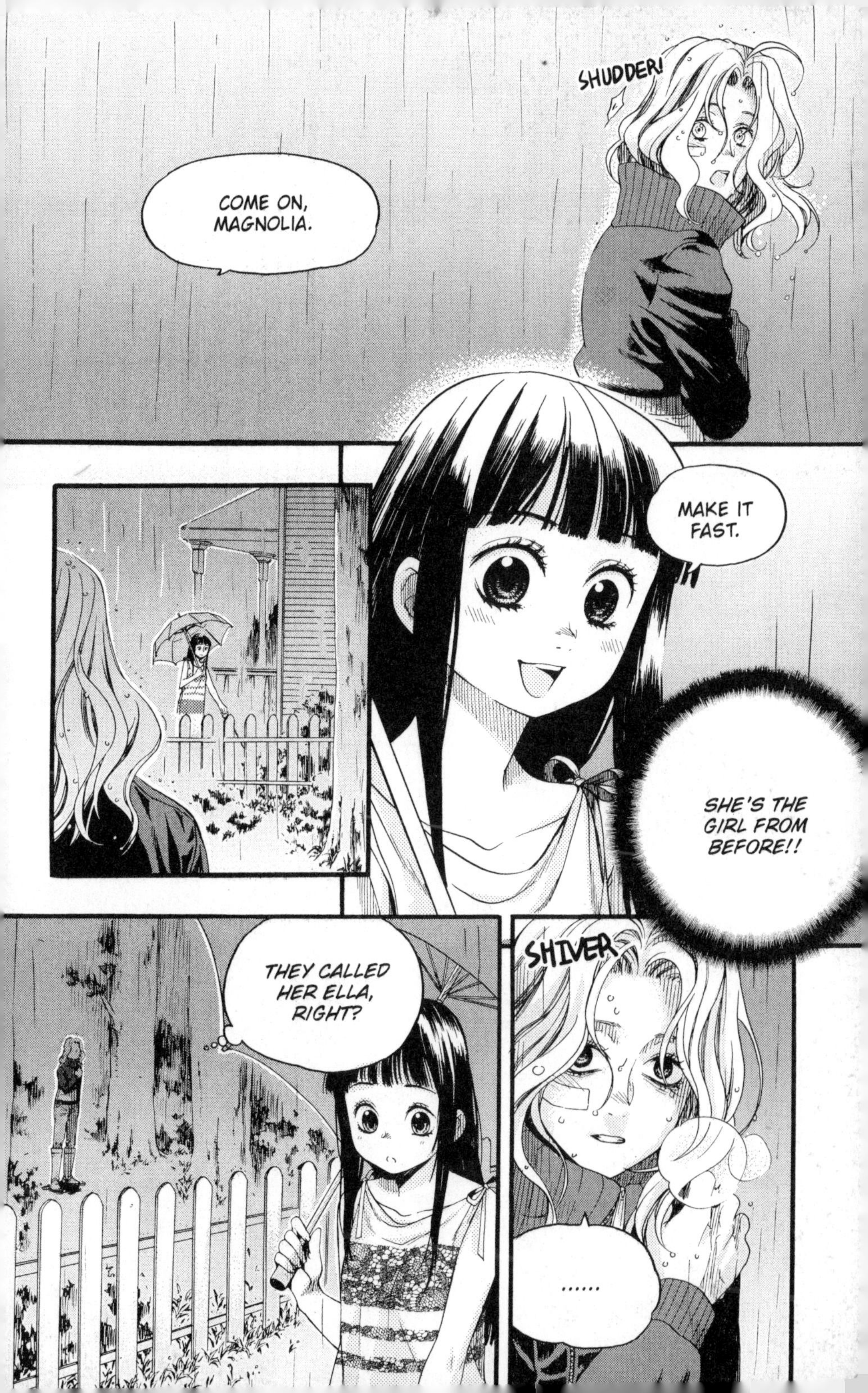

COME ON, MAGNOLIA.
SHUDDER!
MAKE IT FAST.
SHE'S THE GIRL FROM BEFORE!!
THEY CALLED HER ELLA, RIGHT?
SHIVER
......

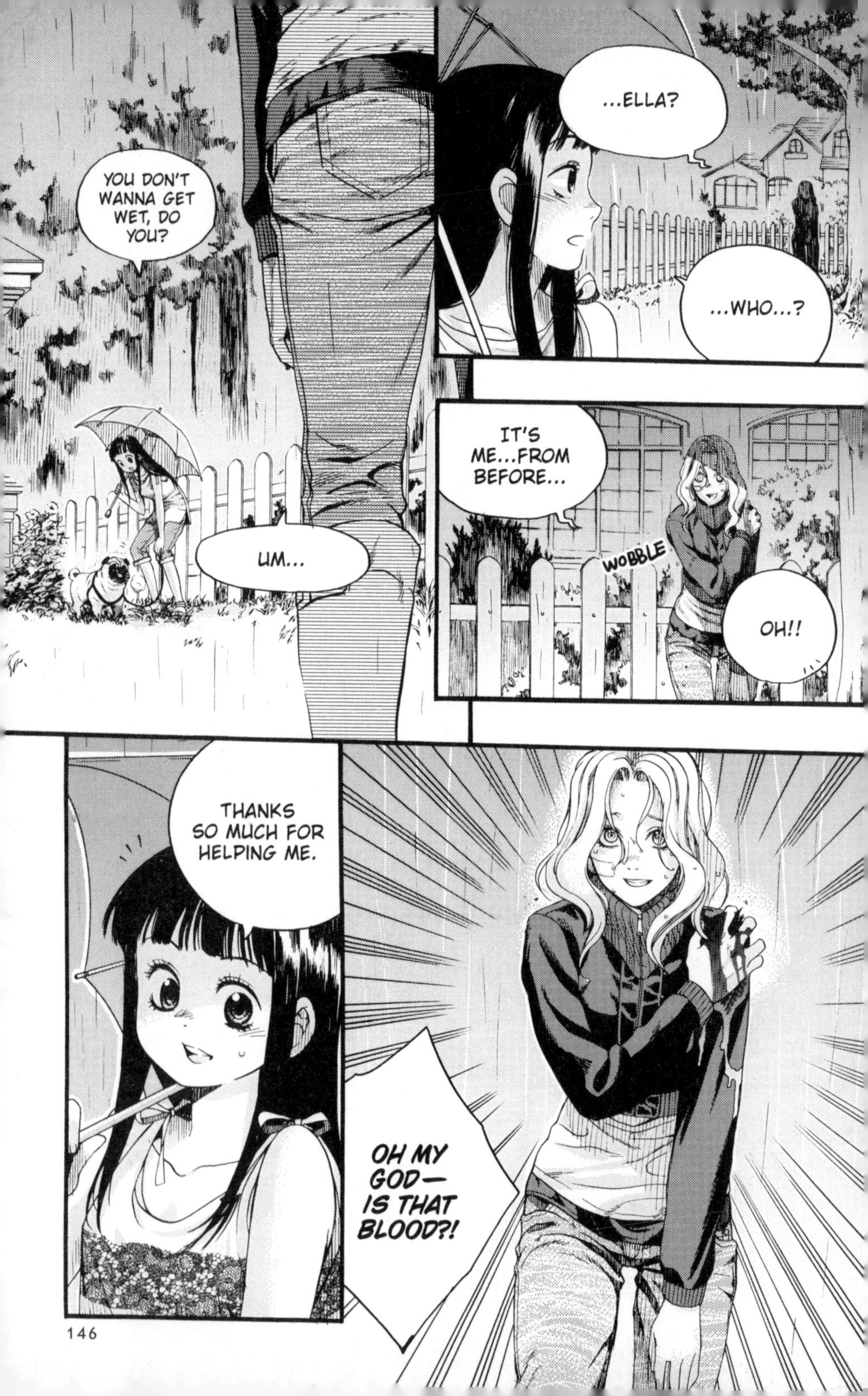
YOU DON'T WANNA GET WET, DO YOU?
UM...
...ELLA?
...WHO...?
IT'S ME...FROM BEFORE...
WOBBLE
OH!!
THANKS SO MUCH FOR HELPING ME.
OH MY GOD— IS THAT BLOOD?!

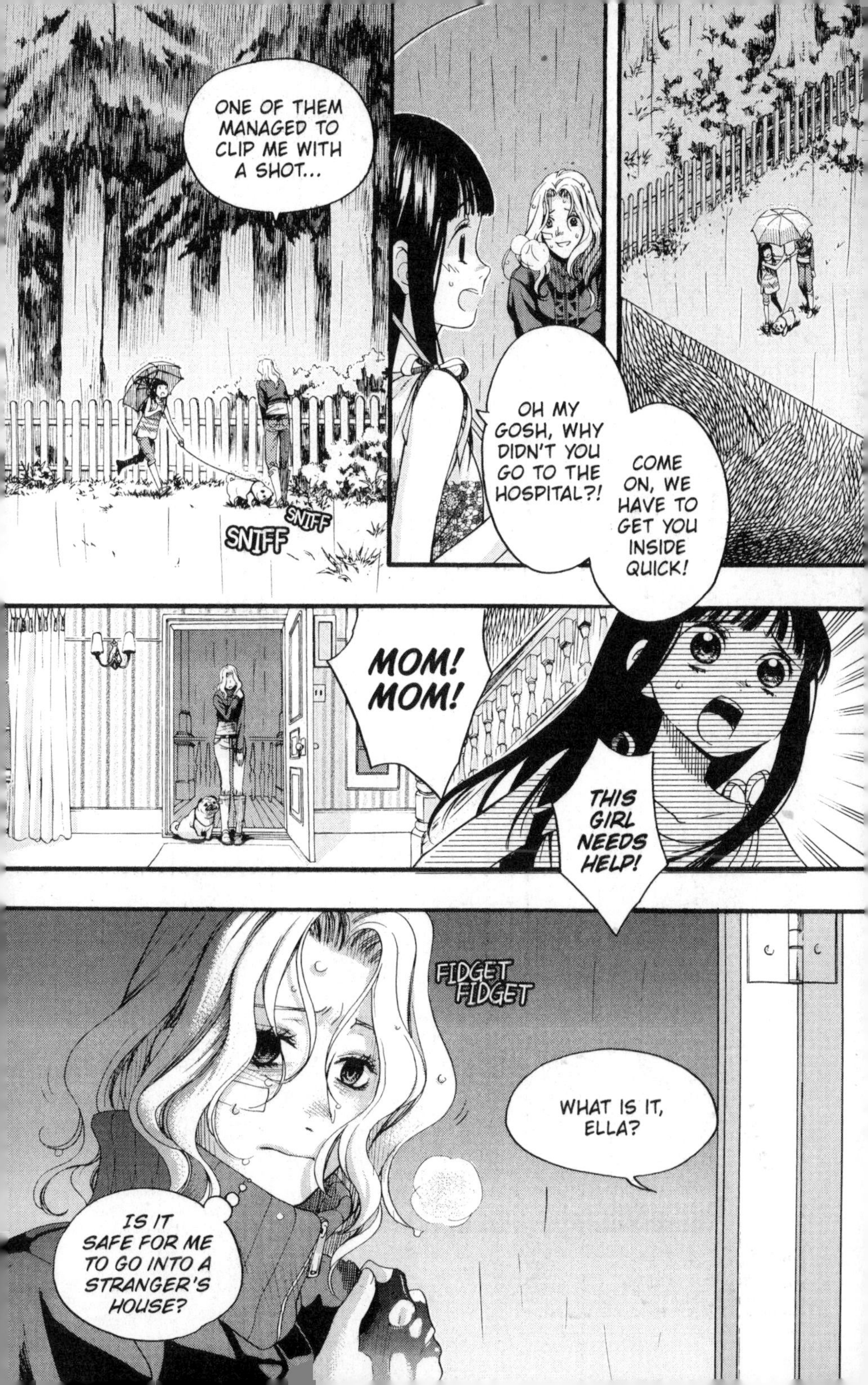

ONE OF THEM MANAGED TO CLIP ME WITH A SHOT...
SNIFF
SNIFF
OH MY GOSH, WHY DIDN'T YOU GO TO THE HOSPITAL?!
COME ON, WE HAVE TO GET YOU INSIDE QUICK!
MOM! MOM!
THIS GIRL NEEDS HELP!
FIDGET FIDGET
WHAT IS IT, ELLA?
IS IT SAFE FOR ME TO GO INTO A STRANGER'S HOUSE?

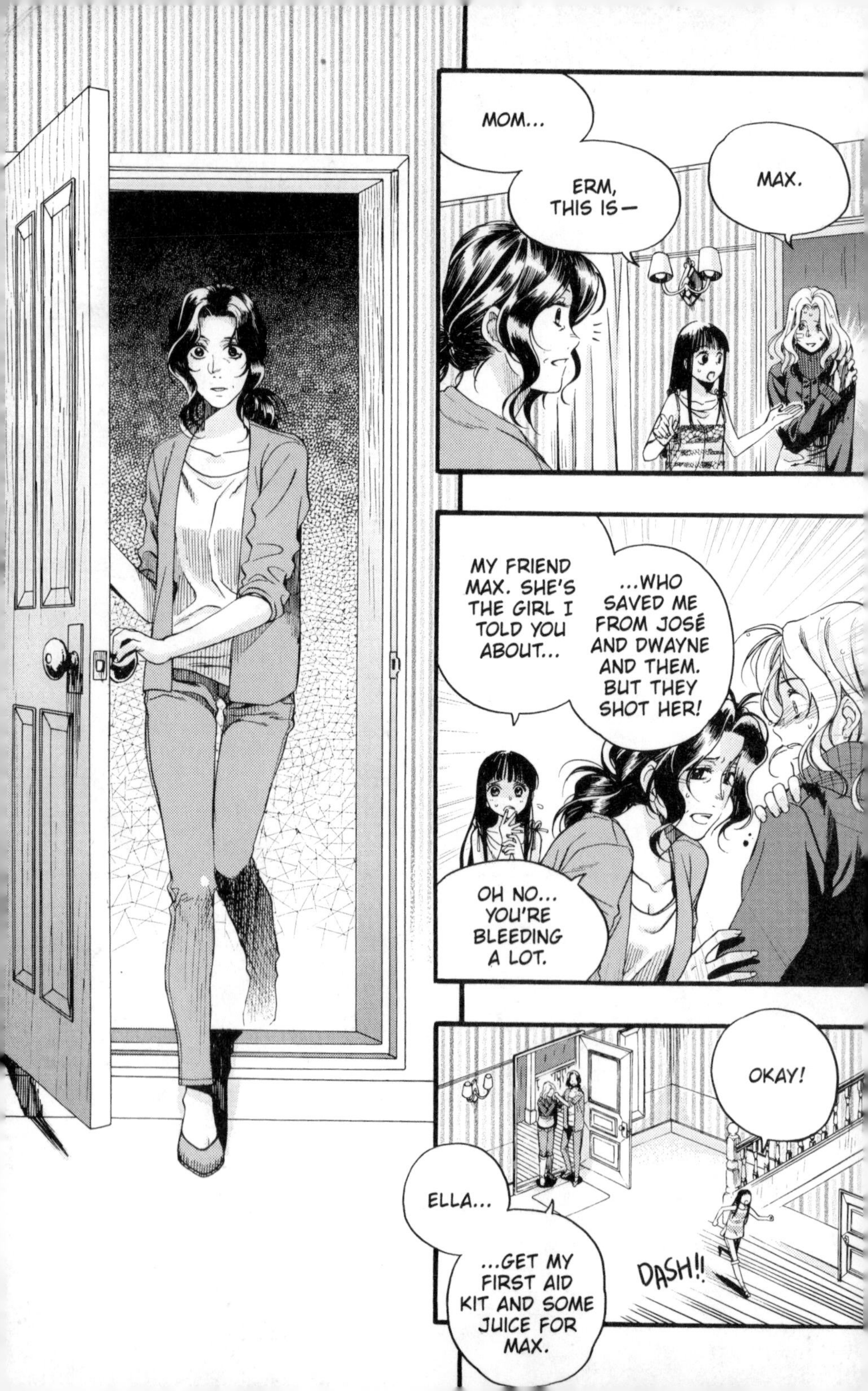
MOM...
ERM, THIS IS—
MAX.
MY FRIEND MAX. SHE'S THE GIRL I TOLD YOU ABOUT...
...WHO SAVED ME FROM JOSÉ AND DWAYNE AND THEM. BUT THEY SHOT HER!
OH NO... YOU'RE BLEEDING A LOT.
ELLA...
...GET MY FIRST AID KIT AND SOME JUICE FOR MAX.
OKAY!
DASH!!

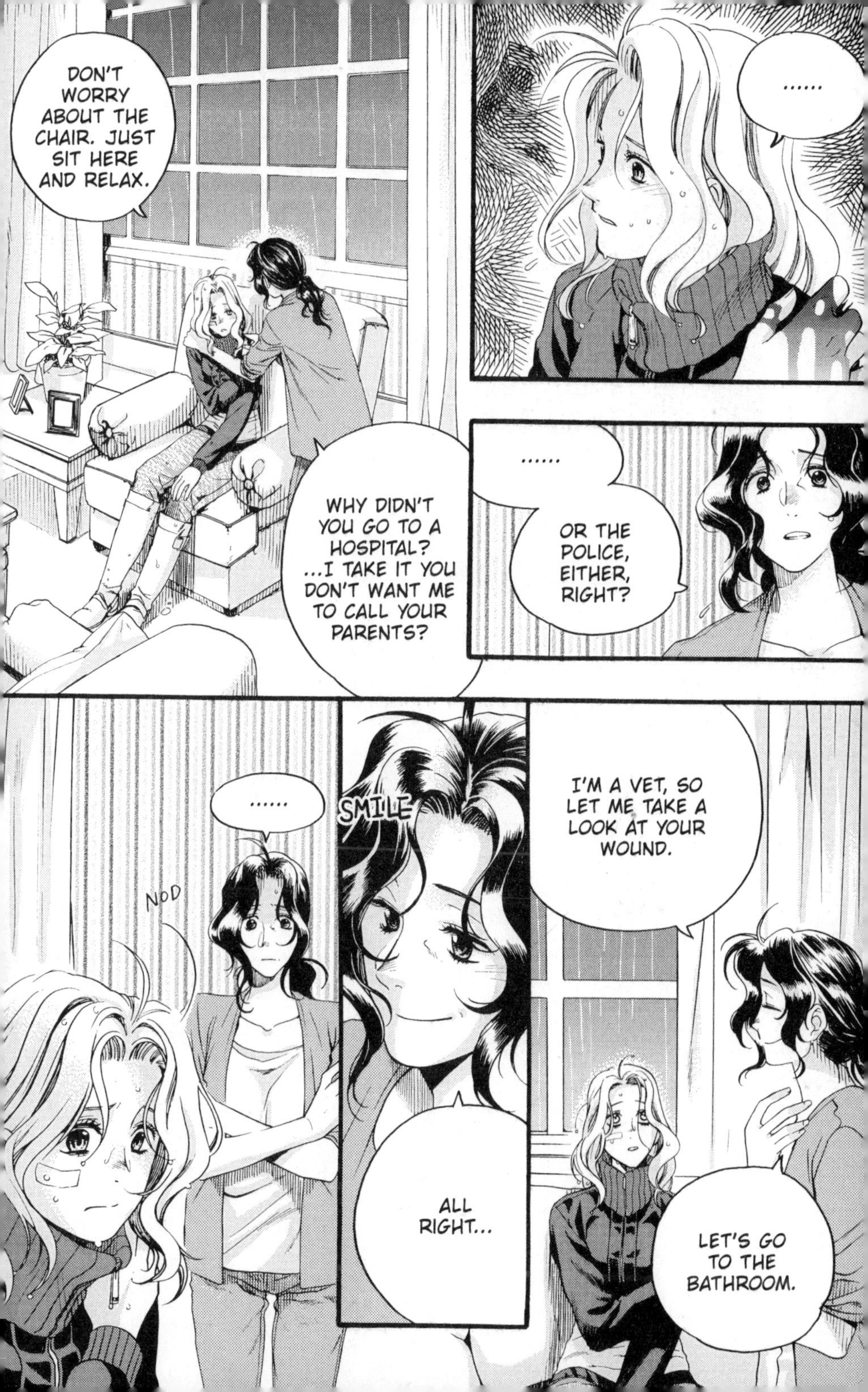
DON'T WORRY ABOUT THE CHAIR. JUST SIT HERE AND RELAX.
......
WHY DIDN'T YOU GO TO A HOSPITAL? ...I TAKE IT YOU DON'T WANT ME TO CALL YOUR PARENTS?
......
OR THE POLICE, EITHER, RIGHT?
......
NOD
SMILE
ALL RIGHT...
I'M A VET, SO LET ME TAKE A LOOK AT YOUR WOUND.
LET'S GO TO THE BATHROOM.

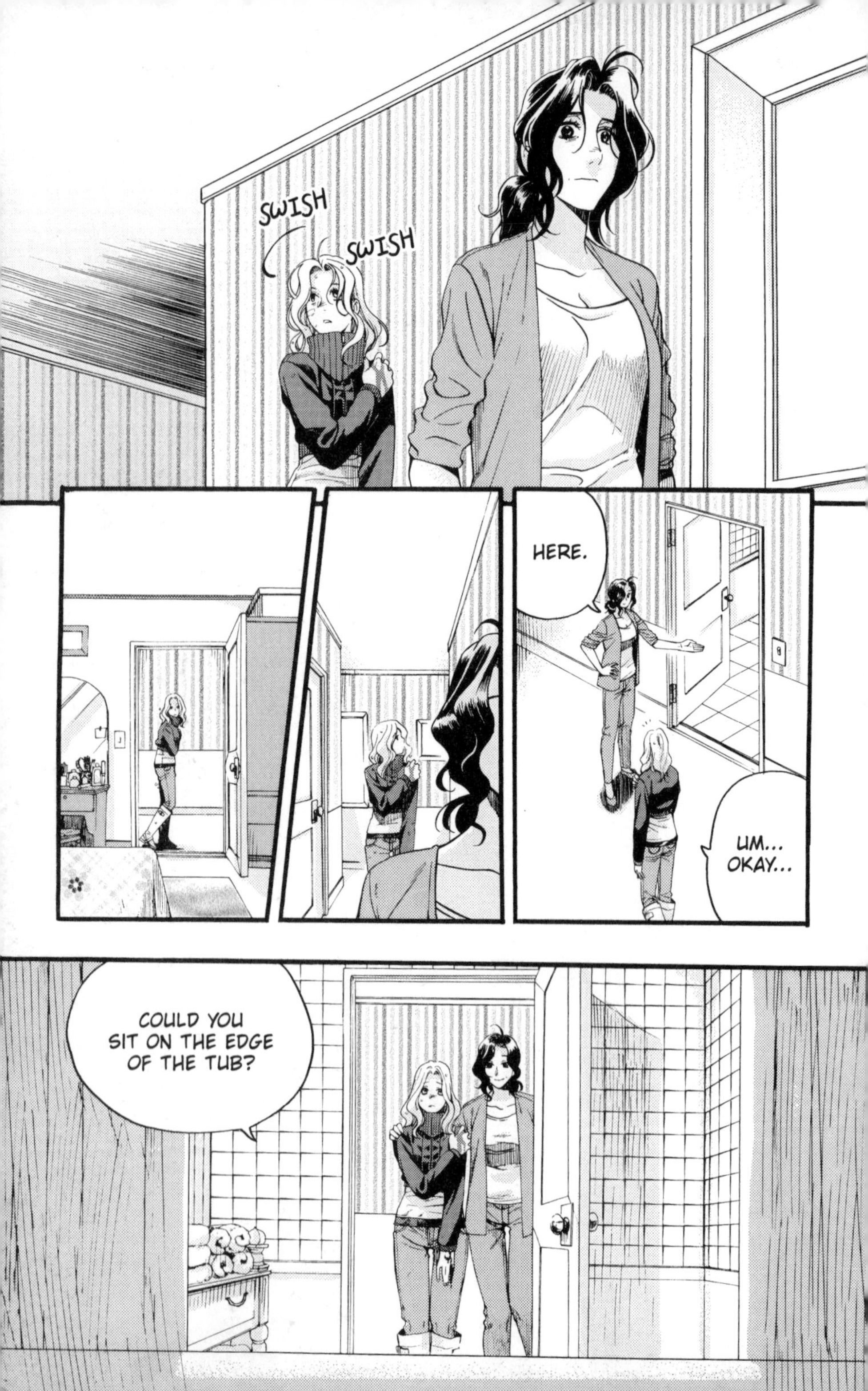
SWISH
SWISH
HERE.
UM... OKAY...
COULD YOU SIT ON THE EDGE OF THE TUB?

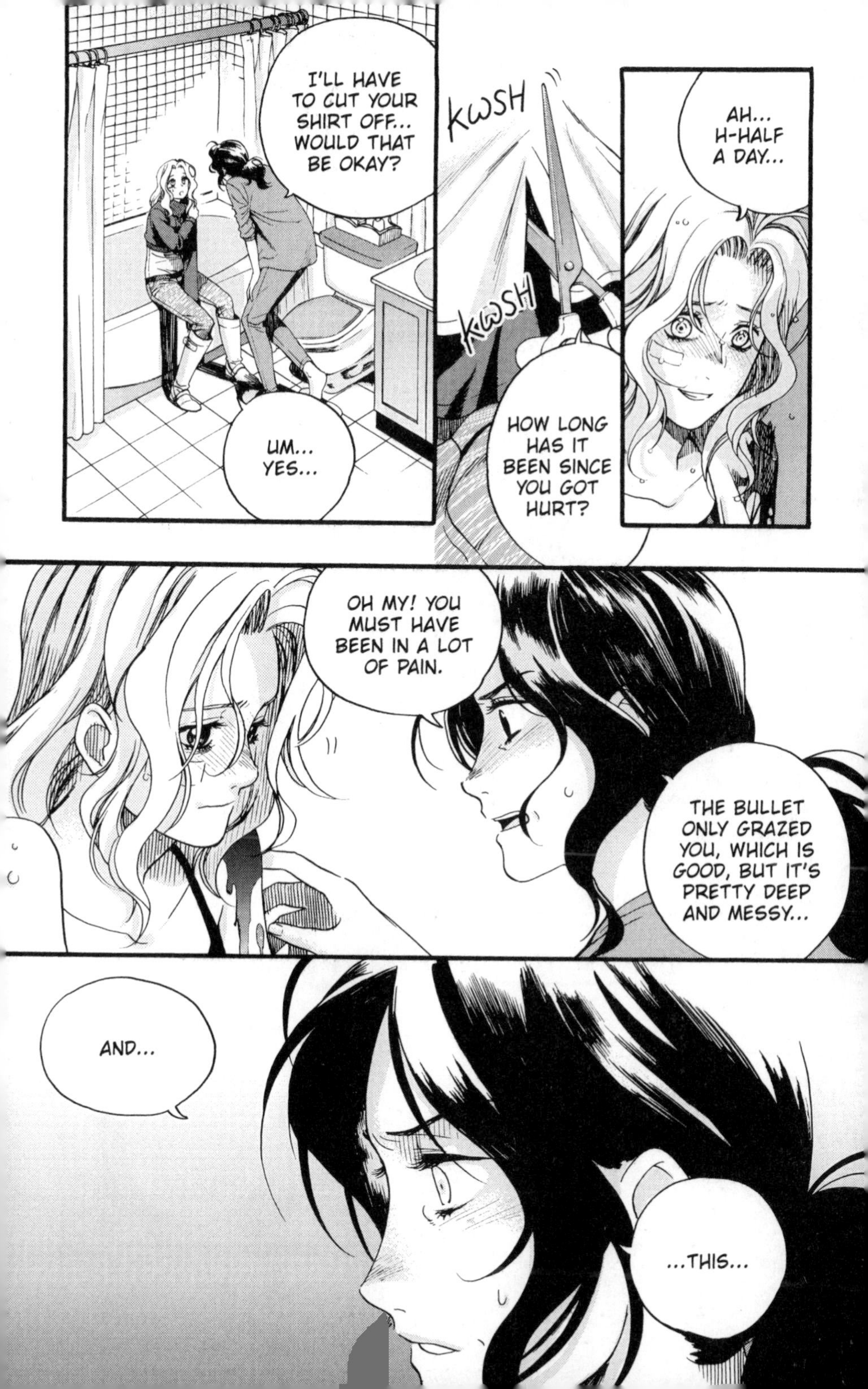
I'LL HAVE TO CUT YOUR SHIRT OFF... WOULD THAT BE OKAY?
UM... YES...
KWSH
KWSH
HOW LONG HAS IT BEEN SINCE YOU GOT HURT?
AH... H-HALF A DAY...
OH MY! YOU MUST HAVE BEEN IN A LOT OF PAIN.
THE BULLET ONLY GRAZED YOU, WHICH IS GOOD, BUT IT'S PRETTY DEEP AND MESSY...
AND...
...THIS...

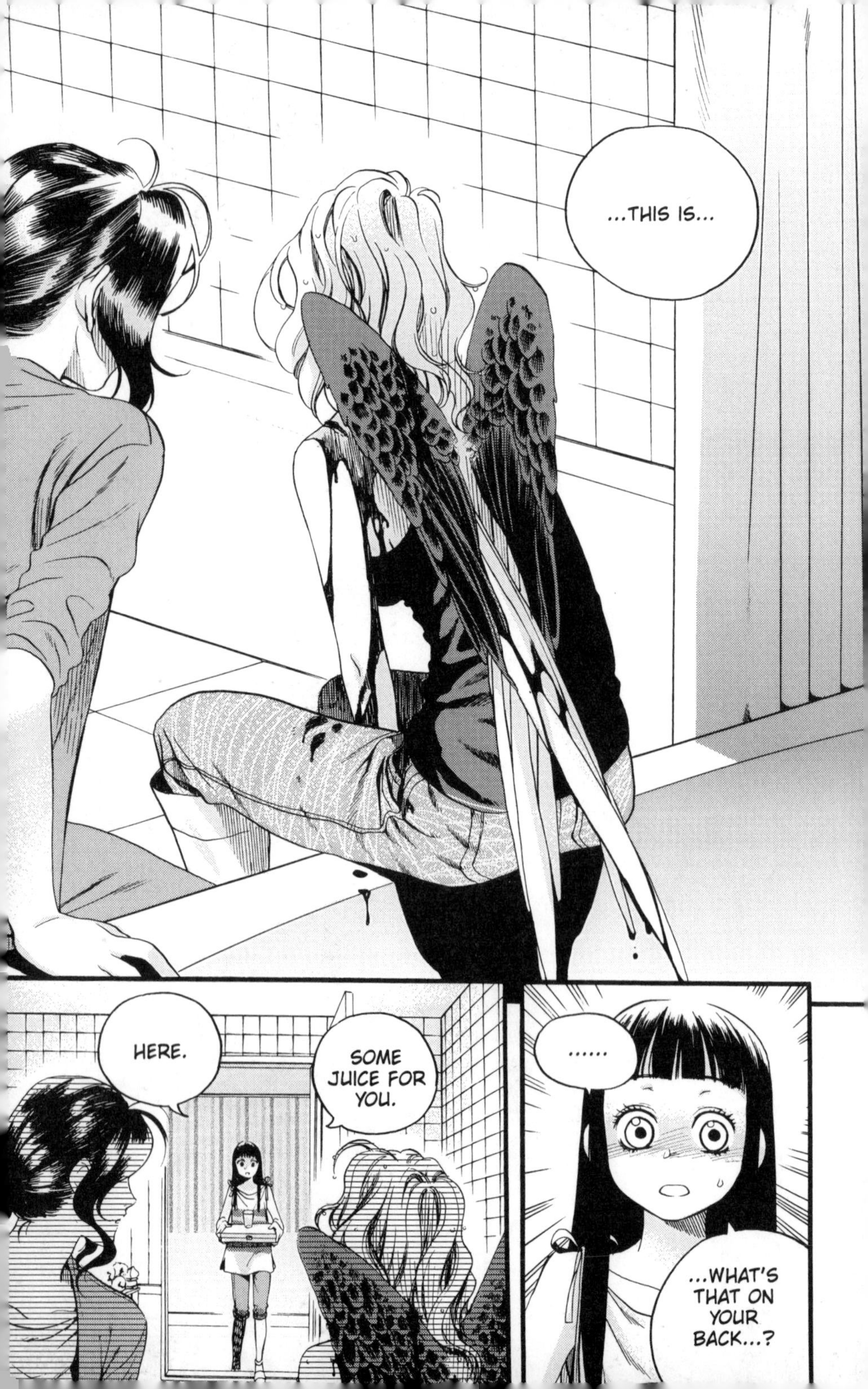
...THIS IS...
HERE.
SOME JUICE FOR YOU.
......
...WHAT'S THAT ON YOUR BACK...?

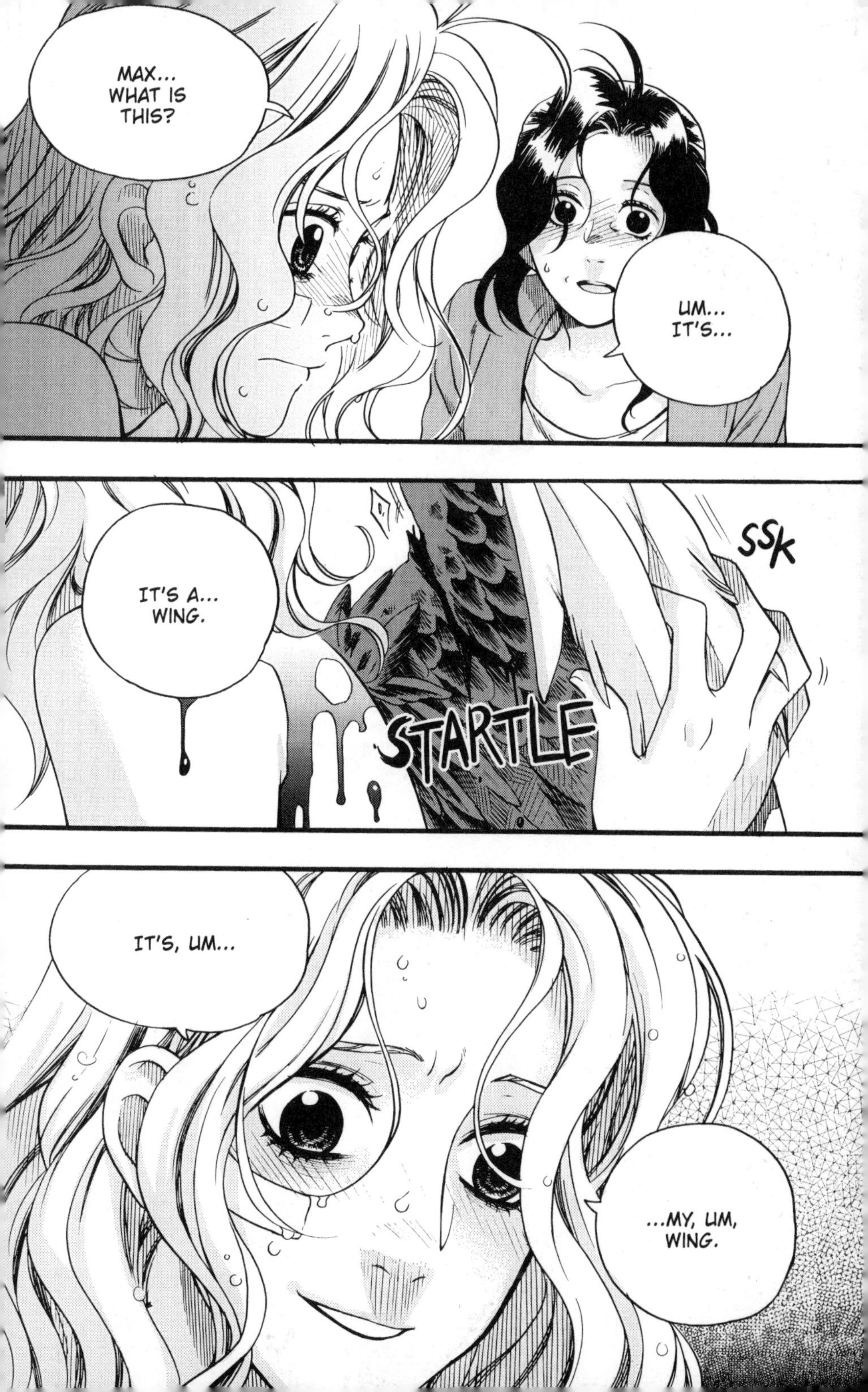
MAX... WHAT IS THIS?
UM... IT'S...
IT'S A... WING.
SSK
STARTLE
IT'S, UM...
...MY, UM, WING.

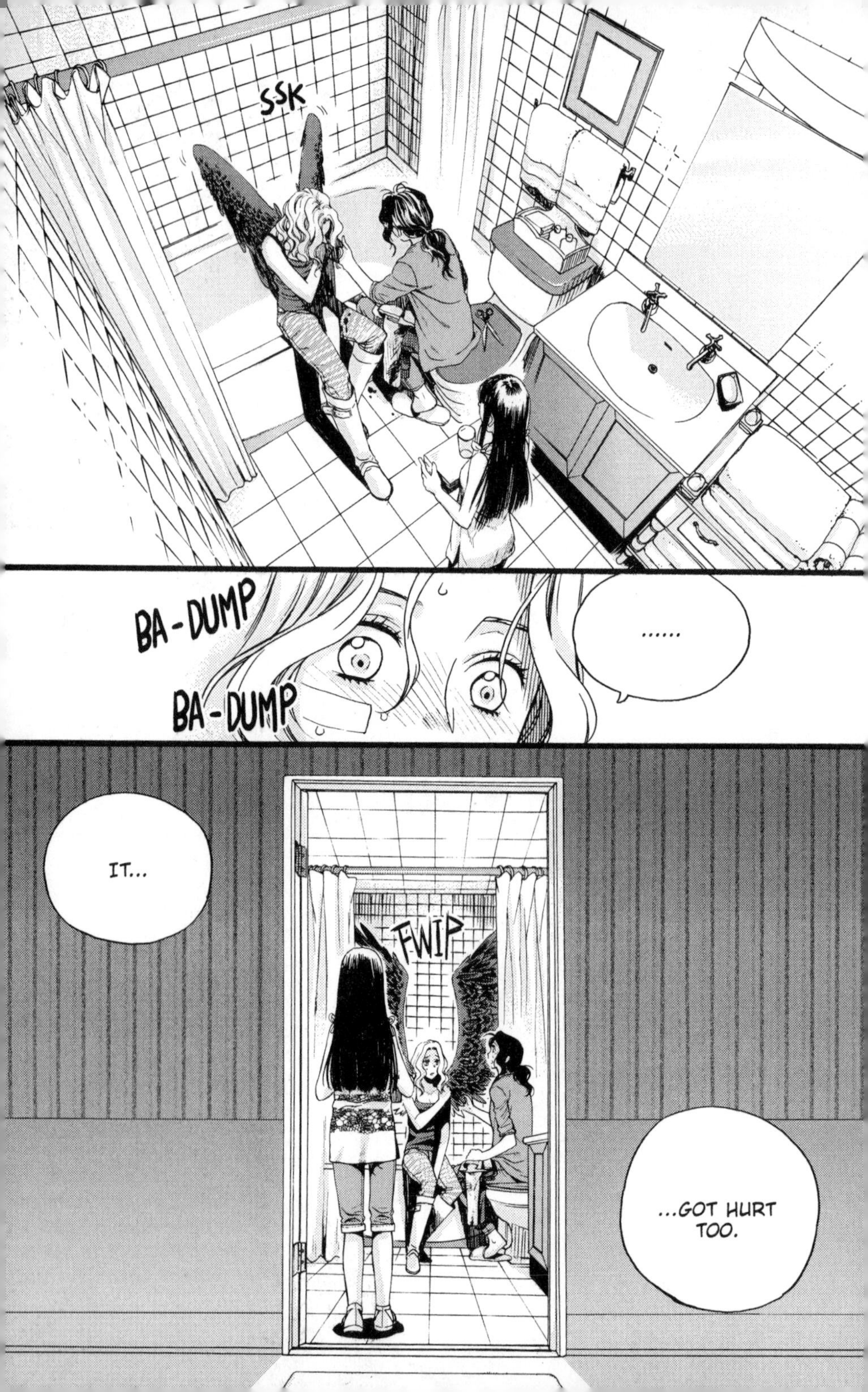
SSK
BA-DUMP
BA-DUMP
......
IT...
FWIP
...GOT HURT TOO.

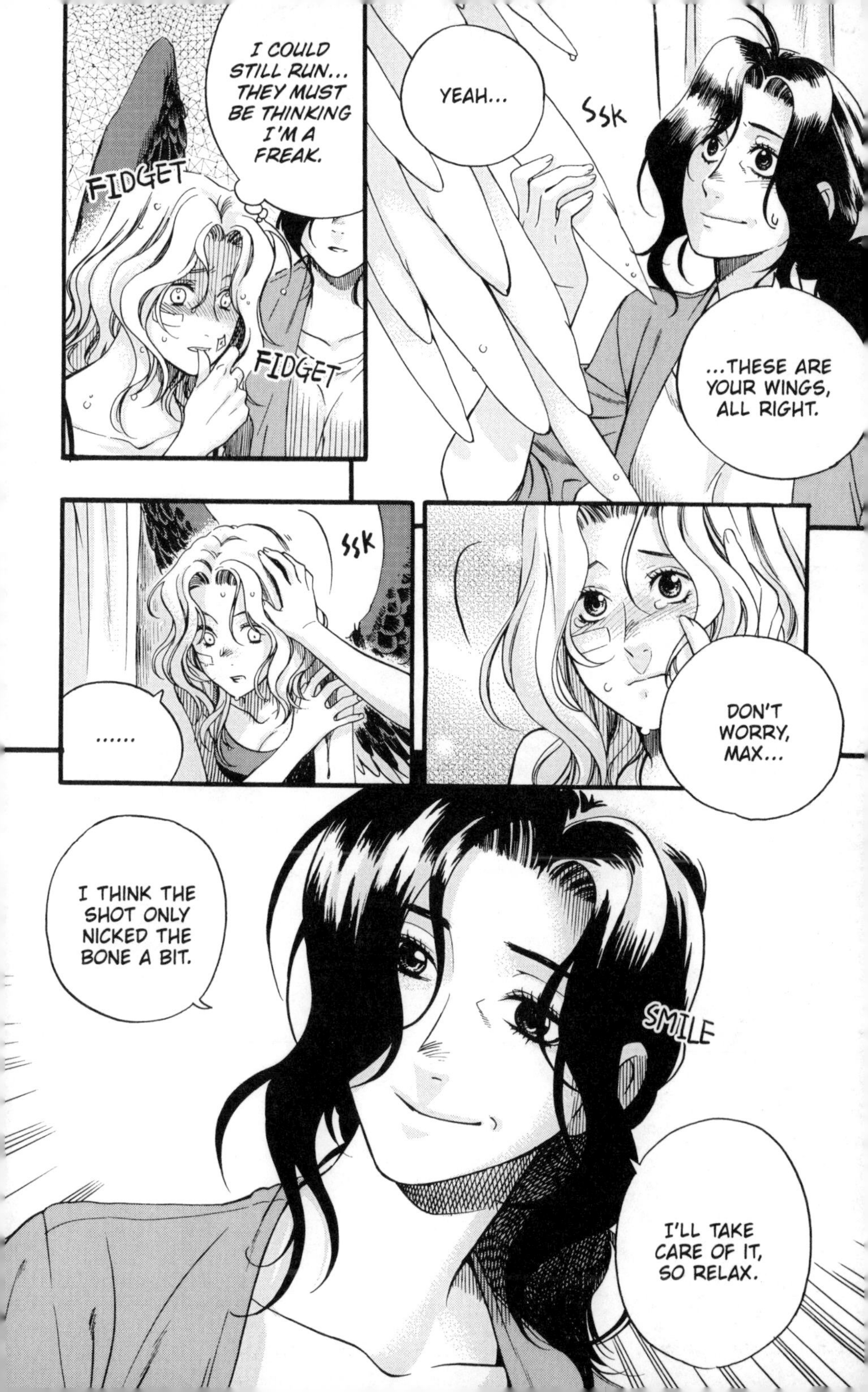
I COULD STILL RUN... THEY MUST BE THINKING I'M A FREAK.
FIDGET
FIDGET
YEAH...
SSK
...THESE ARE YOUR WINGS, ALL RIGHT.
SSK
......
DON'T WORRY, MAX...
I THINK THE SHOT ONLY NICKED THE BONE A BIT.
SMILE
I'LL TAKE CARE OF IT, SO RELAX.

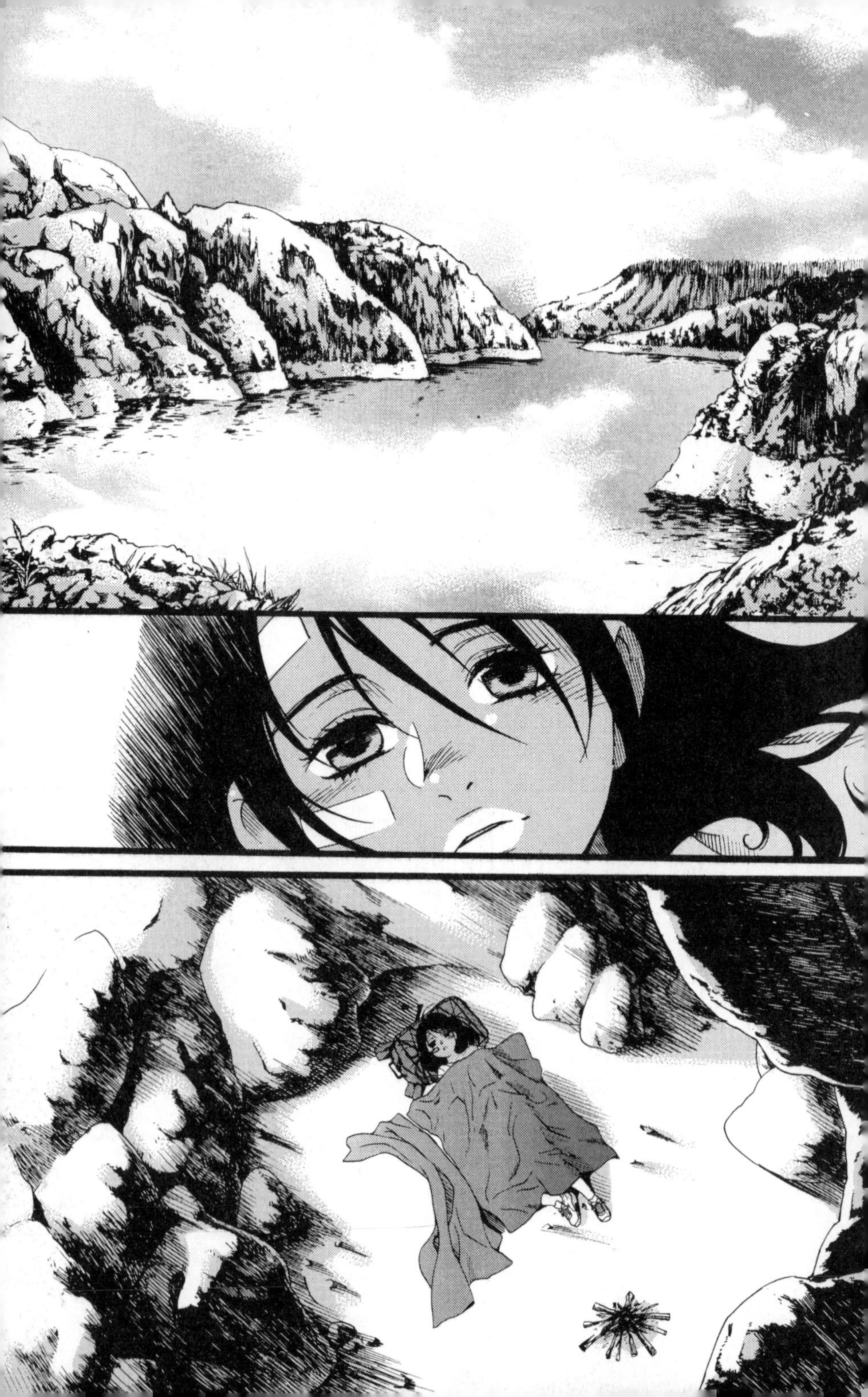

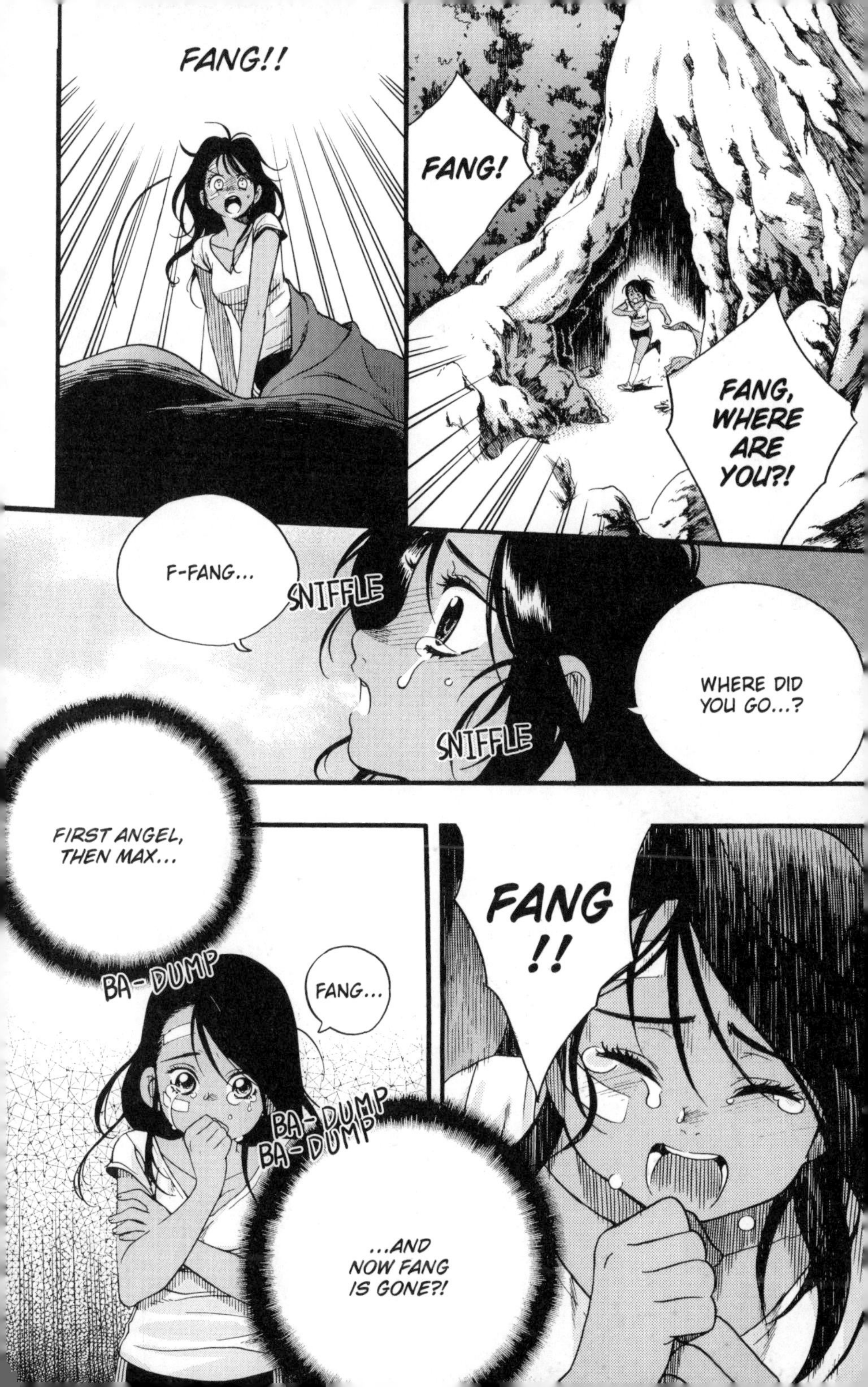
FANG!!
FANG!
FANG, WHERE ARE YOU?!
F-FANG...
SNIFFLE
SNIFFLE
WHERE DID YOU GO...?
FIRST ANGEL, THEN MAX...
BA-DUMP
FANG...
BA-DUMP
BA-DUMP
...AND NOW FANG IS GONE?!
FANG!!

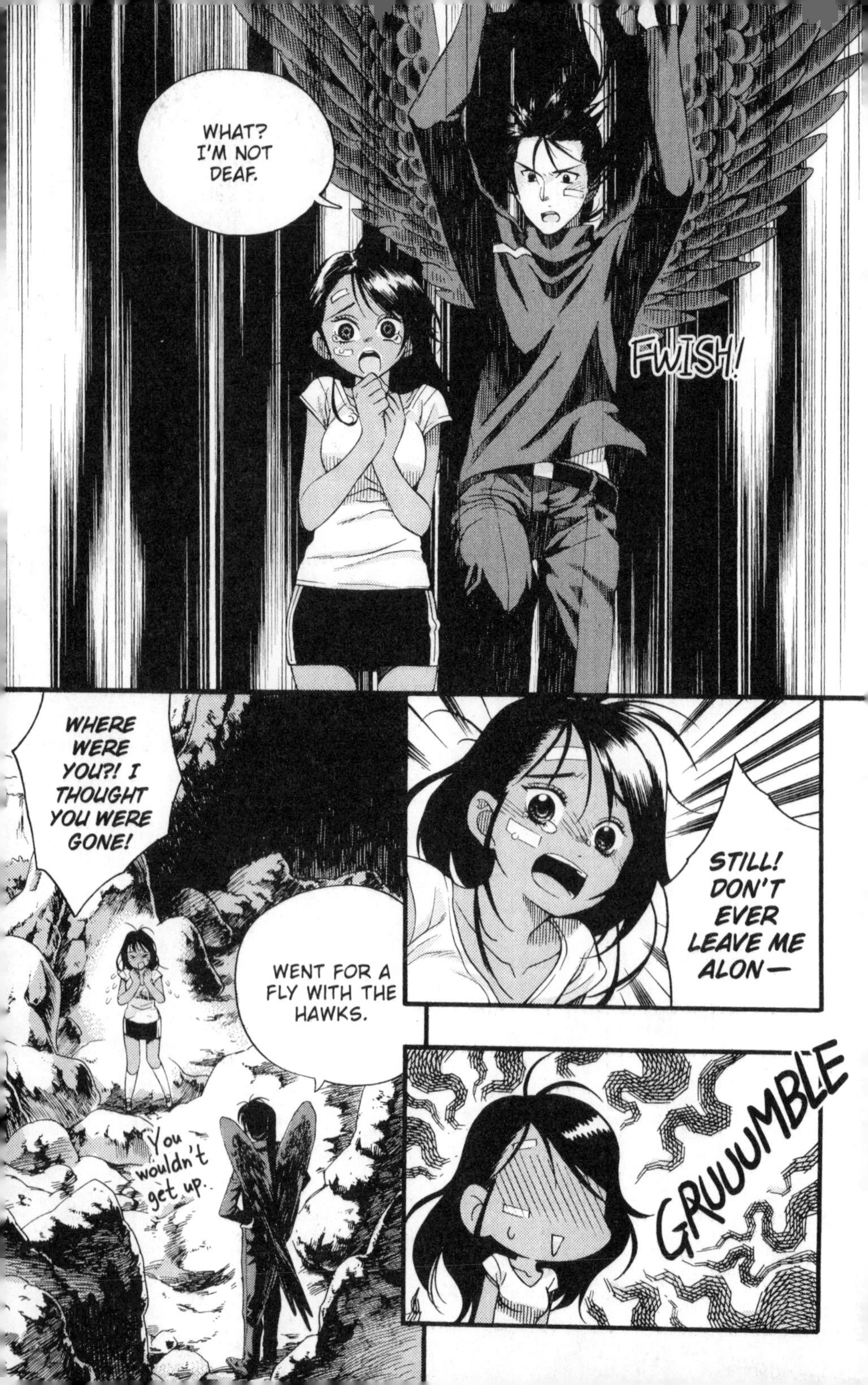
WHAT? I'M NOT DEAF.
FWISH!
WHERE WERE YOU?! I THOUGHT YOU WERE GONE!
WENT FOR A FLY WITH THE HAWKS.
You wouldn't get up..
STILL! DON'T EVER LEAVE ME ALON—
GRUUUMBLE

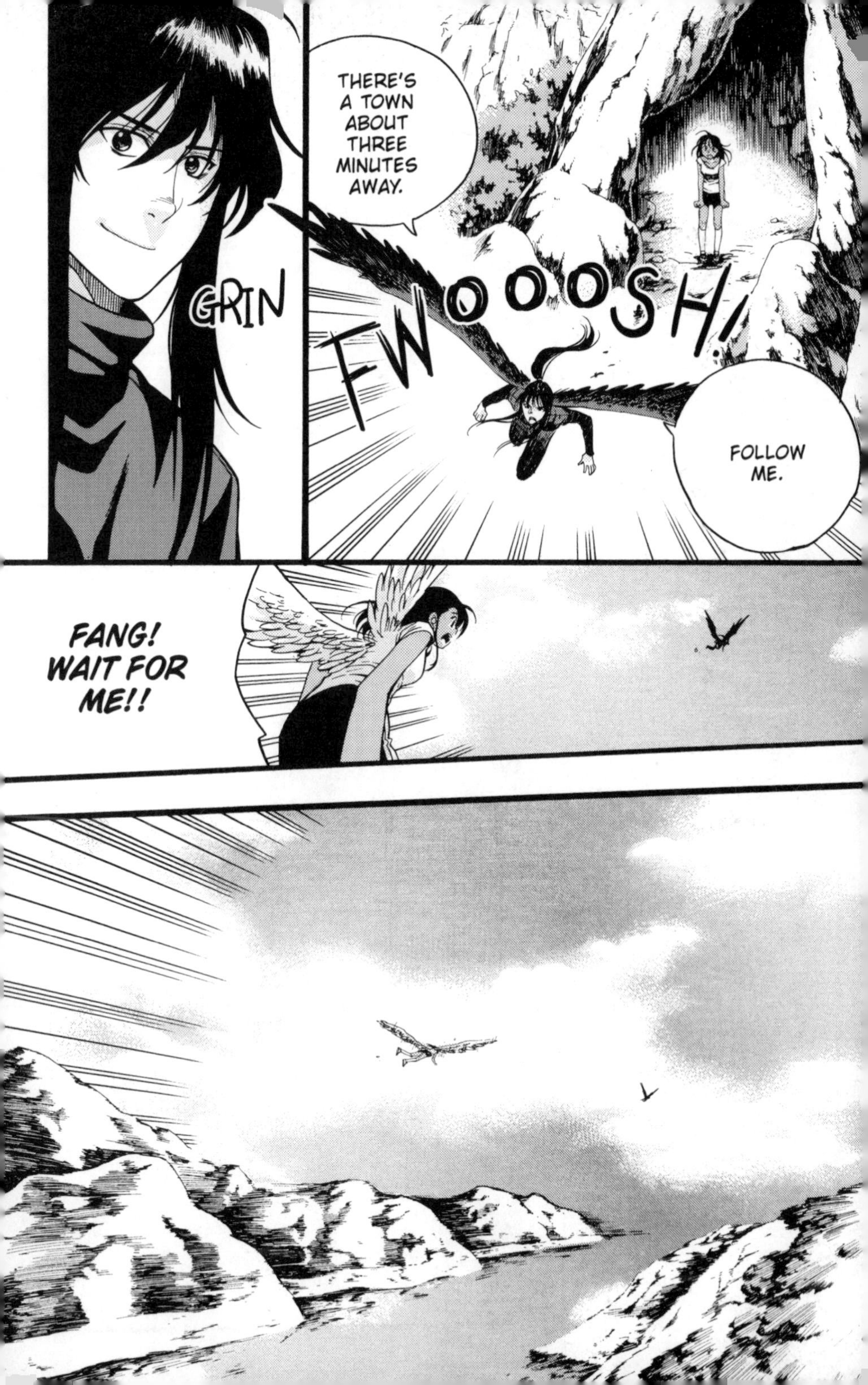
GRIN
THERE'S A TOWN ABOUT THREE MINUTES AWAY.
FWOOOSH!
FOLLOW ME.
FANG! WAIT FOR ME!!

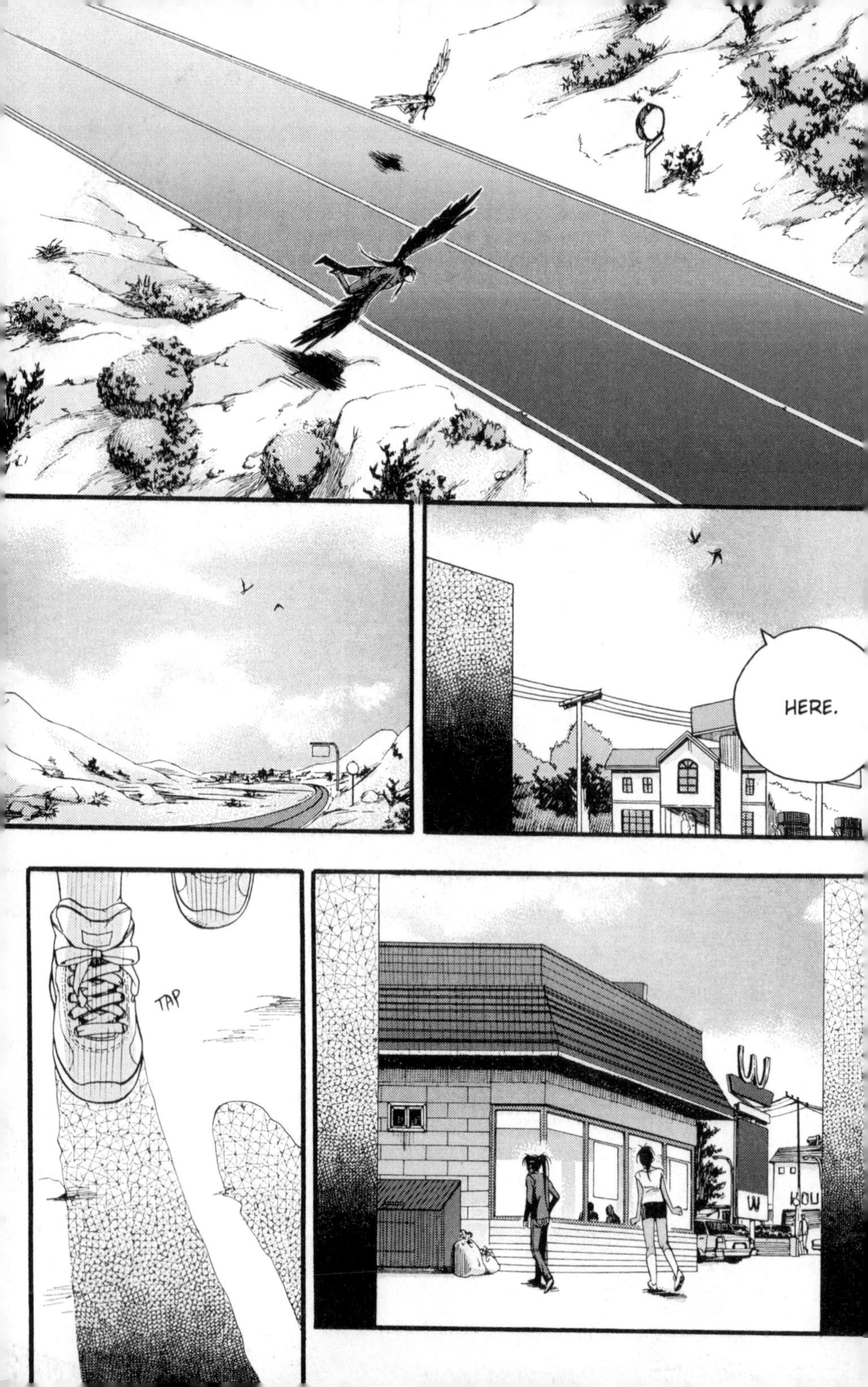
HERE.
TAP
W
W
KOU

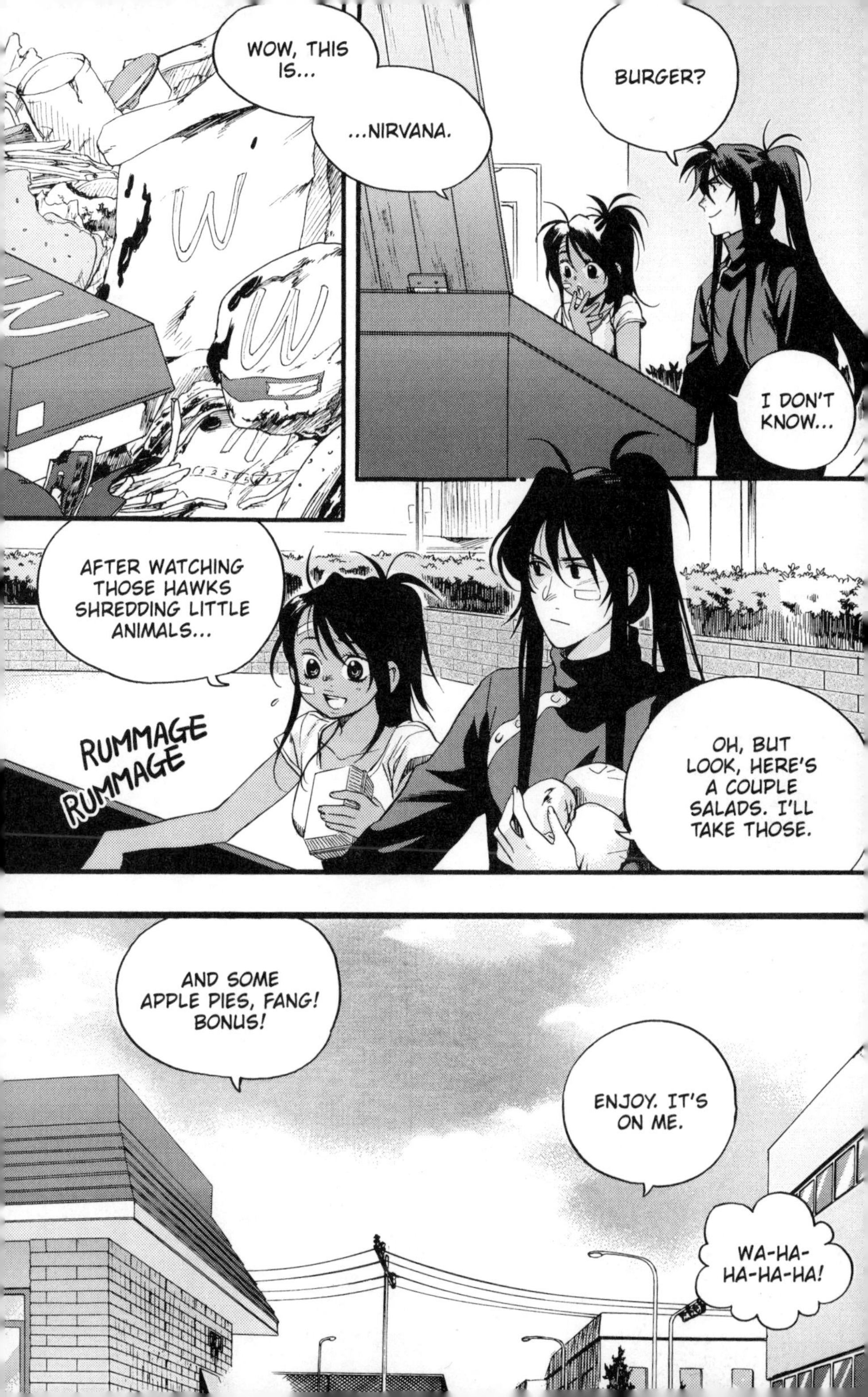
WOW, THIS IS...
...NIRVANA.
BURGER?
I DON'T KNOW...
AFTER WATCHING THOSE HAWKS SHREDDING LITTLE ANIMALS...
RUMMAGE RUMMAGE
OH, BUT LOOK, HERE'S A COUPLE SALADS. I'LL TAKE THOSE.
AND SOME APPLE PIES, FANG! BONUS!
ENJOY. IT'S ON ME.
WA-HA-HA-HA-HA!

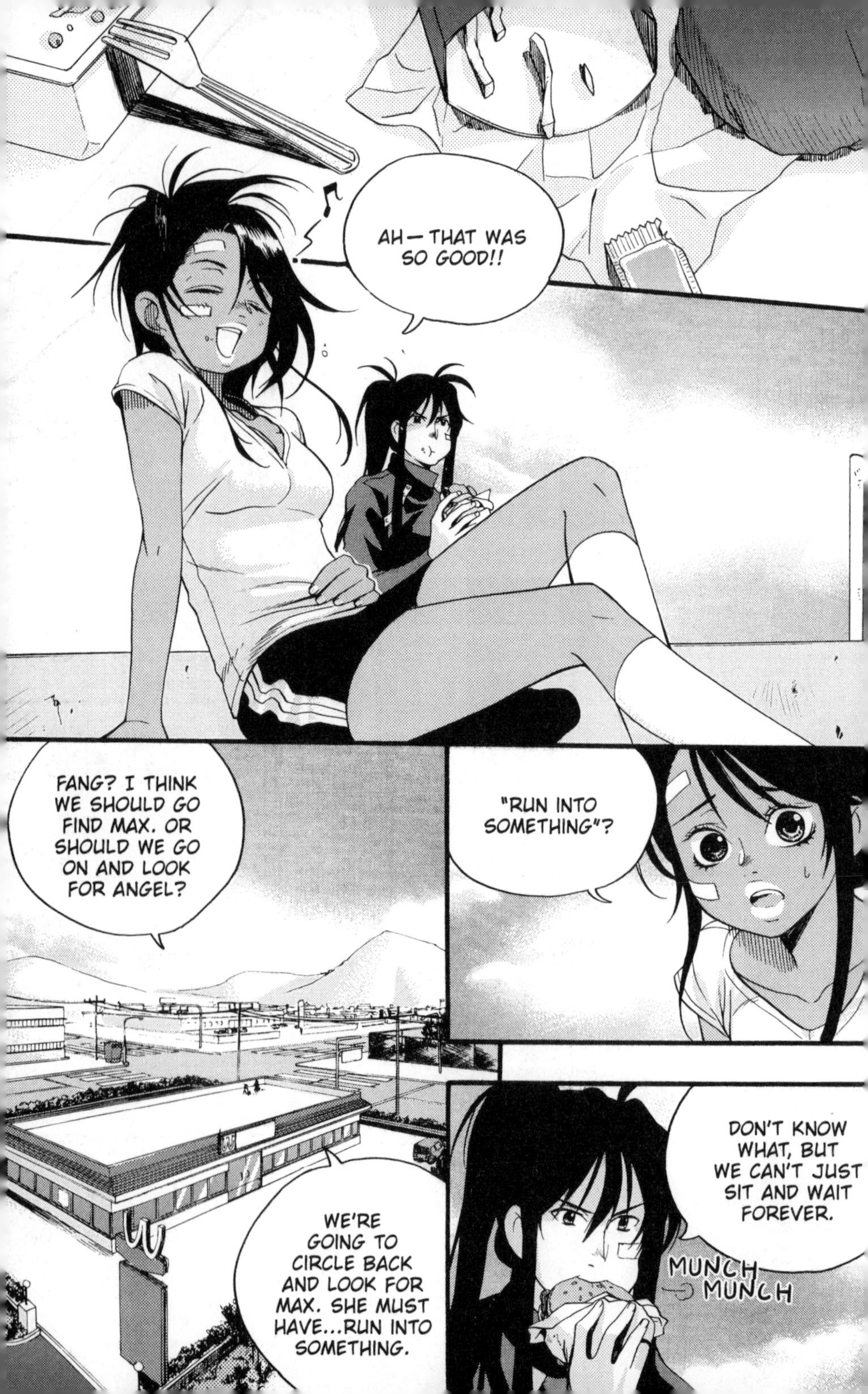
AH— THAT WAS SO GOOD!!
FANG? I THINK WE SHOULD GO FIND MAX. OR SHOULD WE GO ON AND LOOK FOR ANGEL?
"RUN INTO SOMETHING"?
WE'RE GOING TO CIRCLE BACK AND LOOK FOR MAX. SHE MUST HAVE...RUN INTO SOMETHING.
DON'T KNOW WHAT, BUT WE CAN'T JUST SIT AND WAIT FOREVER.
MUNCH MUNCH

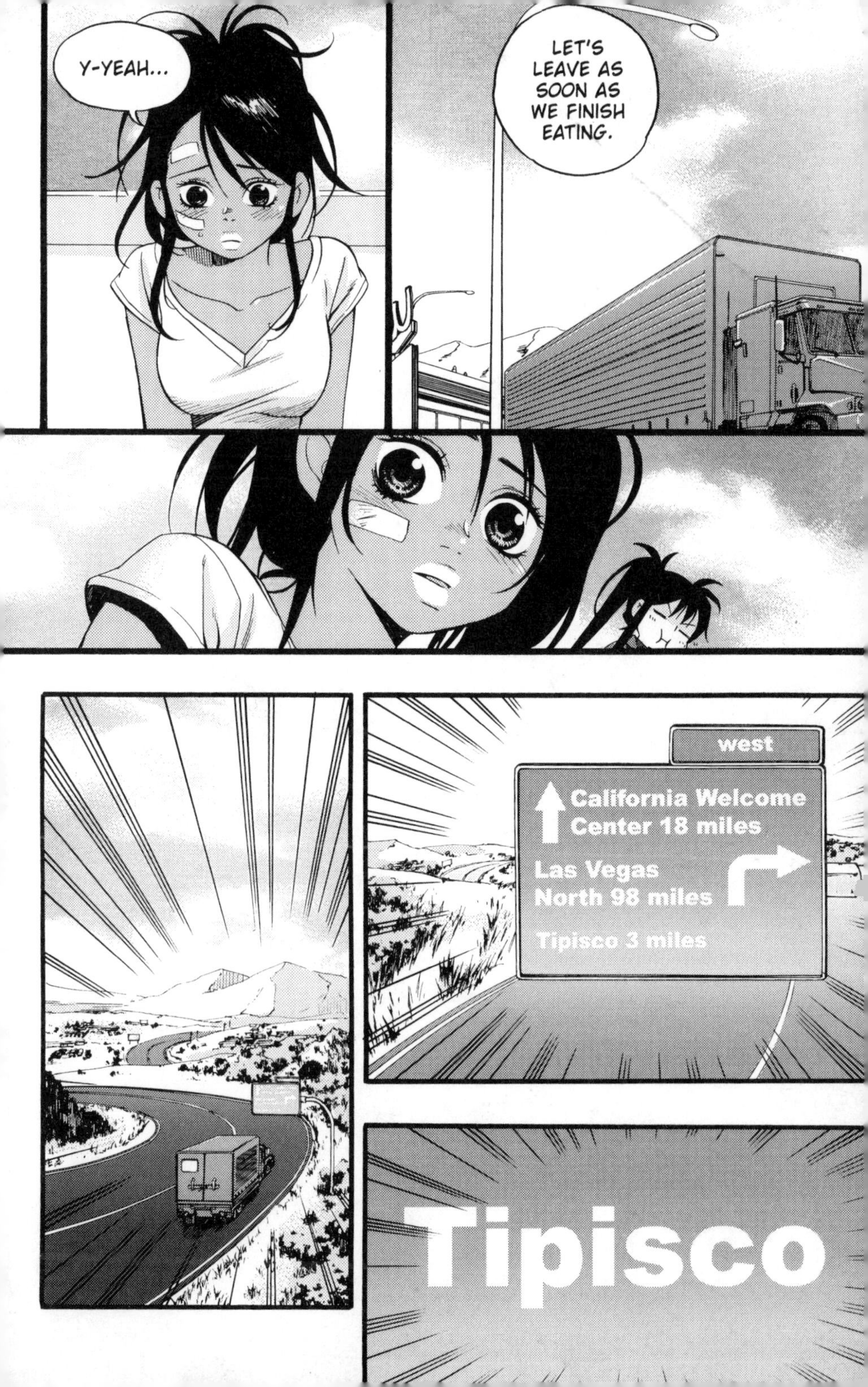
Y-YEAH...
LET'S LEAVE AS SOON AS WE FINISH EATING.
west
California Welcome Center 18 miles
Las Vegas North 98 miles
Tipisco 3 miles
Tipisco

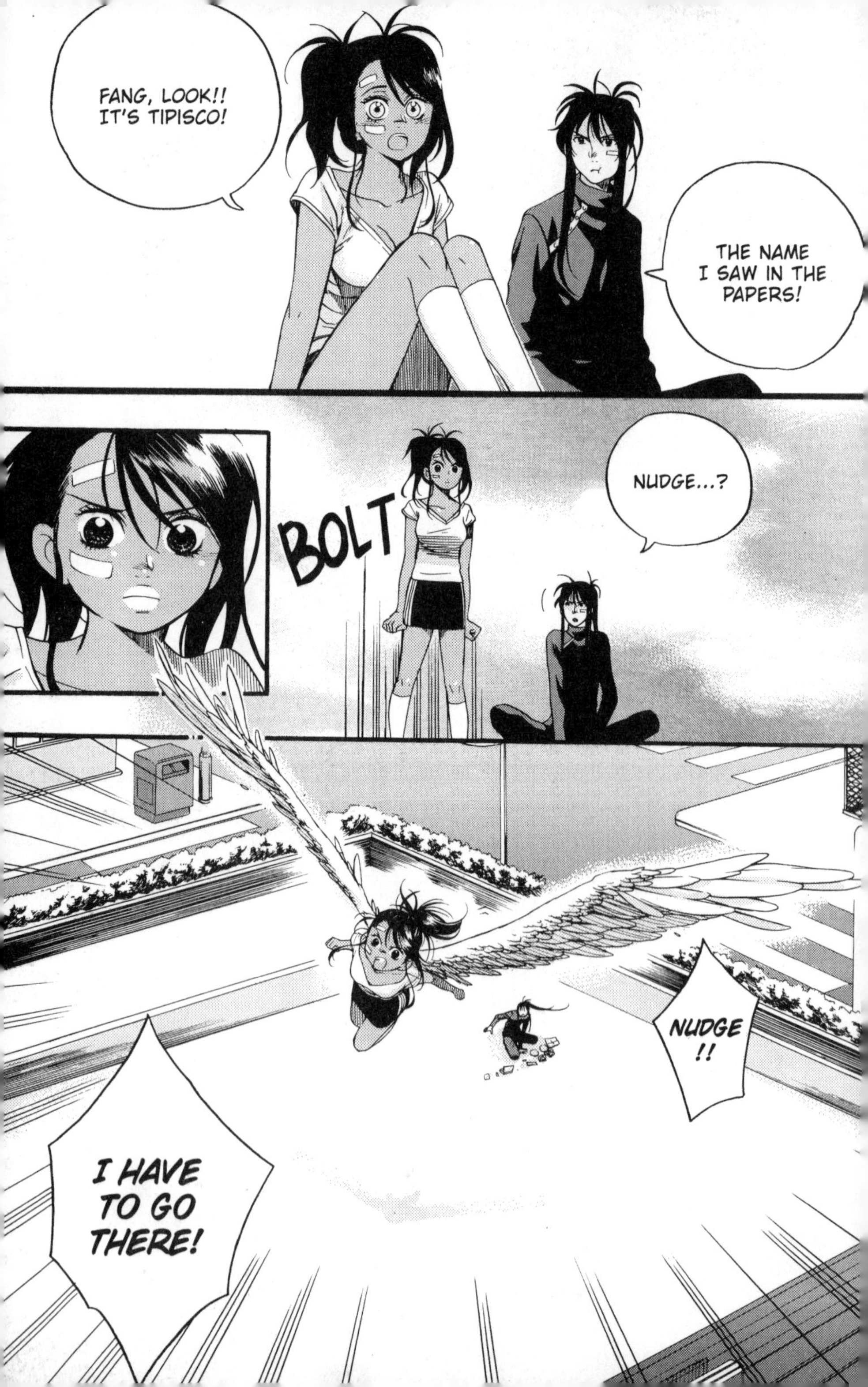
FANG, LOOK!! IT'S TIPISCO!
THE NAME I SAW IN THE PAPERS!
BOLT
NUDGE...?
NUDGE !!
I HAVE TO GO THERE!

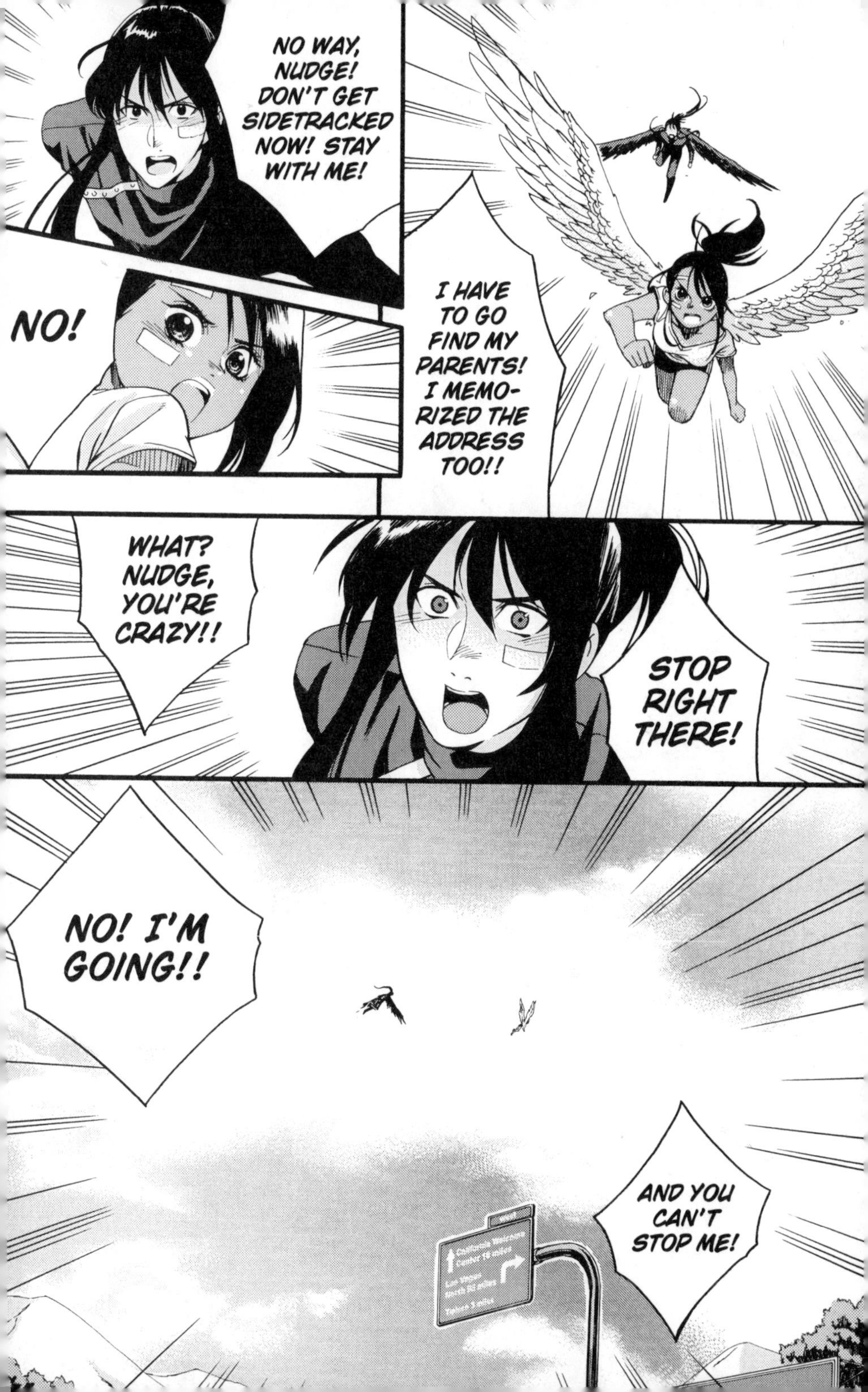
NO WAY, NUDGE! DON'T GET SIDETRACKED NOW! STAY WITH ME!
NO!
I HAVE TO GO FIND MY PARENTS! I MEMO-RIZED THE ADDRESS TOO!!
WHAT? NUDGE, YOU'RE CRAZY!!
STOP RIGHT THERE!
NO! I'M GOING!!
AND YOU CAN'T STOP ME!

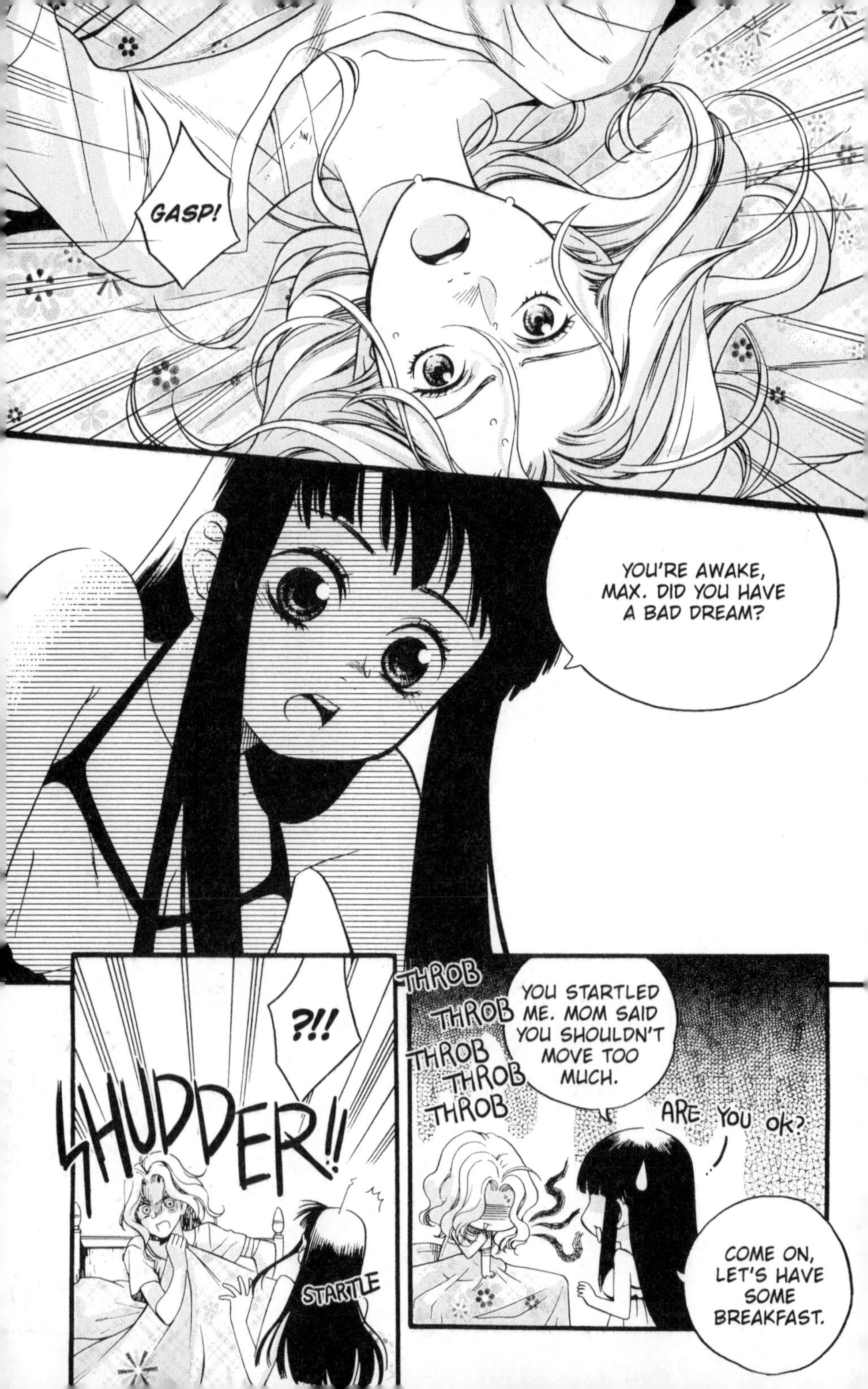
GASP!
YOU'RE AWAKE, MAX. DID YOU HAVE A BAD DREAM?
?!!
SHUDDER!!
STARTLE
THROB THROB THROB THROB THROB
YOU STARTLED ME. MOM SAID YOU SHOULDN'T MOVE TOO MUCH.
ARE YOU OK?
COME ON, LET'S HAVE SOME BREAKFAST.

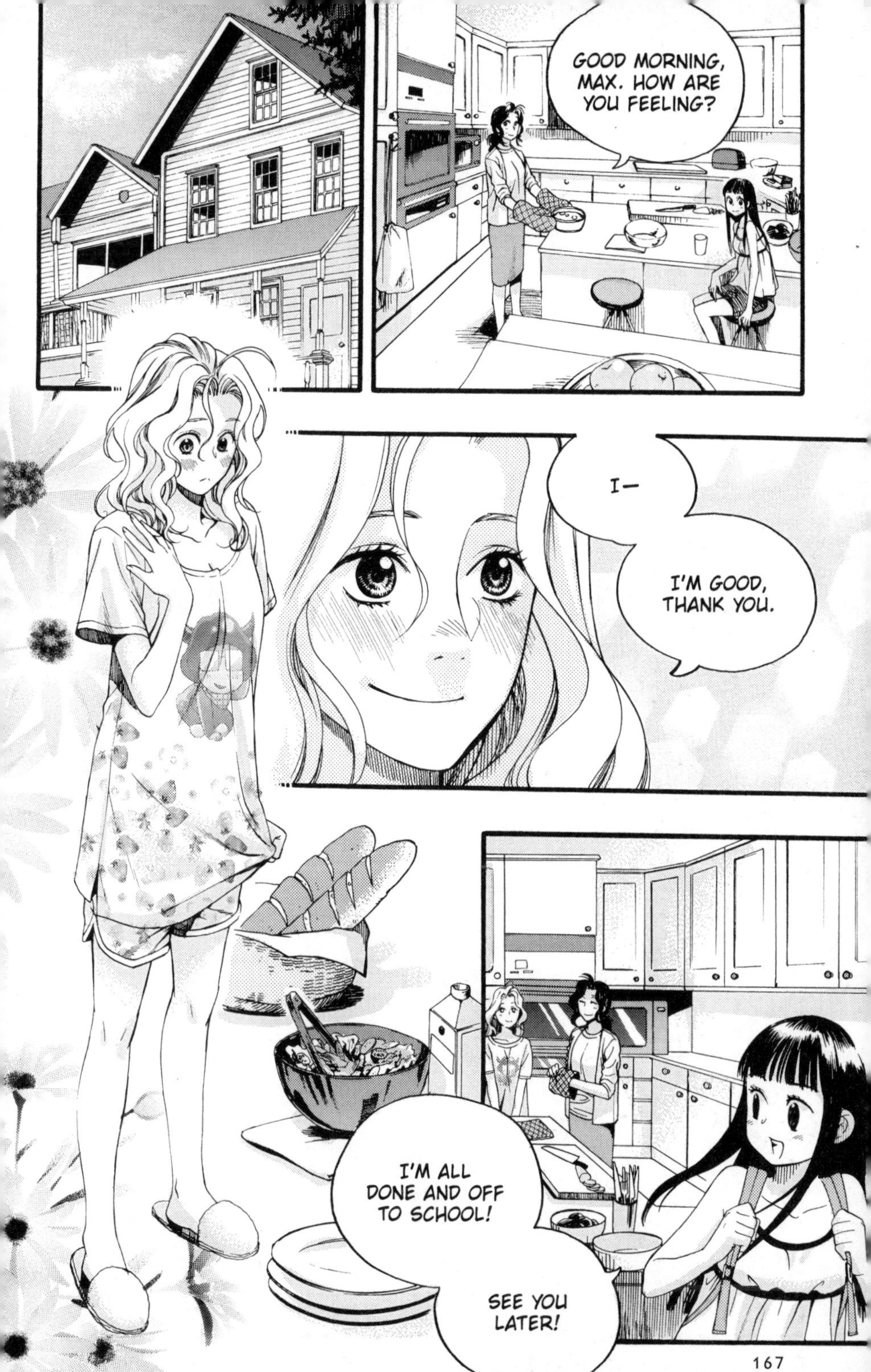
GOOD MORNING, MAX. HOW ARE YOU FEELING?
I—
I'M GOOD, THANK YOU.
I'M ALL DONE AND OFF TO SCHOOL!
SEE YOU LATER!

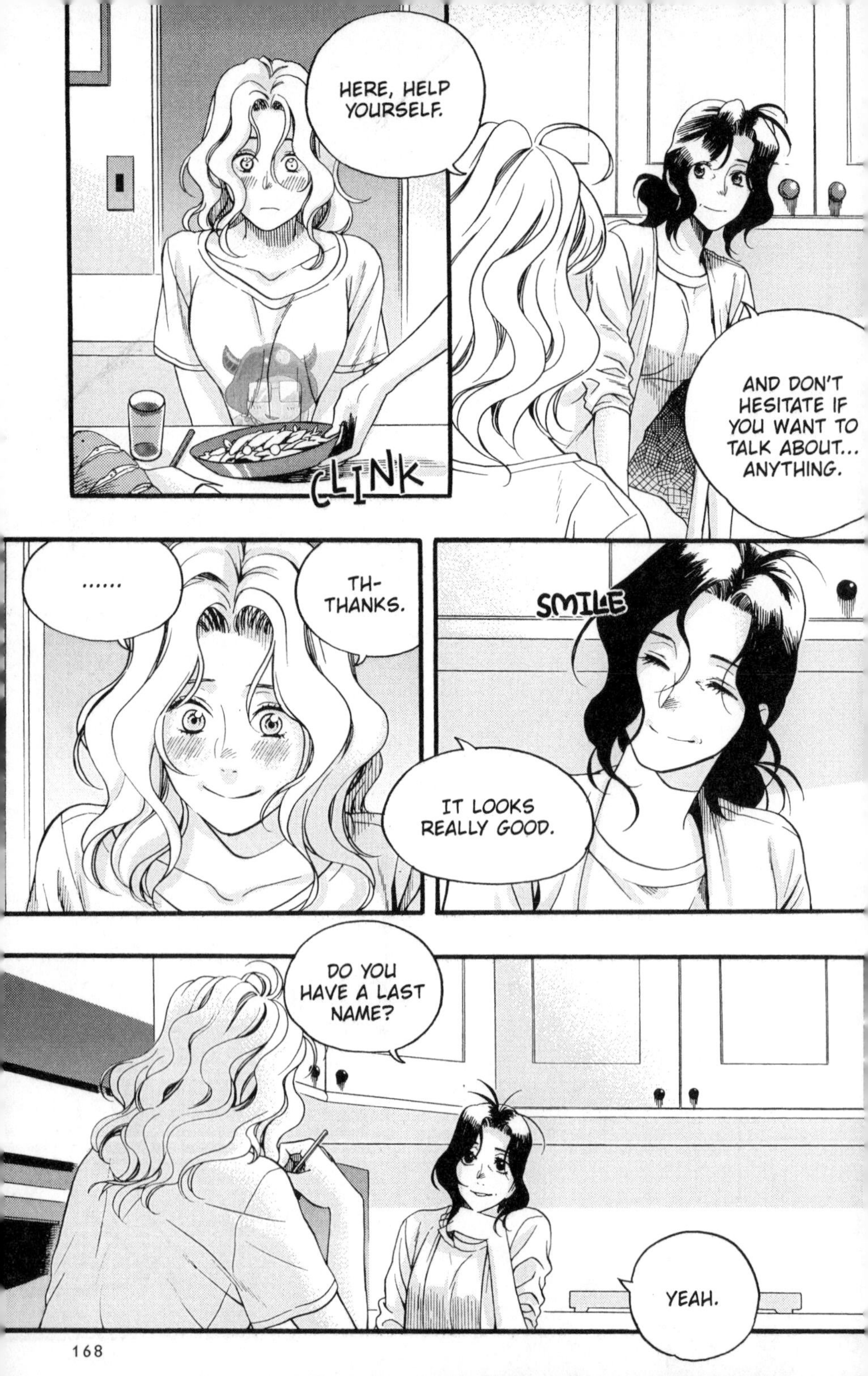
HERE, HELP YOURSELF.
CLINK
AND DON'T HESITATE IF YOU WANT TO TALK ABOUT... ANYTHING.
......
TH- THANKS.
SMILE
IT LOOKS REALLY GOOD.
DO YOU HAVE A LAST NAME?
YEAH.

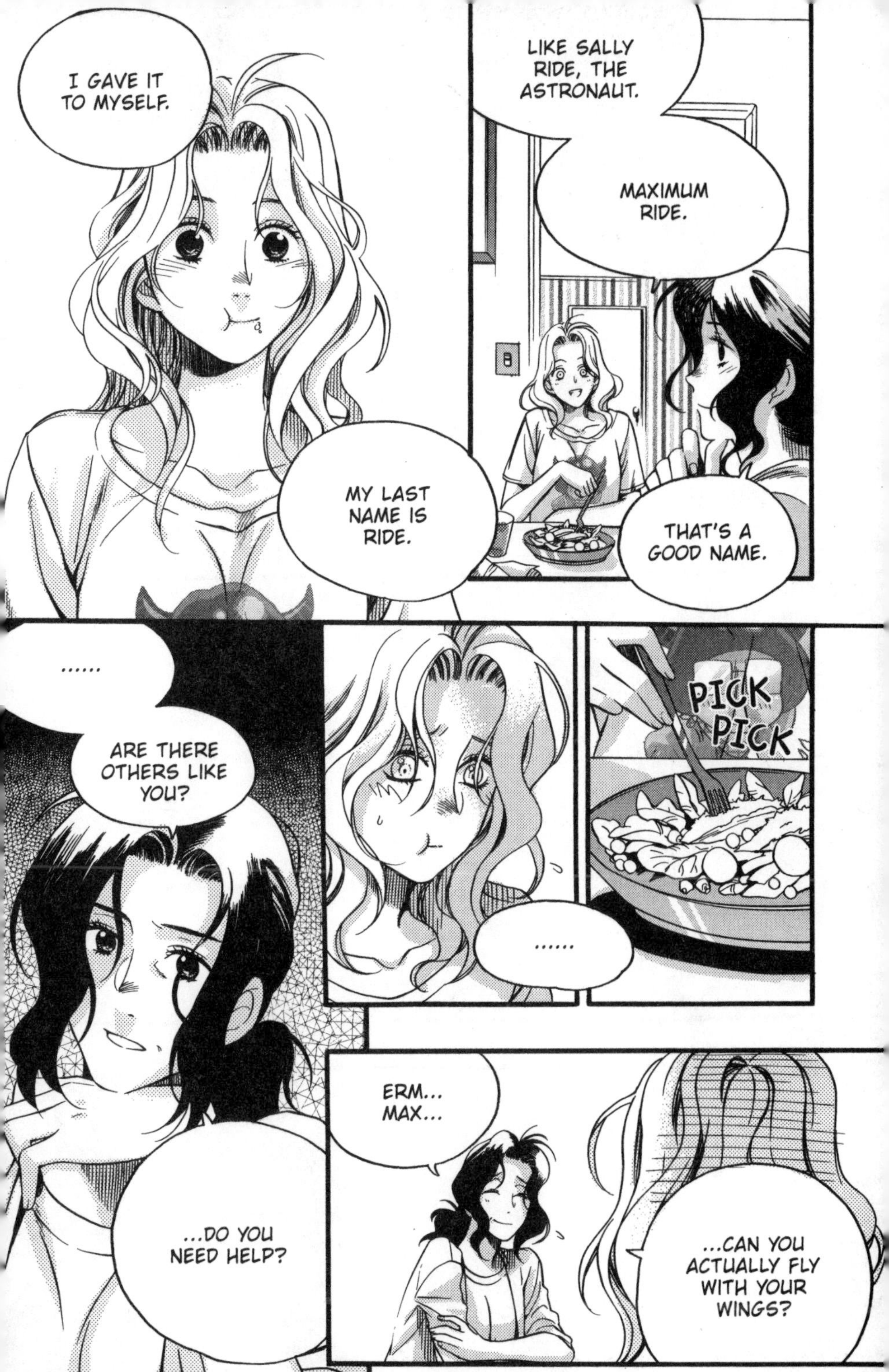
I GAVE IT TO MYSELF.
LIKE SALLY RIDE, THE ASTRONAUT.
MAXIMUM RIDE.
MY LAST NAME IS RIDE.
THAT'S A GOOD NAME.
......
ARE THERE OTHERS LIKE YOU?
...DO YOU NEED HELP?
PICK PICK
......
ERM... MAX...
...CAN YOU ACTUALLY FLY WITH YOUR WINGS?

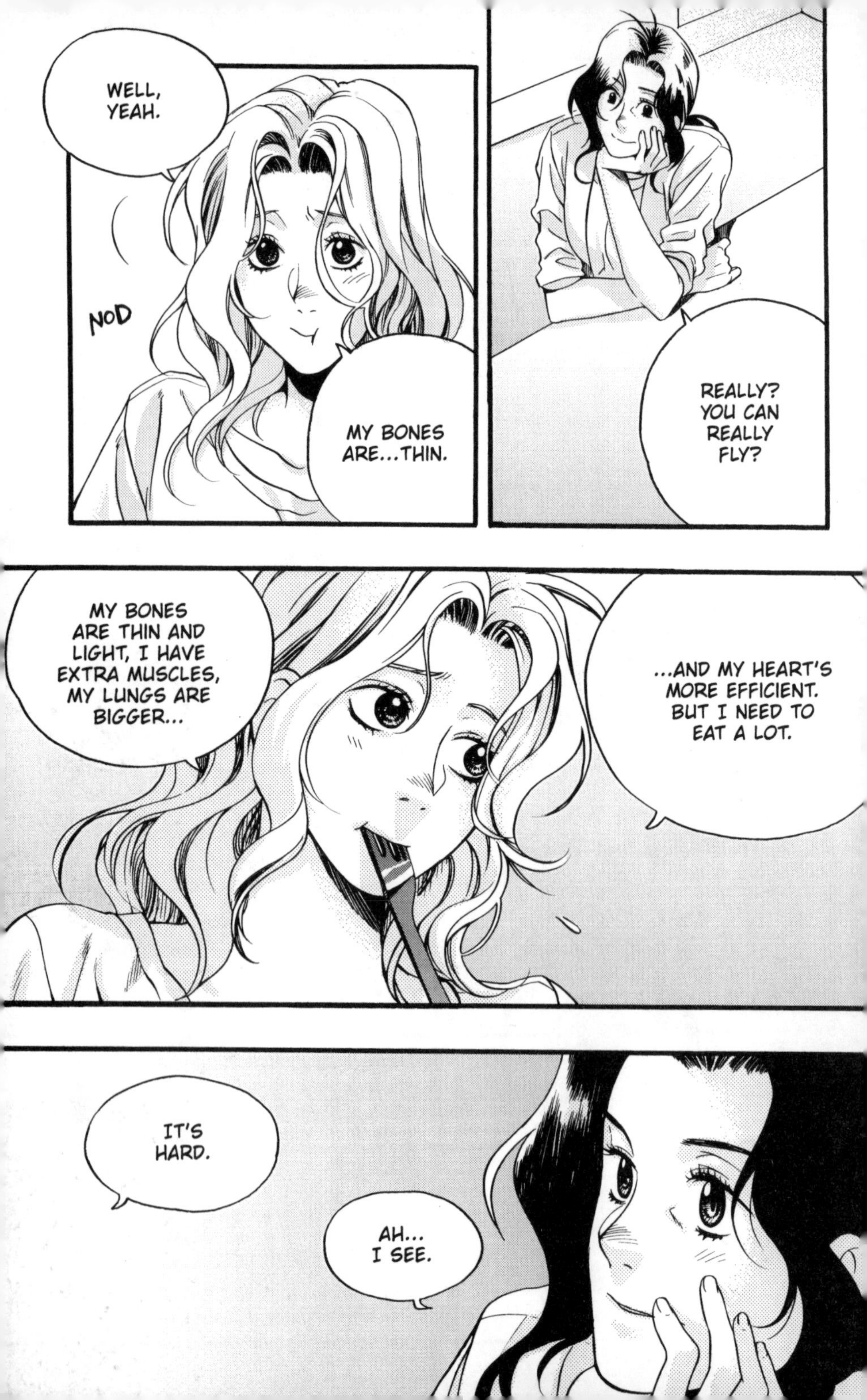
WELL, YEAH.
NOD
MY BONES ARE...THIN.
REALLY? YOU CAN REALLY FLY?
MY BONES ARE THIN AND LIGHT, I HAVE EXTRA MUSCLES, MY LUNGS ARE BIGGER...
...AND MY HEART'S MORE EFFICIENT. BUT I NEED TO EAT A LOT.
IT'S HARD.
AH... I SEE.

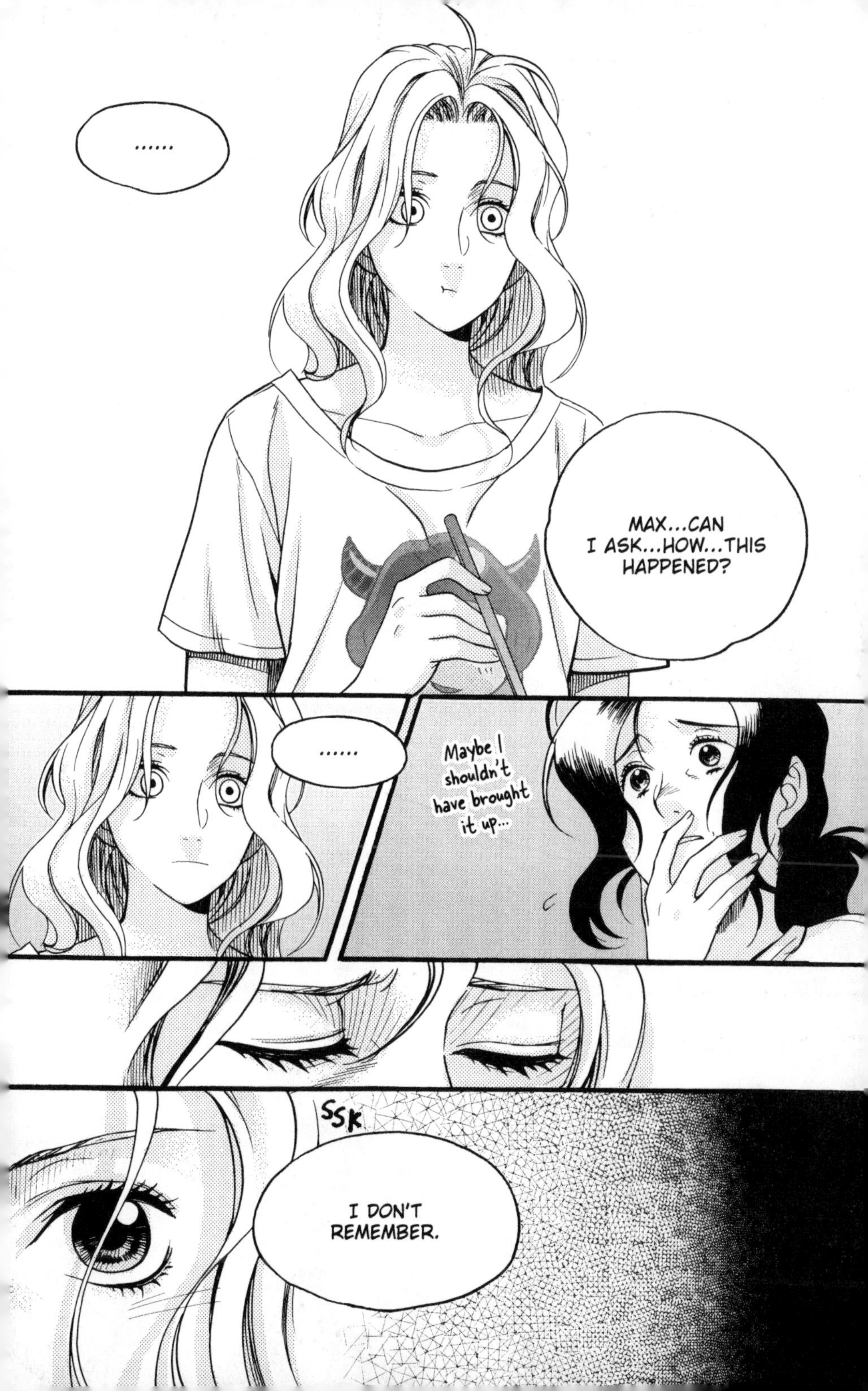

......
MAX...CAN I ASK...HOW...THIS HAPPENED?
......
Maybe I shouldn't have brought it up...
SSK
I DON'T REMEMBER.

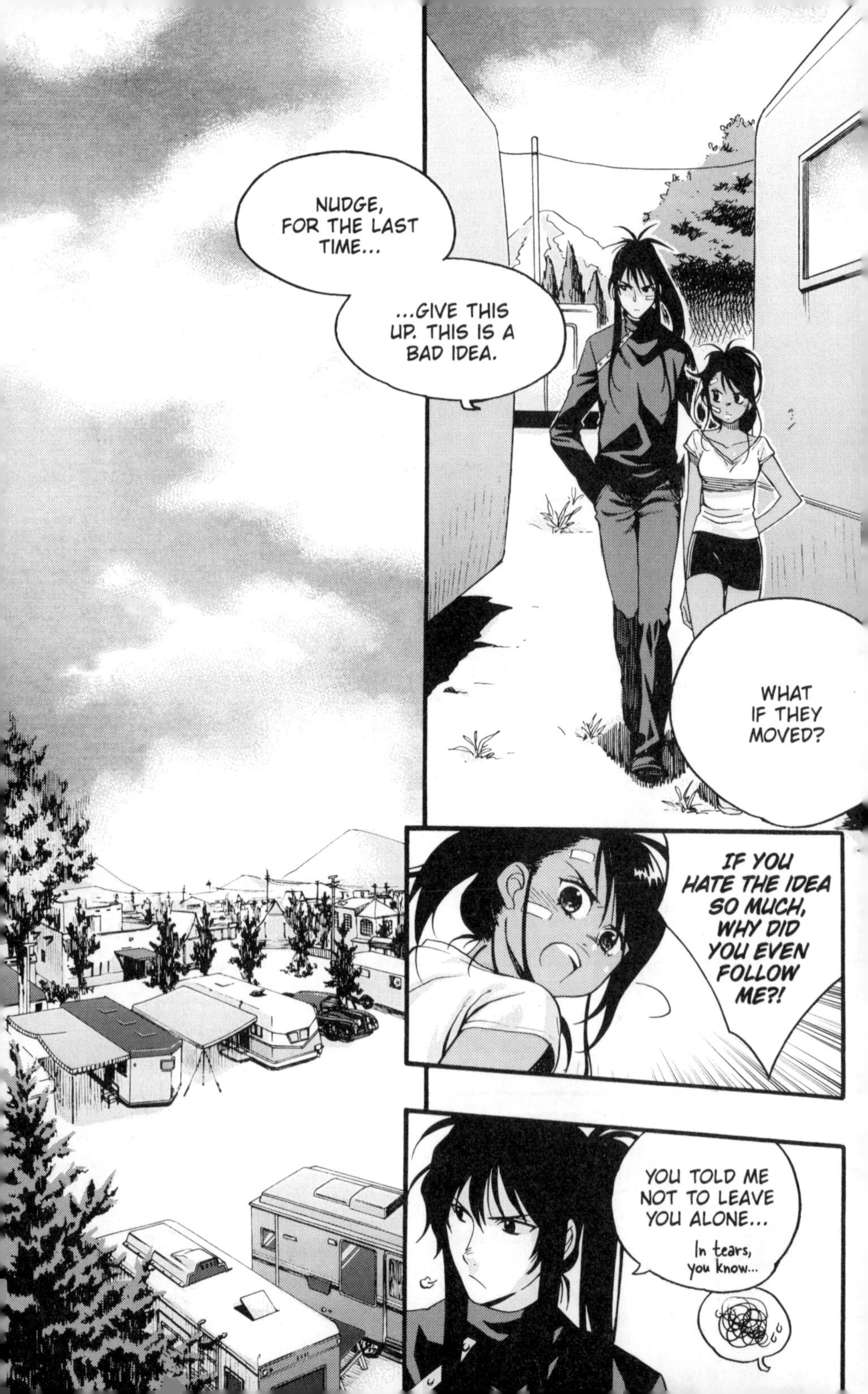
NUDGE, FOR THE LAST TIME...
...GIVE THIS UP. THIS IS A BAD IDEA.
WHAT IF THEY MOVED?
IF YOU HATE THE IDEA SO MUCH, WHY DID YOU EVEN FOLLOW ME?!
YOU TOLD ME NOT TO LEAVE YOU ALONE...
In tears, you know...

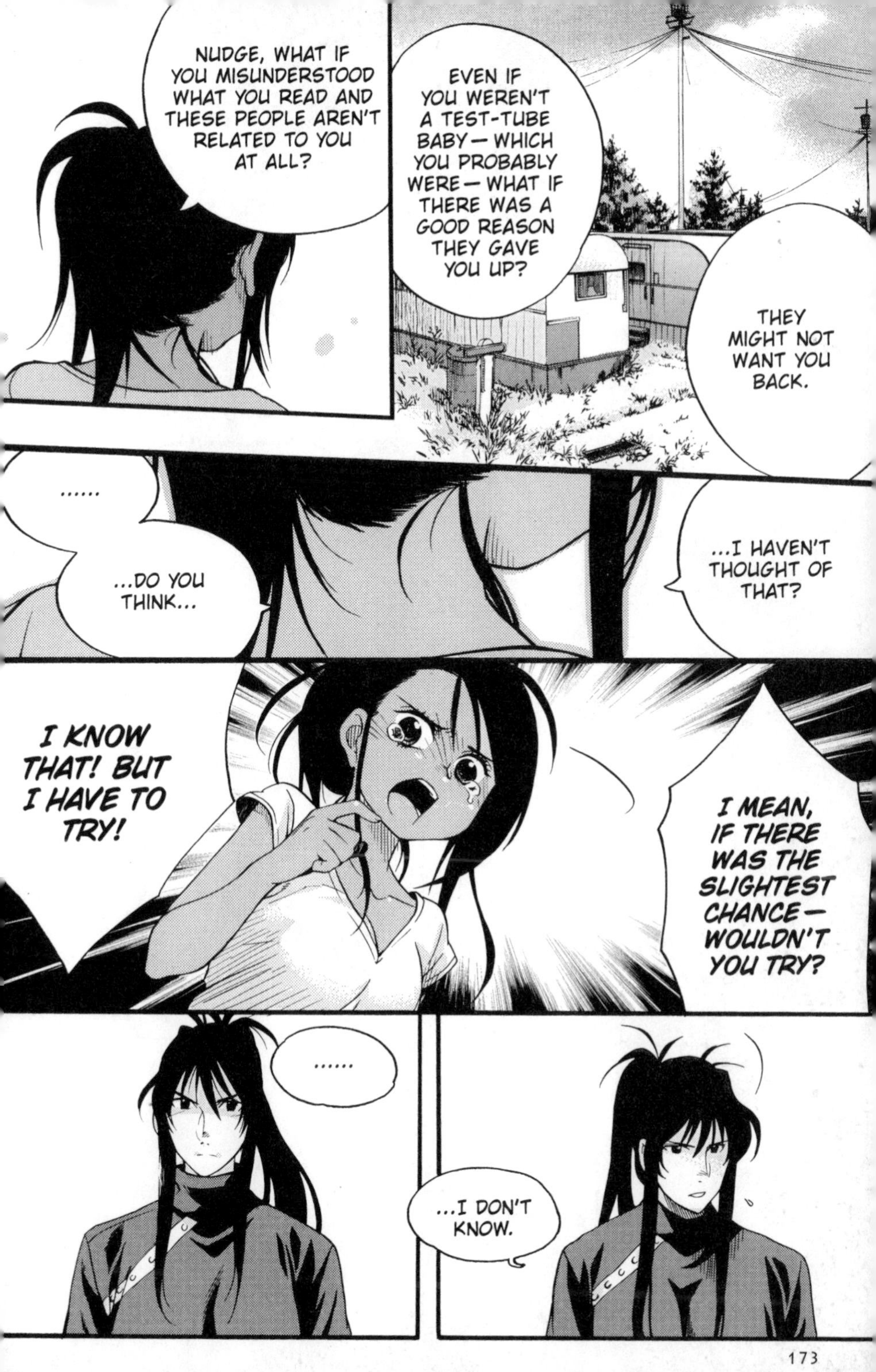
NUDGE, WHAT IF YOU MISUNDERSTOOD WHAT YOU READ AND THESE PEOPLE AREN'T RELATED TO YOU AT ALL?
EVEN IF YOU WEREN'T A TEST-TUBE BABY— WHICH YOU PROBABLY WERE— WHAT IF THERE WAS A GOOD REASON THEY GAVE YOU UP?
THEY MIGHT NOT WANT YOU BACK.
......
...DO YOU THINK...
...I HAVEN'T THOUGHT OF THAT?
I KNOW THAT! BUT I HAVE TO TRY!
I MEAN, IF THERE WAS THE SLIGHTEST CHANCE— WOULDN'T YOU TRY?
......
...I DON'T KNOW.

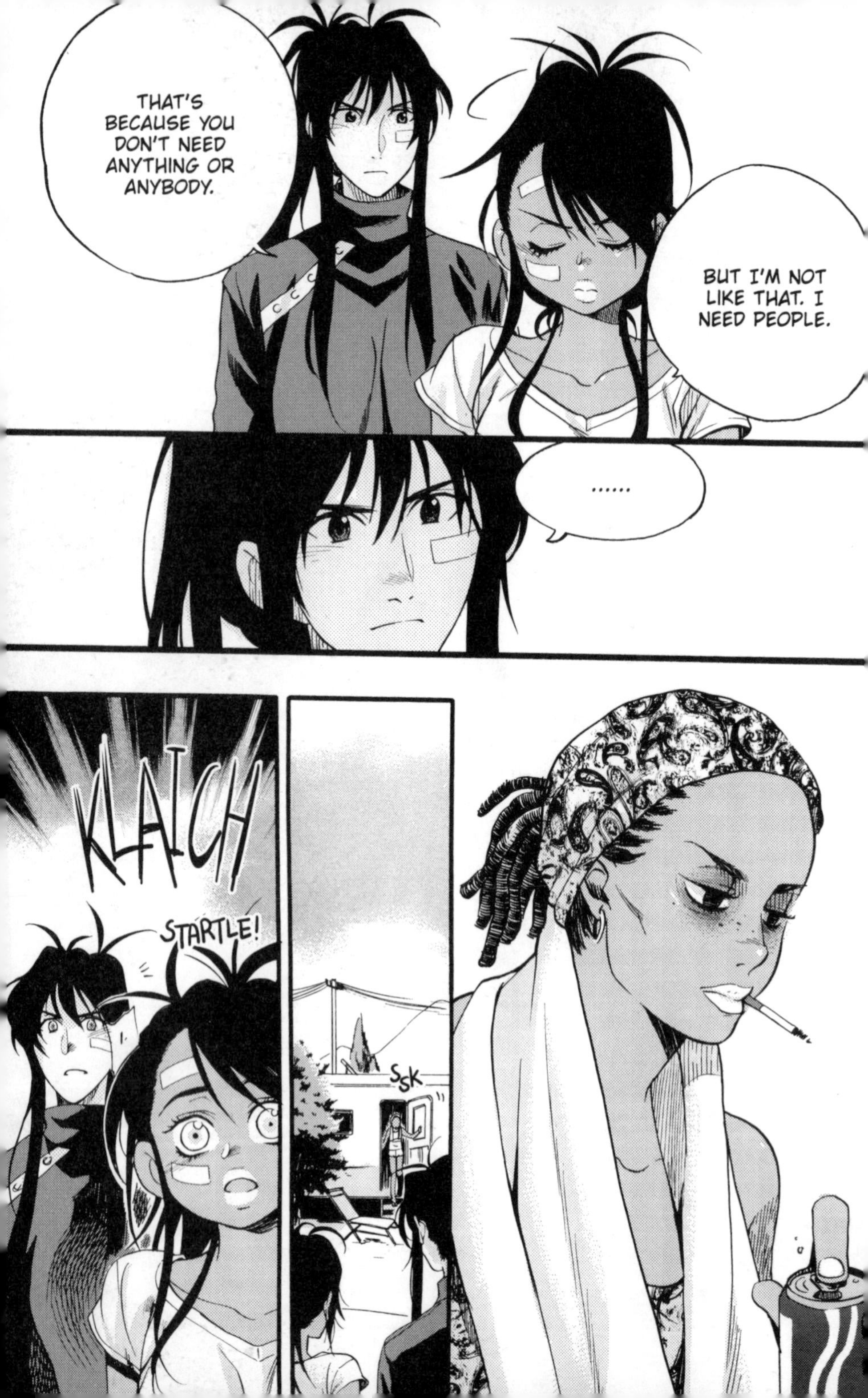
THAT'S BECAUSE YOU DON'T NEED ANYTHING OR ANYBODY.
BUT I'M NOT LIKE THAT. I NEED PEOPLE.
......
KLATCH
STARTLE!
SSK

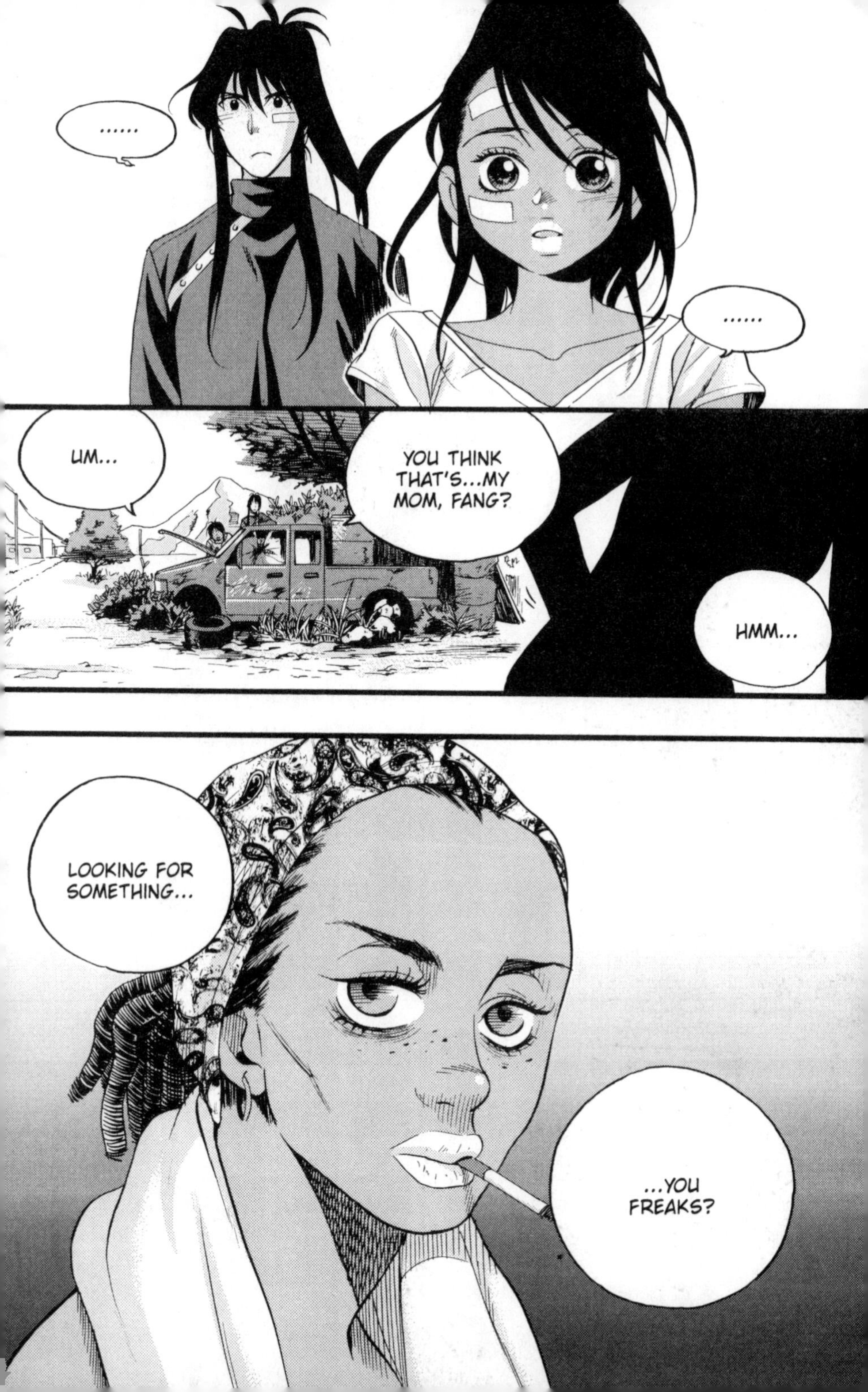
......
......
UM...
YOU THINK THAT'S...MY MOM, FANG?
HMM...
LOOKING FOR SOMETHING...
...YOU FREAKS?

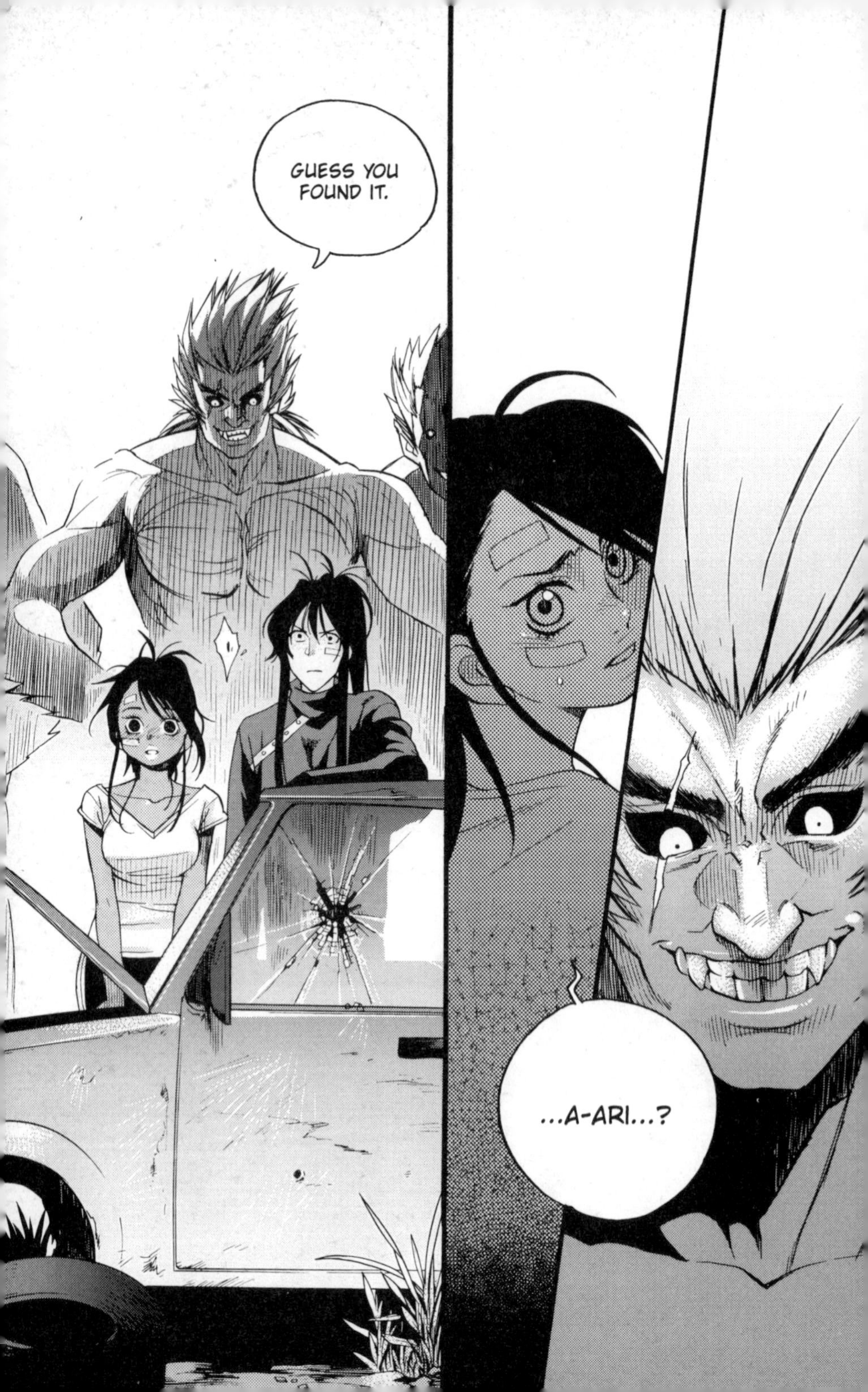
GUESS YOU FOUND IT.
...A-ARI...?

MAXIMUM
RIDE

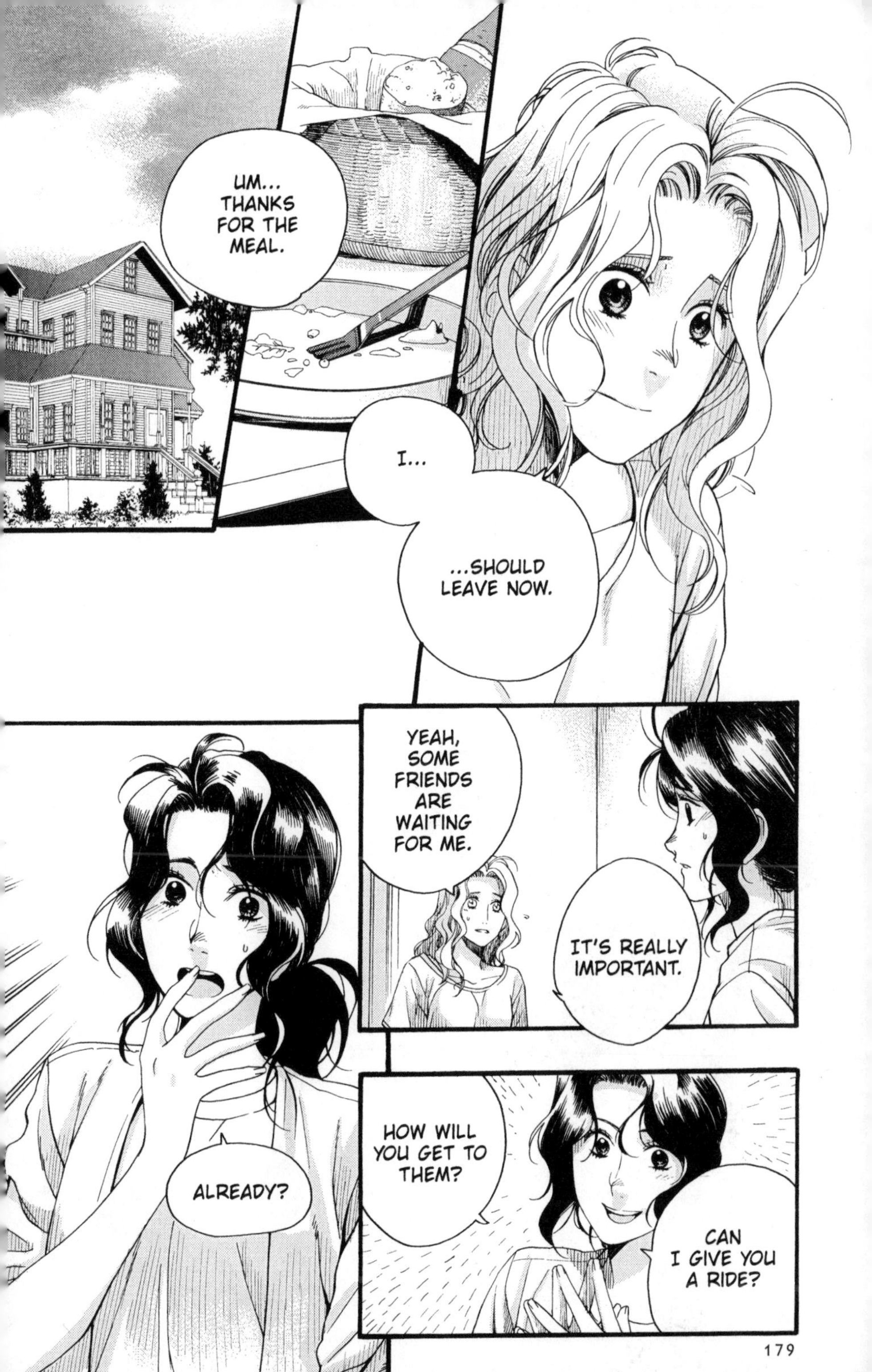
UM... THANKS FOR THE MEAL.
I...
...SHOULD LEAVE NOW.
ALREADY?
YEAH, SOME FRIENDS ARE WAITING FOR ME.
IT'S REALLY IMPORTANT.
HOW WILL YOU GET TO THEM?
CAN I GIVE YOU A RIDE?

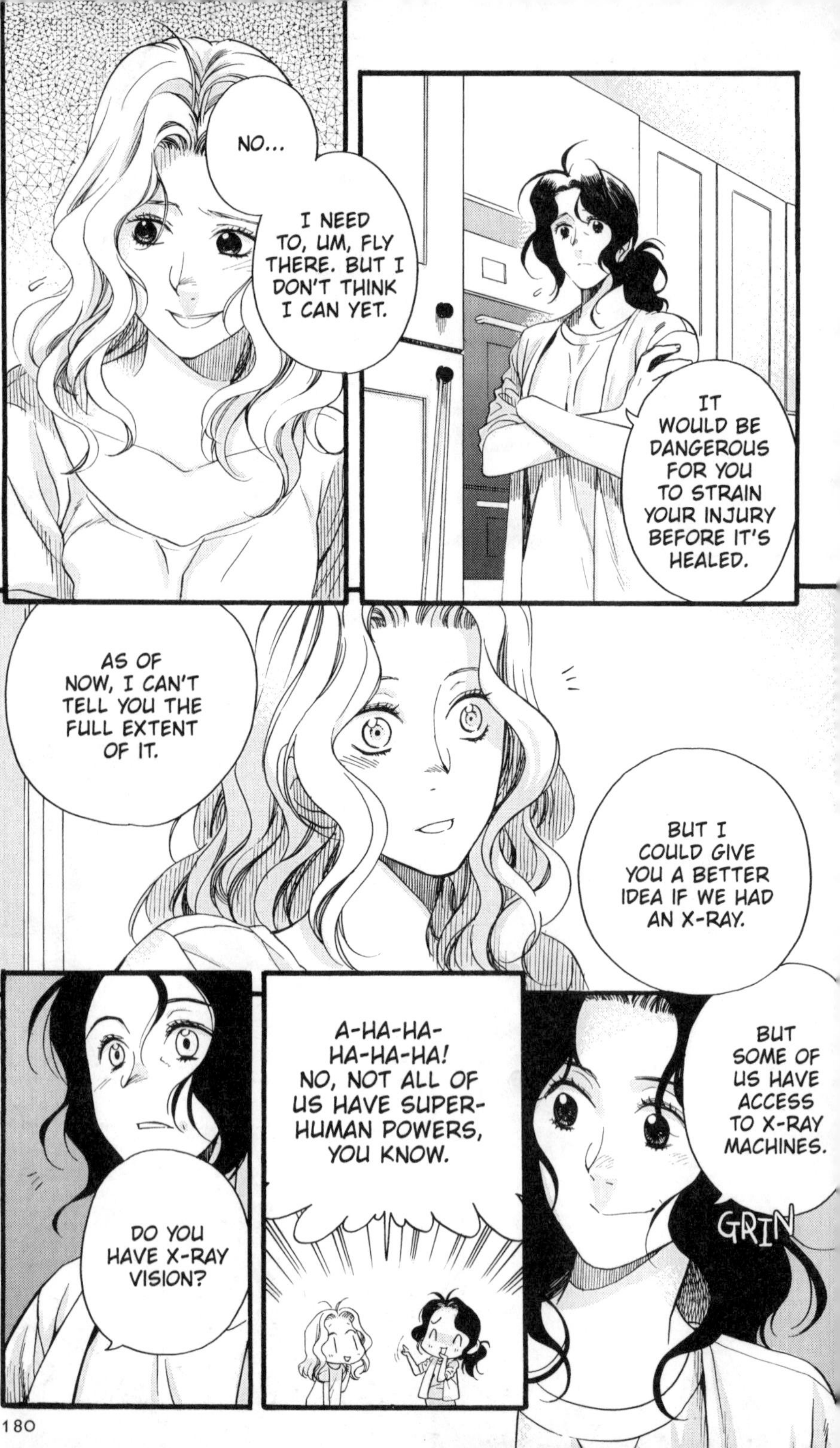
NO...
I NEED TO, UM, FLY THERE. BUT I DON'T THINK I CAN YET.
IT WOULD BE DANGEROUS FOR YOU TO STRAIN YOUR INJURY BEFORE IT'S HEALED.
AS OF NOW, I CAN'T TELL YOU THE FULL EXTENT OF IT.
BUT I COULD GIVE YOU A BETTER IDEA IF WE HAD AN X-RAY.
DO YOU HAVE X-RAY VISION?
A-HA-HA-HA-HA-HA! NO, NOT ALL OF US HAVE SUPER-HUMAN POWERS, YOU KNOW.
BUT SOME OF US HAVE ACCESS TO X-RAY MACHINES.
GRIN

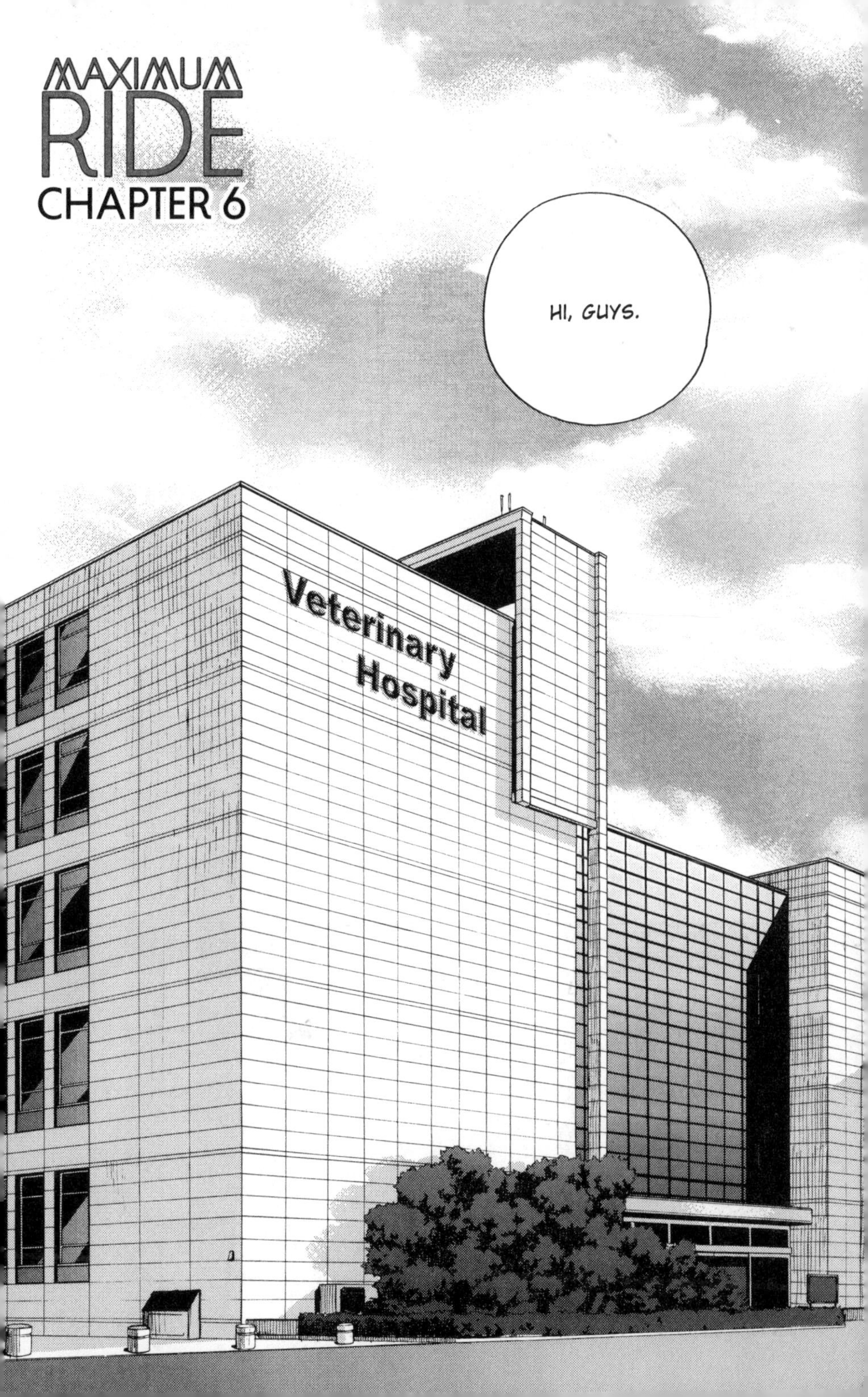
MAXIMUM RIDE
CHAPTER 6
HI, GUYS.
Veterinary Hospital

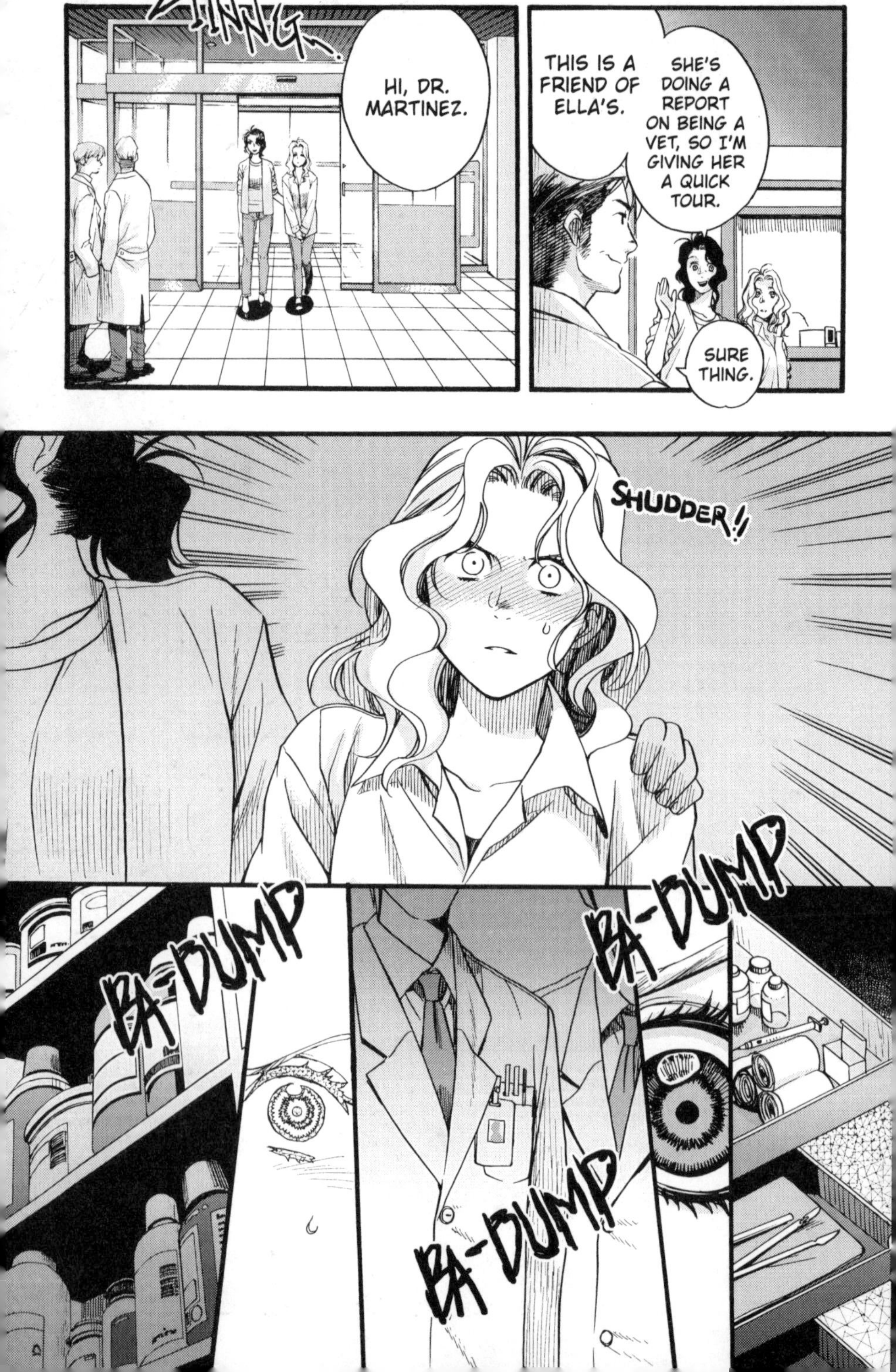
ZIINNG...
HI, DR. MARTINEZ.
THIS IS A FRIEND OF ELLA'S.
SHE'S DOING A REPORT ON BEING A VET, SO I'M GIVING HER A QUICK TOUR.
SURE THING.
SHUDDER!!
BA-DUMP
BA-DUMP
BA-DUMP

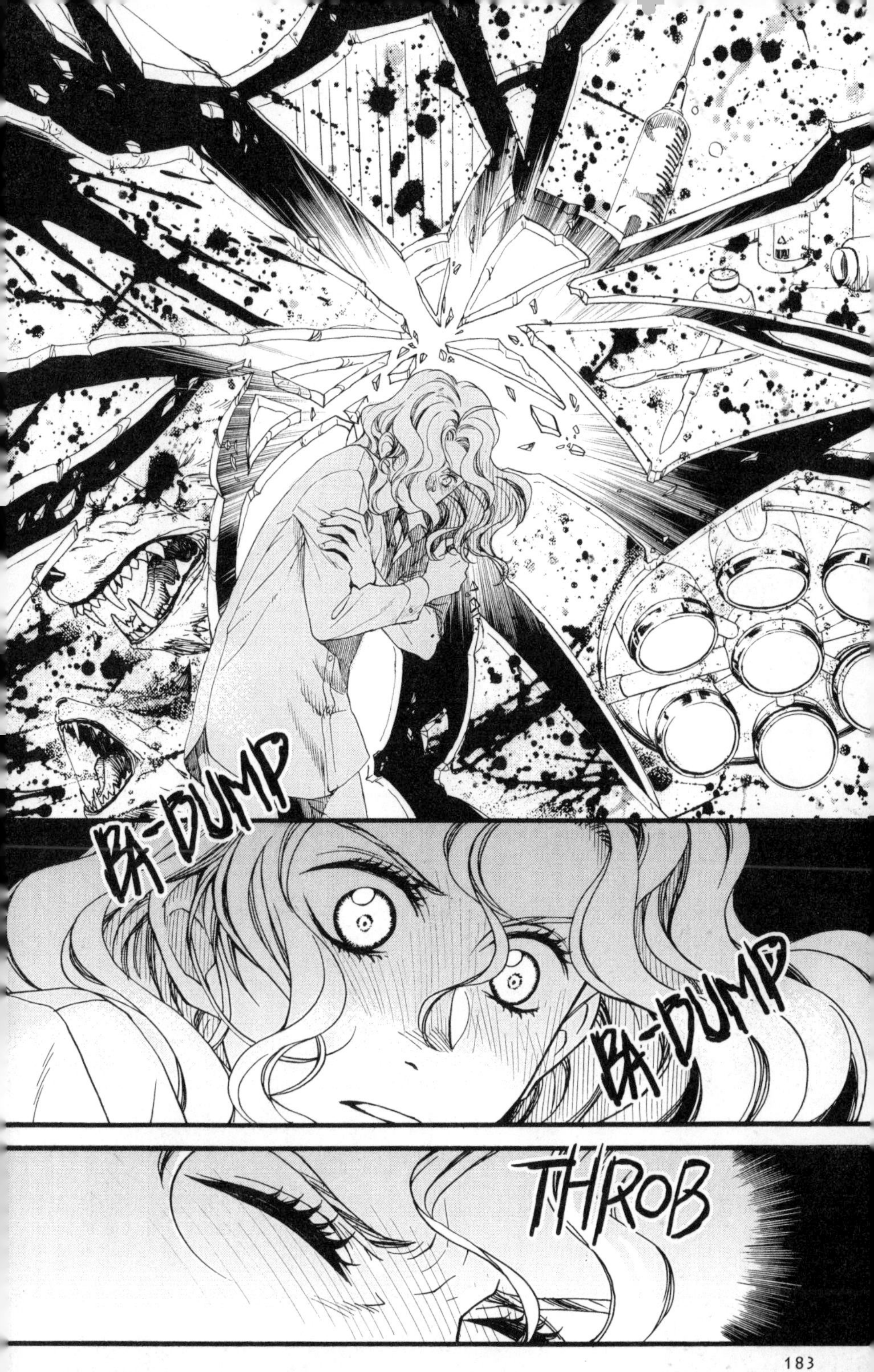
BA-DUMP
BA-DUMP
THROB

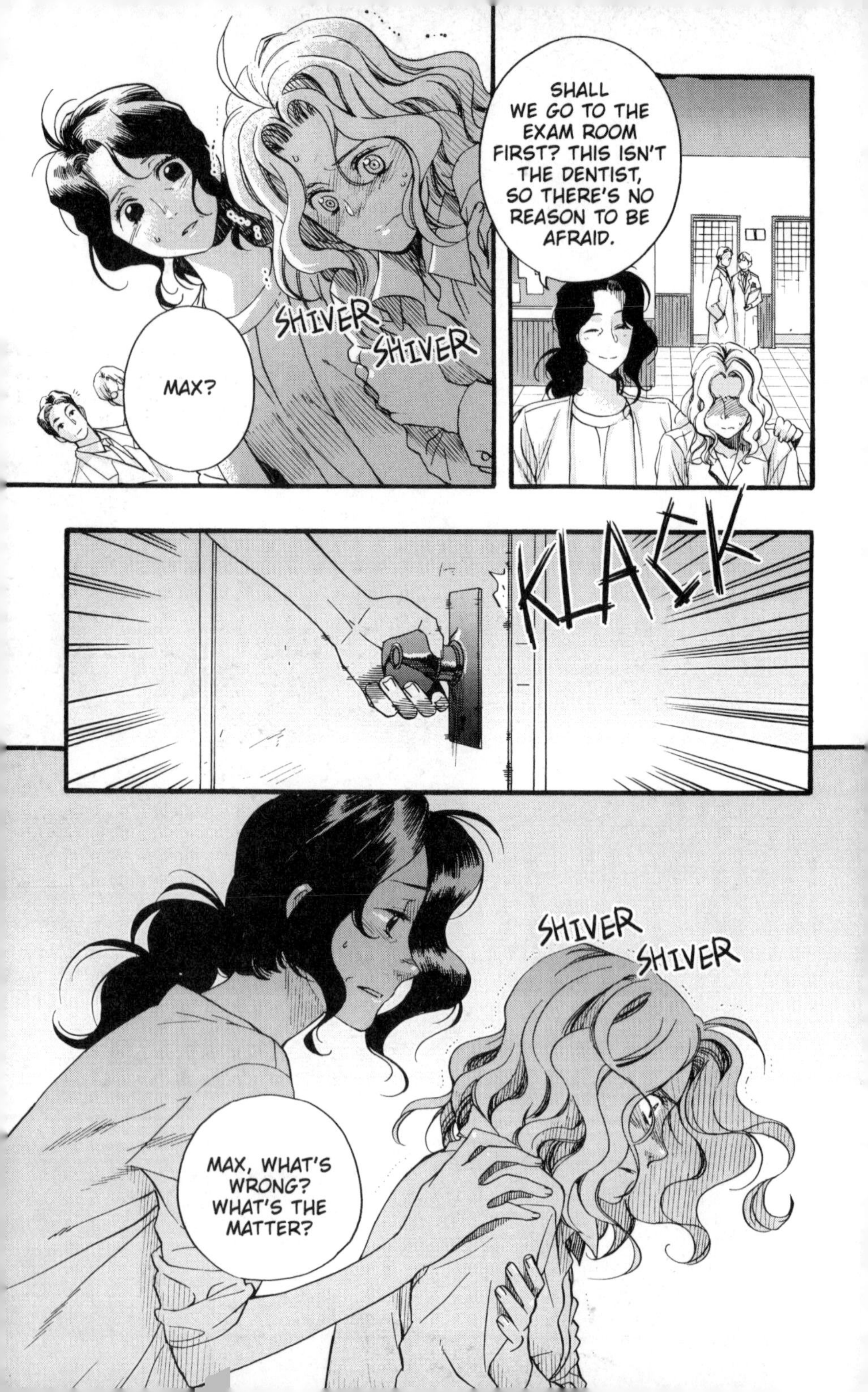
SHIVER SHIVER
MAX?
SHALL WE GO TO THE EXAM ROOM FIRST? THIS ISN'T THE DENTIST, SO THERE'S NO REASON TO BE AFRAID.
KLACK
SHIVER SHIVER
MAX, WHAT'S WRONG? WHAT'S THE MATTER?

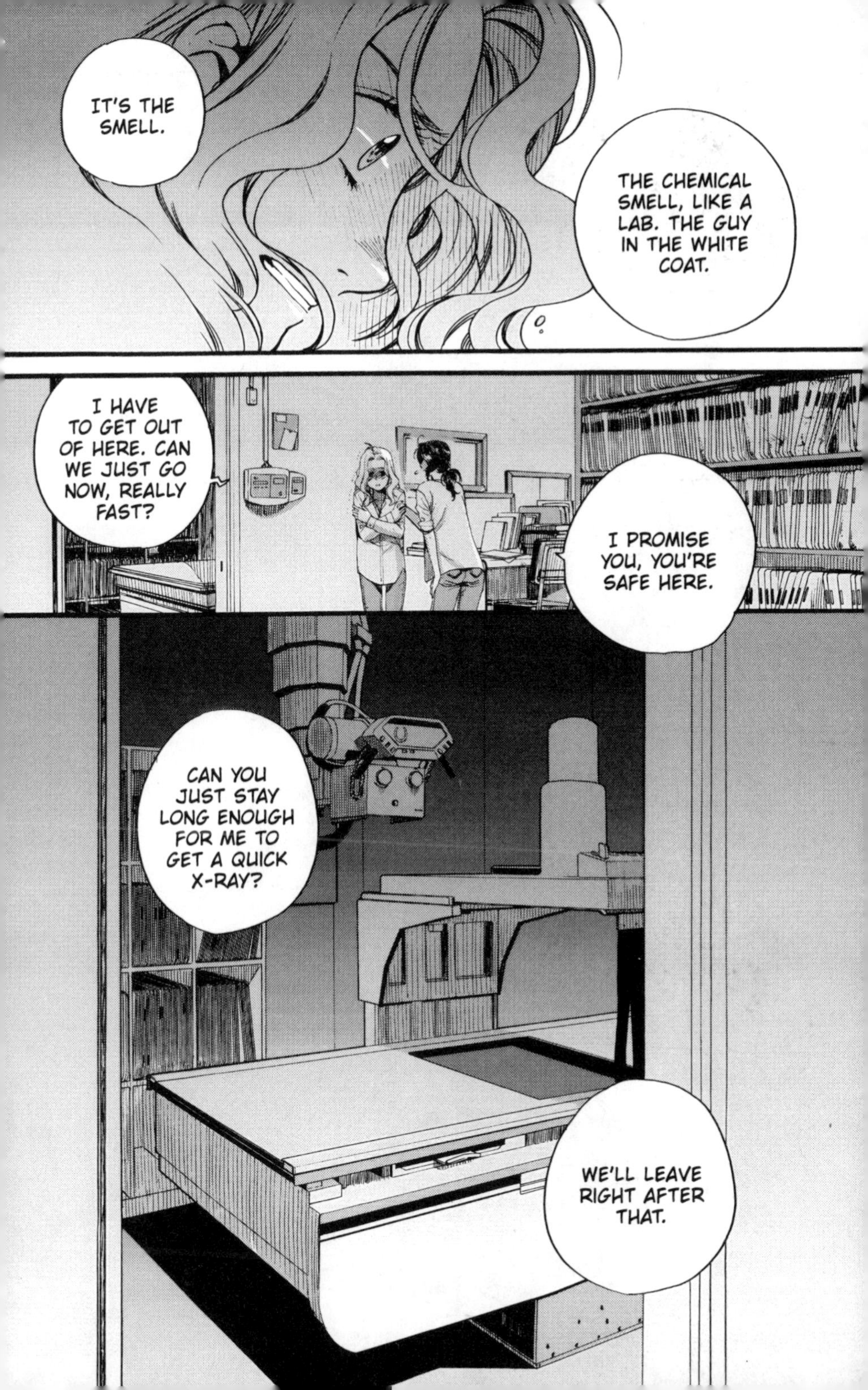
IT'S THE SMELL.
THE CHEMICAL SMELL, LIKE A LAB. THE GUY IN THE WHITE COAT.
I HAVE TO GET OUT OF HERE. CAN WE JUST GO NOW, REALLY FAST?
I PROMISE YOU, YOU'RE SAFE HERE.
CAN YOU JUST STAY LONG ENOUGH FOR ME TO GET A QUICK X-RAY?
WE'LL LEAVE RIGHT AFTER THAT.

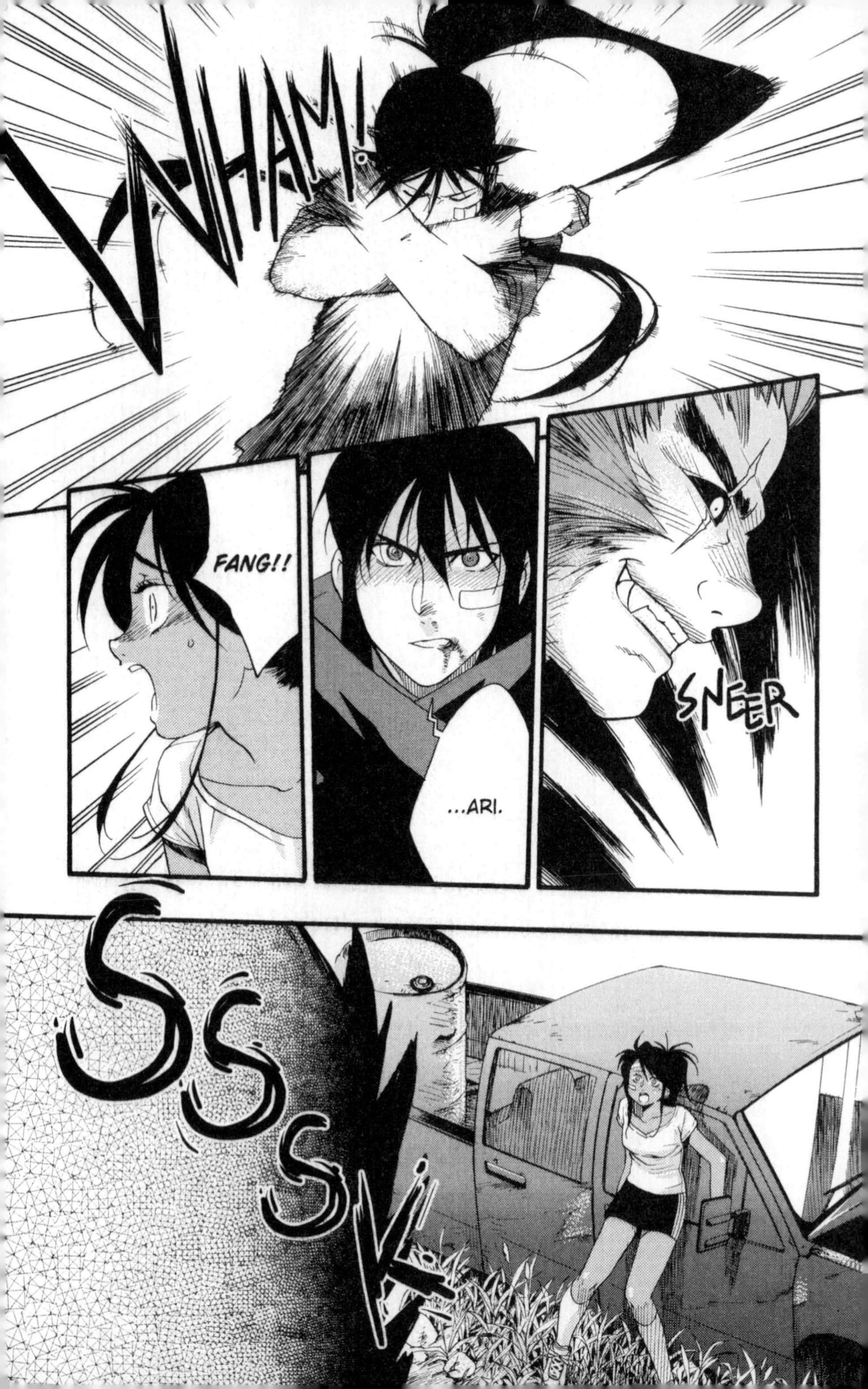
WHAM!
FANG!!
...ARI.
SNEER
SSSK!

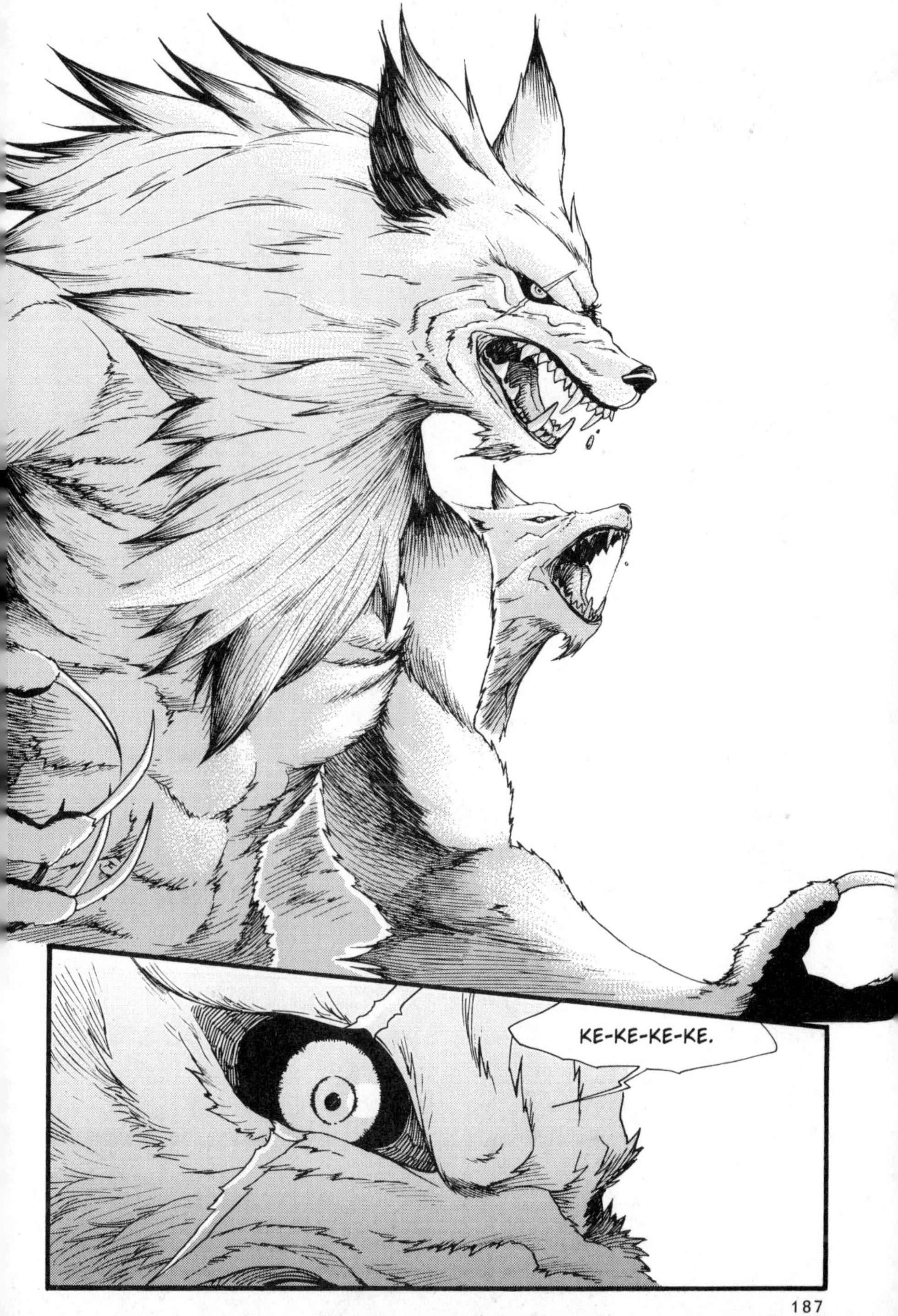
KE-KE-KE-KE.

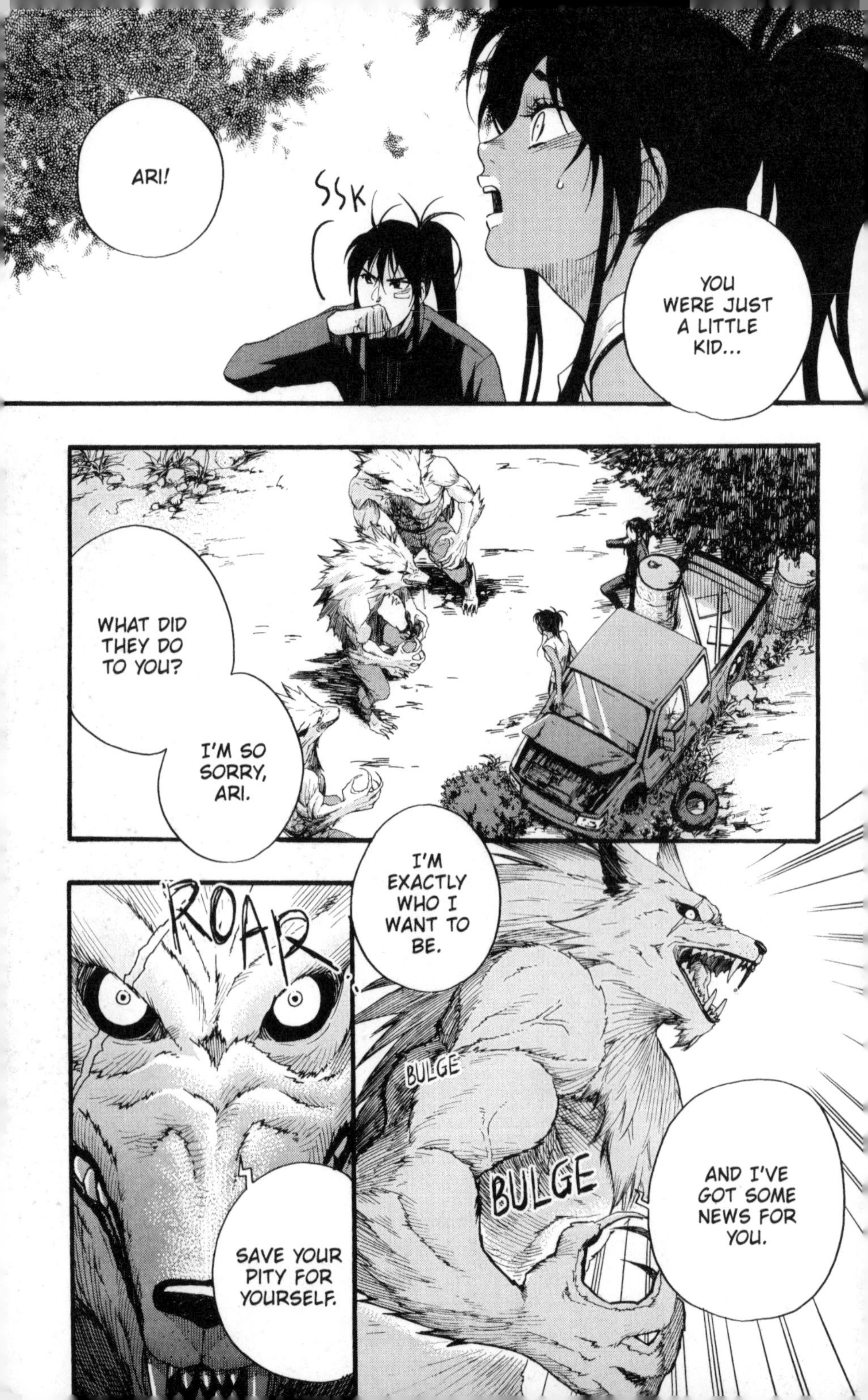
ARI!
SSK
YOU WERE JUST A LITTLE KID...
WHAT DID THEY DO TO YOU?
I'M SO SORRY, ARI.
ROAR
SAVE YOUR PITY FOR YOURSELF.
I'M EXACTLY WHO I WANT TO BE.
BULGE
BULGE
AND I'VE GOT SOME NEWS FOR YOU.

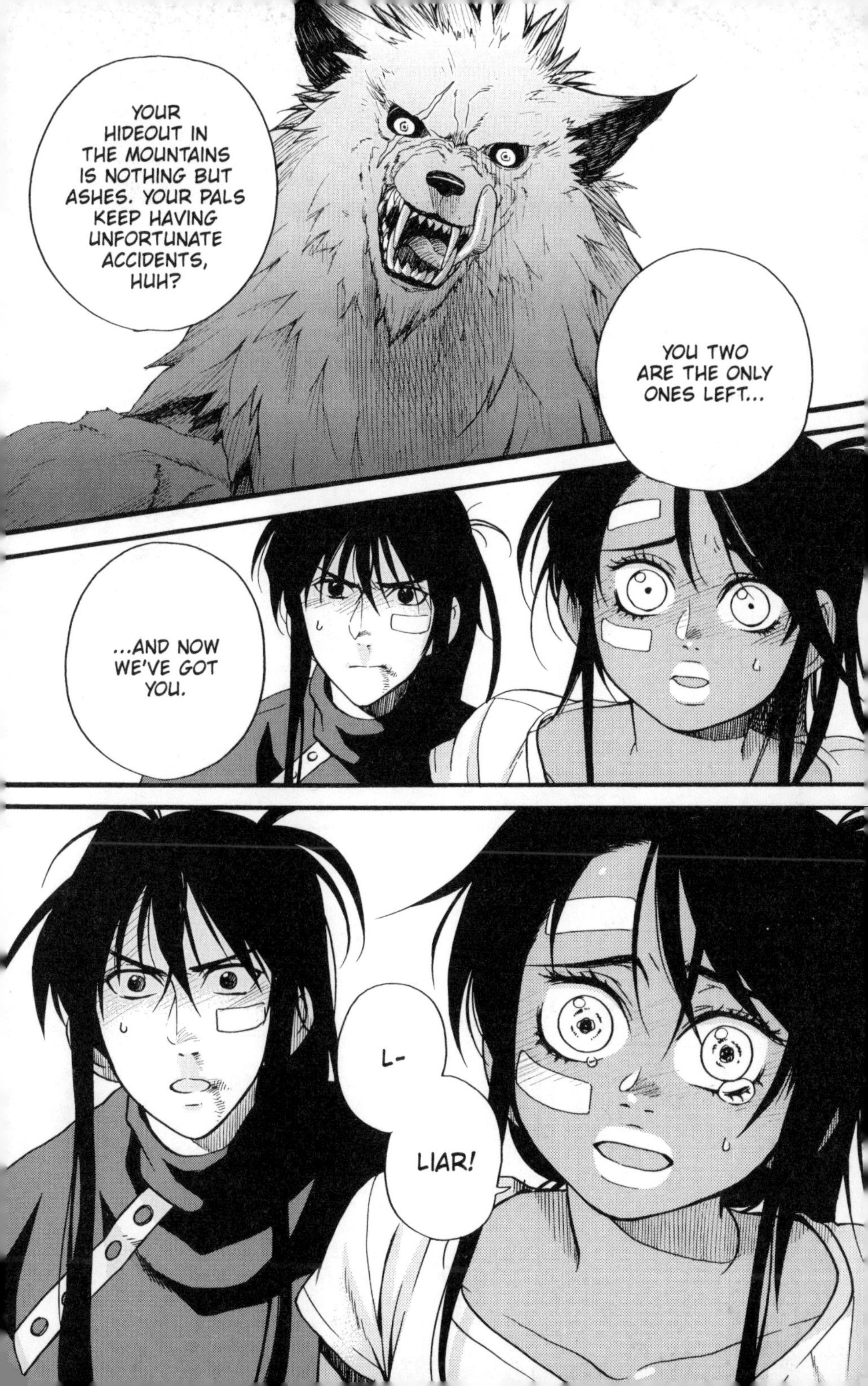
YOUR HIDEOUT IN THE MOUNTAINS IS NOTHING BUT ASHES. YOUR PALS KEEP HAVING UNFORTUNATE ACCIDENTS, HUH?
YOU TWO ARE THE ONLY ONES LEFT...
...AND NOW WE'VE GOT YOU.
L-
LIAR!

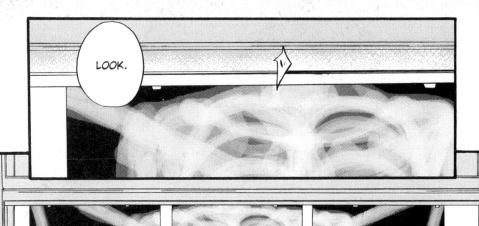

LOOK.

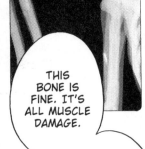

THIS BONE IS FINE. IT'S ALL MUSCLE DAMAGE.

CAN YOU SEE THE TORN TISSUE HERE AND HERE? AND YOUR WING BONES...

...ALL SEEM FINE, WHICH IS GOOD NEWS.

UNFORTUNATELY, MUSCLE DAMAGE USUALLY TAKES LONGER TO HEAL THAN BONES DO.

THOUGH I MUST SAY THE RATE OF YOUR REGENERATION SEEMS STRANGELY FAST.

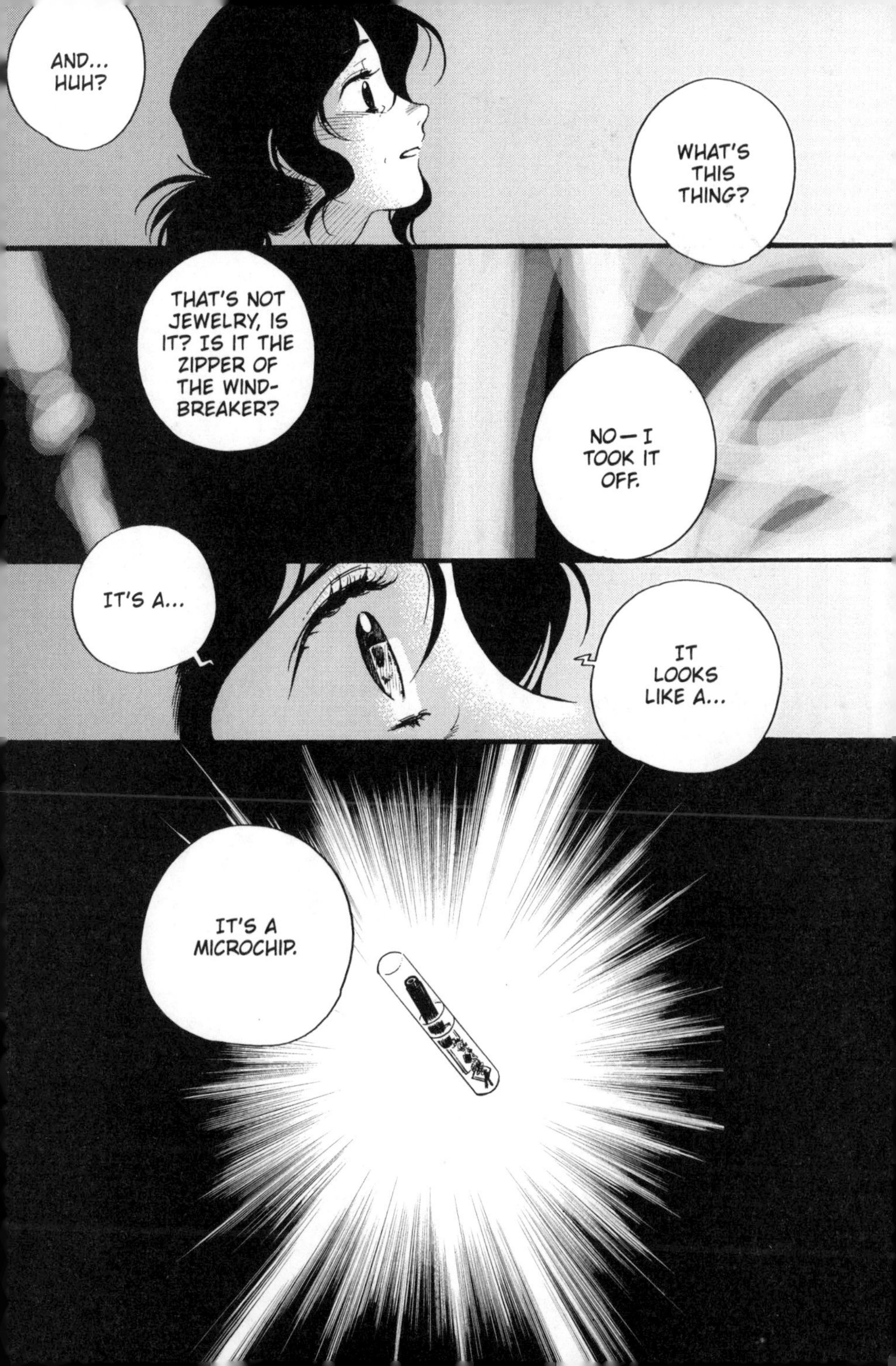
AND... HUH?
WHAT'S THIS THING?
THAT'S NOT JEWELRY, IS IT? IS IT THE ZIPPER OF THE WIND-BREAKER?
NO — I TOOK IT OFF.
IT'S A...
IT LOOKS LIKE A...
IT'S A MICROCHIP.

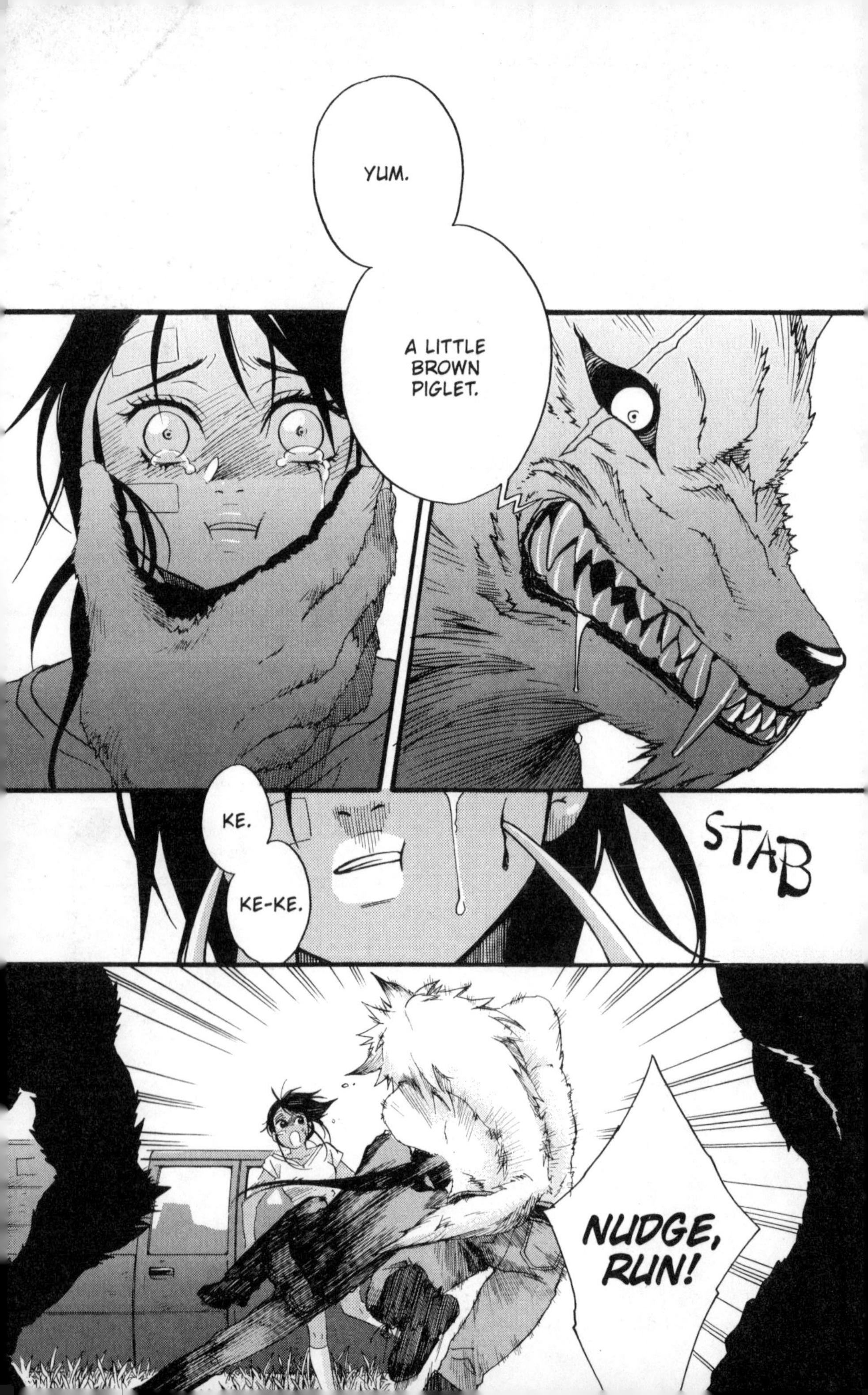
YUM.
A LITTLE BROWN PIGLET.
KE.
KE-KE.
STAB
NUDGE, RUN!

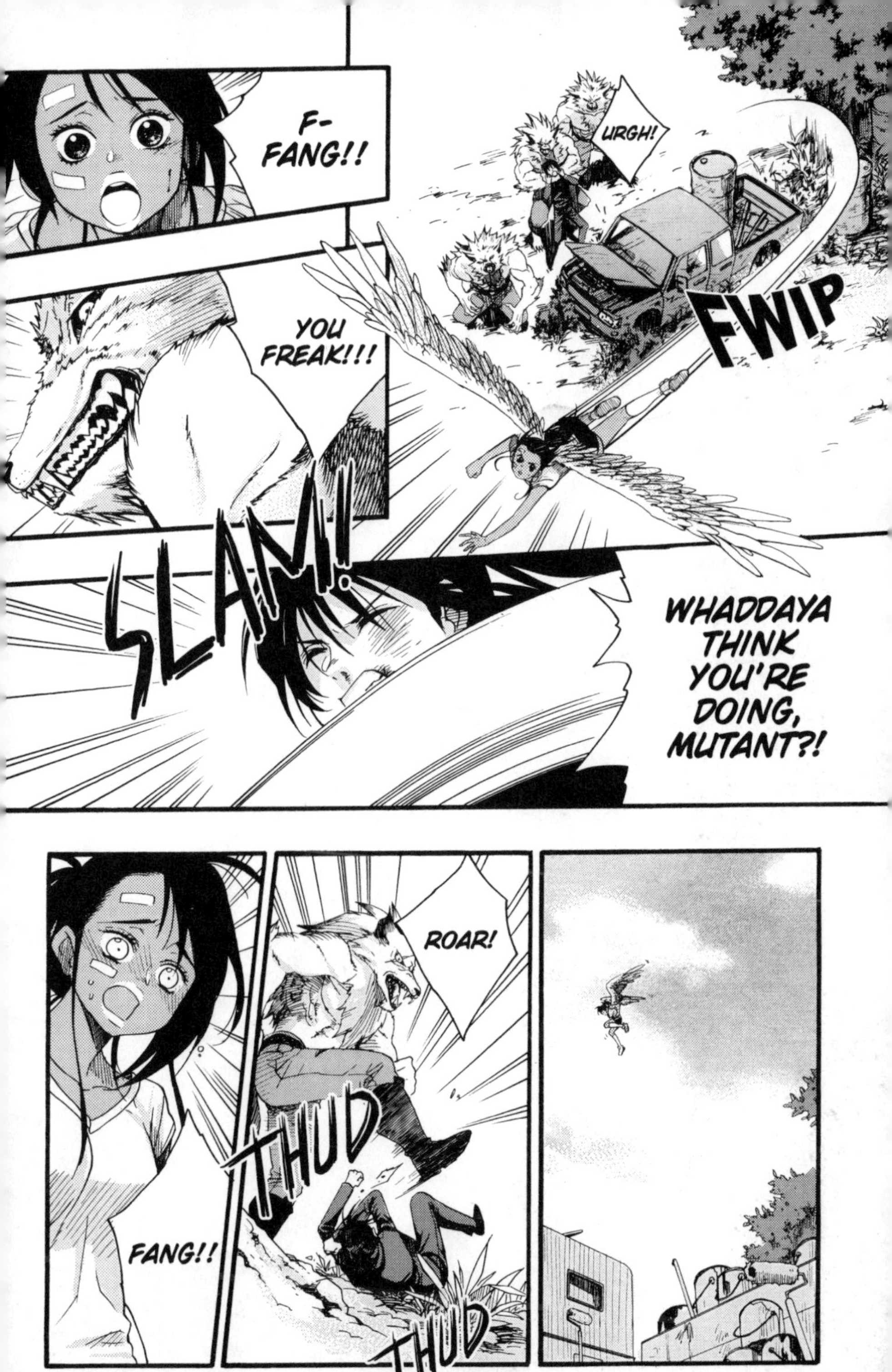
F- FANG!!
YOU FREAK!!!
URGH!
FWIP
SLAM!
WHADDAYA THINK YOU'RE DOING, MUTANT?!
FANG!!
ROAR!
THUD
THUD

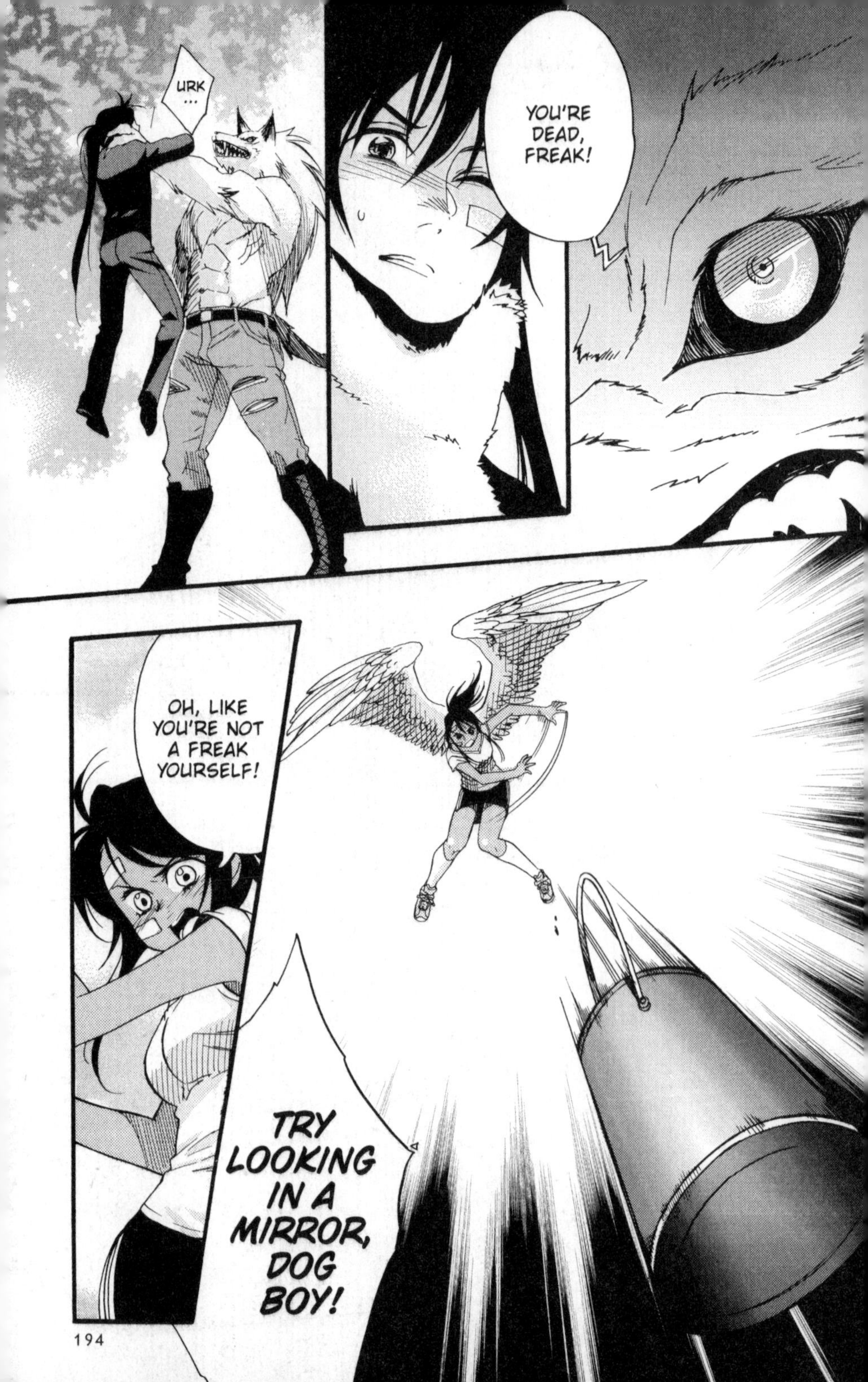
URK ...
YOU'RE DEAD, FREAK!
OH, LIKE YOU'RE NOT A FREAK YOURSELF!
TRY LOOKING IN A MIRROR, DOG BOY!

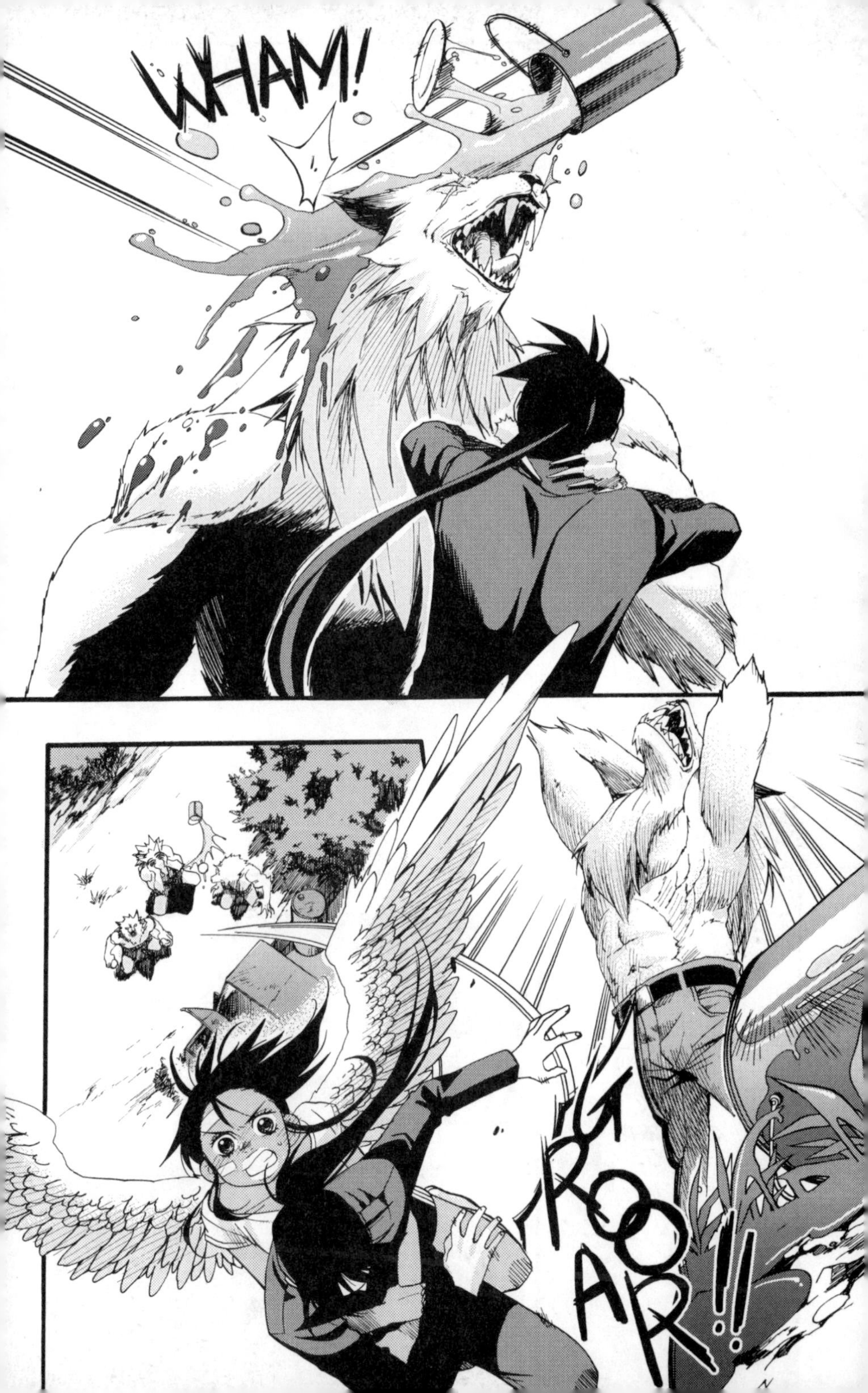
WHAM!
ROOAR!!

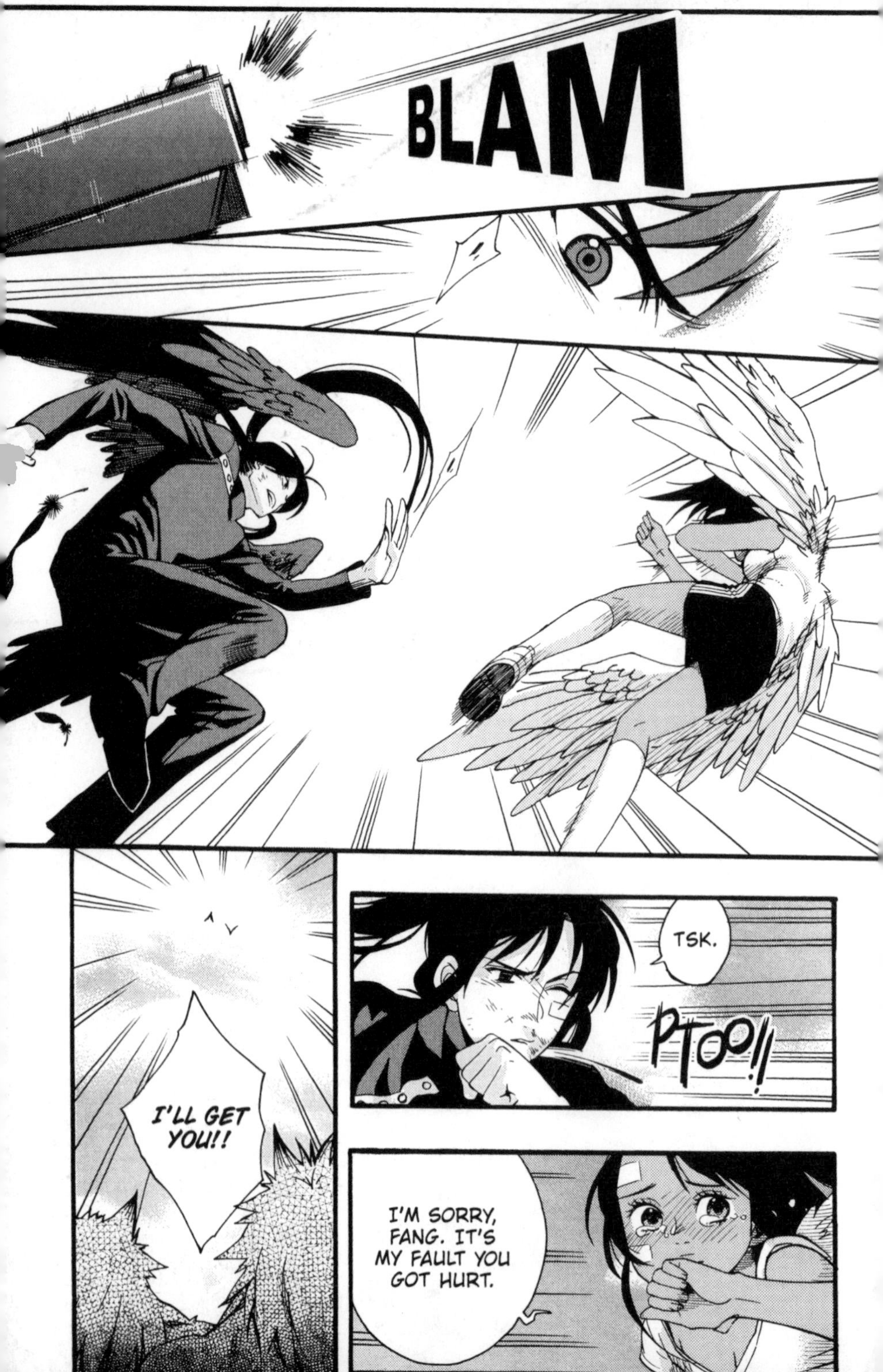
BLAM
I'LL GET YOU!!
TSK.
PTOO!!
I'M SORRY, FANG. IT'S MY FAULT YOU GOT HURT.

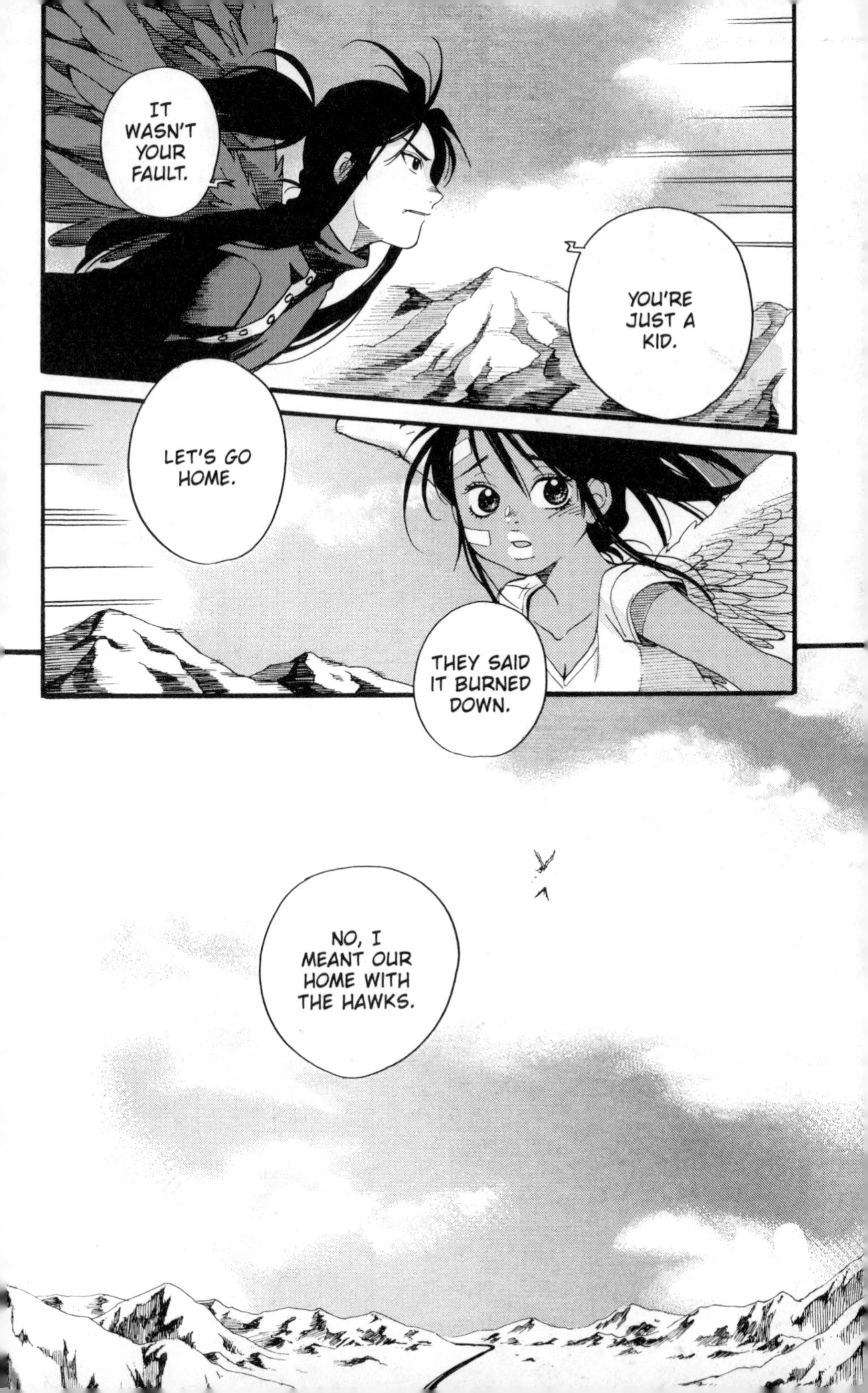
IT WASN'T YOUR FAULT.
YOU'RE JUST A KID.
LET'S GO HOME.
THEY SAID IT BURNED DOWN.
NO, I MEANT OUR HOME WITH THE HAWKS.

WE PUT SOMETHING SIMILAR ON ANIMALS TO IDENTIFY THEM IN CASE THEY GET LOST. YOURS LOOKS LIKE A...

...LIKE THE ONES WE USE ON REALLY EXPENSIVE PETS, SHOW DOGS AND SUCH. THEY HAVE A TRACER IN THEM IN CASE THEY GET STOLEN. THEY CAN BE TRACKED, WHEREVER THEY GO.

I'M NOT SAYING THAT'S WHAT IT IS...

THAT'S JUST WHAT IT LOOKS LIKE.

TAKE IT OUT! PLEASE TAKE IT OUT RIGHT NOW.

SHAKE SHAKE

I DON'T THINK IT CAN BE SURGICALLY REMOVED.

I'M SORRY, MAX.

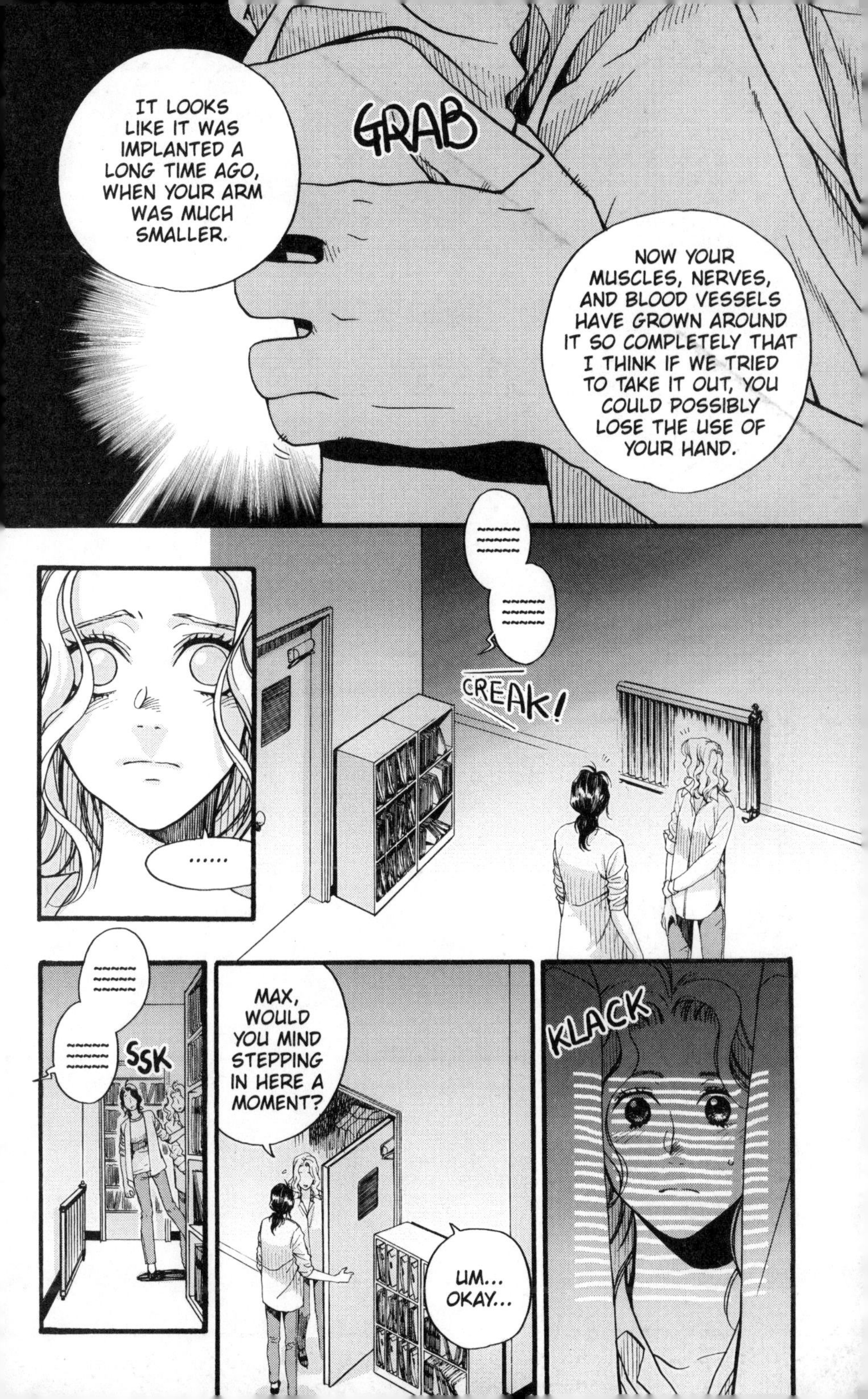
IT LOOKS LIKE IT WAS IMPLANTED A LONG TIME AGO, WHEN YOUR ARM WAS MUCH SMALLER.
GRAB
NOW YOUR MUSCLES, NERVES, AND BLOOD VESSELS HAVE GROWN AROUND IT SO COMPLETELY THAT I THINK IF WE TRIED TO TAKE IT OUT, YOU COULD POSSIBLY LOSE THE USE OF YOUR HAND.
......
CREAK!
SSK
MAX, WOULD YOU MIND STEPPING IN HERE A MOMENT?
UM... OKAY...
KLACK

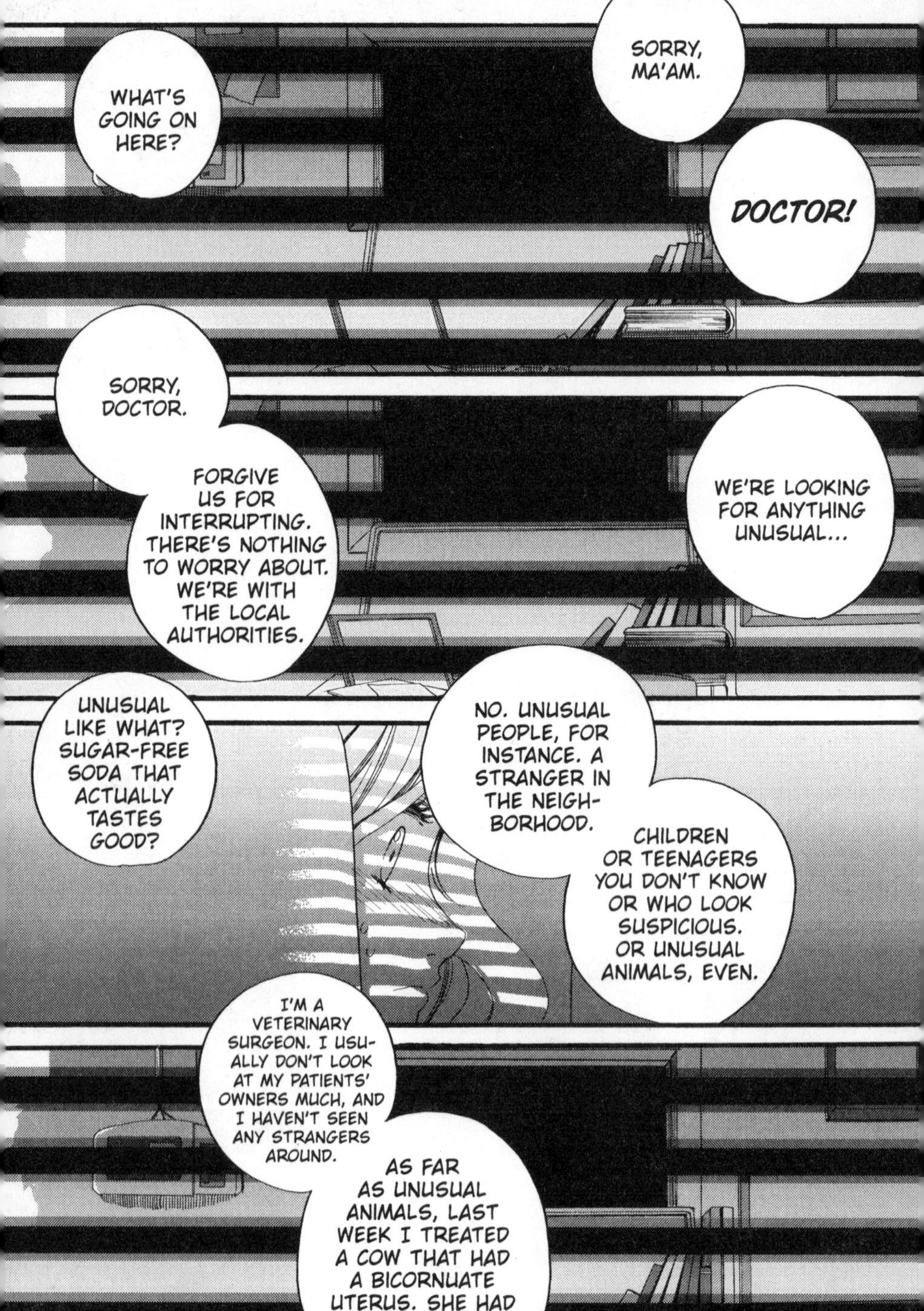
WHAT'S GOING ON HERE?
SORRY, MA'AM.
DOCTOR!
SORRY, DOCTOR.
FORGIVE US FOR INTERRUPTING. THERE'S NOTHING TO WORRY ABOUT. WE'RE WITH THE LOCAL AUTHORITIES.
WE'RE LOOKING FOR ANYTHING UNUSUAL...
UNUSUAL LIKE WHAT? SUGAR-FREE SODA THAT ACTUALLY TASTES GOOD?
NO. UNUSUAL PEOPLE, FOR INSTANCE. A STRANGER IN THE NEIGH-BORHOOD.
CHILDREN OR TEENAGERS YOU DON'T KNOW OR WHO LOOK SUSPICIOUS. OR UNUSUAL ANIMALS, EVEN.
I'M A VETERINARY SURGEON. I USU-ALLY DON'T LOOK AT MY PATIENTS' OWNERS MUCH, AND I HAVEN'T SEEN ANY STRANGERS AROUND.
AS FAR AS UNUSUAL ANIMALS, LAST WEEK I TREATED A COW THAT HAD A BICORNUATE UTERUS. SHE HAD A HEALTHY CALF ON EACH SIDE.

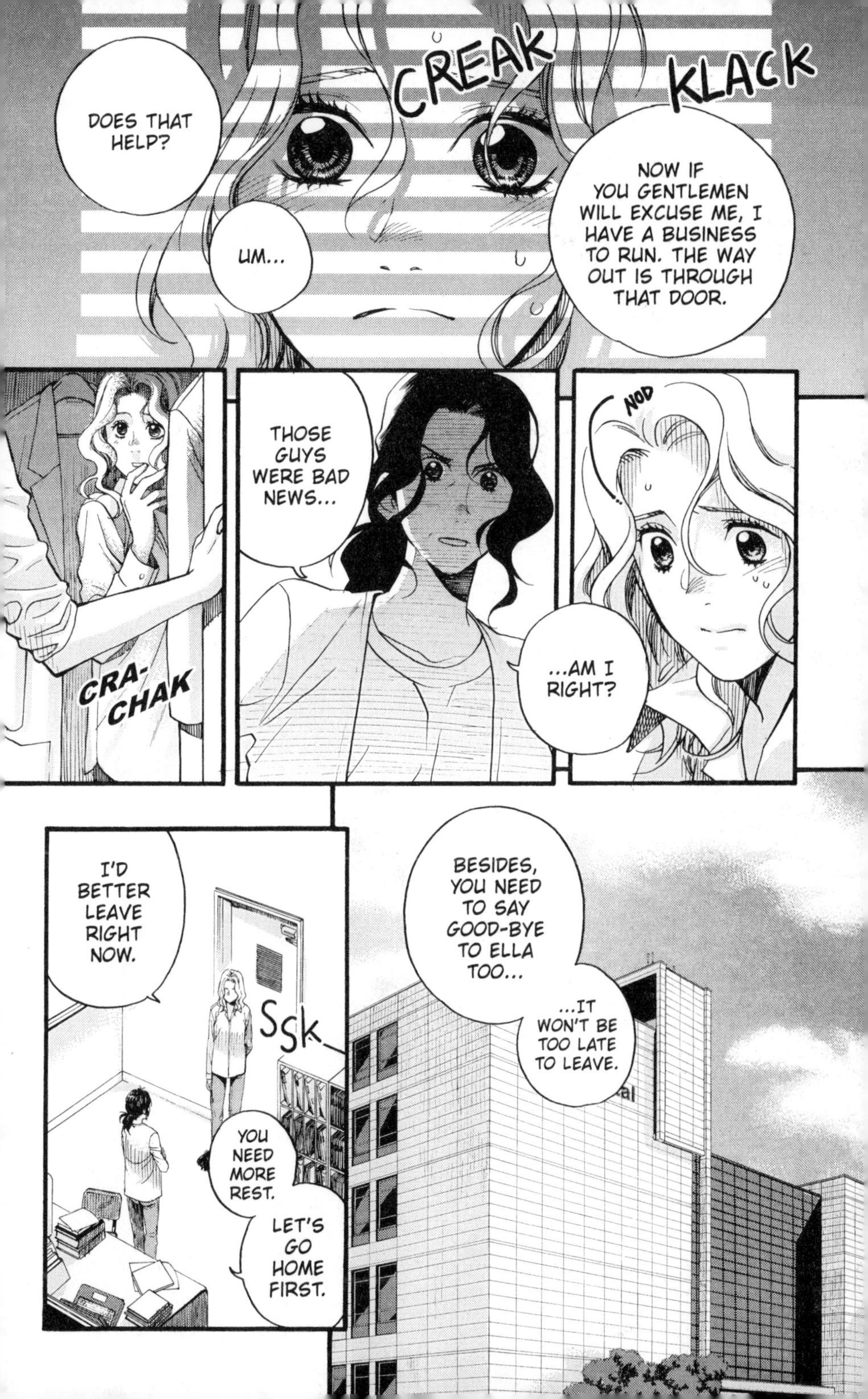
DOES THAT HELP?
UM...
CREAK
KLACK
NOW IF YOU GENTLEMEN WILL EXCUSE ME, I HAVE A BUSINESS TO RUN. THE WAY OUT IS THROUGH THAT DOOR.
CRA-CHAK
THOSE GUYS WERE BAD NEWS...
NOD
...AM I RIGHT?
I'D BETTER LEAVE RIGHT NOW.
SSK
YOU NEED MORE REST.
LET'S GO HOME FIRST.
BESIDES, YOU NEED TO SAY GOOD-BYE TO ELLA TOO...
...IT WON'T BE TOO LATE TO LEAVE.

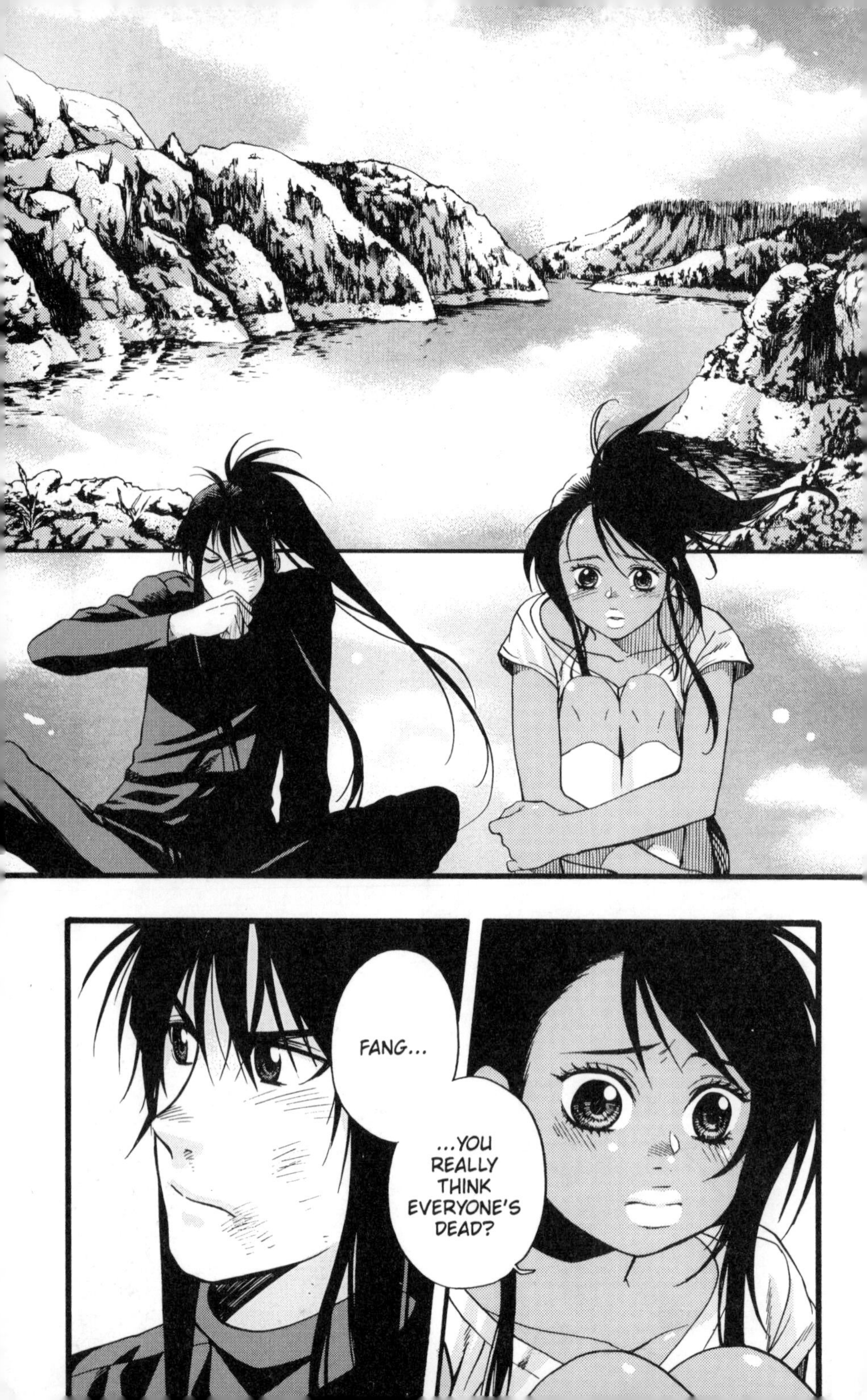
FANG...
...YOU REALLY THINK EVERYONE'S DEAD?

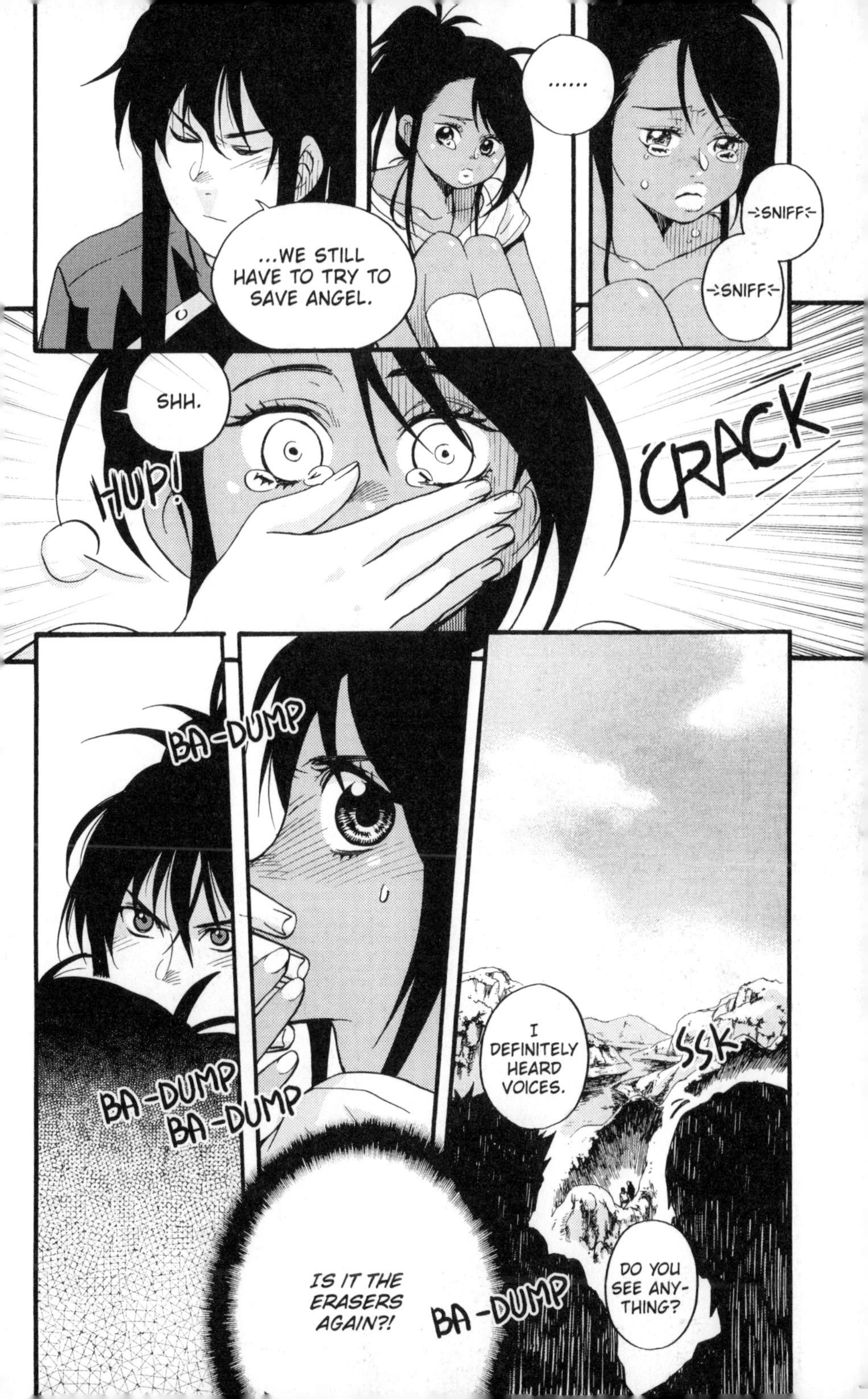

...WE STILL HAVE TO TRY TO SAVE ANGEL.
......
SNIFF
SNIFF
SHH.
HUP!
CRACK
BA-DUMP
BA-DUMP BA-DUMP
I DEFINITELY HEARD VOICES.
SSK
IS IT THE ERASERS AGAIN?!
BA-DUMP
DO YOU SEE ANYTHING?

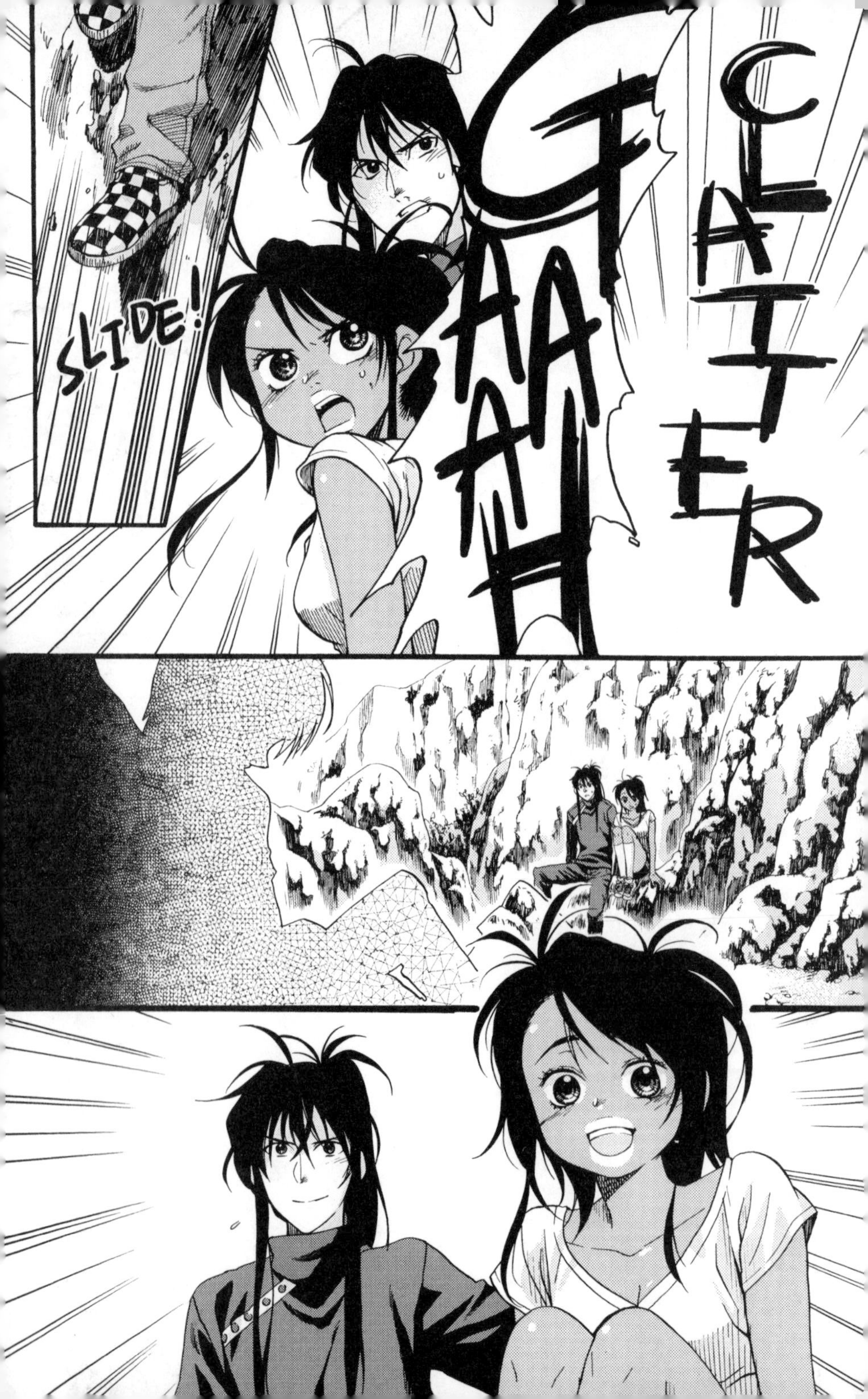
SLIDE!
GAAAAH
CLATTER

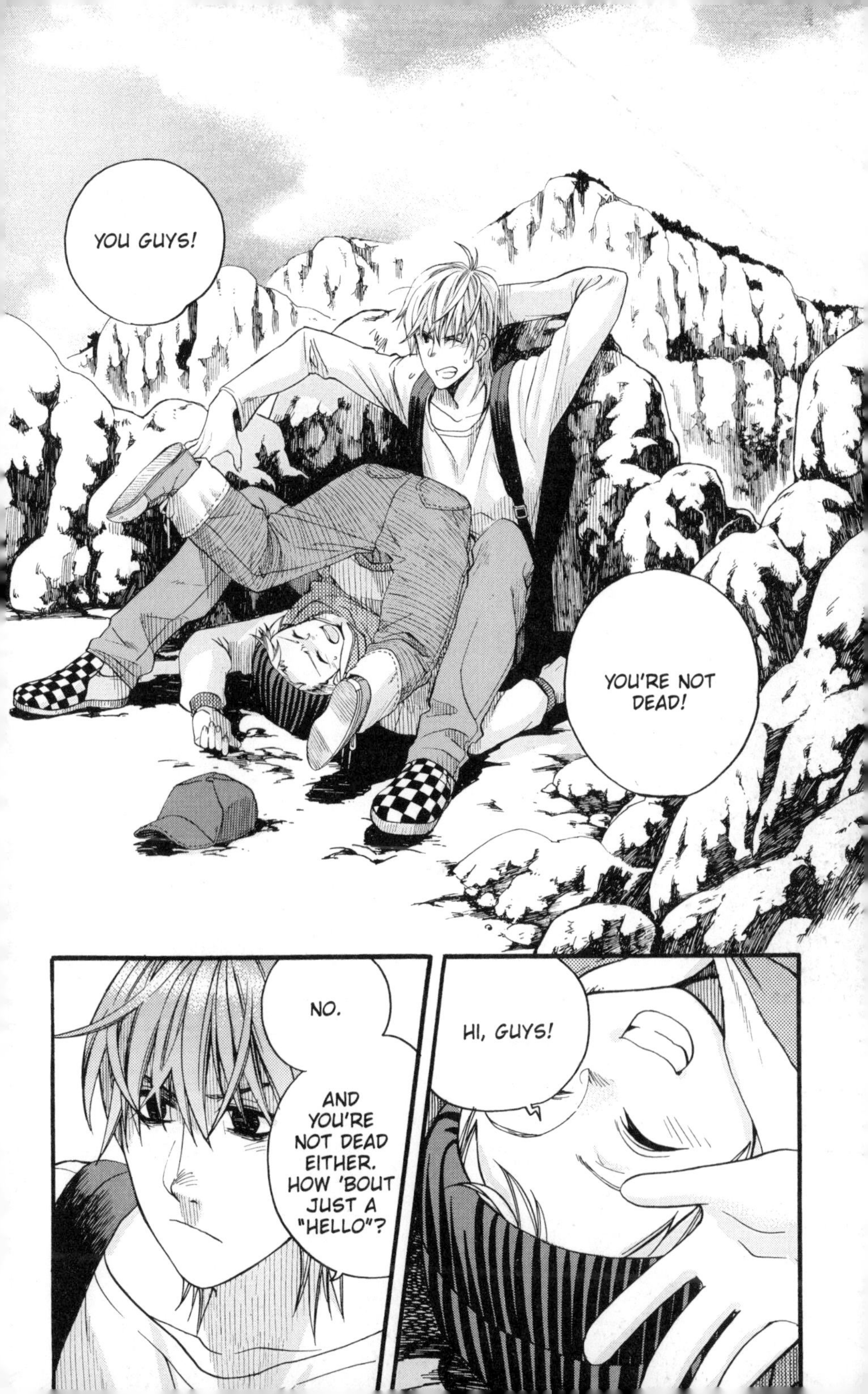
YOU GUYS!
YOU'RE NOT DEAD!
NO.
AND YOU'RE NOT DEAD EITHER. HOW 'BOUT JUST A "HELLO"?
HI, GUYS!

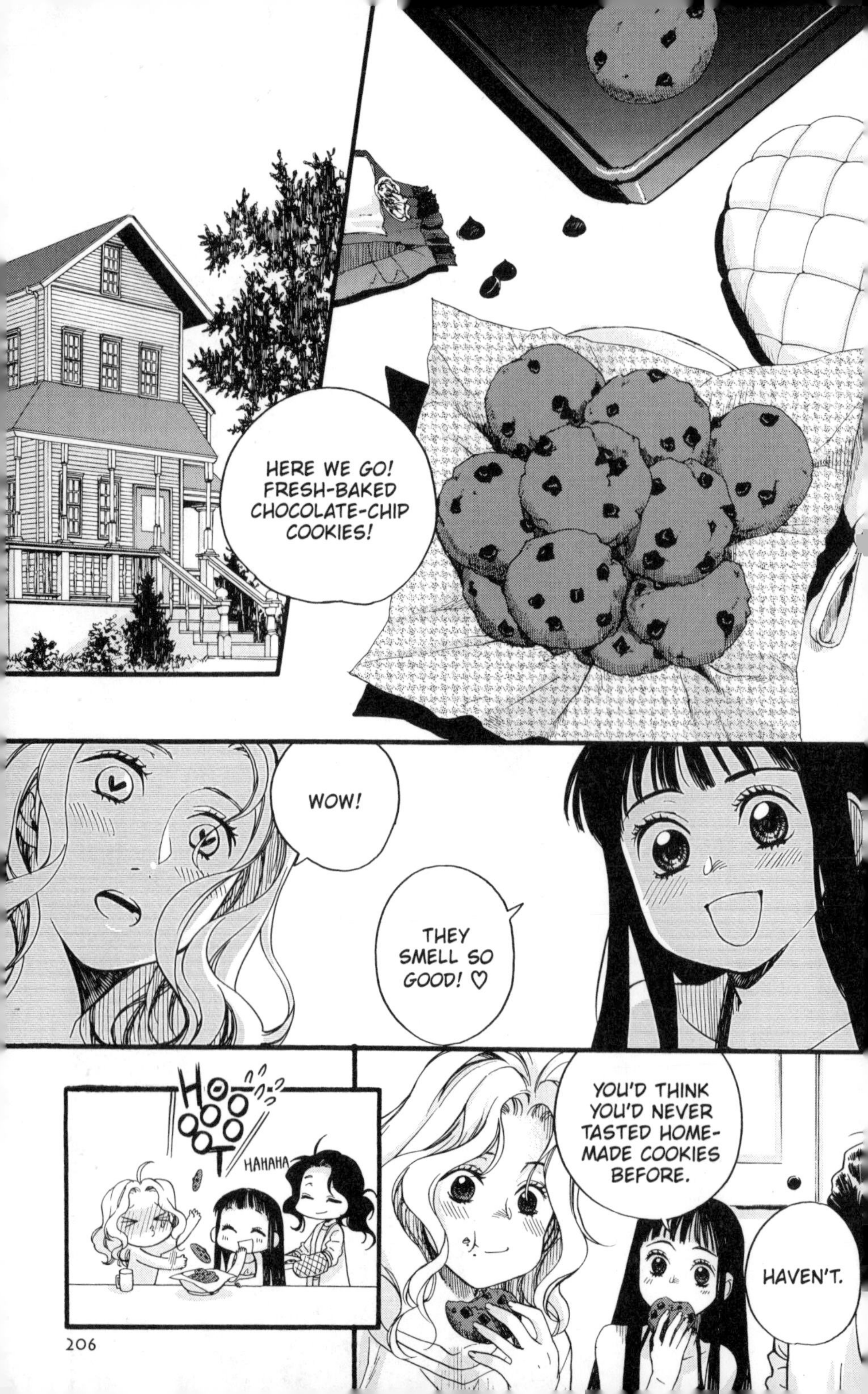
HERE WE GO! FRESH-BAKED CHOCOLATE-CHIP COOKIES!
WOW!
THEY SMELL SO GOOD! ♡
HO-OOOOOT
HAHAHA
YOU'D THINK YOU'D NEVER TASTED HOME-MADE COOKIES BEFORE.
HAVEN'T.

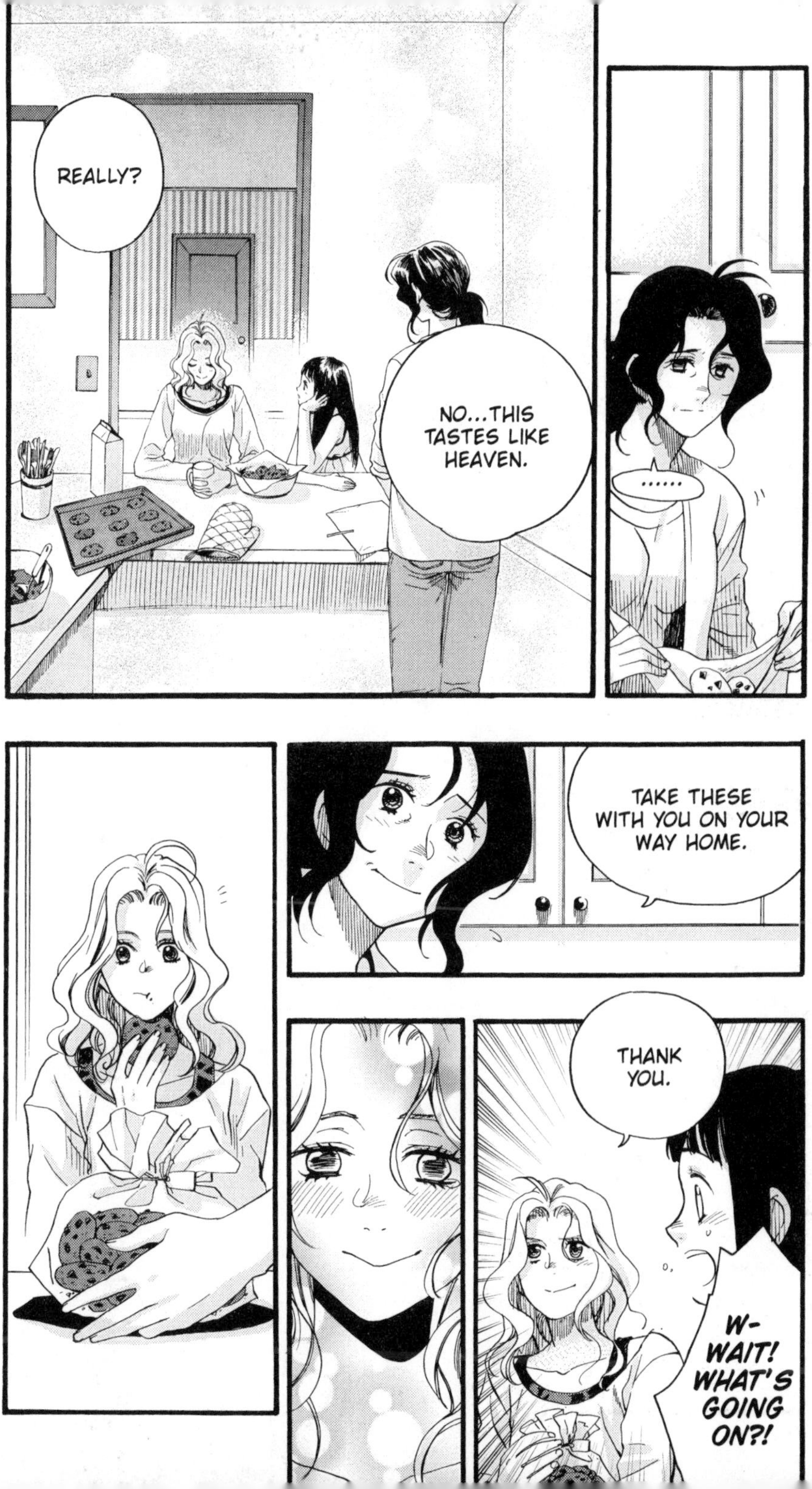
REALLY?
NO...THIS TASTES LIKE HEAVEN.
......
TAKE THESE WITH YOU ON YOUR WAY HOME.
THANK YOU.
W-WAIT! WHAT'S GOING ON?!

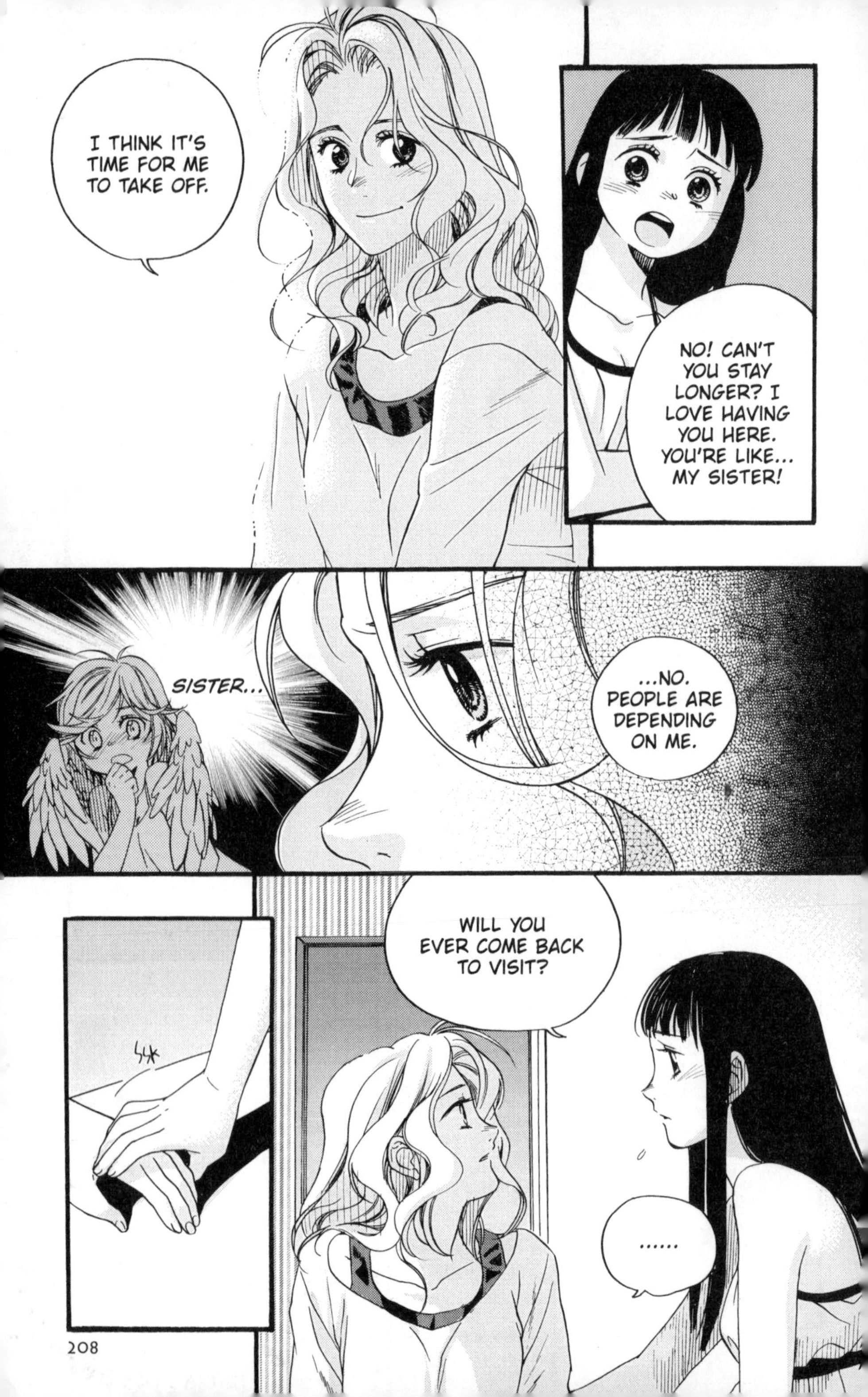
I THINK IT'S TIME FOR ME TO TAKE OFF.
NO! CAN'T YOU STAY LONGER? I LOVE HAVING YOU HERE. YOU'RE LIKE... MY SISTER!
SISTER...
...NO. PEOPLE ARE DEPENDING ON ME.
SSK
WILL YOU EVER COME BACK TO VISIT?
......

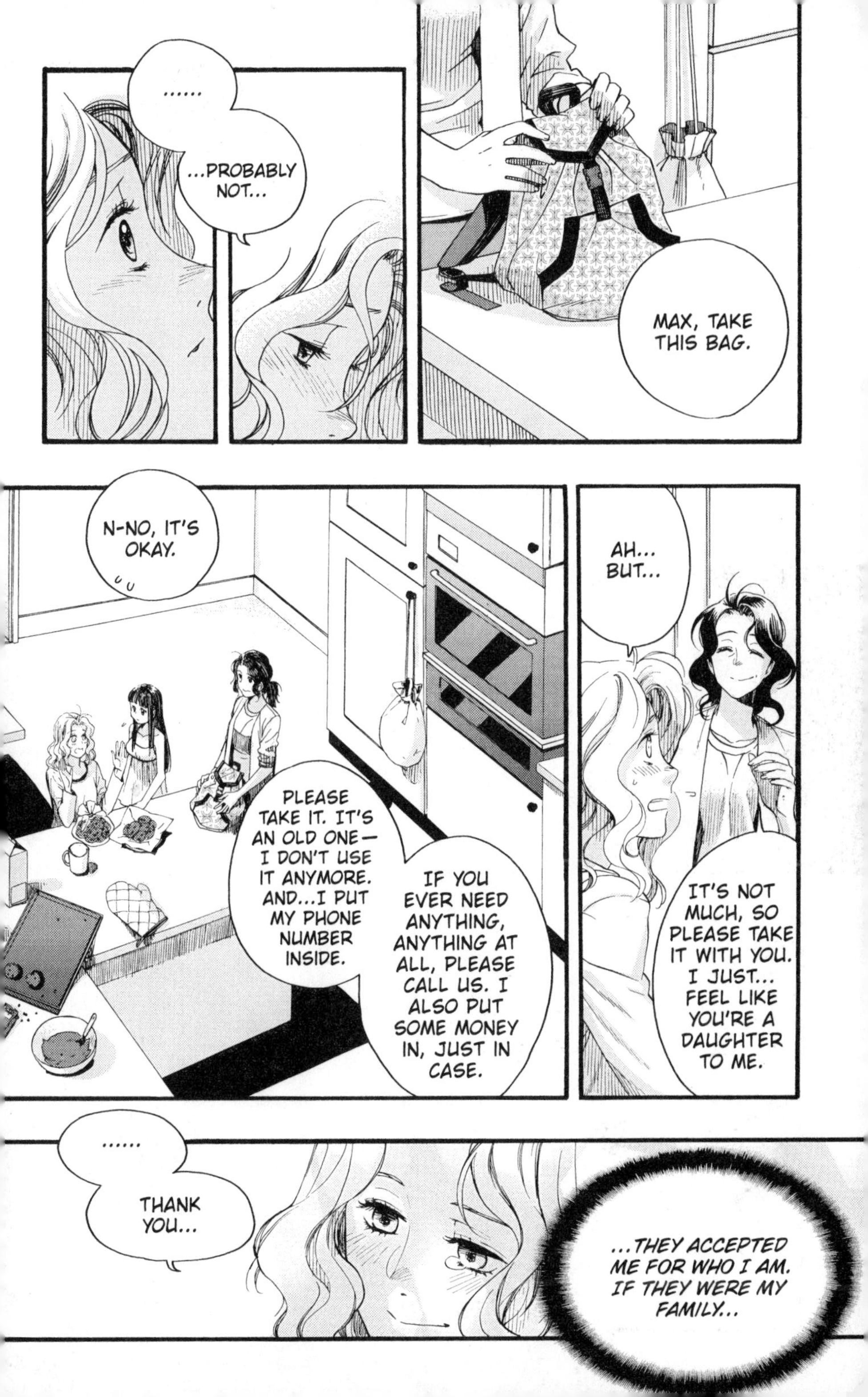
......
...PROBABLY NOT...
MAX, TAKE THIS BAG.
N-NO, IT'S OKAY.
PLEASE TAKE IT. IT'S AN OLD ONE—I DON'T USE IT ANYMORE. AND...I PUT MY PHONE NUMBER INSIDE.
IF YOU EVER NEED ANYTHING, ANYTHING AT ALL, PLEASE CALL US. I ALSO PUT SOME MONEY IN, JUST IN CASE.
AH... BUT...
IT'S NOT MUCH, SO PLEASE TAKE IT WITH YOU. I JUST... FEEL LIKE YOU'RE A DAUGHTER TO ME.
......
THANK YOU...
...THEY ACCEPTED ME FOR WHO I AM. IF THEY WERE MY FAMILY...

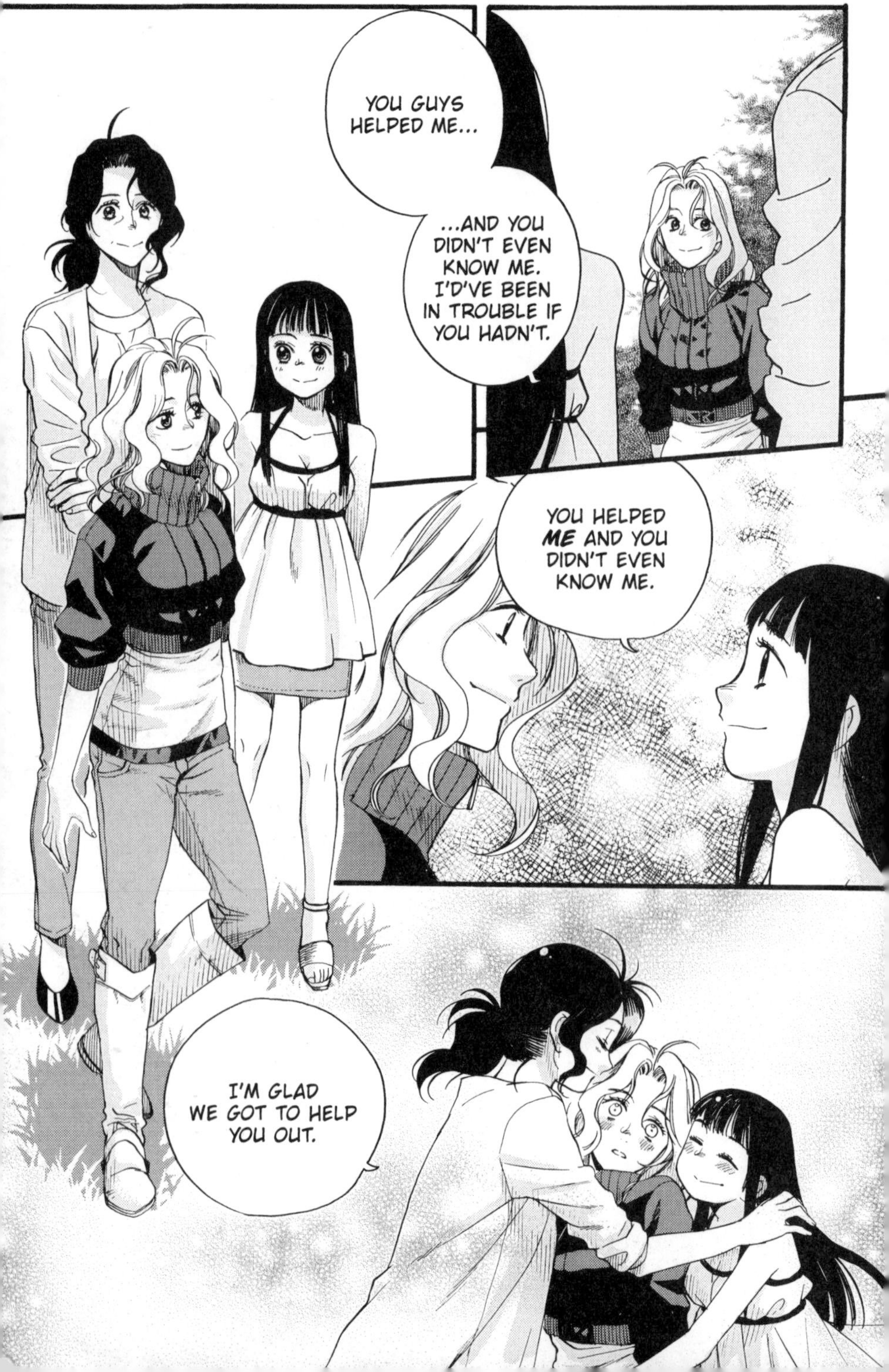
YOU GUYS HELPED ME...
...AND YOU DIDN'T EVEN KNOW ME. I'D'VE BEEN IN TROUBLE IF YOU HADN'T.
YOU HELPED *ME* AND YOU DIDN'T EVEN KNOW ME.
I'M GLAD WE GOT TO HELP YOU OUT.

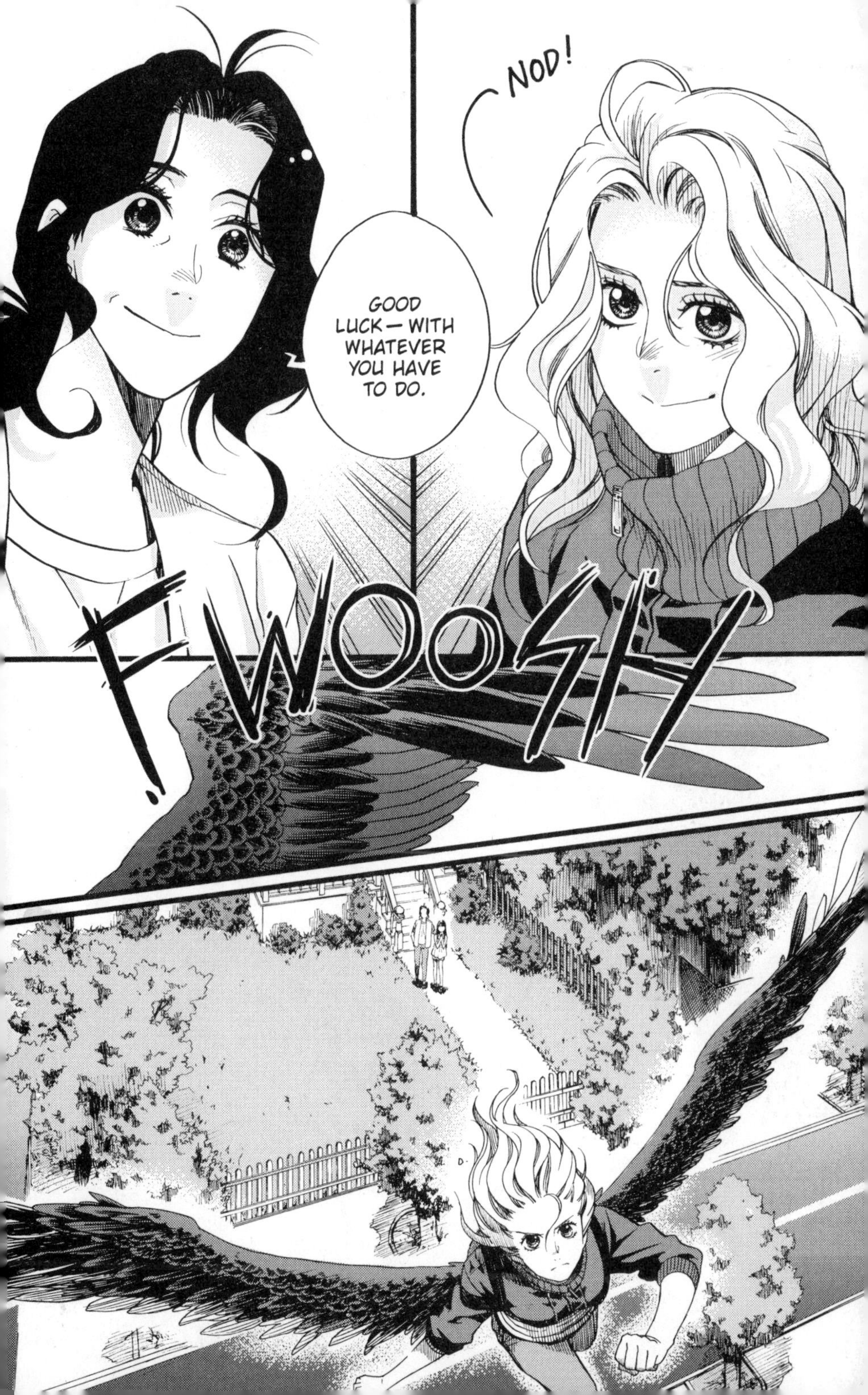
GOOD LUCK—WITH WHATEVER YOU HAVE TO DO.
NOD!
FWOOSH

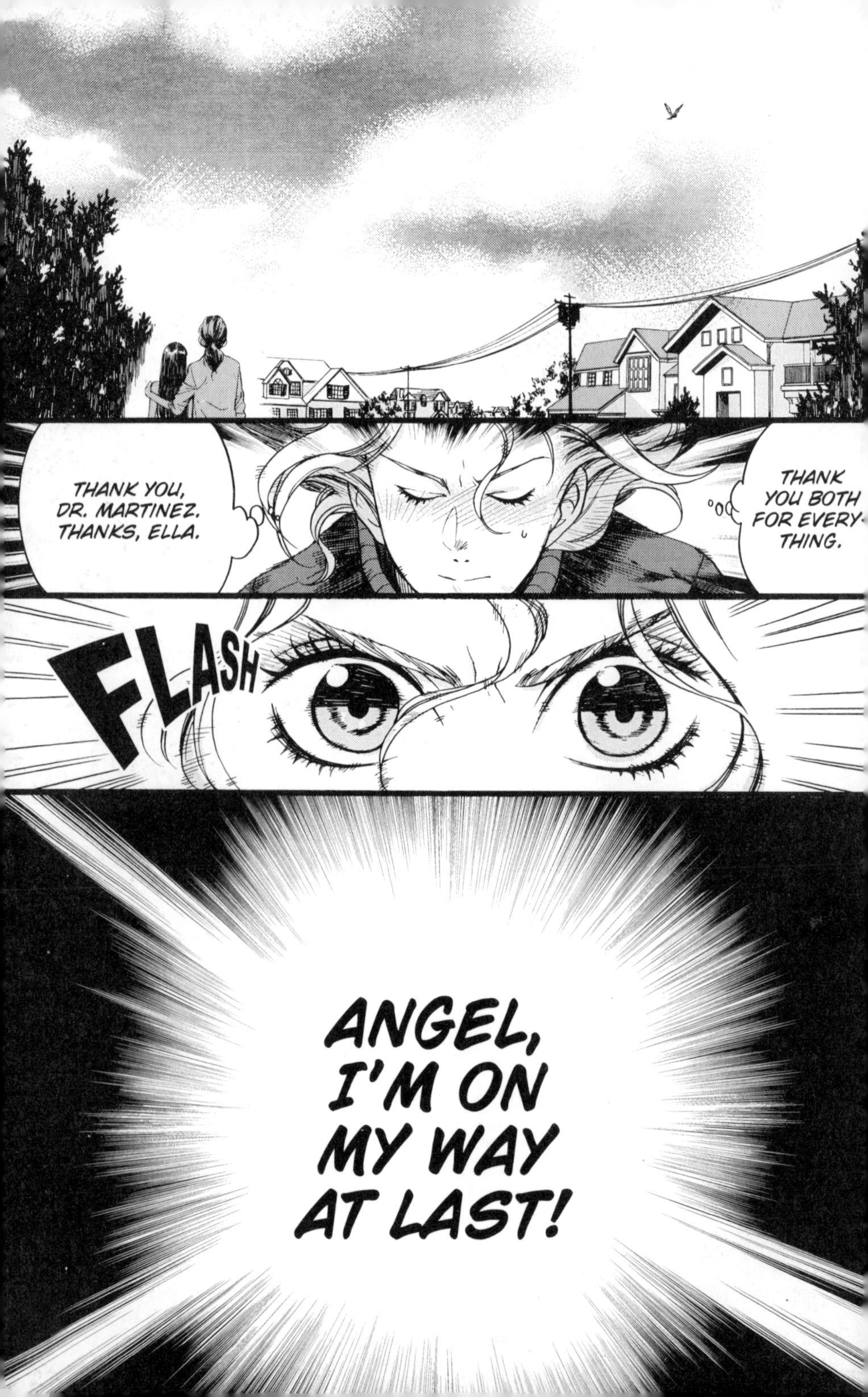

THANK YOU, DR. MARTINEZ. THANKS, ELLA.
THANK YOU BOTH FOR EVERY-THING.
FLASH
ANGEL, I'M ON MY WAY AT LAST!

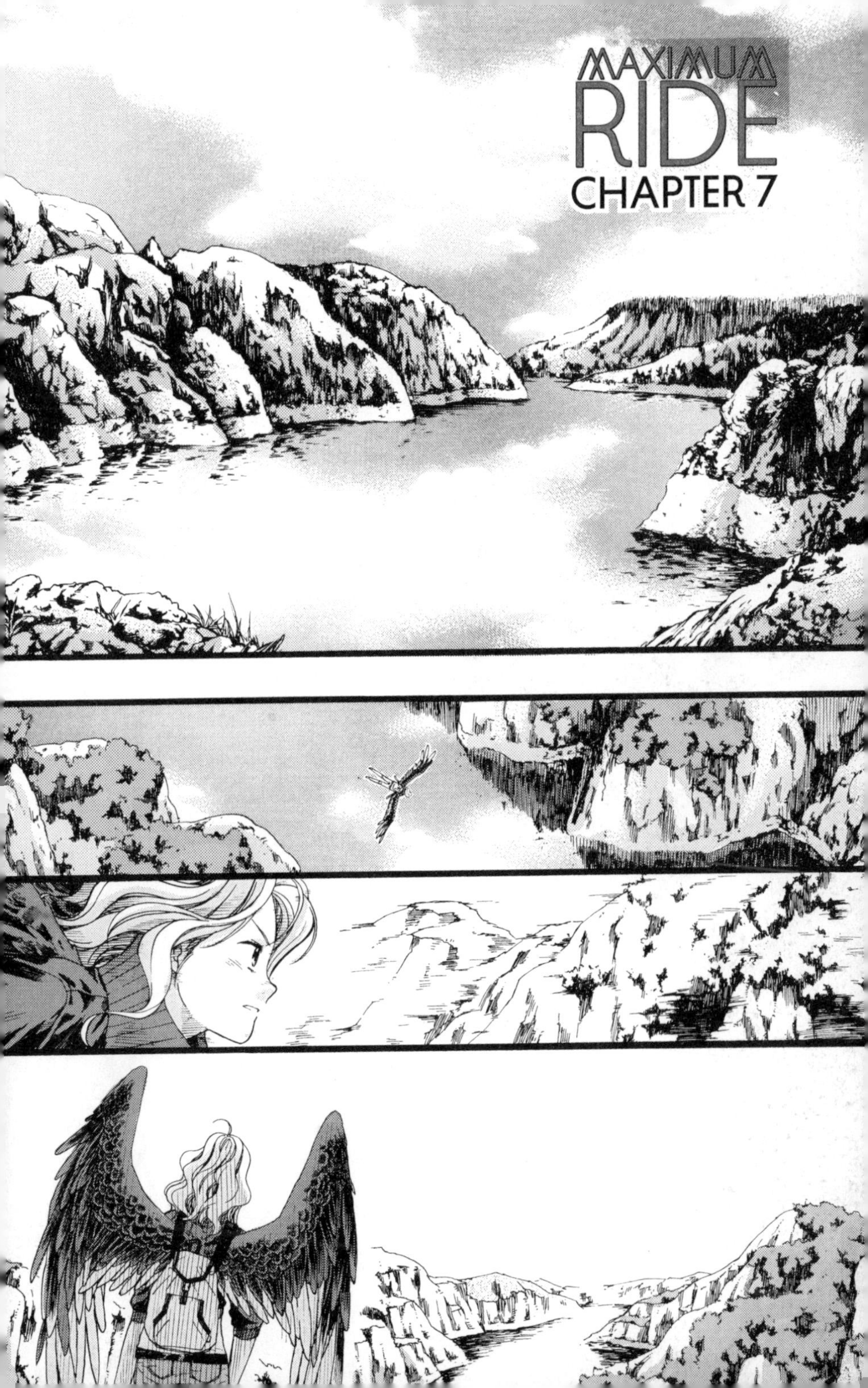
MAXIMUM RIDE
CHAPTER 7

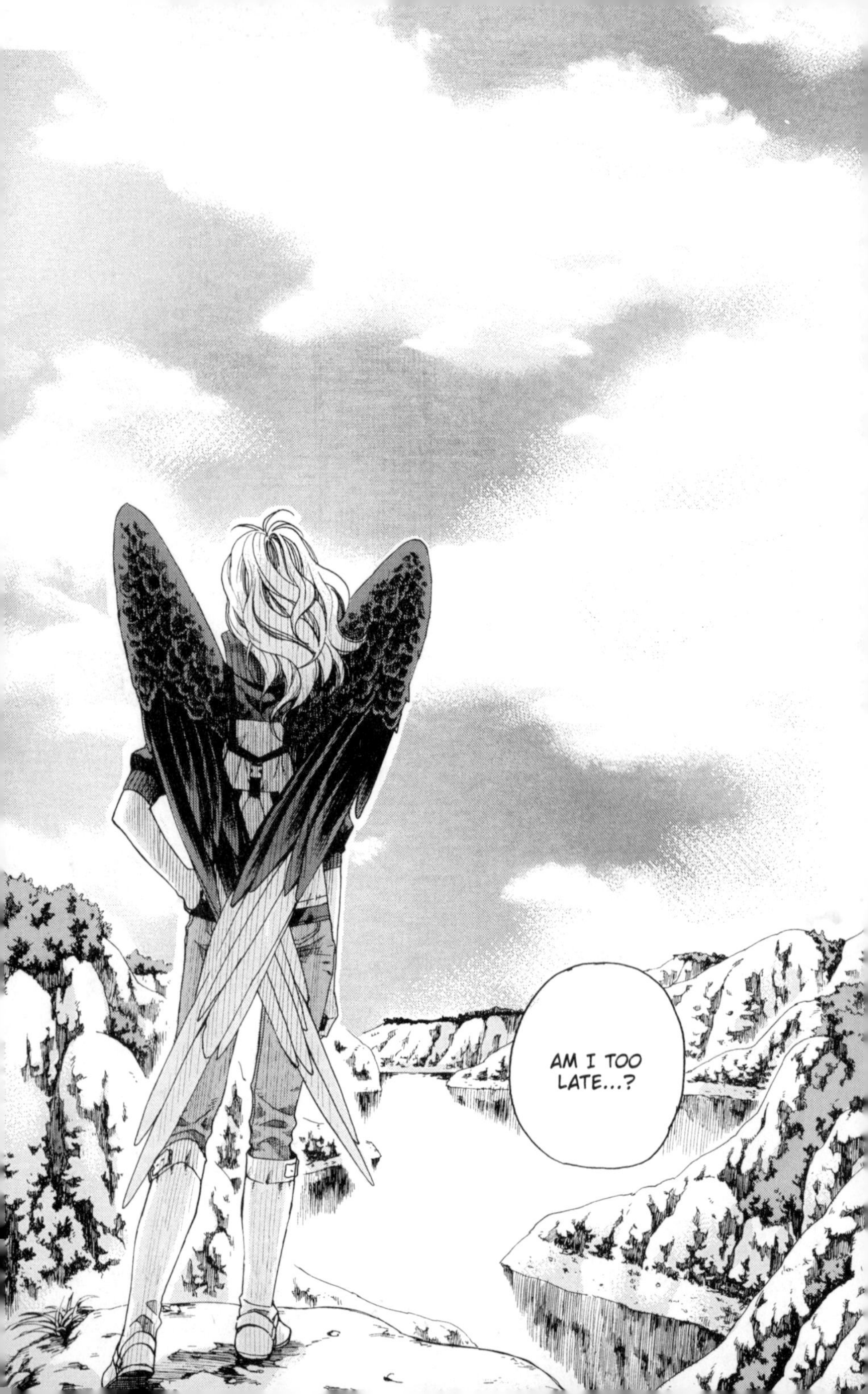
AM I TOO LATE...?

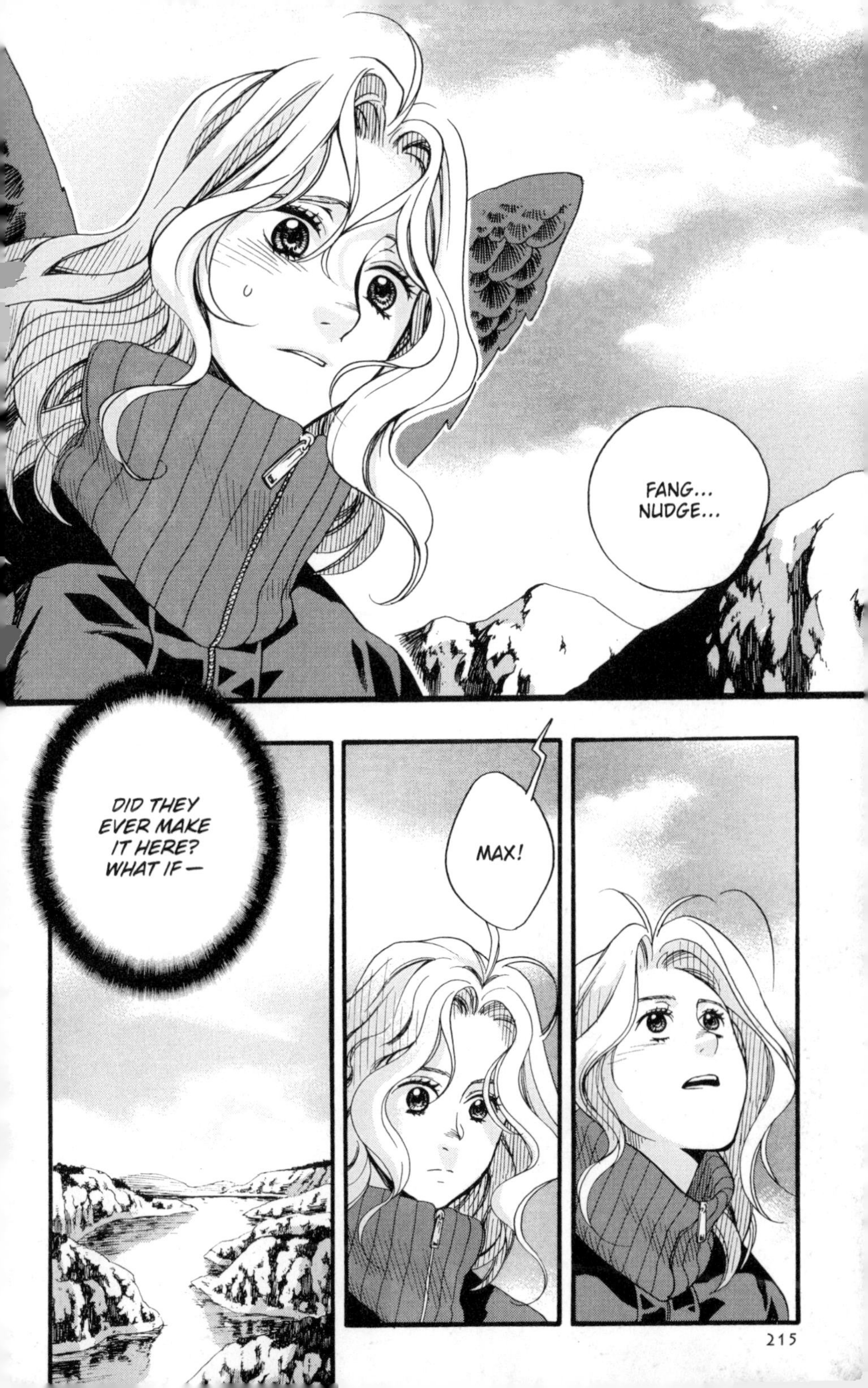
FANG... NUDGE...
DID THEY EVER MAKE IT HERE? WHAT IF—
MAX!

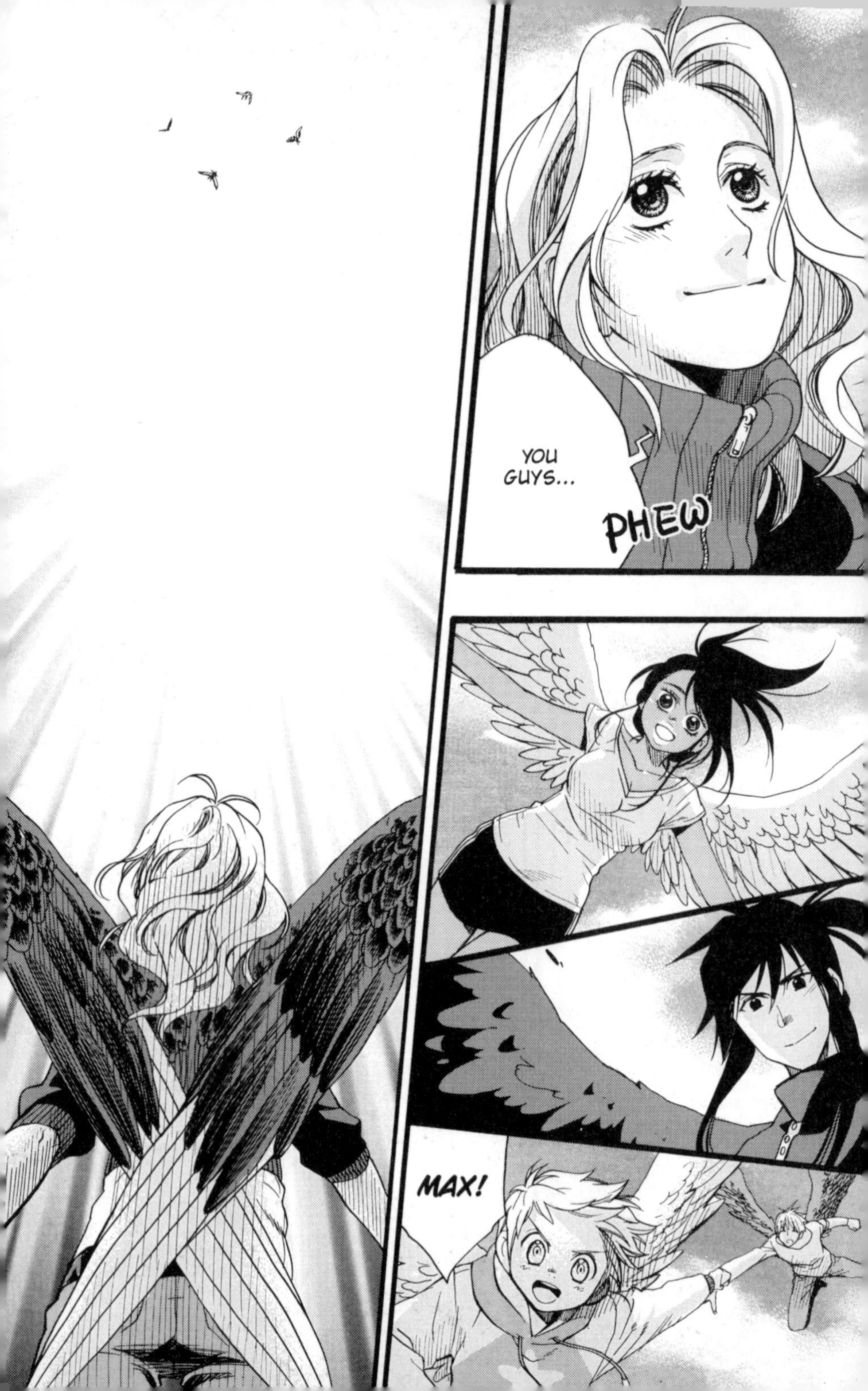
YOU GUYS...
PHEW
MAX!

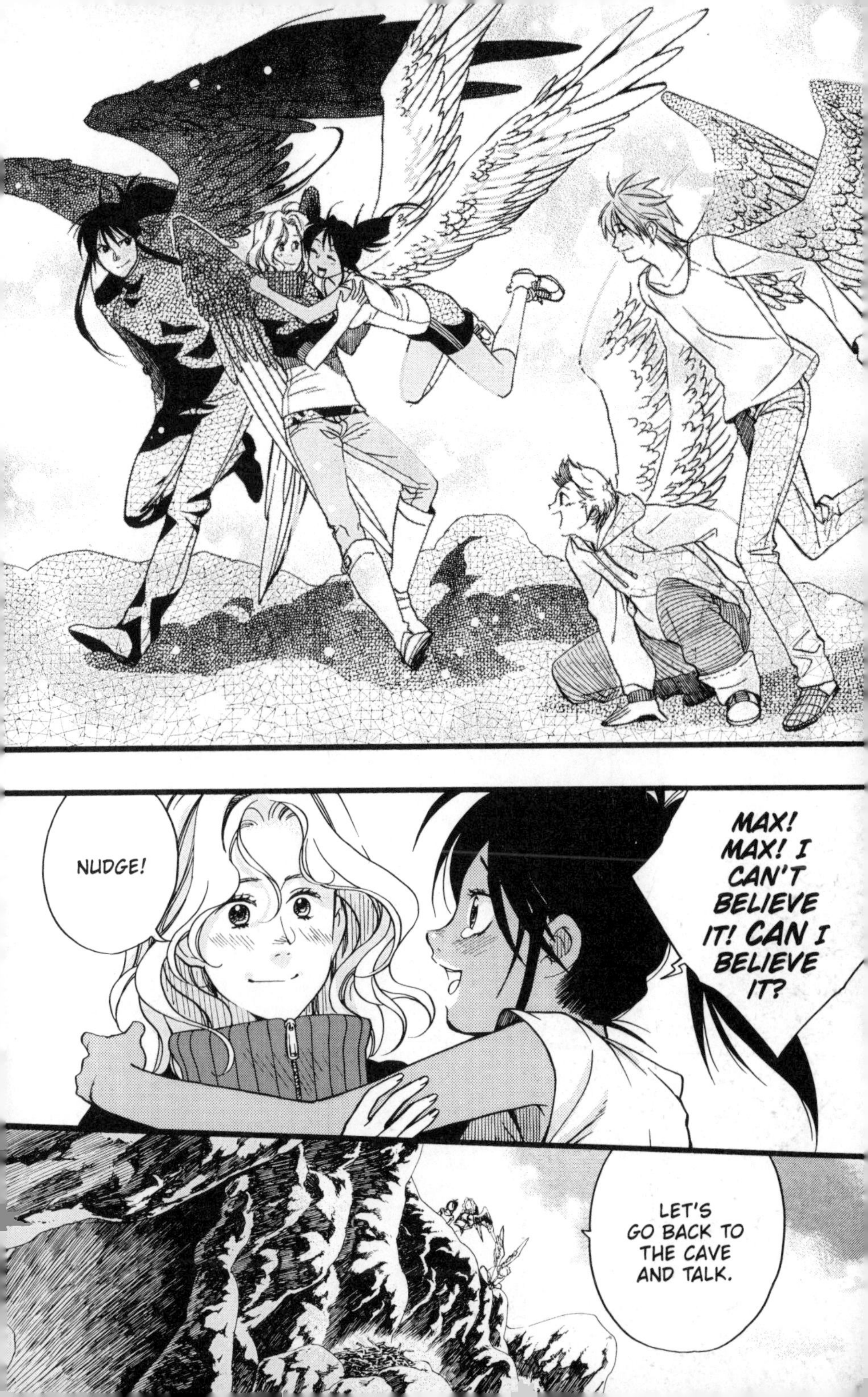
NUDGE!
MAX! MAX! I CAN'T BELIEVE IT! CAN I BELIEVE IT?
LET'S GO BACK TO THE CAVE AND TALK.

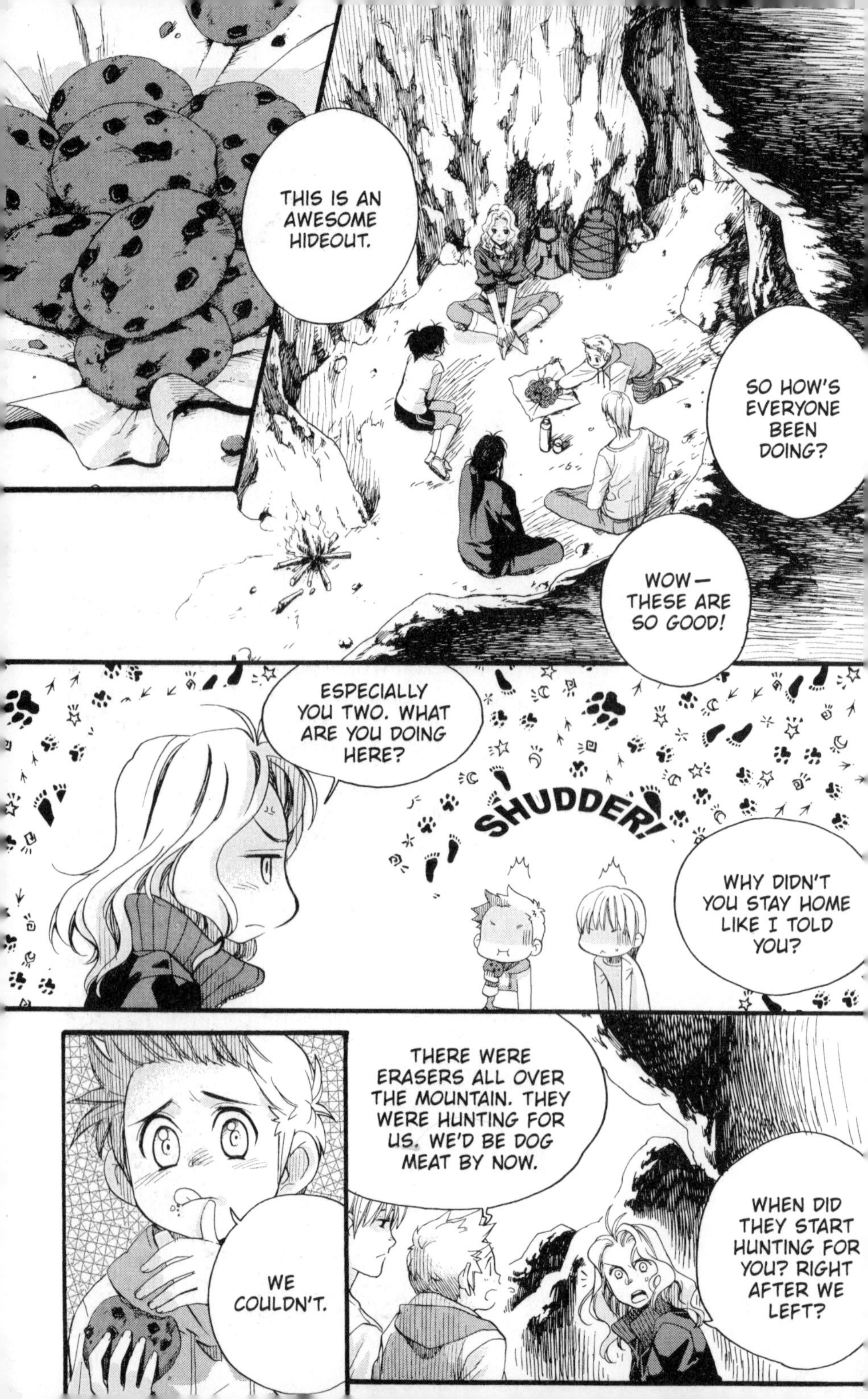
THIS IS AN AWESOME HIDEOUT.
SO HOW'S EVERYONE BEEN DOING?
WOW— THESE ARE SO GOOD!
ESPECIALLY YOU TWO. WHAT ARE YOU DOING HERE?
SHUDDER!
WHY DIDN'T YOU STAY HOME LIKE I TOLD YOU?
WE COULDN'T.
THERE WERE ERASERS ALL OVER THE MOUNTAIN. THEY WERE HUNTING FOR US. WE'D BE DOG MEAT BY NOW.
WHEN DID THEY START HUNTING FOR YOU? RIGHT AFTER WE LEFT?

NO...

WAS IT... WAS IT AFTER THE OIL-SLICK HUMMER CRASH?

OIL-SLICK HUMMER CRASH?!

OR MAYBE IT WAS... AFTER THE BOMB.

NOD

I THINK IT WAS THE BOMB. THAT DEFINITELY SEEMED TO TICK THEM OFF.

BOMB ?!

YOU GUYS SET OFF A BOMB? DIDN'T THAT TELL THE ERASERS EXACTLY WHERE YOU WERE?

YOU SHOULD HAVE STAYED HIDDEN!

BUT THEY ALREADY KNEW WHERE WE WERE!

THEY'D SEEN ALL OF US— THEY KNEW WE WERE IN THE AREA.

......!!

THERE'S A MICROCHIP IN YOUR FORE-ARM.

WELL, I'M GLAD YOU'RE SAFE.

HOW WERE YOU GUYS, FANG AND NUDGE?

SORRY TO KEEP YOU WAITING...

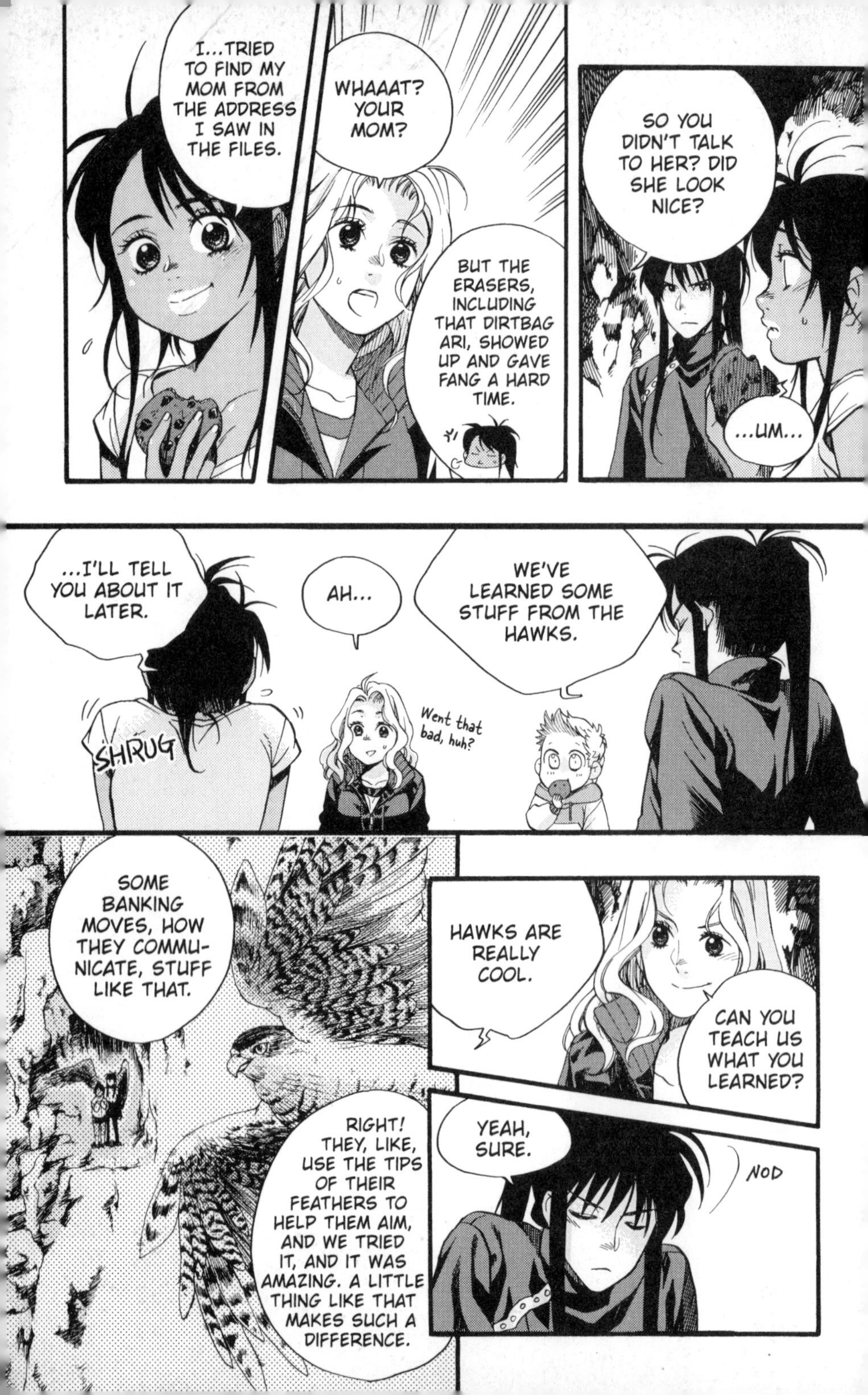
I...TRIED TO FIND MY MOM FROM THE ADDRESS I SAW IN THE FILES.
WHAAAT? YOUR MOM?
BUT THE ERASERS, INCLUDING THAT DIRTBAG ARI, SHOWED UP AND GAVE FANG A HARD TIME.
SO YOU DIDN'T TALK TO HER? DID SHE LOOK NICE?
...UM...
...I'LL TELL YOU ABOUT IT LATER.
SHRUG
AH...
Went that bad, huh?
WE'VE LEARNED SOME STUFF FROM THE HAWKS.
SOME BANKING MOVES, HOW THEY COMMUNICATE, STUFF LIKE THAT.
RIGHT! THEY, LIKE, USE THE TIPS OF THEIR FEATHERS TO HELP THEM AIM, AND WE TRIED IT, AND IT WAS AMAZING. A LITTLE THING LIKE THAT MAKES SUCH A DIFFERENCE.
HAWKS ARE REALLY COOL.
CAN YOU TEACH US WHAT YOU LEARNED?
YEAH, SURE.
NOD

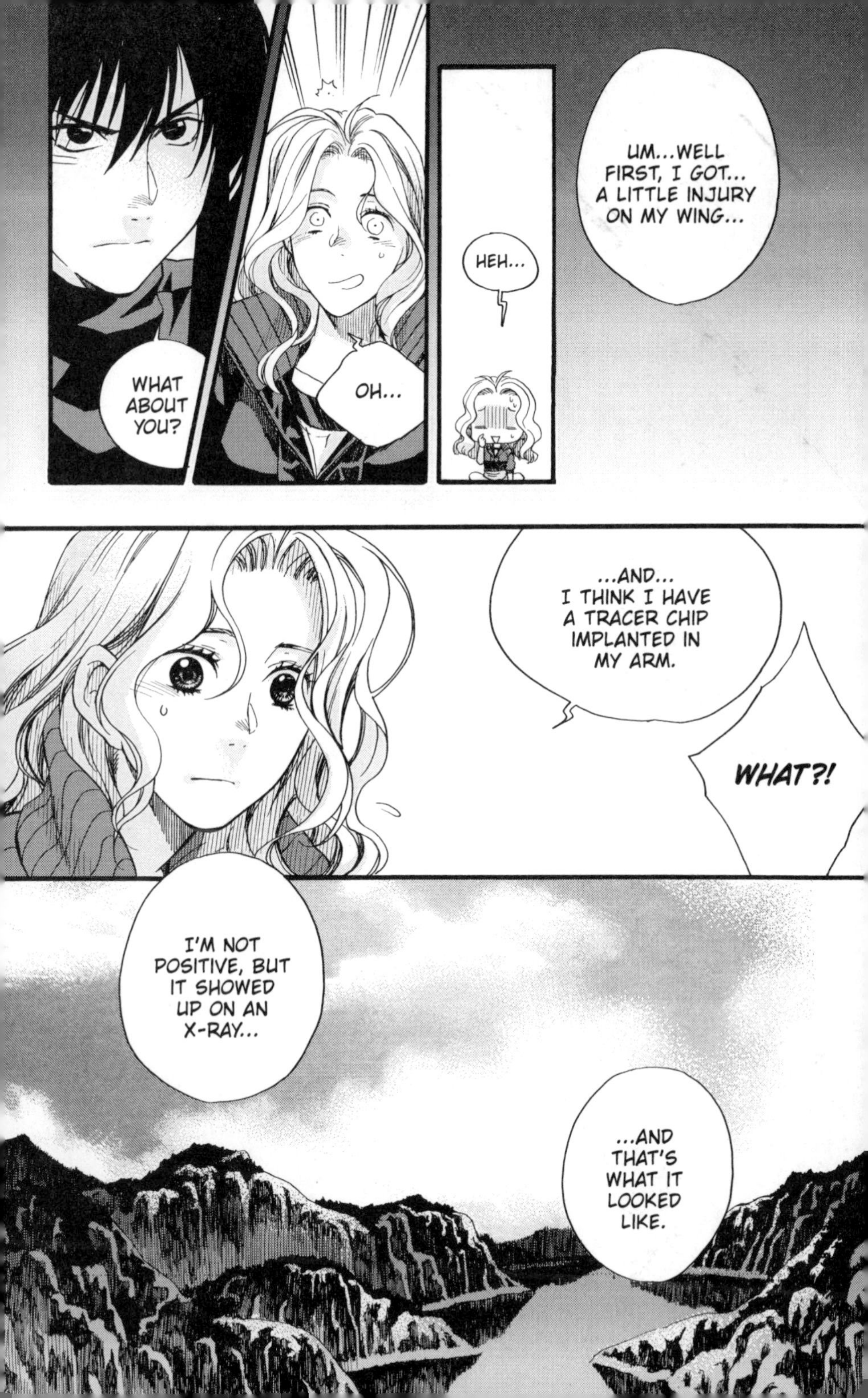
WHAT ABOUT YOU?
OH...
HEH...
UM...WELL FIRST, I GOT... A LITTLE INJURY ON MY WING...
...AND... I THINK I HAVE A TRACER CHIP IMPLANTED IN MY ARM.
WHAT?!
I'M NOT POSITIVE, BUT IT SHOWED UP ON AN X-RAY...
...AND THAT'S WHAT IT LOOKED LIKE.

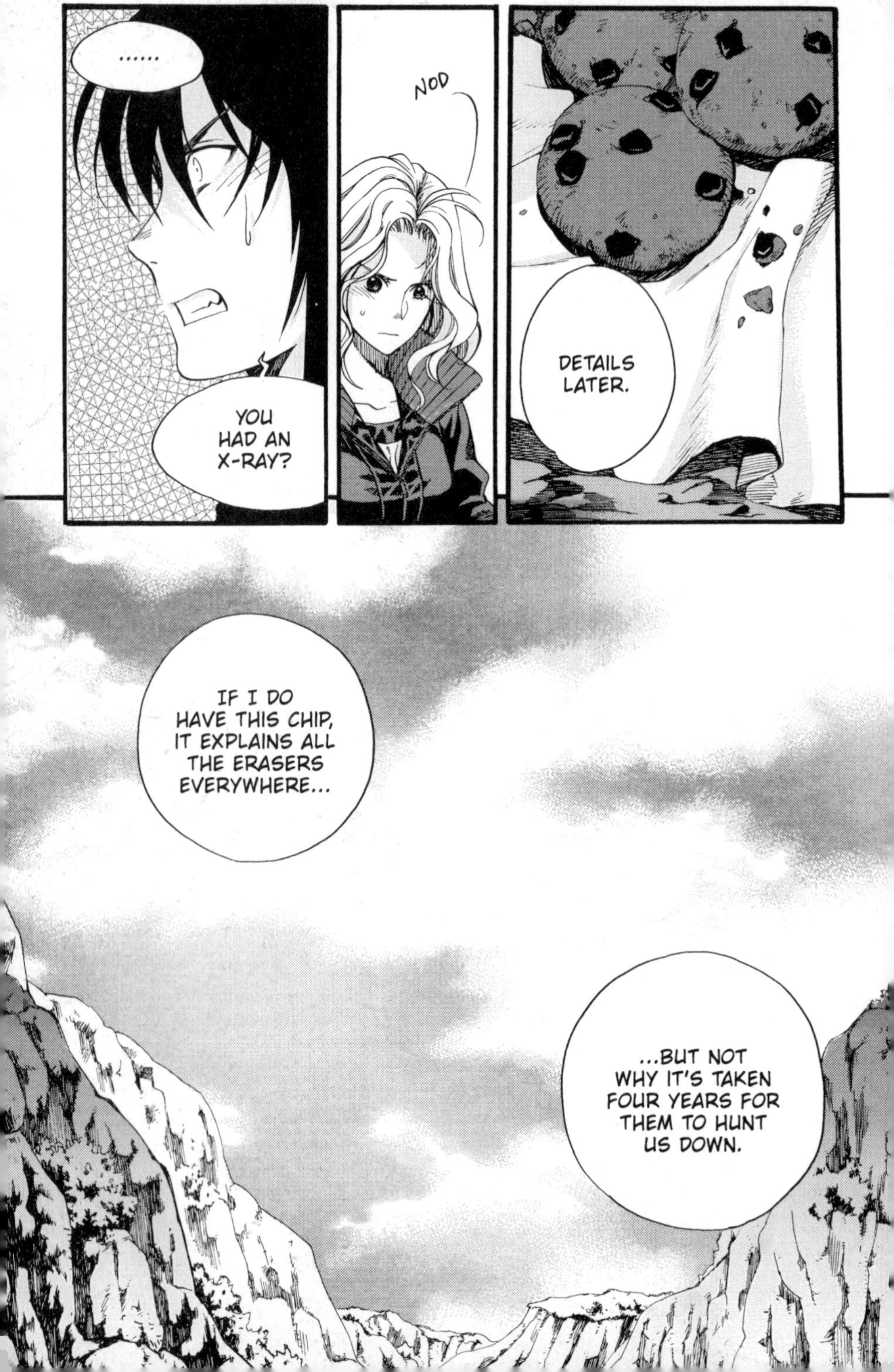
......
YOU HAD AN X-RAY?
NOD
DETAILS LATER.
IF I DO HAVE THIS CHIP, IT EXPLAINS ALL THE ERASERS EVERYWHERE...
...BUT NOT WHY IT'S TAKEN FOUR YEARS FOR THEM TO HUNT US DOWN.

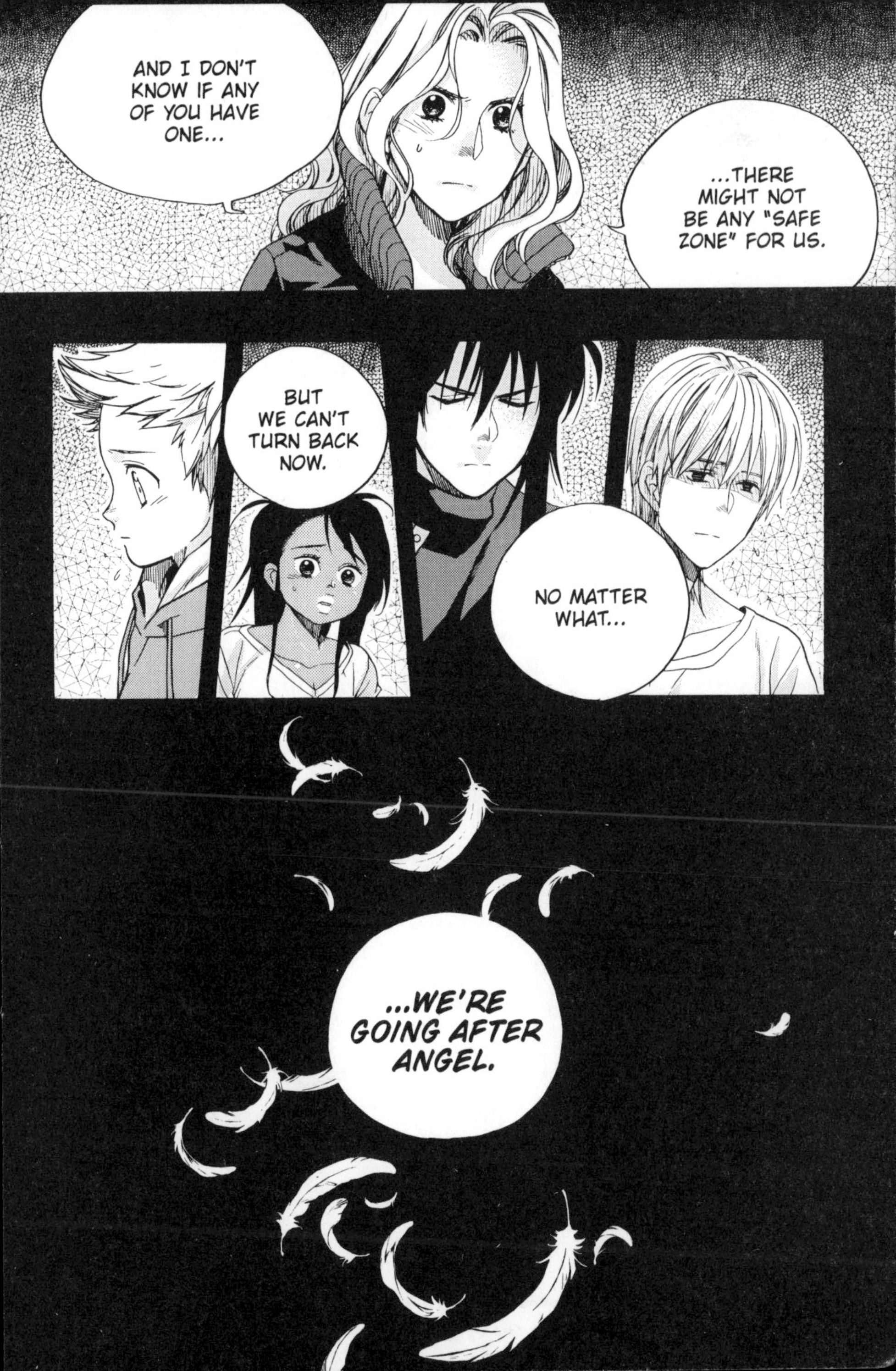
AND I DON'T KNOW IF ANY OF YOU HAVE ONE...
...THERE MIGHT NOT BE ANY "SAFE ZONE" FOR US.
BUT WE CAN'T TURN BACK NOW.
NO MATTER WHAT...
...WE'RE GOING AFTER ANGEL.

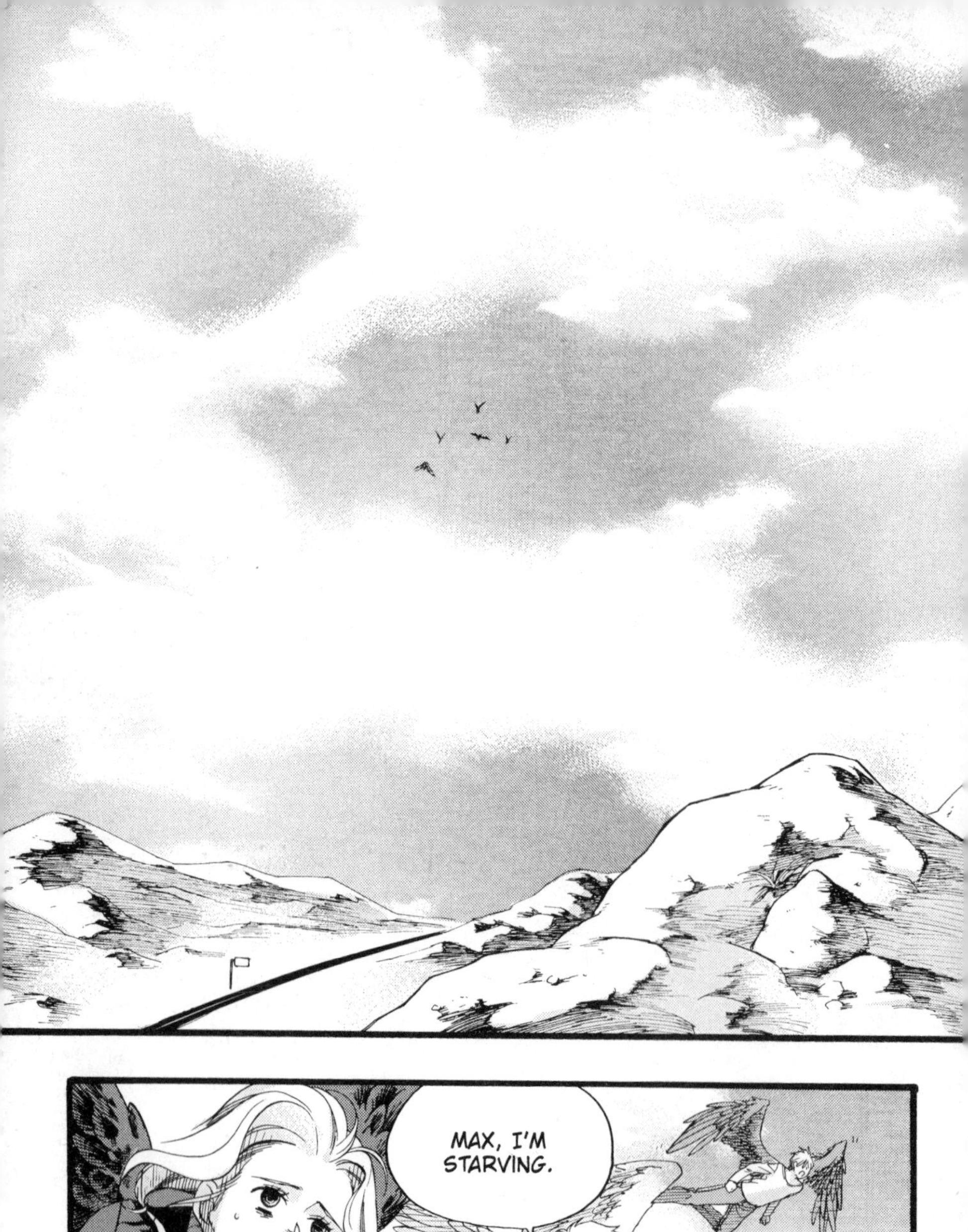

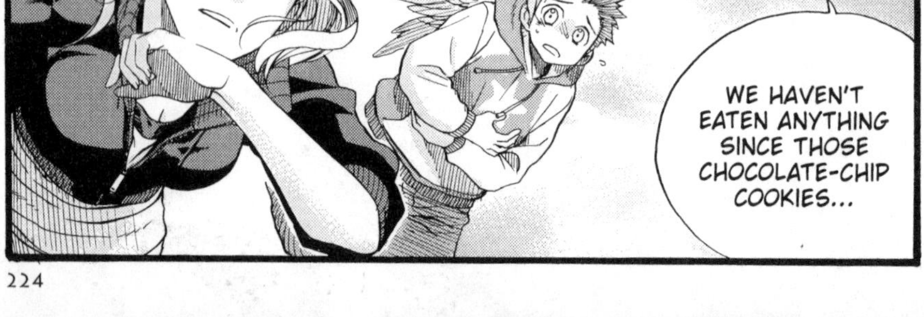
MAX, I'M STARVING.
WE HAVEN'T EATEN ANYTHING SINCE THOSE CHOCOLATE-CHIP COOKIES...

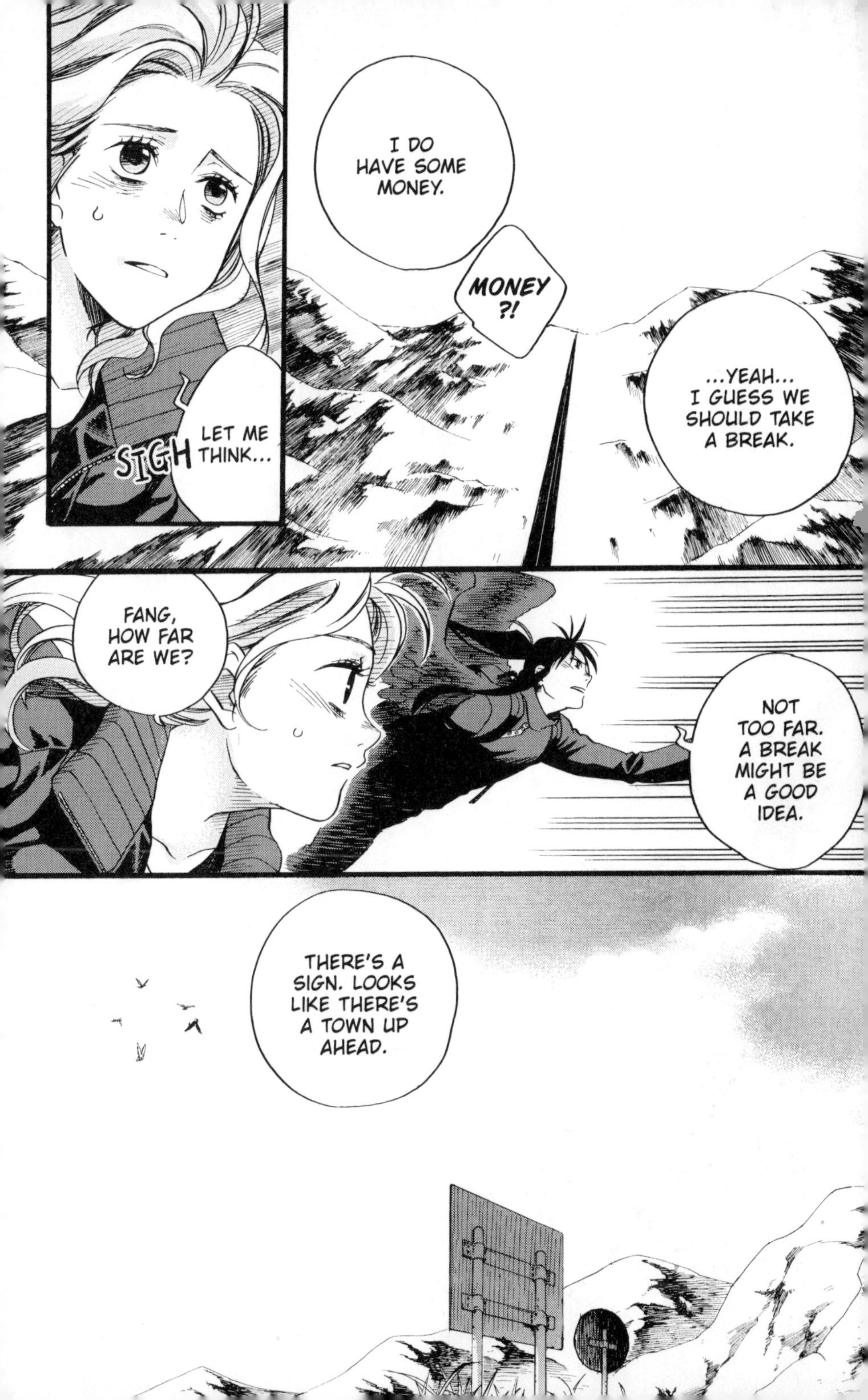

I DO HAVE SOME MONEY.
MONEY ?!
SIGH
LET ME THINK...
...YEAH... I GUESS WE SHOULD TAKE A BREAK.
FANG, HOW FAR ARE WE?
NOT TOO FAR. A BREAK MIGHT BE A GOOD IDEA.
THERE'S A SIGN. LOOKS LIKE THERE'S A TOWN UP AHEAD.

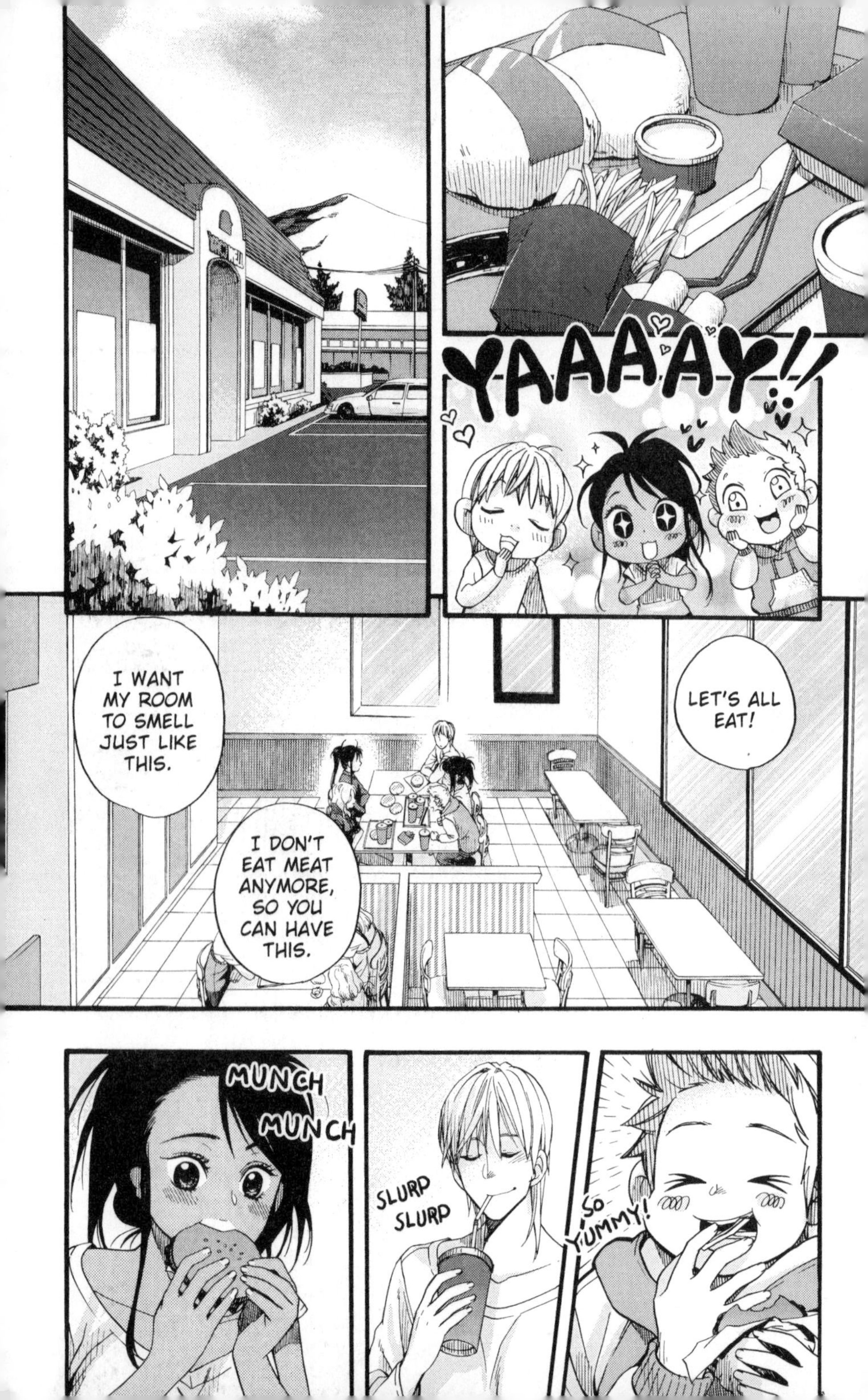
YAAAAY!!
I WANT MY ROOM TO SMELL JUST LIKE THIS.
LET'S ALL EAT!
I DON'T EAT MEAT ANYMORE, SO YOU CAN HAVE THIS.
MUNCH MUNCH
SLURP SLURP
SO YUMMY!

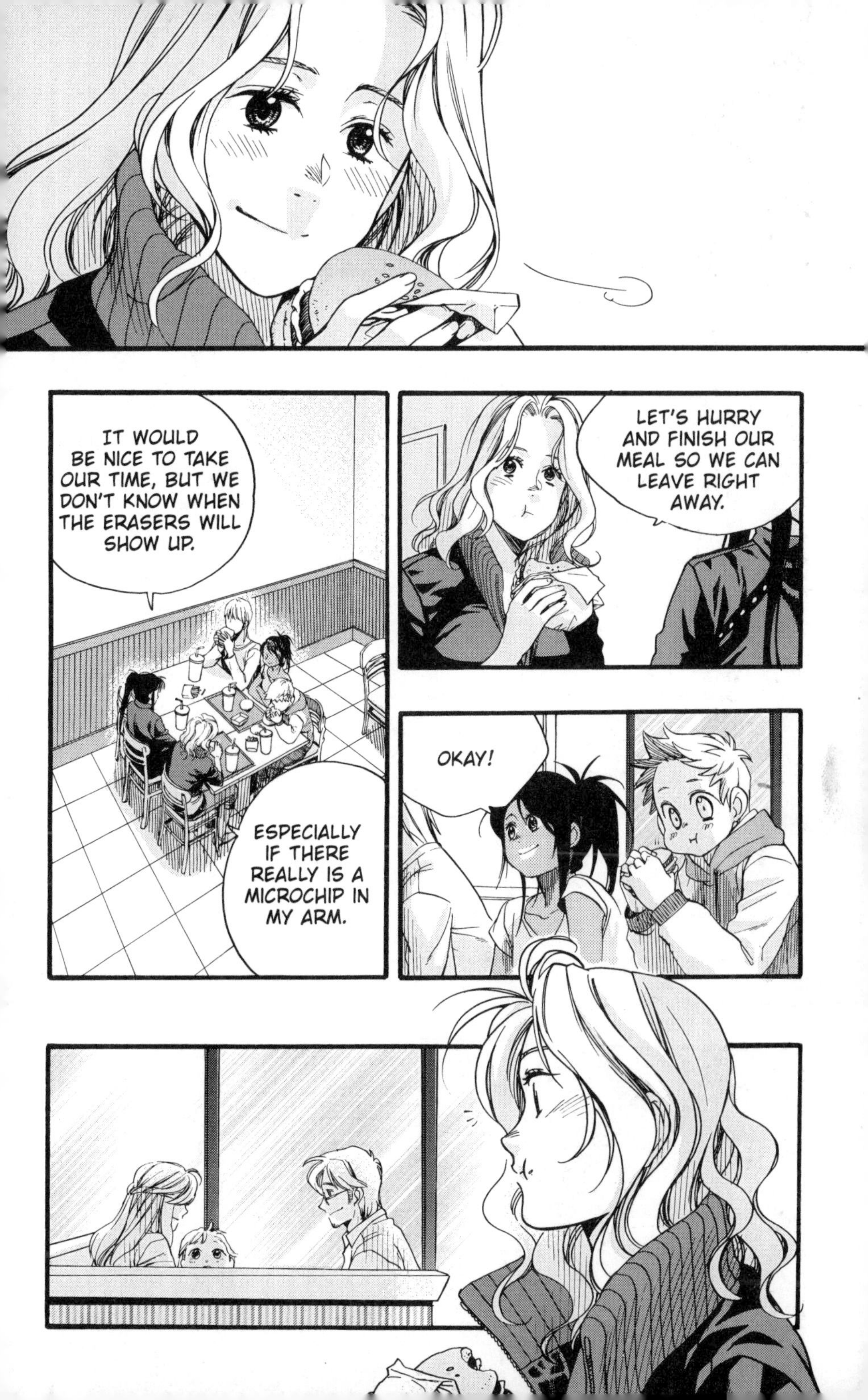
IT WOULD BE NICE TO TAKE OUR TIME, BUT WE DON'T KNOW WHEN THE ERASERS WILL SHOW UP.
ESPECIALLY IF THERE REALLY IS A MICROCHIP IN MY ARM.
LET'S HURRY AND FINISH OUR MEAL SO WE CAN LEAVE RIGHT AWAY.
OKAY!

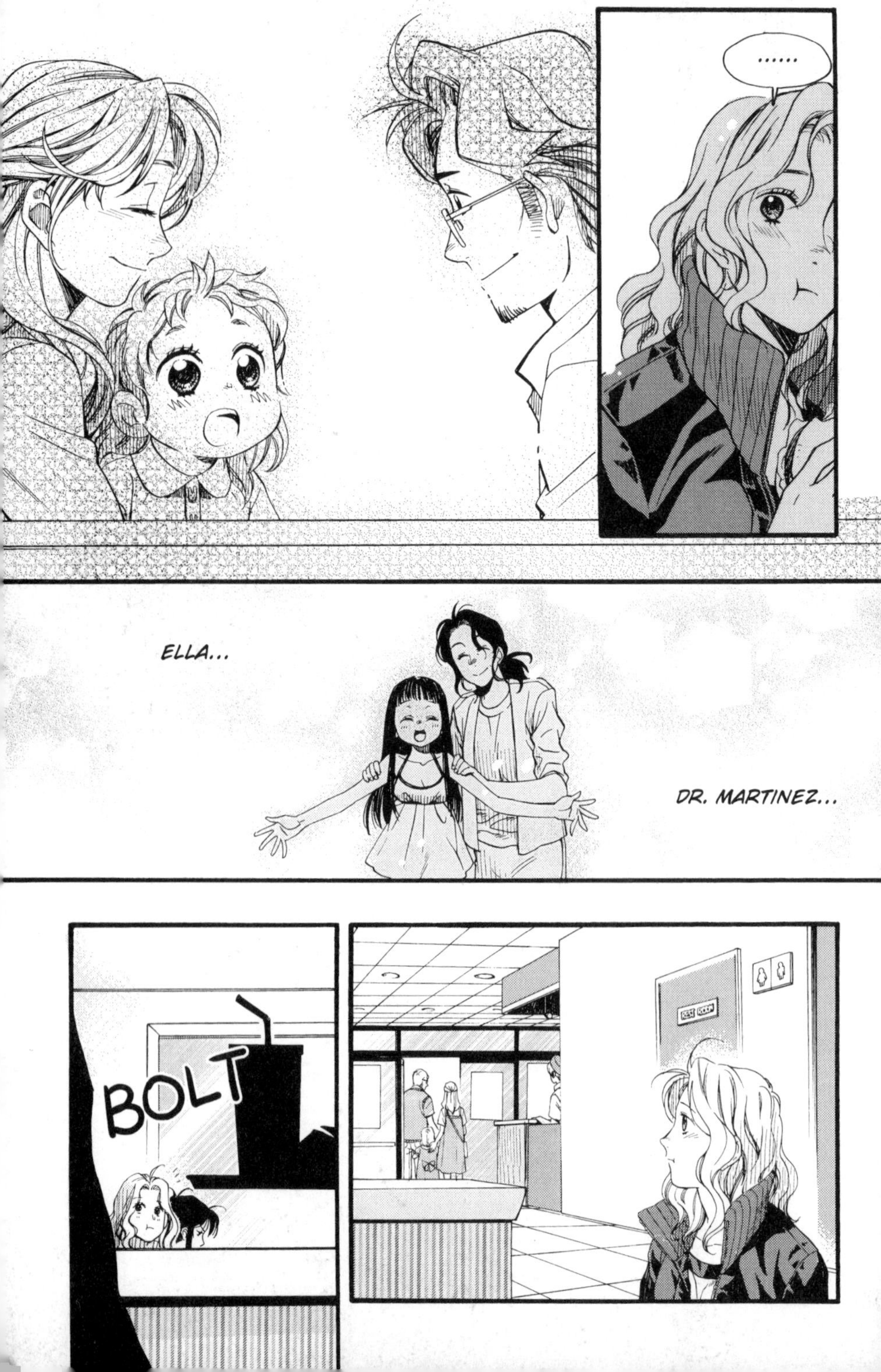
......
ELLA...
DR. MARTINEZ...
BOLT
REST ROOM

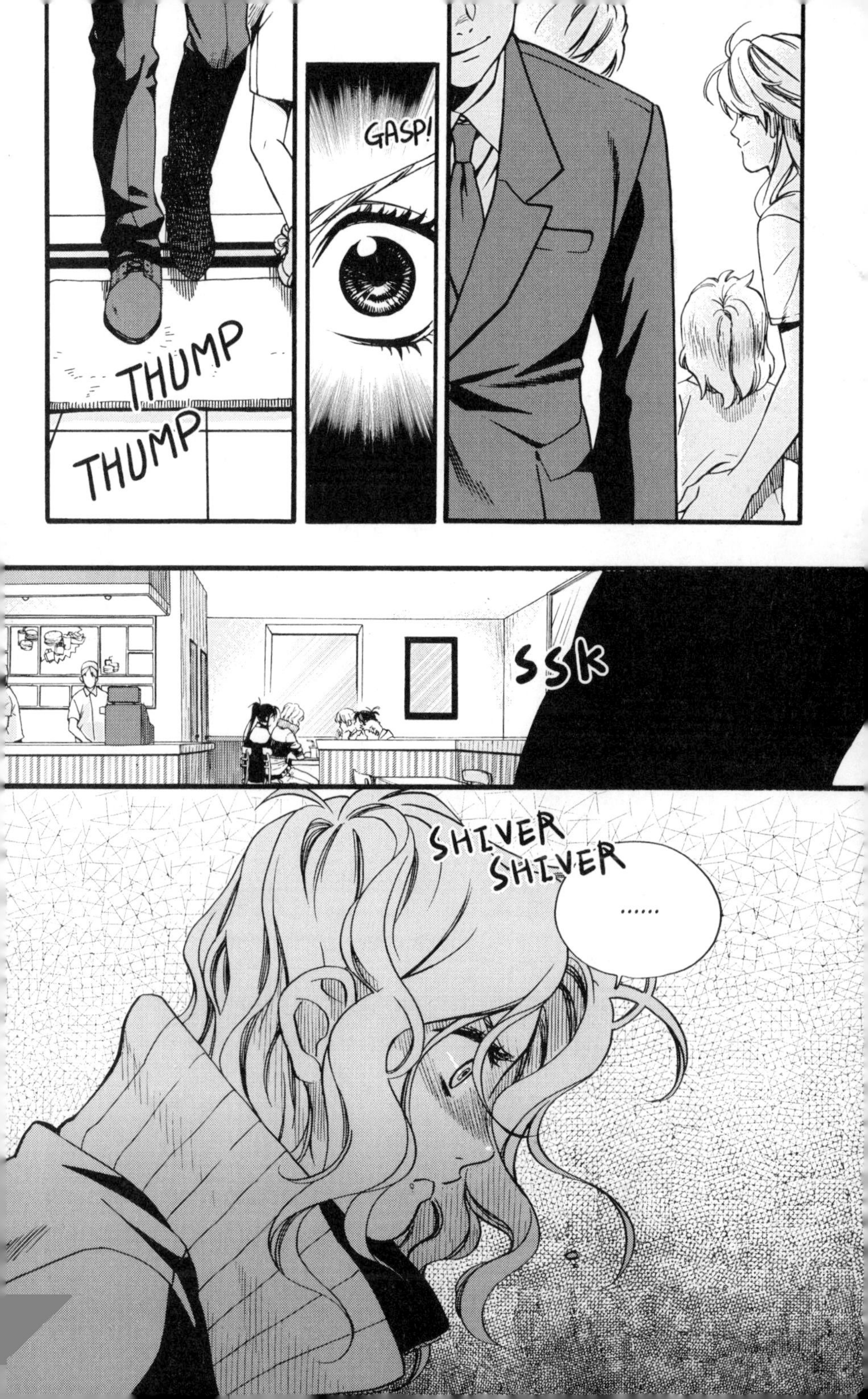
THUMP
THUMP
GASP!
SSK
SHIVER
SHIVER
......

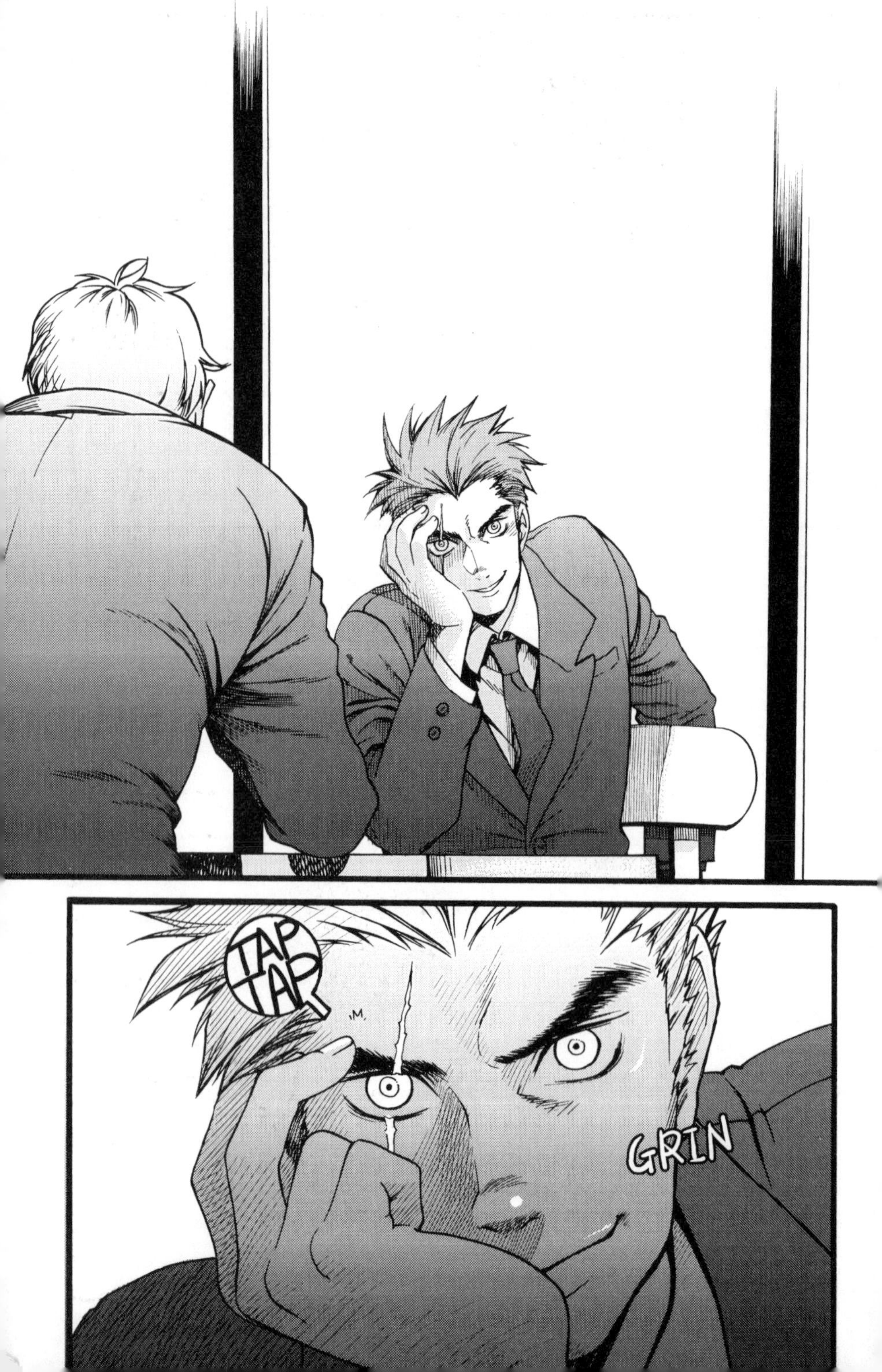
TAP TAP
GRIN

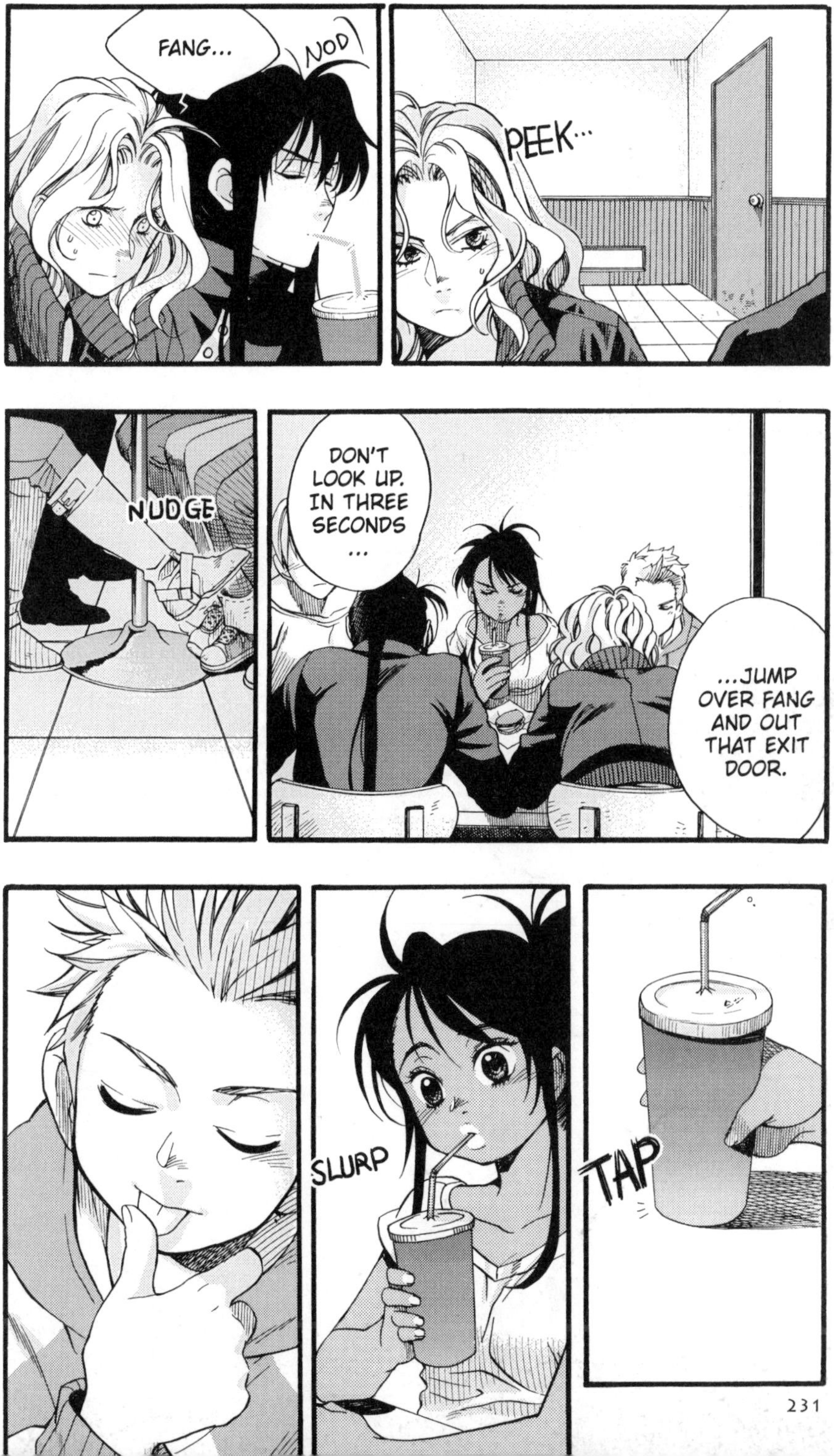
FANG...
NOD
PEEK...
NUDGE
DON'T LOOK UP. IN THREE SECONDS ...
...JUMP OVER FANG AND OUT THAT EXIT DOOR.
SLURP
TAP

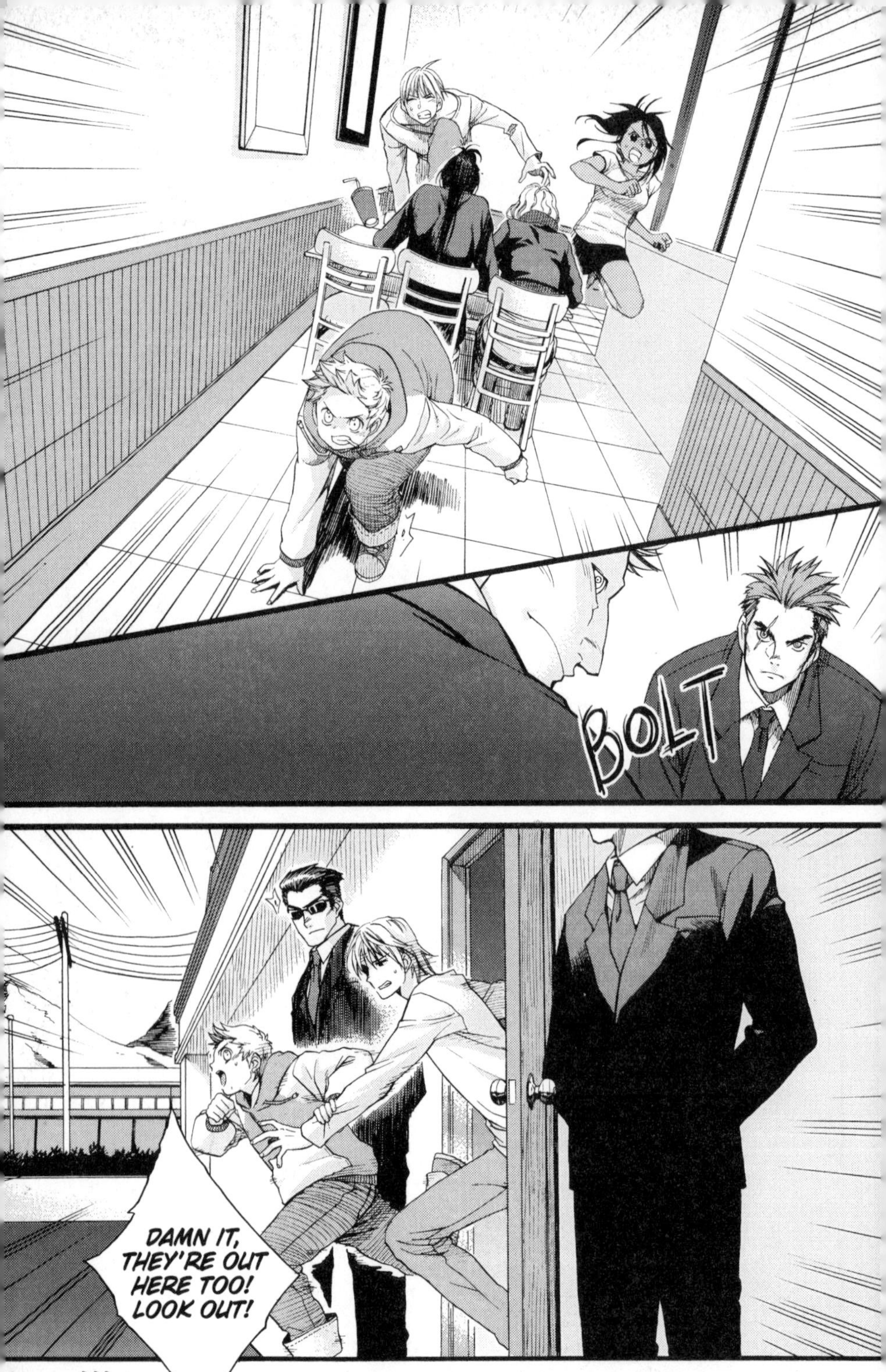
BOLT
DAMN IT, THEY'RE OUT HERE TOO! LOOK OUT!

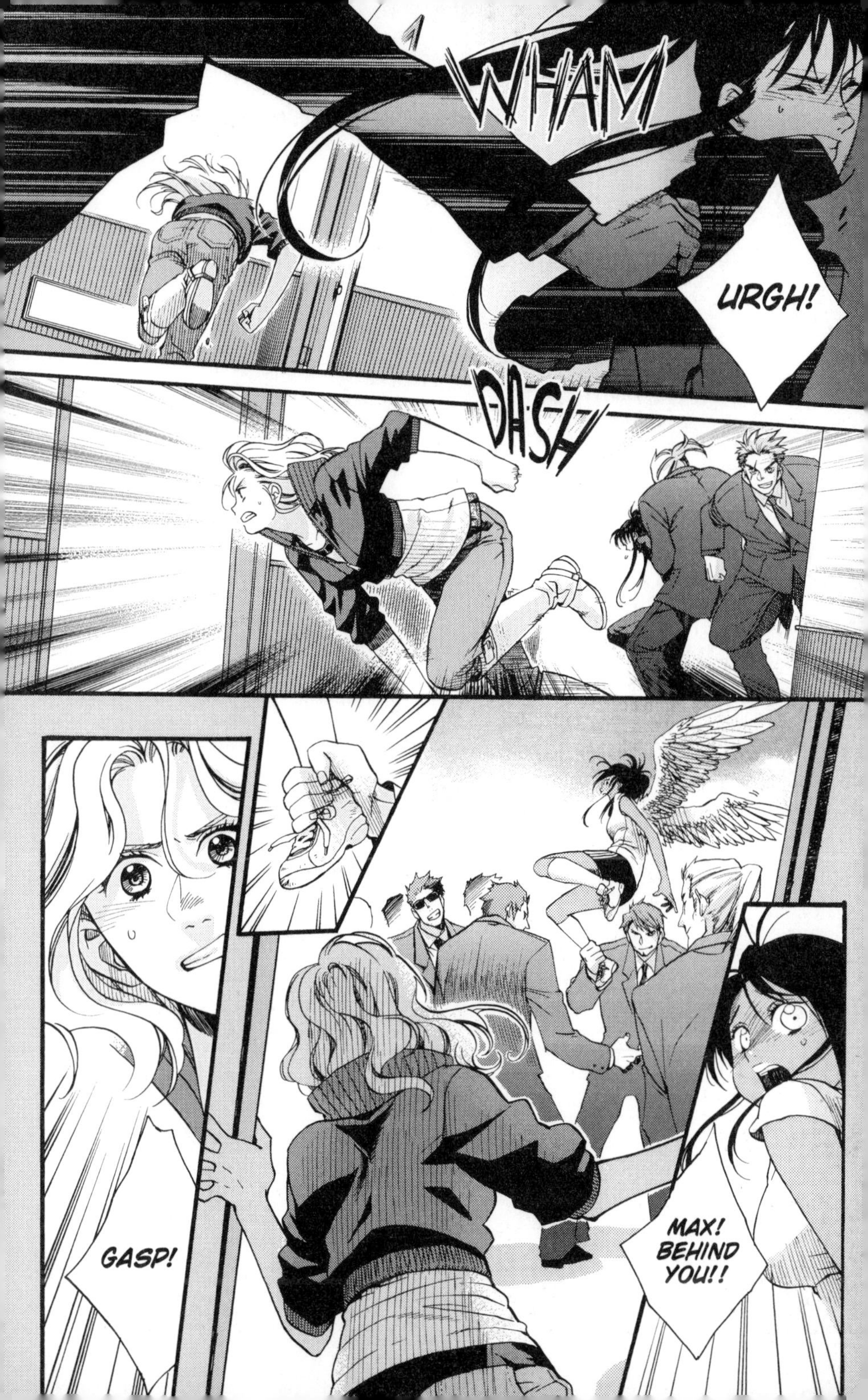
WHAM
URGH!
DASH
GASP!
MAX! BEHIND YOU!!

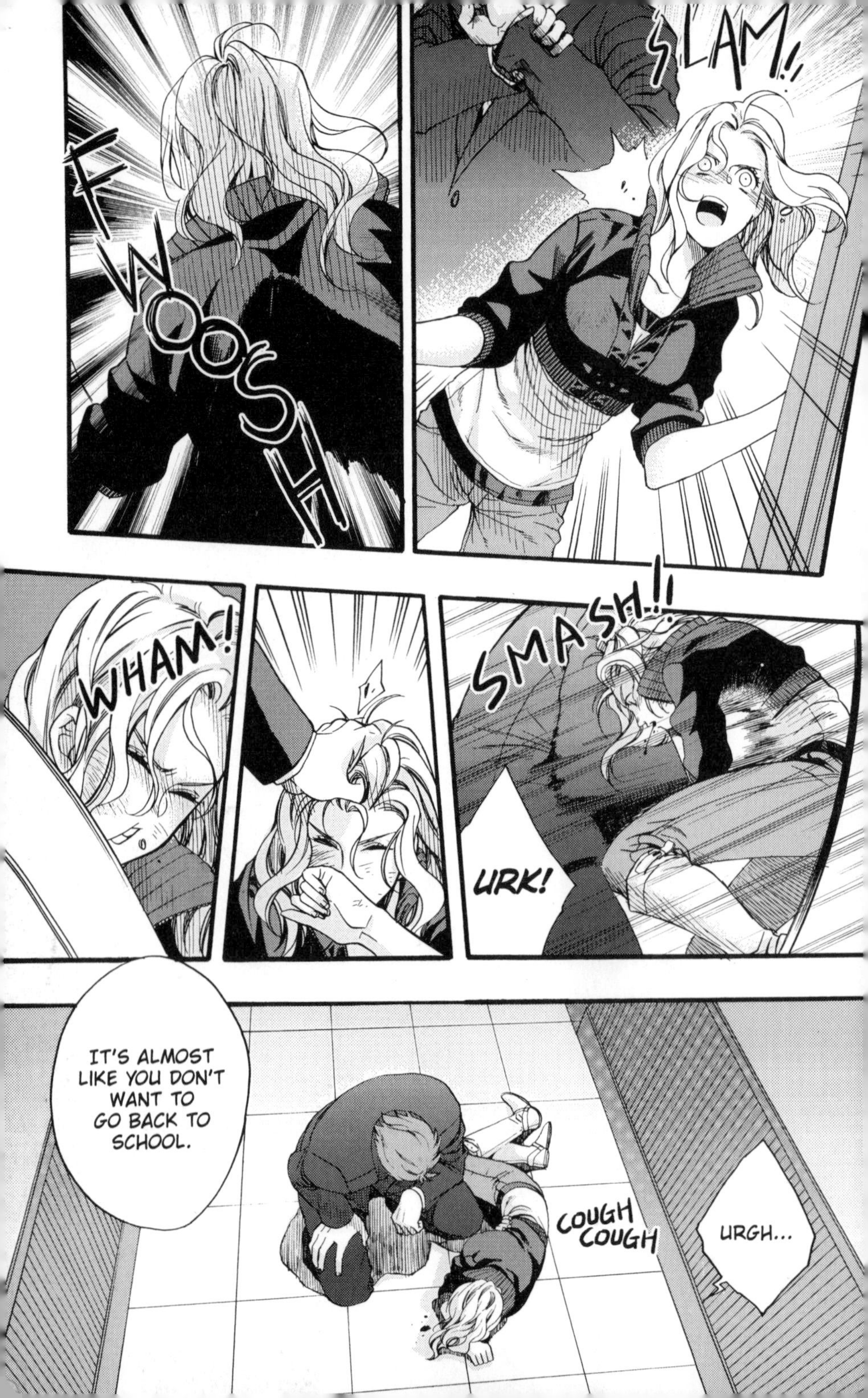
FWOOSH
SLAM!!
WHAM!
SMASH!!
URK!
IT'S ALMOST LIKE YOU DON'T WANT TO GO BACK TO SCHOOL.
COUGH COUGH
URGH...

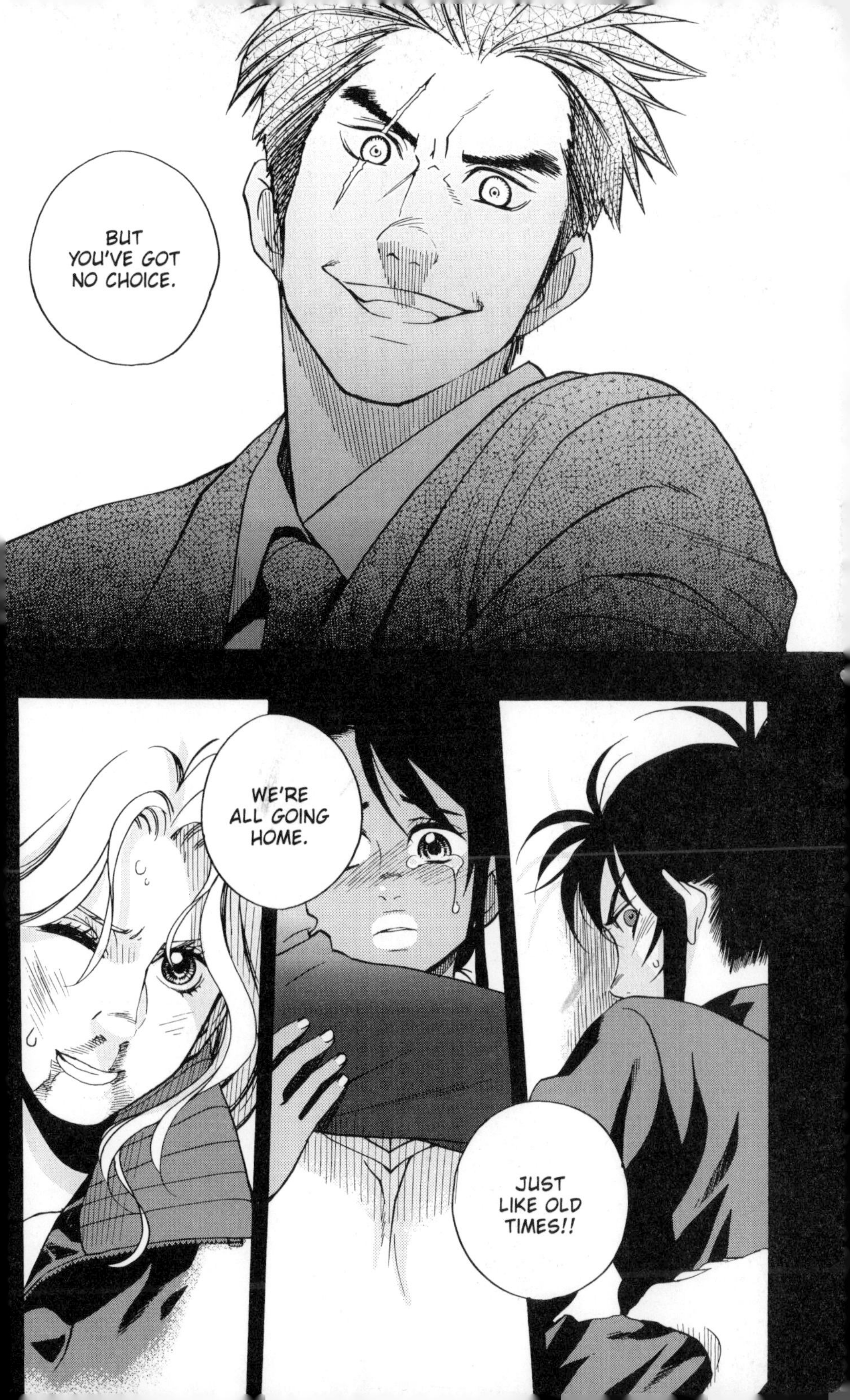
BUT YOU'VE GOT NO CHOICE.
WE'RE ALL GOING HOME.
JUST LIKE OLD TIMES!!

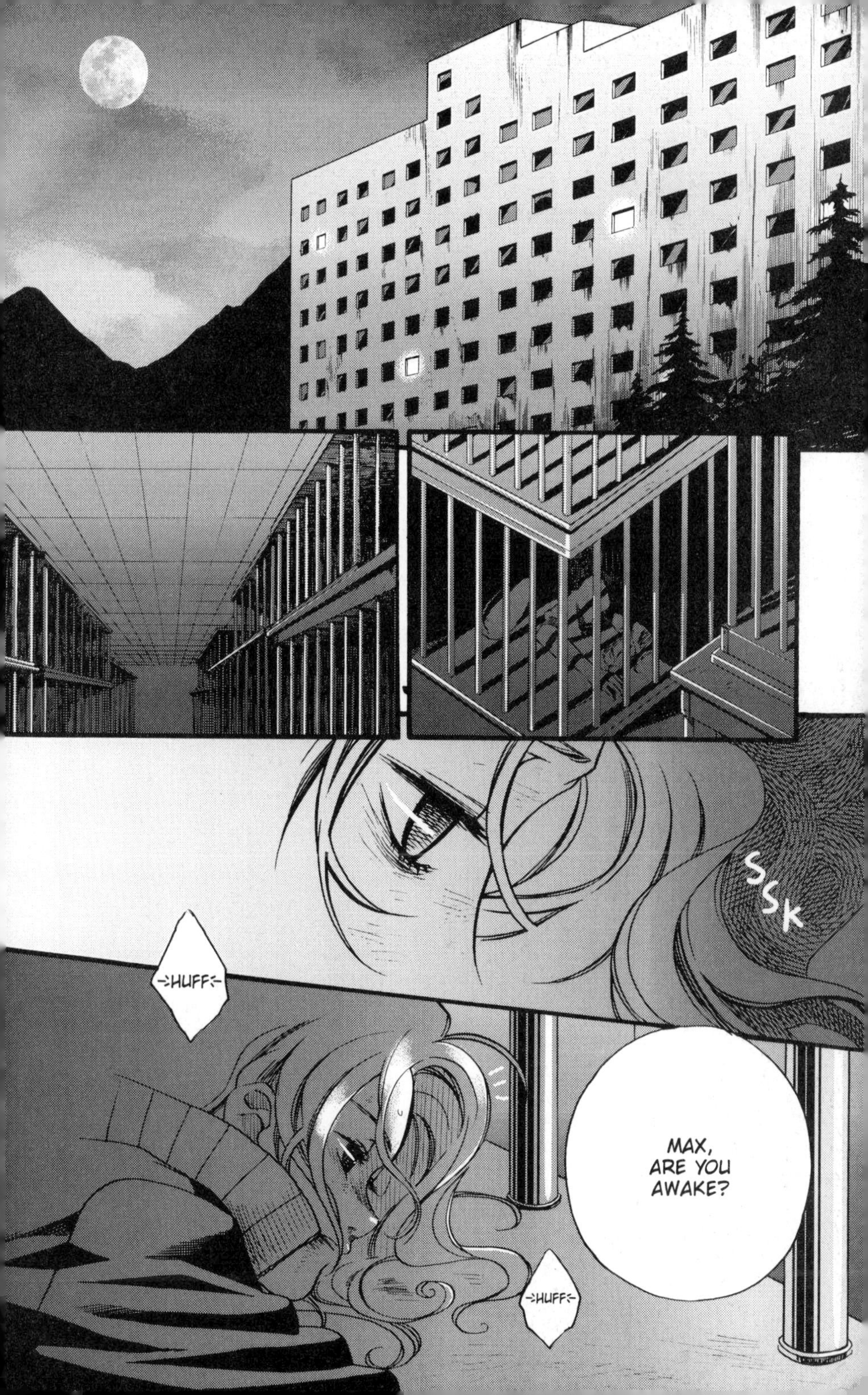
SSK
HUFF
MAX, ARE YOU AWAKE?
HUFF

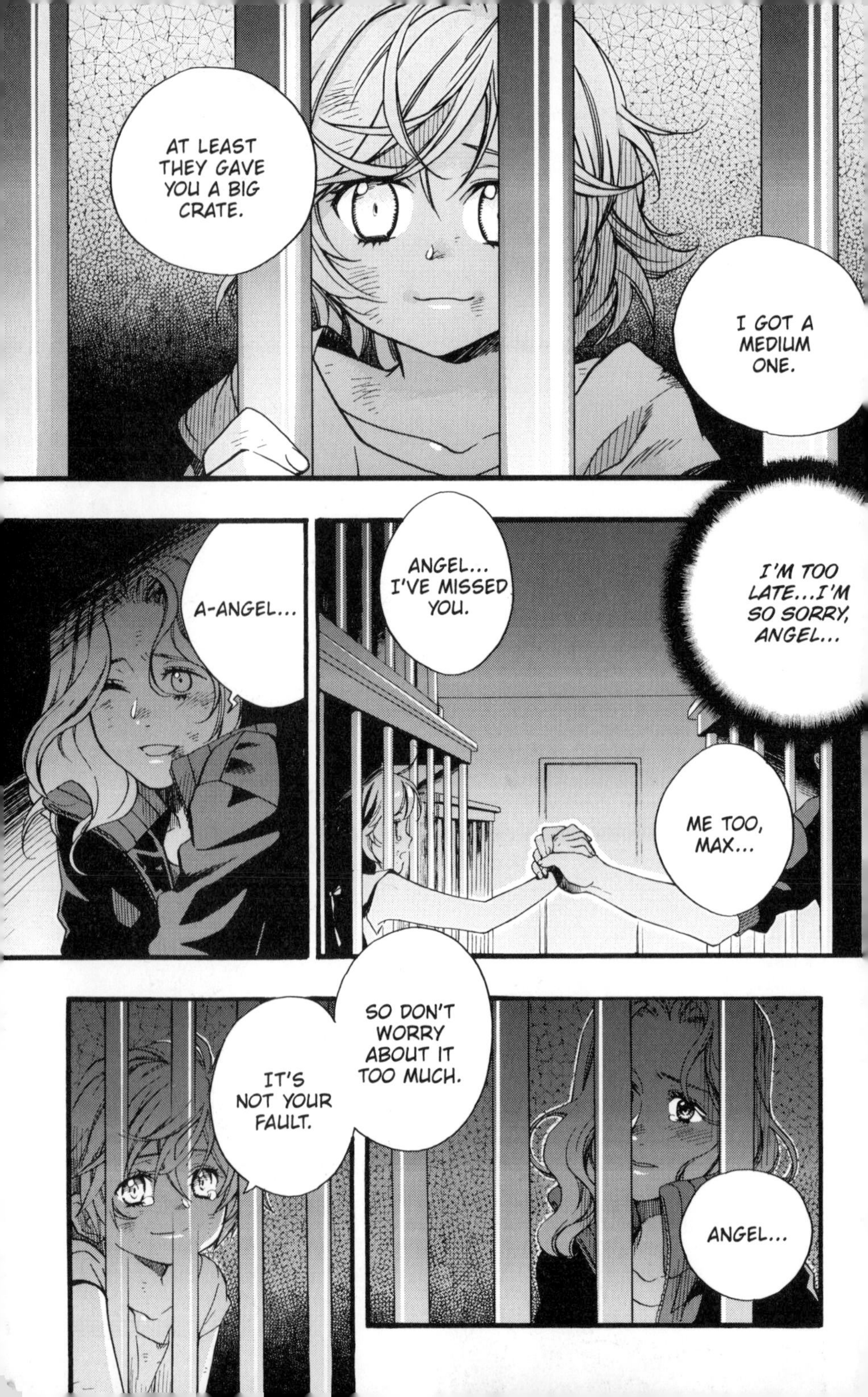
AT LEAST THEY GAVE YOU A BIG CRATE.
I GOT A MEDIUM ONE.
A-ANGEL...
ANGEL... I'VE MISSED YOU.
I'M TOO LATE...I'M SO SORRY, ANGEL...
ME TOO, MAX...
IT'S NOT YOUR FAULT.
SO DON'T WORRY ABOUT IT TOO MUCH.
ANGEL...

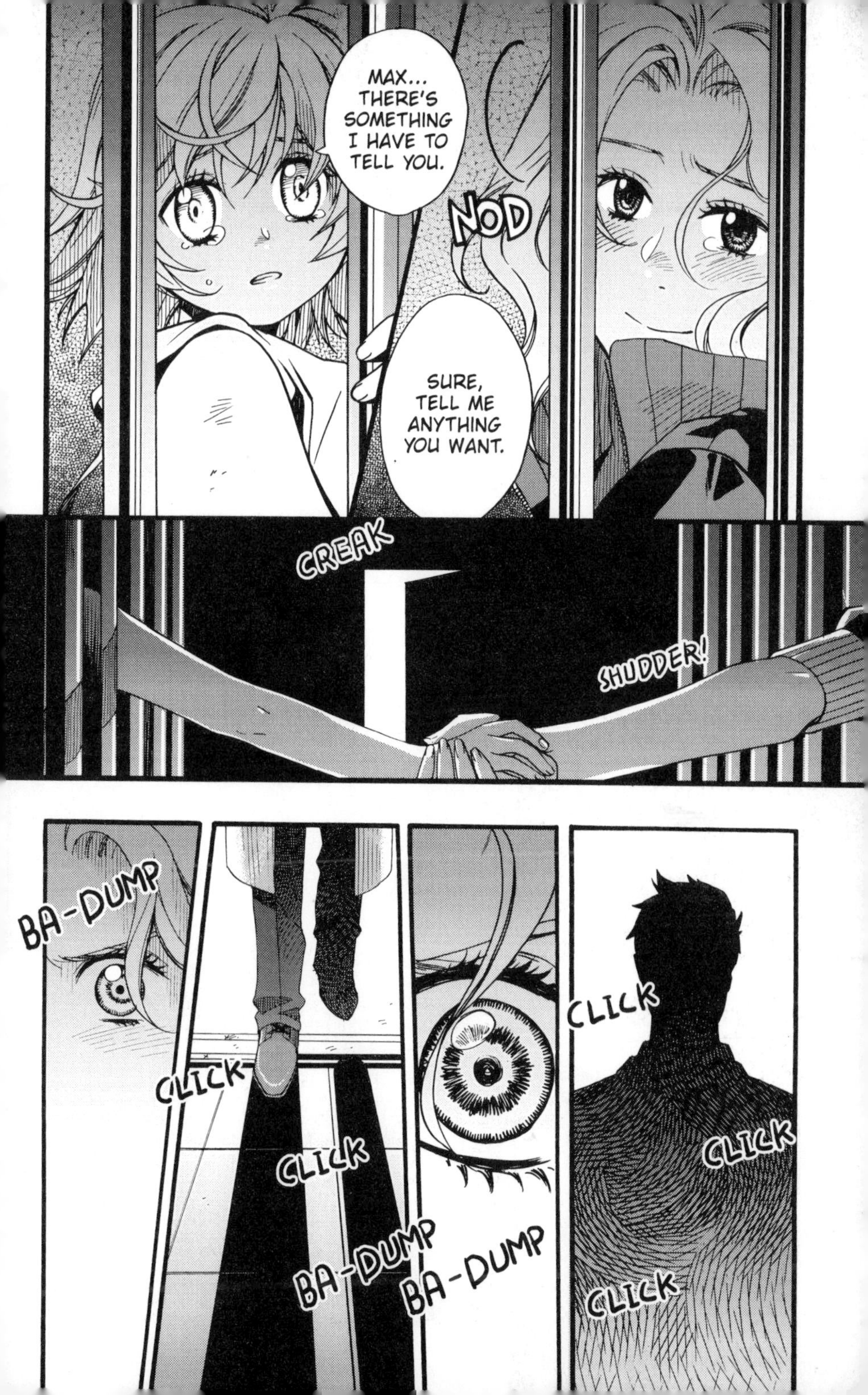
MAX... THERE'S SOMETHING I HAVE TO TELL YOU.
NOD
SURE, TELL ME ANYTHING YOU WANT.
CREAK
SHUDDER!
BA-DUMP
CLICK
CLICK
BA-DUMP
BA-DUMP
CLICK
CLICK
CLICK

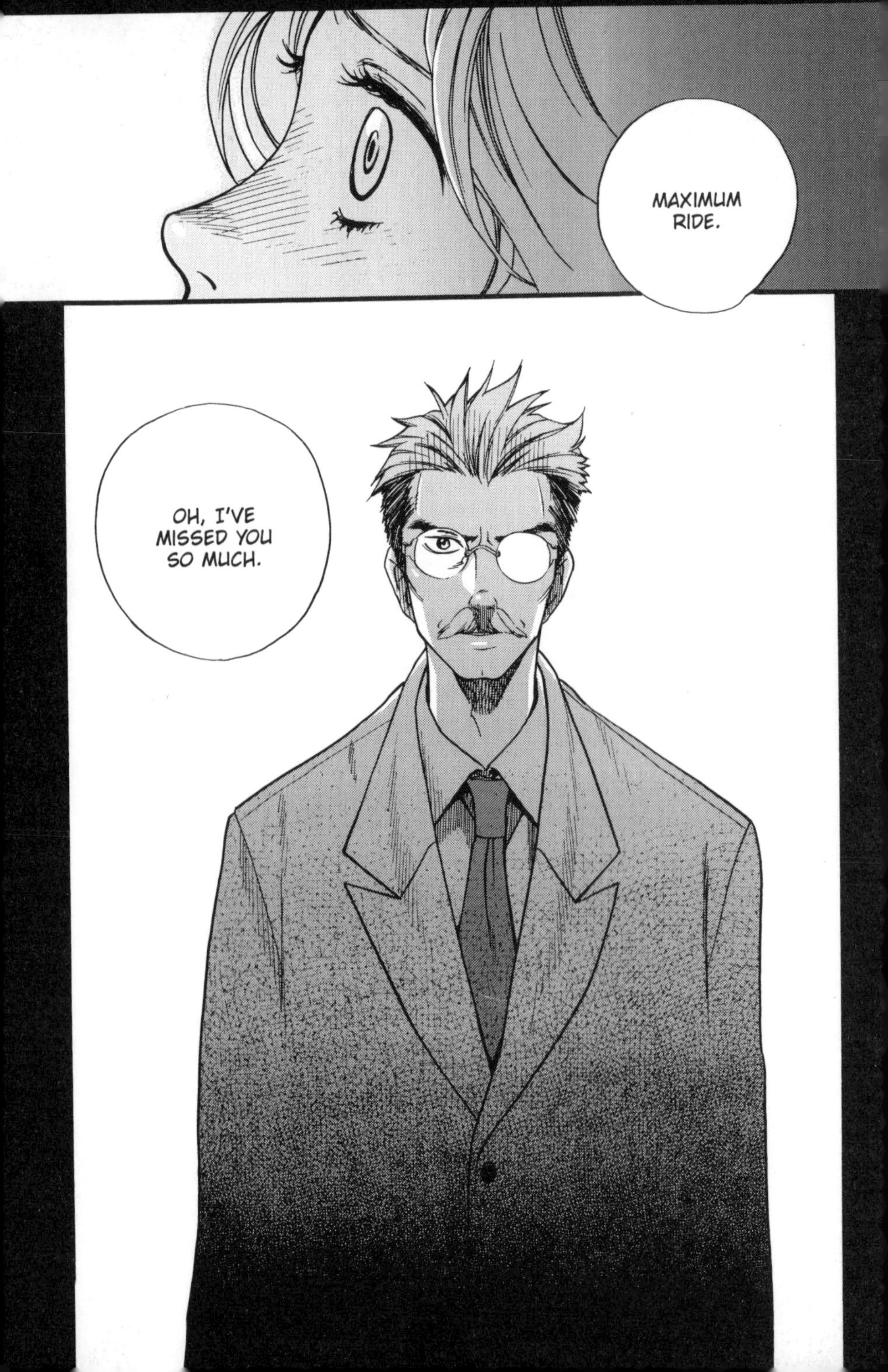
MAXIMUM RIDE.
OH, I'VE MISSED YOU SO MUCH.

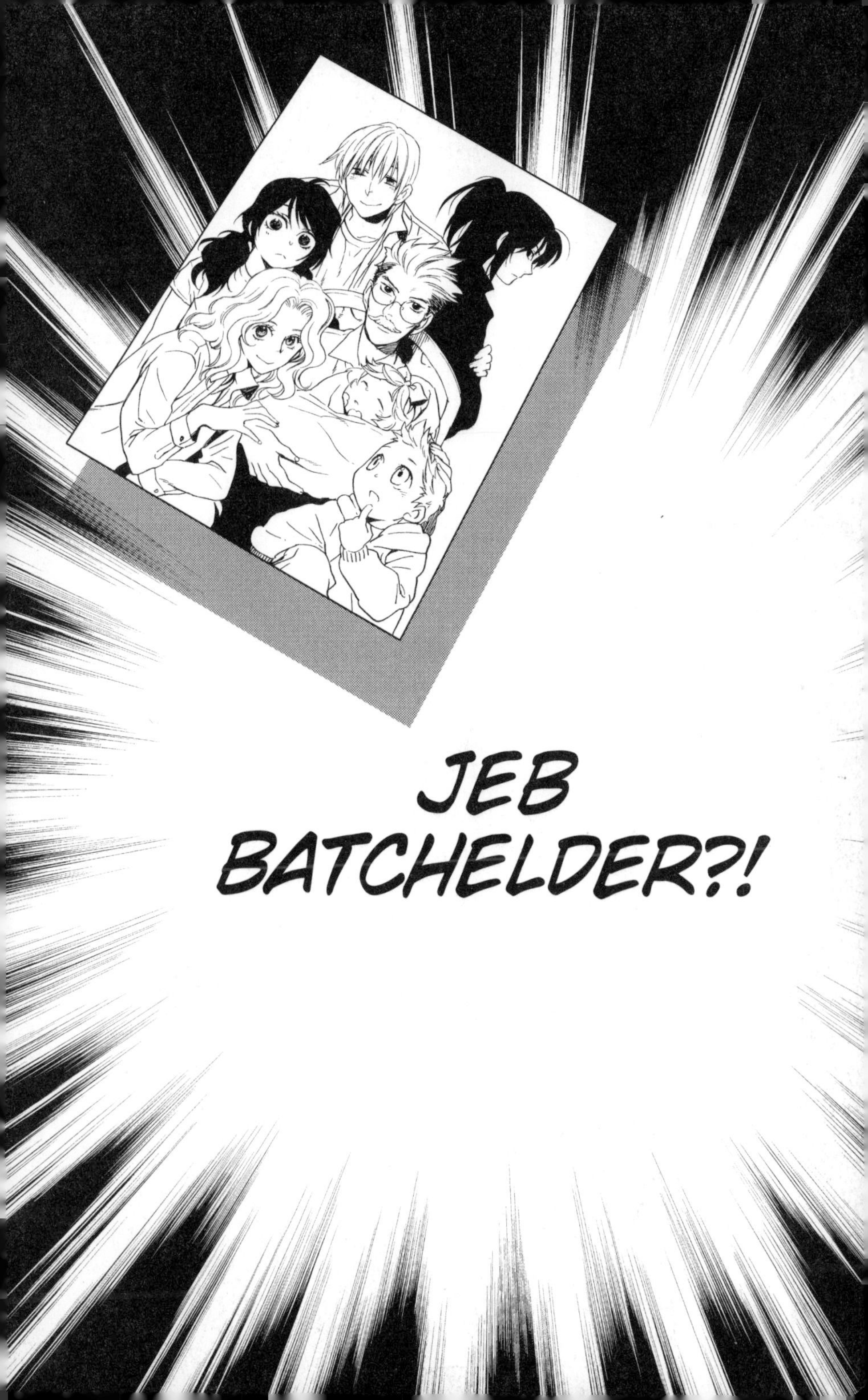
JEB
BATCHELDER?!

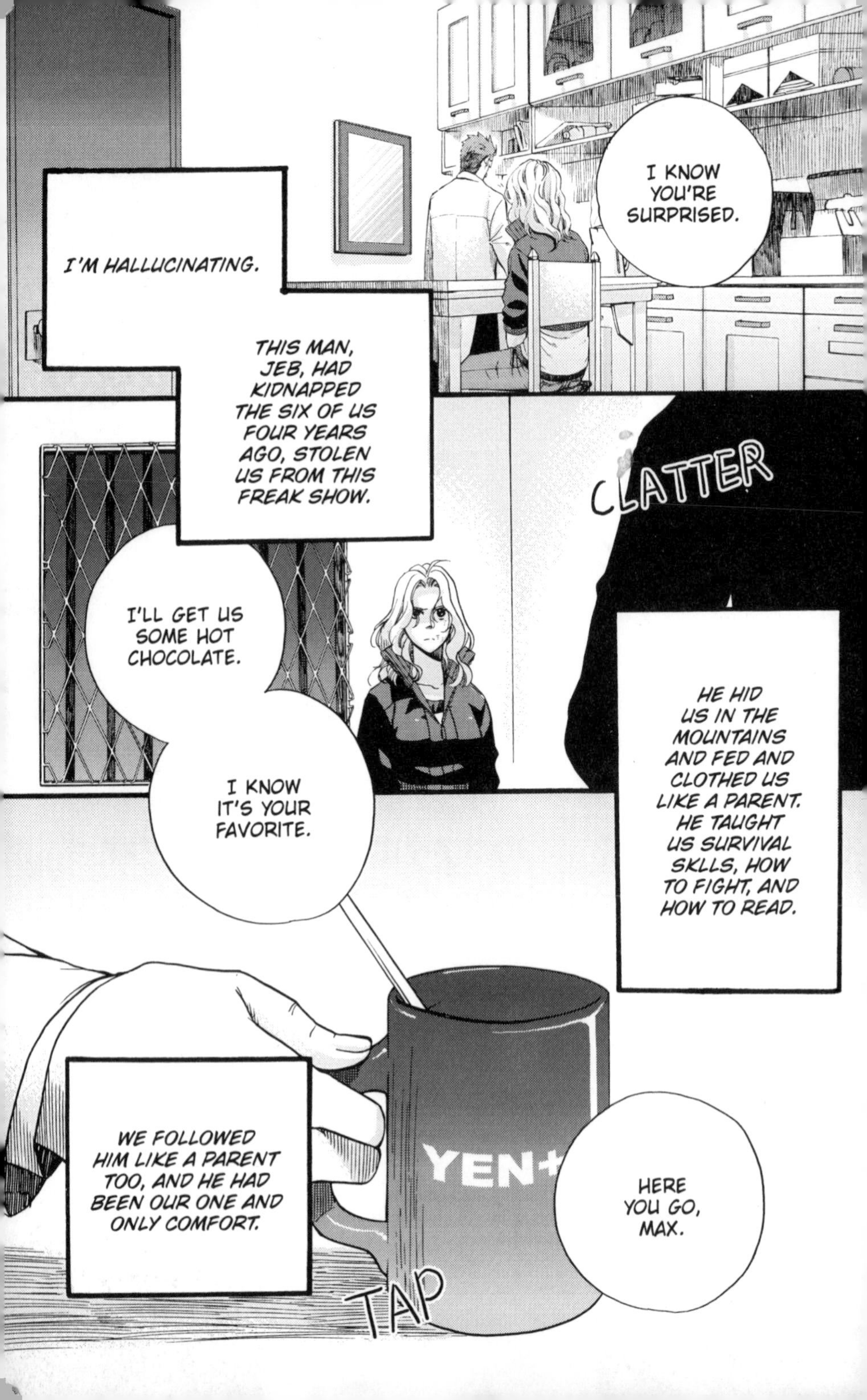
I'M HALLUCINATING.
I KNOW YOU'RE SURPRISED.
THIS MAN, JEB, HAD KIDNAPPED THE SIX OF US FOUR YEARS AGO, STOLEN US FROM THIS FREAK SHOW.
I'LL GET US SOME HOT CHOCOLATE.
CLATTER
HE HID US IN THE MOUNTAINS AND FED AND CLOTHED US LIKE A PARENT. HE TAUGHT US SURVIVAL SKLLS, HOW TO FIGHT, AND HOW TO READ.
I KNOW IT'S YOUR FAVORITE.
WE FOLLOWED HIM LIKE A PARENT TOO, AND HE HAD BEEN OUR ONE AND ONLY COMFORT.
YEN+
HERE YOU GO, MAX.
TAP

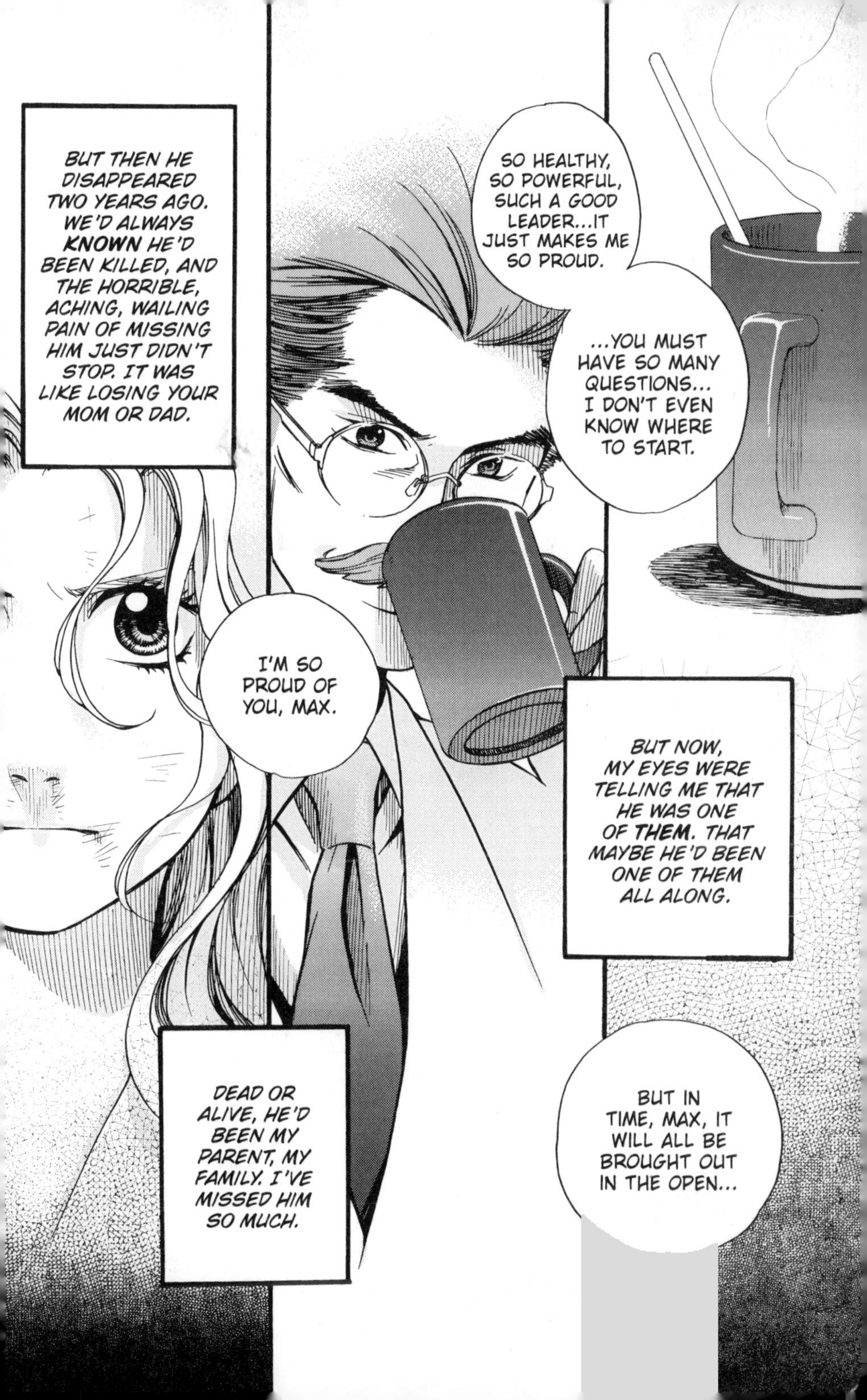
BUT THEN HE DISAPPEARED TWO YEARS AGO. WE'D ALWAYS **KNOWN** HE'D BEEN KILLED, AND THE HORRIBLE, ACHING, WAILING PAIN OF MISSING HIM JUST DIDN'T STOP. IT WAS LIKE LOSING YOUR MOM OR DAD.
I'M SO PROUD OF YOU, MAX.
DEAD OR ALIVE, HE'D BEEN MY PARENT, MY FAMILY. I'VE MISSED HIM SO MUCH.
SO HEALTHY, SO POWERFUL, SUCH A GOOD LEADER...IT JUST MAKES ME SO PROUD.
...YOU MUST HAVE SO MANY QUESTIONS... I DON'T EVEN KNOW WHERE TO START.
BUT NOW, MY EYES WERE TELLING ME THAT HE WAS ONE OF **THEM**. THAT MAYBE HE'D BEEN ONE OF THEM ALL ALONG.
BUT IN TIME, MAX, IT WILL ALL BE BROUGHT OUT IN THE OPEN...

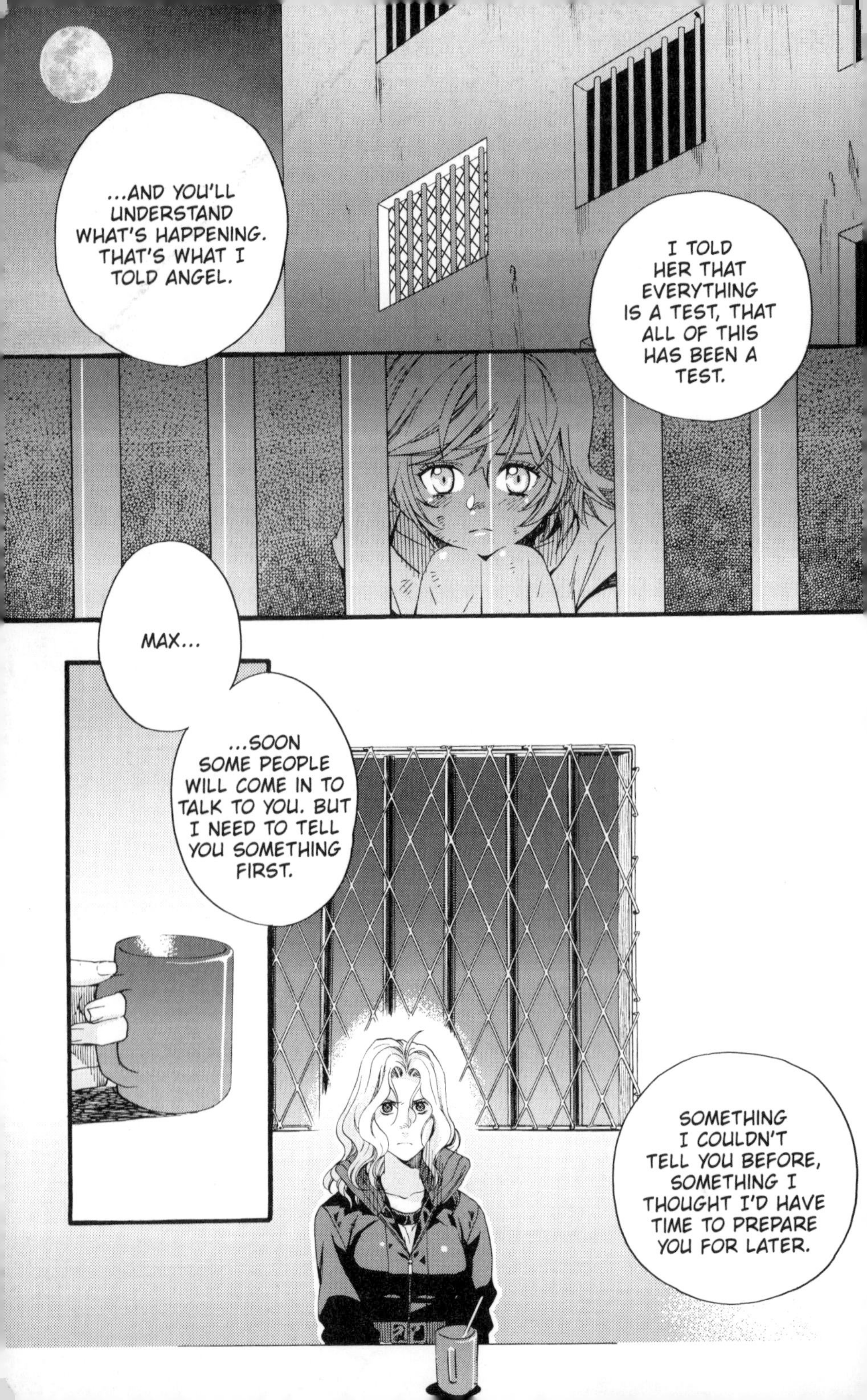
...AND YOU'LL UNDERSTAND WHAT'S HAPPENING. THAT'S WHAT I TOLD ANGEL.
I TOLD HER THAT EVERYTHING IS A TEST, THAT ALL OF THIS HAS BEEN A TEST.
MAX...
...SOON SOME PEOPLE WILL COME IN TO TALK TO YOU. BUT I NEED TO TELL YOU SOMETHING FIRST.
SOMETHING I COULDN'T TELL YOU BEFORE, SOMETHING I THOUGHT I'D HAVE TIME TO PREPARE YOU FOR LATER.

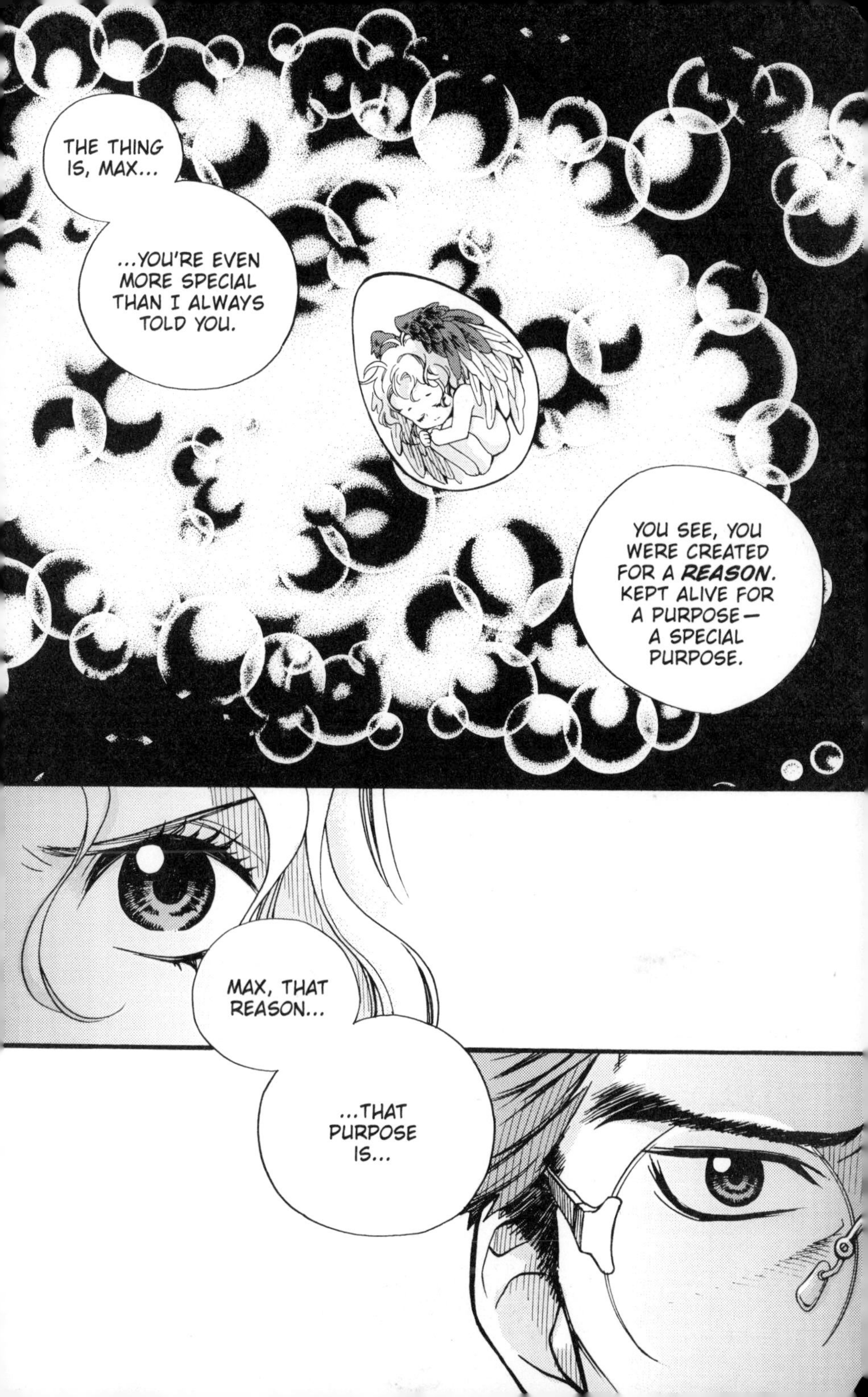
THE THING IS, MAX...
...YOU'RE EVEN MORE SPECIAL THAN I ALWAYS TOLD YOU.
YOU SEE, YOU WERE CREATED FOR A ***REASON***. KEPT ALIVE FOR A PURPOSE— A SPECIAL PURPOSE.
MAX, THAT REASON...
...THAT PURPOSE IS...

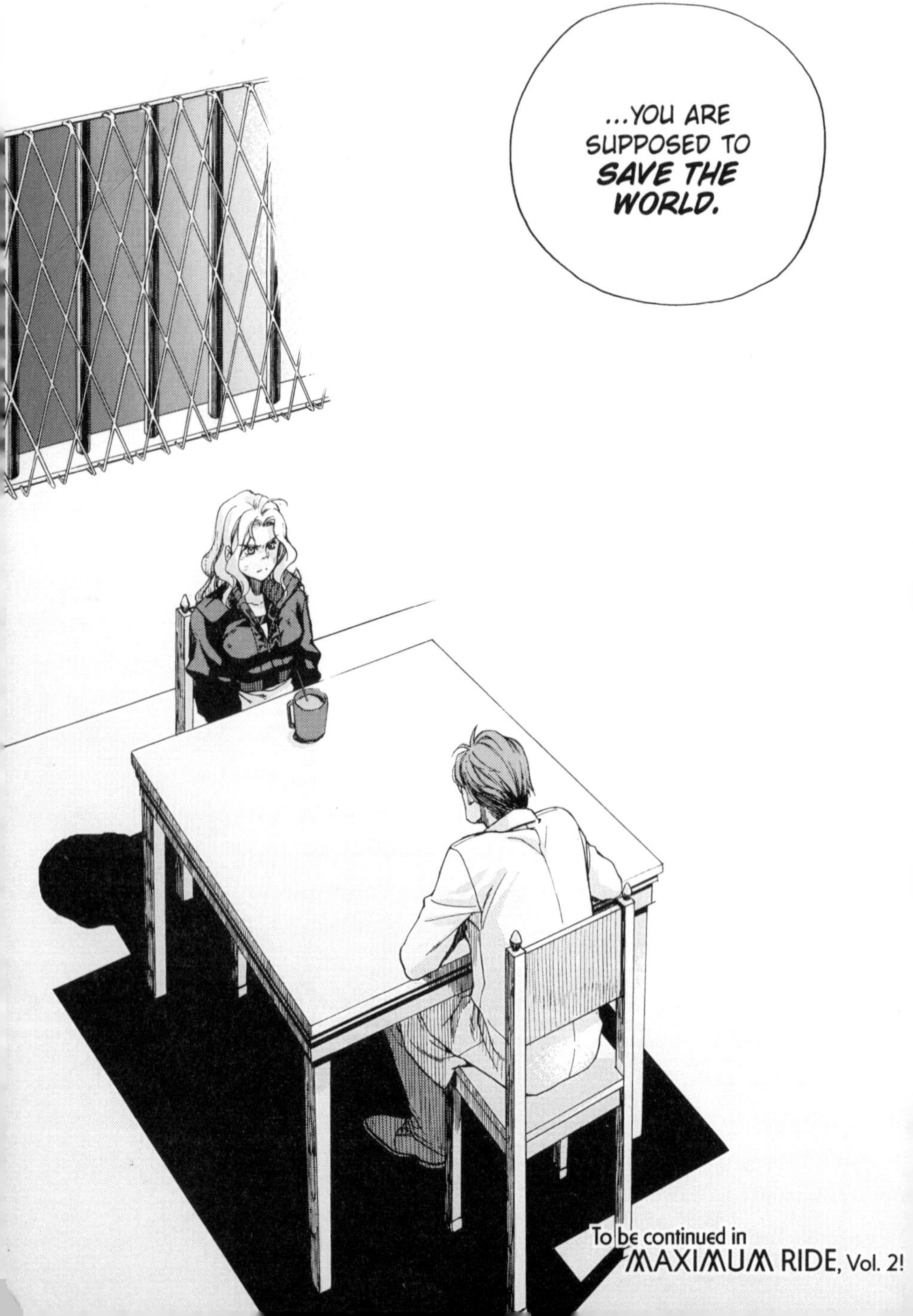
...YOU ARE SUPPOSED TO SAVE THE WORLD.
To be continued in MAXIMUM RIDE, Vol. 2!

Afterword from NaRae Lee ♡

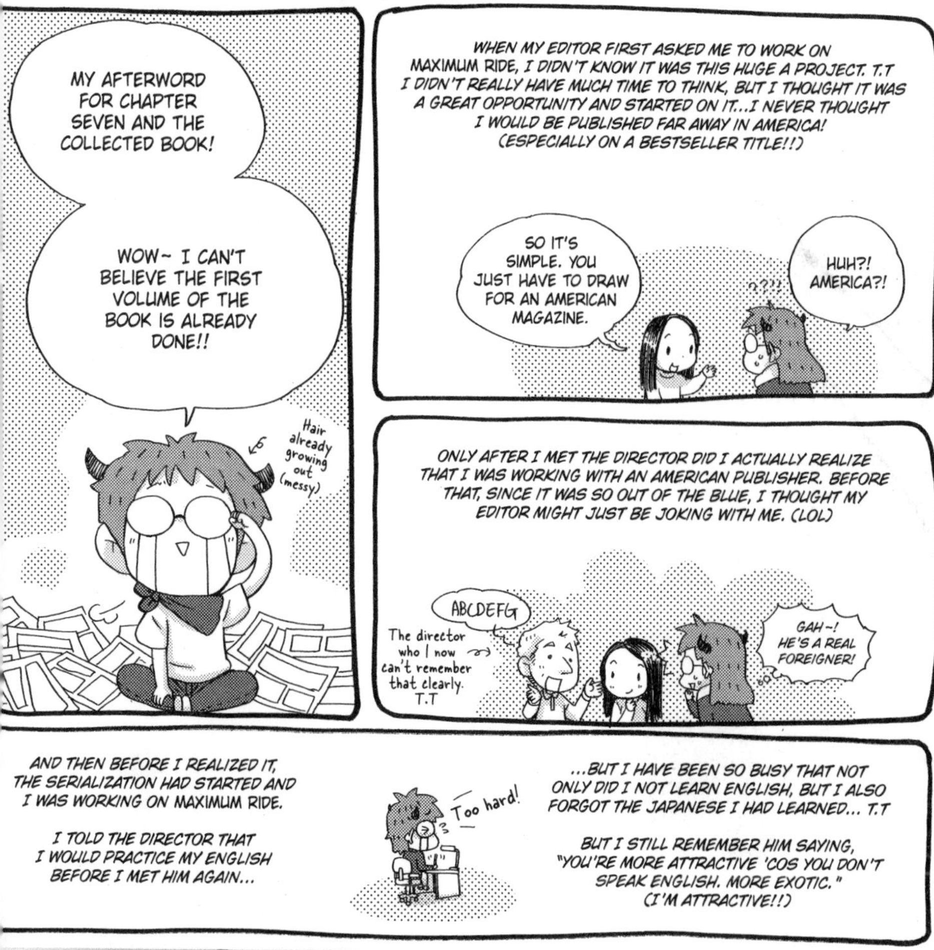
MY AFTERWORD FOR CHAPTER SEVEN AND THE COLLECTED BOOK!
WOW~ I CAN'T BELIEVE THE FIRST VOLUME OF THE BOOK IS ALREADY DONE!!
Hair already growing out (messy)
WHEN MY EDITOR FIRST ASKED ME TO WORK ON MAXIMUM RIDE, I DIDN'T KNOW IT WAS THIS HUGE A PROJECT. T.T I DIDN'T REALLY HAVE MUCH TIME TO THINK, BUT I THOUGHT IT WAS A GREAT OPPORTUNITY AND STARTED ON IT...I NEVER THOUGHT I WOULD BE PUBLISHED FAR AWAY IN AMERICA! (ESPECIALLY ON A BESTSELLER TITLE!!)
SO IT'S SIMPLE. YOU JUST HAVE TO DRAW FOR AN AMERICAN MAGAZINE.
????
HUH?! AMERICA?!
ONLY AFTER I MET THE DIRECTOR DID I ACTUALLY REALIZE THAT I WAS WORKING WITH AN AMERICAN PUBLISHER. BEFORE THAT, SINCE IT WAS SO OUT OF THE BLUE, I THOUGHT MY EDITOR MIGHT JUST BE JOKING WITH ME. (LOL)
ABCDEFG
The director who I now can't remember that clearly. T.T
GAH~! HE'S A REAL FOREIGNER!
AND THEN BEFORE I REALIZED IT, THE SERIALIZATION HAD STARTED AND I WAS WORKING ON MAXIMUM RIDE.
I TOLD THE DIRECTOR THAT I WOULD PRACTICE MY ENGLISH BEFORE I MET HIM AGAIN...
Too hard!
...BUT I HAVE BEEN SO BUSY THAT NOT ONLY DID I NOT LEARN ENGLISH, BUT I ALSO FORGOT THE JAPANESE I HAD LEARNED... T.T
BUT I STILL REMEMBER HIM SAYING, "YOU'RE MORE ATTRACTIVE 'COS YOU DON'T SPEAK ENGLISH. MORE EXOTIC."
(I'M ATTRACTIVE!!)

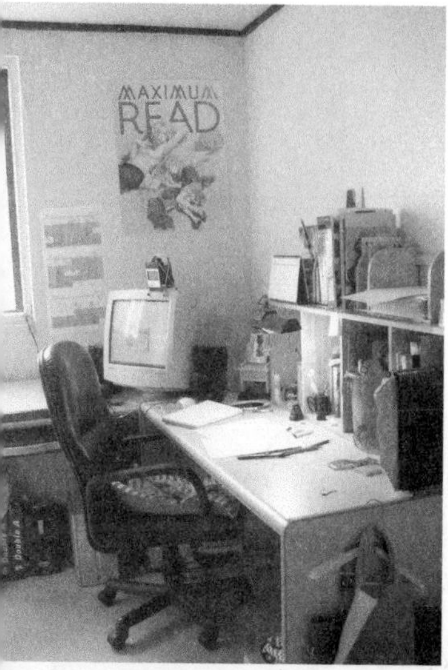
MAXIMUM
READ

<< THE DESK I WORK ON. THIS IS MY ROOM AT MY PARENTS' HOUSE. I USE THE COMPUTER TO DO THE TONING OR TO WORK ON PROJECTS OTHER THAN MAXIMUM RIDE.

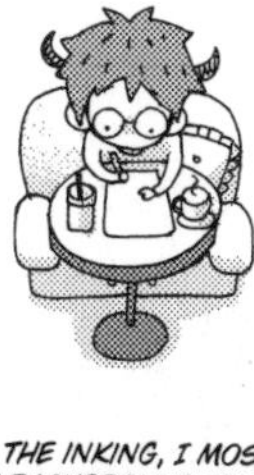

I USED TO PENCIL A LOT AT A NEARBY CAFÉ. IT CAN GET A LITTLE STUFFY IF YOU STAY HOME FOR TOO LONG...

ESPECIALLY IN THE SUMMER, I WENT TO ENJOY THE COOL ICED COFFEE AND THE AIR CONDITIONING!!

AND FOR THE INKING, I MOSTLY WORK AT MY BACKGROUND ASSISTANT FRIEND'S HOUSE. WE GO TO THE SAME SCHOOL NOW AND ALSO WENT TO THE SAME HIGH SCHOOL, SO IT'S COMFY AND NICE. (IS IT JUST COMFY FOR ME?!)

BY THE TIME I START ON THE SECOND VOLUME I WILL HAVE MY OWN STUDIO!

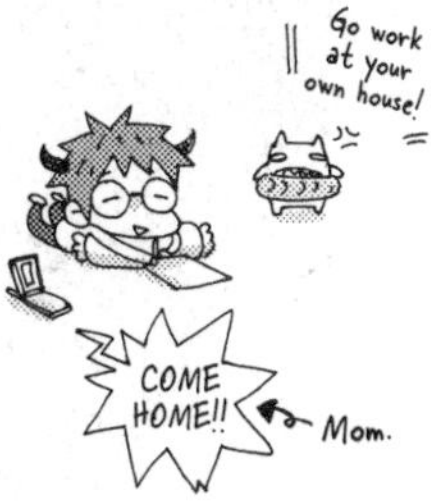
Go work at your own house!
COME HOME!!
Mom.

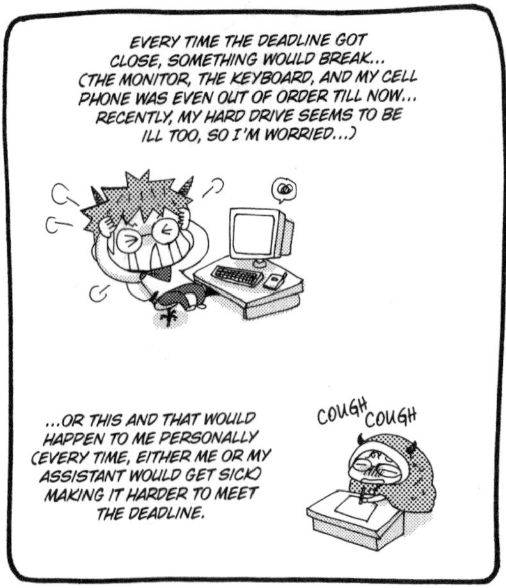
EVERY TIME THE DEADLINE GOT CLOSE, SOMETHING WOULD BREAK... (THE MONITOR, THE KEYBOARD, AND MY CELL PHONE WAS EVEN OUT OF ORDER TILL NOW... RECENTLY, MY HARD DRIVE SEEMS TO BE ILL TOO, SO I'M WORRIED...)
...OR THIS AND THAT WOULD HAPPEN TO ME PERSONALLY (EVERY TIME, EITHER ME OR MY ASSISTANT WOULD GET SICK) MAKING IT HARDER TO MEET THE DEADLINE.
COUGH COUGH

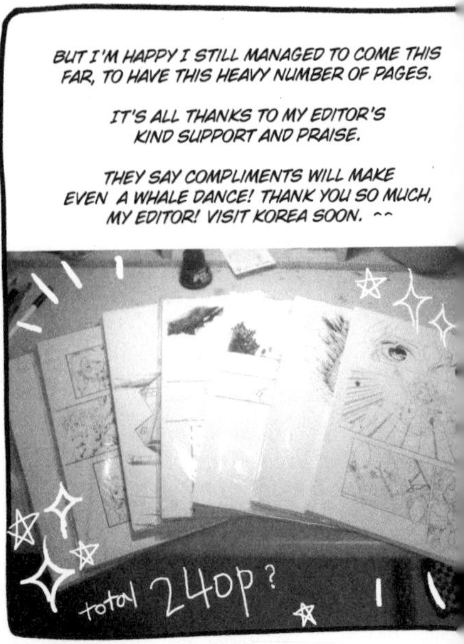
BUT I'M HAPPY I STILL MANAGED TO COME THIS FAR, TO HAVE THIS HEAVY NUMBER OF PAGES.
IT'S ALL THANKS TO MY EDITOR'S KIND SUPPORT AND PRAISE.
THEY SAY COMPLIMENTS WILL MAKE EVEN A WHALE DANCE! THANK YOU SO MUCH, MY EDITOR! VISIT KOREA SOON. ^^
total 240p ?

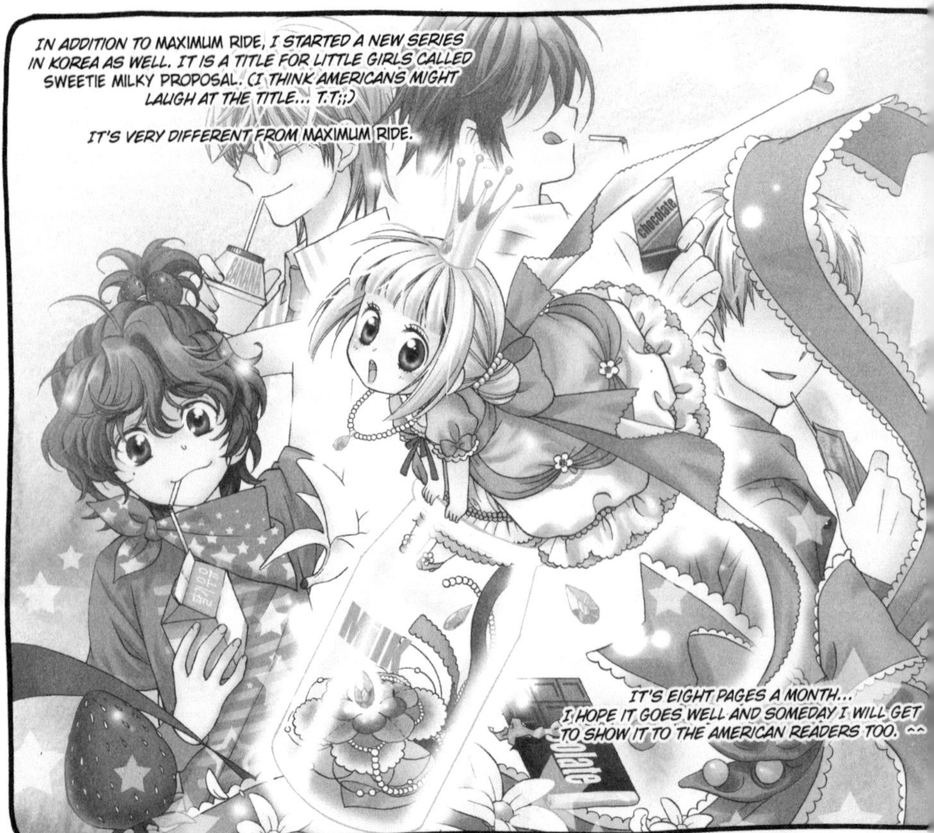
IN ADDITION TO MAXIMUM RIDE, I STARTED A NEW SERIES IN KOREA AS WELL. IT IS A TITLE FOR LITTLE GIRLS CALLED SWEETIE MILKY PROPOSAL. (I THINK AMERICANS MIGHT LAUGH AT THE TITLE... T.T;;)
IT'S VERY DIFFERENT FROM MAXIMUM RIDE.
chocolate
IT'S EIGHT PAGES A MONTH... I HOPE IT GOES WELL AND SOMEDAY I WILL GET TO SHOW IT TO THE AMERICAN READERS TOO. ^^

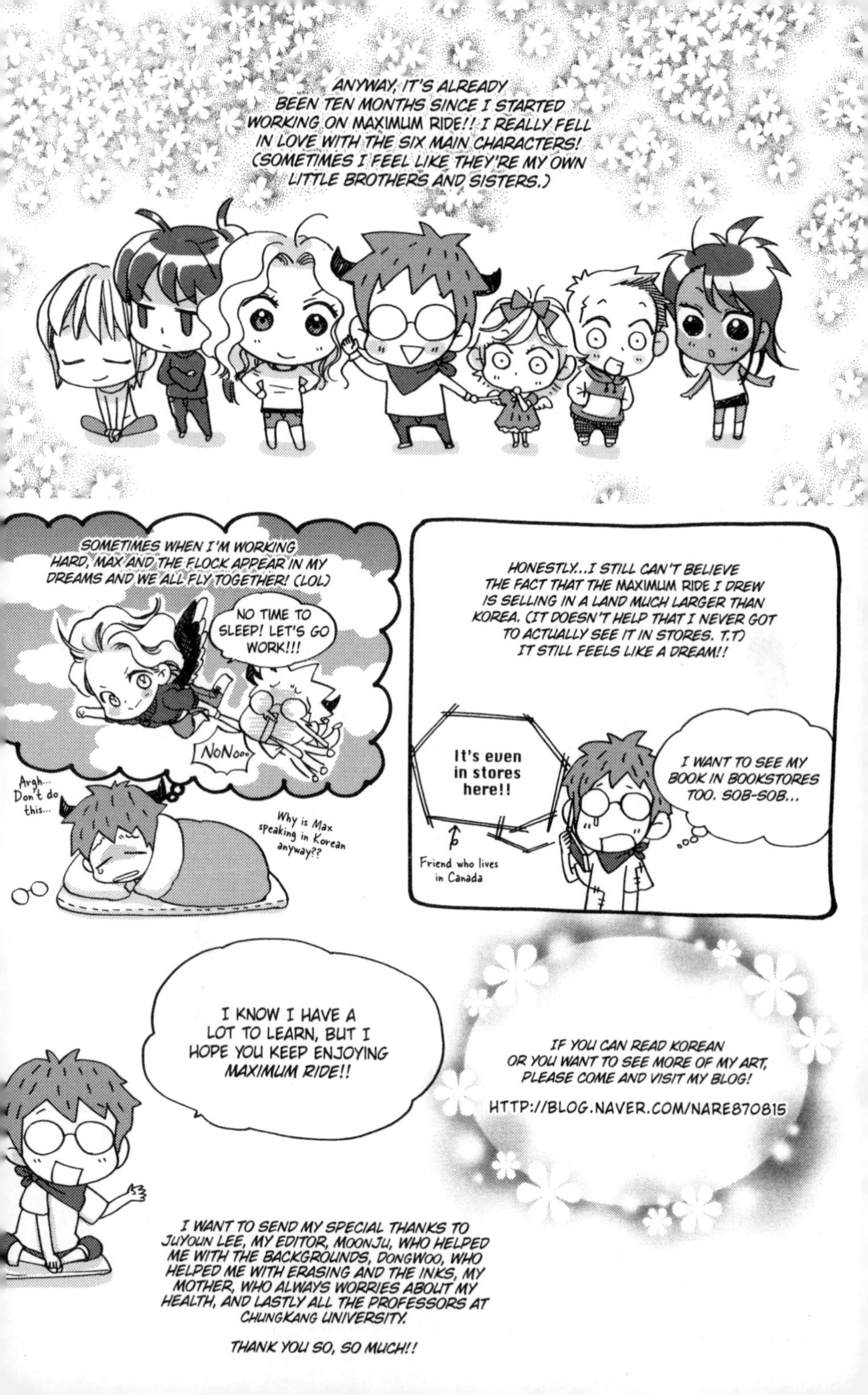

ANYWAY, IT'S ALREADY BEEN TEN MONTHS SINCE I STARTED WORKING ON MAXIMUM RIDE!! I REALLY FELL IN LOVE WITH THE SIX MAIN CHARACTERS! (SOMETIMES I FEEL LIKE THEY'RE MY OWN LITTLE BROTHERS AND SISTERS.)
SOMETIMES WHEN I'M WORKING HARD, MAX AND THE FLOCK APPEAR IN MY DREAMS AND WE ALL FLY TOGETHER! (LOL)
NO TIME TO SLEEP! LET'S GO WORK!!!
NoNooo
Argh... Don't do this...
Why is Max speaking in Korean anyway??
HONESTLY...I STILL CAN'T BELIEVE THE FACT THAT THE MAXIMUM RIDE I DREW IS SELLING IN A LAND MUCH LARGER THAN KOREA. (IT DOESN'T HELP THAT I NEVER GOT TO ACTUALLY SEE IT IN STORES. T.T) IT STILL FEELS LIKE A DREAM!!
It's even in stores here!!
Friend who lives in Canada
I WANT TO SEE MY BOOK IN BOOKSTORES TOO. SOB-SOB...
I KNOW I HAVE A LOT TO LEARN, BUT I HOPE YOU KEEP ENJOYING MAXIMUM RIDE!!
IF YOU CAN READ KOREAN OR YOU WANT TO SEE MORE OF MY ART, PLEASE COME AND VISIT MY BLOG!
HTTP://BLOG.NAVER.COM/NARE870815
I WANT TO SEND MY SPECIAL THANKS TO JUYOUN LEE, MY EDITOR, MOONJU, WHO HELPED ME WITH THE BACKGROUNDS, DONGWOO, WHO HELPED ME WITH ERASING AND THE INKS, MY MOTHER, WHO ALWAYS WORRIES ABOUT MY HEALTH, AND LASTLY ALL THE PROFESSORS AT CHUNGKANG UNIVERSITY.
THANK YOU SO, SO MUCH!!

Read on to enjoy a sneak
preview of MAX,
the flock's latest adventure
from best-selling
author James Patterson.

JAMES PATTERSON

MAX

MAXIMUM RIDE

The Madness Never Stops

Near Los Angeles Basin, California

There.

Devin raised his right arm and focused directly over his wrist. It took less than a millisecond to calculate the trajectory — he didn't have a built-in computer, but his 220 IQ served him well.

He slowly breathed in and out, getting ready to squeeze the trigger between breaths, between heartbeats. His sensitive nose wrinkled as the ever-present smog that hovered over the Los Angeles Basin filled his lungs. He hated to think what the pollutants were doing to his brain cells but accepted that some things were necessary evils.

There.

His light eyes expertly tracked the objects flying overhead: one, two, three, four, five, six. Seven? There was a small seventh object, unexpected but quickly determined to be unimportant. Actually, all of them were unimportant. All but one. The one in front.

He knew they had raptor vision. He merely had extraordinary eyesight. It was good enough. All the same, the crosshairs in the gun sight attached to his wrist made missing an impossibility. He never missed.

That's why they saved him for extraspecial missions like this one.

Many, many others had already failed at this task. Devin felt utter disdain for them. To kill one bird kid — how hard could it be? They were flesh and blood, ridiculously fragile. It wasn't like bullets bounced off them.

Once more Devin raised his arm and observed his prey, catching her neatly in the crosshairs, as if they could pin her to the sky. The flock flew, perfectly spaced, in a large arc overhead, the one called Maximum in front, flanked by the two large males. Then a smaller female. Then a smaller male, and the smallest female.

A little black object, not bird kid shaped, struggled to keep up. Devin couldn't identify it — it hadn't been in his dossier. The closest thing he could imagine was if someone grafted wings onto a small dog or something, as unlikely as that was.

But Max was the only one he was concerned with. It was Max he was supposed to kill, Max whom he kept catching in his sights.

Devin sighed and lowered his arm. This was almost too easy. It wasn't sporting. He loved the chase, the hunt, the split-second intersection of luck and skill that allowed him to exercise his perfection, his inability to miss.

He looked down at what used to be his right hand. One could get used to having no right hand. It was surprisingly easy. And it was so superior to have this lovely weapon instead.

It wasn't as crude as simply having a Glock 18 grafted to the stump of an amputated limb. It was so much more elegant than that, so much more a miracle of design and ingenuity. This weapon was a part of him physically, responsive to his slightest thought, triggered by almost imperceptible nerve firings in the interface between his arm and the weapon.

He was a living work of art. Unlike the bird kids flying in traceable patterns overhead.

Devin had seen the posters, the advertisements. Those naive, do-gooder idiots at the Coalition to Stop the Madness had organized this whole thing, this air show, this demonstration of supposedly "evolved" humans.

Wrong. The bird kids were ill-conceived accidents. He, Devin, was truly an evolved human.

The CSM zealots were wasting their time — and everyone else's. Using the bird kids to promote their own agenda was a typically selfish, shortsighted thing to do. Manipulating and taking advantage of lesser creatures in order to "save" even lesser creatures? It was a joke.

A joke that could not be perpetrated without this flock of examples. And the flock could not survive without its leader.

Once again Devin raised his arm and closed his left eye to focus through the gun sight on his wrist. He angled the Glock a millimeter to the left and smoothly tracked his target as she arced across the sky.

One breath in, one breath out. One heartbeat, two heartbeats, and here we go . . .

PART 1

Freaks and M-Geeks

"And a-one, and a-two —" Nudge said, leaning into a perfect forty-five-degree angle. Her tawny russet wings glowed warmly in the afternoon sunlight.

Behind her, the Gasman made squealing-brakes sounds as he dropped his feet down and slowed drastically. "Hey! Watch gravity in action!" he yelled, folding his wings back to create an unaerodynamic eight-year-old, his blond hair blown straight up by the wind.

I rolled my eyes. "Gazzy, stick to the choreography!" He was sinking fast, and I had to bellow to make sure he heard me. "This is a paying job! Don't blow it!" Okay, they were paying us mostly in doughnuts, but let's not quibble.

Even from this high up, I could hear the exclamations of surprise, the indrawn gasps that told me our captive audience below had noticed one of us dropping like a rock.

I'd give him five seconds, and then I'd swoop down after him. One . . . two . . .

I wasn't sure about this whole air-show thing to begin with, but how could I refuse my own mom? After our last "working vacation" in Ant-freaking-arctica, my mom and a bunch of scientists had created an organization called the Coalition to Stop the Madness, or CSM. Basically, they were trying to tell the whole world about the dangers of pollution, greenhouse gases, dependence on foreign oil — you get the picture.

Already, more than a thousand scientists, teachers, senators, and regular people had joined the CSM. One of the teacher-members had come up with the traveling air-show idea to really get the message out. I mean, Blue Angels, Schmue Angels, but flying mutant bird kids? Come on! Who's gonna pass that up?

So here we were, flying perfect formations, doing tricks, air dancing, la la la, the six of us and Total, whose wings by now had pretty much finished developing. He could fly, at least, but he wasn't exactly Baryshnikov. If Baryshnikov had been a small, black, Scottie dog with wings, that is.

By the time I'd counted to four, the Gasman had ended his free fall and was soaring upward again, happiness on his relatively clean face.

Hanging out with the CSM folks had some benefits, chiefly food and decent places to sleep. And, of course, seeing my mom, which I'd never be able to get enough of, after living the first fourteen years of my life not even knowing she existed. (I explained all this in earlier books, if you want to go get caught up.)

"Yo," said Fang, hovering next to me.

My heart gave a little kick as I saw how the sun glinted off his deeply black feathers. Which matched his eyes. And his hair. "You enjoying being a spokesfreak?" I asked him casually, looking away.

One side of his mouth moved: the Fang version of unbridled chortling.

He shrugged. "It's a job."

"Yep. So long as they don't worry about pesky child-labor laws," I agreed. We're an odd little band, my fellow flock members and I. Fang, Iggy, and I are all fourteen, give or take. So officially, technically, legally, we're minors. But we've been living on our own for years, and regular child-protection laws just don't seem to apply to us. Come to think of it, many regular grown-up laws don't seem to apply to us either.

Nudge is eleven, roughly. The Gasman is eightish. Angel is somewhere in the six range. I don't know how old Total is, and frankly, what with the calculations of dog years into human years, I don't care.

Suddenly, out of nowhere, Angel dropped down onto me with all her forty-one pounds of feathery fun.

"Oof! What are you doing, goofball?" I exclaimed, dipping about a foot. Then I heard it: the high-pitched, all-too-familiar whine of a bullet streaking past my ear, close enough to knock some of my hair aside.

In the next second, Total yelped piercingly, spinning in midair, his small black wings flapping frantically. Angel's quick instincts had saved my life. But Total had taken the hit.

2

In the blink of an eye, I rolled a full 360, spinning in the air, swooping to catch Total and also performing evasive maneuvers that, sadly, I've had way too much practice doing.

"Scatter!" I shouted. "Get out of firing range!"

We all peeled away, our wings moving fast and powerfully, gaining altitude like rockets. I heard applause floating up to me — they thought this was part of the act. Then I looked down at the limp black dog in my arms.

"Total!" I said, holding his chunky little body. "Total!"

He blinked and moaned. "I'm hit, Max. They got me. I guess I'm gonna live fast, die young, and leave a beautiful corpse, huh?"

Okay. In my experience, if you're really hit or seriously hurt, you don't say much. Maybe a few bad words. Maybe grunting sounds. You don't manage pithy quotes.

Quickly I shifted him this way and that, scanning for wounds. He had both ears, and his face was fine. I patted along his wings, which still looked too short to keep him aloft. Bright red blood stained my sleeve, but so far he seemed to be in one unperforated piece.

"Tell Akila," Total gasped, eyelids fluttering, "tell her she's always been the only one." Akila is the Alaskan Malamute Total had fallen for back on the Wendy K., the boat where we lived with a bunch of scientists on our way to Antarctica.

"Shh," I said. "I'm still looking for holes."

"I don't have many regrets," Total rambled weakly. "True, I thought about a career in the theater, once our adventures waned. I know it's just a crazy dream, but I always hoped for just one chance to play the Dane before I died."

"Play the huh?" I said absently, feeling his ribs. Nothing broken. "Is that a game?"

Total moaned and closed his eyes.

Then I found it: the source of the blood, the place where he'd been shot.

"Total?" I said, and got a slight whimper. "You have a boo-boo on your tail."

"What?" He opened his eyes and curled to peer at his short tail. He wagged it experimentally, outrage appearing on his face as he realized a tiny chunk of flesh was missing near the tip. "I'm hit! I'm bleeding! Those scoundrels will pay for this!"

"I think a Band-Aid is probably all you need." I struggled to keep a straight face.

Fang swerved closer to me, big and supremely graceful, like a black panther with wings.

Oh, God. I'm so stupid. Forget I just said that.

"How's he doing?' Fang asked, nodding at Total.

"He needs a Band-Aid," I said. A look passed between me and Fang, full of suppressed humor, relief, understanding, love —

Forget I said that too. I don't know what's wrong with me.

"Got your sniper," Fang went on, pointing downward.

I shifted into battle mode. "One sniper or a whole flotilla of baddies?"

"Only see the one."

I raised an eyebrow. "So, what, we're not worth a whole flotilla anymore?" I looked down at Total. "Wings out, spud. You gotta fly on your own."

Total gathered himself with dignity, extended his wings, and jumped awkwardly out of my arms. He flapped frantically, then with more confidence, and rose to keep up with us.

"What's up?" Iggy had coasted on an updraft for a while, but now he and the others were forming a bird-kid sandwich around me.

"Total's okay," I reported. "One sniper below. Now we gotta go take him out."

Angel's pure-white wing brushed against me. She gave me a sweet smile that melted my heart, and I tried to remember that this kid had many layers, not all of them made of gumdrops and roses.

"Thanks, lamby," I said, and she grinned.

"I felt something bad about to happen," she explained. "Can we go get that guy now?"

"Let's do it," I said, and we angled ourselves downward. Among the many genetic enhancements we sport, the mad scientists who created us had thoughtfully included raptor vision. I raked the land below, almost a mile down, and traced the area where Fang pointed.

I saw him: a lone guy in the window of a building close to the air base. He was tracking us, and we began our evasive actions, dropping suddenly, swerving, angling different ways, trying to be as unpredictable as possible. We're fairly good at being unpredictable.

"Mass zoom?" Fang asked, and I nodded.

"Ig, mass zoom, angle down about thirty-five degrees. Then aim for six o'clock," I instructed. And why was I only giving Iggy instructions? Because Iggy's the only blind one, that's why.

We were moving fast, really fast, dropping at a trajectory that would smash us into the sniper's window in about eight seconds. We'd practiced racing feet-first through open windows a thousand times, one right after the other, bam bam bam. So this was more of a fun challenge than a scary, death-defying act of desperation.

The two things often look very similar in our world.

Seven, six, five, I counted silently.

When I got to four, the window exploded outward, knocking me head over heels.

3

Three days later . . .
Here, in no particular order, is a massively incomplete list of things
that make me twitchy:
1) Being indoors, almost anywhere
2) Places with no easy exits
3) People who promise me tons of "benefits" and assume that
   I don't see right through the crapola to the stark truth that
   actually they want me to do a bunch of stuff for them
4) Being dressed up
So it won't take a lot of imagination on your part to guess how I reacted
to our appointment at a Hollywood talent agency.

"Come in, guys," said the most gorgeous woman I've ever seen.
She flashed glowing white teeth and tossed back her perfect, auburn
hair as she ushered us through the heavy wooden door. "I'm Sharon.
Welcome!"

I could see her trying to avoid looking at our various bruises, scrapes,
and cuts. Well, if you're six feet away from a building when it explodes
at you, you're gonna get a little banged up. Fact of life.

We were in a big office building in Hollywood. If you've been keeping
up with our nutty, action-packed shenanigans, you'll remember how
many incredibly bad experiences we've had inside office buildings.
They're pretty much my least favorite place to be, right after dungeons
and hospitals, but before dog crates and science labs. Call me quirky.

A member of the CSM had a friend who had a friend who had a
cousin who was married to someone who knew someone at this
huge, important Hollywood talent agency and volunteered us for an
interview, without asking us. The CSM thought we spokesbirds were
doing a bang-up job of getting their message out. Emphasis on bang,
given the suicide sniper. But more on that later.

"Come in! Come in!" A short, balding guy in a flashy suit waved us in, big smile in place. I ratcheted up my DEFCON level to orange. "I'm Steve Blackman."

There were four of them altogether, three guys and Sharon with the great hair. She blinked when Total trotted in after us, a small white bandage still covering the tip of his tail. He'd gotten more mileage out of that weensy flesh wound than I've gotten out of broken ribs.

"Good God," I heard Total mutter as he looked at the woman. "She can't be real."

"Max!" said Steve, holding out his hand. "May I call you Max?"

"No." I frowned and looked at his hand until he pulled it back.

The other two guys introduced themselves, and we just stood there, unsmiling. Actually, Nudge smiled a little. She loves stuff like this. She'd even worn a skirt. Angel was wearing a pink tutu over her jeans. My clothes were at least clean and not blood-spattered, which is about as good as it ever gets with me.

"Well!" said Steve, rubbing his hands together. "Let's sit down and get to know each other, huh? Can we get you something to drink? You kids hungry?"

"We're always hungry," said the Gasman seriously.

Steve looked taken aback. "Ah, yes, of course! Growing kids!" He was trying hard not to look at our wings, with limited success. He reached over and tapped a button on his desk, which was so big you could practically land a chopper on it. "Jeff? How about some drinks and snacks in here? Thanks."

"Please, sit down," Sharon said, with another hair toss. I made a mental note to practice doing that in a mirror the next time I saw one. It seemed a useful skill, right up there with roundhouse kicks.

We sat, making sure no one was in back of us or could sneak up on us. I was wound so tight I was about to break out in hives.

A young guy in a purple-striped shirt came in with a tray of sodas, glasses of ice, and little nibbly things on several plates. "They're tapas," he explained. "This one's calamari, and this one's —"

"Thanks a million, Jeff." Steve cut in with a smile. Jeff straightened and left, closing the door quietly behind him. Then, as we fell on the food like hyenas, Steve turned to us again, looking so dang enthusiastic that I wondered how much coffee he'd had this morning. "So! You kids want to be big stars, eh?"

"God, no!" I said, almost spewing crumbs. "No way!"

Oddly, this seemed to throw a petite wrench into the convo.

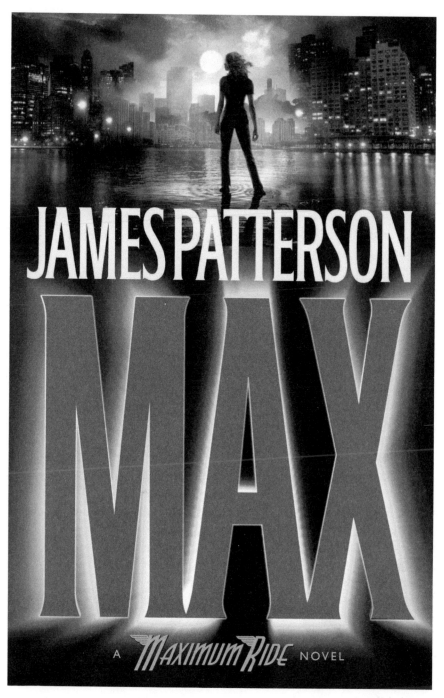

JAMES PATTERSON

MAX

A *MAXIMUM RIDE* NOVEL

AVAILABLE MARCH 16, 2009

MAXIMUM RIDE: THE MANGA ①

JAMES PATTERSON
& NaRae Lee

Adaptation and Illustration: NaRae Lee

Lettering: Abigail Blackman

Yen Press
Hachette Book Group
237 Park Avenue, New York, NY 10017

Visit our Web sites at www.HachetteBookGroup.com and www.YenPress.com.

Yen Press is an imprint of Hachette Book Group, Inc. The Yen Press name and logo are trademarks of Hachette Book Group, Inc.

First Yen Press Edition: January 2009

ISBN-13: 978-0-7595-2951-9

10 9 8 7 6 5 4 3 2 1

BVG

Printed in the United States of America